SIXTH EDITION

TEN STEPS TO ADVANCING COLLEGE READING SKILLS

SIXTH EDITION

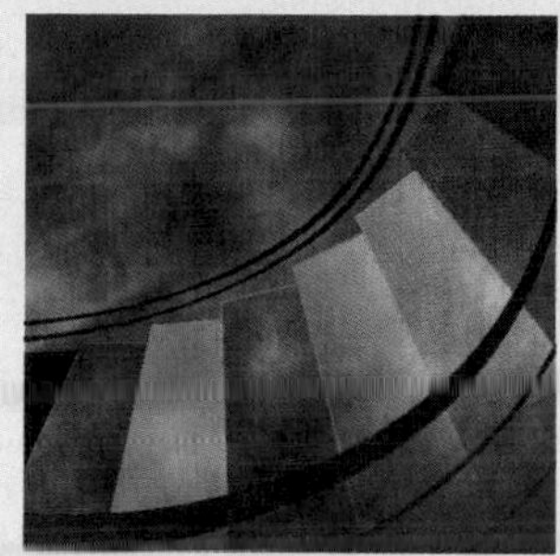

TEN STEPS TO ADVANCING COLLEGE READING SKILLS

JOHN LANGAN

ATLANTIC CAPE COMMUNITY COLLEGE

Books in the Townsend Press Reading Series

Groundwork for College Reading with Phonics
Groundwork for College Reading
Ten Steps to Building College Reading Skills
Ten Steps to Improving College Reading Skills
Ten Steps to Advancing College Reading Skills
Ten Steps to Advanced Reading

Books in the Townsend Press Vocabulary Series

Vocabulary Basics
Groundwork for a Better Vocabulary
Building Vocabulary Skills
Building Vocabulary Skills, Short Version
Improving Vocabulary Skills
Improving Vocabulary Skills, Short Version
Advancing Vocabulary Skills
Advancing Vocabulary Skills, Short Version
Advanced Word Power

Supplements Available for Most Books

Instructor's Edition
Instructor's Manual and Test Bank
Online Exercises

Printed in the United States of America
9 8 7 6 5 4 3

Cover design: Akisia Grigsby

ISBN-13 (Student Edition): 978-1-59194-434-8
ISBN-13 (Instructor's Edition): 978-1-59194-435-5

Send book orders and requests for desk copies or supplements to:

Townsend Press Book Center
439 Kelley Drive
West Berlin, New Jersey 08091

For even faster service, contact us in any of the following ways:

By telephone: 1-800-772-6410
By fax: 1-800-225-8894
By e-mail: cs@townsendpress.com
Through our website: www.townsendpress.com

Contents

Preface: To the Instructor

We all know that many students entering college today do not have the reading skills needed to do effective work in their courses. A related problem, apparent even in class discussions, is that students often lack the skills required to think in a clear and logical way.

The purpose of *Ten Steps to Advancing College Reading Skills,* Sixth Edition, is to develop effective reading and clear thinking. To do so, **Part One** presents a sequence of ten reading skills that are widely recognized as essential for basic and advanced comprehension. The first six skills concern the more literal levels of comprehension:

- Understanding vocabulary in context
- Recognizing main ideas
- Identifying supporting details
- Recognizing implied main ideas
- Understanding relationships that involve addition and time
- Understanding relationships that involve examples, comparison and/or contrast, and cause and effect

The remaining skills cover the more advanced, critical levels of comprehension:

- Making inferences
- Identifying an author's purpose and tone
- Evaluating arguments
- Separating fact from opinion, detecting propaganda, and recognizing errors in reasoning

In every chapter in Part One, the key aspects of a skill are explained and illustrated clearly and simply. Explanations are accompanied by a series of practices, and each chapter ends with four review tests. The last review test consists of a reading selection so that students can apply the skill just learned to real-world reading materials, including newspaper and magazine articles and textbook selections. Together, the ten chapters provide students with the skills needed for both basic and more advanced reading comprehension.

Following each chapter in Part One are **at least six mastery tests for the skill in question.** The tests progress in difficulty, giving students the additional practice and challenge they may need for the solid learning of each skill. While designed for quick grading, the tests also require students to think carefully before answering each question.

Part Two is made up of ten additional readings that will improve both reading and thinking skills. Each reading is followed by *Basic Skill Questions* and *Advanced Skill Questions* so that students can practice all ten skills presented in Part One. In addition, an *Outlining, Mapping,* or *Summarizing* activity after each reading helps students think carefully about the basic content and organization of a selection. *Discussion Questions* then afford instructors a final opportunity to engage students in a variety of reading and thinking skills and thus deepen their understanding of a selection.

Part Three consists of a set of two relationships tests and a series of twenty-five combined-skills tests that review the skills in Part One and help students prepare for the standardized reading test that is often a requirement at the end of a semester.

Part Four serves a variety of purposes. A section on summarizing and outlining offers added instruction and practice in these important techniques. The four additional tests on fact and opinion can be given after students complete their work on Chapter 10 in Part One. Part Four also presents a series of three short textbook selections that instructors can use to give students practice in taking notes. Next, a section on bias provides instruction in a skill that some (but probably not all) instructors will have time to address. Finally, there are writing assignments for all twenty readings in the text. When time permits, asking students to write about a selection will help reinforce the reading and thinking skills they have practiced in the book.

The Appendixes that follow include a pronunciation guide and a limited answer key.

Important Features of the Book

- **Focus on the basics.** The book is designed to explain, in a clear, step-by-step way, the essential elements of each skill. Many examples are provided to ensure that students understand each point. In general, the focus is on teaching the skills—not just on explaining or testing them.

- **Frequent practice and feedback.** Because abundant practice and careful feedback are essential to learning, this book includes numerous activities. Students can get immediate feedback on the practice exercises in Part One and Part Four by turning to the limited answer key at the back of the book. The answers to the review and mastery tests in Part One, the reading questions in Part Two, and the relationships and combined-skills tests in Part Three are in the *Instructor's Manual.*

  The limited answer key increases the active role that students take in their own learning. They are likely to use the answer key in an honest and positive way if they know they will be tested on the many activities and selections for which answers are not provided. (Answers not in the book can be easily copied from the *Instructor's Edition* or the *Instructor's Manual* and passed out at the teacher's discretion.)

- **High interest level.** Dull and unvaried readings and exercises work against learning. Students need to experience genuine interest and enjoyment in what they read. Teachers as well should be able to take pleasure in the selections, for their own good feeling can carry over favorably into class work. The readings in the book, then, have been chosen not only for the appropriateness of their reading level but also for their compelling content. They should engage teachers and students alike.

- **Ease of use.** The logical sequence in each chapter—from explanation to example to practice to review test to mastery test—helps make the skills easy to teach. The book's organization into distinct parts also makes for ease of use. Within a single class, for instance, teachers can work on a new skill in Part One, review other skills with one or more mastery tests, and provide variety by having students read one of the selections in Part Two. The limited answer key at the back of the text also makes for versatility: the teacher can assign some chapters for self-teaching. Finally, the mastery tests—each on its own tear-out page—and the combined-skills tests make it a simple matter for teachers to test and evaluate student progress.

- **Integration of skills.** Students do more than learn the skills individually in Part One. They also learn to apply the skills together through the reading selections in Parts One and Two as well as the combined-skills tests in Part Three. They become effective readers and thinkers through repeated practice in applying a combination of skills.

- **Integrated online resources.** Through the use of TP's acclaimed Learning Center, *Ten Steps to Advancing College Reading Skills,* 6/e, features powerful online components to enhance learning, including:

  1. **Online practice exercises and mastery tests.** Each chapter of the book is supported by additional practice exercises *and* online versions of the book's mastery tests. These materials can be used to reinforce skills taught in the chapter *or* to assess students' learning.

2 **Helpful PowerPoint files.** A comprehensive collection of PowerPoint files covering the book's ten key chapters is available for immediate downloading.

3 **Downloadable Supplements.** Electronic (PDF) versions of the instructor's manual and test bank can be downloaded directly from the Learning Center. These files give you the resources you need whenever and wherever you are—24 hours a day.

4 **Class management controls.** The Learning Center allows you to control which assignments and tests your students can access. It also allows you to create unique assignments for each class you teach, track students' progress, and simplify grading. To learn more, e-mail **cs@townsendpress.com** or visit the Learning Center now at **www.townsendpress.net**.

- **Thinking activities.** Thinking activities—in the form of outlining, mapping, and summarizing—are a distinctive feature of the book. While educators agree that such organizational abilities are important, these skills are all too seldom taught. From a practical standpoint, it is almost impossible for a teacher to respond in detail to entire collections of class outlines or summaries. This book, then, presents activities that truly involve students in outlining, mapping, and summarizing—in other words, that truly make students *think*—and yet enable a teacher to give immediate feedback. Again, it is through continued practice *and* feedback on challenging material that a student becomes a more effective reader and thinker.

- **Supplementary materials.**

Print Supplement

An *Instructor's Edition* is available at no charge to instructors who have adopted the text. It can be obtained quickly by writing or calling Townsend Press (439 Kelley Drive, West Berlin, New Jersey 08091; 1-800-772-6410), by sending a fax to 1-800-225-8894, or by e-mailing Customer Service at **cs@townsendpress.com**. The IE is identical to the student book except that it also provides hints for teachers (starting on the inside front cover of the book), answers to all the practices and tests, and comments on most items. *No other book on the market has such detailed and helpful annotations.*

Online Supplements

Three online supplements are available through the TP website by going to the "Supplements" area for instructors at **www.townsendpress.net**.

1 A combined *Instructor's Manual and Test Bank* includes suggestions for teaching the course, a model syllabus, and readability levels for the text and the reading selections. The test bank contains four additional

mastery tests for each of the ten skills and four additional combined-skills tests—all on letter-sized sheets so they can be copied easily for use with students.

2 PowerPoint presentations.

3 Online exercises.

- **One of a sequence of books.** This text is the fifth in a series of six books.

  Groundwork for College Reading with Phonics and *Groundwork for College Reading* are the basic texts in the series. They are suitable for ESL students and basic adult learners.

  Ten Steps to Building College Reading Skills is often the choice for a first college reading course.

  Ten Steps to Improving College Reading Skills is an intermediate text appropriate for the core developmental reading course offered at most colleges.

  Ten Steps to Advancing College Reading Skills is a higher-level developmental text than the *Improving* book. It can be used as the core book for a more advanced class, as a sequel to *Ten Steps to Improving,* or as a second-semester alternative to it.

  Finally, *Ten Steps to Advanced Reading* is the most advanced text in the series. It can also be used as a sequel (or a second-semester alternative) to either the *Improving* or the *Advancing* text.

  A companion set of vocabulary books, listed on the copyright page, has been designed to go with the *Ten Steps* books. Recommended to accompany this book is *Advancing Vocabulary Skills* (300 words and word parts) or *Advancing Vocabulary Skills, Short Version* (200 words).

  Together, the books and all their supplements form a sequence that should be ideal for any college reading program.

To summarize, *Ten Steps to Advancing College Reading Skills,* Sixth Edition, teaches and reinforces ten essential reading skills. Through an appealing collection of readings and a carefully designed series of activities and tests, students receive extensive guided practice in the skills. The result is an integrated approach to learning that will, by the end of the course, produce better readers and stronger thinkers.

Changes in the Sixth Edition

Changes in this edition include seven new readings, a set of relationships tests, five added combined-skills tests, and a freshening of illustrations and practice materials throughout. In addition, the book will be available in electronic as well as print form, and online support for the book has been expanded.

Acknowledgments

I am grateful for the many helpful suggestions provided by the following reviewers: Nancy Banks, Florida State College at Jacksonville; Donna Clack, Schoolcraft College; Chandler Clifton, Edmonds Community College; Eva Griffin, Community College of Baltimore County, Dundalk; Patricia Hale, Kilgore College; Jacquelin Hanselman, Copper Mountain Community College; Iris Hill, Wake Technical Community College; Jennifer Hurd, Harding University; Heather Kamen, Borough of Manhattan Community College; Dianne F. Kostelny, Northwest Florida State College; Elizabeth Ligon, Florida Memorial University; Margaret Ann Maricle, Cuesta College; Hilda McRaney, Hinds Community College; Joanne Nelson, Hillsborough Community College; Roberta Newman, St. Petersburg College; Betty Payne, Montgomery College; Carol Polo, Cerritos College; Florinda Rodriguez, South Texas College; Diane Schellack, Burlington County College; Judith Schurger, Miami-Dade College; Daniel Strumas, Indian River State College; Karen Waska, Cuesta College; Phyllis West, El Camino College; Paula Wimbish, Hinds Community College; Rosalie Wolf, City College of San Francisco; Paul Wolford, Walters State Community College; and Cheryl Ziehl, Cuesta College.

At Townsend Press, I thank Kathryn Bernstein, Bill Blauvelt, Denton Cairnes, Beth Johnson, Paul Langan, Ruth A. Rouff, and Tanya Savory for the help they provided along the way. And I owe special thanks to two TP editors who brought their exceptional talents to this revision. Barbara Solot is responsible for a layout and full-color text design that are as clear as they are inviting. The result of her artistry is a strikingly attractive book that both students and teachers will appreciate. Janet Goldstein has provided design input along with her usual superb editorial skills. Her insights, coupled with her many years of classroom teaching, have strengthened the clarity and pedagogy of the book.

It is always a special pleasure to work with people who aspire toward excellence. With help from my colleagues in the teaching profession and at Townsend Press, I have been able to create a much better book than I could have managed on my own.

John Langan

Introduction

1 How to Become a Better Reader and Thinker

The chances are that you are not as good a reader as you should be to do well in college. If so, it's not surprising. You live in a culture where people watch an average of *over seven hours of television every day!!!* All that passive viewing does not allow much time for reading. Reading is a skill that must be actively practiced. The simple fact is that people who do not read very often are not likely to be strong readers.

- How much TV do you guess you watch on an average day?

Another reason besides TV for not reading much is that you may have a lot of responsibilities. You may be going to school and working at the same time, and you may have a lot of family duties as well. Given your hectic schedule, you're not going to have much time to read. When you have free time, you're exhausted, and it's easier to turn on the TV than to open up a book.

- Do you do any regular reading (for example, a daily newspaper, weekly magazines, occasional novels)?

- When are you most likely to do your reading?

A third reason for not reading is that school may have caused you to associate reading with worksheets and drills and book reports and test scores. Experts agree that many schools have not done a good job of helping students discover the pleasures and rewards of reading. If reading was an unpleasant experience in school, you may have concluded that reading in general is not for you.

- Do you think that school made you dislike reading, rather than enjoy it?

Here are three final questions to ask yourself:

- Do you feel that perhaps you don't need a reading course, since you "already know how to read"?

- If you had a choice, would you be taking a reading course? (It's okay to be honest.)
- Do you think that a bit of speed reading may be all you need?

Chances are that you don't need to read *faster* as much as you need to read *smarter*. And it's a safe bet that if you don't read much, you can benefit enormously from the reading course in which you are using this book.

One goal of the book is to help you become a better reader. You will learn and practice ten key reading comprehension skills. As a result, you'll be better able to read and understand the many materials in your other college courses. The skills in this book have direct and practical value: they can help you perform better and more quickly—giving you an edge for success—in all of your college work.

The book is also concerned with helping you become a stronger thinker, a person able not just to *understand* what you read but to *analyze* and *evaluate* it as well. In fact, reading and thinking are closely related skills, and practice in thoughtful reading will also strengthen your ability to think clearly and logically. To find out just how the book will help you achieve these goals, read the next several pages.

How the Book Is Organized

The book is organized into five main parts:

Introduction (pages 1–13)

In addition to this chapter, which will give you a good sense of the book, there are two other parts to the introduction. "Some Quick Study Tips" presents four hints that can make you a better student. If I had time to say just four things to incoming college students, based on my thirty years of teaching experience, these are the things I would say. The final part of the introduction, "The Power of Reading," gives four reasons for developing the reading habit and also offers a reading challenge.

Part One: Ten Steps to Advancing College Reading Skills (pages 15–456)

To help you become a more effective reader and thinker, this book presents a series of ten key reading skills. They are listed in the table of contents on pages v and vi. Each chapter is developed in the same way.

- First of all, clear **explanations** and **examples** help you *understand* each skill.
- **Practices** then give you the "hands-on" experience needed to *learn* the skill.
- Closing each chapter are **four review tests**. The first review test provides a check of the information presented in the chapter. The second and third review tests consist of activities that help you practice the skill learned in the chapter. The fourth review test consists of a story, essay, or textbook selection that both gets you reading and gives you practice in the skill learned in the chapter as well as skills learned in previous chapters.
- Following each chapter are **six mastery tests** which gradually increase in difficulty. The tests are on tear-out pages and so can be easily removed and handed in to your instructor. So that you can track your progress, there is a score box at the top of each test. Your score can also be entered into the "Reading Performance Chart" on the inside back cover of the book.

Part Two: Ten Reading Selections (pages 457–574)

The ten reading selections that make up Part Two are followed by activities that give you practice in all of the skills studied in Part One. Each reading begins in the same way. Look, for example, at "The Professor Is a Dropout," which starts on page 459. You'll see two sections that come before the reading itself. The first section, "Preview," gives you an idea of what the reading selection is about. The second one, "Words to Watch," lists some of the challenging words in the selection, together with their meanings.

Note that the vocabulary words in "Words to Watch" are followed by the numbers of the paragraphs in which the words appear. Look at paragraphs 16, 29, and 36 of "The Professor Is a Dropout"; you'll see that each vocabulary word is marked with a small circle (°) in the reading itself.

Activities Following Each Reading Selection

After each selection, there are four kinds of activities that will help you to improve the reading and thinking skills you learned in Part One of the book.

1. The first activity consists of **basic skill questions**—questions involving vocabulary in context, main ideas (including implied main ideas and central points), supporting details, and relationships.

2 The second activity is made up of **advanced skill questions**—ones involving inferences, purpose and tone, argument, and critical reading.

3 The third activity involves **outlining, mapping,** or **summarizing**. Each of these activities will sharpen your ability to get to the heart of a selection and to think logically and clearly about what you read.

4 The fourth activity consists of four **discussion questions**. These questions provide a chance for you to deepen your understanding of each selection.

Part Three: Relationships and Combined-Skills Tests (pages 575–640)

The first chapter in Part Three contains two tests that provide additional practice with the relationships you studied in Chapters 5 and 6.

The second chapter in Part Three consists of short passages that give you practice in all the reading skills taught in the book.

Part Four: For Further Study (pages 641–708)

Part Four contains additional materials that can help improve your reading.

1 The first section, "More about Summarizing and Outlining," provides additional information and activities that your instructor may choose to cover, depending on the needs of the class.

2 The second section, "Additional Tests on Fact and Opinion," contains four 20-item tests that you may take after you have studied Chapter 10, "Critical Reading," in Part One.

3 The third section, "Three Additional Readings," presents a series of short textbook selections that your instructor may assign for note-taking practice.

4 The fourth section, "Understanding Bias," explains how to recognize a speaker's or writer's point of view by looking at word choices.

5 The fifth section, "Writing Assignments," on pages 694–708, presents writing assignments for all twenty reading selections in the book. Reading and writing are closely connected skills, and writing practice will improve your ability to read closely and to think carefully.

Appendixes (pages 709–718)

Following Part Four are appendixes that include a pronunciation guide and a limited answer key.

Helpful Features of the Book

1 The book centers on *what you really need to know* to become a better reader and thinker. It presents ten key comprehension skills and explains the most important points about each one.

2 The book gives you *lots of practice.* We seldom learn a skill only by hearing or reading about it; we make it part of us by repeated practice. There are, then, numerous activities in the text. They are not "busywork," but carefully designed materials that should help you truly learn each skill.

Notice that after you learn each skill in Part One, you progress to review tests and mastery tests that enable you to apply the skill. And as you move from one skill to the next, the reading selections help you practice and reinforce the skills already learned.

3 The selections throughout the book are *lively and appealing.* Dull and unvaried readings work against learning, so subjects have been carefully chosen for their high interest level. Almost all of the selections here are good examples of how what we read can capture our attention. For instance, start reading "The Professor Is a Dropout," which is about the dramatic steps one woman took to educate herself and her children—and try to *stop* reading. Or read "Soft Addictions," which contains surprising findings about the hidden dangers of "normal" activities like drinking coffee, watching TV, and using the Internet. Or read the textbook selection "Effects of the Automobile," which, despite its unexciting title, is full of fascinating—and thought-provoking—details about the many ways that automobiles have changed our daily lives.

4 The readings include *eleven selections from college textbooks.* Therefore, you will be practicing on some materials very much like the ones in your other courses. Doing so will increase your chances of transferring what you learn in your reading class to your other college courses.

How to Use the Book

1 A good way to proceed is to read and review the explanations and examples in a given chapter in Part One until you feel you understand the ideas presented. Then carefully work through the practices. As you finish each one, check your answers with the "Limited Answer Key" that starts on page 713.

For your own sake, *don't just copy in the answers without trying to do the practices!* The only way to learn a skill is to practice it first and then use the answer key to give yourself feedback. Also, take whatever time is needed to figure out just why you got some answers wrong. By using the answer key to help teach yourself the skills, you will prepare yourself for the review and mastery tests at the end of each chapter as well as the other reading tests in the book. Your instructor can supply you with answers to those tests.

If you have trouble catching on to a particular skill, stick with it. In time, you will learn each of the ten skills.

2 Read the selections first with the intent of simply enjoying them. There will be time afterward for rereading each selection and using it to develop your comprehension skills.

3 Keep track of your progress. Fill in the charts at the end of each chapter in Part One and each reading in Part Two. And in the "Reading Performance Chart" on the inside back cover, enter your scores for all of the review and mastery tests as well as the reading selections. These scores can give you a good view of your overall performance as you work through the book.

In summary, *Ten Steps to Advancing College Reading Skills* has been designed to interest and benefit you as much as possible. Its format is straightforward, its explanations are clear, its readings are appealing, and its many practices will help you learn through doing. *It is a book that has been created to reward effort,* and if you provide that effort, you will make yourself a better reader and a stronger thinker. I wish you success.

John Langan

2 Some Quick Study Tips

While it's not my purpose in this book to teach study skills, I do want to give you four quick hints that can make you a better student. The hints are based on my thirty years of experience working with first-year college students and teaching reading and study skills.

TIP 1 The most important steps you can take to succeed in school are to go to every class and take a lot of notes. If you don't go to class, or you go but just sit there without taking notes, chances are you're heading for a heap of trouble.

TIP 2 Let me ask you a question: Which is more important—learning how to read a textbook or learning how to read your instructor?

Write your answer here: ______________________________

You may be surprised at the answer: What is far more important is learning how to read your instructor—to understand what he or she expects you to learn in the course and to know for tests.

I remember becoming a good student in college only after I learned the truth of this statement. And I have interviewed hundreds of today's students who have said the same thing. Let me quote just one of them:

> *You absolutely have to be in class. Then you learn how to read the teacher and to know what he or she is going to want on tests. You could read an entire textbook, but that wouldn't be as good as being in class and writing down a teacher's understanding of ideas.*

TIP 3 Many instructors base their tests mainly on the ideas they present in class. But when you have to learn a textbook chapter, do the following.

First, read the first and last few paragraphs of the chapter; they may give you a good overview of what the chapter is about.

Second, as you read the chapter, look for and mark off definitions of key terms and examples of those definitions.

Third, as you read the chapter, number any lists of items; if there is a series of items and you number the the items *1, 2, 3,* and so on, it will be easier to understand and remember them.

Fourth, after you've read the chapter, take notes on the most important material and test yourself on those notes until you can say them to yourself without looking at them.

TIP 4 Here's another question: Are you an organized person? Do you get out of bed on time, do you get to places on time, do you keep up with school work, do you allow time to study for tests and write papers?

If you are *not* an organized person, you're going to have trouble in school. Here are three steps to take to control your time:

First, pay close attention to the course outline, or *syllabus,* your instructors will probably pass out at the start of a semester. Chances are that the syllabus will give you the dates of exams and tell you when papers or reports are due.

Second, move all those dates onto a *large monthly calendar*—a calendar that has a good-sized block of white space for each date. Hang the calendar in a place where you'll be sure to see it every day—perhaps above your desk or on a bedroom wall.

Third, buy a small notebook and write down, every day, a *"to do" list* of things that need to get done that day. Decide which items are most important, and focus on them first. (If you have classes that day, going to those classes will be "A" priority items.) Carry your list with you during the day, referring to it every so often and checking off items as you complete them.

Questions

1. Of the four hints listed above, which is the most important one for you? Why?

2. Which hint is the second most important for you, and why?

3. You may not realize just how quickly new information can be forgotten. For example, how much class material do you think most people forget in just two weeks? Check (✓) the answer you think is correct.

   ____ 20 percent is forgotten within two weeks

   ____ 40 percent is forgotten within two weeks

   ____ 60 percent is forgotten within two weeks

   ____ 80 percent is forgotten within two weeks

   The truth is that within two weeks most people forget almost 80% of what they have heard! Given that fact, what should you be sure to do in all your classes? ______________________________

3 The Power of Reading

You will become a stronger reader as you practice the comprehension skills presented in this book. But you should take another step as well, and that is to develop the habit of regular reading. Here are four specific reasons why you should develop the reading habit:

Reason 1: Language Power. Research has shown beyond any question that reading and writing are closely connected skills. The more you do of one, the better you'll become at the other. In fact, frequent reading will not only strengthen your grammar and writing style; it will also improve your vocabulary, spelling, and reading speed and comprehension. Once you become a regular reader, all your language and thinking abilities will develop almost automatically!

Reason 2: Entertainment Power. Too many students have done too little reading for pleasure in their lives. You may be one of these students—an unpracticed reader who has never discovered how enjoyable the right kind of reading can be. Perhaps you grew up in a home like mine where a television set dominated the household. Or maybe you were eager to learn about reading when you began school, but then you lost interest. If you were given dull and irrelevant material to read in school, you may have decided (mistakenly) that reading cannot be rewarding for you.

The truth is that reading can open the door to a lifetime of pleasure and adventure. Thrilling stories, unforgettable characters, and powerful life lessons all lie on the other side of the door. If you take the time to walk through that door, chances are you will learn that one of the great experiences of life is the joy of reading for its own sake.

Reason 3: Job Power. Regular reading will increase your chances for job success. In today's world more than ever before, jobs involve the processing of information, with words being the tools of the trade. Studies have found that the better your command of words, the more success you are likely to have. Nothing will give you a command of words as effectively as regular reading.

Reason 4: Human Power. Reading enlarges the mind and the heart. It frees us from the narrow confines of our own experience. Knowing how other people view important matters helps us decide what we ourselves think and feel. Reading also helps us connect with others and realize our shared humanity. The famous novelist C.S. Lewis wrote, "We read in order to know that we are not alone." We become less isolated as we share the common experiences, emotions, and thoughts that make us human. We grow more sympathetic and understanding because we realize that others are like us.

A Special Offer

To promote your reading growth, Townsend Press will send you five books at no charge except for postage and handling. Here are the five books:

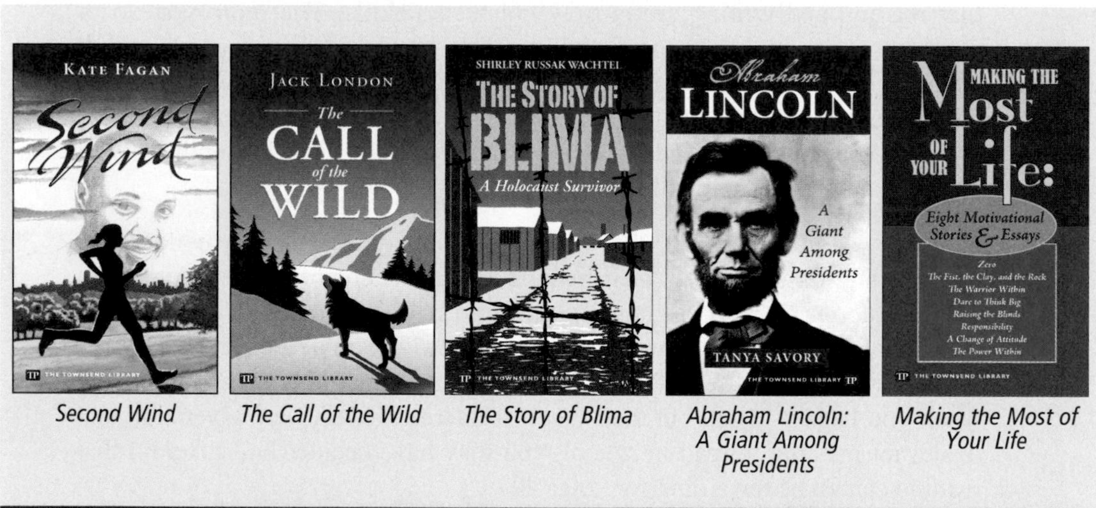

Second Wind | *The Call of the Wild* | *The Story of Blima* | *Abraham Lincoln: A Giant Among Presidents* | *Making the Most of Your Life*

Cut out the actual order form on the following page (not a copy), enclosing five dollars to cover the cost of shipping and handling. You'll then be sent these five very readable books.

ORDER FORM

YES! Please send me copies of *Second Wind, Call of the Wild, The Story of Blima, Lincoln,* and *Making the Most of Your Life*. Enclosed is five dollars to cover the shipping and handling of the books.

Please PRINT the following very clearly. It will be your shipping label.

Name ______________________________

Address ______________________________

City ________________ *State* __________ *Zip* __________

MAIL TO: TP Book Center, 439 Kelley Drive, West Berlin, NJ 08091.

Part One

Ten Steps to Advancing College Reading Skills

1 Vocabulary in Context

If you were asked to define the words *raucous, ubiquitous,* and *advocate,* you might have some difficulty. On the other hand, if you saw these words in sentences, chances are you could come up with fairly accurate definitions. For example, see if you can define the words in *italics* in the three sentences below.

Do not use a dictionary for this work. Instead, in each sentence, try the word you think is the answer. For example, put *boring* or *noisy* or *dangerous* into the sentence in place of *raucous* to see which one makes the best sense. Then, using a capital letter, write, in the space provided, the letter of the answer you have chosen.

___ The homecoming celebration was *raucous*, with people wildly shouting and cheering, blowing whistles, and pounding on drums.

Raucous (rô′kəs) means

A. boring. B. noisy. C. dangerous.

___ Smartphones have become *ubiquitous*; you can see them—and hear them—everywhere.

Ubiquitous (yo͞o-bĭk′wĭ-təs) means

A. unaffordable. B. complicated. C. widespread.

___ Those who *advocate* capital punishment often argue that it prevents crime, but those who oppose it say it has no such effect.

Advocate (ăd′və-kāt′) means

A. support. B. disregard. C. resist.

In each sentence above, the **context**—the words surrounding the unfamiliar word—provides clues to the word's meaning. You may have guessed from the context that *raucous* means "noisy," that *ubiquitous* means "widespread," and that *advocate* means "support."

Using context clues to understand the meaning of unfamiliar words will help you in several ways:

- It will save you time when reading. You will not have to stop to look up words in the dictionary. (Of course, you won't *always* be able to understand a word from its context, so you should always have a dictionary nearby as you read.)
- After you figure out the meaning of a particular word more than once through its context, it may become a part of your working vocabulary. You will therefore add to your vocabulary simply by reading thoughtfully.
- You will get a good sense of how a word is actually used, including any shades of meaning it might have.

Types of Context Clues

There are four common types of context clues:

1 Examples

2 Synonyms

3 Antonyms

4 General Sense of the Sentence or Passage

In the following sections, you will read about and practice using each type. The practices will sharpen your skills in recognizing and using context clues. They will also help you add new words to your vocabulary.

Remember *not* to use a dictionary for these practices. Their purpose is to help you develop the skill of figuring out what words mean without using a dictionary. Pronunciations are provided in parentheses for the words, and a brief guide to pronunciation is on pages 711–712.

1 Examples

If you are given **examples** that relate to an unknown word, you can often figure out its meaning. To understand how this clue works, look again at the sentence on page 17: "The homecoming celebration was *raucous*, with people wildly shouting and cheering, blowing whistles, and pounding on drums." The examples—people wildly shouting and cheering, blowing whistles, and pounding on drums—help you figure out that the word *raucous* means "noisy."

Look also at the cartoon on the next page. What do you think the word *adverse* (ăd′vûrs′) means?

_____ A. known B. pleasant C. harmful

"The only adverse side effect of this prescription is that it will drain your bank account."

Note that the example of an adverse side effect—it will drain the patient's bank account—helps you understand that *adverse* means "harmful."

Check Your Understanding

Now read the items that follow. An *italicized* word in each sentence is followed by examples that serve as context clues for that word. These examples, which are **boldfaced**, will help you figure out the meaning of each word. On each answer line, write the letter of the answer you think is correct. Then read the explanation that follows.

Note that examples are often introduced with signal words and phrases like *for example, for instance, including,* and *such as.*

_____ 1. As they moved westward, early pioneers faced many *tribulations*, such as **scarce food**, **extreme weather**, and **loneliness**.

Tribulations (trĭb′yə-lā′shənz) means

A. criminals. B. hard decisions. C. great difficulties.

Hint: For this and all the exercises in this chapter, actually insert into the sentence the word you think is the answer. For example, substitute *criminals* or *hard decisions* or *great difficulties* in the sentence in place of *tribulations* to see which one fits.

_____ 2. The neighborhood is so *affluent* that most residents have **Olympic-sized swimming pools**, **tennis courts**, and **luxury cars**.

Affluent (ăf′lo͞o-ənt) means

A. wealthy. B. crowded. C. far away.

_____ 3. Each of my coworkers has a strange *idiosyncrasy.* For instance, our receptionist **wears only pink**. The mail clerk **always speaks in a whisper**. And my office mate **lives on peanuts and apples**.

Idiosyncrasy (ĭd′ē-ō-sĭng′krə-sē) means

A. hidden thought. B. unusual goal. C. unusual personal trait.

Explanation

In each sentence, the examples probably helped you to figure out the meaning of the word in italics:

1. In sentence 1, the examples of what the pioneers faced may have helped you realize that *tribulations* means "great difficulties."
2. In sentence 2, the examples—pools, tennis courts, and luxury cars—show that *affluent* means "wealthy."
3. Finally, the examples in sentence 3 indicate that an *idiosyncrasy* is an "unusual personal trait."

PRACTICE 1: Examples

In each of the sentences below, underline the examples that suggest the meaning of the italicized word. Then write the letter of the meaning of that term on the answer line. Note that the last five sentences have been taken from college textbooks.

_____ 1. There was obvious *animosity* between Carmen and Jack—for example, they glared at each other and refused to stay in the same room together.

Animosity (ăn′ə-mŏs′ĭ-tē) means

A. space. B. nothing. C. ill will.

_____ 2. The mayor introduced various *stringent* financial measures, including cutting the police force in half and reducing the pay of all city employees.

Stringent (strĭn′jənt) means

A. minor. B. severe. C. expensive.

_____ 3. The police officer was trying to deal with two *distraught* people at once—a trembling mugging victim and a crying lost child.

Distraught (dĭ-strôt′) means
A. very troubled. B. unhealthy. C. reasonable.

_____ 4. Imagine my *chagrin* when I looked in the mirror right after giving a report in front of the class—and discovered, to my humiliation, that some of the blueberry pie I had eaten for lunch was still on my front teeth.

Chagrin (shə-grĭn′) means
A. embarrassment. B. encouragement. C. pleasure.

_____ 5. Circus performers generally dress in *ostentatious* costumes, with plenty of sequins, feathers, and gold trim to dazzle the eye.

Ostentatious (ŏs′tĕn-tā′shəs) means
A. inexpensive. B. showy. C. athletic.

_____ 6. Unused muscles will begin to *atrophy;* thus a broken leg is noticeably thinner when the cast is removed, and a patient bedridden for too long will lack the lower-body strength needed to stand up.

Atrophy (ăt′rə-fē) means
A. develop. B. be replaced. C. waste away.

_____ 7. *Indigenous* life forms—the cactus and the camel in the desert, the polar bear and the seal in the Arctic, and so on—are suited to their environments in very specific ways.

Indigenous (ĭn-dĭj′ə-nəs) means
A. recent. B. extinct. C. native.

_____ 8. In earlier centuries, people looked with fear upon a number of *innocuous* practices, such as eating tomatoes, taking a bath, and letting a baby kick its legs.

Innocuous (ĭ-nŏk′yo͞o-əs) means
A. dangerous. B. harmless. C. superstitious.

_____ 9. The nonphysical portion of culture includes three *components:* 1) knowledge and beliefs, 2) rules of behavior and values, and 3) signs and language.

Components (kəm-pō′nənts) means
A. questions. B. parts. C. reasons.

_____ 10. *Turbulent* periods in nineteenth-century Europe included the Napoleonic Wars of 1800–1815, the revolutions of 1848, the Crimean War in the 1850s, and the Franco-Prussian War of 1870.

Turbulent (tûr′byə-lənt) means
A. violently disturbed. B. forgotten. C. financially well off.

2 Synonyms

A context clue is often available in the form of a **synonym**: one or more words that mean the same or almost the same as the unknown word. In the sentence on page 17, "Smartphones have become *ubiquitous*; you can see them—and hear them—everywhere," the synonym "everywhere" tells you the meaning of *ubiquitous*. A synonym may appear anywhere in a sentence as a restatement of the meaning of the unknown word.

Look at the cartoon below.

Copyright 2003 by Randy Glasbergen.
www.glasbergen.com
HAPPY FLAKES
GLASBERGEN
"According to the box, this cereal is a panacea.
It will cure everything that's wrong with your life."

Notice that the synonym that helps you understand the word *panacea* is "cure everything."

Check Your Understanding

Each of the following items includes a word or phrase that means the same as the italicized word. Underline the synonym for each italicized word.

1. In the sentence "I actually love the sport of bowling," not only is the word "actually" unnecessary, but the words "the sport of" are also *superfluous* (so͝o-pûr′flo͞o-əs): All the sentence has to say is "I love bowling."

2. That five-year-old girl must have *innate* (ĭ-nāt′) musical talent; playing piano so well at her age requires an inborn gift.

3. Gaining a *mentor* (mĕn′tôr′) is helpful when you are beginning a new job. A wise and trusted adviser can greatly assist your career.

Explanation

In each sentence, the synonym given should have helped you understand the meaning of the word in italics:

1. *Superfluous* means "unnecessary."
2. *Innate* means "inborn."
3. *Mentor* means "wise and trusted adviser."

PRACTICE 2: Synonyms

Each item below includes a word that is a synonym of the italicized word. Write the synonym of the italicized word in the space provided. Note that the last five sentences have been taken from college textbooks.

_______________ 1. I swore not to reveal Anita's secret, but then I did *divulge* (dĭ-vŭlj′) it to my brother.

Hint: What must the speaker have done to Anita's secret?

_______________ 2. The rescue team had *explicit* (ĭk-splĭs′ĭt) directions to the site of the helicopter crash in the mountains. Without such clear directions, they might never have found the place.

_______________ 3. My boss has an *abrasive* (ə-brā′sĭv) personality. It's so irritating that he has trouble keeping friends.

_______________ 4. When I saw the doctor's *somber* (sŏm′bər) expression, I feared that serious news awaited me.

_______________ 5. "This is a *poignant* (poin′yənt) book, as it is filled with touching stories of the author's days in a small Southern town," wrote the reviewer.

_______________ 6. Some consider terrorism the most *heinous* (hā′nəs) crime; others consider treason, torture, or crimes against children the worst evils.

_______________ 7. *Charlatans* (shär′lə-tənz) often get rich when medical science is not yet able to treat a disease effectively. Patients desperate for a cure will try anything, and so they fall into the hands of quacks.

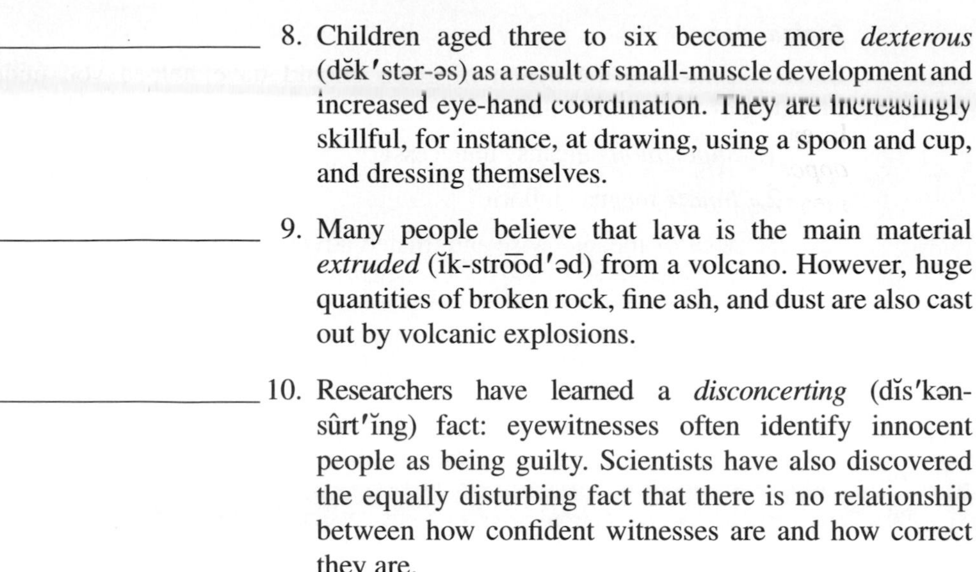

_______________ 8. Children aged three to six become more *dexterous* (dĕk′stər-əs) as a result of small-muscle development and increased eye-hand coordination. They are increasingly skillful, for instance, at drawing, using a spoon and cup, and dressing themselves.

_______________ 9. Many people believe that lava is the main material *extruded* (ĭk-stro͞od′əd) from a volcano. However, huge quantities of broken rock, fine ash, and dust are also cast out by volcanic explosions.

_______________ 10. Researchers have learned a *disconcerting* (dĭs′kən-sûrt′ĭng) fact: eyewitnesses often identify innocent people as being guilty. Scientists have also discovered the equally disturbing fact that there is no relationship between how confident witnesses are and how correct they are.

3 Antonyms

An **antonym**—a word or phrase that means the opposite of another word—is also a useful context clue. Antonyms are sometimes signaled by words and phrases such as *however, but, yet, on the other hand,* and *in contrast.*

Look again at the sentence on page 17, "Those who *advocate* capital punishment often argue that it prevents crime, but those who oppose it say it has no such effect." Here the word *oppose* is an antonym that helps us realize that the word *advocate* means "support."

Look also at the cartoon below.

"Indolent? I'm *not* being indolent! Trying to find something good to watch on TV while eating these chips is *really hard work!*"

Note that the antonym *hard work* helps you figure out that *indolent* must mean "lazy."

Check Your Understanding

In each of the following sentences, underline the word or phrase that means the *opposite* of the italicized word. Then, on the answer line, write the letter of the meaning of the italicized word.

____ 1. The teacher would have achieved better results if she had been as quick to *commend* students for their successes as she was to criticize them for their failures.

Commend (kə-mĕnd′) means
A. blame. B. grade. C. praise.

____ 2. A memo that is brief and to the point is more likely to be read than one that is *verbose* and rambling.

Verbose (vər-bōs′) means
A. argumentative. B. wordy. C. short.

____ 3. Most of my friends' mothers seemed ordinary; mine, however, did such *bizarre* things as spraying green paint on the dead tree in front of our house.

Bizarre (bĭ-zär′) means
A. odd. B. easy. C. dangerous.

Explanation

In the first sentence, the opposite of *commend* is *criticize*; so *commend* means "praise." In the second sentence, *verbose* is the opposite of *brief*, so *verbose* means "wordy." Last, *bizarre* is the opposite of *ordinary*; *bizarre* means "odd."

PRACTICE 3: Antonyms

Each item below includes a word or phrase that is an antonym of the italicized word. Underline the antonym of each italicized word. Then, on the answer line, write the letter of the meaning of the italicized word. Note that the last five items have been taken from college textbooks.

____ 1. My piano teacher's criticism was always *profuse,* but her praise was scarce.

Hint: If the piano teacher's praise was scarce, what must her criticism have been?

Profuse (prə-fyōōs′) means
A. loud. B. well-founded. C. plentiful.

_____ 2. It was hard to know what the speaker was really feeling—was his enthusiasm *feigned* or genuine?

Feigned (fānd) means

A. secret. B. faked. C. formal.

_____ 3. Roberto's mother was *lenient* when he took money from her dresser drawer, but when he stole candy from a drugstore, her punishment was harsh.

Lenient (lē′nē-ənt) means

A. not strict in punishing. B. tough. C. complimentary.

_____ 4. My sister thinks it's *futile* to try to talk my parents into exercising, but I feel it could be useful to show them statistics that tell how beneficial exercise is.

Futile (fyo͞ot′l) means

A. unlikely. B. useless. C. sentimental.

_____ 5. Those who agreed with the mayor's tax proposal were in the majority, but there were also some outspoken *dissidents.*

Dissidents (dĭs′ĭ-dənts) means

A. those in the majority. B. supporters. C. people who disagree.

_____ 6. A *sedentary* lifestyle is a risk to health. Physically active people have a much better chance of avoiding heart disease and premature death.

Sedentary (sĕd′n-tĕr′ē) means

A. free of stress. B. inactive. C. unusual.

_____ 7. The Judeo-Christian religions believe in an *omnipotent* deity, but that is not true of all religions. Some, both ancient and modern, believe in a god or gods whose power is limited.

Omnipotent (ŏm-nĭp′ə-tənt) means

A. helpful. B. invisible. C. all-powerful.

_____ 8. In the United States, there is no *stigma* attached to divorce. Divorce has gained approval as a solution to marital unhappiness.

Stigma (stĭg′mə) means

A. honor. B. shame. C. cost.

_____ 9. The social and environmental influences on aging suggest that if the aging process can be sped up, it can also be *impeded.*

Impeded (ĭm-pēd′ĭd) means

A. recognized. B. slowed down. C. healthy.

_____ 10. The United States has a varied population; it is multicultural, multiracial, and multiethnic. In contrast, Japan's population is *homogeneous*—practically all of its people are ethnic Japanese.

Homogeneous (hō′mə-jē′nē-əs) means
A. Asian. B. large. C. the same throughout.

4 General Sense of the Sentence or Passage

Often, the context of a new word contains no examples, synonyms, or antonyms. In such cases, you must do a bit more detective work; you'll need to look at any clues provided in the information surrounding the word. Asking yourself questions about the passage may help you make a fairly accurate guess about the meaning of the unfamiliar word.

Look at the cartoon below:

"This may not be the opportune time to tell you this, Cranston, but you're fired."

To figure out the meaning of *opportune*, try asking this question: Is this a good time for the boss to tell an injured worker that he's been fired? Since the boss realizes that "this may not be the opportune time," his words to Cranston strongly suggest that *opportune* means "suitable."

Check Your Understanding

Each of the sentences below is followed by a question. Think about each question; then, on the answer line, write the letter of the answer you think is the correct meaning of the italicized word.

_____ 1. One argument against capital punishment is that if an innocent person is executed, the mistake cannot be *rectified.*

(What cannot be done about a mistake as final as an execution?)

Rectified (rĕk′tə-fīd) means

A. remembered. B. predicted. C. corrected.

_____ 2. It took two days for volunteers to *extricate* the little girl from the bottom of the well.

(How would volunteers try to help the trapped girl?)

Extricate (ĕk′strĭ-kāt′) means

A. free. B. delay. C. remember.

_____ 3. Sonya and Liz thought they'd stay good friends forever. But after graduation, their lives *diverged:* Sonya got married, and Liz moved away.

(What relationship did their lives have after graduation?)

Diverged (dĭ-vûrjd′) means

A. came together. B. improved. C. went in different directions.

Explanation

The first sentence provides enough evidence for you to guess that *rectified* means "corrected." *Extricate* in the second sentence means "free." And *diverged* means "went in different directions." (You may not hit on the exact dictionary definition of a word by using context clues, but you will often be accurate enough to make good sense of what you are reading.)

PRACTICE 4: General Sense of the Sentence or Passage

Try to answer the question that follows each item below. Then use the logic of each answer to help you write the letter of the meaning you think is correct. Note that the last five sentences have been taken from college textbooks.

_____ 1. Emily's signature, *embellished* with loops and swirls, was easy to recognize.

(What do loops and swirls do to the signature?)

Embellished (ĕm-bĕl′ĭsht) means

A. hidden. B. decorated. C. made plain.

_____ 2. My three-year-old often fights for her *autonomy* by saying, "I can do it myself."

(What is being fought for with the statement "I can do it myself"?)

Autonomy (ô-tŏn′ə-mē) means

A. sister. B. independence. C. toys.

_____ 3. After lying *dormant* in their burrows every winter, chipmunks come out again in the spring, looking lively but a bit thin.

(How would you describe animals that have been lying in their burrows all winter?)

Dormant (dôr′mənt) means

A. sick. B. busy. C. inactive.

_____ 4. People who suffer from migraine headaches are frequently advised to avoid things that can *precipitate* an attack, such as red wine, chocolate, and some cheeses.

(What do red wine, chocolate, and some cheeses do to a migraine headache?)

Precipitate (prĭ-sĭp′ĭ-tāt′) means

A. trigger. B. prevent. C. follow.

_____ 5. Hector thought his mother's suggestion to use peanut butter to remove the gum from his hair was *ludicrous*—but it worked!

(What is a likely opinion of Hector's mother's suggestion?)

Ludicrous (lo͞o′dĭ-krəs) means

A. practical. B. delicious. C. ridiculous.

_____ 6. Research shows that almost any unpleasant event, such as frustration, foul odors, or high room temperature, can *provoke* aggression.

(What can unpleasant events do to aggression?)

Provoke (prə-vōk′) means

A. imitate. B. bring about. C. eliminate.

_____ 7. Social psychologists agree that attitudes and actions can have a *reciprocal* relationship: Although attitudes may influence actions, actions can also influence attitudes.

(What type of relationship is described?)

Reciprocal (rĭ-sĭp′rə-kəl) means

A. two-way. B. disconnected. C. peaceful.

_____ 8. Forgetting has benefits. The mind's ability to *eradicate* unnecessary information keeps the memory from becoming overloaded.

(What would the mind do to unnecessary information to keep the memory from being overloaded?)

Eradicate (ĭ-răd′ĭ-kāt′) means

A. erase. B. hold on to. C. change.

_____ 9. To test a new drug, subjects in the experimental group are given the drug, while subjects in the control group are given a *placebo* that looks identical.

(What type of substance might the scientists use to show the effects of the real drug?)

Placebo (plə-sē′bō) means

A. surgery. B. dangerous chemical. C. harmless fake drug.

_____ 10. Because of a natural barrier between the blood and brain, many substances cannot leave the blood and *permeate* the brain tissues.

(What does the barrier stop substances from doing?)

Permeate (pûr′mē-āt′) means

A. resemble. B. spread through. C. disappear from.

An Important Point about Textbook Definitions

You don't always have to use context clues or the dictionary to find definitions. Very often, textbook authors provide definitions of important terms. They usually follow a definition with one or more examples to ensure that you understand the word being defined. Here is a short textbook passage that includes definitions and examples:

> [1]In all societies there is some **vertical mobility**—moving up or down the status ladder. [2]The upward movement is called *upward mobility* and the downward movement, *downward mobility*. [3]The promotion of a teacher to the position of principal is an example of upward mobility, and demotion from principal to teacher is downward mobility.

Textbook authors, then, often do more than provide context clues: they set off their definitions in *italic* or **boldface** type, as above. When they take the time to define and illustrate a word, you should assume that the material is important enough to learn.

More about textbook definitions and examples appears on pages 230–231 in the "Relationships II" chapter.

CHAPTER REVIEW

In this chapter, you learned the following:

- To save time when reading, you should try to figure out the meanings of unfamiliar words. You can do so by looking at their *context*—the words surrounding them.
- There are four kinds of context clues: **examples** (marked by words like *for example, for instance, including,* and *such as*); **synonyms** (words that mean the same as unknown words); **antonyms** (words that mean the opposite of unknown words), and **general sense of the sentence** (clues in the sentence or surrounding sentences about what the unknown words might mean).
- Textbook authors typically set off important words in *italic* or **boldface** type and define those words for you, often providing examples as well.

The next chapter—Chapter 2—will introduce you to the most important of all comprehension skills: finding the main idea.

On the Web: If you are using this book in class, you can visit our website for additional practice in understanding vocabulary in context. Go to **www.townsendpress.com** and click on "Learning Center."

REVIEW TEST 1

To review what you've learned in this chapter, answer the following questions by filling in the blank or writing the letter of the correct answer.

1. By using ________________________ to understand the meaning of unfamiliar words, you can save time when reading and help make the words part of your working vocabulary.

_____ 2. In the sentence below, which type of context clue is used for the italicized word?

A. example B. synonym C. antonym

Years ago, high-school boys *aspired* (ə-spīrd′) to be star athletes and high-school girls wished to be popular; neither wanted to be brilliant students.

_____ 3. In the sentence below, which type of context clue is used for the italicized word?

A. example B. synonym C. antonym

In happy couples, each partner both brings and seeks *assets* (ăs′ĕts′); men typically offer status and seek attractiveness; women more often do the reverse.

_____ 4. In the sentence below, which type of context clue is used for the italicized word?

A. example B. synonym C. antonym

Many students are simply *passive* (păs′ĭv) during lectures, but it is more productive to be active, taking notes and asking yourself questions about what is being said.

5. When textbook authors introduce a new word, they often set it off in *italic* or **boldface** type. They also define the word and usually follow it with ________________________ that help make the meaning of the word clear.

REVIEW TEST 2

A. Look at the cartoon below, and then answer the questions that follow.

"Last time the nurse berated me because I'd gained ten pounds. If you promise not to scold me, I'll get on the scale."

_____ 1. Using the context clues in the cartoon, write the letter of the best meaning of *berated* (bĭ-rā′tĭd) in the space provided.

A. complimented B. ignored C. criticized

_____ 2. What kind of context clue helps you understand the meaning of the cartoon?

A. Examples clue B. Synonym clue C. Antonym clue

B. Using context clues for help, write, in the space provided, the letter of the best meaning for each italicized word.

_____ 3. Because of residential segregation, schools in urban areas are often *predominantly* (prĭ-dŏm′ə-nənt-lē) black while those in the suburbs are mostly white.

A. in small part
B. reasonably
C. hopefully
D. mainly

_____ 4. After the funeral, the widow's friends were very *solicitous* (sə-lĭs′ĭ-təs) —they came to see her each day and took turns calling every evening to be sure she was all right.

A. bold
B. concerned
C. annoyed
D. careless

_____ 5. When several members of the president's staff were charged with various crimes, the public's confidence in the government *eroded* (ĭ-rōd′ĭd). Once public trust wears down, it is difficult to rebuild.

A. deteriorated
C. grew
B. healed
D. repeated

C. Using context clues for help, write the definition for each italicized word. Then write the letter of the definition in the space provided. Choose from the definitions in the box below. Each definition will be used once.

A. by chance	B. continuous	C. insulting
D. lack of essentials	E. sociable	

_____ 6. *Deprivation* in early life—poor food, inadequate health care, insufficient education—may be hard to overcome later on.

Deprivation (dĕp′rə-vā′shən) means _______________.

_____ 7. Little Amanda hid shyly behind her mother when she met new people, yet her twin brother, Adam, was very *gregarious.*

Gregarious (grĭ-gâr′ē-əs) means _______________.

_____ 8. During the argument, the angry woman called her husband such *derogatory* names as "idiot" and "fool."

Derogatory (dĭ-rŏg′ə-tôr′ē) means _______________.

_____ 9. The noise in the nursery school classroom was *incessant;* the crying, laughing, and yelling never stopped for a second.

Incessant (ĭn-sĕs′ənt) means _______________.

_____ 10. No one knows how humans acquired the concept of cooking food, but their first experience of cooking was probably *fortuitous;* very likely, some meat fell into a fire by accident.

Fortuitous (fôr-to͞o′ĭ-təs) means _______________.

REVIEW TEST 3

A. Use context clues to figure out the meaning of the italicized word in each of the following sentences, and write your definition in the space provided.

1. Freshmen are often *naive* about college at first, but by their second semester they are usually quite sophisticated in the ways of their new school.

   Naive (nä-ēv′) means ______________________________.

2. If you express yourself clearly the first time you say something, you should not have to *reiterate* it a second time.

   Reiterate (rē-ĭt′ə-rāt′) means ______________________________.

3. The physician could only *conjecture* about the cause of the bad bruise on the unconscious man's head.

   Conjecture (kən-jĕk′chər) means ______________________________.

4. The lawyer tried to confuse the jury by bringing in many facts that weren't *pertinent* to the case.

   Pertinent (pûr′tn-ənt) means ______________________________.

5. When the economy is troubled and weak, the president of the country takes the blame; however, when the economy is *robust*, the president gets the credit.

   Robust (rō-bŭst′) means ______________________________.

B. Use context clues to figure out the meanings of the italicized words in the following textbook passages. Write your definitions in the spaces provided.

[1]Divorce, death, and demands on family members' time can isolate senior citizens, producing deep loneliness which then *adversely* affects their health. [2]Increasingly, doctors are recommending that lonely older Americans acquire pets to help halt their slide into despair, which is *debilitating* physically as well as mentally. [3]Dogs, cats, parakeets, and other sociable pets can provide seniors with companionship. [4]And caring for their dependent pets makes senior citizens feel appreciated and needed—an important factor in preventing *despondency*. [5]Both pets and their owners win in this relationship.

6. *Adversely* (ăd-vûrs′lē) means ______________________________.

7. *Debilitating* (dĭ-bĭl′ĭ-tāt′ĭng) means ______________________________.

8. *Despondency* (dĭ-spŏn′dən-sē) means ______________________________.

[1]One writer, using a *pseudonym* instead of his real name, mailed a typewritten copy of Jerzy Kosinski's novel *Steps* to twenty-eight major publishers and literary agencies. [2]All rejected it, including Random House, which had published the book ten years before and watched it win the National Book Award and sell more than 400,000 copies. [3]The novel came closest to being accepted by Houghton Mifflin, publisher of three other Kosinski novels. [4]"Several of us read your untitled novel here with admiration for writing and style. [5]Jerzy Kosinski comes to mind as a point of comparison.... [6]The drawback to the manuscript, as it stands, is that it doesn't add up to a satisfactory whole." [7]This example is not unusual. [8]Editors' *assessments* of manuscripts can reveal surprising errors and unreliability.

9. *Pseudonym* (so͞od′n-ĭm′) means ______________________.

10. *Assessments* (ə-sĕs′mənts) means ______________________.

REVIEW TEST 4

Here is a chance to apply the skill of understanding vocabulary in context to a full-length selection. In the following article, Sara Hansen suggests a simple way to stay healthy. After reading the selection, answer the vocabulary questions that follow.

Words to Watch

Below are some words in the reading that do not have strong context support. Each word is followed by the number of the paragraph in which it appears and its meaning there. These words are indicated in the article by a small circle (°).

correlation (2): relationship
balk at (3): resist
prone to (3): likely to be affected by
entities (5): creatures
innocuous (8): harmless
lurking (10): lying in wait
hygiene (15): cleanliness

ALL WASHED UP?

Sara Hansen

1 If you've heard it once, you've heard it a thousand times: "Did you wash your hands?" Warnings about the need for hand-washing are given regularly, usually by parents, but proliferate at certain times of year—for example, you'll hear them more often in cold and flu season. The sad truth, though, is that frequent hand-washing is right up there with flossing your teeth on the list of "Things You Know You Ought to Do—but Probably Don't."

2 Why "probably don't"? Research has uncovered a surprising truth: Even though most people have heard that there's a correlation° between hand-washing and staying healthy, they still don't wash their hands thoroughly—or frequently—enough. In fact, the American Society of Microbiology and the Soap and Detergent Association, in a recent study, discovered that 23% of adults observed in public restrooms did not bother to wash their hands at all. Furthermore, those that do wash their hands spend only a few seconds on this activity—insufficient time for the hand-washing to do any good.

3 It's understandable that adults balk° a little at the idea that they should lather up on a regular basis. After all, we consider ourselves fastidious adults, not small children prone to° the sticky messes of childhood. We are not usually smeared with jelly or melted chocolate; we rarely play in the mud. Many adults quite reasonably think, "I'll wash my hands when they need washing—when they're dirty."

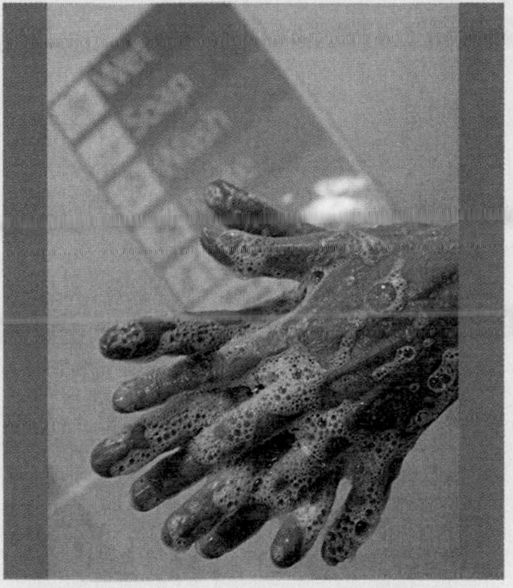

4 Unfortunately, "dirty" is defined by many people as "showing visible signs of dirt." The fact is that in terms of spreading disease, invisible "dirt" is far more dangerous than, say, a streak of mud. In order to understand why, a quick biology lesson is in order.

5 In general, infectious diseases are spread when bacteria and viruses—those microscopic entities° that we lump into the category of "germs"—are transmitted from one person to another. There are three basic ways by which germs can travel:

6 **Direct contact.** Just a few examples of direct contact are shaking hands, kissing, and hugging. Any sort of touching qualifies as direct contact.

7 Most people realize that if they have direct contact with a person who has a cold, they had better wash their hands quickly to avoid being contaminated with that person's cold germs. The problem with that reasoning is that it assumes that healthy people cannot infect you. The exact opposite is true; when you shake hands (or otherwise have direct contact) with those healthy people, you are, in effect, having direct contact with all the people *they* have had recent contact with, and all the people *those* people have had contact with, and on and on. You have no way of knowing whether your healthy friend is transferring someone else's disease-causing germs to you.

8 **Airborne transmission.** Infection can also be spread through the very air we breathe. Germs can hang in the air or be dispersed as moisture droplets—by a cough, a sneeze, or merely the movement of an object. Something as seemingly innocuous° as the sleeve on your doctor's white coat could be laden with dangerous germs, left there by previous patients.

9 **Indirect contact.** Most sneakily of all, germs can survive on an inanimate object, waiting to be picked up by the next person who touches that object. Can you imagine how many such objects you touch over the course of an average day? A few that come to mind instantly are tabletops, pens, phones, ATMs, doorknobs, toilets, light switches, money, supermarket carts, elevator buttons, parking meters, staplers, computer keyboards, and books. Each of those objects and hundreds more may be full of germs capable of causing anything from the common cold to chicken pox to pneumonia. And don't forget how insidious germs are. Because they are invisible to the naked eye, the surface that they inhabit may well look perfectly clean.

10 So now let's return to our original subject: hand-washing. Washing our hands frequently and doing it thoroughly (more on that later), according to the federal Centers for Disease Control and Prevention, is the single most effective way we have of protecting ourselves against the thousands of germs lurking° in our daily environment. Actually, the fact that the germs end up on our hands is not the real problem; it's what we *do* with our hands that puts us in peril. And what is that? We touch our faces—regularly and frequently, without even being aware we are doing it. We rub our eyes, scratch our noses, chew our nails, wipe lipstick off our teeth, and rest our chins on our fists, giving the germs on our hands a convenient bridge directly into our eyes, noses, and mouths, and then straight into our bloodstreams. People who study disease estimate that more than 80 percent of common illnesses develop as a result of face-touching with germ-laden hands.

11 Now that you know *why* hand-washing is so crucial, let's talk about *how*. Yes, you've been washing your hands since you were a toddler, but no, "how to wash your hands" is not a really stupid topic. Too many of us think that a

swipe under the faucet is sufficient. But those few seconds under a faucet are simply not enough to get rid of those pesky germs. Instead, here is what you have to do:

12 **1. Use hot water.** Why hot water? You may have heard "to kill the germs." However, that's not the reason; water hot enough to kill germs would be too hot for you to touch. But there are two genuine reasons. One is that hot water does a better job than cold of dissolving the natural oils on your skin that trap bacteria. The second reason is simply that hot water feels better than cold, leading you to spend more time washing.

13 **2. Use lots of soap, and take time to work up a good lather.** Again, you have probably heard that soap "kills germs." But again, that's not true (unless it's an "antibacterial" soap, and even then, it won't kill viruses). The actual function of soap is to form a thin layer around germs so they can be easily dislodged from your skin. In order to get the full effect, you need plenty of soap, plenty of lather (scrub for a minimum of 20 seconds—some experts say "Long enough to recite the ABCs twice"), and plenty of hot water to wash all the trapped germs down the drain.

14 (By the way, you've undoubtedly seen the many "hand sanitizers" for sale. These small bottles of alcohol-based liquid, conveniently sized for pocket or purse, can be helpful if you need to disinfect your hands and you don't have access to soap and water. But plain old soap-and-water washing is still the most effective, and certainly the cheapest, way of insuring that your hands are clean.)

15 **3. Dry your hands.** The final step in good hand-washing hygiene° is to dry your hands and then exit the washing area without re-contaminating yourself. After all, you've just spent at least 20 seconds carefully washing up. What will happen when you use your nice clean hands to turn off the water faucet and grab the door handle to exit the restroom? That's right—you will pick up brand new germs, many of them left there by people who did not wash *their* hands properly. The solution is simple: grab a paper towel before you turn off the faucet. Use the towel to both turn off the faucet and open the door; then dispose of the towel. Many public restrooms have trash cans right outside the door for this very purpose.

16 How often should you wash your hands? There are some obvious times of day—after you use the restroom, before eating, and before preparing food. But think back to the earlier discussion of where and how we pick up germs, and you'll realize that the more frequently you wash (within reason, of course), the better. In particular, find time to wash up whenever you've been in an area where many people gather, or when you've been handling objects that have been touched by lots of people. Spending a few extra minutes each day washing your hands—and doing it right—will almost certainly save you from the discomfort and inconvenience of preventable illnesses.

Vocabulary Questions

Use context clues to help you decide on the best definition for each italicized word. Then, on the answer line, write the letter of each choice.

_____ 1. In the sentence below, the word *proliferate* (prə-lĭf′ə-rāt′) means

A. slow down.
B. increase.
C. become more surprising.
D. are ignored.

"Warnings about the need for hand-washing are given regularly, usually by parents, but proliferate at certain times of year—for example, you'll hear them more often in cold and flu season." (Paragraph 1)

_____ 2. In the excerpt below, the word *insufficient* (ĭn′sə-fĭsh′ənt) means

A. not enough.
B. more than enough.
C. proper.
D. the best.

". . . most people . . . still don't wash their hands thoroughly—or frequently—enough. . . . Furthermore, those that do wash their hands spend only a few seconds on this activity—insufficient time for the hand-washing to do any good." (Paragraph 2)

_____ 3. In the excerpt below, the word *fastidious* (fă-stĭd′ē-əs) means

A. sloppy.
B. hard-working.
C. successful.
D. fussy about cleanliness.

"It's understandable that adults balk a little at the idea that they should lather up on a regular basis. After all, we consider ourselves fastidious adults, not small children prone to the sticky messes of childhood. We are not usually smeared with jelly or melted chocolate; we rarely play in the mud." (Paragraph 3)

_____ 4. In the sentence below, the word *contaminated* (kən-tăm′ə-nā′tĭd) means

A. surprised.
B. cured.
C. softened.
D. infected.

"Most people realize that if they have direct contact with a person who has a cold, they had better wash their hands quickly to avoid being contaminated with that person's cold germs." (Paragraph 7)

_____ 5. In the sentence below, the word *dispersed* (dĭ-spûrst′) means

A. weakened.
B. described.
C. distributed.
D. remembered.

"Infection can also be spread through the very air we breathe. Germs can be suspended in the air or dispersed as moisture droplets—by a cough, a sneeze, or merely the movement of an object." (Paragraph 8)

______ 6. In the sentence below, the word *laden* (lād′n) means

A. cleansed. C. colored.
B. loaded. D. removed.

"Something as seemingly innocuous as the sleeve on your doctor's white coat could be laden with dangerous germs, left there by previous patients." (Paragraph 8)

______ 7. In the excerpt below, the word *inanimate* (ĭn-ăn′ə-mĭt) means

A. boring. C. very small.
B. non-living. D. wooden.

"Most sneakily of all, germs can survive on an inanimate object, waiting to be picked up by the next person who touches that object. Can you imagine how many such objects you touch over the course of an average day? A few that come to mind instantly are tabletops, pens, phones, ATMs, doorknobs, toilets, light switches, money, supermarket carts, elevator buttons, parking meters, staplers, computer keyboards, and books." (Paragraph 9)

______ 8. In the excerpt below, the word *insidious* (ĭn-sĭd′ē-əs) means

A. sneaky. C. noticeable.
B. violent. D. avoidable.

"And don't forget how insidious germs are. Because they are invisible to the naked eye, the surface that they inhabit may well look perfectly clean." (Paragraph 9)

______ 9. In the sentence below, the word *peril* (pĕr′əl) means

A. a state of disbelief. C. a learning situation.
B. a state of safety. D. a dangerous situation.

"Actually, the fact that the germs end up on our hands is not the real problem; it's what we *do* with our hands that puts us in peril." (Paragraph 10)

______ 10. In the excerpt below, the word *dislodged* (dĭs-lŏjd′) means

A. recognized. C. coated.
B. expanded. D. removed.

"The actual function of soap is to form a thin layer around germs so they can be easily dislodged from your skin. In order to get the full effect, you need plenty of soap, plenty of lather (scrub for a minimum of 20 seconds—some experts say 'Long enough to recite the ABCs twice'), and plenty of hot water to wash all the trapped germs down the drain." (Paragraph 13)

Discussion Questions

1. About how many times a day—and for how long—do you usually wash your hands? Do you think your hand-washing habits will change as a result of reading this selection? Why or why not?

2. Do you agree with Hansen's conclusion that spending more time every day washing your hands will "almost certainly" save you from contracting preventable illnesses? Or are there other factors to take into consideration? Explain.

3. In the course of the selection, Hansen refutes the belief that hot water kills germs. What are some other health theories you've heard that may or may not be true? How could you find out whether or not they *are* true?

4. Hansen points out that frequent hand-washing and flossing one's teeth are two things that people know they ought to do, but probably don't. Can you add some more examples to this list? What do you think are the main reasons people don't do what they should when it comes to questions of health?

Note: Writing assignments for this selection appear on page 696.

Check Your Performance — VOCABULARY IN CONTEXT

Activity	*Number Right*	*Points*		*Score*
Review Test 1 (5 items)	______	× 2	=	______
Review Test 2 (10 items)	______	× 3	=	______
Review Test 3 (10 items)	______	× 3	=	______
Review Test 4 (10 items)	______	× 3	=	______
		TOTAL SCORE	=	______%

Enter your total score into the **Reading Performance Chart: Review Tests** on the inside back cover.

Name ______________________________ Date __________

Section __________ SCORE: (Number correct) _______ x 10 = _______ %

VOCABULARY IN CONTEXT: Mastery Test 1

A. Look at the cartoon below, and then answer the question that follows.

"Your head is going to hurt even more when you get an exorbitant bill from the hospital."

______ 1. Using the context clues in the cartoon, write the letter of the meaning of *exorbitant* (ĭg-zôr′bĭ-tənt) in the space provided.

A. too high B. reasonable C. discounted

B. For each item below, underline the **examples** that suggest the meaning of the italicized word. Then, on the answer line, write the letter of the meaning of that word.

______ 2. We all have our *foibles* (foi′bəlz). Lily, for instance, eats with her mouth open; Earl cracks his knuckles; and Jenelle calls everyone "honey."

A. emotional disturbances C. hobbies
B. minor faults D. good points

______ 3. The company president has an *austere* (ô-stîr′) office: it is furnished with just an ordinary metal desk, an armless chair, and a file cabinet.

A. very plain C. luxurious
B. unclean D. large and roomy

______ 4. If you have a taste for the *macabre* (mə-kä′brə), visit the Chamber of Horrors, an exhibit at Madame Tussaud's Wax Museum in London that features ax murderers, poisoners, and stranglers.

A. gruesome C. historic
B. artistic D. unknown

(Continues on next page)

C. Each item below includes a word or words that are a **synonym** of the italicized word. Write the synonym of the italicized word in the space provided.

_______________ 5. When Kim needed to have a tooth pulled, her boyfriend came along to *bolster* (bōl′stər) her courage. But she was the one who had to support him—he fainted dead away.

_______________ 6. To *forestall* (fôr-stôl′) the need for last-minute cramming, keep up with each course throughout the term. Keeping up will also prevent "test anxiety."

D. Each item below includes a word or words that are an **antonym** of the italicized word. Underline the antonym of each italicized word. Then, on the answer line, write the letter of the meaning of the italicized word.

_____ 7. Automobiles *depreciate* (dĭ-prē′shē-āt′) sharply in a short time. In contrast, real estate will typically increase in value.

A. rust
B. wear out
C. lose value
D. drive

_____ 8. Test results sometimes show that a person who has only a *tenuous* (tĕn′yo͞o-əs) grasp of mathematics nevertheless has very strong verbal abilities.

A. inborn
B. weak
C. acquired
D. surprising

E. Use the **general sense of each sentence** to figure out the meaning of each italicized word. Then, on the answer line, write the letter of the meaning of the italicized word.

_____ 9. Because she enjoyed her work, the new job offer left Elena in a *quandary* (kwŏn′də-rē). She couldn't decide what to do.

A. state of uncertainty
B. state of fear
C. state of anger
D. state of confidence

_____ 10. There is a growing *disparity* (dĭ-spăr′ĭ-tē) between the rich and the poor in the United States. The richest 20 percent of Americans own more than 85 percent of all the nation's wealth.

A. mistrust
B. understanding
C. inequality
D. violence

Name ______________________________ Date __________

Section __________ SCORE: (Number correct) ______ x 10 = ______ %

VOCABULARY IN CONTEXT: Mastery Test 2

A. Look at the cartoon below, and then answer the question that follows.

"I have no motivation to go on a diet, but if I can gain 50 pounds, that will give me the incentive I need."

_____ 1. Using the context clues in the cartoon, write the letter of the meaning of *incentive* (ĭn-sĕn′tĭv) in the space provided.
A. intelligence B. encouragement C. method

B. For each item below, underline the **examples** that suggest the meaning of the italicized word. Then, on the answer line, write the letter of the meaning of that word.

_____ 2. The employees have put up *facetious* (fə-sē′shəs) signs by their desks, such as "A clean desk is the sign of a sick mind," "Don't rush me; I get paid by the hour," and "If you don't believe the dead come back to life, you should see this place at five o'clock."
A. useful
B. humorous
C. expensive
D. insulting

_____ 3. Immigrants to the United States were once urged to *assimilate* (ə-sĭm′ə-lāt′)—to speak only English, to wear American clothes, to eat American food, to adopt American customs.
A. succeed
B. work hard
C. leave
D. blend in

(Continues on next page)

C. Each item below includes a word or words that are a **synonym** of the italicized word. Write the synonym of the italicized word in the space provided.

______________ 4. When Reba lost fifty pounds, there was not just a change in her appearance. Her personality also underwent a *metamorphosis* (mĕt′ə-môr′fə-sĭs)—she became much more outgoing.

______________ 5. Some drivers *circumvented* (sûr′kəm-vĕnt′ĭd) the traffic jam at the bridge. They avoided the tie-up by taking the turnoff a mile back.

D. Each item below includes a word or words that are an **antonym** of the italicized word. Underline the antonym of each italicized word. Then, on the answer line, write the letter of the meaning of the italicized word.

______ 6. Most offices expect employees to wear clothing that is fairly quiet and conservative, so save your *flamboyant* (flăm-boi′ənt) clothes for when you're out with friends.

A. flashy
B. old-fashioned
C. expensive
D. new

______ 7. Someone from outside the group is needed to give an *objective* (əb-jĕk′tĭv) viewpoint. Anyone from the group would be too biased.

A. thoughtless
B. open-minded
C. favorable
D. useful

______ 8. Many people still believe that rubbing butter on a burn will relieve it. However, that practice can actually *exacerbate* (ĭg-zăs′ər-bāt′) the injury.

A. soothe
B. worsen
C. protect
D. cover

E. Use the **general sense of each sentence** to figure out the meaning of each italicized word. Then, on the answer line, write the letter of the meaning of the italicized word.

______ 9. "You keep wandering off into thoughts that are not *germane* (jər-mān′) to your topic," the instructor wrote on my paper. "You must learn to stick to the point."

A. grammatically correct
B. damaging
C. interesting
D. related

______ 10. Stephen King has been a very *prolific* (prə-lĭf′ĭk) writer, sometimes completing two long novels in a single year.

A. secret
B. very productive
C. unimportant
D. very frightening

Name ______________________________ Date __________

Section __________ SCORE: (Number correct) ______ x 10 = ______ %

VOCABULARY IN CONTEXT: Mastery Test 3

A. Look at the cartoon below, and then answer the question that follows.

"Knock it off, honey! I'm trying to learn how to revitalize our relationship!"

_____ 1. Using the context clues in the cartoon, write the letter of the meaning of *revitalize* (re-vīt′l-īz′) in the space provided.
A. put up with B. put an end to C. bring new life to

B. Using context clues for help, write, in the space provided, the letter of the best meaning for each italicized word.

_____ 2. President Calvin Coolidge was so *reticent* (rĕt′ĭ-sənt) that he was nicknamed "Silent Cal."
A. powerful as a speaker C. uncommunicative
B. popular D. well-known

_____ 3. The *paramount* (păr′ə-mount′) duty of the physician is to do no harm. Everything else—even healing—must take second place.
A. successful C. mysterious
B. first D. least

_____ 4. Ideas about *decorum* (dĭ-kôr′əm) change greatly over time. In our society, for instance, until relatively recently, polite people did not appear bareheaded on the street, and a man always tipped his hat to a woman.
A. beauty C. proper behavior
B. physical fitness D. style

(Continues on next page)

_____ 5. The expert witness in the lawsuit chose his words with great care. He didn't want anyone to *misconstrue* (mĭs′kən-stro͞o′) his statements.

A. repeat
B. recall
C. accept
D. misinterpret

_____ 6. The fatty food was so *repugnant* (rĭ-pŭg′nənt) to Fran that she could not force herself to finish the meal.

A. amusing
B. new
C. disgusting
D. surprising

_____ 7. When reporters asked if he would be a mayoral candidate again, the mayor would only *equivocate* (ĭ-kwĭv′ə-kāt′), saying, "Ladies and gentlemen, I still feel that public service is a high calling."

A. predict
B. be purposely unclear
C. clearly deny
D. forget

_____ 8. By forming a *coalition* (kō′ə-lĭsh′ən), the small political parties gained more power in the government than they each had separately.

A. separation
B. publication
C. competition
D. partnership

_____ 9. Some people seek *vicarious* (vī-kâr′ē-əs) experiences. For example, the "stage mother" claims success through her child, and the "peeping Tom," who is emotionally disturbed, gets sexual pleasure from spying on others.

A. varied
B. ordinary
C. indirect
D. inexpensive

_____ 10. The *noxious* (nŏk′shəs) fumes from the chemical spill made people so ill that some had to go to the hospital.

A. permanent
B. silent
C. mild
D. unhealthy

Name ______________________________ Date __________

Section ___________ SCORE: (Number correct) _______ x 10 = _______ %

VOCABULARY IN CONTEXT: Mastery Test 4

Using context clues for help, write, in the space provided, the letter of the best meaning for each italicized word. Note that all of the sentences have been taken from college textbooks.

_____ 1. To carry out his economic programs, Roosevelt had to *contend* (kən-tĕnd′) with a Supreme Court that was deeply opposed to them.

A. travel
B. surrender
C. struggle
D. join

_____ 2. Being unable to write clearly is a *liability* (lī′ə bĭl′ĭ tē) in a business career, in which one must often express opinions and ideas in writing.

A. drawback
B. surprise
C. necessity
D. feature

_____ 3. The idea that off-track betting will work in Alaska because it works in New York is a questionable *analogy* (ə-năl′ə-jē). New York and Alaska may not be alike when it comes to off-track betting.

A. comparison
B. purpose
C. contrast
D. requirement

_____ 4. To *facilitate* (fə-sĭl′ĭ-tāt′) the college admission process, many application forms have been shortened and simplified, and they can be posted on a website, sent by e-mail, or faxed.

A. begin
B. frustrate
C. complicate
D. make easier

_____ 5. There is an *optimum* (ŏp′tə-məm) way to approach each kind of exam question. For a multiple-choice item, for example, first eliminate any clearly wrong answers. For an essay question, jot down an outline first.

A. inconvenient
B. best
C. annoying
D. time-consuming

_____ 6. Studies indicate that a *predisposition* (prē′dĭs-pə-zĭsh′ən) to schizophrenia is inherited. People who are schizophrenic are more likely than others to have schizophrenic children.

A. tendency
B. understanding
C. fear
D. avoidance

_____ 7. By giving military aid to dictatorships in Latin America, the United States has seemed to *sanction* (săngk′shən) their cruel policies.

A. criticize
B. approve of
C. remember
D. create

(Continues on next page)

_____ 8. A *provocative* (prə-vŏk′ə-tĭv) question can be an effective way to open an essay. Students have begun essays with such interesting questions as "What do you think your name means?" and "How long do you think it would take you to count to one billion?"

A. funny
B. arousing interest
C. unanswerable
D. very brief

_____ 9. Manic depression is an emotional disorder in which the patient alternates between feeling delightfully *euphoric* (yo͞o-fôr′ĭk) and being plunged into deep gloom.

A. overjoyed
B. bored
C. exhausted
D. curious

_____ 10. Although relatively few people in the United States lack food desperately, about 36,000,000 American people—approximately 14 percent of the population—live in what is officially *designated* (dĕz′ĭg-nāt′ĭd) as poverty.

A. predicted
B. designed
C. labeled
D. forgotten

Name ______________________ Date ________

Section __________ SCORE: (Number correct) ______ x 10 = ______ %

VOCABULARY IN CONTEXT: Mastery Test 5

A. Using context clues for help, write, in the space provided, the letter of the best meaning for each italicized word. Note that all of the sentences have been taken from college textbooks.

_____ 1. To reduce pollution that causes global warming, many countries are *converting* (kən-vûrt′ĭng) to non-polluting energy sources, such as solar and wind power.

A. growing
B. comparing
C. continuing
D. changing

_____ 2. Marriages are rarely *static* (stăt′ĭk). They continually change as the partners experience and adjust to their own life tasks.

A. successful
B. serious
C. unchanging
D. violent

_____ 3. We now know that two centers in the brain are especially important in controlling hunger. One center *stimulates* (stĭm′yə-lāts′) eating; the other reduces the feeling of hunger.

A. stops
B. finds
C. knows
D. encourages

_____ 4. Those romantic cigarette ads don't exactly claim in words that smoking will make you gorgeous and sexy and give you an exciting life, but that is the *implicit* (ĭm-plĭs′ĭt) message.

A. unfriendly
B. unstated
C. unbelievable
D. healthy

_____ 5. Minor traffic *infractions* (ĭn-frăk′shəns), such as parking in a no-parking zone, are punished by a fine; but a major offense such as drunk driving can put you in jail.

A. violations
B. laws
C. exceptions
D. explanations

(Continues on next page)

B. Use context clues to figure out the meaning of the italicized word in each of the following textbook items. Then write your definition in the space provided.

6. The *prime* sources of protein are animal products, including meat, fish, eggs, milk, and cheese. In addition, some plants, such as soybeans, contain useful proteins.

   Prime (prīm) means ________________________________.

7. An infant learns very quickly to *differentiate* his or her main caretaker from everyone else.

   Differentiate (dĭf′ə-rĕn′shē-āt′) means ________________________.

8. San Quentin prison, which was designed to hold 2,700 prisoners, is so short of space that it *confines* its 5,200 inmates to their cells except for meals and showers.

   Confines (kən-fīnz′) means ______________________________.

9. In *retrospect*, elderly and middle-aged people often conclude that they should have spent more time with their children.

   Retrospect (rĕt′rə-spĕkt′) means ___________________________.

10. Cultural standards influence advertising. For instance, one French ad showed a man's bare arm being grasped by a woman's hand. That ad was *modified* for display in Saudi Arabia. The Saudi version clothed the man's arm in a dark suit sleeve and showed the woman's hand just brushing it.

    Modified (mŏd′ə-fīd′) means ____________________________.

Name ______________________________ Date __________

Section ____________ SCORE: (Number correct) ______ x 10 = ______ %

VOCABULARY IN CONTEXT: Mastery Test 6

A. Five words are **boldfaced** in the textbook passage below. Write the definition for each boldfaced word, choosing from the definitions in the box. Then write the letter of the definition in the space provided.

Be sure to read the entire passage before making your choices. Note that five definitions will be left over.

A. adjust	B. asked about	C. beginning	D. behave
E. death	F. denied	G. disaster	H. filled
I. put forth as a theory	J. said to be caused by		

[1]About 65 million years ago, more than half of all plant and animal species died out. [2]The dinosaurs met their **demise** then, along with large numbers of other animal and plant groups, both terrestrial and marine. [3]Equally important, of course, is the fact that many species survived the disaster. [4]Human beings are descended from these survivors. [5]Perhaps this fact explains why an event that occurred 65 million years ago has captured the interest of so many people. [6]The extinction of the great reptiles is generally **attributed to** this group's inability to **adapt** to some basic change in environmental conditions. [7]What **catastrophe** could have triggered the sudden extinction of the dinosaurs—the most successful group of land animals ever to have lived?

[8]One modern view proposes that about 65 million years ago, a large asteroid or comet about 10 kilometers in diameter collided with the Earth. [9]The impact of such a body would have produced an overwhelming cloud of dust. [10]For many months, the dust-laden atmosphere would have greatly restricted the amount of sunlight that penetrated to the Earth's surface. [11]Without sunlight for plant growth, delicate food chains would collapse. [12]It is further **hypothesized** that large dinosaurs would be affected more negatively by this chain of events than would smaller life forms. [13]In addition, acid rains and global fires may have added to the environmental disaster. [14]It is estimated that when the sunlight returned, more than half of the species on Earth had become extinct.

_____ 1. *Demise* (dĭ-mīz′) means ______________________________.

_____ 2. *Attributed to* (ə-trĭb′yo͞ot-ĭd to͞o) means ______________________________.

_____ 3. *Adapt* (ə-dăpt′) means ______________________________.

_____ 4. *Catastrophe* (kə-tăs′trə-fē) means ______________________________.

_____ 5. *Hypothesized* (hī-pŏth′ĭ-sīzd′) means ______________________________.

(Continues on next page)

B. Five words are **boldfaced** in the textbook passage below. Write the definition for each boldfaced word, choosing from the definitions in the box. Also, write the letter of the definition in the space provided.

Be sure to read the entire passage before making your choices. Note that five definitions will be left over.

A. excited	B. great anger	C. had a strong desire	D. ignored
E. loose	F. seen	G. something very popular	H. straight
I. strict	J. unequaled		

[1]Thanks to the prosperity of the 1920s, Americans had more money for leisure activities than ever before. [2]The 1920s were a decade of contrasts, and popular fiction was no exception. [3]People wanted virtuous heroes and old-time value in their fiction, but a lot of them also wanted to be **titillated**. [4]One of the major publishing trends of the 1920s was the boom in "confession magazines." [5]The rise of the city, the liberated woman, and the impact of the movie industry all relaxed the **stern** Victorian moral standards. [6]Into the vacuum came the confession magazine—borderline pornography with stories of romantic success and failure, divorce, fantasy, and adultery. [7]Writers survived the cuts of the censors by expressing their stories as moral lessons advising readers to avoid similar mistakes in their own lives.

[8]Another **rage** of the 1920s was spectator sports. [9]Because the country **yearned** for individual heroes to stand out larger than life in an increasingly impersonal, organized society, prize-fighting enjoyed a huge following, especially in the heavyweight division, where hard punchers like Jack Dempsey became national idols. [10]Team sports flourished in colleges and high schools, but even then Americans focused on individual superstars, people whose talents or personalities earned them a cult following. [11]Notre Dame emerged as a college football powerhouse in the 1920s, but it was head coach Knute Rockne and his "pep talks" on dedication and persistence which became part of the fabric of American popular culture.

[12]Baseball was even more popular than football. [13]Fans spent countless hours of calculating, memorizing, and quizzing one another on baseball statistics. [14]The sport's superstar was George Herman "Babe" Ruth, the "Sultan of Swat." [15]The public loved Ruth for his **unparalleled** skills as well as his personal weaknesses. [16]While hitting or pitching as nobody had before, Ruth was also known for his huge appetite and his capacity to drink himself into a stupor. [17]His beer belly, like his swing, was unique.

_____ 6. *Titillated* (tĭt′l-āt′ĭd) means ______________________________.

_____ 7. *Stern* (stûrn) means ______________________________.

_____ 8. *Rage* (rāj′) means ______________________________.

_____ 9. *Yearned* (yûrnd) means ______________________________.

_____ 10. *Unparalleled* (ŭn-păr′ə-lĕld′) means ______________________________.

2 Main Ideas

What Is the Main Idea?

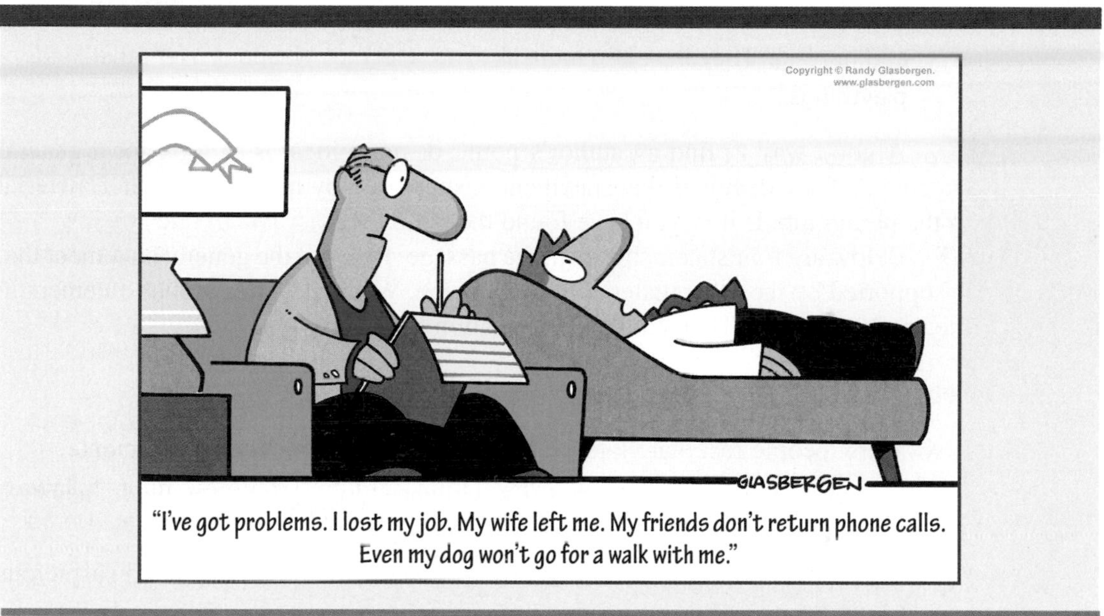

"I've got problems. I lost my job. My wife left me. My friends don't return phone calls. Even my dog won't go for a walk with me."

"What's the point?" You've probably heard these words before. It's a question people ask when they want to know the main idea that someone is trying to express. The same question can guide you as you read. Recognizing the **main idea**, or point, is the most important key to good comprehension. Sometimes a main idea is immediately clear, as in the above cartoon. The point—that the man on the couch has problems—is well supported by the statements about his job, wife, friends, and dog.

To find the main idea of a reading selection, ask yourself, "What's the point the author is trying to make?" For instance, read the paragraph on the following page, asking yourself as you do, "What is the author's point?"

[1]Many people feel that violence on television is harmless entertainment. [2]However, we now know that TV violence does affect people in negative ways. [3]One study showed that frequent TV watchers are more fearful and suspicious of others. [4]They try to protect themselves from the outside world with extra locks on the doors, alarm systems, guard dogs, and guns. [5]In addition, that same study showed that heavy TV watchers are less upset about real-life violence than non-TV watchers. [6]It seems that the constant violence they see on TV makes them less sensitive to the real thing. [7]Another study, of a group of children, found that TV violence increases aggressive behavior. [8]Children who watched violent shows were more willing to hurt another child in games where they were given a choice between helping and hurting. [9]They were also more likely to select toy weapons over other kinds of playthings.

A good way to find an author's point, or main idea, is to look for a general statement. Then decide if that statement is supported by most of the other material in the paragraph. If it is, you have found the main idea.

Below are four statements from the passage. Pick out the general statement that is supported by the other material in the passage. Write the letter of that statement in the space provided. Then read the explanation that follows.

Four statements from the passage:

A. Many people feel that violence on television is harmless entertainment.

B. However, we now know that TV violence does affect people in negative ways.

C. One study showed that frequent TV watchers are more fearful and suspicious of others.

D. They try to protect themselves from the outside world with extra locks on the doors, alarm systems, guard dogs, and guns.

The general statement that expresses the main idea of the passage is _____.

Explanation

Sentence A: The paragraph does not support the idea that TV violence is harmless, so sentence A cannot be the main idea. However, it does introduce the topic of the paragraph: TV violence.

Sentence B: The statement "TV violence does affect people in negative ways" is a general one. And the rest of the passage goes on to describe three negative ways that TV violence affects people. Sentence B, then, is the sentence that expresses the main idea of the passage.

Sentence C: This sentence is about only one study. It is not general enough to include the other studies that are also cited in the paragraph. It is the first supporting idea for the main idea.

Sentence D: This sentence provides detailed evidence for the first supporting idea, which is that frequent TV watchers are more fearful and suspicious of others. It does not cover the other material in the paragraph.

The Main Idea as an "Umbrella" Idea

Think of the main idea as an "umbrella" idea. The main idea is the author's general point; all the other material of the paragraph fits under it. That other material is made up of **supporting details**—specific evidence such as examples, causes, reasons, or facts. The diagram below shows the relationship.

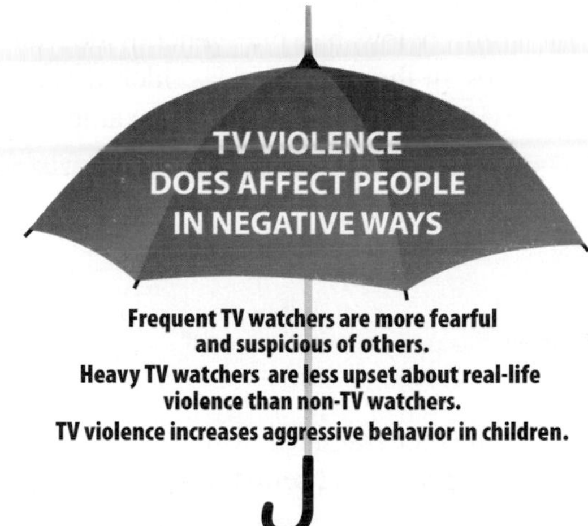

The explanations and activities on the following pages will deepen your understanding of the main idea.

Recognizing a Main Idea

As you read through a passage, you must **think as you read**. If you merely take in words, you will come to the end of the passage without understanding much of what you have read. Reading is an active process, as opposed to watching television, which is passive. You must actively engage your mind, and, as you read, keep asking yourself, "What's the point?" Here are three strategies that will help you find the main idea.

1. Look for **general versus specific ideas**.
2. Use the **topic** to lead you to the main idea.
3. Use **key words** to lead you to the main idea.

Each strategy is explained on the following pages.

1 Look for General versus Specific Ideas

You saw in the paragraph on TV violence that the main idea is a *general* idea supported by *specific* ideas. The following practices will improve your skill at separating general from specific ideas. Learning how to tell the difference between general and specific ideas will help you locate the main idea.

PRACTICE 1

Each group of words below has one general idea and three specific ideas. The general idea includes all the specific ideas. Identify each general idea with a **G** and the specific ideas with an **S**. Look first at the example.

Example

S dishonesty
S greed
G bad qualities
S selfishness

(*Bad qualities* is the general idea which includes three specific types of bad qualities: dishonesty, greed, and selfishness.)

1. ___ handsome
___ appearance
___ well-dressed
___ shabby

2. ___ seafood
___ oysters
___ clams
___ lobster

3. ___ heavy traffic
___ bus not on time
___ alarm didn't go off
___ excuses for being late

4. ___ poor pay
___ mean boss
___ very dull work
___ undesirable job

5. ___ giggling
___ childish behavior
___ tantrums
___ playing peek-a-boo

6. ___ paper cuts
___ minor problems
___ broken nails
___ wrong numbers

7. ___ try to be kinder
___ eat healthier foods
___ go to bed earlier
___ resolutions

8. ___ take stairs instead of elevator
___ ride bike instead of driving
___ exercise opportunities
___ walk instead of riding bus

9. ___ skip breakfast
___ grab a donut mid-morning
___ poor eating habits
___ order supersize portions

10. ___ different goals
___ no common interests
___ dislike each other's friends
___ reasons for breaking up

PRACTICE 2

Write out the answers to each question in the spaces provided. For each question, the answers are specific details that illustrate the general idea, which is underlined.

1. There are many material things in everyday life (appliances, electronic equipment, and the like) that we come to depend upon. What are three things that you would hate to be without?

____

____

____

2. If you were suddenly wealthy, you could hire other people to do tasks that you dislike. What are three specific chores that you'd hand over to somebody else?

____

____

____

3. Most of us enjoy a good movie, but we have different ideas of what makes a film "good." What are three specific qualities that a movie needs in order for you to really like it?

____

____

____

4. We all know people whom we find difficult. Think of a person that you find hard to get along with. Name three specific reasons you find this person difficult.

____

____

____

PRACTICE 3

In the following groups, one statement is the general point, and the other statements are specific support for the point. Identify each point with a **P** and each statement of support with an **S**.

1. ___ The vegetables were soggy and tasteless.
   ___ The chicken was hard to chew.
   ___ The meal was very unpleasant.
   ___ The rolls were rock-hard.

2. ___ The team's best player is averaging over 30 points a game.
   ___ The basketball team is in first place in its division.
   ___ The team has won eight of its first ten games.
   ___ The basketball team is off to a great start.

3. ___ The man doesn't use his turn signals.
   ___ The man drives too fast down narrow residential streets.
   ___ The man is an unsafe driver.
   ___ The man doesn't come to a complete stop at stop signs.

4. ___ Students stay in touch with friends through Facebook and e-mail.
   ___ Students write papers and share class notes online.
   ___ Students do much of their research on the Internet.
   ___ Students have practical uses for computers.

PRACTICE 4

In each of the following groups, one statement is the general point, and the other statements are specific support for the point. Identify each point with a **P** and each statement of support with an **S**.

1. ___ A. Among teenage girls, gossip contributes to bonding.
   ___ B. Political gossip often is leaked to the media as a way of learning how the public is likely to react to a particular policy.
   ___ C. Gossip takes many forms and serves various purposes.
   ___ D. In the business world, gossip can provide insights unavailable through official facts and figures.

2. ___ A. When answering the phone, some people's first words are "Who's this?"
   ___ B. Some people have terrible telephone manners.
   ___ C. Some people never bother to identify themselves when calling someone.
   ___ D. Some people hang up without even saying goodbye.

3. ___ A. Federal law should prohibit banks from giving credit cards to college students.
   ___ B. Credit-card debt is the leading cause of bankruptcy for young Americans.
   ___ C. Taking advantage of the fact that many parents will pay their children's credit-card debts, banks extend excessive credit to students.
   ___ D. When they receive their monthly credit-card bills, many students can pay only the minimum required and so have hefty interest charges on large unpaid amounts.

4. ___ A. Bats are so rarely rabid that a person has a better chance of catching rabies from a cow than from a bat.
   ___ B. Bats, in spite of their bad reputation, are not a danger to human beings.
   ___ C. Bats are afraid of humans and do their best to stay away from them.
   ___ D. Unlike movie vampires, bats do not bite people unless frightened or under attack.

PRACTICE 5

In each of the following groups—all based on textbook selections—one statement is the general point, and the other statements are specific support for the point. Identify each point with a **P** and each statement of support with an **S**.

1. ___ A. Companies that lose lawsuits usually pass the cost along to consumers.
   ___ B. To protect themselves from malpractice suits, doctors now give more patients unneeded tests, which cost hundreds of millions of dollars a year.
   ___ C. The cost of fighting a lawsuit forces some small businesses to close, even when they have successfully defended themselves.
   ___ D. The ever-growing number of lawsuits has had a number of negative consequences.

2. ___ A. Our social roles—whether we're students, employees, visitors, etc.—limit what emotions are acceptable for us to express.
   ___ B. Given the widespread habit of suppressing our emotions, many of us have trouble recognizing what we're really feeling.
   ___ C. Most of us rarely express our deepest emotions because of a variety of factors.
   ___ D. We often hide our emotions rather than display them so as not to seem weak or needy to others.

3. ___ A. Disagreeing parties can accept the status quo, agreeing to just live with the situation as it stands.
   ___ B. When faced with a disagreement, the parties involved have several ways to proceed.
   ___ C. One party may use physical, social, or economic force to impose a solution on the others.
   ___ D. Negotiation, or reaching a mutually acceptable solution, is one means of dealing with conflict.

4. ___ A. With bribes, Prohibition-era bootleggers persuaded politicians, police, and other public officials to ignore the illegal sale of alcoholic beverages.
   ___ B. Prohibition glamorized drinking and made it fashionable for people to drink in illegal bars and break the law.
   ___ C. Prohibition encouraged the formation of organized-crime empires that illegally manufactured, transported, and sold liquor.
   ___ D. Prohibition, which banned alcoholic beverages in the United States from 1920 to 1933, resulted in much illegal activity.

2 Use the Topic to Lead You to the Main Idea

You already know that to find the main idea of a selection, you look first for a general statement. You then check to see if that statement is supported by most of the other material in the paragraph. If it is, you've found the main idea. Another approach that can help you find the main idea is to decide on the topic of a given selection.

The **topic** is the general subject of a selection. It can often be expressed in one or more words. Knowing the topic can help you find a writer's main point about that topic. Paying close attention to the topic of a selection can lead you to the main idea.

Textbook authors use the title of each chapter to state the overall topic of that chapter. They also provide many topics and subtopics in boldface headings within the chapter. For example, here is the title of a chapter in a psychology textbook:

Theories of Human Development (26 pages)

And here are the subtopics:

Psychoanalytic Theories (an 8-page section)

Learning Theories (a 9-page section)

Cognitive Theories (a 9-page section)

If you were studying the above chapter, you could use the topics to help find the main ideas. (Pages 9–10 in this book explain just how to do so, as well as other textbook study tips.)

But there are many times when you are not given topics—with standardized reading tests, for example, or with individual paragraphs in articles or textbooks. To find the topic of a selection when the topic is not given, ask this simple question:

Who or what is the selection about?

For example, look again at the beginning of the paragraph that started this chapter:

> Many people feel that violence on television is harmless entertainment. However, we now know that TV violence does affect people in negative ways.

What, in just a few words, is the above paragraph about? On the line below, write what you think is the topic.

Topic: ____

You probably answered that the topic is "TV violence." As you reread the paragraph, you saw that, in fact, every sentence in it is about TV violence.

The next step after finding the topic is to decide what main point the author is making about the topic. Authors often present their main idea in a single sentence. (This sentence is also known as the **main idea sentence** or the **topic sentence**.) As we have already seen, the main point about TV violence is "we now know that TV violence does affect people in negative ways."

Check Your Understanding

Let's look now at another paragraph. Read it and then see if you can answer the questions that follow.

[1]Recently a family of four was found dead in a suburban home in New Jersey—victims of carbon monoxide. [2]Such cases are tragically common. [3]Carbon monoxide is deadly for many reasons. [4]To begin with, it is created in the most ordinary of ways—by the burning of wood, coal, or petroleum products. [5]Once created, this gas is impossible to detect without instruments: it is colorless, odorless, and tasteless. [6]Also, carbon monoxide mingles with and remains in the air rather than rising and being carried away by the wind. [7]Then, when people unsuspectingly breathe it in, it chokes them, taking the place of the oxygen in their blood. [8]Furthermore, it can do its lethal work in very small quantities: anyone exposed to air that is just 1 percent carbon monoxide for even a few minutes will almost certainly die.

1. What is the *topic* of the paragraph? In other words, what is the paragraph about? (It often helps as you read to look for and even circle a word, term, or idea that is repeated in the paragraph.)

   ____

2. What is the *main idea* of the paragraph? In other words, what point is the author making about the topic? (Remember that the main idea will be supported by the other material in the paragraph.)

   ____

Explanation

As the first sentence of the paragraph suggests, the topic is "carbon monoxide." Continuing to read the paragraph, you see that, in fact, everything in it is about carbon monoxide. And the main idea is clearly that "Carbon monoxide is deadly for many reasons." This idea is a general one that sums up what the entire paragraph is about. It is an "umbrella" statement under which all the other material in the paragraph fits. The parts of the paragraph could be shown as follows:

Topic: Carbon monoxide

Main idea: Carbon monoxide is deadly for many reasons.

Supporting details:
1. Is easily created.
2. Is difficult to detect.
3. Remains in the air.
4. Chokes by taking the place of oxygen in the blood.
5. Deadly even in small quantities.

The following practices will sharpen your sense of the difference between a topic, the point about the topic (the main idea), and supporting details.

PRACTICE 6

Below are groups of four items. In each case, one item is the topic, one is the main idea, and two are details that support and develop the main idea. Label each item with one of the following:

T — for the **topic** of the paragraph
MI — for the **main idea**
SD — for the **supporting details**

Note that an explanation is provided for the first group; reading it will help you do this practice.

Group 1

_____ A. One bite from a piranha's triangular-shaped teeth can sever a person's finger or toe.

_____ B. The piranha.

_____ C. The piranha—only eight to twelve inches long—is an extremely dangerous fish.

_____ D. A school of piranha can strip a four-hundred-pound hog down to a skeleton in just a few minutes.

Explanation

All of the statements in Group 1 are about piranhas, so item B must be the topic. (Topics are easy to identify because they are expressed in short phrases, not complete sentences.) Statements A and D are specific examples of the damage that piranhas can do. Statement C, on the other hand, presents the general idea that piranhas can be extremely dangerous. It is the main idea about the topic of "the piranha," and statements A and D are supporting details that illustrate that main idea.

Group 2

_____ A. Joint custody of a divorced couple's children has become more common.

_____ B. The number of men with sole custody of children has also grown.

_____ C. Alternatives to giving the mother sole child custody have increased in recent years.

_____ D. Alternative child-custody arrangements.

Group 3

_____ A. In later adulthood, we begin to come to terms with our own mortality.

_____ B. Stages of human development.

_____ C. Adolescence is typically a time of identity crisis.

_____ D. According to psychologists, we pass through various stages of human development throughout our lives.

Group 4

_____ A. Kinds of power.

_____ B. Force, which the Italian statesman Machiavelli called "the method of beasts," is the use of physical coercion.

_____ C. Influence, the ability to control or affect the behavior of others, is also a form of power.

_____ D. Power, the ability to control or change the behavior of others, takes different forms.

PRACTICE 7

Following are four paragraphs. Read each paragraph and do the following:

1 Ask yourself, "What seems to be the topic of the paragraph?" (It often helps to look for and even circle a word or idea that is repeated in the paragraph.)

2 Next, ask yourself, "What point is the writer making about this topic?" This will be the main idea. It is stated in one of the sentences in the paragraph.

3 Then test what you think is the main idea by asking, "Is this statement supported by most of the other material in the paragraph?"

> ***Hint:*** When looking for the topic, make sure you do not pick one that is either **too broad** (covering a great deal more than is in the selection) or **too narrow** (covering only part of the selection). The topic and the main idea of a selection must include everything in that selection—no more and no less.
>
> For instance, in the example given in Practice 1, page 58, the topic is "bad qualities." "Character traits" would be too broad, because these would include good qualities as well as bad qualities. "Greed" would be too narrow, since this is only one type of bad quality mentioned.

Paragraph 1

[1] Shocking as it seems, cannibalism is common in the animal world. [2]In species such as the red-back spider, the black widow spider, the praying mantis, and the scorpion, the female commonly eats the male after mating. [3]Another widespread form of cannibalism is size-structured cannibalism, in which large individuals consume smaller ones. [4]Octopus, bats, toads, fish, monitor lizards, salamanders, crocodiles, spiders, crustaceans, birds, mammals, and a vast number of insects have all been observed to engage in size-structured cannibalism. [5]Yet another common form of cannibalism is infanticide. [6]Classic examples include the chimpanzees, where groups of adult males have been observed to attack their infants; and lions, where adult males commonly kill infants when they take over a new harem after replacing the previous dominant males. [7]Also, gerbils and hamsters eat their young if they are stillborn, or if the mothers are especially stressed.

1. What is the *topic* of the paragraph? In other words, what (in one or more words) is the paragraph about? ____________________

_____ 2. What point is the writer making about the topic? In other words, which sentence states the *main idea* of the paragraph? In the space provided, write the number of the sentence containing the main idea.

Paragraph 2

[1]The Great Wall of China is a truly remarkable creation. [2]At 4,500 miles long, taller than five men, and wide enough to allow at least six horses to gallop side by side atop it, the Great Wall is so huge it can be seen from space. [3]The Wall is constructed of four inch blocks made of compressed earth, stone, willow twigs, and the remains of laborers who died among the millions who worked on its construction. [4]The Great Wall follows mountain slopes and has inclines as great as seventy degrees. [5]The paths on the Wall are even more difficult to travel because the steps are of uneven depth, width, and height. [6]Through much of its 2,500-year history, armies marched and camped on the Wall, keeping lookout for invaders and repelling trespassers who dared to pitch ladders to try to mount it. [7]Today the Great Wall is a tourist attraction that brings many visitors to China. [8]Tourists are eager to make the strenuous hike over precarious paths to take in the greatness of its size and history.

1. What is the *topic* of the paragraph? In other words, what (in one or more words) is the paragraph about? ____________________

_____ 2. What point is the writer making about the topic? In other words, which sentence states the *main idea* of the paragraph? In the space provided, write the number of the sentence containing the main idea.

Paragraph 3

[1]At the beginning of the twentieth century, families often hired older women known as chaperones to keep watch over their daughters. [2]These women played an important role in courtship. [3]When a young man asked a girl on a date, he automatically invited her chaperone as well. [4]If a young lady entertained her boyfriend in the parlor, the chaperone did not budge from the room. [5]Because of her responsibilities, the chaperone had the power to make courtship pleasurable or miserable. [6]Some chaperones had soft hearts and gave young lovers some privacy. [7]Others were such sticklers for appearances that they prevented the young couple even from exchanging personal remarks. [8]In addition to being guardians, chaperones sometimes functioned as private eyes. [9]They investigated the backgrounds of gentlemen who called on their charges to see which one would make the best match.

1. What is the *topic* of the paragraph? In other words, what (in one or more words) is the paragraph about? ______________________________

______ 2. What point is the writer making about the topic? In other words, which sentence states the *main idea* of the paragraph? In the space provided, write the number of the sentence containing the main idea.

Paragraph 4

[1]Cardiovascular disease—disease of the heart or blood vessels—is the leading cause of death in the United States, killing about 1 million people a year. [2]Cardiovascular disease is actually a group of disorders. [3]This group includes high blood pressure, or hypertension, which significantly increases the risk of other diseases in the group. [4]Atherosclerosis, or coronary artery disease, is another member of the group. [5]In this cardiovascular disorder, a fatty deposit, plaque, builds up on the walls of the arteries, restricting the flow of blood and causing strain to the heart, which must work harder to pump blood through the narrowed arteries. [6]Sometimes an aneurysm occurs: the artery ruptures. [7]Heart attack—technically, myocardial infarction—is also in this group. [8]It happens when plaque builds up so much that blood flow to the heart is cut off and some heart muscle dies. [9]Congestive heart failure, a chronic disease, is part of the group as well. [10]In this disorder the heart has been weakened and can no longer pump enough blood. [11]Stroke, too, is a cardiovascular disease: it occurs when blood flow to the brain is restricted or cut off.

1. What is the *topic* of the paragraph? In other words, what (in one or more words) is the paragraph about? ______________________________

______ 2. What point is the writer making about the topic? In other words, which sentence states the *main idea* of the paragraph? In the space provided, write the number of the sentence containing the main idea.

3 Find and Use Key Words to Lead You to the Main Idea

Sometimes authors make it fairly easy to find their main idea. They announce it using **key words**—verbal clues that are easy to recognize. One group of these is **list words**, which tell you a list of items will follow. For example, the main idea in the paragraph about TV violence was stated like this: "However, we now know that TV violence does affect people in negative ways." The expression *negative ways* helps you zero in on your target: the main idea. You realize that the paragraph will most likely be about specific ways that TV violence affects people. As you read on and see the series of negative effects, you know your assumption about the main idea was correct.

Here are some common word groups that often announce a main idea. Note that each of them contains a word that ends in **s**—a plural that suggests the supporting details will be a list of items.

List Words

several kinds (or ways) of	several causes of	some factors in
three advantages of	five steps	among the results
various reasons for	a number of effects	a series of

When expressions like these appear in a sentence, look carefully to see if that sentence might be the main idea. Chances are a sentence containing list words will be followed by a list of major supporting details.

Note: Many other list-word expressions are possible. For example, a writer could begin a paragraph with a sentence containing "four kinds of" or "some advantages of" or "three reasons for." So if you see a sentence with a word group like the ones above, you've probably found the main idea.

Check Your Understanding

Underline the list words in the following sentences.

Hint: Remember that list words usually end in ***s***.

Example Emotional decisions can be divided into two main types.

1. At least five job trends deserve watching in today's world.
2. Pathologists identify four different stages of cancer in the body.
3. Several steps can be effective in helping people deal with prejudice.
4. Winners of presidential elections share various traits in common.
5. Giving birth to and raising a child will require a number of adjustments in the parents' lives.

Explanation

You should have underlined the following groups of words: *five job trends, four different stages, several steps, various traits,* and *a number of adjustments.* Each of these phrases tells you that a list of details may follow.

In addition to list words, addition words can alert you to the main idea. **Addition words** are generally used right before supporting details. When you see this type of clue, you can assume that the detail it introduces fits under the umbrella of a main idea.

Here are some of the addition words that often introduce supporting details and help you discover the main idea.

Addition Words

one	to begin with	also	further
first (of all)	for one thing	in addition	furthermore
second(ly)	other	next	last (of all)
third(ly)	another	moreover	final(ly)

Check Your Understanding

Reread the paragraph about TV violence, underlining the addition words that alert you to supporting details.

[1]Many people feel that violence on television is harmless entertainment. [2]However, we now know that TV violence does affect people in negative ways. [3]One study showed that frequent TV watchers are more fearful and suspicious of others. [4]They try to protect themselves from the outside world with extra locks on the doors, alarm systems, guard dogs, and guns. [5]In addition, that same study showed that heavy TV watchers are less upset about real-life violence than non-TV watchers. [6]It seems that the constant violence they see on TV makes them less sensitive to the real thing. [7]Another study, of a group of children, found that TV violence increases aggressive behavior. [8]Children who watched violent shows were more willing to hurt another child in games where they were given a choice between helping and hurting. [9]They were also more likely to select toy weapons over other kinds of playthings.

Explanation

The words that introduce each new supporting detail for the main idea are *One*, *In addition*, and *Another*. When you see these addition words, you realize the studies are all being cited in support of an idea—in this case, that TV violence affects people in negative ways.

That main idea includes the list words *negative ways*, which suggest that the supporting details will be a list of negative ways TV violence affects people. In this and many paragraphs, list words and addition words often work hand in hand.

The following chapter, "Supporting Details," includes further practice in the words and phrases that alert you to the main idea and the details that support it. But what you have already learned here will help you find main ideas.

Locations of the Main Idea

Now you know how to recognize a main idea by (1) distinguishing between the general and the specific, (2) identifying the topic of a passage, and (3) using key words. You are ready to find the main idea no matter where it is located in a paragraph.

A main idea may appear at any point within a paragraph. Very commonly, it shows up at the beginning, as either the first or the second sentence. However, main ideas may also appear further within a paragraph or even at the very end.

Main Idea at the Beginning

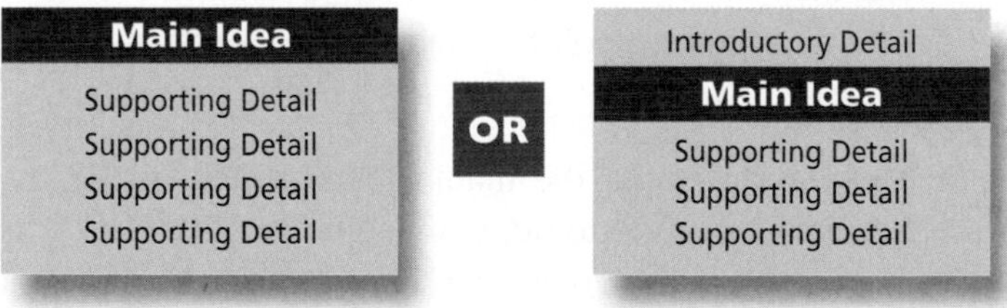

In textbooks, it is very common for the main idea to be either the first or the second sentence of a paragraph.

See if you can underline the main idea in the paragraph on the following page.

[1]People tend to cling to their first impressions, even if they are wrong. [2]Suppose you mention the name of your new neighbor to a friend. [3]"Oh, I know him," your friend replies. [4]"He seems nice at first, but it's all an act." [5]Perhaps this appraisal is off-base. [6]The neighbor may have changed since your friend knew him, or perhaps your friend's judgment is simply unfair. [7]Whether the judgment is accurate or not, once you accept your friend's evaluation, it will probably influence the way you respond to the neighbor. [8]You'll look for examples of the insincerity you've heard about, and you'll probably find them. [9]Even if this neighbor were a saint, you would be likely to interpret his behavior in ways that fit your expectations.

In this paragraph, the main idea is in the *first* sentence. All the following sentences in the paragraph provide a detailed example of how we cling to first impressions.

Check Your Understanding

Now read the following paragraph and see if you can underline its main idea:

[1]For shy people, simply attending class can be stressful. [2]Several strategies, though, can lessen the trauma of attending class for shy people. [3]Shy students should time their arrival to coincide with that of most other class members—about two minutes before the class is scheduled to begin. [4]If they arrive too early, they may be seen sitting alone or, even worse, may actually be forced to talk with another early arrival. [5]If they arrive late, all eyes will be upon them. [6]Before heading to class, shy students should dress in the least conspicuous manner possible—say, in the blue jeans, sweatshirt, and sneakers that 99.9 percent of their classmates wear. [7]That way they won't stand out from everyone else. [8]They should take a seat near the back of the room. [9]But they shouldn't sit at the very back, since instructors sometimes make a point of calling on students there.

Explanation

In the above paragraph, the main idea is stated in the *second* sentence. The first sentence introduces the topic, shy people in class, but it is the idea in the second sentence—several strategies can lessen the trauma of attending class for shy people—that is supported in the rest of the paragraph. So keep in mind that the first sentence may simply introduce or lead into the main idea of a paragraph.

Hint: Very often, a contrast word like *however, but, yet,* or *though* signals the main idea, as in the paragraph you have just read.

Main Idea in the Middle

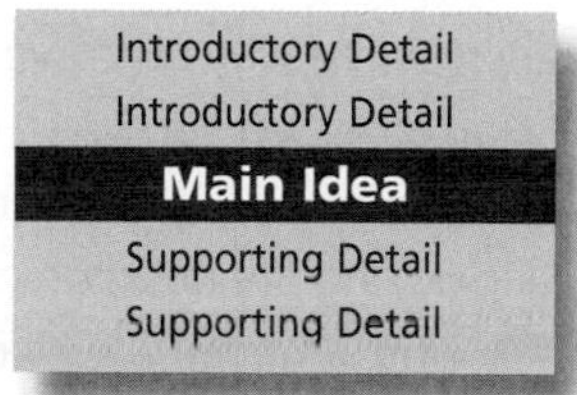

The main idea at times appears in the middle of a paragraph. Here is an example of a paragraph in which the main idea is somewhere in the middle. Try to find it and underline it. Then read the explanation that follows.

> [1]A television ad for a new sports car showed scenes of beautiful open country that suggested freedom and adventure. [2]The car never appeared in the ad at all. [3]An ad for a hotel chain showed a romantic couple in bed together. [4]They were obviously on vacation and having a leisurely, romantic, sexy morning. [5]As these ads suggest, advertisers often try to sell products and services by associating them with positive images rather than by providing relevant details about the product or service. [6]An ad giving the car's gas mileage, safety rating, or repair frequency would be more important to a buyer, but it might not draw the viewer's interest as much as beautiful scenery. [7]Similarly, details on the hotel's prices and service would be more informative than images of a glamorous vacation. [8]But the romantic couple gets people's attention and associates the hotel in viewers' minds with a good time.

If you thought the fifth sentence states the main idea, you were correct. The first four sentences introduce the topic of advertisers and provide specific examples of the main idea. The fifth sentence then presents the writer's main idea, which is that advertisers often try to sell their products by associating them with appealing images rather than with relevant details. The rest of the paragraph continues to develop that idea.

Main Idea at the End

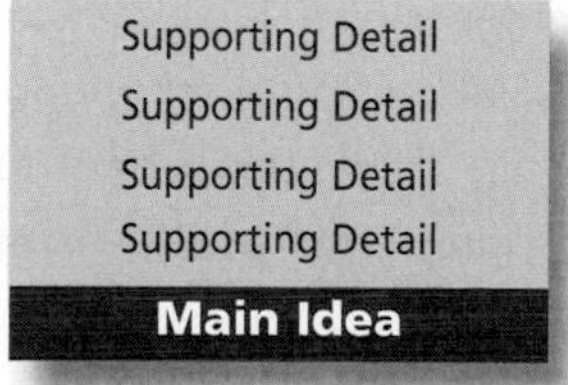

Sometimes all the sentences in a paragraph will lead up to the main idea, which is presented at the end. Here is an example of such a paragraph.

[1]At the end of the twentieth century, with the economy booming and unemployment at historic lows, the American economy was a job-producing marvel. [2]Opportunities for workers seemed endless; college students were getting bonuses from companies before they started working, and older workers were planning early retirement. [3]The first decade of the twenty-first century was entirely different. [4]From the 9/11 terrorist attacks to surges in oil prices to bank failures and financial losses on Wall Street and in the housing market, millions either lost their jobs or feared they would. [5]They watched helplessly as the value of their houses and retirement savings declined. [6]At the end of the first decade of the twenty-first century, the United States endured the Great Recession, the worst economy in seventy years. [7]**In less than a decade, Americans experienced the best and worst of times.**

Main Idea at the Beginning and the End

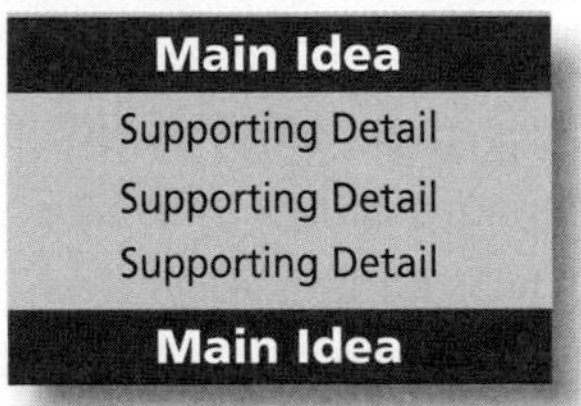

At times an author may choose to state the main idea near the beginning of the paragraph and then emphasize it (as a conclusion) by restating it in other words later in the paragraph. In such cases, the main idea is at both the beginning and the end. Such is the case in the following paragraph.

> [1]**An important result of medical advances is an increase in the number of conditions thought to be of medical concern.** [2]In the not-too-distant past, birth and death usually occurred at home. [3]Family members and friends were there or close by. [4]Now most people are born and die in a hospital, surrounded by bright lights and expensive machines. [5]People who were addicted to alcohol or drugs were once considered sinful or lacking in willpower. [6]Now they are considered "sick." [7]Problems that used to be accepted as part of life—baldness, wrinkles, small breasts, sleeplessness—are now deemed proper matters for medical attention. [8]Some criminologists have even defined antisocial behavior as a medical problem. [9]Lawbreakers of all kinds, from the shoplifter to the mass murderer, may potentially be labeled "sick." [10]**Because of current medical knowledge, what were once thought to be problems of life or of character are now considered medical issues.**

Note that the main idea—because of medical advances, more problems are considered medical issues—is expressed in different words in the first and last sentences.

PRACTICE 8

The main ideas of the following paragraphs appear at different locations—in the beginning, somewhere in the middle, or at the end. Identify each main idea by filling in its sentence number in the space provided.

_____ 1. [1]Many people think of thieves as clever. [2]In reality, thieves can be remarkably foolish. [3]One evening, a Los Angeles woman was walking her miniature poodle when a man came up behind her, pushed her to the ground, grabbed the plastic bag she was holding, and drove away. [4]Afterward, when asked about the mugging, the woman cheerfully commented, "I only wish there had been more in the bag." [5]The woman had used the bag when she cleaned up her dog's messes. [6]In Baltimore, an even dumber burglar broke into a house while the woman who lived there was home, ransacked the place, and, having found only $11.50 in cash, demanded that the victim write him a check for $30. [7]When the woman asked to whom she should make the check payable, the thief gave his own name, in full. [8]He was arrested a few hours later. [9]But an Oklahoma thief may have been dumbest of all. [10]Charged with purse-snatching, he decided to act as his own attorney. [11]At his trial, he cross-examined the victim: "Did you get a good look at my face when I took your purse?" [12]Not surprisingly, he was convicted.

_____ 2. [1]For 250 million years, reptiles—which appeared on Earth long before the first mammals—have been fighting over territory. [2]Today, human beings do battle over property as well. [3]But the reptiles' way of fighting is generally more civilized and humane than the humans'. [4]Lizards will take a few rushes at one another to test which one is stronger. [5]After a few passes, the loser rolls over on his back to signal defeat. [6]The winner allows him to leave unharmed. [7]Rattlesnakes, similarly, will duel over territory. [8]But they do it with their necks twined together so that they cannot injure each other with their fangs. [9]Humans, of course, generally fight with the intent of injuring one another. [10]The victor often seems to feel he hasn't really won until he's wounded and humiliated his opponent, if not killed him.

_____ 3. [1]If asked to describe ourselves, most of us would not answer that we are mostly water, but that's exactly what we are. [2]A 150-pound person is actually 100 pounds of water and only 50 pounds of everything else. [3]Our blood plasma is 92% water, and our brains are 75% water. [4]We use the expression "dry as a bone," but in fact our bones are not dry at all—they are about 20% water.

[5]Our "inner sea" is constantly in motion, flowing through us every moment, bringing food and oxygen to our cells, carrying away wastes, lubricating our joints, cushioning our brains and regulating our temperatures. [6]If the percentage of water in our bodies drops even 1 or 2 percent, we feel thirsty. [7]A drop of 10% is usually fatal. [8]Every day, we lose about two and a half quarts of water. [9]Surprisingly, we replace less than half this lost water through drinking. [10]The rest we replenish with food which, just like us, is mostly water. [11]A tomato, for example, is over 87% water, which is released into the body when we eat it.

_____ 4. [1]As the rates of obesity and related diseases such as diabetes, stroke, heart disease, and kidney failure continue to rise in this country, it's become evident that the Standard American Diet, with its walloping portions of sugar, salt, and fat, is largely to blame. [2]But the problem with our diet isn't confined to what we eat. [3]What we drink is as problematic. [4]And what we drink is soda. [5]Soda is a vehicle for delivering large amounts of sugar, often in the form of high fructose corn syrup. [6]The American Heart Association recommends that adult women consume no more than 5 teaspoons of added sugar (meaning sugar that does not naturally occur in whole foods) a day, adult men no more than 9 teaspoons, and children no more than 3 teaspoons. [7]In contrast, a 12-ounce bottle or can of Coca-Cola contains 9.75 teaspoons of added sugar. [8]And of course most people with the soda habit drink more than one bottle or can a day. [9]They drink it with meals and as a snack. [10]They purchase 42-ounce super-sized drinks that contain 30 teaspoons of added sugar. [11]Most dangerously of all, they feed sodas to their children instead of wholesome foods. [12]Those unfortunate kids begin early on to experience the sugar spikes and insulin resistance that lead to Type 2 diabetes, a dangerous disease once known as "adult onset" diabetes. [13]Today it is epidemic among children. [14]If we're truly concerned about the future of our increasingly obese, unhealthy society, eliminating sodas from our diet is a good place to start.

The Central Point

Just as a paragraph may have a main idea, a longer selection may have a **central point**, also known as a **central idea** or **thesis**. The longer selection might be an essay, a reading, or a section of a textbook chapter. You can find a central point in the same way that you find a main idea—by identifying the topic (which is often suggested by the title of the selection) and then looking at the supporting material. The paragraphs within the longer reading will provide supporting details for the central point.

Check Your Understanding

In the following essay, the central point is stated in one sentence. See if you can find and underline this sentence. Then write its number in the space provided.

Peer Pressure

[1]We often hear about the dangers of peer pressure to teenagers. [2]Teens take drugs, skip school, get drunk, or have sex to impress their friends. [3]However, there is another, perhaps equally bad, effect of peer pressure. [4]Desperate to conform to their friends' values, teens may give up their interests in school, in hobbies, and even in certain people.

[5]Teens may lose or hide their interest in school in order to be like their friends. [6]They adopt a negative attitude in which school is seen as a battlefield, with teachers and other officials regarded as the enemy. [7]In private, they may enjoy certain teachers, but in front of their friends, they put on a sarcastic or hostile act. [8]In addition, teenagers may stop participating in class. [9]They may refuse to join in class discussions, even when the topic interests them. [10]They may decide it is cool to show up without the assigned homework. [11]If their peers demand it, they may interfere with others' learning by disrupting class. [12]Conforming also means not joining in after-school activities.

[13]Teenagers also give up private pleasures and hobbies to be one of the crowd. [14]Certain pastimes, such as writing poems, practicing piano, reading books, or joining an after-school club may be off-limits because the crowd laughs at them.

[15]Most sadly, teenagers sometimes give up the people they love in order to be accepted. [16]If necessary, they sacrifice the old friend who no longer dresses well enough, listens to the wrong kind of music, or refuses to drink or take drugs. [17]Potential boyfriends or girlfriends may be rejected, too, if the crowd doesn't like their looks or values. [18]Teens can even cut their families out of their lives if they are too poor, too conventional, or too different from their friends' parents.

_____ is the number of the sentence that states the central point.

Explanation

The central point is a general statement that covers all or most of the details in a reading. To find the central point of the essay above, look first at its topic. Since the title is "Peer Pressure," and every paragraph is about that subject, we can say "peer pressure" is the topic. Then decide on what point is being made about the topic by looking at the major details of the essay. The first major detail, presented in the second paragraph, is about giving up interest in school as a result of peer pressure. The next major detail, in the third paragraph, is about giving up interest in hobbies; and the third major detail, in the fourth paragraph, is about giving up interest in certain people.

The central point, then, will be a general statement that covers all of the major details presented. As is often the case, the central point is stated in the first paragraph. Sentence 4 in that paragraph expresses the idea that peer pressure may cause students to give up interest in school, in hobbies, and in certain people.

PRACTICE 9

The author has stated the central point of the following textbook selection in one sentence. Find that sentence, and write its number in the space provided.

Prewriting Strategies

[1]Prewriting refers to strategies you can use to generate ideas before starting the first draft of a paper. [2]Prewriting techniques have various advantages. [3]They encourage imaginative exploration and therefore also help you discover what interests you most about your subject. [4]Having such a focus early in the writing process keeps you from plunging into your initial draft without first giving some thought to what you want to say. [5]Prewriting thus saves you time in the long run by keeping you on course.

[6]Prewriting can help in other ways, too. [7]When we write, we often interfere with our ability to generate material because we continually critique what we put down on paper. [8]"This makes no sense," "This is stupid," "I can't say that," and other critical thoughts pop into our minds. [9]Such negative, self-critical comments stop the flow of our thoughts and reinforce the fear that we have nothing to say and aren't very good at writing. [10]During prewriting, you deliberately ignore your internal critic. [11]Your purpose is simply to get ideas down on paper without evaluating their effectiveness. [12]Writing without immediately judging what you produce can be liberating. [13]Once you feel less pressure, you'll probably find that you can generate a good deal of material. [14]And that can make your confidence soar.

[15]One final advantage of prewriting: The random associations typical of prewriting tap the mind's ability to make unusual connections. [16]When you prewrite, you're like an archaeologist going on a dig. [17]On the one hand, you may not unearth anything; on the other hand, you may stumble upon one interesting find after another. [18]Prewriting helps you appreciate—right from the start—this element of surprise in the writing process.

_____ is the number of the sentence that states the central point.

A Final Thought

Whether we are readers, writers, listeners, or speakers, the "heart" of clear communication is the main idea, or point, and the support for the main idea. Look at the following diagram:

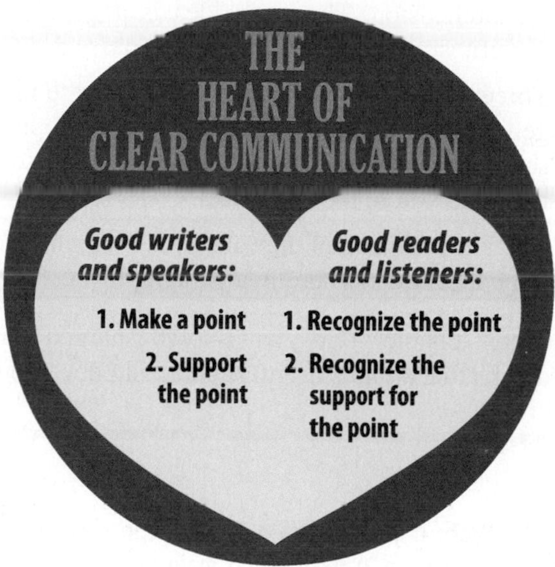

The diagram underscores the importance of the most important of all reading skills: the ability to identify main ideas. The diagram also shows that the ability to identify supporting details for the main idea is an almost equally important skill.

CHAPTER REVIEW

In this chapter, you learned the following:

- Recognizing the main idea is the most important key to good comprehension. The main idea is a general "umbrella" idea; all the specific supporting material of the passage fits under it.
- Three strategies that will help you find the main idea are to 1) look for general versus specific ideas; 2) use the topic (the general subject of a selection) to lead you to the main idea; 3) use key words—verbal clues that lead you to the main idea.
- The main idea often appears at the beginning of a paragraph, though it may appear elsewhere in a paragraph.

The next chapter—Chapter 3—will sharpen your understanding of the specific details that authors use to support and develop their main ideas.

On the Web: If you are using this book in class, you can visit our website for additional practice in recognizing main ideas. Go to **www.townsendpress.com** and click on "Learning Center."

REVIEW TEST 1

To review what you've learned in this chapter, answer the following questions by filling in the blank or writing the letter of the correct answer.

1. To become an active reader, you need to think as you read by constantly asking yourself the question, "What is the ______________?"

2. One strategy that will help you find the main idea is to look for the ____________________—the general subject of a selection.

______ 3. What kind of writing typically provides many topics and subtopics that will help you find main ideas?

A. Magazines B. Fiction books C. Textbooks

4. *Two benefits, three reasons, four steps, five effects* are all examples of ____________________ that can help you find main ideas.

5. While a main idea may appear at any point within a paragraph, in textbooks it most often appears at the ______________________.

REVIEW TEST 2

A. In each of the following groups, one statement is the general point, and the other statements are specific support for the point. Identify each point with a **P** and each statement of support with an **S**.

1. ____ A. In urban areas, infant mortality is 25 percent higher than the national average.

____ B. Urban children face greater risks than other children.

____ C. Forty percent of urban children live below the poverty level.

____ D. Between 30 and 50 percent of urban children are inadequately immunized.

2. ___ A. The night before a fox hunt, "earth stoppers" roam the countryside filling in fox holes and other burrows to prevent a hunted fox from escaping underground.

___ B. During the hunt, the fox is pursued—sometimes for hours—by dozens of hounds followed by mounted hunters; a fox caught by hounds is torn apart.

___ C. Many fox hunters practice "blooding," a ritual in which blood from a killed fox is smeared on the cheeks of children attending their first hunt.

___ D. There are good reasons to find fox hunting bizarre and cruel.

B. Each group of statements below includes one topic, one main idea, and two supporting details. In the space provided, label each item with one of the following:

T — for the **topic** of the paragraph
MI — for the **main idea**
SD — for the **supporting details**

Group 1

_____ A. Lack of exercise leads to "older" joints and muscles.

_____ B. Signs of aging.

_____ C. Smoking and spending a great deal of time in the sun lead to wrinkling.

_____ D. Everyday habits can produce signs of aging.

Group 2

_____ A. Many students now do much of their learning using online computers.

_____ B. Modern technology is changing the very nature of our educational system.

_____ C. Technology's effect on education.

_____ D. Students have begun to use wireless reading devices that can hold the information contained in thousands of books.

REVIEW TEST 3

A. The main idea appears at various places in the following paragraphs. Write the number of each main idea in the space provided.

______ 1. [1]Individuals sometimes develop amazing strengths by uniting to overcome trouble. [2]At the end of World War II, for example, a group of six children who had lost their parents, their homeland, and their native language were freed from a concentration camp. [3]They were so strongly attached to one another that they refused to be separated even when one became ill with a contagious disease. [4]In the refugee hostel, they resisted being singled out for treats. [5]At mealtimes, each made certain the other five had food before eating. [6]Only after several months had passed and they knew their safety was assured did they show the competitiveness and need for attention normal children do.

______ 2. [1]Among the tasks of public schools is the teaching of reading, writing, and arithmetic. [2]Evidence makes clear, though, that public schools often do not succeed in teaching the basic skills. [3]As many as one young adult in three is functionally illiterate—that is, unable to read at an eighth-grade level. [4]The rate of functional illiteracy among minority youth is even higher than the national average: about 40 percent. [5]Few seventeen-year-olds can express their thoughts effectively in writing. [6]Even when their spelling and grammar are adequate, they use short, childlike sentences and cannot organize coherent paragraphs. [7]And although young adults can perform basic mathematical operations, they have trouble using these operations to solve problems. [8]Less than half can read a federal income tax table, and just 1 percent can balance a checkbook.

______ 3. [1]After experiencing an extremely shocking event, some people will continue to reexperience it through dreams and recollections. [2]They may even reexperience it through a flashback—the sudden feeling that one is back in the traumatic experience. [3]They may also feel a sense of emotional "numbness," as if their bodies have shut down in order to protect them from further emotional damage. [4]They may avoid any stimuli that remind them of the traumatic event. [5]This collection of symptoms, called posttraumatic stress disorder (PTSD), afflicts people who have experienced any of various seriously damaging experiences. [6]PTSD is best known because of its association with Vietnam and Iraqi War veterans. [7]But it is also often found in individuals who have been victims of violent crimes such as rape or extreme child abuse.

B. (4.) The author has stated the central point of the following textbook selection in one sentence. Find that sentence, and write its number in the space provided.

A Medical Mystery

[1]Medical researchers were perplexed. [2]Reports were coming in from all over the country indicating that women, who live longer than men, were twice as likely to die after coronary bypass surgery. [3]Medical records at one hospital showed that of almost 2,300 coronary bypass patients, 4.6 percent of the women died as a result of the surgery, compared with only 2.6 percent of the men.

[4]Initial explanations were based on biology. [5]Coronary bypass surgery involves taking a blood vessel from one part of the body and stitching it to a coronary artery on the surface of the heart. [6]This operation was supposedly more difficult to perform on women because of their smaller hearts and coronary arteries. [7]But researchers who tested this theory soon found that the operation was not more difficult to perform on women.

[8]As the researchers continued to probe, a surprising answer slowly unfolded: The cause of the greater number of deaths of women after bypass surgery was sexual discrimination by physicians. [9]They simply did not take the chest pains of their women patients as seriously as those of their men patients. [10]Physicians were ten times more likely to give men exercise stress tests and radioactive heart scans. [11]And they sent men to surgery on the basis of abnormal stress tests but waited until women showed clear-cut symptoms of coronary heart disease before recommending surgery. [12]Being referred for surgery later in the course of the disease decreases the chances of survival.

_____ is the number of the sentence that states the central point.

REVIEW TEST 4

Here is a chance to apply your understanding of main ideas to a textbook passage. Read the passage below, and then answer the questions on main ideas that follow. There are also vocabulary questions to help you continue practicing the skill of understanding vocabulary in context.

Words to Watch

Below are some words in the reading that do not have strong context support. Each word is followed by the number of the paragraph in which it appears and its meaning there. These words are indicated in the article by a small circle (°).

tangible (1): concrete
afloat (7): out of difficulty
perception (7): judgment
longitudinal survey (7): a study that follows the same people over a period of time

HOW DUAL-EARNER COUPLES COPE

Diane E. Papalia and Sally Wendkos Olds

1 The growing number of marriages in which both husband and wife are gainfully employed presents both opportunities and challenges. A second income raises some families from poverty to middle-income status and makes others affluent. It makes women more independent and gives them a greater share of economic power, and it reduces the pressure on men to be providers; 47 percent of working wives contribute half or more of family income. Less tangible° benefits may include a more equal relationship between husband and wife, better health for both, greater self-esteem for the woman, and a closer relationship between a father and his children.

2 However, this way of life also creates stress. Working couples face extra demands on time and energy, conflicts between work and family, possible rivalry between spouses, and anxiety and guilt about meeting children's needs. Each role makes greater or lesser demands at different times, and partners have to decide which should take priority when. The family is most demanding, especially for women, when there are young children. Careers are especially demanding when a worker is getting established or being promoted. Both

kinds of demands frequently occur in young adulthood.

3 Men and women tend to be stressed by different aspects of the work-family situation. Among 314 spouses with relatively high income and education, husbands were more likely to suffer from overload (perhaps because they had not been socialized to deal with domestic as well as occupational responsibilities). Women, on the other hand, were more likely to feel the strain of conflicting role expectations—for example, the need to be aggressive and competitive at work but compassionate and nurturing at home.

4 Temporary withdrawal from social interaction after a busy workday helped settle men down and softened the effects of overload. "Talking things over" seemed to worsen their stress, perhaps because they were uncomfortable expressing feelings or because the outcome of such discussions might be even greater demands. For both men and women, the most successful way of coping was rethinking the way they looked at the situation.

5 Dual-income couples fall into three patterns: conventional, modern, and role sharing. In a conventional marriage, both partners consider household chores and childcare "women's work." The husband may "help," but his career comes first; he earns more than his wife and sees it as "her choice" to add outside employment to her primary domestic role. In modern couples, the wife does most of the housework, but the husband shares parenting and wants to be involved with his children.

In the role-sharing pattern, characteristic of at least one-third of dual-income marriages, both husband and wife are actively involved in household and family responsibilities as well as careers. However, even among such couples, tasks tend to be gender-typed: wives buy the groceries and husbands mow the lawn.

Men, on average, earn more and have more powerful positions than women. But in general, the burdens of the dual-earner lifestyle fall most heavily on the woman. Women tend to work more hours—20 percent more in industrialized countries and 30 percent more in less developed countries. Women put in a longer "second shift" at home, as well. Although men's participation has been increasing, even husbands in non-traditional marriages still do 6 only one-third of the domestic work. A Swedish study found that working women with three or more children put in one and a half times as many hours as men at home and on the job. A father is most likely to take on childcare when his work schedule is different from his wife's.

7 Women's personal activities tend to suffer more than men's, probably owing to the disproportionate time they put into domestic work, and in the long run the compromises women make to keep the dual-earner lifestyle afloat° may weaken the marriage. An unequal division of work may have contributed to the higher degree of marital distress reported by wives in a study of three hundred mostly managerial and professional dual-earner couples. On the other hand, unequal roles are not necessarily seen as inequitable; it may be a perception° of unfairness that contributes most to marital instability. A national longitudinal survey° of 3,284 women in two-income families found greater likelihood of divorce the more hours the woman worked, but only when the wife had a nontraditional view of marriage. Nontraditional wives who work full time may feel more resentment of their husbands' failure to share equally in household tasks, whereas traditional wives may be more willing to accept additional burdens.

What spouses perceive as fair may 8
depend on how much money the wife's earnings contribute, whether she thinks of herself as someone who supplements her husband's income, and what meaning and importance she and her husband place on her work. Whatever the actual division of labor, couples who agree on that division and who enjoy a more harmonious, caring, involved family life are more satisfied than those who don't.

Family-friendly policies in the 9
workplace can help alleviate the strains experienced by dual-earner families. A flexible work environment is one that could include part-time, flextime, and shared jobs. Supportive companies might also provide more at-home work (without loss of fringe benefits), more affordable high-quality childcare, and tax credits or other assistance to let new parents postpone returning to work. One encouraging change is the Family and Medical Leave Act, which requires businesses with fifty or more workers to offer twelve weeks of unpaid leave for the birth or adoption of a child.

Reading Comprehension Questions

Vocabulary in Context

_____ 1. In the sentence below, the word *socialized* (sō′shə-līzd′) means
A. afraid.
B. taught through experience.
C. paid well.
D. strong enough.

"Among 314 spouses with relatively high income and education, husbands were more likely to suffer from overload (perhaps because they had not been socialized to deal with domestic as well as occupational responsibilities)." (Paragraph 3)

_____ 2. In the sentence below, the word *conventional* (kən-vĕn′shə-nəl) means
A. convenient.
B. happy.
C. traditional.
D. modern.

"In a conventional marriage, both partners consider household chores and childcare 'women's work.'" (Paragraph 5)

_____ 3. In the excerpt below, the word *disproportionate* (dĭs′prə-pôr′shə-nĭt) means
A. unequal in size.
B. too short.
C. equal.
D. late.

"Women's personal activities tend to suffer more than men's, probably owing to the disproportionate time they put into domestic work . . . " (Paragraph 7)

_____ 4. In the sentence below, the word *inequitable* (ĭn-ĕk′wĭ-tə-bəl) means
A. fair.
B. surprising.
C. ideal.
D. unequal.

"On the other hand, unequal roles are not necessarily seen as inequitable; it may be a perception of unfairness that contributes most to marital instability." (Paragraph 7)

Main Ideas

_____ 5. The main idea of paragraphs 1 and 2 is the
A. first sentence of paragraph 1.
B. second sentence of paragraph 1.
C. first sentence of paragraph 2.
D. last sentence of paragraph 2.

_____ 6. The main idea of paragraph 3 is its
A. first sentence.
B. second sentence.
C. third sentence.

_____ 7. The main idea of paragraph 5 is its
A. first sentence.
B. second sentence.
C. third sentence.
D. last sentence.

_____ 8. The main idea of paragraph 6 is its
A. first sentence.
B. second sentence.
C. third sentence.
D. fourth sentence.

_____ 9. The topic of paragraph 9 is
A. companies that support at-home work.
B. the strains experienced by dual-earner families.
C. family-friendly policies in the workplace.
D. the Family and Medical Leave Act.

_____ 10. The main idea of paragraph 9 is its
A. first sentence.
B. second sentence.
C. third sentence.
D. last sentence.

Discussion Questions

1. Discuss some of the challenges in a dual-income marriage. Draw upon your own experience if you are married, or use the example of a married couple you know.
2. Discuss some of the benefits in a dual-income marriage. Again, draw upon your own experience if you are married, or use the example of a married couple you know.
3. The author states, "Dual-income couples fall into three patterns: conventional, modern, and role sharing." What view of marriage did your family have as you grew up? How did that view affect your family's lifestyle? If you're married, which view do you and your spouse have?
4. How do you think dual-earner marriages affect children? What, if anything, can spouses who both work outside the home do to ensure that their children receive the time and attention they deserve?

Note: Writing assignments for this selection appear on pages 696–697.

Check Your Performance — MAIN IDEAS

Activity		*Number Right*	*Points*		*Score*
Review Test 1	(5 items)	______	× 2	=	______
Review Test 2	(16 items)	______	× 2.5	=	______
Review Test 3	(4 items)	______	× 5	=	______
Review Test 4	(10 items)	______	× 3	=	______
			TOTAL SCORE	=	______ %

Enter your total score into the **Reading Performance Chart: Review Tests** on the inside back cover.

Name ______________________________ Date __________

Section __________ SCORE: (Number correct) ______ x 5 = ______ %

MAIN IDEAS: Mastery Test 1

A. In each of the following groups, one statement is the general point, and the other statements are specific support for the point. Identify each point with a **P** and each statement of support with an **S**.

1. ___ A. While traveling in different countries, there are some things to do and some things to avoid doing.

   ___ B. In Tibet, you should greet people by sticking out your tongue, the same way as the natives do.

   ___ C. In Japan, you should not look at a person directly in the eye for more than a few seconds, which the Japanese consider rude.

   ___ D. In Greece, you should refrain from waving your hand to say goodbye because hand-waving is regarded as an insult.

2. ___ A. By relieving tension, laughing can prevent an angry eruption.

   ___ B. Instead of allowing anger to build, a person should deal with anger-arousing situations as they arise.

   ___ C. Sometimes the best way to deal with particular people or situations that arouse anger is to avoid them as much as possible.

   ___ D. Different coping strategies can help people to curb their anger.

3. ___ A. In ancient Greece, women could not vote or hold public office.

   ___ B. The women of ancient Greece lived under very strict constraints in family and civic life.

   ___ C. A wife in ancient Greece was expected to do little else than bear and raise children and be a housekeeper.

   ___ D. After marriage, a woman had no independent standing; she was her husband's responsibility.

(Continues on next page)

B. Each group of statements below includes one topic, one main idea, and two supporting details. In the space provided, label each item with one of the following:

T — for the **topic** of the paragraph
MI — for the **main idea**
SD — for the **supporting details**

Group 1

_____ A. Through its life and death, a tree will serve a variety of important functions.

_____ B. Functions of a tree.

_____ C. While alive, a tree provides food, nesting sites, shade, wind protection, and concealment for wildlife.

_____ D. After a tree begins to die, stored nutrients are released, and it continues to provide protection and food for many forms of plant and animal life.

Group 2

_____ A. In cultures where most working people are thin and tanned from outdoor labor, being pale and overweight indicates wealth and high status.

_____ B. Physical signs of wealth.

_____ C. At some points in history, long fingernails for men and women demonstrated that, unlike common laborers, the person did not have to work with his or her hands.

_____ D. In different societies and stages of history, different physical attributes have indicated a person's status.

Name ______________________________ Date __________

Section __________ SCORE: (Number correct) ______ x 5 = ______ %

MAIN IDEAS: Mastery Test 2

A. In each of the following groups—all based on textbook selections—one statement is the general point, and the other statements are specific support for the point. Identify each point with a **P** and each statement of support with an **S**.

1. ___ A. In the summer, tenement apartments were so hot the Boston Board of Health recommended that mothers take their babies to the rooftops at night.

   ___ B. For many immigrants in the late 19th century, their first American home was less appealing than the place they had left behind.

   ___ C. In the winter, the tenements were so cold that people went to work even when they were sick just so they could get warm.

   ___ D. One tenement had 170 children but only a 14-foot-square yard for them to play in.

2. ___ A. There were ten women in the House of Representatives in 1970 and only one woman in the Senate.

   ___ B. In North Carolina, only a virgin could charge a man with rape.

   ___ C. Divorced women were regarded as high risks by insurance companies, and they had trouble getting credit cards.

   ___ D. In the early 1970s, women still had a long way to go in terms of gaining equal rights.

3. ___ A. The introduction of firearms in Europe in the 1300s had a great impact on road travel.

   ___ B. Firearms allowed fourteenth-century travelers to protect themselves from highwaymen who robbed and assaulted travelers.

   ___ C. In the 1300s, most road travelers (being right-handed) wore their weapons on their left side so they could draw the weapon easily, leading to the common practice of keeping to the right side of the road.

   ___ D. Later in the fourteenth century, villages and towns began to hire men who could use firearms to protect travelers on sections of roadway; this practice was the forerunner of modern highway patrols.

(Continues on next page)

B. Each group of statements below includes one topic, one main idea, and two supporting details. In the space provided, label each item with one of the following:

T — for the **topic** of the paragraph
MI — for the **main idea**
SD — for the **supporting details**

Group 1

_____ A. Certain behaviors are considered especially serious signs that a child may later engage in violent criminal acts.

_____ B. "Red flags" in childhood for future criminal behavior.

_____ C. Cruelty to animals, such as beating or torturing pets, is often a sign of serious psychological problems in children.

_____ D. Children who show a fascination with setting fires have a strong tendency to later engage in violent criminal behavior.

Group 2

_____ A. Adults seek out spicy or bitter foods to stimulate their smaller supply of taste buds.

_____ B. Sensitivity to flavors.

_____ C. The difference in the sensitivity to flavors between children and adults lies in the taste buds, the tiny taste receptors that line the tongue.

_____ D. Young children's tongues are loaded with taste buds and are especially sensitive; therefore, sour or spicy flavors seem too intense to them.

Name ______________________________ Date __________

Section ____________ SCORE: (Number correct) _______ x 20 = _______ %

MAIN IDEAS: Mastery Test 3

The main idea may appear at any place within each of the five paragraphs that follow. Write the number of each main idea sentence in the space provided.

______ 1. [1]A century ago, medical practice left much to be desired. [2]In the late 1800s, surgeons still operated with bare hands, wearing the same clothes they had worn on the street. [3]Their shoes carried into the surgery room the debris of the streets and hospital corridors. [4]Spectators were often permitted to observe operations, gathering around the patient within touching distance of the incision. [5]Surgeons used surgical dressings made from pressed sawdust, a waste product from the floors of sawmills. [6]Surgical instruments were washed in soapy water, but not heat-sterilized or chemically disinfected. [7]The mortality rate following operations in many hospitals was as high as 90 percent.

______ 2. [1]Police officers complain that many of the criminals they arrest end up very soon on the streets to commit crimes again. [2]Judges argue that because of the technicalities of the law, they are forced to free many defendants, some of whom may be guilty as charged. [3]Government officials lament that they don't have the funds or space to build new prisons. [4]And many citizens charge that the police, the judges, or the government officials are not doing their jobs well. [5]Clearly, the way the huge problem of crime is being handled angers and frustrates many segments of our society.

______ 3. [1]When we speak of a "close friend," we usually mean an intimate friend, not a friend who is standing close by. [2]However, according to researchers who study human behavior, there are in fact four "distance zones" in human interaction. [3]Intimate distance is the closest zone, eighteen inches or less. [4]This is the zone of making love, for instance, and also of physical confrontations ("in your face!"). [5]Second is personal distance, eighteen inches to four feet, which is used for everyday conversations with friends. [6]Then there is social distance, four to seven feet, which we use for most interactions with strangers, such as buying something in a store. [7]The fourth zone is public distance, twelve feet or more. [8]A public speaker or a singer at a concert is usually at least twelve feet from the nearest audience members.

(Continues on next page)

_____ 4. [1]Have you ever wondered why products come in the colors they do? [2]For instance, why is toothpaste often green or blue and shampoo often golden-yellow? [3]Manufacturers pick the colors that are associated with qualities consumers value in certain products. [4]For example, it's known that blue symbolizes purity to most people and that green is refreshing. [5]These are both desirable qualities in toothpastes. [6]Manufacturers also know that golden-yellow symbolizes richness (as in real gold or egg yolks), so they frequently choose this color for shampoos and cream rinses—products in which consumers value richness. [7]Baby products, such as body lotion, are often tinted pink because that is a color commonly associated with softness and gentleness—the very qualities consumers want for a baby's care.

_____ 5. [1]On most days, we are surrounded by faces. [2]In a public place, our eyes flicker automatically to the faces around us. [3]We instinctively look for information, clues about other people's thoughts and feelings. [4]And yet, beyond the most obvious impressions (we recognize the person; we find the person attractive), faces tell us next to nothing. [5]As the poet William Blake wrote, "The human mask is forged in iron." [6]Glancing at the faces of strangers, we cannot begin to guess what turmoil or ecstasy is hidden behind those carefully composed features. [7]There may be the despair of mental illness, or relief over a friend's healing; the trauma of lost employment, or the excitement of a promotion; the heartbreak of a spouse's betrayal, or the joy of new love; the anguish over a suffering child, or the delight of an eagerly anticipated pregnancy. [8]Some of the people whose faces surround us have wakened that day wondering how they could possibly go on, how they could survive another day of crushing internal pain. [9]Others are moving through the day joyful, filled with elation. [10]But their features, transformed into iron masks, betray none of this. [11]We move by one another silently, curiously looking for evidence that is not there.

Name ______________________________ Date __________

Section __________ SCORE: (Number correct) ________ x 20 = ________ %

MAIN IDEAS: Mastery Test 4

The main idea may appear at any place within each of the five paragraphs that follow. Write the number of each main idea sentence in the space provided.

_____ 1. [1]One writer spent nine hundred hours over the course of eight years watching the action in singles bars and learning about male-female relationships. [2]Although men may think of themselves as the aggressors, says this writer, it is really women who make the decisions when a courtship is beginning. [3]He has observed that women are the ones who pick a potential mate out of the crowd. [4]They position themselves near the man they've selected and, with a glance or a smile, invite him to make contact. [5]Similarly, as conversation begins, the woman initiates each increasingly intimate stage. [6]Her continuing eye contact, moving closer, and touching the man all signal her permission for him to make further advances. [7]In most cases, the woman's signals are so subtle that the man is only subconsciously aware of them.

_____ 2. [1]In everyday advertising, one observes many obvious attempts to package and sell products and ideas (toothpaste, aspirin, presidential candidates) through clever tactics to influence consumers. [2]Many people claim that such blatant attempts at persuasion are so pitifully obvious that they are not much affected by them. [3]Nevertheless, the sales of one cigarette brand increased seven times during a four-year period of heavy advertising. [4]A toy company increased its sales twenty-four times after it began to advertise extensively on television. [5]And one venerable but nearly forgotten cereal brand experienced a sudden 30 percent increase in sales when a well-known natural-foods enthusiast began plugging this rather bland cereal. [6]There are many other advertising success stories as well. [7]It appears that tremendous numbers of consumers are influenced by advertising, despite their claims to the contrary.

_____ 3. [1]Pedal error occurs when the driver of an automobile mistakenly presses down on the accelerator instead of the brake pedal. [2]This leads to unintended acceleration, which, in turn, can frequently result in an accident. [3]It seems as though stepping on the wrong pedal would be an unlikely occurrence. [4]However, an analysis of pedal error shows that this mistake is easier to make than you might think. [5]A driver sometimes turns his upper body a little to the left at the same moment that he moves his right foot toward the brake pedal. [6]The driver might turn his upper body to the right to look in the left

(Continues on next page)

side mirror or to reach for his seatbelt. [7]Or, if he is in reverse, he might look over his left shoulder to make sure that it is safe to back up. [8]This turning of the upper body could cause his right foot to move slightly to the right. [9]As he unconsciously moves his foot to the right, he may end up hitting the accelerator rather than the brake. [10]Instead of stopping and remaining stationary, the car in fact begins to accelerate. [11]Believing that his foot is on the brake, the driver presses his foot down harder in an effort to stop the car. [12]Obviously, this action only makes the problem worse.

______ 4. [1]Of the many problems American pioneer women faced, perhaps the most unusual was insects. [2]One of the most terrifying assaults of nature involved grasshoppers. [3]Swarms would appear suddenly, in huge clouds, and devour everything in sight. [4]If a housewife tried covering her garden with gunnysacks, the bugs simply went under them, or ate their way through them. [5]After they ate the crops, the grasshoppers moved into the barns and houses. [6]They ate all the food and devoured clothing, window curtains, furniture, fence boards, and cabin sidings. [7]In the summer, flies or gnats swarmed over everything. [8]In a desperate attempt to drive away mosquitoes, plainswomen burned buffalo chips—they could stand the smell better than the bugs could. [9]In the Southwest, women were instructed to place their beds at least two feet away from the walls, lest they wake up covered with scorpions. [10]Fleas were also a terrible problem, and some settlers burned their houses down when the fleas became too burdensome. [11]But American settlers had a yen for permanence, and a sturdy house that lasted forever was also a permanent abode for vermin.

______ 5. [1]The American author Mark Twain is famous for the humor in his writing. [2]His novels, stories, and essays have brought laughter to millions. [3]However, Twain's own life in the sixteen years leading up to his death in 1910 was marked more by sorrow than humor, as he faced several personal tragedies. [4]He had invested a significant amount of money in the development of a mechanical typesetting machine. [5]In 1894 the project failed, and his investment was lost. [6]In addition, a publishing company that he had begun ten years earlier went bankrupt. [7]So at the age of 59, this once-rich man went on a two-year worldwide lecture tour in order to earn money. [8]He took his wife with him on this tour but left his three daughters at home in Hartford, Connecticut. [9]While he was gone, his favorite daughter, Susy, died of meningitis, an inflammation of the brain and spinal cord. [10]Although his wife, Olivia, was ten years younger than he, she had a long history of health problems and died in 1904. [11]In December 1909, just five months before Twain's own death, his daughter Jean died. [12]Only one of his three daughters outlived him.

Name ______________________________ Date __________
Section __________ SCORE: (Number correct) ______ x 25 = ______ %

MAIN IDEAS: Mastery Test 5

A. The main idea may appear at any place within each of the three paragraphs that follow. Write the number of each main idea sentence in the space provided.

______ 1. [1]Just as there are rules of the road for drivers of cars, trucks, and buses, there are "rules of the sidewalk" for pedestrians. [2]The sociologist Erving Goffman points out that, for one thing, pedestrians on a sidewalk keep to their right, relative to an imaginary dividing line in the middle of the sidewalk. [3]Thus people sort themselves into lanes going in opposite directions, as on a vehicular roadway. [4]And people who are walking slowly often tend to stay closer to the buildings, while to their left, in a "passing lane," are the people who are moving more quickly. [5]Also, like drivers, pedestrians scan the route ahead so that they can swerve around obstacles—say, a puddle or a hole in the walkway—and so that they will not collide with anyone else. [6]If a head-on collision seems possible, pedestrians will make eye contact and maneuver to keep out of each other's way. [7]Goffman notes one obvious difference, though: rules of the road are often codified in laws and regulations, whereas rules of the sidewalk are informal social customs.

______ 2. [1]When labor-management disputes are reported on news broadcasts, listeners sometimes think that mediation and arbitration are simply two interchangeable words for the same thing. [2]But mediation and arbitration are very different processes, with different outcomes, though both involve the use of a neutral third party. [3]In mediation, the third party (called a mediator) is brought in to assist in the negotiations so that the opponents will keep talking to each other. [4]Mediators can only make suggestions about how to resolve a dispute; neither side is obliged to accept them. [5]In arbitration, on the other hand, the third party—the arbitrator—is called in to settle the issue, and the arbitrator's decision is final and binding on both sides.

______ 3. [1]A biological virus can attach itself to a human host cell and take charge, using the cell's functions to make the substances needed to form new virus particles, which then leave that cell and spread, repeating the process in other cells. [2]Biological viruses cause many diseases—some minor, like the common cold; but some life-threatening, like polio or AIDS. [3]Biological viruses may kill the host cell or make the cell itself malignant, or the virus may set off a dangerously violent response in the immune system. [4]Biological viruses reproduce and spread in various ways, and they may be very hard to

(Continues on next page)

treat because they can take forms that the immune system cannot detect. [5]Computer viruses are programs designed to attach themselves to ordinary software, take it over, and then reproduce and spread. [6]A computer virus can do its damage by attacking the startup program, at which point antivirus devices cannot yet detect it; or by attacking the operating system; or by attacking applications such as databases. [7]In any case, the virus can distort or kill computer memory. [8]A computer virus, as the name implies, is very much like a biological virus.

B. (4.) The author has stated the central point of the following textbook selection in one sentence. Find that sentence, and write its number in the space provided.

Bug Protection

[1]Almost all insects will flee if threatened. [2]Many insects, however, have more specialized means of defense. [3]Roaches and stinkbugs, for example, secrete foul-smelling chemicals that deter aggressors. [4]Bees, wasps, and some ants have poisonous stings that can kill smaller predators and cause pain for larger ones. [5]The larvae of some insects have hairs filled with poison. [6]If a predator eats one of these larvae, it may suffer a toxic reaction. [7]Insects that defend themselves by unpleasant or dangerous chemicals gain two advantages. [8]On one hand, they often deter a predator from eating them. [9]On the other hand, predators learn not to bother them in the first place.

[10]Other insects gain protection by mimicry, or similarity of appearance. [11]In one kind of mimicry, insects with similar defense mechanisms look alike, and predators learn to avoid them all. [12]Bees and wasps mimic each other in this way. [13]In another kind of mimicry, insects with no defenses of their own mimic the appearance of stinging or bad-tasting insects. [14]Predators avoid the mimic as well as the insect with the unpleasant taste or sting. [15]For example, syrphid flies look like bees but do not sting.

[16]Another kind of defense based on appearance is camouflage, or the ability to blend into surroundings. [17]Many kinds of insects and animals have distinctive color markings that make them difficult to see. [18]Predators have trouble locating prey that looks like its background. [19]An insect is more likely to survive and produce offspring if it is camouflaged than if it is not.

_____ is the number of the sentence that states the central point.

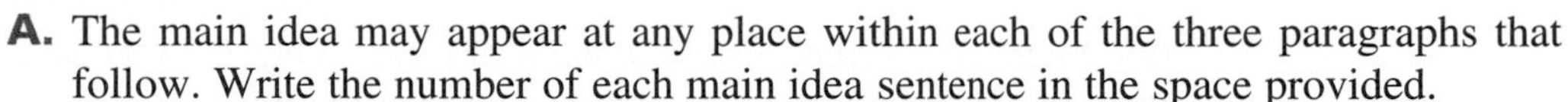
Name ____ Date __________
Section ____________ SCORE: (Number correct) _______ x 25 = _______ %

MAIN IDEAS: Mastery Test 6

A. The main idea may appear at any place within each of the three paragraphs that follow. Write the number of each main idea sentence in the space provided.

______ 1. [1]An old saying has it that "Many hands make light the work." [2]Thus we might expect that three individuals can pull three times as much as one person and that eight can pull eight times as much. [3]Research reveals that persons individually average 130 pounds of pressure when tugging on a rope. [4]However, in groups of three, they average 351 pounds (only 2.5 times the solo rate); and in groups of eight, only 546 pounds (less than 4 times the solo rate). [5]One explanation is that faulty coordination produces group inefficiency. [6]However, when subjects are blindfolded and believe they are pulling with others, they also slacken their effort. [7]Apparently when we work in groups, we cut down on our efforts, a process termed social loafing.

______ 2. [1]Criminal and civil cases, the two types of court cases, differ in significant ways. [2]Criminal cases involve the enforcement of criminal laws, that is, laws against acts such as murder and robbery. [3]The case is brought by a government—a state or the federal government—against someone who is charged with committing a crime. [4]The government, then, is the prosecutor, and the accused is the defendant. [5]The defendant will be found "guilty" or "not guilty," usually by a jury. [6]A civil case involves a legal dispute between individuals and organizations, such as businesses. [7]One party to the case, the plaintiff, has filed a complaint against the other party, the defendant. [8]Civil lawsuits arise, for example, over personal injuries (as in automobile accidents), disagreements about contracts, and—more and more often these days—medical malpractice. [9]There is no verdict of "guilty" or "not guilty" in a civil case; instead, a jury, a judge, or a panel of judges will decide in favor of the plaintiff or the defendant.

______ 3. [1]In one tribe in New Guinea, aggression is encouraged in boys from early infancy. [2]The child cannot obtain nourishment from his mother without carrying on a continuous battle with her. [3]Unless he grasps the nipple firmly and sucks vigorously, his mother will withdraw it and stop the feeding. [4]In his frantic effort to get food, the child frequently chokes—an annoyance to both himself and his mother. [5]Thus the feeding situation itself is "characterized by anger and struggle rather than by affection and reassurance" (Mead, 1939). [6]The people of another New Guinea tribe are extremely peaceful and do

(Continues on next page)

everything possible to discourage aggression. [7]They regard all instances of aggression as abnormal. [8]A similar tribe—the Tasaday of the Philippines—has been discovered. [9]These people are extremely friendly and gentle. [10]They possess no weapons for fighting or food-gathering; in fact, they are strict vegetarians who live off the land. [11]Evidence of this sort suggests that, rather than being basically aggressive animals, human beings are peaceful or aggressive depending upon their early childhood training.

B. (4.) The author has stated the central point of the following textbook selection in one sentence. Find that sentence, and write its number in the space provided.

[1]Those who are fortunate enough not to live in poverty may equate "being poor" with "not having enough money to buy the things I'd like." [2]Certainly, being poor does mean doing without many of life's material pleasures. [3]But the impact of poverty goes far beyond the inability to buy goods.

[4]One fundamental effect of poverty is that the poor often live in substandard housing. [5]They rent from landlords who may neglect the property, even to a criminal extent. [6]The houses are often unsafe, with dangerous electrical wiring, non-functioning plumbing, and inadequate heat.

[7]Poverty also profoundly affects people's ability to receive an education. [8]Public schools in poor areas are under-funded, poorly staffed, and supplied with outdated textbooks and sparse supplies. [9]Classrooms are crowded and often chaotic; the schools function more as warehouses than as places of education. [10]Children coming out of these schools are inadequately prepared for college, so they rarely advance beyond high school.

[11]A third way in which poverty profoundly affects people's lives is in the area of employment. [12]Without the career preparation that quality education provides, poor people are often qualified only for jobs with no future, no benefits, and a high chance of being laid off. [13]When the poor do lose their jobs, they must deal with the tangled mess of unemployment insurance and welfare, adding stress and the increasing sense of failure to their lives.

_____ is the number of the sentence that states the central point.

3 Supporting Details

In Chapter 2 you worked on the most important reading skill—finding the main idea. A closely related reading skill is locating *supporting details*—the added information that is needed for you to make sense of a main idea.

This chapter describes supporting details and presents three techniques that will help you take study notes on main ideas and their supporting details: outlining, mapping, and summarizing.

What Are Supporting Details?

Supporting details are reasons, examples, facts, steps, or other kinds of evidence that explain a main idea. In the cartoon shown above, the main idea is that "I know why I don't lose weight." The joke in the cartoon is that the man's supporting details—big meals, snacks, beer, and not exercising—may make him *happy*, but they don't make him *healthy*.

On the next page is a paragraph with strong support for its point.

A Paragraph with Strong Support

In the paragraph below, three major details support the main idea that the penny should be phased out of our economy. As you read the paragraph, try to identify and check (✓) the three major details.

[1]"A penny saved is a penny earned," the old saying goes. [2]But there are now good reasons for our government to phase the penny out of the economy, allowing the nickel to stand as the lowest-valued coin. [3]For one thing, pennies take up more space than they are worth. [4]We can all recall a time when we needed a nickel, dime, or quarter to make an important phone call, buy a vending machine snack, or make a photocopy, and all we could come up with was a fistful of useless pennies. [5]Pennies are also a nuisance to the business community. [6]According to the National Association of Convenience Stores, 5.5 million hours and 22 million dollars are wasted by businesses on the extra time and effort it takes to handle pennies. [7]Finally, keeping pennies in circulation costs the nation as a whole. [8]The manufacturing, storage, and handling expenses involved in a penny's production and distribution add up to considerably more than the one cent it is worth.

Check Your Understanding

See if you can complete the basic outline below that shows the three major details supporting the main idea.

Main idea: Our government should phase the penny out of the economy.

Supporting detail 1: ______________________________

Supporting detail 2: ______________________________

Supporting detail 3: ______________________________

Explanation

You should have added 1) pennies take up more space than they are worth; 2) pennies are a nuisance to the business community, and 3) pennies cost the nation as a whole. These major supporting details help you fully understand the main idea. To read effectively, then, you must learn to recognize main ideas and the details that support these ideas.

Outlining

Preparing an outline of a passage often helps you understand and see clearly the relationship between a main idea and its supporting details. Outlines start with a main idea (or a heading that summarizes the main idea), followed by supporting details. There are often two levels of supporting details—major and minor. The **major details** explain and develop the main idea. In turn, the **minor details** help fill out and make clear the major details.

Below is the paragraph on TV violence that appeared in Chapter 2. Its supporting details are *factual evidence* found in two studies. Reread the paragraph, and put a check (✓) next to the each of three major supporting details.

> [1]Many people feel that violence on television is harmless entertainment. [2]However, we now know that TV violence does affect people in negative ways. [3]One study showed that frequent TV watchers are more fearful and suspicious of others. [4]They try to protect themselves from the outside world with extra locks on the doors, alarm systems, guard dogs, and guns. [5]In addition, that same study showed that heavy TV watchers are less upset about real-life violence than non-TV watchers. [6]It seems that the constant violence they see on TV makes them less sensitive to the real thing. [7]Another study, of a group of children, found that TV violence increases aggressive behavior. [8]Children who watched violent shows were more willing to hurt another child in games where they were given a choice between helping and hurting. [9]They were also more likely to select toy weapons over other kinds of playthings.

Check Your Understanding

Now see if you can fill in the missing items in the following outline of the paragraph, which shows both major and minor details.

Main idea: We now know that TV violence does affect people in negative ways.

Major detail 1: Frequent TV watchers are more fearful and suspicious of others.

Minor detail: Protect themselves with extra locks, alarms, dogs, and guns.

Major detail 2: ____

____

Minor detail: Constant violence on TV makes them less sensitive to the real thing.

Major detail 3: ______________________________

Minor detail: ______________________________

____

Explanation

You should have added two major supporting details: (2) Heavy TV watchers are less upset about real-life violence than non-TV watchers; (3) TV violence increases aggressive behavior in children. And to the third major supporting detail you should have added the minor detail that children watching violent shows are more likely to choose toy weapons instead of other playthings.

Notice that just as the main idea is more general than its supporting details, major details are more general than minor ones. For instance, the major detail "Frequent TV watchers are more fearful and suspicious of others" is more general than the minor details about people protecting themselves with "extra locks on the doors, alarm systems, guard dogs, and guns," which illustrate the major detail.

Outlining Tips

The following tips will help you prepare outlines:

TIP 1 Look for words that tell you a list of details is coming. Here are some common list words:

List Words

several kinds of	various causes	a few reasons
a number of	a series of	three factors
four steps	among the results	several advantages

For example, look again at the main ideas in the two paragraphs already discussed and underline the list words:

- But there are now good reasons for our government to phase the penny out of the economy.
- In fact, we now know that TV violence does affect people in negative ways.

Here the words *good reasons* and *negative ways* each tell us that a list of major details is coming. But you will not always be given such helpful signals that a list of details will follow. For example, there are no list words in the paragraph on page 67 with this main idea: "Shocking as it seems, cannibalism is common in the animal world." However, you will want to note such list words when they are present, because they help you to understand quickly the basic organization of a passage.

TIP 2 Look for words that signal major details. Such words are called **addition words**, and they will be explained further on pages 186–187. Here are some common addition words:

Addition Words

one	to begin with	also	further
first (of all)	for one thing	in addition	furthermore
second(ly)	other	next	last (of all)
third(ly)	another	moreover	final(ly)

✓ *Check Your Understanding*

Now look again at the selection on TV violence on page 105:

1. The word *one* (in *One study*) signals the first major supporting detail.
2. What addition words introduce the second major supporting detail?

   ____

3. What addition word introduces the third major supporting detail?

   ____

And look again at the selection on phasing out the penny on page 104:

1. What words introduce the first major detail?________________
2. What word introduces the second major detail? ________________
3. What word introduces the third major detail? ________________

Explanation

In the selection on TV violence, the second major detail is introduced by the words *In addition*, and the third major detail by the word *Another*. In the selection on phasing out the penny, the first major detail is introduced by the words *For one thing*; the second major detail by the word *also*; and the third major detail by the word *Finally*.

TIP 3 When making an outline, put all supporting details of equal importance at the same distance from the margin. In the outline on TV violence on pages 105–106, the three major supporting details all begin at the same distance from the left margin. Likewise, the minor supporting details are all indented at a slightly greater distance from the margin. You can therefore see at a glance the main idea, the major details, and the minor details.

Check Your Understanding

Put appropriate numbers *(1, 2, 3)* and letters *(a, b)* in front of the items in the following outline.

Main idea

    ___ **Major detail**

        ___ Minor detail

        ___ Minor detail

    ___ **Major detail**

        ___ Minor detail

        ___ Minor detail

    ___ **Major detail**

Explanation

You should have put a *1, 2,* and *3* in front of the major details and an *a* and *b* in front of the minor details. Note that an outline proceeds from the most general to the most specific, from main idea to major details to minor details.

The practice that follows will give you experience in finding major details, in separating major details from minor details, and in preparing outlines.

PRACTICE 1

Read and then outline each passage. Begin by writing in the main idea, and then fill in the supporting details. The first outline requires only major details; the second calls for you to add minor details as well.

A. [1]*Merriam Webster's Collegiate Dictionary* defines *intimacy* as a state of "very close association, contact, or familiarity." [2]Researchers have identified four kinds of intimacy. [3]The first kind is physical. [4]Fortunate children are continually nourished by physical intimacy: being rocked, fed, hugged, and held. [5]As we grow older, we hug, shake hands, and continue to seek physical intimacy of all kinds. [6]Intimacy can also come from intellectual sharing. [7]When you engage another person in an exchange of important ideas, a kind of closeness develops that can be powerful and exciting. [8]Another kind of intimacy is emotional: exchanging important feelings. [9]Sharing personal information can both reflect and create feelings of closeness. [10]Last, shared activities can be seen as a dimension that achieves intimacy. [11]Shared activities can include everything from working side by side at a job or in a study group or meeting regularly for exercise workouts.

Main idea: ______________________________

____

Major detail 1: ______________________________

____

Major detail 2: ______________________________

____

Major detail 3: ______________________________

____

Major detail 4: ______________________________

____

B. [1]A crowd is a temporary, relatively unorganized gathering of people. [2]Since a wide range of behavior is covered by the concept, sociologist Herbert Blumer distinguishes among four basic types of crowds. [3]The first, a casual crowd, is a collection of people with little in common except for participating in a common event, such as looking through a department-store window. [4]The second, a conventional crowd, is a number of people who have assembled for some specific purpose, such as attending a baseball game or concert. [5]Members of a conventional crowd typically act in accordance with established norms. [6]The third, an expressive crowd, is a group of people who have gotten together for self-stimulation and personal satisfaction, such as a religious revival or a rock festival. [7]And fourth, an acting crowd is an excited, explosive collection of people, including those who engage in rioting, looting, or other forms of aggressive behavior in which established norms carry little weight.

Main idea: According to sociologist Herbert Blumer, there are ____________

____

Major detail 1: ______________________________________

____

Minor detail: ______________________________________

Major detail 2: ______________________________________

____

Minor detail: ______________________________________

Major detail 3: ______________________________________

____

Minor detail: ______________________________________

Major detail 4: ______________________________________

____

Minor detail: ______________________________________

____

Study Hint: At times you will want to include minor details in your study notes; at other times, it may not be necessary to do so. If you are taking notes on one or more textbook chapters, use your judgment. It is often best to be aware of minor details but to concentrate on writing down the main ideas and major details.

Mapping

Students sometimes find it helpful to use maps rather than outlines. **Maps**, or diagrams, are highly visual outlines in which circles, boxes, or other shapes show the relationships between main ideas and supporting details. Each major detail is connected to the main idea, often presented in the form of a title. If minor details are included, each is connected to the major detail it explains.

Check Your Understanding

Read the following passage, and then see if you can complete the map and the questions that follow.

[1]Weber says that there are three types of authority from which governments gain their right to command. [2]One type of authority is based on tradition. [3]Kings, queens, feudal lords, and tribal chiefs do not need written rules in order to govern. [4]Their authority is based on long-standing customs and is handed down through generations from parent to child. [5]People may also submit to authority because of charisma, the exceptional personal quality of an individual. [6]Such leaders as Napoleon and Gandhi illustrate authority that derives its legitimacy from charismatic personalities. [7]The political systems of industrial states are based largely on a third type of authority: legal authority. [8]These systems derive legitimacy from a set of explicit rules and procedures that spell out the ruler's rights and duties. [9]Typically, the rules and procedures are put in writing. [10]The people grant their obedience to "the law." [11]It specifies procedures by which certain individuals hold offices of power, such as governor or president or prime minister. [12]But the authority is vested in those offices, not in the individuals who temporarily hold the offices.

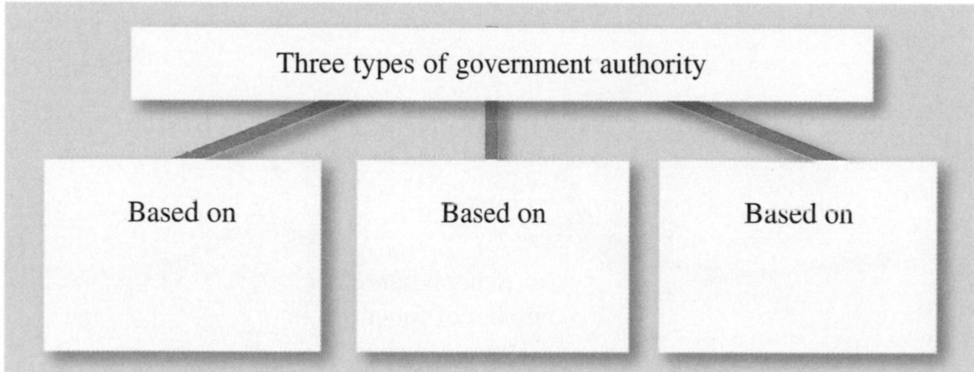

Which word or words introduce:

1. The first major detail? ____________________
2. The second major detail? ____________________
3. The third major detail? ____________________

Explanation

The map sets off the major details in a very visual way. You see at a glance what Weber's three types of governmental authority are based on: tradition, charisma, and law. The words that introduce the major details are *One*, *also*, and *third*.

PRACTICE 2

Read each passage, and then complete the maps that follow. The main ideas are given so that you can focus on finding the supporting details. The first passage requires only major details. The second passage calls for you to add both major and minor details.

A. [1]Schools serve a number of functions in American society. [2]Because most students are unmarried, high schools and colleges act as matchmaking institutions. [3]It is at school that many young people find their future spouses. [4]Schools also establish social networks. [5]Some adults maintain friendships from high school and college; others develop networks that benefit their careers. [6]Another function of schools is to provide employment. [7]With 53 million students in grade and high schools, and another 15 million enrolled in colleges, U.S. education is big business. [8]Primary and secondary schools provide jobs for 2.9 million teachers, while another million work in colleges and universities. [9]Moreoever, schools help stabilize employment. [10]To keep millions of young people in school is to keep them out of the labor market, protecting the positions of older workers.

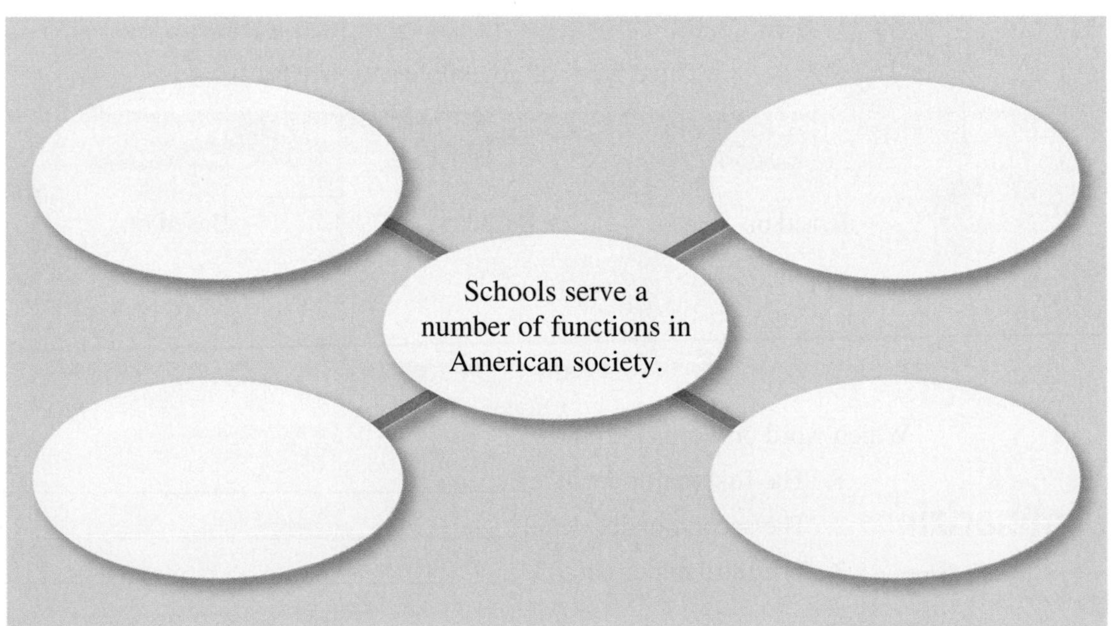

B. [1]In India, which has the largest number of cattle in the world, why is the slaughter of cows forbidden when there are many poor and starving people? [2]Some social scientists have pointed out that the sacred cows serve several important, practical functions. [3]First, they produce oxen, which Indian farmers desperately need to plow their fields and pull their carts. [4]In addition, cows benefit people when they die naturally. [5]Their beef is eaten by the poor lower castes, and their hides are used by non-Hindu Indians to maintain one of the world's largest leather industries. [6]Third, the cows produce an enormous amount of manure, which is used as fertilizer and cooking fuel. [7]Fourth, the cows are easy to raise. [8]They are tireless scavengers, eating garbage, stubble, and grass between railroad tracks, in ditches, and on roadsides. [9]Thus, it costs nothing to raise the cows, and they provide many things of value.

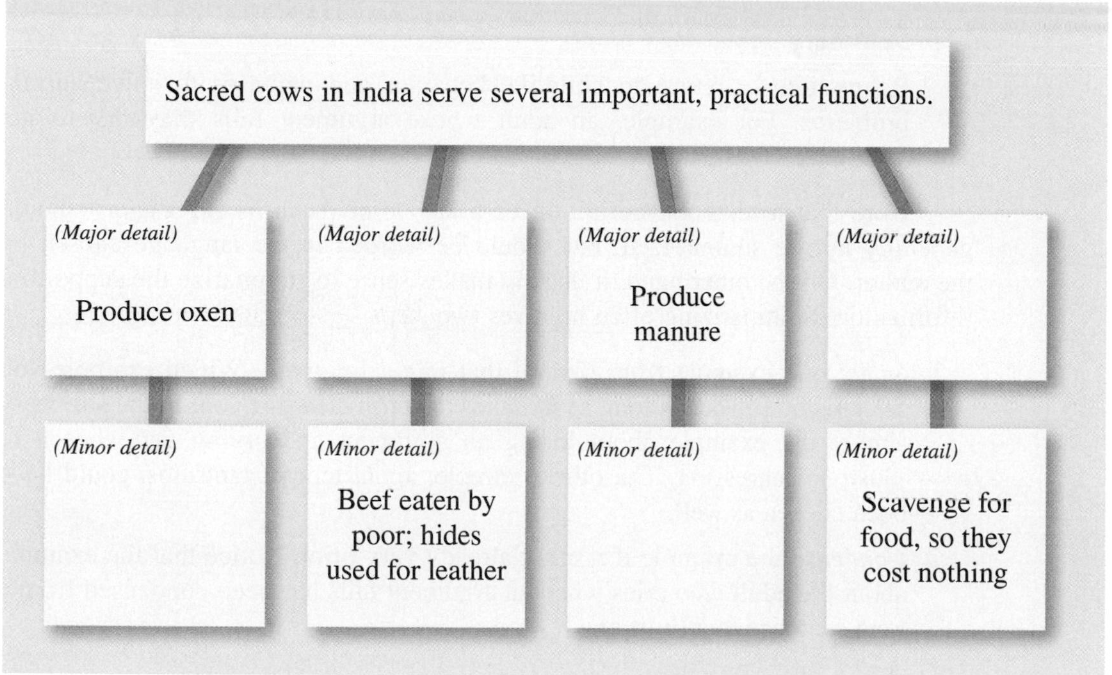

Summarizing

A **summary** is the reduction of a large amount of information to its most important points. The length and kind of summary will depend upon one's purpose as well as the material in question. Often, a summary will consist of a main idea and its major supporting details. As a general guideline, a paragraph might be reduced to a sentence or two, an article might be reduced to a paragraph, and a textbook chapter might be reduced to about three pages of notes.

One of the most common types of summarizing occurs when you are taking study notes on textbook material. Very often you will find it helpful to summarize examples of key terms. For instance, look at the following textbook passage and the summary that follows.

> [1]People under severe stress may react to their problems with **regression**, a return to childlike behavior and defenses. [2]Adults who cry when their arguments fail may expect those around them to react sympathetically, as their parents did when they were children. [3]Other adults may use temper tantrums in a similar way. [4]In both examples, people are drawing on childish behaviors to solve current problems, in the hope that someone will respond to them the way adults did when they were children. [5]Inappropriate as it may seem, such immature and manipulative behavior often works—at least for a while.

Summary

Regression—a return to childlike behavior and defenses to solve current problems. For example, an adult whose argument fails may cry to get sympathy.

Note that a textbook definition of a key term (such as *regression*) should generally not be summarized, but should be worded in the language chosen by the author. On the other hand, it usually makes sense to summarize the supporting information. Summarizing often involves two steps:

1. *Select* one example from several that might be given. Which example you select is up to you, as long as it makes the term clear for you. In the summary above, the example about losing an argument and crying was chosen to illustrate regression. The other example, about temper tantrums, could have been chosen as well.
2. *Condense* the example if it's not already very brief. Notice that the example about the adult who cries when an argument fails has been condensed from a long sentence to a short one.

A definition of a key term followed by one condensed example is a very useful way to take notes—especially in introductory college courses, where many terms are defined and illustrated.

> ***Study Hint:*** If you have a textbook chapter to learn, very often you can get the information you need by doing two things: 1) writing down the definitions in the chapter and summarized examples of the definitions, and 2) writing down lists of major supporting details and any minor details that you think are important.

Check Your Understanding

Read the selection below, taken from an introductory textbook for a college social science course. As is often the case in such introductory texts, a new term is presented and then followed by an extended example. Complete the study notes by circling the answer choice that best summarizes that example.

[1]The tendency for members to be so intent on maintaining group agreement that they overlook or put aside the flaws in their decision is called **groupthink**. [2]Once a tentative decision has been made, members withhold information or opinions that might cast doubt on that course of action. [3]They do not want to be seen as criticizing their colleagues or as "rocking the boat." [4]If outside experts raise questions about the wisdom of their decision, members unite in opposing and discrediting the new information. [5]A classic example of "groupthink" occurred more than 50 years ago, during President Kennedy's administration. [6]Kennedy sought the advice of a small group of trusted advisers in deciding whether to support the Bay of Pigs invasion of Cuba in 1961—an attempt by a force of Cuban exiles to overthrow the government of Fidel Castro. [7]Although several advisers had strong objections to the plan, not one expressed doubts. [8]As far as Kennedy knew, his advisers were unanimously in favor. [9]The invasion was a military and public relations disaster.

Study notes

Groupthink—the tendency for members to be so intent on maintaining group agreement that they overlook or put aside the flaws in the group's decision.

Example—

A. During Kennedy's administration, the Bay of Pigs invasion of Cuba in 1961 was a military and public relations disaster.
B. A classic example occurred during President Kennedy's administration.
C. Kennedy went ahead with the disastrous Bay of Pigs invasion because advisers withheld their objections.

Explanation

Useful study notes should clearly show how an example illustrates a new term. In the case of the paragraph above, the notes should include the key point that Kennedy's advisers overlooked the flaws in a decision. Only answer C includes the idea that advisers withheld their objections in order to seem unanimously in favor of the Bay of Pigs invasion, which turned out to be a disaster. Answer A tells about the results of the Bay of Pigs invasion, but says nothing about how the advisers withheld their true opinions. Answer B also makes no mention of what the advisers did. It refers to the example so generally that the event isn't even mentioned.

PRACTICE 3

Read each textbook selection below. Then complete the study notes by circling the letter of the answer that best summarizes an example of the term being defined.

A. [1]People are often motivated by the direct object of a desire, such as food or water. [2]A **secondary reinforcer** is something one learns to desire through association with other, direct rewards. [3]It is referred to as secondary not because it is less important, but because it is learned. [4]A rat learns to get food by pressing a bar; then a buzzer is sounded every time the rat presses the bar and gets food. [5]Even if the rat stops getting the food, it will continue to press the bar just to hear the buzzer. [6]Although the buzzer by itself has no value to the rat, it has become a secondary reinforcer. [7]For humans, money is a secondary reinforcer. [8]Money is just paper or metal, but through its association with food, clothing, and other objects of desire, it becomes a powerful reward. [9]Children come to value money only after they learn that it will buy such things as candy, something that has direct value to them. [10]Then the money becomes a secondary reinforcer, something they have learned to want.

Study notes

Secondary reinforcer—something one learns to desire through association with other, direct rewards.

Example—

A. People are motivated by the direct objects of their desires, such as food, water, clothing, and candy.

B. Money is desired not for its own sake but because of its association with direct rewards of desire.

C. After a rat learns to get food by pressing a bar, a buzzer is sounded every time the rat presses the bar to get food.

B. [1]According to one sociologist, virtually every organization includes "higher participants" (such as the administrators) and "lower participants" (the rank and file). [2]**Coercive organizations** are among the most common types of organizations. [3]Prisons, concentration camps, and custodial mental hospitals are examples of coercive organizations. [4]In each, force or the threat of force is used to achieve the organization's main goal: keeping the inmates in. [5]The inmates obviously do not enjoy being imprisoned; they will run away if they have the chance. [6]They are alienated from the organization and do not support its goals at all. [7]Understandably, the higher participants—such as prison administrators—have to act tough toward the inmates, seeking compliance by threatening solitary confinement if they try to escape. [8]In brief, in this kind of organization, coercion, or force, is the main form of power used, and the involvement by lower participants is alienating.

Study notes

Coercive organizations—organizations in which force or the threat of force is used to achieve the main goal: keeping in inmates, who are alienated from the organization.

Example—

A. Every organization includes "higher participants" (such as administrators) and "lower participants" (rank and file).

B. In coercive organizations, force is the main form of power used, and the involvement by lower participants is alienating.

C. In a prison, inmates will run away if they can, and the administrators seek obedience by threatening solitary confinement.

PRACTICE 4

Read each textbook selection below. Then take study notes by 1) writing down the key term and its definition, 2) selecting an example that makes the definition clear, and 3) writing that example in your notes, condensing it if possible.

A. [1]A **Pyrrhic victory** is a victory won at enormous cost. [2]A good example of such a victory is provided by the person whose name the term comes from: Pyrrhus, a Greek mercenary general who invaded Italy and attacked the Romans in 281 B.C. [3]Pyrrhus defeated the Roman army sent against him, but his own army suffered terrible losses. [4]"One more such victory and I am ruined," he exclaimed. [5]The Battle of Borodino in 1812 was another classic instance of a Pyrrhic victory. [6]Napoleon's invading French army defeated a defending Russian army near Moscow and occupied the city. [7]But the French suffered so greatly from the battle and the winter that followed that the invasion turned into a disaster that cost Napoleon his throne.

Study notes

A Pyrrhic victory—______________________________

Example—______________________________

____

____

B. [1]To protect their self-esteem, some people will practice **suppression**, which is a deliberate attempt to avoid stressful thoughts. [2]For instance, Jeff wants to avoid thinking about an argument he had with his girlfriend. [3]To keep it out of his mind, he spends as much of his time as possible hanging out with his buddies, talking about and playing sports. [4]An elderly woman whose husband has died keeps herself busy with chores and volunteer work. [5]Scarlett O'Hara in the novel and movie *Gone with the Wind* is among the more famous practitioners of suppression. [6]Remember her line "I shall think about it tomorrow"? [7]Scarlett was suppressing her unpleasant thoughts.

Study notes:

______________________ — ______________________

____

Example—____________________________________

____

A Final Note

This chapter has centered on supporting details as they appear in well-organized paragraphs. But keep in mind that supporting details are part of readings of any length, including selections that may not have an easy-to-follow list of one major detail after another. Starting with the reading at the end of this chapter (page 125), you will be given practice in answering all kinds of questions about key supporting details. These questions will develop your ability to pay close, careful attention to what you are reading.

CHAPTER REVIEW

In this chapter, you learned the following:

- Major and minor details provide the added information you need to make sense of a main idea.
- List words and addition words can help you to find major and minor supporting details.
- Outlining, mapping, and summarizing are useful note-taking strategies.
- Outlines show the relationship between the main idea, major details, and minor details of a passage.
- Maps are very visual outlines.
- Writing a definition and summarizing an example is a good way to take notes on a new term.

The next chapter—Chapter 4—will show you how to find implied main ideas and central points.

On the Web: If you are using this book in class, you can visit our website for additional practice in recognizing supporting details. Go to **www.townsendpress.com** and click on "Learning Center."

REVIEW TEST 1

To review what you've learned in this chapter, answer each of these questions about supporting details by filling in the blank.

1. Two key reading skills that go hand in hand are finding the main idea and identifying the major and minor ________________ that support the main idea.
2. **List words**—words such as *several kinds of, four steps, three factors,* and *four reasons*—are important words to note because they alert you that a list of ____________________ is coming.

3. A traditional outline shows at a glance the relationship between ______________ and supporting details; it is a very helpful way to take textbook study notes.

4. Another good way to take study notes is to use a ______________—a highly visual outline that uses circles, boxes, and other shapes to set off main ideas and supporting details.

5. Very often textbook study notes will include definitions of key terms and summaries of ______________ that make those key terms clear and understandable.

REVIEW TEST 2

A. (1–5.) Answer the supporting-detail questions that follow the passage. Note that the main idea is boldfaced.

> [1]**When a teenager becomes pregnant, the odds are stacked against her and her baby in a variety of ways.** [2]To begin with, the babies of teen moms are at increased risk for premature birth and low birth weight, which can lead to lifelong medical problems. [3]Also, children of teen moms are at higher risk for abuse. [4]Reports of abuse or neglect occur twice as often in families headed by a teen mom as in other families. [5]In addition, teen moms are unlikely to complete their educations. [6]Less than a third of girls who have a baby before age 18 earn a high-school degree. [7]Only 15 percent of teen moms earn a college degree before the age of 30. [8]Finally, the future prospects for children of teen moms are bleak. [9]Boys born to teen moms are 13 percent more likely to end up in prison than other boys. [10]Girls born to teen mothers are 22 percent more likely to become teen moms themselves.

____ 1. The major details of the paragraph are
A. facts.
B. examples.
C. reasons.

2. What addition word introduces the second major detail? ______________

3. What addition word introduces the third major detail? ______________

____ 4. Sentence 8 provides
A. a major detail.
B. a minor detail.

____ 5. Sentences 9 and 10 provide
A. major details.
B. minor details.

B. (6–10.) Outline the following paragraph by completing the main idea and filling in the missing major and minor details. Note that addition words introduce the major details.

[1]Do you sometimes feel cold, or hot, while others around you seem comfortable? [2]Don't worry—you are not alone. [3]Weight is one of many biological factors that affect how warm or cold you feel: the more body fat you have, the greater the amount of insulation, so you tend not to be as cold. [4]Muscle mass is another factor affecting our body temperature. [5]The more muscular you are, the better your body will be at regulating temperature. [6]Moreover, diet affects body temperature. [7]People with a poor diet who don't get enough essential nutrients may find themselves feeling cold and tired because their body is not getting the "fuel" it needs to work efficiently. [8]In addition, age is a biological factor to consider. [9]As people age, their declining hormonal systems don't produce as many hormones as when they were younger. [10]As a result, the elderly often feel colder. [11]Finally, stress is a factor affecting people's body temperature: tenseness could reduce your circulation, making you feel colder.

Main idea: ______________________________ affect how warm or cold you feel.

Major detail 1: ______________________________

Minor detail: More body fat means more insulation.

Major detail 2: ______________________________

Minor detail: ______________________________

Major detail 3: Diet

Minor detail: Poor diet can make body feel cold and tired.

Major detail 4: Age

Minor detail: Declining hormonal systems can make elderly feel colder.

Major detail 5: ______________________________

Minor detail: Tenseness can reduce circulation and make you feel colder.

REVIEW TEST 3

A. (1–4.) Map the following passage by filling in the main idea and the major supporting details.

[1]Functional illiteracy—the inability to read and write well enough to carry out everyday activities—is a complex social problem that stems from several sources. [2]One source of the problem is our educational system. [3]Our schools are too quick to pass children from one grade to the next even when their learning is woefully deficient. [4]Even teachers who care may not want to "buck the system" by refusing to pass along students who have not yet learned important basic skills. [5]The community also contributes to functional illiteracy. [6]Local businesses and agencies, indifferent to education, do not work with schools toward improving children's motivation and learning. [7]Another source is the home. [8]Millions of children grow up with illiterate parents who do not give them the opportunity or encouragement to learn language skills. [9]In all too many homes, a television is turned on much of the time, but there are few if any books to interest children in reading.

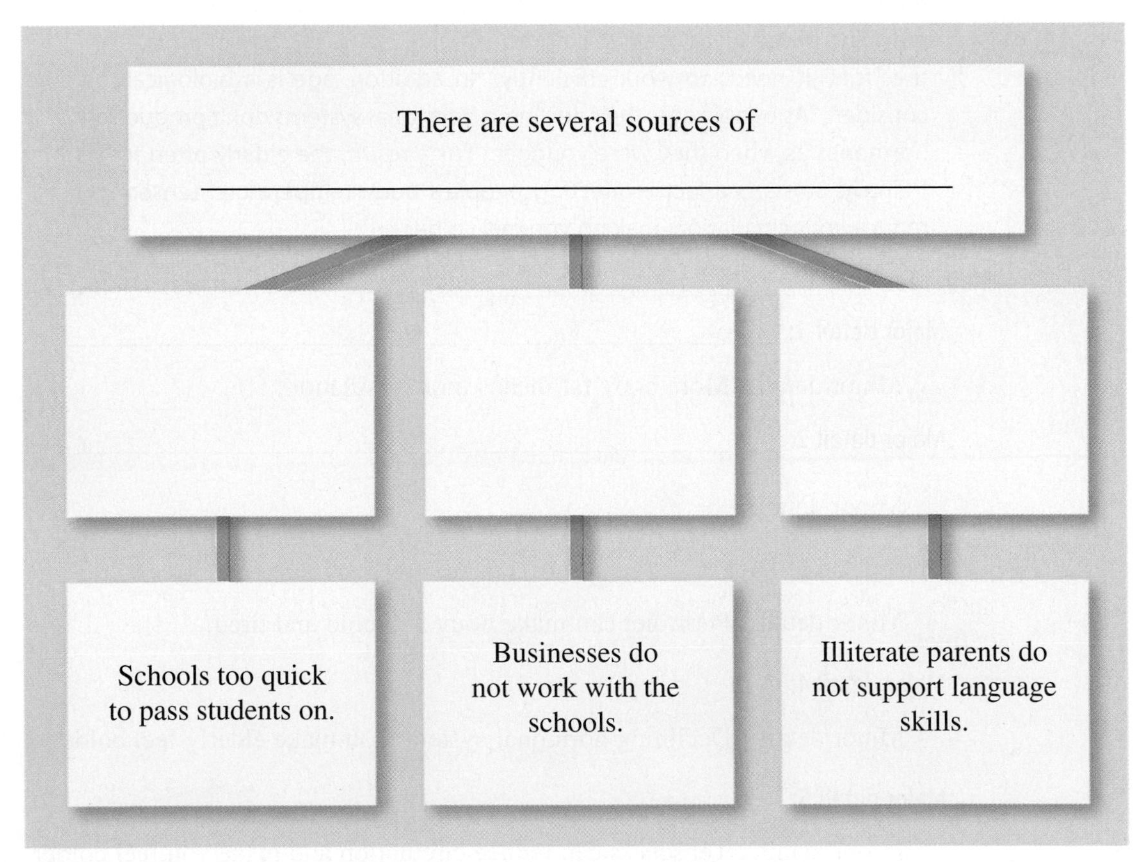

There are several sources of

____

Schools too quick to pass students on.	Businesses do not work with the schools.	Illiterate parents do not support language skills.

B. (5–9.) Outline the following passage by filling in the main idea, the major supporting details, and the one missing minor detail.

> [1]There are three recognized mechanisms of heat transfer. [2]One is **conduction**, which is heat transferred through matter by molecular activity. [3]For instance, anyone who has touched a metal spoon that was left in a hot pan has discovered that heat was conducted through the spoon. [4]A second mechanism of heat transfer is **convection**. [5]This is the transfer of heat by mass movement or circulation within a substance. [6]The boiling water in a pan on a stove demonstrates transfer of heat by convection. [7]As the water at the bottom of the pan is heated, it expands and becomes lighter, so it rises. [8]At the same time, the cooler, denser water near the top sinks to the bottom, where it then is heated and rises. [9]A third mechanism of heat transfer is **radiation.** [10]Radiation is heat that travels out in all directions from its source. [11]It does not need a medium (such as the spoon or the water) to travel through. [12]For example, it is by radiation that the sun's heat travels through the vacuum of space and reaches the earth.

Main idea: ____.

Major detail: ____

____

Minor detail: spoon left in hot pan

Major detail: ____

____

Minor detail: ____

Major detail: ____

____

Minor detail: the sun

C. (10.) Read the textbook selection below. Then complete the study notes by circling the letter of the answer choice that best summarizes the example of the term being defined.

> [1]Some animals exhibit **warning coloration**, bright coloring that protects the animals by warning predators of a distasteful and often poisonous meal. [2]Since poisoning your predator is little comfort if you have already been eaten, the bright colors declare: "Eat me at your own risk." [3]After a single unpleasant experience, predators avoid these conspicuous prey. [4]For instance, a toad that tries to eat a yellow and black bee and gets stung will avoid brightly colored bees in the future. [5]A bird that eats the distasteful, colorful monarch butterfly will no longer be tempted to dine on monarchs.

Study notes

Warning coloration—the bright coloring sometimes shared by different species that effectively warns predators of a distasteful and often poisonous meal.

Example—

A. Since poisoning your predator is little comfort if you're eaten, the bright colors warn your predator beforehand.
B. After being stung when trying to eat a bee, a toad will avoid brightly colored bees.
C. Different species of dangerous animals have similar warning coloration, such as the bee.

REVIEW TEST 4

When Miranda left for school at a faraway university, she thought that all her dreams were on their way to coming true. Then, once disappointment set in, friends began suggesting she check out her local community college. Soon, Miranda's life had completely turned around.

Read the selection, and then answer the supporting-detail questions that follow. To help you continue to strengthen your work on the skills taught in previous chapters, there are also questions on vocabulary in context and main ideas.

Words to Watch

Below are some words in the reading that do not have strong context support. Each word is followed by the number of the paragraph in which it appears and its meaning there. These words are indicated in the article by a small circle (°).

culinary (3): cooking
gourmet (3): fine food
diversity (10): variety
ecstatic (11): thrilled, overjoyed

NOW MORE THAN EVER: COMMUNITY COLLEGES

Daniel Wister

1 A few years ago, Miranda left home for college at a big four-year university nearly 1500 miles away from the city where she grew up. She had big dreams of being the first person to graduate from college in her family and even bigger dreams of becoming a successful professional some day. At first, Miranda was certain that nothing could get in the way of her dreams coming true. However, Miranda had barely been on campus for more than a few months before she started seeing her high hopes, and her dreams, fade.

2 To begin with, Miranda wasn't particularly comfortable with being so far away from home right after high school. She felt awkward living with a roommate she had never met, and she became increasingly homesick. Making matters worse, Miranda's family didn't have enough money to fly her home more than once during the school year. And that was just the beginning of Miranda's problems. During her second semester, she realized that she really didn't know why she had picked the major she'd picked. She had chosen history because she'd always been kind of interested in the past, but now she wasn't so sure about her decision. However, at a tuition rate of nearly $12,000 a year, Miranda felt pressured to stick with her choice. After all, she had taken out some serious student loans, and she didn't want to waste money by enrolling in a variety of classes in order to make up her mind. Miranda couldn't afford the luxury of taking the time to find out what she really wanted to do with her life.

Then Miranda realized that she 3
would need a job in order to help pay for all the added expenses of attending college that her loans didn't cover. Her parents sent some extra money now and then, but it was never nearly enough. Miranda hoped she could work three days a week and take a few of her classes at night or on Saturday. However, Miranda found out that very few night or weekend classes were offered. Compounding her problems, Miranda was beginning to realize that she was not particularly interested in her chosen major, after all. What she had discovered was that she really wanted to major in culinary° arts and become a chef. Gourmet° cooking and creating new recipes had always been a passion of Miranda's. But a culinary arts degree wasn't even offered at her university. Miranda's grades began to drop, and soon she lost interest in college altogether. Finally, at the end of her freshman year, Miranda dropped out. She returned home without a degree but with thousands of dollars to

repay for her confusing and upsetting experience at the university. And all her dreams had disappeared.

4 So what's the moral of this story? That it's a bad idea to go to college? Hardly. The moral is more along the lines of, "Consider your options before committing to a four-year school." More and more high school graduates are now turning to community colleges for either their associate degrees or their first two years of college education. Although community college education used to have a reputation for being second best, that is definitely no longer the case. Today, in fact, four out of ten college students who go on to graduate from four-year institutions begin their education in community colleges. With more than 1600 community colleges nationwide and 11 million people enrolled in them, these schools are the fastest growing institutions in higher education. Why are they so popular? Well, consider the rest of Miranda's story.

5 After working full-time at an unfulfilling job for over a year to help pay off her student loans, Miranda was ready to make a change and move on with her life. She was still interested in a culinary arts degree, but this time she didn't want to leave home or spend so much money. She definitely didn't want to take out another loan. Friends had told her about the culinary arts program at the local community college. When Miranda looked into it, she was amazed to see that tuition was only a little over $1200 a semester! That was about *five times* less expensive than the tuition at the university had been. In fact, community colleges nationwide average only $3000 a year, less than a quarter of what it costs to attend many universities. In addition, now Miranda could live at home, avoiding the huge added expense of living on campus.

6 However, Miranda still wanted to continue working part time in order to pay for school on her own and to eventually save for a car. After her experience at the university, Miranda was afraid that she'd have no choice but to put school off until she had saved all the money she needed. But when she looked at a class schedule, she was relieved to see that nearly all the classes she needed to take were also offered in the evenings. Some were even available on weekends. Because nearly *80 percent* of students who attend community college work either full or part time,

most schools arrange classes to fit busy schedules. Miranda realized she could easily fit a part-time working schedule around all her classes.

7 Now, looking at the community college catalog, Miranda wished she had started college there in the first place. She noticed that there were nearly twice as many degrees offered. There was everything from architectural engineering to sign language to web technology. And because classes were so inexpensive, she could have sampled a number of classes before deciding on what exact career she wanted to pursue. The fact is, nearly 70 percent of all college students end up changing majors. Now, if Miranda decided to change her focus from culinary arts, it wouldn't be a big deal—or a big waste of money. And speaking of money, Miranda's college, like most community colleges, was located near the center of the city where she lived. It would be easy and inexpensive to reach by public transportation (unlike a 1500-mile flight!) until she had saved enough for a car. Miranda began to understand why these schools were called "community" colleges.

8 When Miranda began her classes at the college, she worried that her teachers might not be as good as those at a four-year university. What Miranda discovered was a pleasant surprise. These professors weren't better or worse, but they were definitely different. Some of her culinary arts teachers actually worked as chefs in addition to teaching one or two classes a semester. And one of her teachers owned the most popular restaurant in the city! It was a great experience to learn from master chefs who knew exactly what a student needed to know in order to be successful. The years, even decades, of hands-on experience that many of her teachers had was something that Miranda felt was invaluable—and yet the classes were so inexpensive. Also, Miranda found that some of her full-time teachers seemed to have more time for her and her fellow students. In general, this is true at community colleges, because teachers are not required to do research or write papers and books the way they are at four-year universities. All of their time at the community college is devoted solely to teaching.

Miranda had also been concerned that she would be older than most of 9
the students in her classes since she had spent several years working and was now in her 20s. At the university, nearly all the students were the same age. Not so at the community college. In many of her classes, students ranged in age from 18 to 65! Miranda became good friends with a 64-year-old woman who said she wanted to open a cupcake bakery when she retired. Miranda also met plenty of people her own age who had not been certain what they wanted to do when they graduated from high school. Some had taken a few years between high school and college to explore and consider their options. Others, like Miranda, had tried four-year schools and realized that direction was not for them.

In addition to the broad age range at 10
her college, Miranda was also impressed by the diversity° of the students. Because most community colleges offer courses

for developing English-language skills in reading and writing, they attract students for whom English is a second language. These students often need basic courses before progressing on to their career classes. Also, because all community colleges have an open-door policy (meaning no one with a high-school diploma can be turned away, regardless of GPA), Miranda met a number of students who had not done very well in high school, but still wanted a college degree. These students were determined to "re-do" themselves and prove that they could be successful and well educated in spite of their pasts.

11 When Miranda graduated, less than two years after beginning the culinary arts program, the job placement office at the college helped her set up some interviews. Because many of the teachers in the program actually worked at or owned restaurants, they knew where and when jobs were opening. Two of Miranda's chef/teachers let her use them as references. Miranda was ecstatic° when she was offered a job at an upscale French restaurant within three weeks of graduating. Community colleges are often more successful than four-year schools when it comes to placing their graduates in jobs shortly after graduation. This is because many of the degrees offered at two-year schools are in big demand. Popular community college programs such as nursing and computer science have a nearly 100 percent job placement rate.

Today, Miranda has worked her way 12
up to sous-chef (one step away from head chef) at the French restaurant. And on weekends she helps out her now-retired classmate in the cupcake bakery. She's not entirely certain that she has any natural talent for decorating cupcakes, but it's a lot of fun and pretty tasty, too. And because Miranda has now finished two years of college, she can transfer to a four-year university as a junior if she decides one day that she'd like to continue her education. Already, Miranda has begun thinking about getting her bachelor's degree in business administration so that she can be better prepared to open her own restaurant some day. So much for faded dreams!

Reading Comprehension Questions

Vocabulary in Context

______ 1. In the sentence below, the word *compounding* (kŏm-pound′ĭng) means
A. increasing.
B. creating.
C. solving.
D. without.

"Compounding her problems, Miranda was beginning to realize that she was not particularly interested in her chosen major, after all." (Paragraph 3)

Central Point and Main Ideas

______ 2. Which sentence best expresses the central point of this selection?
A. Many students are surprised by how difficult it is to adjust to college.
B. Community colleges offer more opportunities than four-year colleges, and the teachers have more time to teach.
C. For a number of reasons, a community college is a better choice for some students than a four-year college.
D. Four-year schools are often far more expensive and demanding than community colleges.

______ 3. The main idea of paragraph 5 is that
A. Miranda had to work at an unfulfilling job to save money.
B. friends helped Miranda see the advantages of attending community college.
C. Miranda found out how affordable attending community college could be.
D. it is not necessary to take out student loans when attending community college.

Supporting Details

______ 4. Which of the following is **not** a reason that Miranda was worried about attending a community college?
A. She was worried that she would be older than most of her fellow students.
B. She was afraid that she'd have to put off school until she had saved enough money to pay for classes during the day.
C. She was afraid that community college professors wouldn't be as good as those at a four-year university.
D. She thought that living at home might distract her from her studies.

_____ 5. When Miranda looked at a community college catalog, she

A. realized that switching majors wasn't as big a deal as it had been at a four-year school.
B. decided to sample a number of courses before deciding on a major.
C. felt unsure whether she really wanted to pursue a major in culinary arts.
D. noticed that there were about the same number of degrees offered as at four-year schools.

_____ 6. According to the author, the reason many professors at community colleges have more time for their students than professors at four-year schools do is that

A. they teach only part-time.
B. classes at community colleges tend to be smaller than classes at four-year schools.
C. they don't have to write papers and books to keep their teaching positions.
D. they usually live in the community, so they don't have to commute far to work.

_____ 7. According to the selection, which community college programs have the highest job placement rate?

A. Culinary arts and law enforcement
B. Computer science and nursing
C. Drafting and interior design
D. Early childhood education and dental assisting

8–10. Add the details missing in the following partial outline of the first seven paragraphs of the reading. Do so by filling in each blank with the letter of one of the sentences in the box below.

Details Missing from the Outline

A. When looking into the possibility of community college, Miranda made several unexpected discoveries.
B. For a number of reasons, Miranda did not like attending a four-year school.
C. Class schedules were actually designed to fit the schedules of working students.

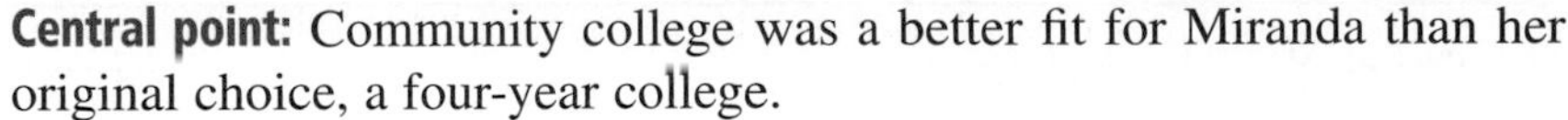

Central point: Community college was a better fit for Miranda than her original choice, a four-year college.

A. ______

1. Miranda didn't feel comfortable at the school.
   a. She wasn't used to living with a stranger.
   b. Home was too far away and she couldn't afford to fly home.
2. Because tuition was so expensive, Miranda felt pressured to quickly choose a major.
3. Miranda quickly discovered that she had chosen the wrong major for her.
4. Miranda realized she wouldn't be able to fit classes around a job.

B. ______

1. Tuition was far less than what she had paid at the four-year college.
2. ______
3. More degrees were offered, including the degree Miranda was interested in.
4. The college was very close to her home.

Discussion Questions

1. Has reading this selection changed your opinion of community colleges? Explain.
2. As the author points out, community college education has grown rapidly in popularity recently. Why do you think a two-year degree has become more popular?
3. The article mentions that 70 percent of college students end up changing their majors. What might account for this high percentage? Have you decided what you want to study in college? If so, how did you arrive at this decision?
4. Sometimes people judge community colleges unfairly because of their policy of allowing anyone with a high-school diploma to attend. Do you think that the open-door policy of community colleges makes these colleges better—or worse? Why?

Note: Writing assignments for this selection appear on page 697.

Check Your Performance **SUPPORTING DETAILS**

Activity		*Number Right*		*Points*		*Score*
Review Test 1	(5 items)	______	×	2	=	______
Review Test 2	(10 items)	______	×	3	=	______
Review Test 3	(10 items)	______	×	3	=	______
Review Test 4	(10 items)	______	×	3	=	______
				TOTAL SCORE	=	______%

Enter your total score into the **Reading Performance Chart: Review Tests** on the inside back cover.

Name ____________________ Date __________

Section __________ SCORE: (Number correct) ______ x 10 = ______ %

SUPPORTING DETAILS: Mastery Test 1

A. Answer the supporting-detail questions that follow the textbook passage.

[1]People who have no or low self-control share common traits. [2]First, they seem to have an unwillingness or inability to defer gratification. [3]Given a choice between getting five dollars today or fifteen dollars if they wait sixty days, they'll take the five dollars today. [4]People with weak self-control often pursue immediate gratification through such risky behaviors as too much smoking, drinking, or gambling, as well as by engaging in unprotected sex with strangers. [5]Second, they lack persistence in a course of action. [6]They prefer actions that are simple and easy, such as getting money without working or obtaining sex without establishing a relationship. [7]They tend to have poor work records, high rates of absenteeism when employed, unstable marital and family relationships, and other problems caused by an unwillingness to "work" at life. [8]At school, they usually learn little and quit early. [9]They lack all skills that require practice and training—they won't know how to fix a car or play a trumpet. [10]Finally, people with a lack of self-control are selfish. [11]Self-centered, indifferent, and insensitive to the suffering and needs of others, they impose loss and suffering on others. [12]They wreak havoc on all in their path without a qualm.

_____ 1. The first sentence provides
- A. the main idea.
- B. a major detail.
- C. a minor detail.

_____ 2. Sentences 3 and 4 provide
- A. the main idea.
- B. major details.
- C. minor details.

_____ 3. Sentence 5 provides
- A. the main idea.
- B. a major detail.
- C. a minor detail.

_____ 4. How many major supporting details does the paragraph include?
- A. Two
- B. Three
- C. Four
- D. Five

(Continues on next page)

B. (5–10.) Complete the outline of the following textbook passage by filling in the main idea and the major supporting details.

[1]According to social researcher Herbert Gans, there are five basic types of urban dwellers. [2]First are the cosmopolites—the intellectuals, professionals, and artists who have been attracted to the city. [3]They value the city's conveniences and cultural benefits. [4]The second type is the singles. [5]Roughly between the ages of 20 and their early 30s, the singles have not decided to settle in the city permanently. [6]For them, urban life is a stage in their life course. [7]Businesses and services, such as singles bars and apartment complexes, cater to their needs and desires. [8]After they marry, many singles move to the suburbs. [9]The next type of urban dweller is the ethnic villagers. [10]Feeling a sense of identity, working-class members of the same ethnic group band together. [11]They form tightly knit neighborhoods that resemble villages and small towns. [12]Family- and peer-oriented, they try to isolate themselves from the dangers and problems of urban life. [13]A fourth type of urban dweller is the deprived. [14]Destitute, emotionally disturbed, and having little income, education, or work skills, the deprived live in neighborhoods that are more like urban jungles than urban villages. [15]Some of them stalk those jungles in search of prey. [16]Neither predator nor prey has much hope for anything better in life—for themselves or for their children. [17]Finally, there are the trapped. [18]Some were trapped when an ethnic group "invaded" their neighborhood and they could not afford to move. [19]Others are "downwardly mobile"; they started in a higher social class but because of mental or physical illness, alcohol or other drug addiction, or other problems, they drifted downward. [20]Many are elderly and are not wanted elsewhere. [21]Like the deprived, the trapped suffer from high rates of assault, mugging, and rape.

Main idea: ____

____

Major detail 1: ______________________________________

Major detail 2: ______________________________________

Major detail 3: ______________________________________

Major detail 4: ______________________________________

Major detail 5: ______________________________________

Name ______________________________ Date __________

Section ___________ SCORE: (Number correct) _______ x 10 = _______ %

SUPPORTING DETAILS: Mastery Test 2

A. Answer the supporting-detail questions that follow the textbook passage.

[1]A variety of factors influence people's eating habits. [2]One such factor is social influences. [3]For example, when you eat with friends, on average you linger two or three times as long as you would if eating alone, and you eat almost twice as much. [4]Someone wants dessert, so you have one, too. [5]Our expectations also affect our eating. [6]Even the name of the food can influence our appetite. [7]What we now call Chilean sea bass used to be called Patagonian tooth fish. [8]Changing the name greatly increased sales. [9]Another fish, orange roughy, used to be called slimehead. [10]Would anyone go to a restaurant and order a yummy plate of slimehead? [11]Yet another influence is portion size. [12]If someone serves you a large meal, do you feel obligated to eat most of it? [13]If you dine at an all-you-can-eat buffet, do you try to get your money's worth? [14]In one study, people at a convention of nutrition experts (who you might think would know better) were asked to serve themselves ice cream. [15]Those who were given a large bowl gave themselves almost one-third more ice cream than those given a smaller bowl. [16]In another study, customers at a movie theater were given a free box of popcorn, either a large box (120g) or a huge one (240g). [17]Afterward, researchers weighed the remainder to determine how much people ate. [18]People ate significantly more if they were given a huge box, even if the popcorn was very stale—14 days old!

_____ 1. In general, the major details of this paragraph are
- A. kinds of foods we eat.
- B. factors affecting what we eat.
- C. research findings about eating.
- D. eating habits.

_____ 2. Specifically, the major details of the paragraph are
- A. social influences, expectations, and portion size.
- B. lingering after meals, the names of foods, and large meals.
- C. examples, studies, influences.
- D. expectations, influences, experiments.

_____ 3. Sentence 1 provides
- A. the main idea.
- B. a major detail.
- C. a minor detail.

_____ 4. Sentence 7 provides
- A. the main idea.
- B. a major detail.
- C. a minor detail.

(Continues on next page)

_____ 5. Sentence 11 provides
A. the main idea.
B. a major detail.
C. a minor detail.

6. *Fill in the blank:* Slimehead is the original name of the fish now known as ____________________.

B. (7–10.) Complete the outline of the following textbook passage by filling in the missing supporting details.

[1]There are two main forms of survey, and each has its own advantages. [2]One type of survey is the interview. [3]An interview can obtain a high response rate because people find it more difficult to turn down a personal request for an interview than to throw away a written questionnaire. [4]In addition, a skillful interviewer can go beyond written questions and probe for a subject's underlying feelings and reasons. [5]Questionnaires, the second main form of survey, also have two advantages. [6]They are cheaper than interviews, especially when large samples are used. [7]Moreover, since the questions are written, the researcher knows that there is a guarantee of consistency, whereas five interviewers can ask the same question in five different ways.

Main idea: There are two main forms of survey, and each has its own advantages.

1. ____

   a. ____

      ____

   b. Can go beyond written questions

2. ____

   a. ____

      ____

   b. Guarantee of consistency (since questions are written)

Name ______________________________ Date __________

Section __________ SCORE: (Number correct) _______ x 10 = _______ %

SUPPORTING DETAILS: Mastery Test 3

A. Answer the supporting-detail questions that follow the textbook passage.

[1]More has been written on the fall of Rome than on the death of any other civilization. [2]While scholars are still debating this issue today, most agree that a number of factors led to Rome's demise at the hands of Germanic attackers in 476 A.D. [3]First, Rome was vulnerable to outside attackers because of internal political instability. [4]The Roman constitution did not have a clear law of succession. [5]As a result, each time a ruler died, civil war would break out—killing thousands and causing great political struggle. [6]Another factor that made Rome ripe for conquest was severe economic turmoil. [7]Rome's economy relied heavily upon slave labor. [8]However, years of harsh work and poor living conditions reduced the population of Rome's slaves. [9]Fewer slaves working on farms meant that the empire had fewer goods for trade and less food for its citizens. [10]Rome was also weakened by a lack of manpower. [11]The empire's long borders required more soldiers than were available to protect it from attack. [12]In addition, the need for soldiers abroad meant that there were fewer people to keep peace and order within the empire.

_____ 1. The main idea is expressed in sentence
- A. 1.
- B. 2.
- C. 4.
- D. 12.

_____ 2. The major supporting details of this paragraph are
- A. events.
- B. effects.
- C. theories.
- D. factors.

_____ 3. The second major detail of the paragraph is introduced in sentence
- A. 2.
- B. 4.
- C. 6.
- D. 8.

_____ 4. The third major detail of the paragraph is introduced in sentence
- A. 7.
- B. 8.
- C. 9.
- D. 10.

(Continues on next page)

_____ 5. Sentence 12 provides
A. the main idea.
B. a major detail.
C. a minor detail.

B. (6–10.) Complete the map of the following textbook passage by filling in the missing major supporting details.

[1]A good many factors influence whether a situation is seen as too crowded. [2]Duration is one factor. [3]For instance, people typically find it easier to tolerate a brief exposure to high-density conditions, such as a ride on a crowded elevator, than prolonged exposure on a cross-country bus. [4]A second factor is predictability. [5]People typically find crowded settings even more stressful when they are unable to predict them. [6]A third factor has to do with frame of mind. [7]There are times when individuals welcome solitude and other times when they prefer the presence of others. [8]A fourth factor involves the environmental setting. [9]People generally report that they can tolerate crowding better in impersonal settings, such as a shopping center or an airline terminal, than in a home or apartment. [10]Finally, people's attitude toward a situation determines how they feel about crowding. [11]If people are fearful and antagonistic—or excited and friendly—crowding tends to intensify the feelings. [12]Crowding makes a doctor's waiting room and a subway car all the more unpleasant, whereas it makes a football game and a party all the more enjoyable. [13]And even though a crowded New York subway car turns people off, a crowded San Francisco cable car, crammed with people hanging over the sides, is defined as a "tourist attraction."

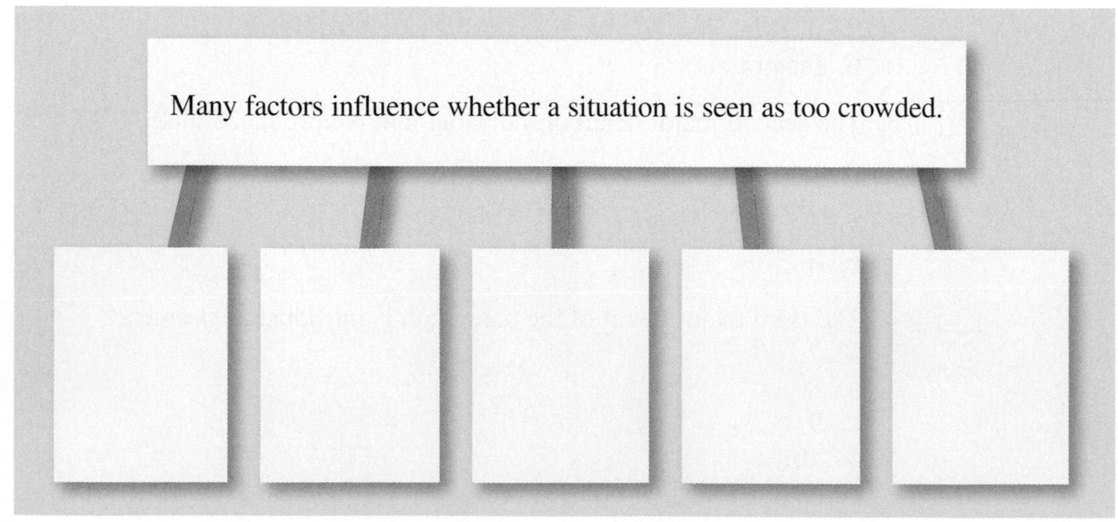

Name ______________________________ Date __________

Section __________ SCORE: (Number correct) _______ x 10 = _______ %

SUPPORTING DETAILS: Mastery Test 4

A. (1–6.) Complete the outline of the following textbook passage by filling in the main idea and the major supporting details.

[1]Psychologists believe that people progress through a sequence of stages as they make changes in their lives. [2]The first stage of change is precontemplation. [3]Whether or not they're aware of a problem behavior, people in this stage have no intention of making a change in the next six months. [4]Busy college students in good health, for instance, might never think about getting more exercise. [5]The second stage of change is contemplation. [6]Individuals in this stage are aware they have a problem behavior, but are torn between the positives of the new behavior and the amount of time and energy required to change. [7]For instance, students in a health class may start thinking about exercising but struggle to balance potential benefits with the effort of getting up early to jog or go to the gym. [8]In the next stage—preparation—people intend to change a problem behavior in the next month. [9]Some focus on a master plan. [10]For instance, they might look into fitness classes, gyms, or other options for working out. [11]Others might start by making small changes, such as walking to classes rather than taking a campus shuttle bus. [12]Next comes the action stage—people are modifying their behavior according to their plan. [13]For instance, they might be jogging or working out at the gym three times a week. [14]In the maintenance stage, individuals have continued to work at changing their behavior and have avoided relapse for at least six months. [15]Lastly comes the termination stage. [16]While it may take two to five years, a behavior becomes so deeply ingrained that a person can't imagine abandoning it. [17]More than eight in ten college seniors who exercise regularly remain as active, or even more active, after graduation.

Main idea: ______________________________

____

Major detail 1. ______________________________

Major detail 2. ______________________________

Major detail 3. ______________________________

Major detail 4. ______________________________

Major detail 5. ______________________________

Major detail 6. Termination

(Continues on next page)

B. (7–10.) Complete the map of the following textbook passage.

[1]There have always been homeless people in the United States. [2]But the homeless of today are more visible to the general public because they are much more likely to sleep on the streets or in other public places. [3]Today's homelessness has arisen from at least three social forces. [4]One is the increased shortage of inexpensive housing for the poor because of diminishing government subsidy of such housing. [5]Another social force is the decreasing demand for unskilled labor. [6]This decrease, which has occurred since the 1980s, has resulted in extremely high unemployment among young men in general and African Americans in particular. [7]A third social force is the decrease in public welfare benefits that has taken place over the last two decades. [8]These three social forces have enlarged the ranks of the extremely poor, thereby increasing the chances of these people becoming homeless.

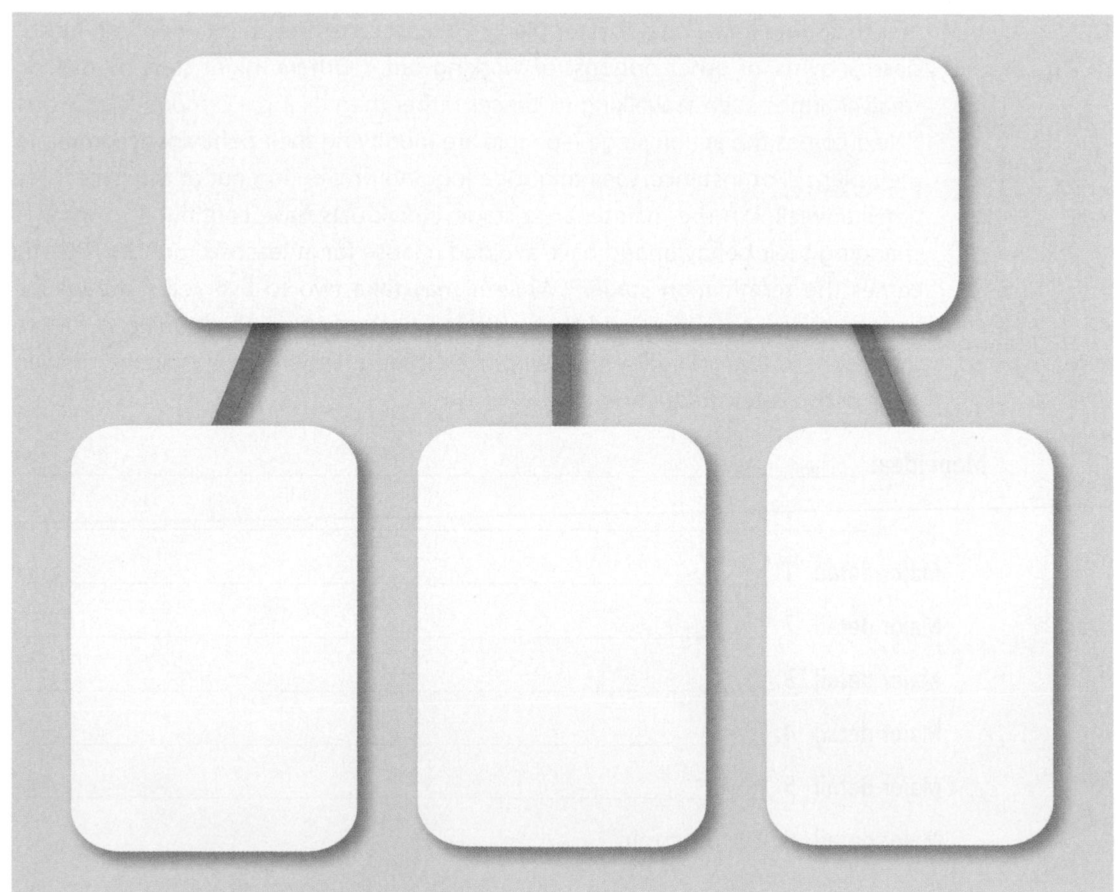

Name ______________________ Date __________

Section __________ SCORE: (Number correct) ______ x 10 = ______ %

SUPPORTING DETAILS: Mastery Test 5

A. Answer the supporting-detail questions that follow the textbook passage.

[1]*Heuristics* (pronounced *hyoo-ris'tiks*) are rules of thumb that help us to simplify problems. [2]They do not guarantee a solution, but they may bring it within reach. [3]A very simple heuristic method is hill-climbing. [4]In this process, we try to move continually closer to our final goal without ever digressing or going backward. [5]On a multiple-choice test, for example, one useful strategy in answering each question is to eliminate the alternatives that are obviously incorrect. [6]Even if this does not leave you with the one correct answer, you are closer to a solution. [7]Or in trying to balance a budget, each reduction in expenses brings you closer to the goal and leaves you with a smaller deficit to deal with. [8]Another heuristic method is the creation of subgoals. [9]By setting subgoals, we can often break a problem into smaller, more manageable pieces, each of which is easier to solve than the problem as a whole. [10]A student whose goal is to write a history paper might set subgoals by breaking down the work into a series of separate tasks: choosing a topic, doing the research, preparing an outline, writing the first draft, editing, rewriting, and so on.

_____ 1. The main idea is expressed in sentence
- A. 1.
- B. 3.
- C. 4.
- D. 8.

_____ 2. The major supporting details of this paragraph are
- A. events.
- B. reasons.
- C. methods.
- D. questions.

_____ 3. The first major detail of the paragraph is introduced in sentence
- A. 2.
- B. 3.
- C. 4.
- D. 5.

_____ 4. The second major detail of the paragraph is introduced in sentence
- A. 5.
- B. 7.
- C. 8.
- D. 10.

(Continues on next page)

5–6. Complete the following study notes that summarize the paragraph.

Heuristics—rules of thumb that help us to simplify problems

1. Hill-climbing—try to move continually closer to final goal without digressing.

   Example—______________________________

   ____

2. Creation of subgoals—break a problem into smaller, more manageable pieces.

   Example—______________________________

   ____

B. (7–10.) Complete the map of the following textbook passage by filling in the main idea and the missing major details.

[1]Public speaking is very different from everyday conversation. [2]First of all, speeches are much more structured than a typical informal discussion. [3]A speech usually imposes strict time limitations on the speaker. [4]In addition, for most situations, speeches do not allow listeners to interrupt with questions or commentary. [5]Another difference to keep in mind when speaking to groups is that public speaking generally requires more formal language. [6]Slang, jargon, and bad grammar have little place in public speeches. [7]Audiences usually react negatively to speakers who do not elevate and polish their language when giving a public talk. [8]A third significant difference between public and private discussion is that public speaking requires a different method of delivery. [9]Unlike casual conversation, which is usually quiet, effective public speakers adjust their voices to be heard clearly throughout the audience. [10]Speaking to a group also requires the speaker to assume a more erect posture and avoid distracting mannerisms and verbal habits.

Name ______________________ Date ________

Section __________ SCORE: (Number correct) ______ x 10 = ______ %

SUPPORTING DETAILS: Mastery Test 6

A. (1–3.) The main idea of the following textbook passage is **boldfaced**. Complete the map below by filling in the three major details, including brief explanations of each detail.

[1]In Latin, *plagiarism* means "kidnapper." [2]To plagiarize means to use another person's words or ideas as if they were one's own original creations. [3]Quite simply, it is theft. [4]Common thieves steal material goods that legally belong to others and then use this property as it if were rightfully theirs. [5]Plagiarists do the same with words and ideas. [6]**This theft can occur in three forms: global, patchwork, and incremental.** [7]Global plagiarism is stealing all the words and ideas from another source and passing them off as one's own. [8]This is the most blatant kind of plagiarism and is considered to be grossly unethical. [9]Patchwork plagiarism occurs when words and ideas are pilfered from several sources and then patched together. [10]In other words, instead of copying everything from one single source, the thief copies word for word from several sources. [11]In global and patchwork plagiarism, entire sections are copied verbatim. [12]A third kind of plagiarism, incremental plagiarism, occurs when small portions (choice words or phrases) are borrowed from different parts of one source without proper credit being given.

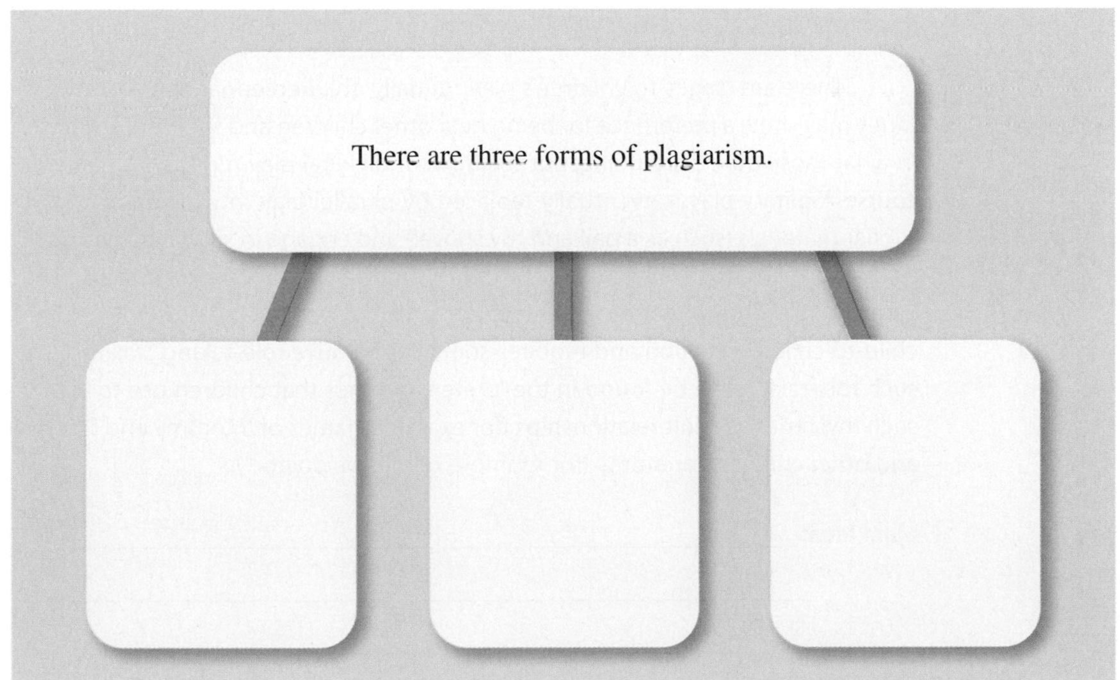

(Continues on next page)

B. (4–6.) Outline the following textbook passage by filling in the main idea and the two major supporting details.

[1]What causes forgetting? [2]Research has established that most forgetting occurs because of interference from other information, which can take place in two ways. [3]In proactive interference, prior information inhibits our ability to remember new information. [4]For instance, if you have a new locker combination each year, you may have difficulty remembering it because you keep recalling the old one. [5]In retroactive interference, new information inhibits our ability to remember old information. [6]Now that you finally know your new locker combination, you may find that you have forgotten the old one. [7]In both cases, we forget because competing information displaces the information we are trying to retrieve.

Main idea: ______________________________

____

1. ______________________________

2. ______________________________

C. (7–10.) Outline the following textbook passage by filling in the main idea and the major supporting details, including brief explanations of each detail.

Note: The number of answer lines given does not indicate the number of major details in the passage.

[1]There are stages to children's play. [2]Initially, children engage in solitary play. [3]They may show a preference for being near other children and show some interest in what those others are doing, but their own individual play runs an independent course. [4]Solitary play is eventually replaced by parallel play, in which children use similar materials (such as a pail and toy shovel) and engage in similar activity (such as digging sand), typically near one another; but they hardly interact at all. [5]By age 3, most children show at least some cooperative play, a form that involves direct child-to-child interaction and requires some cooperative role-taking. [6]Examples of such role-taking can be found in the "pretend" games that children use to explore such mysteries as adult relationships (for example, games of "Mommy and Daddy") and other children's anatomy (for example, games of "doctor").

Main idea: ______________________________

____

____

____

____

4 Implied Main Ideas

© 2000 Randy Glasbergen.
GLASBERGEN
"Kenny hasn't spoken to me in two months, he won't return my calls, and he's been seeing one of my friends. Do you think I should break up with him?"

In Chapters 2 and 3, you learned the two basic parts of anything you read: a *main idea* and the *supporting details* that explain and develop that idea. As you have seen, the main idea may be clearly stated in one sentence of a selection.

However, sometimes the main idea may be **implied**—only suggested by the supporting details and not clearly stated in one sentence. The reader must figure out the implied main idea by considering the supporting details. In the above cartoon, you can figure out the main idea by noting the details: the speaker's boyfriend hasn't spoken to her in two months, won't return her calls, and is dating one of her friends. The clearly implied idea is that *he* has already broken up with *her*!

This chapter offers practice in finding implied main ideas, both in paragraphs and in longer selections.

Implied Main Ideas in Paragraphs

Sometimes a selection lacks a sentence that directly states the main idea. In such cases, the author has simply decided to let the details of the selection suggest the main idea. You must figure out what that implied idea is by deciding upon the point all the details support. For example, read the following paragraph.

> [1]Slashing their swords wildly, swordfish swim through schools of fish, trying to slice as many as possible; then they feast. [2]When hooked by fishermen, they have been known to fight nonstop for three or four hours. [3]They have pulled some fishermen to their deaths, and if they are not clubbed senseless when captured, they will slash fishermen on deck. [4]A puncture wound made by a swordfish bill means a severe and nearly instantaneous infection. [5]Their sword, which is a bony extension of the upper jaw, is deadly sharp on the sides and can grow to a length of four or five feet. [6]It is a weapon backed up by five hundred pounds of sleek, muscular fish. [7]Swordfish have even been known to attack boats, driving their swords right through the hull and at times sinking them.

You can see that no sentence in the paragraph is a good "umbrella" statement that covers all of the other sentences. To decide on the main idea, we must ask the same three questions we've already used to find main ideas:

- "Who or what is this paragraph about?" That will be the topic.
- "What is the main point the author is trying to make about that topic?"
- And when we think we know the main point, we can test it by asking, "Does *all or most* of the material in the paragraph support this idea?"

In the paragraph above, all of the details are about swordfish, so that must be the topic. Which of the following statements expresses the general point that the author is trying to make about swordfish? Check (✓) the answer you think is correct.

_____ A. Swordfish will attack entire schools of fish.

_____ B. Swordfish will fight for hours when hooked and have even pulled some fisherman to their deaths.

_____ C. A swordfish bill can cause severe infections and even sink a boat.

_____ D. Swordfish are aggressive, dangerous fish.

The details reveal the author's general point to be answer D: swordfish are aggressive, dangerous fish. All the other statements above are supporting details for this main idea—each tells of a way in which swordfish are aggressive and dangerous. Although the main idea is not directly stated, it is clearly implied by all the material in the paragraph.

Figuring Out Implied Main Ideas in Paragraphs

Remember, to find implied main ideas, it often helps to decide on the topic first. Do so by asking yourself, "Who or what is the selection about?" After you find the topic, then ask yourself, "What is the author's main point about the topic?"

Check Your Understanding

Read the selection below, and then try to answer the questions that follow.

[1]All writers get bogged down now and then. [2]Accept the fact that sooner or later writer's block will happen to you. [3]When it does, one response is to try to write something—no matter how awkward or imprecise it may seem. [4]Just jot a reminder to yourself in the margin ("Fix this," "Redo," or "Ugh!") to fine-tune the section later. [5]Another way to deal with a writing snag is leave a blank space—a spot for the right words when they finally come to mind at a later time. [6]Then move on to an easier section, see if you can write that, and then return to the challenging part. [7]It may also help to reread—to yourself or out loud—what you've already written. [8]Regaining a sense of the large context may be enough to overcome writer's block. [9]You might also try talking your way through a troublesome section. [10]Like most people, you probably speak more easily than you write; by speaking aloud, you tap this oral fluency and put it to work in your writing.

_____ 1. What is the topic of the above paragraph?
- A. Writer's block
- B. Writing and talking
- C. The writing process
- D. Rereading your writing

_____ 2. Which statement best expresses the unstated main idea of the paragraph?
- A. Writing is not easy.
- B. There are various ways to deal with writer's block.
- C. Talking about what you are trying to write may help you break out of a writing snag.
- D. Write easier sections of a paper first and come back later to a harder section.

Explanation

The topic, referred to directly or indirectly in several sentences, is writer's block. The implied main idea about writer's block is that there are various ways to deal with it. Statement A, "Writing is not easy," is too broad, and statements C and D are too narrow—each referring to only one specific way to deal with writer's block.

When you think you have determined an implied main idea, test youself by asking, "Does all or most of the material in the paragraph support this idea?" Almost the entire paragraph above is made up of practical suggestions for responding to writer's block.

PRACTICE 1

Read each paragraph, and then answer the questions that follow. Remember to find a topic by asking "Who or what is the selection about?" and to find an implied main idea by asking "What is the author's point about the topic?"

> ***Hint:*** Noticing addition words (such as *first, another, also, moreover,* and *finally*) will help you identify the major supporting details that can suggest the main idea.

Paragraph 1

[1]Which way do you prefer to learn? [2]Some people find it easier to understand what they see in print than what they hear. [3]Others find it easier to understand things they hear. [4]Some people prefer seeing a picture to reading words. [5]Think about your own learning preferences. [6]For example, imagine that you need to get from your home to someplace you have never been before. [7]What would be the easiest way for you to find the place? [8]Some people want to *look* at a map. [9]Others prefer to *read* a list of step-by-step directions. [10]Still others prefer to be *told* a list of step-by-step directions so that they can *hear* them. [11]Know what is best for you.

_____ 1. What is the topic of the above paragraph?
- A. Learning preferences
- B. Learning through hearing
- C. Learning through pictures
- D. Learning through print

_____ 2. Which statement best expresses the unstated main idea?
- A. Some people understand better by reading something rather than hearing it.
- B. Some people learn best by seeing a picture rather than reading words.
- C. Directions that are helpful for one person may not be helpful for another.
- D. People should be aware of and take advantage of their learning preferences.

Paragraph 2

[1]According to Dale Carnegie, one way to make people feel important is to remember their names. [2]Greeting people by name makes them feel liked and valued. [3]So does greeting them warmly and enthusiastically. [4]Convey delight when you see or hear from someone you know, Carnegie advises. [5]In conversations, allow people to talk about themselves: their experiences, their views, their goals, their work, their hobbies, their relationships. [6]Encourage them by listening attentively, asking questions, and otherwise showing interest. [7]Also, be generous with your praise. [8]Compliment people—not falsely, but in genuine appreciation of their accomplishments and merits.

_____ 1. What is the topic of the above paragraph?

A. Ways to greet people
B. Ways to make people feel important
C. The values of attentive listening
D. The benefits of providing compliments

_____ 2. Which statement best expresses the unstated main idea?

A. Greeting people by name makes them feel liked and valued.
B. Compliment people in a sincere way.
C. Dale Carnegie has suggested a number of ways to make people feel important.
D. In conversations, allow people to talk about themselves.

Paragraph 3

[1]Flextime, or flexibility of working hours, has become popular in recent years. [2]The most obvious advantage is less absenteeism. [3]When employees can choose working hours that meet their needs, they are less likely to take time off. [4]Another advantage of flextime is more efficient use of the physical plant. [5]The additional hours that a company is "open for business" could mean higher productivity and greater profits. [6]Finally, giving employees a choice of working hours permits them more control over their work environment, leading to increased job satisfaction and less turnover.

_____ 1. What is the topic of the above paragraph?

A. Giving employees a choice
B. Absenteeism at work
C. Flextime
D. The most popular employee benefits

______ 2. Which statement best expresses the unstated main idea?

A. Flextime leads to increased job satisfaction and higher productivity.
B. People who can choose their working hours are less likely to take time off.
C. Companies have found that flextime keeps employee turnover down.
D. Companies have found that flextime has several advantages.

PRACTICE 2

The main idea of each of the following paragraphs is unstated, and each paragraph is followed by four sentences. In the space provided, write the letter of the sentence that best expresses each unstated main idea.

Remember to consider carefully all of the information given and to ask yourself the following two questions:

- Who or what is the selection about? In other words, what is the topic?
- What is the author's main point about that topic? In other words, what is the implied main idea?

Then test your answer by asking:

- Does *all or most* of the material in the paragraph support this idea?

Paragraph 1

[1]The most common means of communication for insects is chemical. [2]Pheromones are chemicals with which an insect influences the behavior of other insects in its group. [3]For example, the queen bee, on her flight from the hive, secretes a pheromone that attracts drones, whose sole function is to mate with the queen. [4]Ants secrete pheromones that mark a trail from the nest to a food source. [5]Only members of the ant's own colony recognize the trail. [6]Fireflies communicate during the mating season not with chemicals but by flashing a light. [7]The female of each species emits a special series of flashes that males of her species recognize. [8]Other insects communicate by tapping, rubbing, or stroking each other. [9]Sometimes these are part of an elaborate courtship ritual. [10]Perhaps the most complex of all forms of insect communication is the dance of the honeybee. [11]When a forager bee finds a source of nectar, she returns to the hive and does a "waggle dance." [12]The dance lets other bees know where the food is.

_____ Which statement best expresses the unstated main idea of the paragraph?

A. Research has shown that animals do not communicate as people do.
B. All creatures need to communicate with each other.
C. Insects communicate through chemicals, visual signals, certain kinds of touching, and motions.
D. Insects have ways of communicating with each other about food sources.

Paragraph 2

[1]Cosmetic surgery is often presented as easy and painless, not like surgery at all but rather like dyeing hair or putting on nail polish. [2]This idea is reflected in casual, lighthearted terms like "tummy tuck." [3]But the risks of cosmetic surgery include an adverse reaction to the anesthesia used, excessive bleeding, and postoperative infection. [4]Also, muscles and nerves can be damaged during the surgery, and the patient may be paralyzed or may even, in rare instances, die. [5]Even if the patient recovers well, there is also the risk of an unacceptable result—that is, the patient looks worse, not better—in which case further surgery may be needed, perhaps several times. [6]Finally, even a reasonably successful outcome may be disappointing because it does not miraculously change the patient's whole life: a prettier nose, say, will not ensure fame, fortune, or romance.

_____ Which statement best expresses the unstated main idea of the paragraph?

A. People often get cosmetic surgery in hopes of improving their romantic lives.
B. Merely looking more attractive is not a good enough reason to get cosmetic surgery.
C. Cosmetic surgery is riskier than it's often portrayed to be.
D. Casual, lighthearted terms like "tummy tucks" should be eliminated from cosmetic surgery advertising.

Paragraph 3

[1]In some countries defeated by Nazi Germany during World War II, almost the entire Jewish population was murdered. [2]But in Denmark, the story was different. [3]After the Nazis took over Denmark in April 1940, complaints from the Danish people prevented the Germans from freely pursuing Danish Jews. [4]Then, in August 1943, the Nazis made demands that the Danes take action against the Jews. [5]Unwilling to obey, every important government official resigned. [6]When the German military commander decided to send Danish Jews to concentration camps, average citizens in Denmark began hiding Jews in their homes until they could be moved to the coast. [7]Also, the Danish church, royal family, and a variety of organizations protested the new German policy. [8]In the end, Danish fishermen succeeding in transporting

about seven thousand Jews to Sweden. [9]When the Germans moved the five hundred Danish Jews they found to a concentration camp, the Danish people kept up a public outcry and sent food and clothing packages to help save their countrymen. [10]All but about one hundred Danish Jews survived the war.

_____ Which statement best expresses the unstated main idea of the paragraph?

A. The Nazis were determined to take widespread action against the Danish Jews.

B. Danish fishermen were the real heroes in saving their Jewish fellow citizens.

C. Jews in other European countries could have been saved if their fellow citizens had acted as the Danes did.

D. The Danish people, acting with their government, saved thousands of Jewish lives by refusing to cooperate with Nazi invaders.

Putting Implied Main Ideas into Your Own Words

When you read, you often have to **infer**—figure out on your own—an author's unstated main idea. The implied main idea that you come up with should cover all or most of the details in the paragraph.

Check Your Understanding

See if you can find and write the topic of the paragraph below. Then write the implied main idea in your own words. Finally, read the explanation that follows.

Hints: Remember that you can help yourself identify the topic and main idea if you (1) look for repeated words as you read and (2) try to mark major supporting details. Major details are often signaled by such common addition words as the following:

Addition Words

one	to begin with	also	further
first (of all)	for one thing	in addition	furthermore
second(ly)	other	next	last (of all)
third(ly)	another	moreover	final(ly)

[1]Nonverbal messages are more emotionally powerful than verbal ones. [2]Nonverbal behaviors tell people about our emotional state. [3]When we want to convey how we feel about someone, language often fails us. [4]Nonverbal messages

are also more universal than verbal ones. [5]Members of different linguistic groups must spend a lot of time and effort to learn each other's verbal codes, but they can communicate instantly by smiling or wrinkling their faces in disgust. [6]Some researchers have shown a number of emotions to be expressed in the same way by members of different cultural groups. [7]Last, nonverbal messages are more continuous and natural than spoken language. [8]Because gestures and body movements flow into one another without obvious beginnings and endings, they seem to be a more natural part of our existence than words.

What is the topic of this paragraph? ______________________________

What is the implied main idea of this paragraph? ______________________

____

Explanation

One key to the topic here is the phrase *nonverbal messages*, which is repeated through the paragraph. The other key to the topic is the list of major details in the paragraph. Two of the details are signaled by addition words (*also* in "Nonverbal messages are also" and *Last* in "Last, nonverbal messages are"). Here are the three major details in the paragraph.

- Nonverbal messages are more emotionally powerful than verbal ones.
- They are more universal.
- They are more continuous and natural.

What do those three major details have in common? They're all about nonverbal messages (or behaviors), so that phrase can be considered the topic. And the author's main point about that topic could be stated like this: *Nonverbal messages have several advantages over verbal ones.*

PRACTICE 3

In the spaces provided, fill in the topic of each paragraph. Then, using your own words, write the implied main ideas of the paragraphs.

Hints:

1. To find the topic, it often helps to look for repeated words in a paragraph.
2. To identify the topic and main idea, mark major supporting details as you read. These major details are often signaled by such common addition words as the ones shown in the box on the previous page.

A. [1]Why do fashions occur in the first place? [2]One reason is that some cultures, like that of the United States, value change: What is new is good. [3]And so, in many modern societies, clothing styles change yearly, while people in traditional societies may wear the same style for generations. [4]A second reason is that many industries promote quick changes in fashions to increase sales. [5]A third reason is that fashions usually trickle down from the top. [6]A new style may occasionally originate from lower-status groups, as blue jeans did. [7]But most fashions come from upper-class people, who like to adopt some style or artifact as a badge of their status. [8]They cannot monopolize most status symbols for long, however. [9]Their style is adopted by the middle class and may be copied or modified for use by lower-status groups, offering many people the prestige of possessing a high-status symbol.

Topic: ____________________

Implied main idea: ____________________

____

B. [1]A hurricane is a relatively flat system of winds rotating around a center where the atmospheric pressure is abnormally low. [2]This system can be hundreds of miles across and usually brings heavy rains along with its powerfully strong winds. [3]As with a hurricane, air pressure at the center of a tornado is very low; but a tornado is a violently rotating column or "funnel" of air, usually reaching down from a thundercloud, and is typically only a few hundred yards across. [4]Wind speeds in a hurricane are about 75 to 150 miles per hour, but the wind speed in a tornado might be 300 miles per hour. [5]A hurricane may last for one or more days; a tornado lasts only a few minutes. [6]Locally, tornadoes are even more destructive than hurricanes.

Topic: ____________________

Implied main idea: ____________________

____

C. [1]During the American Revolution, the British army far outnumbered the American colonial army, and the British frequently fought with cannons, while the Americans had very few of them. [2]However, the British troops had to fight more than three thousand miles away from home, which meant that reinforcements, money, and supplies took months to reach the battlefront. [3]Americans fought in their own territory, which was undeveloped and unfamiliar to the British, and American troops were supported by local and French supplies stationed nearby. [4]The British forces were more likely to fight in straight lines across the battlefield, kneeling down in the open to reload their weapons. [5]American troops also used linear tactics, but they were just as likely to fight using the cover of trees and buildings. [6]Whenever the British retreated from a battle, they would do so in single file, and this allowed the colonists to sneak around the British formation to pick off more soldiers.

[7]Perhaps the most important difference between the two armies, however, was that of motivation. [8]The British troops fought to control the colonists and secure wealth for the English king. [9]The Americans fought for freedom and the defense of their homeland, and every colonial soldier had a high personal stake in the war's outcome.

Topic: ______________________________

____

Implied main idea: ______________________________

____

Implied Central Ideas in Longer Passages

More often than not, authors of essays, articles, and textbook selections will state their central points or ideas in much the same way as they state their main ideas in a single paragraph. Occasionally, however, the central point will be implied rather than stated directly.

As you learned in Chapter 2, you can find a central point in the same way you find a main idea—by looking for a topic and considering the supporting material. The central idea that you come up with should cover all or most of the details in the passage.

Check Your Understanding

Read the following selection. Then, in the space provided, see if you can write the letter of the sentence that best expresses the unstated central idea.

Modifying Behavior

[1]Can people modify their own behavior? [2]The answer is yes.

[3]The first thing to do is to decide what behavior you want to acquire—the desired "target" behavior. [4]What if you want to get rid of some behavior? [5]Behavior modification specialists emphasize a positive approach called "ignoring." [6]Much better results are achieved when the emphasis is on the new behavior to be acquired rather than on the behavior to be eliminated. [7]For example, instead of setting a target of being less shy, you might define the target behavior as becoming more outgoing or more sociable. [8]Other possible target behaviors are behaving more assertively, studying more, and getting along better with your roommate. [9]In each case, you have focused on the behavior that you want to acquire rather than on the behavior that you want to reduce or eliminate.

[10]The next step is to define the target behavior precisely: What exactly do you mean by "assertive" or by "sociable"? [11]One way to do this is to imagine situations in which the target behavior could be performed. [12]Then describe in writing these situations and the way in which you now respond to them. [13]For example, in the case of shyness, you might write: "When I am sitting in the lecture hall, waiting for class to begin, I don't talk to the people around me." [14]Next, write down how you would rather act in that situation: "Ask the people sitting next to me how they like the class or the professor; or ask if they have seen any particularly good movies recently."

[15]The last step—which gets to the heart of self-modification—is to provide yourself with a positive reinforcer that is gained only upon specific improvements in the target behavior. [16]You may be able to use the same reinforcer that now maintains your undesirable behavior, or you may want to pick a new reinforcer. [17]Researchers use the example of a student who wanted to improve his relationship with his parents. [18]He first counted the times he said something pleasant to them and then rewarded himself for improvement by making his favorite pastime, playing pool, dependent on predetermined increases in the number of pleasant remarks he made. [19]You can also use tokens: Give yourself one token for every thirty minutes of studying, and cash in those tokens for reinforcement. [20]For instance, the privilege of going to a movie might require ten tokens.

_____ Which sentence best expresses the implied central idea of the entire selection?

A. Research has taught us a great deal about behavior modification.
B. Positive reinforcement is the key step in behavior modification.
C. Emphasis should be placed on acquiring a new behavior rather than eliminating an old one.
D. By following several steps, you can modify your behavior.

Explanation

The central point is a general statement that covers all or most of the details in a reading. To find the central point of the essay above, look first at its topic. Since the title is "Modifying Behavior," and every paragraph is about that subject, we can say "Modifying Behavior" is the topic. Then decide on what point is being made about the topic by looking at the major details of the essay. The first major detail, presented in the second paragraph, is deciding what behavior you want to acquire. The next major detail, in the third paragraph, is defining just what that desired behavior would be. The third major detail, in the fourth paragraph, is providing a positive reinforcer for that desired behavior.

The central point, then, will be a general statement that covers all of the details presented. That statement can be expressed simply as "By following several steps, you can modify your behavior."

PRACTICE 4

The central idea of the following passage is implied rather than stated, and the passage is followed by four sentences. In the space provided, write the letter of the sentence that best expresses the unstated central idea.

[1]If exercise could be packed into a pill, it would be the single most widely prescribed and beneficial medicine in the nation. [2]In a survey, eight in ten undergraduates realized that physical activity can prevent heart disease and prevent and treat obesity. [3]However, fewer than half knew that it maintains bone density and can help prevent diabetes.

[4]With regular exercise, your heart muscles become stronger and pump blood more efficiently. [5]Your heart rate and resting pulse slow down. [6]Your blood pressure may drop slightly from its normal level.

[7]Exercise thickens the bones and can slow the loss of calcium that normally occurs with age. [8]Physical activity increases flexibility in the joints and improves digestion and elimination. [9]It speeds up metabolism and builds lean body mass, so the body burns more calories and body fats decrease. [10]It heightens sensitivity to insulin (a great benefit for diabetics) and may lower the risk of developing diabetes. [11]In addition, exercise enhances clot-dissolving substances in the blood, helping to prevent strokes, heart attacks, and pulmonary embolisms (clots in the lungs), and it helps lower the risk of certain cancers. [12]Regular exercise can actually extend your lifespan and sharpen your memory and mind.

[13]Even your eyes benefit from physical activity. [14]Individuals who exercise three or more times a week may reduce by 70 percent their risk of age-related macular degeneration, which destroys the sharp central vision needed for tasks such as reading and driving.

_____ Which sentence best expresses the implied central idea of the entire selection?

A. Few undergraduates realize all the health benefits of exercise.
B. Nothing is better than exercise to help your body function at its best.
C. Science needs to develop a pill that will provide all the benefits of exercise.
D. Exercise can make your heart pump more efficiently and improve your digestion and elimination.

CHAPTER REVIEW

In this chapter, you learned the following:

- At times authors imply, or suggest, a main idea without stating it clearly in one sentence. In such cases, you must figure out that main idea by considering the supporting details.
- To find implied central points in longer reading selections, you must again look closely at the supporting material.

The next chapters—Chapters 5 and 6—will explain common ways that authors organize their material.

On the Web: If you are using this book in class, you can visit our website for additional practice in recognizing implied main and central ideas. Go to **www.townsendpress.com** and click on "Learning Center."

REVIEW TEST 1

To review what you've learned in this chapter, complete each of the following sentences.

1. At times authors ____________, or suggest, a main idea without stating it clearly in one sentence.

2. To figure out an implied idea, it often helps to determine the ____________ of the paragraph by asking, "Who or what is this paragraph about?"

3. After you figure out what you think is the implied main idea of a paragraph, test yourself by asking, "Does all or most of the material in the paragraph ____________ this idea?"

4. Just as a paragraph has a main idea, a longer selection has a central ____________ that is supported by all or most of the material in the selection.

5. The central point of a long selection may be stated directly, or it may be ____________.

REVIEW TEST 2

A. Look at the cartoon below, and then, in the space provided, answer the question that follows.

_____ 1. Which sentence best expresses the implied main idea of the cartoon?

A. The speaker has become dependent on pills.
B. The speaker has major health problems.
C. The speaker has decided to stop taking pills.
D. The speaker's doctor has ordered her to take the pills.

B. In the space provided, write the letter of the sentence that best expresses the implied main idea of each of the following paragraphs.

_____ 2. [1]One of the most common sleep disorders is insomnia. [2]Such things as noise, light, temperature, stress, nasal congestion, allergies, indigestion, pain, worrying, and the snoring of a sleep partner are factors that contribute to insomnia, which affects about 58 percent of American adults in any given year. [3]In narcolepsy, another sleep disorder, a person has sudden and irresistible "sleep attacks" that last about fifteen minutes. [4]Sleep paralysis sometimes accompanies narcoleptic episodes. [5]Apnea is a dangerous sleep disorder in which the air passages are obstructed, causing cessation of breathing as often as ten times an hour or more. [6]This dangerous disorder can lead to high blood pressure, heart attacks, and strokes. [7]Three other sleep disorders—sleep terrors, bed-wetting, and sleepwalking—occur during deep sleep, are more common among children, and may be related to immaturity of the nervous system.

A. Many things contribute to insomnia.
B. There are a number of sleep disorders.
C. Apnea presents several dangers to a person who has it.
D. Several sleep disorders are more common among children.

______ 3. [1]For many working-class couples, the first baby in the family arrives just nine months after marriage. [2]They hardly have time to adjust to being husband and wife before being thrust into the demanding roles of mother and father. [3]The result can be financial problems, bickering, and interference from in-laws. [4]The young husbands may not be ready to "settle down," and they resent getting less attention from their wives. [5]In contrast, middle-class couples often postpone the birth of their first child, which gives them more time to adjust to each other. [6]On average, their first baby arrives three years after marriage. [7]Their greater financial resources also work in their favor, making life as parents a lot easier and the marriage more pleasant.

A. Couples may have a good deal of difficulty in adjusting to their roles as husband and wife.
B. Middle-class couples postpone having children for several reasons.
C. Social class makes a significant difference in how couples adjust to the arrival of children.
D. Financial resources are a major key to the success of a marriage.

C. (4.) In the space provided, write out, in your own words, the implied main idea of the following paragraph.

[1]There is a story about a prisoner sentenced to a life of punitive labor—all day long he turned the crank of a machine that provided light for a nearby city.

[2]It was monotonous, tedious, unending toil. [3]But when he looked out the small window of the prison he could see illuminated lights on the horizon. [4]Even though he was exhausted each evening, he knew he'd spent his day in a useful enterprise.

[5]After years of work, another inmate told him: "You're a fool! [6]You're not creating light—that's from the electric generator across town. [7]When you turn that crank, all you're doing is pushing paddles through sand in a drum. [8]What you've been doing is completely worthless."

[9]As it turned out, this was true—the crank was unrelated to the production of light.

[10]When the prisoner believed he was doing something useful, he'd felt at peace; but when his illusion was burst, he grew despondent, eventually sickened, and died.

Implied main idea: ______________________________

____

REVIEW TEST 3

A. In the space provided, write the letter of the sentence that best expresses the implied main idea of each of the following paragraphs.

_____ 1. [1]Have you ever caught yourself dozing off after lunch, while trying to work or study? [2]A common reaction to the body's natural mid-day sleepiness is to consume caffeine or sugar, but these remedies will only provide temporary energy and increase fatigue later on. [3]Studies show that "power naps" of twenty to thirty minutes reduce stress, increase energy, and improve mental focus. [4]In fact, the brains of people who nap regularly are more active than those of people who don't. [5]Naps can also decrease the risk of heart disease. [6]Experts agree that you should take a nap at the same time each day, approximately eight hours after waking up in the morning, and eight hours before going to sleep at night. [7]Your nap shouldn't last longer than thirty minutes; otherwise, you will enter a deeper sleep that will make you feel groggy and listless. [8]If you suffer from a severe lack of sleep, naps will not fix your problem, but they will aid you more than artificial stimulants. [9]If you are still not convinced that naps are good for you, consider the example set by these creative people: Albert Einstein, Thomas Edison and Winston Churchill. [10]All of these men were nap enthusiasts known for their great accomplishments. [11]A coincidence? [12]Take a nap and find out!

A. Einstein, Edison, and Churchill all owed their success to their habit of taking daily naps.
B. People who don't benefit from an afternoon nap are not doing it correctly.
C. A healthy way to regain energy during the day is to take a short, well-timed afternoon nap.
D. The abuse of caffeine and sugar is a major health problem for many people.

_____ 2. [1]Filmmakers know that our attention is most likely to be drawn to the central portion of the movie screen. [2]We expect elements within the frame to be balanced, with dominant elements near the center or slightly above the center, in the case of most medium shots. [3]When a director's purpose is to achieve realism, most shots will be balanced in this way since that is what he or she knows the audience expects. [4]But when a sense of drama is needed, the "norm" is usually violated. [5]Dominant figures or elements may be placed near the edge of the screen, perhaps even fading out of the picture. [6]To create a sense of dominance or power, important elements may be emphasized by placing them in the top third of the screen. [7]Also, using a low camera angle can make a figure on the screen appear more dominant or menacing, as it looks down on us or on other characters or objects. [8]The opposite effect can be achieved by placing characters in the lower portion of the frame. [9]Characters placed this way look especially vulnerable or helpless, and even more so if the rest of the screen is empty or stark in contrast to the lonely figure at the bottom of the screen.

A. Filmmakers use different areas of the screen and camera angles to communicate ideas and moods.
B. There are several steps filmmakers must take to complete a film.
C. Filmmakers use the central portion of the movie screen when presenting realistic situations.
D. Artists in all fields use tricks of the trade in their work.

B. (3.) In the space provided, write out, in your own words, the implied main idea of the following paragraph.

[1]Many people think of the hippopotamus as a harmless, playful beast. [2]But it kills more people per year than crocodiles and poisonous snakes combined. [3]Hippos have been known to upset boats and kill the swimming passengers, using their strong jaws and sharp teeth to attack and rip their victims apart. [4]In one case, a hippo turned over a canoe carrying a safari hunter, and ripped off the man's head and shoulders. [5]These fierce animals also pose a considerable threat on land, since they feel particularly vulnerable out of water. [6]If you get between a hippo and its favorite river, or between a mother and its calf, then watch out! [7]A hippo can weigh over five thousand pounds and can run as fast as eighteen miles per hour, which makes it a difficult predator to escape. [8]People can usually avoid danger by keeping their distance from these creatures. [9]However, some hippos in Niger, Africa, recently went out of their way to make trouble. [10]Traveling in marauding hordes, these rogue animals threatened fishermen, destroyed rice fields, and attacked cattle. [11]The government was forced to kill the animals before they did any more damage.

Implied main idea: ______________________________

____

C. (4.) The central idea of the following passage is implied rather than stated, and the passage is followed by four sentences. In the space provided, write the letter of the sentence that best expresses the unstated central idea.

> [1]Although it is only 3 percent of the population, the upper class possesses more than half of the wealth in the United States. [2]This class consists of both the old rich and the new rich. [3]The old rich are families, such as the Rockefellers, that have been wealthy for generations. [4]Examples of the new rich include Bill Gates of Microsoft, TV talk show host Oprah Winfrey, and the founder of Amazon, Jeff Bezos.
>
> [5]People in the upper-middle class are distinguished from those above them primarily by their lesser wealth and power and from those below them by their highly successful and profitable careers as doctors, lawyers, midsized business owners, and corporate executives. [6]Many have advanced degrees and live comfortably with sky-high incomes, the envy of their professional peers.
>
> [7]The middle class comprises the largest class in the United States and is much more diverse in occupation than the upper-middle class. [8]It is made up of people with college educations or at least high-school diplomas. [9]They work in low- to mid-level white-collar occupations as average professionals, small-business owners, salespersons, managers, teachers, secretaries, bank clerks, and cashiers. [10]They have achieved the middle-class dream of owning a suburban home.
>
> [11]The working class consists mainly of those who have little education and whose jobs are manual and carry little prestige. [12]The working class is also marked by having more part-time workers and union members than other classes. [13]Some working-class people, such as construction workers, carpenters, and plumbers, are skilled workers and may make more money than some members of the middle class, such as secretaries and teachers. [14]Other working-class people are unskilled, such as migrant workers, janitors, and dishwashers. [15]There are also many women in this class working as domestics, cleaners, and waitresses.
>
> [16]The lower class is characterized by joblessness and poverty. [17]It includes the chronically unemployed, welfare recipients, and the impoverished aged. [18]These people suffer the indignity of living in rundown houses, wearing old clothes, eating cheap food, and lacking proper medical care. [19]Very few have finished high school. [20]They may have started out in their youth with poorly paying jobs that required little or no skill, and their earning power began to drop when they reached their late twenties.

_____ 4. Which sentence best expresses the implied central idea of the passage?

A. People in the United States work at a wide range of jobs that pay a variety of incomes.

B. It is unfair that the upper class possesses more than half of the wealth in the United States.

C. In order to be considered middle- or upper-class, a person must have a college education.

D. On the basis of income and education, people in the United States can be divided into a number of social classes.

REVIEW TEST 4

Remember what your teachers used to tell you about how to study? You probably were told to sit in one place, probably at a desk with a good light over your left shoulder, and focus on only one subject at a time. But, as Benedict Carey explains, these ideas might be just the opposite of what you *should* be doing when you need to learn new material.

To help you continue to strengthen your skills, the reading is followed by questions not only on implied ideas and central points but also on what you've learned in previous chapters.

Words to Watch

Below are some words in the reading that do not have strong context support. Each word is followed by the number of the paragraph in which it appears and its meaning there. These words are indicated in the article by a small circle (°).

cognitive (4): having to do with reasoning or mental processes
auditory (8): relating to the process of hearing
Falstaff (9): a funny, talkative character in several of Shakespeare's plays
neural scaffolding (11): supports that help the brain retain information
aesthetic (17): artistic
intuitive (17): instinctive
subsequently (24): later
connotation (28): implied meaning

FORGET WHAT YOU KNOW ABOUT GOOD STUDY HABITS

Benedict Carey

1 Every September, millions of parents try a kind of psychological witchcraft to transform their summer-glazed campers into fall students, their video-bugs into bookworms. Advice is cheap and all too familiar: Clear a quiet work space. Stick to a homework schedule. Set goals. Set boundaries. Do not bribe (except in emergencies).

2 And check out the classroom. Does Junior's learning style match the new teacher's approach? Or the school's philosophy? Maybe the child isn't "a good fit" for the school.

3 Such theories have developed in part because of sketchy education research that doesn't offer clear guidance. Student traits and teaching styles surely interact; so do personalities and at-home rules. The trouble is, no one can predict how.

4 Yet there are effective approaches to learning, at least for those who are motivated. In recent years, cognitive° scientists have shown that a few simple techniques can reliably improve what matters most: how much a student learns from studying.

5 The findings can help anyone, from a fourth grader doing long division to a retiree taking on a new language. But they directly contradict much of the common wisdom about good study habits, and they have not caught on.

6 For instance, instead of sticking to one study location, simply alternating the room where a person studies improves retention. So does studying distinct but related skills or concepts in one sitting, rather than focusing intensely on a single thing.

"We have known these principles for some time, and it's intriguing that schools don't pick them up, or that people don't learn them by trial and error," said Robert A. Bjork, a psychologist at the University of California, Los Angeles. "Instead, we walk around with all sorts of unexamined beliefs about what works that are mistaken." 7

Take the notion that children have specific learning styles, that some are "visual learners" and others are auditory°; some are "left-brain" students, others "right-brain." In a recent review of the relevant research, published in the journal *Psychological Science in the Public Interest*, a team of psychologists found almost zero support for such ideas. "The contrast between the enormous popularity of the learning-styles approach within education and the lack of credible evidence for its utility is, in our opinion, striking and disturbing," the researchers concluded. 8

Ditto for teaching styles, researchers say. Some excellent instructors caper in front of the blackboard like summer-theater Falstaffs°; others are reserved to the point of shyness. "We have yet to 9 identify the common threads between teachers who create a constructive learning atmosphere," said Daniel T. Willingham, a psychologist at the University of Virginia and author of the book *Why Don't Students Like School*?

10 But individual learning is another matter, and psychologists have discovered that some of the most hallowed advice on study habits is flat wrong. For instance, many study skills courses insist that students find a specific place, a study room or a quiet corner of the library, to take their work. The research finds just the opposite. In one classic 1978 experiment, psychologists found that college students who studied a list of 40 vocabulary words in two different rooms—one windowless and cluttered, the other modern, with a view of a courtyard—did far better on a test than students who studied the words twice, in the same room. Later studies have confirmed the finding, for a variety of topics.

11 The brain makes subtle associations between what it is studying and the background sensations it has at the time, the authors say, regardless of whether those perceptions are conscious. It colors the terms of the Versailles Treaty with the wasted fluorescent glow of the dorm study room, say; or the elements of the Marshall Plan with the jade-curtain shade of the willow tree in the backyard. Forcing the brain to make multiple associations with the same material may, in effect, give that information more neural scaffolding°.

12 "What we think is happening here is that, when the outside context is

varied, the information is enriched, and this slows down forgetting," said Dr. Bjork, the senior author of the two-room experiment.

Varying the type of material studied in a single sitting—alternating, for example, among vocabulary, reading and speaking in a new language—seems to leave a deeper impression on the brain than does concentrating on just one skill at a time. Musicians have known this for years, and their practice sessions often include a mix of scales, musical pieces, and rhythmic work. Many athletes, too, routinely mix their workouts with strength, speed, and skill drills. 13

The advantages of this approach to studying can be striking, in some topic areas. In a study recently posted online by the journal *Applied Cognitive Psychology*, Doug Rohrer and Kelli Taylor 14 of the University of South Florida taught a group of fourth graders four equations, each to calculate a different dimension of a prism. Half of the children learned by studying repeated examples of one equation, say, calculating the number of prism faces when given the number of sides at the base, then moving on to the next type of calculation, studying repeated examples of that. The other half studied mixed problem sets, which included examples of all four types of calculations grouped together. Both groups solved sample problems along the way, as they studied.

15 A day later, the researchers gave all of the students a test on the material, presenting new problems of the same type. The children who had studied mixed sets did twice as well as the others, outscoring them 77 percent to 38 percent. The researchers have found the same in experiments involving adults and younger children.

16 "When students see a list of problems, all of the same kind, they know the strategy to use before they even read the problem," said Dr. Rohrer. "That's like riding a bike with training wheels." With mixed practice, he added, "each problem is different from the last one, which means kids must learn how to choose the appropriate procedure—just like they had to do on the test."

17 These findings extend well beyond math, even to aesthetic° intuitive° learning. In an experiment published last month in the journal *Psychology and Aging*, researchers found that college students and adults of retirement age were better able to distinguish the painting styles of 12 unfamiliar artists after viewing mixed collections (assortments, including works from all 12) than after viewing a dozen works from one artist, all together, then moving on to the next painter.

18 The finding undermines the common assumption that intensive immersion is the best way to really master a particular genre or type of creative work, said Nate Kornell, a psychologist at Williams College and the lead author of the study. "What seems to be happening in this case is that the brain is picking up deeper patterns when seeing assortments of paintings; it's picking up what's similar and what's different about them," often subconsciously.

19 Cognitive scientists do not deny that honest-to-goodness cramming can lead to a better grade on a given exam. But hurriedly jam-packing a brain is akin to speed-packing a cheap suitcase, as most students quickly learn—it holds its new load for a while; then most everything falls out.

20 "With many students, it's not like they can't remember the material" when they move to a more advanced class, said Henry L. Roediger III, a psychologist at Washington University in St. Louis. "It's like they've never seen it before."

21 When the neural suitcase is packed carefully and gradually, it holds its contents for far, far longer. An hour of study tonight, an hour on the weekend, another session a week from now: such so-called spacing improves later recall, without requiring students to put in more overall study effort or pay more

attention, dozens of studies have found.

22 No one knows for sure why. It may be that the brain, when it revisits material at a later time, has to relearn some of what it has absorbed before adding new stuff—and that that process is itself self-reinforcing.

23 "The idea is that forgetting is the friend of learning," said Dr. Kornell. "When you forget something, it allows you to relearn, and do so effectively, the next time you see it."

24 That's one reason cognitive scientists see testing itself—or practice tests and quizzes—as a powerful tool of learning, rather than merely assessment. The process of retrieving an idea is not like pulling a book from a shelf; it seems to fundamentally alter the way the information is subsequently° stored, making it far more accessible in the future.

25 Dr. Roediger uses the analogy of the Heisenberg uncertainty principle in physics, which holds that the act of measuring a property of a particle (position, for example) reduces the accuracy with which you can know another property (momentum, for example): "Testing not only measures knowledge but changes it," he says—and, happily, in the direction of more certainty, not less.

26 In one of his own experiments, Dr. Roediger and Jeffrey Karpicke, also of Washington University, had college students study science passages from a reading comprehension test, in short study periods. When students studied the same material twice, in back-to-back sessions, they did very well on a test given immediately afterward, then began to forget the material.

27 But if they studied the passage just once and did a practice test in the second session, they did very well on one test two days later, and another given a week later.

28 "Testing has such bad connotation°; people think of standardized testing or teaching to the test," Dr. Roediger said. "Maybe we need to call it something else, but this is one of the most powerful learning tools we have."

29 Of course, one reason the thought of testing tightens people's stomachs is that tests are so often hard. Paradoxically, it is just this difficulty that makes them such effective study tools, research suggests. The harder it is to remember something, the harder it is to later forget. This effect, which researchers call "desirable difficulty," is evident in daily life. The name of the actor who played Linc in *The Mod Squad*? Francie's brother in *A Tree Grows in Brooklyn*? The name of the co-discoverer, with Newton, of calculus?

30 The more mental sweat it takes to dig it out, the more securely it will be subsequently anchored.

31 None of which is to suggest that these techniques—alternating study environments, mixing content, spacing study sessions, self-testing, or all the above—will turn a grade-A slacker into a grade-A student. Motivation matters. So do impressing friends, making the hockey team, and finding the nerve to text the cute student in social studies.

32 "In lab experiments, you're able to control for all factors except the one

you're studying," said Dr. Willingham. "Not true in the classroom, in real life. All of these things are interacting at the same time."

33 But at the very least, the cognitive techniques give parents and students, young and old, something many did not have before: a study plan based on evidence, not schoolyard folk wisdom or empty theorizing.

Reading Comprehension Questions

Vocabulary in Context

_____ 1. In the excerpt below, the word *hallowed* (hăl′ōd) means

A. unusual.
B. inventive.
C. highly respected.
D. based on research.

"But individual learning is another matter, and psychologists have discovered that some of the most hallowed advice on study habits is flat wrong." (Paragraph 10)

_____ 2. In the excerpt below, the word *paradoxically* (păr′ə-dŏks′ĭ-kəl-ē) means

A. understandably.
B. strangely enough.
C. unfortunately.
D. reliably.

"Of course, one reason the thought of testing tightens people's stomachs is that tests are so often hard. Paradoxically, it is just this difficulty that makes them such effective study tools, research suggests." (Paragraph 29)

Central Point and Main Ideas

_____ 3. Which sentence best expresses the central point of the selection?

A. A few simple techniques can improve students' ability to learn new material.
B. Research has shown that people should study in different places, study mixed problem sets, and not cram for tests.
C. People should be aware of and practice study techniques that are based on solid evidence, not folk wisdom or unproved theories.
D. Despite the enormous popularity of the learning-styles approach in education, there is little evidence that it is useful.

_____ 4. Which of the following best expresses the main idea of paragraphs 8–9?
A. Experts do not agree on which learning or teaching style is most effective.
B. Just as students have a range of learning styles, teachers have varied teaching styles.
C. There is no proof that children actually have learning styles.
D. Because teachers can be either outgoing or shy, children's learning styles are difficult to identify.

_____ 5. The main idea of paragraphs 13–15 is best expressed in
A. the first sentence of paragraph 13.
B. the second sentence of paragraph 14.
C. the first sentence of paragraph 15.
D. the last sentence of paragraph 15.

Supporting Details

_____ 6. TRUE OR FALSE? The author believes that some students are "visual learners," while others are "auditory" learners.

_____ 7. The author compares varying the type of material studied in a single setting to
A. riding a bike with training wheels.
B. giving the brain more neural scaffolding.
C. the way musicians mix scales, musical pieces, and rhythmic work in a practice session.
D. speed-packing a cheap suitcase.

_____ 8. When studying for a test, the author recommends
A. cramming.
B. studying the same material twice in the same quiet room.
C. requiring students to put in more overall study effort.
D. spacing out periods of study over a week or so.

Implied Main Ideas

_____ 9. The implied main idea of paragraphs 10–12 is that

A. it's not necessary for students to find a specific place, like a study room or a quiet corner of the library, in which to study.

B. although experts have long advised students to find one specific place to study, research shows that students retain information better when they vary the places in which they study.

C. scientists have learned that the brain makes subtle associations between what it is studying and the background sensations it has at the time.

D. students who studied a list of 40 vocabulary words in two rooms did better on a test than students who studied the words twice in the same room.

_____10. The entire selection suggests that

A. most educators closely follow the latest news in psychological research.

B. the principles of effective studying are by now widely known.

C. many teachers and students still hold mistaken beliefs about studying.

D. researchers now have a clear idea how student traits and teaching styles interact.

Discussion Questions

1. After reading this selection, do you plan to change the way you study? If so, which piece of Carey's advice would you be most likely to follow? Explain.

2. Carey admits that the study techniques he presents, which contradict common wisdom about good study habits, have not been widely accepted. Why do you think this is the case?

3. The author notes that there are excellent instructors who are very outgoing, as well as other excellent instructors who are very reserved. A psychologist is quoted as saying, "We have yet to identify the common threads between teachers who create a constructive learning atmosphere." From your experience, can you identify any "common threads" between excellent instructors you have known?

4. Although Carey concedes that "the thought of testing tightens people's stomachs," he calls testing one of the most powerful learning tools we have. Do you agree or disagree? Explain.

Note: Writing assignments for this selection appear on page 698.

Check Your Performance

IMPLIED MAIN IDEAS

Activity		*Number Right*		*Points*		*Score*
Review Test 1	(5 items)	______	×	2	=	______
Review Test 2	(4 items)	______	×	7.5	=	______
Review Test 3	(4 items)	______	×	7.5	=	______
Review Test 4	(10 items)	______	×	3	=	______
				TOTAL SCORE	=	______%

Enter your total score into the **Reading Performance Chart: Review Tests** on the inside back cover.

Name ______________________________ Date __________

Section ____________ SCORE: (Number correct) ________ x 25 = ________ %

Implied Main Ideas: Mastery Test 1

In the space provided, write the letter of the sentence that best expresses the implied main idea of each of the following paragraphs.

_____ 1. [1]One form of jumping to conclusions is putting words into a speaker's mouth. [2]Because we are so sure of what others mean or are going to say, we simply don't listen to what they actually say. [3]Sometimes we don't even hear them out. [4]Instead of listening, we leap to a meaning that they may not have intended to communicate. [5]Another form of jumping to conclusions is rejecting others' ideas too early as boring or misguided. [6]We decide that others have nothing valuable or useful to say. [7]We simply tune out and hear nothing because we decide early on that we can spend our mental effort in a better way.

A. We "tune out" in several ways.
B. For several reasons, we might find it difficult to listen to others.
C. There is more than one way to jump to conclusions.
D. Communication problems are common in relationships.

_____ 2. [1]The first farm animals were sheep and goats, the most suitable species for driving in small flocks while people might still be traveling. [2]For millennia wild animals had been slaughtered on the spot, but then some bright person realized that sheep and goats could be captured and driven home, thereby saving the effort of dragging their carcasses. [3]Evidently, once the animals were alive at home, it became clear that they could be kept alive for longer periods to serve as dietary insurance policies—ready meat on the hoof. [4]It was only a matter of time before stocks of sheep and goats were kept alive to reproduce so that there might be a continuous supply without hunting.

A. Little by little, humans came to own and breed livestock.
B. Sheep and goats were the most suitable species for traveling flocks.
C. At first, humans slaughtered wild animals on the spot and dragged them home.
D. Keeping livestock is easier than hunting.

_____ 3. [1]The divorce rate in the United States is estimated to be as high as 57.7 percent, and the average length of new marriages is 26 months. [2]Sixty-two percent of our citizens are obese. [3]Emotional neglect of children has increased 330 percent in the last decade. [4]One in four women has been sexually molested. [5]Suicide is on

(Continues on next page)

the rise. [6]One out of every six people in America will have a serious, function-impairing episode of depression in a lifetime. [7]Antidepressant and anxiety-reducing remedies are now a multibillion-dollar business. [8]Violence is evident everywhere, and 25 percent of us fall prey to violent crimes. [9]Teenagers commit about four thousand murders a year. [10]Half of our children have experimented with alcohol by the time they reach the eighth grade, and a fourth have experimented with drugs.

A. American society is overmedicated.
B. American society is troubled in many ways.
C. American society is marked by too much violence.
D. Children and teenagers are at risk in American society.

______ 4. [1]When an eyewitness is asked a question by a police officer or an attorney, the wording of the question can affect the way the witness recalls the information. [2]In one experiment, the participants were shown a film of two cars crashing into each other. [3]Some were then asked the question, "About how fast were the cars going when they *smashed into* each other?" [4]On average, these people estimated the speed to be 41 miles per hour. [5]Another group was asked, "About how fast were the cars going when they *bumped into* each other?" [6]This group estimated the speed at about 37 miles per hour. [7]For a third group, the word *contacted* was used instead of *bumped into*. [8]The average estimated speed for this group was only 32 miles per hour. [9]When the witness is a child, the likelihood of error is even greater because children's memories are highly vulnerable to the influence of others. [10]In one experiment, 5- to 7-year-old girls who had just had a routine physical examination were shown an anatomically explicit doll. [11]The girls were shown the doll's genital area and asked, "Did the doctor touch you here?" [12]Three of the girls who did not have a vaginal or anal exam said that the doctor had in fact touched them in the genital area, and one of those three made up the detail "The doctor did it with a stick."

A. The recall of information by an eyewitness can be influenced by the person asking the questions.
B. Eyewitnesses often deliberately invent details in an effort to please the person questioning them.
C. Witnesses interpreted the word "smashed" differently than they interpreted the words "bumped" or "contacted."
D. The testimony of eyewitnesses should not be admitted in court.

Name ______________________________ Date __________

Section __________ SCORE: (Number correct) ______ x 25 = ______ %

Implied Main Ideas: Mastery Test 2

In the space provided, write the letter of the sentence that best expresses the implied main idea of each of the following paragraphs.

_____ 1. [1]It is difficult to do the intense, active thinking that clear writing demands. [2](Perhaps television has made us all so passive that the active thinking necessary in both writing and reading now seems doubly hard.) [3]It is frightening to sit down before a blank sheet of paper and know that an hour later, nothing on it may be worth keeping. [4]It is frustrating to discover how much of a challenge it is to transfer thoughts and feelings from one's head onto a sheet of paper. [5]It is upsetting to find that an apparently simple writing assignment often turns out to be complicated. [6]But writing is not an automatic process: we will not get something for nothing, and we cannot expect something for nothing.

A. Writing is hard work.
B. Writing offers rich rewards.
C. Anything worthwhile requires patience and effort.
D. Television is making active thinking more difficult than ever.

_____ 2. [1]In college, students experience a lot of stress around exam time. [2]Knowing that, researchers took saliva samples from healthy college students before, during, and after final exams. [3]They tested the saliva for the presence of a substance which fights infection. [4]The tests showed that the infection-fighter was at its lowest level during the exam period. [5]In addition, many of the students developed colds during final exams. [6]In a related study, older adults who were receiving flu shots were interviewed. [7]About half of those adults reported living with a high degree of stress. [8]Six months after receiving the shot, blood tests showed that the group that had reported having little stress in their lives had a far higher degree of immunity than the highly-stressed group. [9]The adults living with more stress were at much greater risk for catching flu.

A. Flu epidemics could be eliminated if more people would learn how to deal with stress.
B. College students who do not prepare ahead of time for exams are more likely to get sick.
C. Older adults often have to cope with a high degree of stress.
D. Apparently, the more stressed a person is, the lower his or her immunity to disease.

(Continues on next page)

_____ 3. [1]Primary relationships—with our relatives, friends, or neighbors—are very precious to us. [2]As research has shown, they are particularly helpful when we are going through stressful life events. [3]They help ease recovery from heart attacks, prevent childbirth complications, make child rearing easier, lighten the burden of household finances, and cushion the impact of job loss by providing financial assistance and employment information. [4]However, secondary relationships have their own special benefits. [5]Our close friends may not help us, for instance, get as good a job as our acquaintances can. [6]Our friends move in the same social circle as we do, but our acquaintances, to whom we have only weak ties, move in different circles. [7]As a result, we may already be aware of the job openings known to our friends, but we may not know of the many other job opportunities our acquaintances can tell us about.

A. Primary relationships and secondary relationships each have their own special benefits.
B. Primary and secondary relationships are necessary for our very survival.
C. Secondary relationships can be invaluable if we are looking for jobs.
D. We would probably not be able to get through stressful life events without primary relationships.

_____ 4. [1]The United States buys goods from other nations at such a frenzied pace that it has become the largest debtor nation in the world. [2]When you add up what we pay for the products we buy from other nations and what we receive for the products we sell to those nations, at the end of the year we end up about $600 billion short. [3]Year after year, we sell less than we buy. [4]These mountains of debt have been piling up, and this cannot go on indefinitely. [5]Just as individuals must repay what they borrow or else get into financial trouble—and perhaps financial ruin—so it is with nations. [6]To finance the **national debt** (the total amount the U.S. government owes), we pay about $180 billion a year in interest. [7]These billions are money that we cannot use to build schools and colleges, hire teachers, pay for medical services or job programs for the poor, operate Head Start, or pay for any other services that help to improve our quality of life.

A. Government officials have refused to tell American citizens the truth about our financial crisis.
B. America imports many more products than it exports.
C. It is possible for entire countries as well as individuals to get into financial trouble.
D. Our huge national debt has gotten us in financial trouble and threatens our quality of life.

Name ______________________ Date __________

Section __________ SCORE: (Number correct) ______ x 25 = ______ %

IMPLIED MAIN IDEAS: Mastery Test 3

A. In the space provided, write the letter of the sentence that best expresses the implied main idea of each of the following paragraphs.

_____ 1. [1]When a person does something that causes you discomfort or inconvenience, you may think of him or her as being a jerk—or perhaps some other more colorful label. [2]Seeing a person as a "jerk" puts the person in an entirely negative light. [3]Such labeling involves overgeneralizing, perhaps on the basis of only a single event. [4]In reality, we all perform our share of "jerklike" behaviors. [5]But if we label someone else as the jerk, we see ourselves as being somewhat superior. [6]We then feel more justified in becoming angry with this person, since he or she is the essence of badness, rather than just a person who chose a behavior that we consider to be undesirable.

A. People may use a negative label for someone who causes discomfort or inconvenience.
B. It is unfair to label someone negatively on the basis of a single event.
C. We tend to judge others in ways that make us feel superior.
D. To justify our own anger or discomfort, we may use unfair labels that make us feel superior.

_____ 2. [1]Feedback to workers should be timely. [2]Timely feedback is that which occurs soon after a behavior occurs—the sooner the better. [3]Although an annual performance evaluation may be important for other reasons, it is not very effective as a feedback mechanism. [4]The feedback must also be accurate. [5]To maintain motivation and performance, give positive feedback to people doing the best work and negative feedback to people doing the poorest work. [6]If people receive inappropriate feedback, the entire system looks foolish and will fail. [7]It is also discouraging to give the same feedback to everyone. [8]Not everyone can be doing the best job (or the worst, either). [9]If everyone receives the same feedback, then the feedback becomes meaningless, or worse. [10]If the better workers are receiving the same feedback as the poorer workers, the better workers may become unmotivated, and their performance may drop. [11]Why perform well if you earn the same feedback (and rewards) as those doing less well?

A. Positive feedback is a very useful tool in managing motivation and performance.
B. To be effective, job feedback must be timely and accurate.
C. An annual performance evaluation is a poor feedback tool.
D. To be timely, feedback should be given as soon as possible after what is being evaluated takes place.

(Continues on next page)

_____ 3. [1]Criminal courts in most jurisdictions are very busy. [2]The large number of people arrested and prosecuted, the limited availability of defense attorneys to help an accused person prepare and offer a defense, and the overcrowded courts create a heavy caseload demand on everyone associated with criminal justice—prosecutors, public and private defenders, and judges. [3]The result of the crowded court calendars, court delays, and clogged caseloads is that most cases do not go to trial at all. [4]Most are "settled" through guilty pleas, pleas arranged among the prosecutor, defense attorney, the accused, and the judge. [5]Guilty pleas are induced through negotiations whereby the defendant pleads guilty to reduced charges in exchange for a lenient sentence, that is, a lighter sentence than the judge would normally give after conviction at trial. [6]This entire process is generally known as plea-bargaining, or plea negotiation.

A. Crime is a major problem in the United States.
B. In plea-bargaining, defendants plead guilty to lesser charges in exchange for a more lenient sentence.
C. Because of heavy court caseloads, most cases are settled through plea-bargaining.
D. The criminal courts are crowded because a large number of people are arrested.

B. (4.) Write out, in your own words, the implied main idea of the following paragraph.

[1]Nowadays Americans worry more, for example, about being murdered by others than about killing ourselves, even though twice as many Americans commit suicide every year than are murdered. [2]We worry about being struck by lightning during a thunderstorm, while more than 10 times as many Americans die from falling out of bed. [3]We are more afraid of dying in an airline accident than on the highway, although more than 500 times as many people die in car wrecks as in plane crashes. [4]We wring our hands over getting bird flu and mad cow disease, which have not killed a single person in the United States. [5]But we are not shaken up over the likelihood of getting the common flu, which annually contributes to 36,000 deaths in the United States. [6]We are not scared, either, by the cholesterol in our hamburger that contributes to heart disease, killing 700,000 Americans a year.

Implied main idea: ______________________________

____

____

Name ______________________________ Date __________

Section ____________ SCORE: (Number correct) _______ x 25 = _______ %

IMPLIED MAIN IDEAS: Mastery Test 4

A. In the space provided, write the letter of the sentence that best expresses the implied main idea of each of the following paragraphs.

_____ 1. [1]"Anybody can go to college if he or she really wants to. [2]I didn't have any money, but I worked nights, lifted myself up by my bootstraps, and got a college degree. [3]If I could do it, anyone can!" [4]Is that assumption necessarily true? [5]What if a person has a large family to support and is living up to or beyond the limits of his or her income? [6]What if a person hasn't had the good fortune to be born with great mental abilities? [7]The exceptions could go on and on. [8]"I work because I need the money. [9]Wendy shouldn't be working here. [10]Her husband makes good money, so she doesn't even have to work." [11]Isn't this person assuming that what is true for one is true for all? [12]Couldn't there be other reasons for working besides the quest for money? [13]How about the need to socialize with others or the need to make a contribution? [14]Every individual's situation is different.

A. Not everybody can go to college if he or she really wants to.
B. What is true for one person or situation is never true for anyone else.
C. What is true for one person in a situation may or may not be true for someone else.
D. People are more alike than they realize.

_____ 2. [1]Every wage earner covered under the Social Security Act pays a tax; the employer also pays a tax, which is equal to that paid by the employee. [2]The amount that one can expect to receive each month in old-age insurance benefits depends on one's average monthly earnings. [3]Also, the size of the benefits depends on the number of years one has worked. [4]If a person retires at 65, the monthly benefits are greater than if he or she retires at 62. [5]These benefits are a retirement annuity. [6]In other words, they are paid to the wage earner from the date of retirement to the time he or she dies. [7]In addition, when a wage earner dies, Social Security provides payments to his or her spouse, to dependent parents, and to children until they are 18 years of age (21 if they are in school). [8]Further, payments are made to a wage earner (and dependents) if he or she is totally disabled and unable to work.

A. Social Security pays retirement annuities, which are paid to the wage earner from the date of retirement until death.
B. Both wage earners and employers make payments to Social Security.
C. The government makes direct payments to various individuals and institutions.
D. A complicated set of rules governs the funding and payment of Social Security.

(Continues on next page)

B. Write out, in your own words, the implied main idea of the following paragraphs.

3. [1]Our senses of sight, hearing, taste, and smell are constantly bombarded by stimuli. [2]These stimuli are stored in our sensory memory, where they remain for just a fraction of a second. [3]When we look up a phone number and remember it long enough to dial it, we are using another form of memory, our short-term memory. [4]Ideal for briefly remembering such small chunks of information, short-term memory decays quickly, which is why we would probably have to look up that same phone number again if we needed it a few hours later. [5]The third type of memory is long-term memory, where we store information that we've judged as important. [6]Our long-term memories can last a lifetime.

   Implied main idea: ______________________________

   ____

   ____

4. [1]For an older person who lives alone, having a dog in the house or apartment provides companionship. [2]Physical contact with a dog can also be helpful. [3]Patting a dog has been shown to lower the blood pressure of both the human and the dog. [4]A dog owner frequently talks to the pet, and talking helps keep the owner's mind active. [5]In addition, the dog depends on the person for its survival. [6]Being needed by another living creature creates a sense of purpose in a senior citizen's life. [7]The dog must be fed and walked at regular intervals. [8]This helps the person maintain a daily routine and stay physically active in older age. [9]Dog walking also encourages the owner to have contact with other human beings.

   Implied main idea: ______________________________

   ____

   ____

Name ______________________________ Date __________

Section __________ SCORE: (Number correct) ______ x 25 = ______ %

IMPLIED MAIN IDEAS: Mastery Test 5

A. In the space provided, write the letter of the sentence that best expresses the implied main idea of each of the following paragraphs.

______ 1. [1]A line graph shows changes, especially changes over specific time periods. [2]It might show outdoor temperatures hour by hour, or weight loss week by week. [3]Bar graphs display and compare amounts: the higher or longer a bar, the greater the amount. [4]A bar graph might show, for instance, the number of male and female smokers in several age groups, or death rates from various causes. [5]A circle or "pie" graph shows parts of a whole. [6]Each sector of the circle—each wedge of the pie—is one part. [7]Circle graphs are often used for budgets: 50 percent for rent, 25 percent for food, and so on. [8]They're also used for polls: for instance, 45 percent "yes," 40 percent "no," and 15 percent "undecided."

A. The sectors of a circle graph look like wedges of a pie.
B. Line graphs, bar graphs, and circle graphs are used to show different kinds of information.
C. Line graphs are the most useful kind of graph.
D. We often see line graphs, bar graphs, and circle graphs in newspapers, magazines, and textbooks.

______ 2. [1]One condition of society that lies at the roots of political conflict in America is scarcity. [2]Society has limited resources, but people have unlimited appetites, so there is never enough money in even the wealthiest countries. [3]This scarcity creates conflict over how the available resources will be distributed. [4]How will taxes be used? [5]Who will be eligible for welfare benefits? [6]How much will those eligible for benefits receive? [7]These issues best demonstrate the conflict over scarcity. [8]The other condition of society that creates political conflict is differences in values. [9]People don't see things the same way and therefore bring to politics a wide range of conflicting values—about abortion, the environment, defense spending, crime and punishment, the poor, the economy, and almost everything else imaginable.

A. Political conflict in America is rooted in two general conditions of society.
B. People view politics in differing ways.
C. Conflict in America is a natural outcome of our many differences in values.
D. Because of the scarcity of available resources, conflict is inevitable.

______ 3. [1]*Verbal irony*, which is often tongue-in-cheek, involves a discrepancy between the words that are spoken and what is actually meant. [2]For example, "I just heard you got the highest grade on the final exam. [3]I guess that news ruined your day." [4]If the ironic comment is designed to be hurting or insulting, it qualifies as *sarcasm*. [5]An illustration is the comment "Congratulations! You failed the final exam." [6]In *dramatic irony*, the discrepancy is between what the

(Continues on next page)

speaker says and what the author means or what the audience knows. [7]For instance, in Shakespeare's *King Lear*, the old king gives all his wealth to two cold-blooded daughters who flatter and manipulate him with false words; he then entrusts himself to their care. [8]He banishes the daughter who so truly loves him that she will tell him nothing but the truth. [9]The audience watches Lear make this catastrophic misjudgment and waits for tragedy to unfold.

A. Irony occurs in several forms.
B. Shakespeare made good use of irony.
C. Sarcasm is a type of irony with a biting quality.
D. Dramatic irony adds power to a work of fiction.

B. Read the following textbook passage and, in the space provided, write the letter of the sentence that best expresses the implied main idea.

_____ 4. [1]In early human history, life used to be short, and women gave birth to many children. [2]Because only women get pregnant, carry a child for nine months, give birth, and nurse, for a considerable part of their lives women were limited in what they could do. [3]To survive, an infant needed a nursing mother. [4]With a child at her breast or in her womb and one on her hip or on her back, a woman was encumbered physically. [5]Thus women everywhere took on the tasks associated with the home and child care, while men took over hunting large animals and other tasks that required more speed and longer absence from the base camp.

[6]Men gained both power and prestige. [7]They made and controlled the weapons used for hunting and warfare. [8]They left the camp to hunt animals, returning triumphantly with prey. [9]Leaving the camp, they also made contact with other tribes and accumulated possessions in trade. [10]Men also gained prestige by returning with prisoners from warfare. [11]In contrast, little prestige was given to the routine activities of women, who didn't do such showy and triumphant things and were not seen as risking their lives for the group. [12]The men's weapons, their items of trade, and the knowledge they gained from their contacts with other groups became sources of power.

[13]The result was that men took over society, creating a fundamental change in the relations of the sexes. [14]As women became subject to the decisions of men, men justified their dominance. [15]They developed the idea that because biology gives men superior strength, it also imbues manhood with superiority. [16]To avoid "contamination" by females, who had become a lower class of people, men shrouded some of their activities in secrecy and established rules and rituals that excluded women.

A. Men's dominance in society is rooted in biology.
B. In early human history, women everywhere took on the tasks associated with the home and child care.
C. Because they were physically stronger than women, men came to believe that they were superior to women.
D. It is natural for women today to feel inferior to men.

Name ______________________________________ Date __________

Section ___________ SCORE: (Number correct) _______ x 50 = _______ %

IMPLIED MAIN IDEAS: Mastery Test 6

In the space provided, write the letter of the sentence that best expresses the implied main idea of each of the textbook passages that follow.

______ 1. [1]According to recent research, bad moods descend upon us an average of three out of every ten days. [2]The most effective way to banish a sad or bad mood is by changing what caused it in the first place—if you can figure out what made you upset and why. [3]"Most bad moods are caused by loss or failure in work or intimate relationships," says psychologist Randy Larsen. [4]"The questions to ask are: What can I do to fix the failure? [5]What can I do to remedy the loss? [6]Is there anything under my control that I can change? [7]If there is, take action and solve it." [8]Rewrite the report. [9]Ask to take a makeup exam. [10]Apologize to the friend whose feelings you hurt. [11]If there's nothing you can do, accept what happened and focus on doing things differently next time. [12]"In our studies, resolving to try harder actually was as effective in improving mood as taking action in the present," says Larsen.

[13]Another way of changing a bad mood is to change the way you think about what happened—by putting a positive spin on it. [14]This technique, called *cognitive reappraisal*, or *reframing*, helps you look at a setback in a new light: What lessons did it teach you? [15]What would you have done differently? [16]Could there be a silver lining or hidden benefit?

[17]If you can't identify or resolve the problem responsible for your emotional funk, the next-best solution is to concentrate on altering your negative feelings. [18]For example, try setting a quick, achievable goal that can boost your spirits with a small success. [19]Clean out your drawer; sort through the piles of paper on your desk; send an e-mail or text message to an old friend.

[20]Another good option is to start exercising. [21]In studies of mood regulation, exercise consistently ranks as the single most effective strategy for banishing bad feelings. [22]Numerous studies have confirmed that aerobic workouts, such as walking or jogging, significantly improve mood. [23]Even nonaerobic exercise, such as weight lifting, can boost spirits, improve sleep and appetite, and produce feelings of mastery and accomplishment.

A. Some mood-boosting strategies are more effective than others.

B. Most bad moods are caused by loss or failure at work or in intimate relationships and can be relieved through cognitive reappraisal or exercise.

C. Learning effective mood-boosting, mood-regulating strategies can help us pull ourselves out of an emotional slump.

D. The most important thing to ask when suffering from a bad mood is "What can I do to fix the failure or remedy the loss?"

(Continues on next page)

______ 2. [1]What's the best way to improve children's performance in the classroom? [2]According to a recent study published in the journal *Pediatrics*, children who had more than 15 minutes of recess a day showed better behavior in class than those who had little or none. [3]Although disadvantaged children were more likely to be denied recess, the association between better behavior and recess time held up even after researchers controlled for a number of variables, including sex, ethnicity, public or private school, and class size. [4]The lead researcher, Dr. Romina M. Barros, believes the findings are important because many schools do not view recess as essential to education. [5]In the *Pediatrics* study, 30 percent of school children were found to have little or no daily recess. [6]Also, teachers often punish children by taking away recess privileges. [7]That strikes Dr. Barros as illogical. [8]"Recess should be part of the curriculum," she says. [9]"You don't punish a kid by having them miss math class, so kids shouldn't be punished by not getting recess." [10]In a similar study, Harvard researchers found that the more physical fitness tests children passed, the better they did on academic tests. [11]The study, of 1,800 middle-school students, suggests that children can benefit academically from physical activity during gym class and recess.

[12]These findings are echoed by laboratory studies. [13]Young rats denied opportunities for rough-and-tumble play develop numerous social problems in adulthood. [14]They fail to recognize social cues and the nuances of rat hierarchy; they aren't able to mate. [15]By the same token, people who play as children "learn to handle life in a much more resilient and vital way," said Dr. Stuart Brown, the author of the new book *Play: How It Shapes the Brain, Opens the Imagination and Invigorates the Soul.* [16]Brown calls play "a fundamental biological process" and works with educators and legislators to promote the importance of preserving playtime in schools. [17]"From my viewpoint, it's a major public health issue," he says. [18]"Teachers feel like they're under huge pressures to get academic excellence to the exclusion of having much fun in the classroom. [19]But playful learning leads to better academic success than the skills-and-drills approach."

A. Recent studies suggest that children can benefit academically from playtime at school.
B. According to one researcher, many schools do not view recess as essential to education.
C. Laboratory studies with rats echo the idea that play is important for children.
D. Because teachers are under huge pressure to get academic excellence, they often fail to let children have fun in the classroom.

5 Relationships I

Authors use two common methods to show relationships and make their ideas clear. The two methods—**transitions** and **patterns of organization**—are explained in turn in this chapter. The chapter also explains two common types of relationships:

- Relationships that involve **addition**
- Relationships that involve **time**

Transitions

Look at the following items and put a check (✓) by the one that is easier to read and understand:

___ The weather at the North Pole is truly extreme. The average winter temperature is more than 20 degrees below zero.

___ The weather at the North Pole is truly extreme. First of all, the average winter temperature is more than 20 degrees below zero.

You probably found the second item easier to understand. The words *First of all* make it clear that the writer plans on explaining two or more ways the weather is extreme. **Transitions** are words or phrases (like *first of all)* that show relationships between ideas. They are like signs on the road that guide travelers. Or they can be seen as "bridge" words, carrying the reader across from one idea to the next:

The weather at the North Pole is truly extreme. **First of all,** the average winter temperature is more than 20 degrees below zero.

Two major types of transitions are words that show addition and words that show time.

Words That Show Addition

Once again, put a check (✓) beside the item that is easier to read and understand:

___ A virus cannot move or grow. It can reproduce only inside a cell of another organism.

___ A virus cannot move or grow. Furthermore, it can reproduce only inside a cell of another organism.

In the first item, we're not sure of the relationship between the two sentences. The word *furthermore* in the second item makes the relationship clear: The author is listing two altogether different qualities of a virus. One quality is that it cannot move or grow; a *second* quality is that it can reproduce only inside another organism. *Furthermore* and words like it are known as addition words.

"I can't marry you, Henry. First of all, you're too tall for me. In addition, I don't like pink."

Addition words signal added ideas. These words tell you a writer is presenting one or more ideas that continue along the same line of thought as a previous idea. Like all transitions, addition words help writers organize their information and present it clearly to readers. In the cartoon on the previous page, the words *In addition* introduce a *second* reason Henry's proposal is being rejected.

Here are some common words that show addition:

Addition Words

one	to begin with	also	further
first (of all)	for one thing	in addition	furthermore
second(ly)	other	next	last (of all)
third(ly)	another	moreover	final(ly)

Examples

The following examples contain addition words. Notice how these words introduce ideas that *add to* what has already been said.

- We communicate to exchange information. We *also* communicate to develop relationships.
- Tiger sharks eat fish, squid, sea turtles, seals, and smaller sharks. *Moreover,* they have been known to swallow car license plates and gasoline cans.
- Consumers today want much more information about food products than they did twenty or more years ago. Why? *For one thing,* they are much more aware of nutrition than they used to be.

PRACTICE 1

Complete each sentence with a suitable addition word from the box above. Try to use a variety of transitions.

> ***Hint:*** Make sure that each addition word or phrase that you choose fits smoothly into the flow of the sentence. Test each choice by reading the sentence aloud.

1. An important dental warning sign is a tooth that shows sensitivity to hot or cold. ______________________ sign is bleeding gums.

2. Paranoid people often believe that someone is plotting against them. They may _______________________ believe that everyone is staring at them and talking about them.

3. A two-thousand-year-old tomb in England contained remnants of a wooden board game. _______________________, the tomb contained a set of surgical instruments.

4. A person in a crowd is less likely to offer help in an emergency than a person by himself. One reason is that he may be afraid of embarrassing himself by overreacting to the situation. A _________________ reason is that he may assume that a better-qualified person will respond.

5. Education has a very real effect on one's earning power. A recent survey showed that high-school dropouts earned an average of $18,900 annually, while high-school graduates earned $25,900. _________________, adding a college degree brought the average salary up to $45,400.

Words That Show Time

Put a check (✓) beside the item that is easier to read and understand:

___ I fill in the answers to the test questions I'm sure I know. I work on the rest of the exam.

___ First I fill in the answers to the test questions I'm sure I know. Then I work on the rest of the exam.

The words *First* and *Then* in the second item clarify the relationship between the sentences. The writer begins work on the rest of the exam *after* answering the questions that he or she is sure about. *First, then,* and words like them are time words.

"First Goldilocks ate Papa Bear's porridge. Next she ate Momma Bear's porridge. Finally she ate Baby Bear's porridge. Then her cholesterol dropped 14 points!"

Time words indicate a time relationship; they tell us *when* something happened in relation to when something else happened. They help writers organize and make clear the order of events, stages, and steps in a process. In the above cartoon, the words *First*, *Next*, *Finally*, and *Then* indicate when each of the events happened in the story.

Here are some common words that show time:

Time Words

before	immediately	when	until
previously	next	whenever	often
first (of all)	then	while	frequently
second (ly)	following	during	eventually
third (ly)	later	as (soon as)	final(ly)
now	after	by	last (of all)

Note: Some additional ways of showing time are dates ("In 1890 . . . ," "Throughout the 20th century . . . ," "By 2018 . . .") and other time references ("Within a week . . . ," "by the end of the month . . . ," "in two years . . .").

Examples

The following examples contain time words. Notice how these words show us *when* something takes place.

- *During* the last ice age, there were huge icebergs in the ocean as far south as Mexico.
- I cross the street *whenever* I see someone coming toward me whose name I've forgotten.
- *Before* assuming something you read on the Internet is true, remember that anyone can post information there.

Helpful Tips about Transitions

Here are two points to keep in mind about transitions.

TIP 1 Some transition words have the same meaning. For example, *also, moreover,* and *furthermore* all mean "in addition." Authors typically use a variety of transitions to avoid repetition.

TIP 2 In some cases the same word can serve as two different types of transitions, depending on how it is used. For example, the word *first* may be used as an addition word to show that the author is beginning to list a series of ideas, as in the following sentences:

> Plant researchers have developed promising new types of apples. *First,* the apples are disease-resistant and don't need pesticides. *Moreover,* . . .

First may also be used to signal a time sequence, as in this sentence:

> When you feel anger building up within you, take several steps to deal with it. *First,* start to breathe slowly and deeply. *Second,* . . .

PRACTICE 2

Complete each sentence with a suitable time word from the box on the previous page. Try to use a variety of transitions.

> ***Hint:*** Make sure that each time word or phrase that you choose fits smoothly into the flow of the sentence. Test each choice by reading the sentence aloud.

1. Tension headaches generally begin in the morning or early afternoon. They ____________________ worsen during the day.

2. ____________________ a great white shark was spotted a half-mile off shore, lifeguards made everyone get out of the water.

3. ____________________ the summer, our dog Floyd spends most of his day sprawled on the cool tiles of the kitchen floor, panting and drooling.

4. San Francisco tailor Levi Strauss originally made jeans from canvas. It wasn't ____________________ the early 1860s that he started using a softer fabric imported from France, which in the United States was called denim.

5. Advances in medical technology have forced doctors to redefine when death actually occurs. ____________________ such advances, the definition of death had seemed fairly simple.

Patterns of Organization

You have learned that transitions show the relationships between ideas in sentences. In the same way, **patterns of organization** show the relationships between supporting details in paragraphs, essays, and chapters. It helps to recognize the common patterns in which authors arrange information. You will then be better able to understand and remember what you read.

The rest of this chapter discusses two major patterns of organization:

- The **list of items pattern**
  (Addition words are often used in this pattern of organization.)
- The **time order pattern**
  (Time words are often used in this pattern of organization.)

Noticing the transitions in a passage can often help you become aware of its pattern of organization. Transitions can also help you locate the major supporting details.

1 The List of Items Pattern

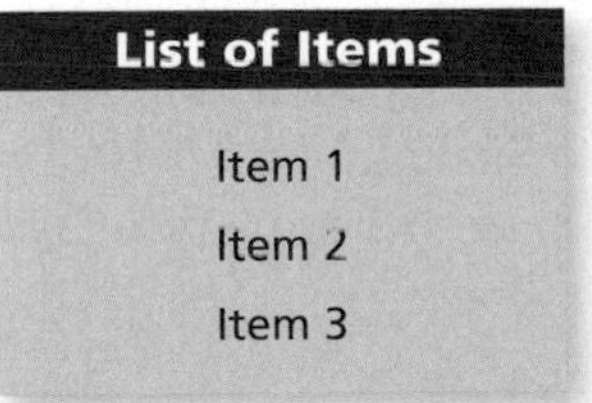

To get a sense of the list of items pattern, try to arrange the following sentences in a logical order. Put a *1* in front of the sentence that should come first, a *2* in front of the sentence that comes next, a *3* in front of the third sentence, and a *4* in front of the sentence that should come last. The result will be a short paragraph. Use the addition words as a guide.

___ Another is the mythical Atlas, who was pictured holding up the heavens in an early collection of maps; ever since, *atlas* has meant any book of maps.

___ The names of many people, real and fictional, have become permanent parts of the English language.

___ A third name-turned-word is that of John Montagu, the Earl of Sandwich, who got the idea of putting a piece of meat between two slices of bread; the result was the sandwich that bears his name.

___ One is Joseph Guillotin, a physician, who invented a machine for cutting off condemned prisoners' heads—the guillotine.

This paragraph begins with the main idea: "The names of many people, real and fictional, have become permanent parts of the English language." The next three sentences go on to list people whose names have become parts of the language, resulting in the pattern of organization known as a *list of items*. The transitions *One, Another,* and *third* each introduce one of the names being listed and indicate their order. Here is the whole paragraph in its correct order:

> [1]The names of many people, real and fictional, have become permanent parts of the English language. [2]One is Joseph Guillotin, a physician, who invented a machine for cutting off condemned prisoners' heads—the guillotine. [3]Another is the mythical Atlas, who was pictured holding up the heavens in an early collection of maps; ever since, *atlas* has meant any book of maps. [4]A third name-turned-word is that of John Montagu, the Earl of Sandwich, who got the idea of putting a piece of meat between two slices of bread; the result was the sandwich that bears his name.

A **list of items** refers to a series of reasons, examples, or other details that support an idea. The items have no time order, but are listed in whatever order the author prefers. Addition words are often used in a list of items to tell us that other supporting points are being added to a point already mentioned. Textbook authors frequently organize material into lists of items, such as a list of types of financial institutions, symptoms of iron deficiency, or reasons for alcohol abuse by college students.

Addition Words Used in the List of Items Pattern

one	to begin with	also	further
first (of all)	for one thing	in addition	furthermore
second(ly)	other	next	last (of all)
third(ly)	another	moreover	final(ly)

Check Your Understanding

The paragraph below is organized as a list of items. Complete the outline of the list by first filling in the missing part of the main idea. Then add to the outline the three major details listed in the paragraph.

To help you find the major details, do two things to the paragraph:

- Underline the addition words that introduce the major details in the list;
- Number (*1, 2, . . .*) each item in the list.

[1]Self-disclosure is revealing information about oneself. [2]Meaningful self-disclosure includes three important elements. [3]First of all, it must be done on purpose. [4]If you accidentally mention to a friend that you're thinking about quitting a job, that is not self-disclosure. [5]Second, the information must be significant. [6]Telling trivial facts, opinions, or feelings—that you like fudge, for example—hardly counts as disclosure. [7]The third requirement is that the information being shared is private. [8]There's nothing noteworthy about telling others that you are depressed or happy if they already know that.

Main idea: Meaningful self-disclosure includes ______________________

____

1. ______________________________
2. ______________________________
3. ______________________________

Explanation

The main idea is that meaningful self-disclosure includes three important elements. (At times you may also express the main idea in a short heading: the heading here could be "Elements in meaningful self-disclosure.") Following are the three elements you should have added to the outline:

1. Done on purpose. (This element is signaled with the addition phrase *First of all).*
2. Significant. (This element is signaled by the addition word *Second).*
3. Private. (This element is signaled by the addition word *third.)*

PRACTICE 3

A. The following passage uses a listing pattern. Outline the passage by filling in the main idea and the major details.

> ***Hint:*** Underline the addition words that introduce the items in the list, and number the items.

[1]All of us, at one time or another, have said something to someone that we regretted. [2]Researchers have discovered five general categories of "regrettable comments." [3]The most common kind of regrettable comment is the blunder. [4]Examples are forgetting someone's name or getting it wrong, or asking, "How's your mother?" and hearing the reply, "She died." [5]The next most common category is direct attack—a generalized criticism of the other person or of his or her family or friends. [6]Another type of regrettable remark is the negative group reference, which often contains racial or ethnic slurs. [7]The fourth category is direct and specific criticism such as "You never clean house" or "You shouldn't go out with that guy." [8]The final type of regrettable comment is saying too much. [9]It includes telling other people's secrets or telling hurtful things said by others.

Main idea: ______________________________

____

1. ______________________________
2. ______________________________
3. ______________________________
4. ______________________________
5. ______________________________

B. The following passage uses a listing pattern. Complete the map of the passage by filling in the main idea and the missing major and minor details.

[1]Preventive medicine sounds ideal as a way of ensuring good health and reducing costs, but how do you actually prevent something from happening? [2]A number of practitioners and health planners have figured out ways of putting preventive medicine into practice. [3]Primary prevention consists of actions that keep a disease from occurring at all. [4]An example would be childhood vaccinations against polio, measles, and smallpox. [5]Secondary prevention involves detection before a disease comes to the attention of the physician. [6]An example would be self-examination by women for breast cancer. [7]Finally, tertiary prevention devotes itself to preventing further damage from already existing disease. [8]Keeping a diabetic on insulin and controlling pneumonia so it does not lead to death are examples of tertiary prevention.

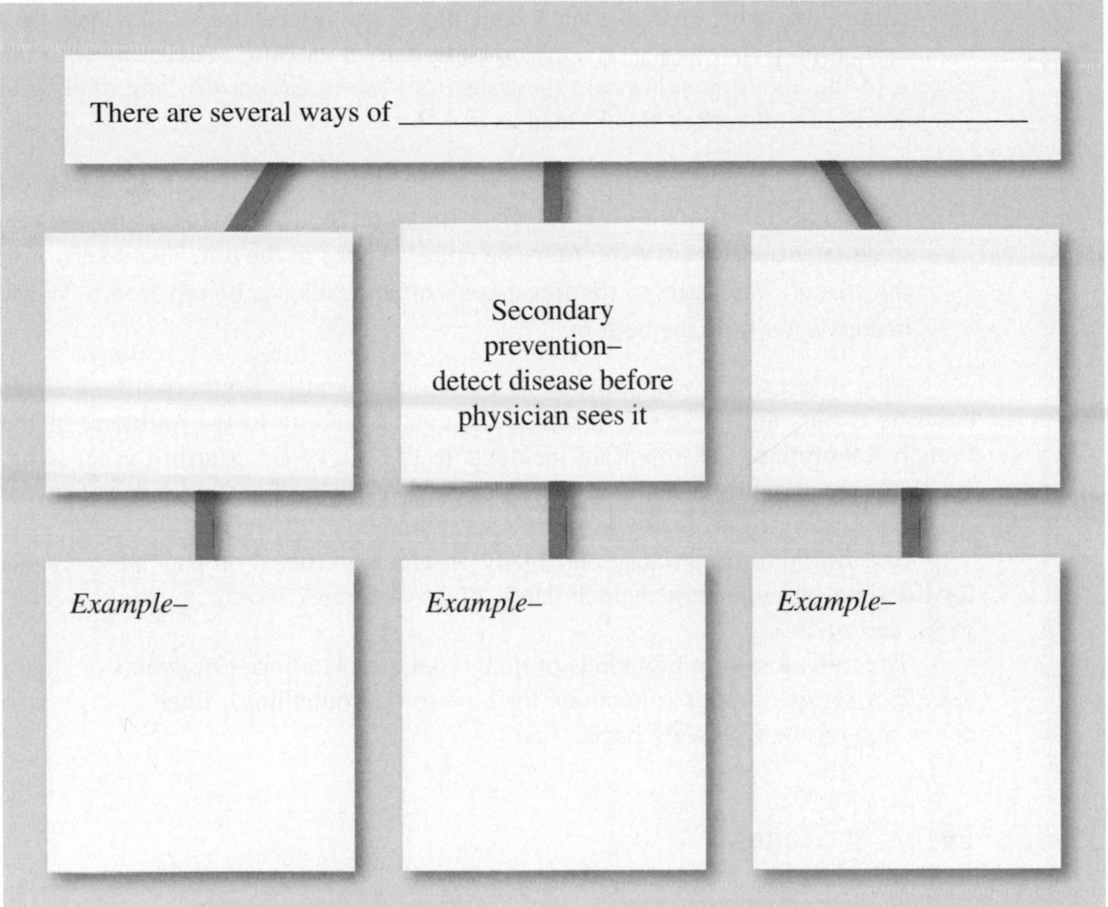

2 The Time Order Pattern

To get a sense of the time order pattern, try to arrange the following sentences in a logical order. Put a *1* in front of the sentence that should come first, a *2* in front of the sentence that comes next, and a *3* in front of the sentence that should come last. The result will be a short paragraph. Use the time words as a guide.

___ The water then begins to expand and rise, to be replaced by cold water from the upper regions of the pot.

___ In the convection process, water at the bottom of a heated pot increases in temperature and begins to move faster.

___ Eventually, after this heated water gets to the top, it cools off and sinks, to be replaced by newly heated water from the bottom.

Authors usually present events and processes in the order in which they happen, resulting in a pattern of organization known as **time order**. Clues to the pattern of the above sentences are the transitions *(then, Eventually,* and *after)* that show time. The sentences should read as follows:

> [1]In the convection process, water at the bottom of a heated pot increases in temperature and begins to move faster. [2]The water then begins to expand and rise, to be replaced by cold water from the upper regions of the pot. [3]Eventually, after this heated water gets to the top, it cools off and sinks, to be replaced by newly heated water from the bottom.

As a student, you will see time order used frequently. Textbooks in all fields describe events and processes, such as the events leading to the outbreak of the French Revolution; the important incidents in the life of Dr. Martin Luther King, Jr.; the steps in filing a lawsuit; the process involved in digesting a meal; or the stages in recovering from the death of a loved one.

In addition to time transitions, many of which are listed on page 189, signals for the time order pattern include dates, times, and such words as *stages, series, steps,* and *process.*

The two most common kinds of time order are (1) a series of events or stages and (2) a series of steps (directions for how to do something). Each is discussed below and on the following pages.

Series of Events or Stages

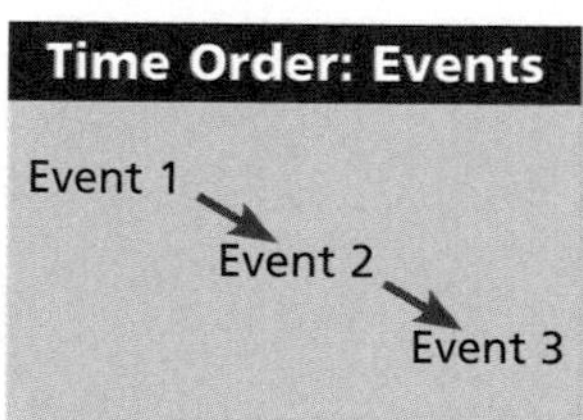

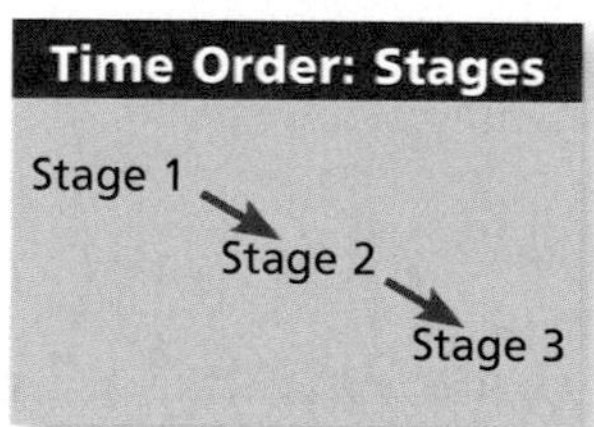

Check Your Understanding

On the next page is a paragraph that is organized according to time order. Complete the outline of the paragraph by listing the missing stages in the order in which they happen.

To help you find the stages, do two things to the paragraph:

- Underline the words that introduce each stage;
- Number (*1, 2, . . .*) each stage.

[1]The study of volunteers in sleep laboratories has led researchers to believe that humans go through four different stages of sleep in a normal night's rest. [2]After falling asleep, people enter stage 1 sleep, also called "light sleep" or "REM" (rapid eye movement) sleep. [3]During this stage the sleeper's brain waves are irregular, and the person is easily awakened. [4]The next period of sleep, stage 2 sleep, is marked by bursts of fast brain-wave activity called "spindles." [5]Then, during stage 3 sleep, the spindles disappear, and brain waves become long and slow. [6]Last, the deepest level of sleep, during which the sleeper is hardest to awaken, occurs during stage 4 sleep. [7]Extremely slow brain waves known as delta waves are present during this deep-sleep phase.

Main idea: Researchers believe that humans go through four different stages of sleep in a normal night's rest.

1. ______________________________

   ____

2. ______________________________

   ____

3. Stage 3—spindles disappear; brain waves become long and slow.

4. ______________________________

   ____

Explanation

You should have added these points to the outline:

1. Stage 1—light, or REM, sleep: irregular brain waves; easily awakened.
2. Stage 2—burst of fast brain-wave activity called "spindles."
4. Stage 4—deepest level: very slow brain waves called "delta waves"; most difficult to awaken.

As emphasized by the transitions *After, next, Then*, and *Last* (and the stage numbers 1, 2, 3, and 4), the relationship between the points is one of time: The first stage happens *after* the person falls asleep. The second stage happens *next*, and so on.

PRACTICE 4

The following passage describes a sequence of events. Outline the paragraph by filling in the main idea and major details. Note that the major details are signaled by time words and dates.

Hint: Underline the time word or words that introduce each major detail, and number each major detail.

[1]World War II was a massive military conflict that eventually involved most of the world's nations. [2]While dozens of events led up to the war, four were particularly significant. [3]In January 1933, in the midst of growing unrest over food shortages and unemployment, Adolf Hitler was named chancellor of Germany. [4]Three years later, in defiance of the terms of the treaty which had ended World War I, Hitler threateningly moved troops into the area of Germany that bordered France. [5]Next, in March 1938, Germany seized control of Austria and established a Nazi government there. [6]Hoping that Hitler would be satisfied with these gains, the European powers did not challenge him. [7]Finally, on September 1, 1939, Hitler launched an invasion of Poland. [8]Two days later, France and Britain declared war on Germany, thus marking the official start of World War II.

Main idea: ____.

1. ____
2. ____
3. ____
4. ____

PRACTICE 5

The following passage describes a series of stages. Complete the map of the paragraph by writing the main idea in the top box and filling in the four major details (the stages).

[1]We can think of the scientific method in terms of four stages, which are usually carried out by different scientists, sometimes many years apart. [2]The first stage is the formulation of a problem. [3]The scientist may have a theory, perhaps only a hunch, about some aspect of nature but cannot come to a definite conclusion without further study. [4]The next stage is observation and experiment,

activities which are carried out with extreme care. [5]Facts about nature are the building blocks of science and the ultimate proof of its results. [6]This insistence on the importance of accurate, objective data is what sets science apart from other modes of intellectual effort. [7]The third stage is interpretation, which may lead to a general rule, or it may be a more ambitious attempt to account for what has been found in terms of how nature works. [8]The last stage is testing the interpretation, which involves making new observations or performing new experiments to see whether the interpretation correctly predicts the results. [9]If the results agree with the predictions, the scientist is clearly on the right track.

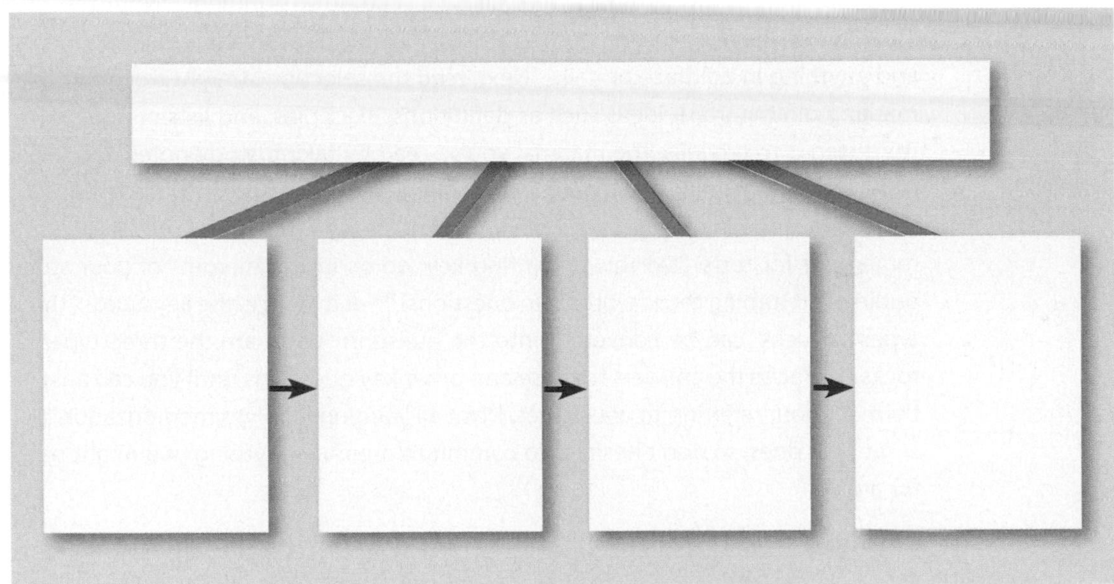

Series of Steps (Directions)

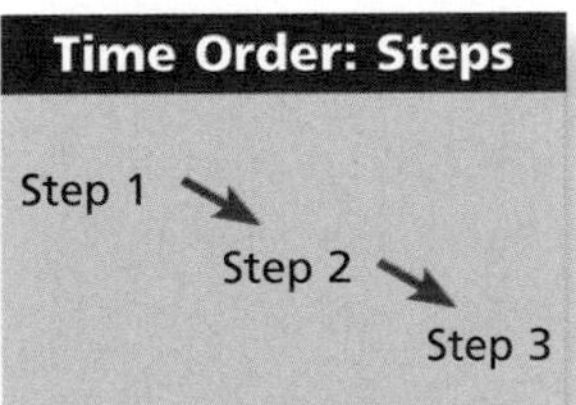

When authors give directions, they use time order. They explain step 1, then step 2, and so on through the entire series of steps that must be taken toward a specific goal.

Check Your Understanding

Below is a paragraph that gives directions. Complete the outline of the paragraph by filling in the main idea and listing the missing steps in the correct sequence. To help yourself identify each step, do two things to the paragraph:

- Underline the time words that introduce each item in the sequence;
- Number (*1, 2, . . .*) each step in the sequence.

[1]If you mention the word PROM to people, they are going to think of a high-school rite of passage. [2]In fact, PROM is also the name of a proven study method. [3]The first step in this system is to *preview* a reading assignment. [4]Note the title and read the first and last paragraphs; also look quickly at headings and subheads and anything in boldface or italic. [5]Next, *read* the selection straight through while marking off important ideas such as definitions, examples, and lists of items. [6]The third step is to *organize* the material you've read by taking study notes on it. [7]Get all the important ideas down on paper in outline form, relating one idea to another as much as possible. [8]Last of all, *memorize* the study notes that you will need to remember for tests. [9]Do this by writing key words in the margins of your study outline and turning those words into questions. [10]For instance, the key words "three types of rocks" can be converted into the question "What are the three types of rocks?" [11]Recite the answers to these and other key questions until you can answer them without referring to your notes. [12]Not all learning involves memorization, but some of it does, so don't hesitate to commit to memory anything you might need for a test.

Main idea: ____________________

1. ____________________
2. ____________________
3. ____________________
4. ____________________

Explanation

You should have added the main idea—"PROM is a proven study method"—and the following steps to the outline:

1. Preview a reading assignment. (The author signals this step with the time word *first.)*
2. Read the selection straight through, marking off important ideas as you do. (This step is signaled with the time word *Next.)*

3. Organize the material you've read by taking study notes on it. (This step is signaled with the time word *third.*)
4. Memorize the study outline by turning key words into questions. (The author signals this last step with the time transition *Last of all.*)

As indicated by the transitions used, the relationship between the steps is one of time: The second step happens *after* the first, and so on.

PRACTICE 6

The following passage gives directions involving several steps that must be done in order. Complete the map below by writing the main idea in the top box and filling in the three missing steps.

Hint: Underline the time words that introduce each step in the sequence, and number each step.

[1]When you feel overwhelmed by a heavy workload, there are several steps you can take to gain control. [2]The first is to list as quickly as possible everything that needs to get done. [3]This can mean jotting down on paper as many ideas you can think of in ten minutes, without worrying about order or form. [4]Second, divide the tasks into three groups: what has to be done immediately, what can be done within the next week or so, and what can be postponed till a later date. [5]Next, break each task down into the exact steps you must take to get it done. [6]Then, as on a test, do the easiest ones first and go back to the hard ones later. [7]Instead of just worrying about what you ought to be doing, you'll be getting something done. [8]And you'll be surprised at how easily one step leads to another.

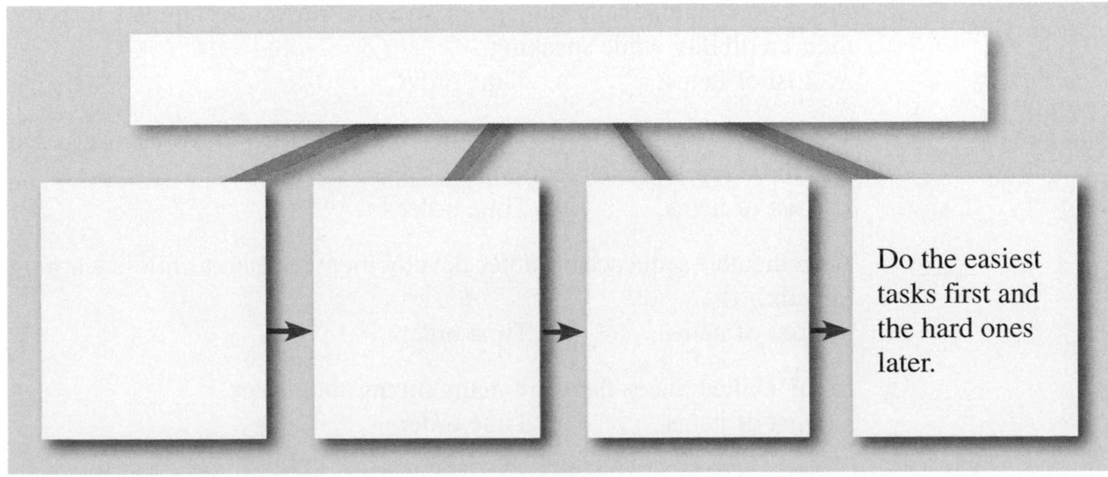

A Note on Main Ideas and Patterns of Organization

A paragraph's main idea often indicates its pattern of organization. For example, here's the main idea of the paragraph you just read: "When you feel overwhelmed by a heavy workload, there are several steps you can take to gain control." The words *several steps* suggest that this paragraph will be organized according to time order. Another good example is the main idea of the earlier paragraph about self-disclosure: "Meaningful self-disclosure includes three important elements." The words *three important elements* suggest that this paragraph will be a list of three items.

Paying close attention to the main idea, then, can often give you a quick sense of a paragraph's pattern of organization. Try, for instance, to guess the pattern of the paragraph with this main idea:

> While there are thousands of Internet chat groups, they all fall into three basic categories.

The statement that Internet chat groups "fall into three basic categories" is a strong indication that the paragraph will list those categories. The main idea helps us realize that the paragraph will be a list of three items.

PRACTICE 7

Most of the main ideas below have been taken from college textbooks. In the space provided, write the letter of the pattern of organization that each main idea suggests.

_____ 1. The story of the Gold Rush begins with a carpenter noticing several bright bits of yellow mineral near a sawmill on a California ranch.
A. List of items B. Time order

_____ 2. Speakers should take advantage of specific, proven techniques to boost their credibility while speaking.
A. List of items B. Time order

_____ 3. Traditionally, efforts to prevent the abuse of drugs have been divided into three types of intervention.
A. List of items B. Time order

_____ 4. A predictable sequence of motor development leads to a child's learning to walk.
A. List of items B. Time order

_____ 5. In the United States there are many myths about rape.
A. List of items B. Time order

_____ 6. Less dependence on foreign oil is only one of many benefits of energy-efficient automobiles.
A. List of items B. Time order

_____ 7. Few products last forever; most go through a product life cycle, passing through four distinct stages in sales and earnings.
A. List of items B. Time order

_____ 8. The American colonists that remained loyal to the British crown did so for a number of reasons.
A. List of items B. Time order

_____ 9. Progressive muscle relaxation is a procedure in which each of several muscle groups in turn is systematically contracted and relaxed.
A. List of items B. Time order

_____10. Three questions, if explored carefully, will carry us a long way to deciding what moral action to take in the very human dilemmas in which we find ourselves caught.
A. List of items B. Time order

Three Final Points

1 While many passages have just one pattern of organization, often the patterns are mixed. For example, you may find that part of a passage uses a list of items pattern, and another part of the same passage uses a time pattern.

2 You may have noted that when an author presents a series of events or stages or steps, that series is itself a list of items. For example, look at this time order passage:

> [1]To find a job, follow these key steps. [2]**First of all**, tell everyone you know that you're looking for work. [3]Most jobs are found through word-of-mouth, rather than newspaper advertisements. [4]**Second**, call a potential employer and ask to schedule an interview. [5]Be sure you sound friendly and enthusiastic on the phone. [6]The **next** step is the interview itself. [7]Dress nicely, be on time, and answer your interviewer's questions fully and politely. [8]**Finally**, send your interviewer a thank-you note in a day or two. [9]That doesn't guarantee you'll get the job, but it will add to the positive impression you've already made.

The above passage is indeed made up of a list of items. But what makes it a time order passage is that the list of items appears not at random, but in a *time sequence*. Realizing that there is a time sequence will help you achieve your study purpose, which is probably to take effective notes on the material.

3 Remember that not all relationships between ideas are signaled by transitions. An author may present a list of items, for example, without using addition words. So as you read, watch for the relationships themselves, not just the transitions.

CHAPTER REVIEW

In this chapter, you learned how authors use transitions and patterns of organization to make their ideas clear. Just as transitions show relationships between ideas in sentences, patterns of organization show relationships between supporting details in paragraphs and longer pieces of writing.

You also learned two common kinds of relationships that authors use to make their ideas clear:

- **Addition relationships**
  - — Authors often present a list or series of reasons, examples, or other details that support an idea. The items have no time order, but are listed in whatever order the author prefers.
  - — Transition words that signal such addition relationships include *for one thing, second, also, in addition,* and *finally.*
- **Time relationships**
  - — Authors usually discuss a series of events or steps in the order in which they happen, resulting in a time order.
  - — Transition words that signal such time relationships include *first, next, then, after,* and *last.*

The next chapter—Chapter 6—will help you learn three other important kinds of relationships: definition-example, comparison and/or contrast, and cause-effect.

On the Web: If you are using this book in class, you can visit our website for additional practice in understanding relationships that involve addition and time. Go to **www.townsendpress.com** and click on "Learning Center."

REVIEW TEST 1

To review what you've learned in this chapter, fill in the blanks in the following items.

1. ____________________ are words or phrases (like *first of all* or *another* or *then* or *finally*) that show the relationships between ideas. They are like signs on the road that guide travelers.

2. Words such as *for one thing, also,* and *furthermore* are known as ____________________ words. They tell us the writer is presenting one or more ideas that continue the same line of thought as a previous idea.

3. Words such as *then, next,* and *after* are known as ____________________ words. They tell us *when* something happened in relation to when something else happened.

4. Transitions show the relationships between ideas in sentences. Patterns of organization show the relationships between ____________________ in a paragraph or longer passage.

5. The main idea of a paragraph often indicates its ____________________ ____.

REVIEW TEST 2

A. (1–2.) What kinds of transitions are used in the following cartoons?

"Sorry, Boss, I can't take anything else on right now. For one thing, I can't even find my computer."

_____ 1. A. addition B. time

_____ 2. A. addition B. time

B. Fill in each blank with one of the words in the box. Use each transition once. Then write the letter of the word in the space provided.

A. after	B. also	C. before

______ 3. Many students today have very little access to books in their homes. They ______________ have no quiet, comfortable place to read, free from the televisions that are turned on loud a good deal of the time.

______ 4. ______________ the invention of television, people probably spent more of their leisure time reading.

______ 5. ______________ people are fired, it is common for them to lapse into a period of mental pain and depression. Many experience a sharp sense of loss—both of the job they held and of the coworkers and friends they knew as part of the job.

C. Read the textbook paragraph below, and then answer the questions that follow.

[1]To turn a corpse into a mummy, ancient Egyptians first washed the body with water from the Nile River. [2]Next they removed all organs except the heart, which was thought to house a person's spirit. [3]Following organ removal, they rinsed the body cavity with wine, stuffed it, and covered the body with salty powder. [4]After the body dried in this powder for thirty-five to forty days, they replaced the stuffing with salty powder and linen soaked in a plant-derived glue. [5]Then they closed all incisions, covered the skin with glue, wrapped the entire body in linen, and placed a mask (of either the dead person or an Egyptian god) on the mummy's head. [6]Finally, they placed the mummy inside a coffin (decorated to resemble a person) and sealed the coffin inside a tomb, along with food and other items that they believed the dead person would need or desire in the afterlife.

______ 6. The relationship of sentence 2 to sentence 1 is one of
A. addition. B. time.

7. The key transition word in sentence 4 is ______________.

8. The key transition word in sentence 5 is ______________.

9. The key transition word in sentence 6 is ______________.

______ 10. The paragraph is organized as a
A. list of items.
B. series of events or stages.

REVIEW TEST 3

A. Fill in each blank with the appropriate transition from the box. Use each transition once.

A. first	B. next	C. until	D. while

[1]I do not like to write. [2]In fact, I dislike writing so much that I have developed a series of steps for postponing the agony of doing writing assignments. [3](1)________________, I tell myself that to proceed without the proper equipment would be unwise. [4]So I go out to buy a new pen. [5]This kills at least an hour. [6](2)________________ I begin to stare at the blank page. [7]Before long, however, I realize that writing may also require thought; so I begin to think deeply about my subject. [8]Soon I feel drowsy. [9]This naturally leads to the conclusion that I need a nap because I can't throw myself into my writing (3)________________ I am at my very best. [10]After a refreshing nap, I again face the blank page. [11]It is usually at this stage that I actually write a sentence or two—disappointing ones. [12]I wisely decide that I need inspiration, perhaps from an interesting magazine or a television movie. [13]If thoughts of my writing assignment should interfere (4)________________ I am reading or watching TV, I comfort myself with the knowledge that, as any artist knows, you can't rush these things.

_____ 5. The pattern of organization of the above selection is
A. list of items. B. time order.

B. Below are the beginnings of five passages. Label each one with the letter of its pattern of organization. (You may find it helpful to underline the transition or transitions in each item.)

A List of items
B Time order

_____ 6. [1]There are certain steps which, taken in order, will help you remember your dreams. [2]The first step is to place a notebook and pen beside your bed. [3]The second is to make up your mind, before going to sleep, that you will remember what you are going to dream. . . .

_____ 7. [1]Weeds may seem harmful in the garden, but they have great value in nature. [2]Some so-called weeds serve as food. [3]Dandelions, for instance, are often eaten as greens. [4]Other weeds are sources of drugs, medicines, and dyes. [5]Also, many weed seeds make up an important part of the diet of songbirds, game birds, and other types of wildlife. . . .

______ 8. [1]*The Glass Menagerie,* the well-known play by Tennessee Williams, opens with the narrator of the play. [2]Tom introduces himself, briefly discusses the play, and explains that the other characters will be his mother, his sister, and a gentleman caller. [3]Tom then walks onto the set of a dining room and takes a seat, and his mother, Amanda, begins to speak. . . .

______ 9. [1]People considering adopting a dog or cat should ask themselves a few important questions. [2]First of all, do they really want the responsibility of caring for an animal for the next ten to fifteen years? . . .

______10. [1]Abraham Lincoln took an unusual path to the Presidency. [2]He lost his first job and then declared bankruptcy. [3]Later on, he suffered a nervous breakdown. . . .

REVIEW TEST 4

We usually think of addictions as being habits involving harmful substances that can destroy our lives. But what about some of our common day-to-day habits? Can spending too much time on the Internet or drinking too much coffee be considered an addiction? And if so, can these "soft addictions" actually disrupt our lives?

To help you continue to strengthen your skills, the reading is followed by questions on what you've learned not only in this chapter but also in previous chapters.

Words to Watch

Below are some words in the reading that do not have strong context support. Each word is followed by the number of the paragraph in which it appears and its meaning there. These words are indicated in the article by a small circle (°).

transfixed (4): fascinated
proliferation (6): a large number or abundance of something
indispensable (10): necessary or very important

SOFT ADDICTIONS

Tim Bashard

1 What images come into your mind when you think of the word *addiction*?

2 Most people would respond to that question with something dramatic: a junkie nodding off in a crack house; tearful confessions at an AA meeting; a celebrity going off to rehab; a smoker lighting one cigarette from the burning butt of another.

3 Those are images of the "hard addictions"—addictions to drugs, alcohol, and nicotine. Those are the addictions that can and do destroy countless lives, families, and careers. They're the images that make the headlines, the TV shows, and the movies.

4 But there are other addictions whose images are less dramatic. Think of a group of teens swigging their bottles of Red Bull, or a home where the television is never turned off, or a person sitting transfixed° for hours in front of a computer screen. Are these people addicted in the same way a person is chemically addicted to heroin, whiskey, or nicotine? Most people would say not. And yet, giving up their use of caffeine, television, or the Internet would cause these people intense anxiety and discomfort. Is this dependence also a form of addiction?

5 According to a growing number of experts, the answer is yes. Behavioral scientists are increasingly interested in the concept of "soft addictions," which are defined as everyday habits that have gotten powerful enough to interfere with normal life. And dependence on caffeine, television, and the Internet are three of the most common forms of "soft addictions."

6 Having a cup of coffee in the morning has been a part of many adults' daily routine for generations. In our grandparents' day, that cup was most likely made from powdered instant coffee, and it yielded about 60 milligrams of caffeine. Such a modest intake of caffeine would have little addictive effect. But in today's fast-paced world, it's routine to indulge in several caffeinated pick-me-ups during the day. And those aren't your grandfather's cup of Maxwell House. The proliferation° of sleek coffee shops like Starbucks has made "designer coffee" chic. A "tall" (12 ounce) brewed coffee from Starbucks has 260 milligrams of caffeine. A "grande" cup provides 330 milligrams, and a "venti" a whopping 415 milligrams. The caffeine content of drinks such as lattes and cappuccinos depends on whether they contain a single, double, or triple shot of espresso—each shot equals 75 milligrams. And, of course, today's Americans are not getting their caffeine fix from coffee alone. A 12-ounce Diet Coke, for instance, provides about 45 milligrams of caffeine, and a Mountain Dew as much as 55 milligrams. Then

there are the so-called "energy drinks," which are basically delivery systems for high doses of sugar and caffeine. Monster, Red Bull, and Rockstar, three of the most popular brands, each provide about 80 milligrams of caffeine per bottle.

7 The bottom line is that a great many people are consuming massive quantities of caffeine on a daily basis, and that their need for caffeine has become a soft addiction. Their choice of coffee or soda or an energy drink has ceased to be merely a pleasant beverage. The caffeine these drinks provide has become a necessity. When caffeine addicts wake up in the morning, the first thing they think of is getting that initial caffeine hit. Until they have had it, they tend to be grouchy, groggy, and unwilling to interact with people. If they are in a situation where their caffeinated beverage of choice isn't available, they become almost frantic. They are nervous and shaky, often have a raging headache, and cannot concentrate on anything until they've found a caffeine source. This cycle often repeats itself in mid-afternoon and early evening, when the need for more caffeine hits. They have to take breaks, even if it means neglecting their work or interrupting an important conversation, to seek out another caffeine fix. At day's end, their brains are still buzzing with the effects of caffeine, and they sleep poorly. They awaken groggy and ill-tempered, and the cycle begins again.

8 Television viewing is another activity that can slip over the line from a harmless pastime to a soft addiction. Again, in the past, excessive TV watching was less common. There were only a few major networks, so the choices of what to view were limited. Today, by contrast, the choices are almost limitless, including hundreds of cable channels, network shows, and instant-view movies. According to the most recent AC Nielsen study, the average American watches 34 hours of TV a week, plus another three to six hours of taped programs. That adds up to the equivalent of a 40-hour workweek. And of course, that's only the *average* viewer, meaning that half of all viewers watch more—sometimes much, much more. In some cases, it's almost impossible to measure how much television a person actually watches, because the TV is on virtually all the time.

9 But why does excessive TV watching qualify as a "soft addiction," when we would not use that term to describe most other leisure activities, such as gardening or playing tennis? The answer is in the way TV addicts describe their own feelings about their habit. Unlike the way gardeners or tennis players describe their hobbies, TV mega-watchers report that they feel unhappy about the amount they watch, but are powerless to stop it. They say that their excessive TV watching has damaged their social lives—that they see less and less of their friends and even family. They report that after watching a lot of TV, they feel *less* relaxed, less happy, and less able to concentrate than they were before. But because watching TV is their go-to activity when they're feeling depressed, their response to feeling unhappy is to watch more TV.

10 A final soft addiction is one that did not exist a generation ago. In only a few short decades, the Internet has become an indispensable° part of almost everyone's daily life. The advantages have been enormous. Communication has become easier than ever before, and ordinary men and women now have access to a literally limitless world of information.

11 But it is that very quality—the unlimited promise of the Internet—that has made it so addictive. A person can sit down at his laptop—or pick up his smartphone or open his tablet—fully intending to look up one simple fact. But to enter the Internet is to fall down a bottomless rabbit hole of possibilities. There are e-mails to read, instant messages to respond to, Facebook statuses to like or update, and headlines to look over. A friend on the other side of the world may suddenly appear on Skype. There are urgent invitations to join games, to sign petitions, to watch cute kitten videos. The minute that our person intended to spend looking up that one fact can easily turn into hours as he is sucked into the endless tunnel of facts and entertainment.

12 For a person who has difficulty setting limits on his Internet usage, time spent online can easily get out of control. Like television watching, an Internet addiction can cut into time spent with real-world friends, healthful physical exercise, and the development of offline social skills. While the promise of the Internet is enormous, it is at the end of the day just a glowing screen in a dark room. After hours of interacting with that screen, the Internet addict, like the TV addict, is likely to feel vaguely depressed, with a sense of having accomplished very little.

13 While hard addictions to drugs or alcohol are clearly very serious, soft addictions can be far from harmless. Whenever any activity—even drinking coffee, watching TV, or using the Internet—gets out of control, it can upset the balance that people should aim for in everyday life. It's often said that "knowledge is power." We would all benefit from knowing whether any of our everyday habits have become soft addictions.

Reading Comprehension Questions

Vocabulary in Context

_____ 1. In the excerpt below, the words *the equivalent of* (thē ĭ-kwĭvə-lənt ŭv) mean

A. the rest of.
B. the pleasure of.
C. a substitute for.
D. the same amount as.

"According to the most recent AC Nielsen study, the average American watches 34 hours of TV a week, plus another three to six hours of taped programs. That adds up to the equivalent of a 40-hour workweek." (Paragraph 8)

Central Point and Main Ideas

_____ 2. Which sentence best expresses the central point of the selection?

A. Everyday habits that become something we can't live without, like caffeine or television, are harmless and not real addictions.
B. Most people watch far too much television and waste too much time on the Internet.
C. Common habits like watching TV or needing caffeine in the morning can become "soft addictions" that may affect our lives in negative ways.
D. Addictions to drugs, alcohol, and cigarettes are far more dangerous than addictions to everyday habits.

_____ 3. Which sentence best expresses the main idea of paragraph 7?

A. Many people drink far too much caffeine.
B. Those who are addicted to caffeine continue to get their "fixes" all day long and even into the evening.
C. People who are dependent on caffeine often suffer from headaches, grogginess, and moodiness.
D. Although it is considered a "soft addiction," caffeine dependency can create real physical and emotional problems.

_____ 4. Which sentence best expresses the main idea of paragraph 11?

A. The Internet is addictive because it offers endless possibilities for information and entertainment.

B. People often go online to look up one small bit of information and then end up spending hours and hours surfing the Internet.

C. Too much time spent online checking Facebook statuses, watching videos of cute kittens, and playing games can lead to Internet addiction.

D. Internet possibilities are endless, ranging from playing games with a friend across town to chatting on Skype with a friend across the continent.

Supporting Details

_____ 5. According to the selection, the caffeine content of designer coffee drinks, such as lattes and cappuccinos, can be measured by

A. whether or not they are made from powdered instant coffee.

B. the number of shots of espresso each drink contains.

C. the size of the cup each drink is served in.

D. the price Starbucks charges for each drink.

_____ 6. Television addicts agree with all of the following *except*

A. they feel less relaxed and happy than before they watch a lot of TV.

B. they now see less of their friends and family.

C. they feel unable to stop watching TV.

D. they fear that excessive TV watching damages their eyesight.

Transitions

_____ 7. The relationship of the first half of the sentence below to the second half is one of

A. addition.

B. time.

"When caffeine addicts wake up in the morning, the first thing they think of is getting that initial caffeine hit." (Paragraph 7)

_____ 8. Which word from the following sentence indicates an addition transition?

A. *is*

B. *another*

C. *over*

D. *from*

"Television viewing is another activity that can slip over the line from a harmless pastime to a soft addiction." (Paragraph 8)

Patterns of Organization

_____ 9. The pattern of organization in paragraph 2 is one of
A. list of items.
B. time order.

_____ 10. Paragraph 7 is organized mainly as a
A. list of items.
B. series of events in time order.

Discussion Questions

1. Bashard begins his article by asking, "What images come into your mind when you think of the word *addiction*?" What images come into *your* mind when you hear that word? And after having read this article, would you say those images have changed at all?

2. Bashard describes the Internet as an "endless tunnel of facts and entertainment." Have you ever gotten sucked into this tunnel? What draws you into the Internet, and why is it so hard to leave sometimes?

3. It's safe to say that caffeine, television, and the Internet are not the only everyday addictions in our society. Can you think of other soft addictions that many of us indulge in that can affect us negatively?

4. Some people would disagree with the author and say that these pastimes are not really addictions. They would argue that since TV, coffee, and the Internet can't actually destroy one's life (as drugs and alcohol can), they're not worth worrying about seriously. What do you think?

Note: Writing assignments for this selection appear on pages 698–699.

Check Your Performance — RELATIONSHIPS I

Activity		*Number Right*	*Points*		*Score*
Review Test 1	(5 items)	______	× 2	=	______
Review Test 2	(10 items)	______	× 3	=	______
Review Test 3	(10 items)	______	× 3	=	______
Review Test 4	(10 items)	______	× 3	=	______
		TOTAL SCORE		=	______%

Enter your total score into the **Reading Performance Chart: Review Tests** on the inside back cover.

Name ______________________________ Date __________

Section __________ SCORE: (Number correct) ______ x 10 = ______ %

RELATIONSHIPS I: Mastery Test 1

A. Fill in each blank with an appropriate transition from the box. Use each transition once. Then, in the space provided, write the letter of the transition you have chosen.

A. after	B. another	C. for one thing
D. later	E. soon	

Hint: Make sure that each word or phrase that you choose fits smoothly into the flow of the sentence. Test your choices by reading each sentence to yourself.

_____ 1. [1]A philosopher once said that life is "nasty, brutish, and short." [2]He might have been writing about early English settlers in the American colonies. [3]__________________, the majority of the new arrivals died quickly. [4]They were wiped out by malaria, typhoid, and dysentery. [5]Children born in the colonies had a short life expectancy as well. [6]Half of them died before they reached the age of 20. [7]Furthermore, the chances were slim that a colonist would have a long, happy marriage. [8]Most marriages ended within seven years, due to the death of one partner.

_____ 2. [1]The female hummingbird does all the work of raising its young. [2]It collects tiny bits of leafy material, which it then weaves together with silk from spider webs to form a nest the size of a ping-pong ball. [3]When the nest is ready, it lays two eggs no larger than jelly beans. [4]______________ the babies hatch, the mother catches tiny spiders and insects to feed them.

_____ 3. [1]Online social networks, designed to help friends connect and meet new people, have been very competitive. [2]One early network, Friendster, began in 2002. [3]Then the social network Myspace was launched and soon attracted more people. [4]In 2004, Facebook started and four years ______________ was the most popular social networking site. [5]Now Facebook has more than a billion active users worldwide.

_____ 4. [1]A man who pleaded guilty to illegal trading of $20 million with Swiss banks received a $30,000 fine and a suspended sentence. [2]A few days later, the same judge heard ______________ case, one in which an unemployed shipping clerk pleaded guilty to stealing a television set worth $100. [3]The judge sentenced the clerk to one year in jail.

(Continues on next page)

_____ 5. [1]Suppose a fish dies and settles to the bottom of a lake. [2]The bottom is covered with soft sediments—fine materials, such as sand or mud. [3]The fish's body sinks into this material, and water currents sweep over the fish and gradually bury it. [4]Other sediments then settle on top, and the soft parts of the fish ____________________ decay. [5]But the bones are left buried in sediment. [6]More and more layers of sediment pile up. [7]Water may add minerals that act like glue. [8]Over numerous years, the old sediments harden into rock. [9]And inside the rock is a fossil—the bones of the fish.

B. (6–9.) Fill in each blank with an appropriate transition word from the box. Use each transition once.

A. also	B. final	C. first of all
D. second		

[1]A review of the ways the United States deals with its garbage reveals the ongoing problems that we face in getting rid of and limiting our waste. [2](6)____________________, most of the 500,000 tons of waste generated each day in the United States is buried in landfills. [3]Landfills are expensive to construct, fill up rapidly, and can contaminate ground water. [4]A (7)____________________ method, incineration, is cheaper and theoretically can pay for itself by producing energy in the form of electricity or steam. [5]The initial construction expense, however, is enormous, and mechanical problems are common. [6](8)____________________ disturbing is the potential threat incinerators pose to public health because of the dangerous toxic gases they emit during burning. [7]The (9)____________________ and most important way to deal with our garbage problem lies in recycling—a process that can reduce the amount of garbage produced in the first place. [8]It has been estimated that up to 80 percent of our garbage can be eliminated through separation and recycling. [9]To succeed, this method will have to be much more widely used than it is now.

_____10. The pattern of organization of the above selection is

A. list of items.
B. time order.

Name ______________________________ Date __________

Section __________ SCORE: (Number correct) ______ x 10 = ______ %

RELATIONSHIPS I: Mastery Test 2

A. Fill in each blank with an appropriate transition from the box. Use each transition once. Then, in the spaces provided, write the letter of the transition you have chosen.

A. after	B. also	C. another
D. before	E. eventually	

_____ 1. [1]_______________ going to the doctor's office, write down all your questions. [2]Then, when you are face to face with the doctor, use this list of questions to find out everything you want to know about your condition.

_____ 2. [1]The legend of Faust tells of a scholar who is approached by the Devil. [2]The Devil successfully tempts Faust to sell his soul in exchange for power and knowledge. [3]For a while, Faust enjoys all sorts of pleasures; _______________, though, he dies and becomes the Devil's property for eternity.

_____ 3. [1]A chimp by the name of Sherman participated in an interesting math experiment. [2]He was given two pairs of cups containing chocolates. [3]One pair contained five candies—three in one cup and two in the other. [4]The second pair held only four candies—three in one and only one in the other. [5]Sherman chose the pair of cups with the most chocolates 90 percent of the time. [6]_______________ chimp, Lana, can match the numbers 1, 2, or 3 with a picture of the matching number of boxes 80 percent of the time.

_____ 4. [1]According to people who have survived long falls, the acceleration of gravity is heart-stoppingly fast. [2]A body accelerates roughly twenty miles an hour for every second it's in the air. [3]In just one second, it's falling twenty miles an hour. [4]_______________ two seconds, speed is up to forty miles an hour, and so on, up to a hundred and thirty miles an hour, when the body is said to reach terminal velocity.

_____ 5. [1]Some strange and disturbing events have happened around extra-high-voltage electrical lines. [2]The lines often glow a weird blue. [3]___________, they can cause unconnected fluorescent bulbs to light up. [4]Perhaps more scary, however, is the fact that many people near the extra-high-voltage lines have gotten unexpected shocks. [5]People living near such wires, for instance, have complained about getting shocks when touching wire fences or farm machines. [6]Some have even complained of receiving shocks from damp clotheslines and while sitting on the toilet.

(Continues on next page)

B. Read the passage and then answer the question that follows.

[1]The modern police department of today is the product of hundreds of years of evolution. [2]The origins of policing can be traced back to England in the twelfth century. [3]During this time, criminals were tracked down by groups of armed citizens led by the "Shire Reeve"—"leader of the county." [4]Our modern word *sheriff* is derived from these early words. [5]Centuries later, as towns grew, law enforcement fell to the hands of bailiffs, or watchmen. [6]The bailiff's job was to alert people to theft by yelling loudly when a crime occurred. [7]Once alerted, townsfolk would track down the culprit—often beating and torturing him on the spot. [8]This system worked with limited success until the 1720s, when gin was invented. [9]Then, the availability of cheap alcohol increased crime and created the need for better law enforcement. [10]Finally, in 1829 Robert Peel created the first true police force by securing funds and hiring a thousand handpicked officers. [11]Peel's "bobbies" were given uniforms and instructed to patrol London's streets. [12]Eventually, they became the model for police departments worldwide.

_____ 6. The main pattern of organization of the passage is
A. list of items. B. time order.

C. (7–10.) Fill in each blank with an appropriate transition word from the box. Use each transition once. Then answer the question that follows.

A. during	B. finally	C. then

[1]Salmon may migrate thousands of miles, but no matter how far they go, they (7)_______________ return to the rivers in which they were spawned, to produce the next generation. [2]Their journey is an amazing feat. [3]One of the longest of those return journeys is in the Yukon River in Canada, where salmon travel nearly two thousand miles. [4]They travel day and night, with occasional rests in quiet pools. [5]At first, they swim at speeds of ten to twenty miles a day, but (8)_______________ accelerate to as much as sixty miles a day, using their strong tails to propel them. [6](9)_______________ their entire journey, they eat nothing. [7]After a month, they arrive at their birthplace, sickly and battered. [8]The female soon deposits her eggs, and the male, waiting nearby, releases his sperm. [9]Within days, both adults will die.

_____ 10. The pattern of organization of the above selection is
A. list of items. B. time order.

Name ______________________________ Date __________

Section ___________ SCORE: (Number correct) _______ x 10 = _______ %

RELATIONSHIPS I: Mastery Test 3

A. (1–5.) Arrange the scrambled sentences below into a logical paragraph by numbering them *1, 2, 3,* and *4* in an order that makes sense. Then, in the space provided, write the letter of the pattern of organization used.

Note that transitions will help you by clarifying the relationships between sentences.

___ For one thing, alcohol consumption begins in junior high school or earlier.

___ Experimentation with marijuana and mind-altering pills of all sorts also seems commonplace.

___ Today's students have to confront the reality that drug use is all around them.

___ Last, tobacco consumption is everywhere, despite the fact that it is illegal for those under 18 to purchase cigarettes.

_____ 5. The pattern of organization of the above selection is

A. list of items.

B. time order.

B. Read the passage and then answer the question that follows. You may find it helpful to underline transitions as you read.

[1]On its way to becoming the most recognized brand name on Earth, Coca-Cola has gone through lots of changes. [2]Coke was invented in 1886 by an Atlanta pharmacist named John Pemberton, who mixed it in a copper pot and sold it as a headache remedy. [3]A few years later, in 1899, a couple of businessmen bought the rights to bottle and sell the beverage. [4]Coke grew steadily in popularity, soon becoming the world's best-selling soft drink. [5]In the 1980s, Diet Coke was introduced, quickly becoming the world's best-selling diet soda. [6]This success was followed by Coca-Cola's decision to change the original Coke formula. [7]Although people had loved "new" Coke in taste tests, real-world consumers angrily rejected any change in the taste of their favorite soft drink. [8]In less than three months, the embarrassed Coca-Cola company returned to its original formula. [9]Having learned its lesson, Coca-Cola now introduces new varieties of its old favorite, such as Vanilla Coke, Coke Zero, and Diet Coke with Lemon.

_____ 6. The pattern of organization of the above selection is

A. list of items.

B. time order.

(Continues on next page)

C. (7–10.) Read the textbook passage below, and then answer the question and complete the outline.

[1]Researchers have debated for many years about what causes people to commit crimes. [2]Today many theories exist, among them the popular explanation that crime is caused by the celebration of violence in our culture. [3]This approach argues that the glamorous portrayal of violence on TV and in movies encourages young people to become criminals. [4]Another theory holds that crime is the result of social and economic inequalities. [5]If class, racial, and social differences were eliminated, the theory goes, then crime would disappear. [6]A third popular explanation is that psychological reasons account for criminal actions. [7]Children who receive poor or inadequate parenting are more likely to become criminals because they have never received a solid grounding in conventional social and moral behavior. [8]Yet another theory suggests that crime is caused by biological factors. [9]According to this point of view, biology, genetics, and nutrition are all elements that can lead people to a life of crime. [10]There is no absolute evidence to disprove any of these theories, and conventional wisdom suggests that all of them may have some validity.

_____ 7. The pattern of organization of the above selection is
A. list of items.
B. time order.

8–10. Complete the outline of the passage.

Main idea: ____

____

Major supporting details:

1. ____

____

2. Social and economic inequalities
3. ____
4. Biological factors

Name ______________________________ Date ___________

Section ___________ SCORE: (Number correct) _______ x 10 = _______ %

RELATIONSHIPS I: Mastery Test 4

A. (1–5.) Arrange the scrambled sentences below into a logical paragraph by numbering them *1, 2, 3,* and *4* in an order that makes sense. Then, in the space provided, write the letter of the pattern of organization used.

Note that transitions will help you by clarifying the relationships between sentences.

___ Last of all, let any intruding thoughts drift away as you repeat the word or phrase continually for ten to twenty minutes.

___ Physician Herbert Benson's antidote to stress, which he calls the "relaxation response," involves a few simple steps.

___ Next, close your eyes and concentrate on a single word or a phrase—or perhaps a favorite prayer.

___ First of all, assume a comfortable position, breathe deeply, and relax your muscles from feet to face.

_____ 5. The pattern of organization of the above selection is
- A. list of items.
- B. series of events or stages.
- C. series of steps (directions).

B. Read the passage below and answer the question that follows.

[1]Water evaporates from the seas, rivers, lakes, trees, and land surfaces, adding moisture to the atmosphere. [2]When the moisture in the air cools, it condenses to form water droplets or ice crystals. [3]As these droplets and crystals become larger, they fall toward the earth as precipitation—rain, snow, hail, etc. [4]Some evaporate while falling, or they fall on tree leaves and evaporate; but some reach the ground. [5]A portion of the water that reaches the ground evaporates. [6]As water accumulates on the ground, some of it runs off to form rivers and lakes, with most eventually flowing back to the sea. [7]Evaporation from all of these surfaces completes the water cycle. [8]Water in the atmosphere is recycled every two weeks.

_____ 6. The purpose of the above selection is to
- A. list forms of water.
- B. list types of evaporation.
- C. describe stages in the water cycle.
- D. describe a series of events in the history of the Earth.

(Continues on next page)

C. (7–10.) Complete the map of the following textbook passage by filling in the missing main idea and major and minor details.

[1]Monogamy, the practice of each person marrying one other person in his or her lifetime, is just one of several types of marriage that occur throughout the world. [2]A separate but related form of marriage is serial monogamy, which allows a person to have several spouses in a lifetime, but only one at a time. [3]The practice of polygamy allows persons to have multiple spouses at the same time. [4]There are two forms of polygamy. [5]One variety is polygyny, in which one man has several wives at once. [6]The other is polyandry, in which a woman may have multiple husbands.

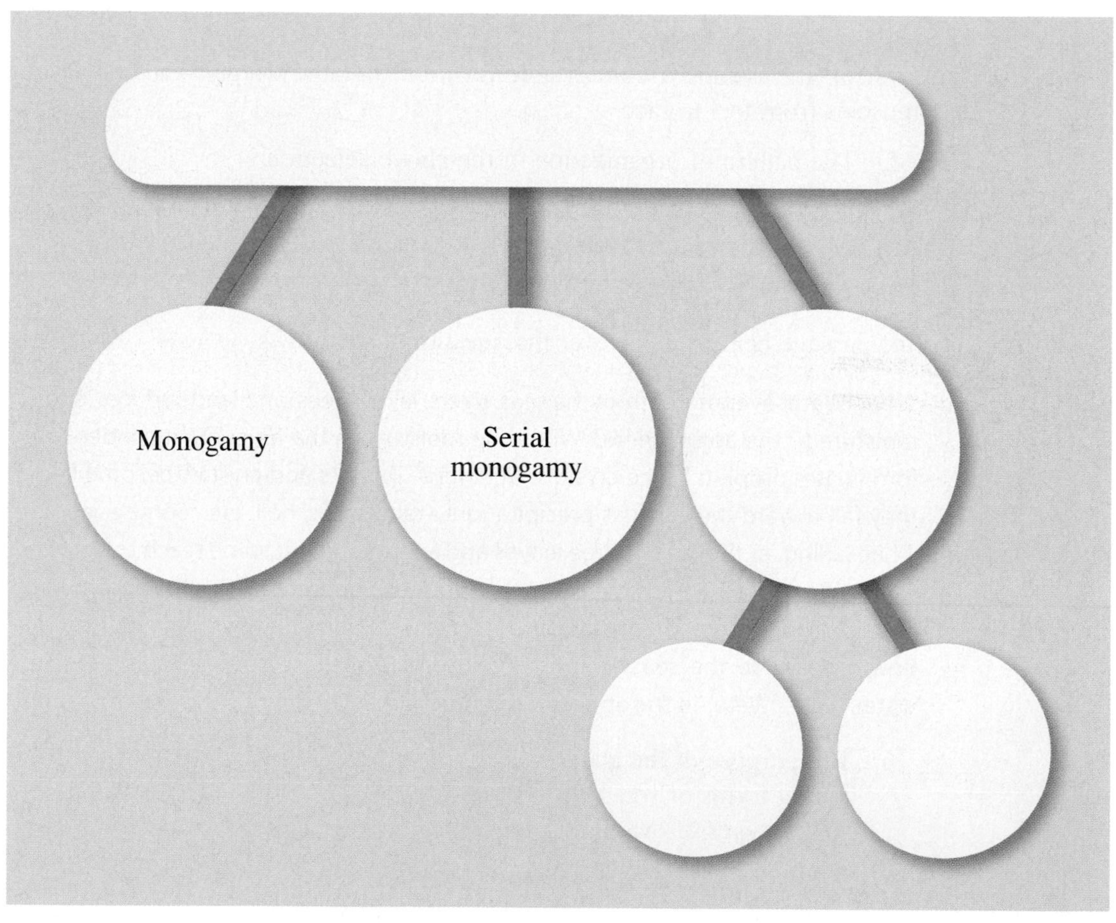

Name ______________________________ Date __________

Section __________ SCORE: (Number correct) ______ x 10 = ______ %

RELATIONSHIPS I: Mastery Test 5

Read each textbook passage and then answer the questions or follow the directions provided.

A. [1]When a president needs to appoint someone to the Supreme Court, the first step is to find a list of good candidates. [2]Next, the president shortens the list, considering the political impact of each candidate's appointment and his or her fitness to serve. [3]Then each candidate on the short list is thoroughly investigated by the Federal Bureau of Investigation. [4]Weighing numerous political and ideological factors, as well as the chances for Senate confirmation, the president formally nominates a candidate. [5]The nominee meets informally with members of the Senate Judiciary Committee. [6]The committee then holds a formal hearing, takes a vote, and passes the nomination on to the full Senate. [7]Finally, the full Senate then approves or rejects the nomination by a simple majority vote.

_____ 1. The pattern of organization of the above selection is
A. list of items.
B. time order.

2. A transition that introduces one of the major details of the paragraph is
______________________________.

B. [1]What causes people to join groups? [2]One reason is for security, a factor that leads people to form neighborhood-watch groups. [3]Another common reason for joining a group is a desire to be with others who share one's interests and values. [4]Some people, for instance, join computer support groups to share ideas, knowledge, and software. [5]Managers may join service groups, such as Rotary Clubs, to exchange ideas with other managers. [6]Individuals may also form groups to acquire power that is difficult if not impossible to attain alone. [7]Membership in a union or employee association, for example, provides workers with influence that they lack as individual employees. [8]Goal accomplishment is a further reason people join groups. [9]Mountain climbers and astronauts generally function in groups.

_____ 3. The pattern of organization of the above selection is
A. list of items.
B. time order.

4. A transition that introduces one of the major details of the paragraph is
______________________________.

(Continues on next page)

C. [1]There are three main ways people respond to those who offend or annoy them. [2]One of the most common ways people deal with negative situations is through passive behavior. [3]Passive people are those who do not share their opinions, feeling, or emotions when they are upset. [4]Instead of trying to get an offensive individual to stop hurting them, passive people will often remain silent, allowing the unfair or unkind actions to continue. [5]Another way people address a negative situation is through aggressive behavior. [6]Aggressive people lash out at those who have hurt them—with little regard for the situation or the feelings of those they are attacking. [7]Aggressive behavior is judgmental, harsh, and hurtful. [8]The final way of dealing with conflicts is through assertive behavior. [9]Assertive people, like those who are aggressive, also actively address the cause of their problem—but they do it differently. [10]Instead of yelling at the person who has offended them, assertive people will discuss what has annoyed them, and then work to find a way to fix it.

_____ 5. The pattern of organization of the above selection is
A. list of items.
B. time order.

6. The transition that signals the third major detail is _______________.

7–10. Complete the map of the paragraph.

Name ______________________________ Date __________

Section __________ SCORE: (Number correct) ______ x 10 = ______ %

RELATIONSHIPS I: Mastery Test 6

Read each textbook passage and then answer the questions or follow the directions provided.

A. [1]Consumer products are commonly divided into categories that reflect buyers' behavior. [2]One category is convenience goods (such as milk and newspapers) and convenience services (such as fast-food restaurants), which are consumed rapidly and regularly. [3]They are relatively inexpensive and must be purchased frequently and with little expenditure of time and effort. [4]Another category is shopping goods (such as stereos and tires) and shopping services (such as insurance). [5]Shopping goods and services are more expensive and are purchased less frequently than convenience goods and services. [6]Consumers often compare brands, sometimes in different stores. [7]The last category is specialty goods (such as wedding gowns) and specialty services (such as catering for wedding receptions). [8]Specialty goods are extremely important and expensive purchases. [9]Consumers usually decide on precisely what they want and will accept no substitutes. [10]They will often go from store to store, sometimes spending a great deal of money and time to get a specific product.

_____ 1. The pattern of organization of the above selection is
A. list of items. B. time order.

2. The second major detail is signaled with the transition ____________.

_____ 3. The total number of major details is
A. two. B. three. C. four.

B. [1]Although people move through courtship in different ways, researchers have identified a number of stages common to the process. [2]First, relationships begin when two individuals feel attraction toward each other. [3]In this early stage, both people show interest in each other and choose to spend time together. [4]Then, after a period of "dating," both partners declare themselves a couple, telling their friends and relatives about the new person in their lives. [5]Next, couples make a commitment to each other. [6]Here, expectations become more serious, and partners agree to have an exclusive relationship with each other. [7]Eventually, both partners begin coordinating their activities so that they function as a couple in important matters. [8]In this stage, schedules, finances, and career plans are mutually decided. [9]Finally, the couple makes a permanent commitment to marry or cohabitate.

_____ 4. The pattern of organization of the above selection is
A. list of items. B. time order.

(Continues on next page)

5–7. Three of thc transitions that introduce the major details of the paragraph are

_______________ _______________ _______________.

C. [1]Jargon—a specialized vocabulary used by a particular group, such as lawyers, teenagers, or musicians—has several benefits for group members. [2]One benefit of jargon is that it provides a way of setting insiders apart from outsiders because only the insiders know what it means. [3]Teens, borrowing from Internet shorthand, enjoy leaving their parents in the dark with remarks like "BRB" (be right back), "YTB!" (you're the best!), or "BTW" (by the way). [4]Another benefit is that jargon strengthens the ties between insiders. [5]They use it to communicate only with each other, not with anyone else. [6]Musicians know their fellow performers will know that an "axe" is a guitar, a "busker" is a street musician, and "woodshedding" means "practicing." [7]In addition, jargon is an important way for a group to maintain its identity and project a clear form of authority. [8]Clients want to think lawyers know more about the law than they do, so they feel some reassurance when lawyers talk about "statutes" (laws), "billable hours" (how the lawyer will charge them), and "plaintiff" (the person bringing a case against another). [9]Last, jargon gives individual group members a sense of belonging, and so it raises their self-esteem.

_____ 8. The pattern of organization of the above selection is
A. list of items.
B. time order.

9–10. Complete the outline of the paragraph.

Main idea: Jargon has several benefits for group members.

1. Provides a way of setting insiders apart from outsiders
   Example—teens use shorthand like "BRB" for "be right back."
2. ______________________________________
   ____
   Example—Musicians know "woodshedding" means "practicing."
3. Maintains a group identity and projects a clear form of authority
   Example—lawyers will say "statutes" instead of "laws."
4. ______________________________________
   ____

6 Relationships II

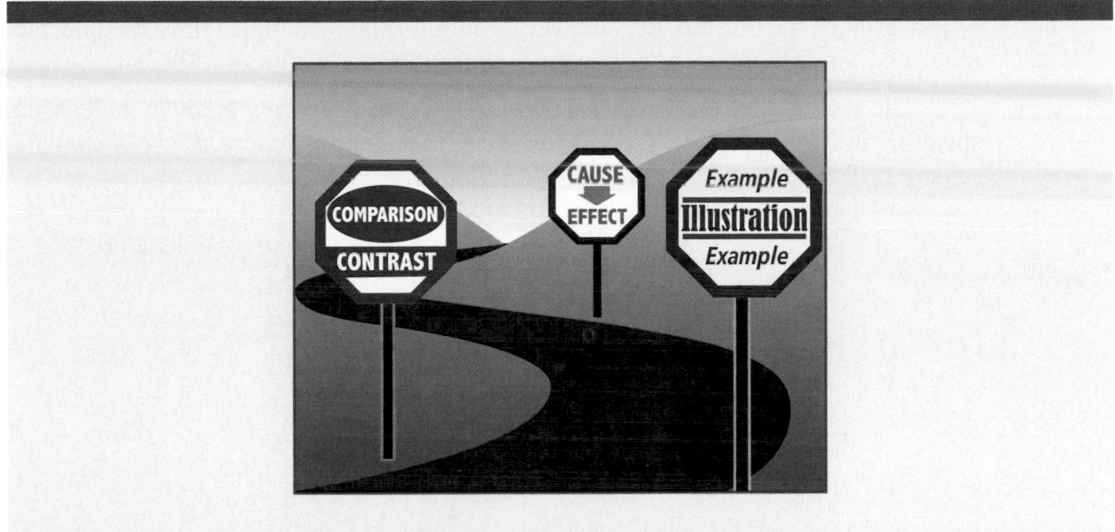

In Chapter 5, you learned how authors use transitions and patterns of organization to show relationships and make their ideas clear. You also learned about two common types of relationships:

- Relationships that involve **addition**
- Relationships that involve **time**

In this chapter, you will learn about three other types of relationships:

- Relationships that involve **illustration**
- Relationships that involve **comparison and contrast**
- Relationships that involve **cause and effect**

1 Illustration

Words That Show Illustration

Put a check (✓) beside the item that is easier to understand:

___ Certain types of anxiety are very common. Most people feel anxious at the thought of speaking in front of a large group.

___ Certain types of anxiety are very common. For example, most people feel anxious at the thought of speaking in front of a large group.

The second item is easier to follow. The words *For example* make it clear that speaking in front of a large group is one type of common anxiety. *For example* and other words and phrases like it are illustration words.

"He's been acting strange lately. For instance, when I ask him to sit, he actually sits."

Illustration words indicate that an author will provide one or more *examples* to develop and clarify a given idea. In the above cartoon, the owner gives an example of his dog's strange behavior—the dog actually obeys a command!

Here are some common words that introduce examples:

Illustration Words

(for) example	including	(as an) illustration	one
(for) instance	specifically	to illustrate	once
such as	to be specific		

Examples

The following items contain illustration words. Notice how these words signal that one or more *examples* are coming.

- Birds sing for various reasons, *such as* to proclaim territory, to signal hunger, or to attract a mate.
- As obesity becomes more common in the United States, the rates for related health problems, *including* diabetes among children, have soared.
- Some common beliefs about the United States are really myths. *For example*, Betsy Ross did not design the American flag.

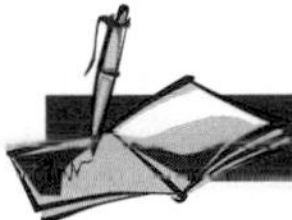

PRACTICE 1

Complete each item with a suitable illustration word or phrase from the box on the previous page. Try to use a variety of transitions.

> ***Hint:*** Make sure that each word or phrase that you choose fits smoothly into the flow of the sentence. Test each choice by reading the sentence aloud.

1. Throughout history, men have chosen to marry for different reasons. In ancient Sparta, _________________, men needed wives solely for childbearing.

2. Common courtesies, ________________ saying *please* and *thank you,* are becoming less and less common.

3. Sometimes drivers don't seem to be paying full attention to their driving. _________________, this morning I saw people driving while talking on cell phones, combing their hair, and glancing at newspapers.

4. Color in the workplace can serve a functional purpose. _____________, different colors can be used to mark secure and unsecured areas, areas where visitors are and are not allowed, or various levels of safety and danger.

5. We have come to understand in recent years how the English language is riddled with sexism. Most blatant is the generic "he," which excludes women from whatever group is being discussed, _________________ in the line "When a college student studies for an exam, he should be sure to review all his lecture notes."

Illustration words are common in all types of writing. One way they are used in textbooks is in the pattern of organization known as the definition and example pattern.

The Definition and Example Pattern

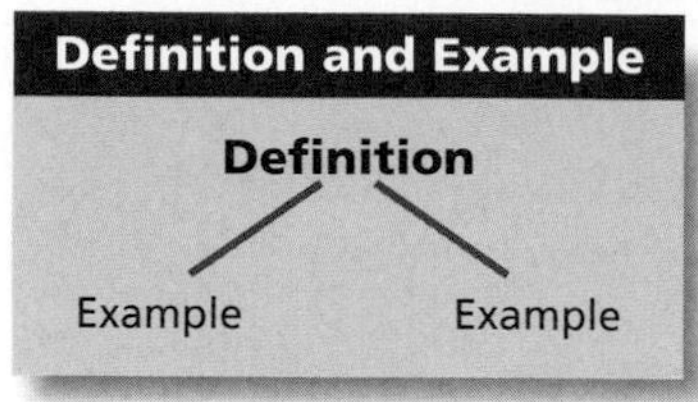

To get a sense of the definition and example pattern, try to arrange the following sentences in an order that makes sense. Put a *1* in front of the sentence that should come first, a *2* in front of the sentence that comes next, and a *3* in front of the sentence that should be last. The result will be a short paragraph. Then read the explanation that follows.

___ For instance, a football player recovering from an operation may want to return to his team, yet he also knows that he may limp for the rest of his life if he is injured again.

___ An approach-avoidance conflict is a situation in which someone is both attracted to and repelled by the same goal.

___ People who feel loyal to their present employer but are interested in a new and better job are another example.

This paragraph begins with a definition: "An approach-avoidance conflict is a situation in which someone is both attracted to and repelled by the same goal." The second sentence clarifies the meaning of *approach-avoidance conflict* with an example: "For instance, a football player recovering from an operation may want to return to his team, yet he also knows that he may limp for the rest of his life if he is injured again." The third sentence then provides a second example: "People who feel loyal to their present employer but are interested in a new and better job are another example." The second and third sentences include the illustration words *For instance* and *example.* As you can see, the **definition and example pattern of organization** includes just what its name suggests: a definition and one or more examples.

An Important Study Hint: Good textbook authors want to help readers understand the important ideas and terms in a subject—whether it is psychology, sociology, business, biology, or any other field. Such authors often take time, then, to include key definitions. The ideas and terms being defined are usually set off in *italic* or **boldface** type, and the definitions are signaled by such words as *is, are, is called, termed*, and *refers to*. Here are some definitions from a variety of textbooks:

- A method for the gradual removal of fearful associations is sometimes referred to as **desensitization**.

- The amount of current that actually flows in a wire is measured in a unit called the **ampere**, or **amp**.
- A court's **jurisdiction** is its authority to hear cases of a particular type.
- **Microwaves** are electromagnetic waves whose wavelengths range from about one meter to one millimeter.
- Leading experts define **sales promotion** as an action-focused marketing event whose goal is a direct impact on the behavior of a firm's customers.
- The most important fact in describing any atom is the **atomic number**—the number of protons in its nucleus.

(***Note:*** Sometimes a dash is used to signal a definition.)

If an author defines a term, you can assume that it is important enough to learn. So when reading and taking notes on a textbook, always do two things:

1) Write down key definitions.
2) Write down a helpful example for each definition. When a definition is general and abstract, examples are often essential to help make its meaning clear.

Check Your Understanding

The following paragraph defines a term, explains it a bit, and then gives an example of it. After reading the paragraph, see if you can answer the questions that follow.

[1]Rick and Mia are having an argument. [2]Rick says, "America is a land of endless opportunity. [3]People should make it on their own. [4]That is why welfare should be abolished. [5]No one deserves a handout, and if a person is not making it in life, he has only himself to blame." [6]Mia replies, "What nonsense! [7]You are nothing but a hard-hearted Scrooge. [8]I am disappointed in you." [9]Who is making a better argument here—Rick or Mia? [10]You may be surprised to hear that Rick is making a better argument. [11]He is presenting a strong point of view—a point of view lacking in compassion, but an argument nonetheless. [12]Mia, on the other hand, is not addressing the argument at all. [13]Instead, she is attacking Rick. [14]Her "argument" is known as *argumentum ad hominem*—Latin for "argument to the person"; it substitutes a personal attack for a response to the issue at hand. [15]Consider also a father who argues with his son about the dangers of smoking, only to have his son point out that his father is or was a smoker. [16]The son's response is a personal attack and not a valid counterargument.

What term is being defined? ______________________

Which sentence contains the definition? ______________________

In which sentence does the first example begin? ______________________

In what sentence does a second example appear? ______________________

Explanation

The term *argumentum ad hominem* is explained in sentence 14. The first example of such an argument begins in the first sentence, with the argument of Rick and Mia. The second example appears in the last two sentences of the selection.

PRACTICE 2

Each of the following passages includes a definition and one or more examples. Underline the term being defined. Then, in the spaces provided, write the number of the definition sentence and the number of the sentence where each example begins.

A. [1]The self-handicapping strategy is a technique for making up protective excuses ahead of time. [2]Research has shown that people use this strategy often. [3]For instance, they'll offer an excuse before they take an exam, saying, "I had to work, so I didn't get much studying done. [4]I may not do very well." [5]Or in advance of a social occasion, they might say, "I didn't get much sleep last night, so I'm probably not going to have anything interesting to say." [6]In either case, the excuse planted ahead of time takes the heat off the individual and places the blame on the circumstance.

Definition ________ *Example 1* ________ *Example 2* ________

B. [1]A loss leader is a product or service that sells at a loss but generates customer interest that can lead to a later profit. [2]As an illustration, supermarkets sell food staples such as sugar or milk at less than the cost at which they were purchased in order to draw customers to their businesses. [3]Inkjet printers are generally sold at a loss, with the manufacturer hoping that customers will come back to buy the overpriced ink cartridges. [4]As long as a small initial loss can lead to a big profit on the back end, loss leaders will continue to appear.

Definition ________ *Example 1* ________ *Example 2* ________

2 Comparison and Contrast

Words That Show Comparison

Put a check (✓) beside the item that is easier to understand:

___ The computerized scanner has streamlined the supermarket checkout line. Computerized fingerprint identification allows the police to do in seconds what once took two hours.

___ The computerized scanner has streamlined the supermarket checkout line. Similarly, computerized fingerprint identification allows the police to do in seconds what once took two hours.

The first item makes us wonder, "What has supermarket work got to do with police work?" In the second item, the transition word *similarly* makes it clear that the author is *comparing* the benefits of computerization in both types of work. *Similarly* and words like it are comparison words.

"What do you mean you can't marry me? We're perfect for each other. We look exactly alike, and we both love to swim."

Comparison words signal similarities. Authors use a comparison transition to show that a second idea is *like* the first one in some way. In the above cartoon, the words *alike* and *both* indicate that a comparison is being made: if the two goldfish are so much like each other, they deserve to be together.

Here are some common words that show comparison:

Comparison Words

(just) as	both	in like fashion	in a similar fashion
(just) like	equal(ly)	in like manner	in a similar manner
alike	resemble	similar(ly)	(in) the same way
same	likewise	similarity	(in) common

Examples

The sentences below contain comparison words. Notice how these words show that things are *alike* in some way.

- *Both* alligators and crocodiles use nerve-packed bumps in their jaws to sense the movement of nearby prey.
- Surveys show that women who work outside the home and stay-at-home moms are *equally* concerned about their children's welfare.
- Many thousands of plant species are in danger of vanishing from the Earth. *Likewise*, up to five thousand species of animals could soon be extinct.

PRACTICE 3

Complete each sentence with a suitable comparison word or phrase from the box above. Try to use a variety of transitions.

1. A swarm of locusts looks ____________________ a massive dark cloud moving across the sky.
2. As a young boy, Raymond was often beaten by his parents. Unfortunately, he now treats his own children ______________________.
3. ____________________ people put their best foot forward for romance, birds show off their skills or looks during courtship.
4. My cousin, who gets around in a wheelchair, had kitchen counters built at a convenient height for him. ______________________, he created a flower container garden at a height he can easily reach.
5. American films are enormously popular in almost every country. ______________________, American clothing styles influence fashions around the world.

Words That Show Contrast

Put a check (✓) beside the item that is easier to understand:

___ The company pays the manager handsomely. He doesn't do much work.

___ The company pays the manager handsomely even though he doesn't do much work.

The first item is puzzling: does the company pay the manager well *because* he doesn't do much work? The second item makes it clear that the company pays the manager well *even though* he doesn't do much work. *Even though* and other words and phrases like it are contrast words.

"The main difference between us is that I spend all my money on shoes."

Contrast words signal that an author is pointing out differences between subjects. A contrast word shows that two things *differ* in one or more ways. Contrast words also inform us that something is going to *differ from* what we might expect. In the above cartoon, the speaker uses the contrast word *difference* to signal a major distinction between the two insects.

Here are some common words that show contrast:

Contrast Words

but	instead (of)	even though	difference
yet	in contrast	as opposed to	different(ly)
however	on the other hand	in spite of	differ (from)
although	on the contrary	despite	unlike
nevertheless	converse(ly)	rather than	while
still	opposite		

Examples

The sentences below contain contrast words. Notice how these words signal that one idea is *different from* another idea.

- Women communicate *differently* in the workplace than men do.
- *Although* the cost of attending college has tripled over the last twenty years, sources of financial aid have decreased.
- The average person can safely tolerate ten bee stings for each pound of body weight. This means that the average adult could withstand more than a thousand stings. *However,* one sting can cause death in a person who is allergic to such stings.

PRACTICE 4

Complete each sentence with a suitable contrast word or phrase from the box on the previous page. Try to use a variety of transitions.

1. People are capable of making some adjustment to a constant noise level. ______________________, if the noise exceeds eighty-five to ninety decibels, their productivity will decrease over the course of the workday.
2. ________________________ Americans claim to be concerned with fitness, the typical adult can't climb a flight of steps without getting short of breath.
3. ________________________ perennial plants, which return year after year, annuals survive for only one season.
4. Most American-born college students cannot converse in a foreign language. ____________________, it is a rare student in Europe who cannot speak at least one language besides his or her own.
5. The most effective bridge from low levels of reading ability to higher levels is pleasure reading. ____________________, this is exactly the kind of reading that is missing from the lives of many students.

Comparison and contrast transitions are often used in paragraphs organized in the comparison and/or contrast pattern.

The Comparison and/or Contrast Pattern

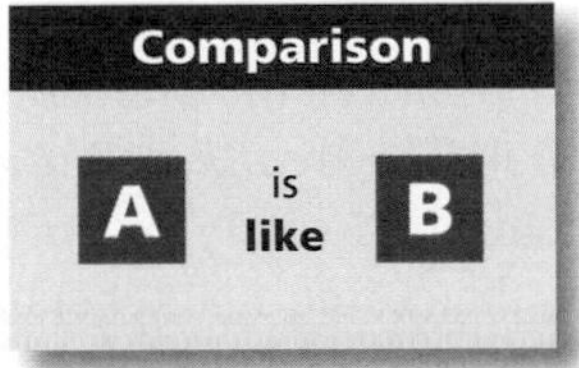

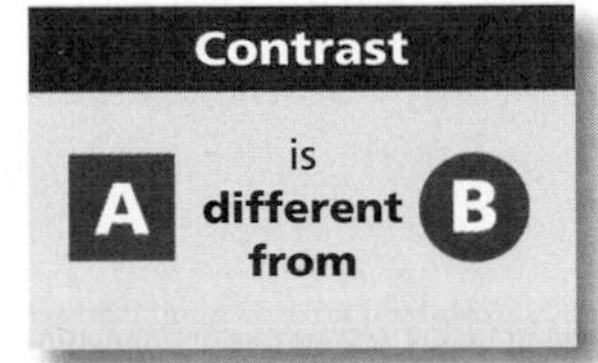

To get a sense of the comparison and/or contrast pattern, try to arrange the following sentences in an order that makes sense. Put a *1* in front of the sentence that should come first, a *2* in front of the sentence that comes next, and a *3* in front of the sentence that should be last. The result will be a short paragraph. Then read the explanation that follows.

___ They are alike in offering health-care services for patients suffering from injury or disease.

___ Hospices and hospitals are much more different than they are similar.

___ However, the goal of a hospital is to make patients well, while the concern of a hospice is to relieve the pain and suffering of dying patients.

The first sentence of this paragraph is the general one, the one with the main idea: "Hospices and hospitals are much more different than they are similar." The word *different* suggests a comparison and/or contrast pattern of organization. The comparison word *alike* and the contrast words *However* and *while* in the other two sentences show that hospices and hospitals are being both compared *and* contrasted: "They are alike in offering health-care services for patients suffering from injury or disease. However, the goal of a hospital is to make patients well, while the concern of a hospice is to relieve the pain and suffering of dying patients."

The **comparison-contrast pattern** shows how two things are alike or how they are different, or—as in this example—both. When things are **compared**, their similarities are pointed out; when they are **contrasted**, their differences are discussed (for example, the different goals of a hospital and a hospice). Comparison or contrast transitions will signal what an author is doing.

Authors frequently find it useful to compare and contrast. Here are three examples:

- The author of a psychology text contrasts genuine and artificial facial expressions. He explains that smiles resulting from actual joy involve the outer muscles that surround the eyes, while smiles used to hide negative emotions tend to involve the muscles around the lips.
- The author of a sociology text compares and contrasts the political beliefs of Catholics, Protestants, and Jews. In most policy issues, he notes, the three groups hold similar opinions. Catholics and fundamentalist Protestants

oppose abortion more strongly than the other groups, while Catholics and Jews are more supportive of food programs for the poor than are most Protestants.

- The author of an economics text contrasts the philosophies of two men, Adam Smith and Karl Marx. In his book *The Wealth of Nations*, Smith argues for a free-market economy that is controlled solely by supply and demand. In the book *Das Kapital*, Marx argues that a free-market economy exploits workers, and proposes an economy that the workers control.

Check Your Understanding

In the following paragraph, the main idea is stated in the first sentence. As is often the case, the main idea suggests a paragraph's pattern of organization. Here the transition *different* is a hint that the paragraph may be organized in a comparison and/or contrast pattern. Read the paragraph and answer the questions below. Then read the explanation that follows.

> [1]The feeling of awe is mostly different from the feeling of fear. [2]In both cases, we may feel a sense of being overwhelmed, of confronting someone or something much more powerful than ourselves. [3]But awe is a positive feeling, an expansive feeling. [4]While fear makes us want to run away, awe makes us want to draw closer even as we hesitate to get too close. [5]When we are in awe, we stand open-mouthed in appreciation of something greater than ourselves rather than being anxious about it. [6]To stand at the edge of a steep cliff and look down is to experience fear. [7]We want to get out of that situation as quickly and safely as we can. [8]In contrast, to stand securely on a mountaintop and look around us is to feel awe. [9]We could linger there forever.

1. Is this paragraph comparing, contrasting, or both? ____________________

2. What two things are being compared and/or contrasted? ______________

   ____

3. What are four of the comparison and/or contrast signal words used in the paragraph? ____

Explanation

This paragraph is both comparing and contrasting—it discusses both a similarity and differences. The two things being compared and contrasted are (1) awe and (2) fear. One comparison transition is used—*both*. Five contrast transitions are used—*different, But, While, rather than,* and *In contrast*.

PRACTICE 5

The following passages use the pattern of comparison and/or contrast. Read each passage and answer the questions that follow.

A. [1]The difference between work and play is in the purpose of and reward for performing an activity. [2]Work has a definite purpose. [3]Something is being accomplished when work is performed. [4]Some resource such as raw material or information is being changed. [5]Play, however, need not have a purpose; sometimes people engage in play for its own sake. [6]The rewards for work are mainly external ones. [7]Money may be the most common external reward; others are recognition and promotion. [8]In contrast, the rewards for play are internal ones: satisfaction, enjoyment, a sense of achievement.

Check (✓) the pattern that is used in this passage:

___ Comparison

___ Contrast

___ Comparison and contrast

What two things are being compared, contrasted, or compared *and* contrasted?

1. ____________________ 2. ____________________

B. [1]The similarity in causes and characteristics of the First and Second World Wars was more than superficial. [2]Both were triggered by threats to the balance of power, and both were conflicts between peoples, entire nations, rather than between governments. [3]On the other hand, there were notable differences between the two conflicts. [4]The methods of warfare in the Second World War had little in common with those of the earlier conflict. [5]Instead of the trench warfare of the First World War, the Second had bombing and sudden air attacks on civilian populations as well as on military installations. [6]Thus, to a much greater degree than in the First World War, those at home shared with soldiers the dangers of the war. [7]Finally, this war was not greeted with the almost universal, naive enthusiasm that had marked the outbreak of the other. [8]Men and women still remembered the horrors of the First World War. [9]They entered the Second with determination, but also with a keener appreciation of the frightful devastation that war could bring than their predecessors had possessed.

Check (✓) the pattern that is used in this passage:

___ Comparison

___ Contrast

___ Comparison and contrast

What two things are being compared, contrasted, or compared *and* contrasted?

1. ____________________ 2. ____________________

3 Cause and Effect

Words That Show Cause and Effect

Put a check (✓) beside the item that is easier to understand:

___ The young woman decided to go away to school. Her boyfriend began talking about getting married.

___ The young woman decided to go away to school because her boyfriend began talking about getting married.

In the first item, we're not sure about the relationship between the two sentences. Did the young woman's boyfriend discuss marriage because she decided to go away to school? Or was it the other way around? The word *because* in the second item makes it clear that the young woman decided to go away to school *as a result of* her boyfriend's interest in marriage. *Because* and words like it are cause and effect words.

GLASBERGEN
"The explanation is that you've been eating too much pepperoni pizza, Mr. Jones."

GLASBERGEN
"Your problem is the result of not drinking enough water."

Cause and effect words signal that the author is explaining *the reason why* something happened or *the result of* something happening. In the first cartoon above, the doctor is explaining that the reason Mr. Jones is covered with red spots is that he's been eating too much pepperoni pizza. In the second cartoon, the result of not drinking enough water is that the patient has turned into a cactus!

Here are some common words that show cause and effect:

Cause and Effect Words

therefore	so	owing to	because (of)
thus	(as a) result	effect	reason
(as a) consequence	results in	cause	explanation
consequently	leads to	if . . . then	accordingly
due to	since	affect	

Examples

The following examples contain cause and effect words. Notice how these words introduce a *reason* for something or the *results* of something.

- The first street traffic lights were created in 1920 by a Detroit policeman. He picked the colors red, yellow, and green *because* railroads used them.
- In England during the sixteenth century, the color red was thought to be helpful to the sick. *Consequently,* patients were dressed in red nightgowns.
- Don't eat an egg that has a crack in it. The *reason* is that the egg may be contaminated.

PRACTICE 6

Complete each sentence with a suitable cause and effect word or phrase from the box above. Try to use a variety of transitions.

1. The __________________ many people support organic farming is that it is less destructive to the environment than farming with chemicals and pesticides.
2. If you're taking an antibiotic, you must continue taking it until all the pills are gone. Failure to do so could __________________ in a relapse or in the emergence of resistant bacteria strains.
3. Human behavior is so complicated that we are not always aware of the ____________________s of our own actions.
4. Although reduced-fat foods may sound healthy, the fat is often replaced by carbohydrates that may _________________ weight gain.

5. Information overload is all around us, coming with terrifying speed via the Internet as well as fax, phone, text messaging, e-mail, and scores of cable channels. ______________________ so much information bombards us constantly, we fail to remember a great deal of it.

Cause and effect transitions often signal the cause and effect pattern of organization.

The Cause and Effect Pattern

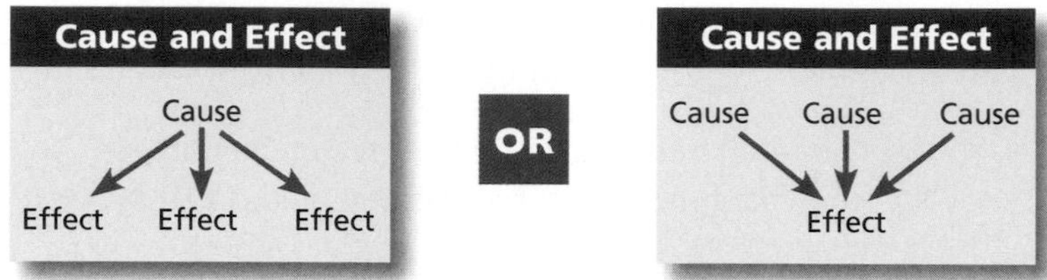

To get a sense of the cause and effect pattern, try to arrange the following sentences in an order that makes sense. Put a *1* in front of the sentence that should come first, a *2* in front of the sentence that comes next, and a *3* in front of the sentence that should be last. The result will be a short paragraph. Then read the explanation that follows.

___ As a result, federal authorities required that ships carry enough lifeboats to save everyone on board.

___ The sinking of the ship *Titanic* led to safer sea travel.

___ When the *Titanic* sank, many died because there were too few lifeboats.

As the words *led to, because,* and *As a result* suggest, this paragraph is organized in a cause and effect pattern. The paragraph begins with the general idea: "The sinking of the ship *Titanic* led to safer sea travel." Next comes the detailed explanation: "When the *Titanic* sank, many died because there were too few lifeboats. As a result, federal authorities required that ships carry enough lifeboats to save everyone on board."

Information in a **cause-effect pattern** addresses the questions "Why does a behavior or event happen?" and/or "What are the results of a behavior or event?" An author may then discuss causes, or effects, or both causes and effects.

Authors usually don't just tell what happened; they try to tell about events in a way that explains both *what* happened and *why.* A textbook section on the sinking of the ship *Titanic,* for example, would be incomplete if it did not include the cause of the disaster—going at high speed, the ship collided with an iceberg. Or if the number of people out of work in the country increases, journalists may not simply report the increase. They may also explore the reasons for and effects of that increase.

Check Your Understanding

Read the paragraph below and see if you can answer the questions about cause and effect. Then read the explanation to see how you did.

[1]The number of unmarried couples who are cohabiting (living together) has increased from about half a million in 1970 to over 7.5 million today. [2]Why are these couples choosing cohabitation rather than marriage? [3]One explanation may be the high divorce rates in America. [4]Cohabitation may not last longer than marriage, but its ending is easier to deal with. [5]It does not entail the emotional and financial hassles of going through a divorce. [6]Another cause of cohabitation is that it costs much less to cohabit. [7]Marriage requires stable employment, financial security, home ownership, and money for a wedding. [8]Not surprisingly, the financially better-off are more likely to get married. [9]But the less affluent are more likely to cohabit because it costs little to do so. [10]A third reason is a growing acceptance of cohabitation. [11]It is no longer a stigma to cohabit. [12]Most Americans now approve of a couple's right to live together outside of marriage if they so choose. [13]Finally, cohabitation provides a variety of options. [14]A couple can exist in a casual, temporary, or convenient relationship that involves little commitment. [15]They can extend this intimate relationship for as long as they enjoy being together. [16]They can use it as a permanent alternative to marriage. [17]Or they can use it as a stepping stone to marriage at some future date.

1. What is the single *effect* being discussed in the paragraph?

   ____

2. What are the four *causes* discussed?

   A. ______________________________

   B. ______________________________

   C. ______________________________

   D. ______________________________

3. What are the three cause and effect transitions are used in the paragraph?

   ____

Explanation

The paragraph begins with the main idea: "The number of unmarried couples who are cohabiting (living together) has increased from about half a million in 1970 to over 7.5 million today." That point, or effect, is then supported by four causes: (1) the high divorce rates in America; (2) the lower cost of cohabitation; (3) a growing acceptance of cohabitation; and (4) the variety of options that cohabitation provides. The cause and effect transitions used are *explanation, cause,* and *reason.*

Note that even in the cause and effect pattern—or any other pattern—addition words may be used to introduce supporting details and show their order. Each cause in the above paragraph, for example, is introduced by an addition word: "*One* explanation ... *Another* cause ... A *third* reason ... *Finally*."

PRACTICE 7

A. Read the paragraph below, looking for one effect and four causes (the four major supporting details of the paragraph). Then complete the diagram that follows.

[1]There are a number of motivations for shoplifting. [2]Poverty is one cause, shown both by the evidence that poor people are more likely than others to shoplift and by the fact that shoplifting becomes more common when unemployment is high. [3]A second reason for shoplifting is frugal customers, ones who can afford to buy the things they need but are driven to steal them by a desire to stretch their budget. [4]Another explanation is the sense of excitement and fun that shoplifters experience when committing the crime. [5]Yet another cause, especially among youngsters, is the desire for social acceptance; when asked why they shoplift, many young people say, "Because my friends are doing it."

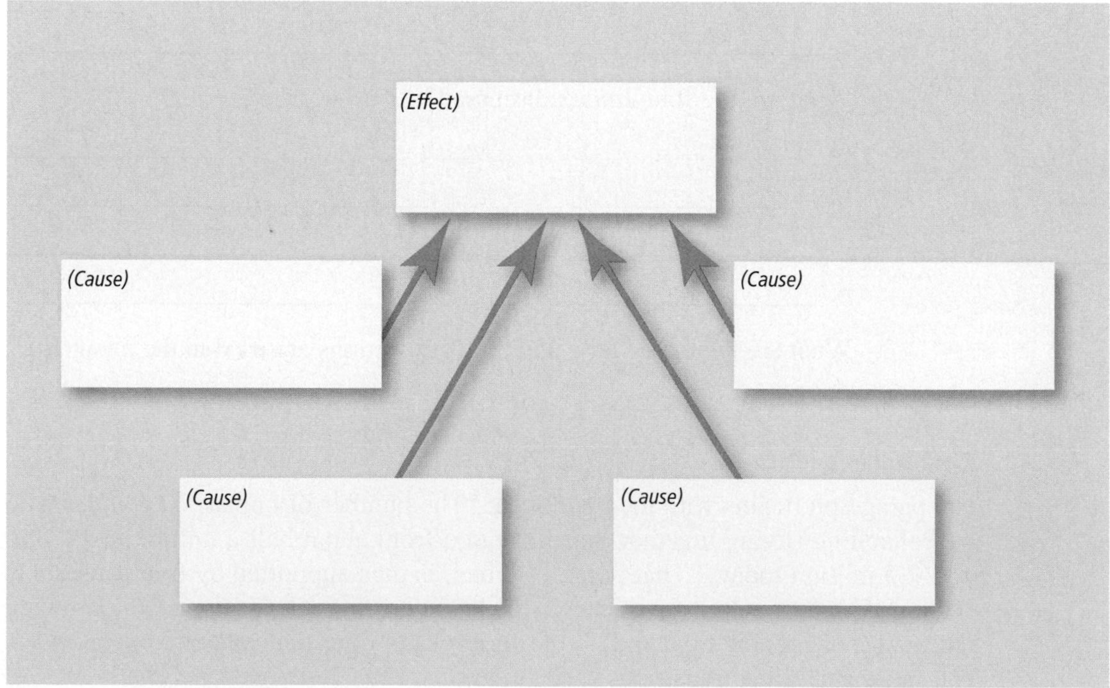

B. Read the paragraph below, looking for the one effect and the two causes. Then complete the outline that follows.

> [1]The number of humans on Earth continues to rise dramatically. [2]One reason is technology. [3]A hundred years ago, it was not unusual to find countries with infant mortality rates over 50 percent. [4]Today, however, infants in even the most impoverished countries have well over an 80 percent chance to live. [5]Technological advances have also reduced the death rate by eliminating fatal diseases such as smallpox, improving crop yields, and devising new means of distributing food. [6]Another major cause of the population explosion is the changing rates of deaths and births. [7]In underdeveloped countries, people depend on their children for support and security. [8]Parents typically have had many children to ensure that a few will survive. [9]But the decline in death rates has now resulted in the population in these countries growing rapidly. [10]In many affluent countries, such as Japan and the United States, the birthrate is actually declining, but because the death rate is declining even faster, their populations continue to grow.

Main idea *(the effect):* ______________________________

____

Major supporting details *(the causes):*

1. ______________________________
2. ______________________________

A Note on Main Ideas and Patterns of Organization

As mentioned in Chapter 5, a paragraph's main idea often indicates its pattern of organization. Try, for instance, to guess the pattern of the paragraph with this main idea:

> Norms are the standards of behavior accepted as appropriate in a society.

This sentence defines the word *norms.* A definition suggests that the author may be using the definition and example pattern. In fact, the paragraph continues with these sentences:

> For example, in Europe, it is normal for meat to be eaten with the fork facing down in the left hand. In America, however, the fork is transferred to the right hand after the meat is cut.

The words *For example* indicate that the material that follows is an example of a norm.

Recognizing a main idea, and the pattern of organization that may be implied in a main idea, are both helpful steps in understanding the material in the paragraph.

PRACTICE 8

Most of the main ideas below have been taken from college textbooks. In the space provided, write the letter of the pattern of organization that each suggests.

_____ 1. Depressed economic times often lead to an increase in spouse abuse and divorce.
A. Definition and example B. Comparison and/or contrast C. Cause and effect

_____ 2. While Randy Jarvis and Octavio Ruiz live only a few miles from one another, their lives are so different that they might as well be living in separate countries.
A. Definition and example B. Comparison and/or contrast C. Cause and effect

_____ 3. A franchise is a business arrangement in which an individual obtains rights from a larger company to sell a well-known product or service.
A. Definition and example B. Comparison and/or contrast C. Cause and effect

_____ 4. Because of the high cost of raising a family and of housing, two-income families have become a way of life in America.
A. Definition and example B. Comparison and/or contrast C. Cause and effect

_____ 5. White-collar crimes refer to crimes that respectable people of high social status commit in the course of their occupations.
A. Definition and example B. Comparison and/or contrast C. Cause and effect

_____ 6. A high-fat meal and a high-carbohydrate meal may provide the same food energy, but they affect the appetite differently.
A. Definition and example B. Comparison and/or contrast C. Cause and effect

_____ 7. Among the reasons that people daydream are to help tolerate boredom and to discharge hostile feelings.
A. Definition and example B. Comparison and/or contrast C. Cause and effect

_____ 8. The jobs created by small businesses differ from those created by big companies in several key respects.
A. Definition and example B. Comparison and/or contrast C. Cause and effect

_____ 9. Monotremes are mammals that lay eggs; the duck-billed platypus, which lives only in Australia, is one of the two types of monotremes that are alive today.

A. Definition and example B. Comparison and/or contrast C. Cause and effect

_____ 10. When an Egyptian pharoah died, some of his slaves were killed and entombed with him. This practice resulted from the belief that he would need servants in the afterlife.

A. Definition and example B. Comparison and/or contrast C. Cause and effect

A Final Point

Keep in mind that a paragraph or passage may often be made up of more than one pattern of organization. For instance, the paragraph in this chapter on page 232 explaining the term *loss leader* uses a definition and example pattern. The term is defined and examples are given; the examples are selling sugar and milk below cost to attract customers and selling inkjet printers at a loss so customers will buy expensive cartridges. But the explanations of how loss leaders work incorporate a cause-effect pattern—the loss leaders are used because of the positive effects they have.

Or consider the following passage:

[1]According to the United Nations, women in poor countries have lives very different from, and worse than, the lives of men in those countries. [2]For one thing, women have much lower literacy rates than men. [3]In South Asia, females' literacy rates are only around 50 percent of males'. [4]In addition, women lag far behind in education. [5]The females' rates for secondary education represent 72 percent of the men's rates and, for college education, only 51 percent. [6]Also, women in poor countries have fewer opportunities for paid employment. [7]There are only fifty-eight women employees for every one hundred men, and they are paid considerably less. [8]Women not gainfully employed are far from idle, however. [9]In fact, they usually work an average of twelve hours a day, while men work only eight hours.

The paragraph uses a contrast pattern: Women in poor countries are contrasted with men in the same countries. It also uses a list of items pattern, listing points of contrast between the men and women regarding literacy, education, employment, and hours of work. Pages 275–280 offer practice on passages with more than one pattern of organization.

CHAPTER REVIEW

In this chapter, you learned about three kinds of relationships that authors use to make their ideas clear:

- **Definitions and examples**
  - — To help readers understand the important ideas and terms in a subject, textbook authors often take time to include key definitions (often setting them off in *italic* or **boldface**) and examples of those definitions. When reading a textbook, it is usually a good idea to mark off both definitions and examples.
  - — Transition words that signal the definition and example pattern include *for example, for instance, to illustrate,* and *such as.*
- **Comparison and/or contrast**
  - — Authors often discuss how two things are alike or how they are different, or both.
  - — Transition words that signal comparisons include *alike* and *similar.*
  - — Transition words that signal contrasts include *but, however,* and *in contrast.*
- **Cause and effect**
  - — Authors often discuss the reasons why something happens or the effects of something that has happened.
  - — Transition words that signal causes include *reason* and *because.*
  - — Transition words that signal effects include *therefore, consequently,* and *as a result.*

Note that pages 274–280 list and offer practice in all the transitions and patterns of organization you have studied in "Relationships I" and "Relationships II."

The next chapter—Chapter 7—will sharpen your ability to make inferences in reading.

On the Web: If you are using this book in class, you can visit our website for additional practice in understanding relationships that involve examples, comparison or contrast, and cause and effect. Go to **www.townsendpress.com** and click on "Learning Center."

REVIEW TEST 1

To review what you've learned in this chapter, choose the best answer or fill in the blank for the following items.

_____ 1. Words such as *for example, for instance,* and *such as* are known as
A. illustration words.
B. definition words.
C. cause-and-effect words.

_____ 2. Words such as *just as, similarly,* and *in the same way* are known as
A. illustration words.
B. comparison words.
C. contrast words.

_____ 3. Words such as *however, on the other hand,* and *differs from* are known as
A. illustration words.
B. contrast words.
C. cause-and-effect words.

_____ 4. Words such as *therefore, as a result,* and *reason* are known as
A. definition words.
B. contrast words.
C. cause-and-effect words.

5. In textbooks, definitions of key terms are often followed by one or more _____________________ that help make those definitions clear.

REVIEW TEST 2

A. Fill in each blank with one of the words in the box. Use each word once. Then write the letter of the word in the space provided.

A. because	**B.** despite	**C.** even though
D. for instance	**E.** similarly	

_____ 1. Many products are named after specific individuals. ________________, the man who created the Tootsie Roll named it after his daughter, whom he had nicknamed Tootsie.

_____ 2. ____________________ a learning disability which made it difficult for her to learn to read, Darla worked hard and became a successful businesswoman.

_____ 3. It's important to keep candy out of the reach of dogs ____________________ an overdose of chocolate can kill a dog quickly.

_____ 4. Some people hate driving small cars ____________________ the gas mileage is far superior to that of a large, luxurious "gas-guzzler."

_____ 5. In one study, men and women who merely walked for a half hour to an hour every day at a fast but comfortable pace cut their health risks by half or more. ____________________, a study of five hundred women between the ages of 42 and 50 found that as little as three brisk twenty-minute walks each week can lower the risk of heart disease.

B. Below are the beginnings of five passages. Label each one with the letter of its pattern of organization. (You may find it helpful to underline the transition or transitions in each item.)

A Definition and example
B Comparison and/or contrast
C Cause and effect

_____ 6. [1]Preventive medicine is like changing a car's oil. [2]Just as we must change the oil regularly for a car to operate smoothly, we must have regular checkups with our doctors. . . .

_____ 7. [1]A fetus can be affected by all kinds of sensory stimulation while in the mother's womb. [2]A bright light shining on the mother's abdomen will cause the fetus to raise its hands over its eyes. [3]Loud sounds will make it cover its ears. . . .

_____ 8. [1]Jungles are areas of land that are densely overgrown with tropical trees and other vegetation. [2]In South America, for instance, the Amazon is the largest jungle. . . .

_____ 9. [1]Although American culture stresses the importance of a strong mother-child relationship, traditional Samoan families do not see the relationship as essential. [2]Rather than having just one family, many Samoan children are passed around among several foster families during childhood, with no apparent negative effect.

_____10. [1]We can prevent soil from being blown away by wind or from being washed away by rain simply by planting bushes and trees on the land. [2]The roots of these plants penetrate the soil; consequently, it is held in place. . . .

REVIEW TEST 3

Read each item and answer the questions that follow.

A. Look at the following cartoon:

"You need to swallow without chewing. Sending big chunks of food into your bloodstream leads to your arteries opening wider, which increases blood flow to the brain. As a result, you become smarter and more successful."

_____ 1. The pattern of organization used by the speaker in this cartoon is
A. definition and example.
B. contrast.
C. comparison.
D. cause and effect.

2. One transition that signals the pattern of organization is _____________ _____________________________________.

B. [1]In the world of politics, "dirty tricks" are unethical tactics—lies, slander, and innuendo/insinuations—used to destroy or at least damage a political opponent. [2]For instance, in 2002, the race for the U.S. Senate seat in Georgia pitted Max Cleland, a decorated Vietnam War veteran who had lost both legs and an arm in a grenade attack, against Saxby Chambliss, who had used up four student deferments to avoid service in Vietnam and finally sought and received a medical disqualification for a bad knee. [3]As he campaigned in the wake of the September 11, 2001, terrorist attacks, Chambliss accused Cleland of being "soft on terrorism." [4]Chambliss ran a TV ad showing a photograph of Cleland next to ones of Iraqi dictator Saddam Hussein and terrorist Osama bin Laden. [5]The message was clear: Max Cleland was somehow on the side of the terrorists. [6]In the atmosphere of fear that then gripped the nation, Chambliss' dirty trick worked: War hero Max Cleland lost his Senate seat to a man who had taken steps to stay out of harm's way during a national conflict. [7]Another example concerns Republican John McCain's first run for the presidency, during the 2000 primaries. [8]McCain was, like Cleland, a decorated Vietnam veteran. [9]He had been a prisoner of war for six years. [10]In the heated primary contest in South Carolina, which pitted McCain against George W. Bush, a series of dirty tricks were unleashed against McCain. [11]A number of fictitious stories were spread about McCain, specifically that the Bangladeshi daughter he and his wife had adopted was, in fact, his illegitimate black child; that he had been driven crazy by his years as a POW; that his wife was a drug addict; and that he had betrayed his fellow POWs in Vietnam. [12]The dirty tricks worked; McCain lost the nomination to George W. Bush.

_____ 3. The main pattern of organization of the paragraph is
- A. definition and example.
- B. comparison and/or contrast.
- C. cause and effect.

4. One transition that signals the pattern of organization of this paragraph is ______________________________.

C. [1]Young children and very elderly people represent opposite extremes of the life cycle, but their similarities are striking. [2]All children are physically and mentally dependent on others. [3]Likewise, many elderly people need assistance with eating and dressing. [4]Just as a toddler cannot be left unsupervised at home, an older person suffering from dementia must be under constant watch. [5]Both are apt to fall, although the danger for an elderly person is much greater than for a child, whose extra padding protects him or her from injury. [6]Interestingly, however, the young and old possess more proportional body fat than a normal adult. [7]Both groups are at greater risk for physical abuse, disease and illness, and all medication must be modified to fit their unique needs. [8]Because the health concerns of children and elderly can be radically different from those of adults, medical practice for these patients has developed into two special branches, pediatrics and geriatrics. [9]Socially, children and senior citizens share a common plight, usually depending on others to get them out of the house. [10]Elderly people who still work can face job discrimination, and many establishments have "no-children" policies. [11]In addition, children and the elderly often find that their opinions do not hold as much weight in society as those of adults, and they frequently have decisions made for them.

_____ 5. The main pattern of organization of the paragraph is
A. definition and example.
B. comparison and/or contrast.
C. cause and effect.

6. One transition that signals the pattern of organization of this paragraph is ______________________________.

D. [1]Doing something nice for someone can affect us in an interesting way—it can make us like that person better. [2]In experiments, doing a favor for another subject or tutoring a student usually increases liking of the person helped. [3]In 1793, Benjamin Franklin tested the idea that doing a favor has the effect of increasing liking. [4]As clerk of the Pennsylvania General Assembly, he was disturbed by opposition from another important legislator. [5]Franklin set out to win him over:

> [6]Having heard that he had in his library a certain very scarce and curious book I wrote a note to him . . . requesting he would do me the favour of lending it to me for a few days. [7]He sent it immediately and I return'd it in about a week, expressing strongly my sense of the favour. [8]When we next met in the House he spoke to me (which he had never done before), and with great civility; and he ever after manifested a readiness to serve me on all occasions, so that we became great friends and our friendship continued to his death.

_____ 7. The main pattern of organization of the paragraph is
A. definition and example.
B. comparison and/or contrast.
C. cause and effect.

8. One transition that signals the pattern of organization of this paragraph is ______________________________.

E. [1]Animals know their environment by direct experience only. [2]In contrast, humans crystallize their knowledge and feelings in symbolic representations. [3]Using those written symbols, they accumulate knowledge and pass it on to further generations of humans. [4]Animals feed themselves where they find food, but humans, coordinating their efforts with the efforts of others through language, often feed themselves abundantly and with food prepared by a hundred hands and brought from great distances. [5]Animals exercise limited control over each other. [6]However, humans, again by employing symbols, establish laws and ethical systems.

______ 9. The main pattern of organization of the paragraph is
A. definition and example.
B. comparison and/or contrast.
C. cause and effect.

10. One transition that signals the pattern of organization of this paragraph is ______________________________.

REVIEW TEST 4

Here is a chance to apply your understanding of relationships and patterns of organization to a passage from a college textbook: *Looking Out, Looking In,* Tenth Edition, by Ronald B. Adler and Neil Towne. The reading may make you think twice the next time you hear yourself saying, "I just *knew* that would happen."

To help you continue to strengthen your skills, the reading is followed by questions not only on what you've learned in this chapter but also on what you've learned in previous chapters.

Words to Watch

Below are some words in the reading that do not have strong context support. Each word is followed by the number of the paragraph in which it appears and its meaning there. These words are indicated in the article by a small circle (°).

phenomenon (1): an observable fact or event
preconceptions (3): opinions or ideas formed about something before experiencing it
peers (5): equals; people of the same social standing
sabotage (5): undermine; damage
disposition (6): frame of mind

THE INFLUENCE OF THE SELF-FULFILLING PROPHECY

Ronald B. Adler and Neil Towne

1 The self-concept is such a powerful force on the personality that it not only determines how you see yourself in the present but also can actually influence your future behavior and that of others. Such occurrences come about through a phenomenon° called the self-fulfilling prophecy.

2 A **self-fulfilling prophecy** occurs when a person's expectations of an event make the event more likely to occur than would otherwise have been true. Self-fulfilling prophecies occur all the time, although you might never have given them that label. For example, think of some instances you may have known.

- You expected to become nervous and botch a job interview and later did so.
- You anticipated having a good (or terrible) time at a social affair and found your expectations being met.
- A teacher or boss explained a new task to you, saying that you probably wouldn't do well at first. You did not do well.
- A friend described someone you were about to meet, saying that you wouldn't like the person. The prediction turned out to be correct—you didn't like the new acquaintance.

In each of these cases, there is a good chance that the event occurred because it was predicted to occur. You needn't have botched the interview, the party might have been boring only because you helped make it so, you might have done better on the job if your boss hadn't spoken up, and you might have liked the new acquaintance if your friend hadn't given you preconceptions°. In other words, what helped each event occur was the expectation of it. 3

Types of Self-Fulfilling Prophecies

There are two types of self-fulfilling prophecies. *Self-imposed prophecies* occur when your own expectations influence your behavior. In sports you've probably "psyched" yourself into playing either better or worse than usual, so that the only explanation for your unusual performance was your attitude. Similarly, you've probably faced an audience at one time or another with a fearful attitude and forgotten your remarks, not because you were unprepared, but because you said to yourself, "I know I'll blow it." 4

Research has demonstrated the power of self-imposed prophecies. In one study, people who considered themselves incompetent proved less likely to pursue rewarding relationships 5

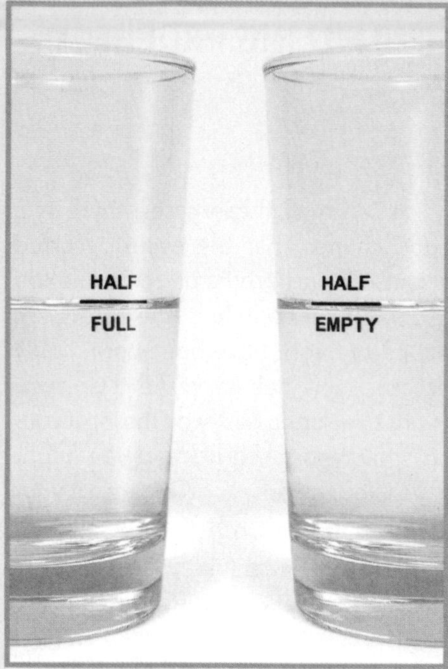

with others. Compared to their more confident peers°, they were also more likely to sabotage° existing relationships. On the other hand, students who perceived themselves as capable achieved more academically. In another study, subjects who were sensitive to social rejection tended to expect rejection, perceive it where it might not have existed, and act as if it had occurred even when it did not. Such a response strains relationships and can result in exactly what the sensitive person was trying to avoid—rejection. Research also suggests that communicators who feel anxious about giving speeches seem to create self-fulfilling prophecies about doing poorly that cause them to perform less effectively. The self-fulfilling prophecy also operates on the job. For instance, salespeople who view themselves as being effective communicators are more successful than those who view themselves as less effective, despite the fact that there was no difference in the approach that members of each group used with customers. In other words, the apparent reason why some salespeople are successful is that they expect to succeed.

Self-imposed prophecies operate 6
in many ways that affect everyday communication. You've had the experience of waking up in an irritable mood and saying to yourself, "This will be a bad day." After you made such a decision, you may have acted in ways that made it come true. If you approached a class expecting to be bored, you most probably did lose interest, owing partly to a lack of attention on your part. If you avoided the company of others because you expected they had nothing to offer, your expectations would have been confirmed—nothing exciting or new did happen to you. However, if you approached the same day with the idea that it could be a good one, this expectation probably would have been met also. Researchers have found that putting a smile on your face, even if you're not in a good mood, can lead to a more positive disposition°. Likewise, if you approach a class determined to learn something, you probably will—even if it's how not to instruct students! Approach many strangers with the idea that some of them will be good to know, and you'll most likely make some new friends. In these cases and ones like them, your attitude has a great deal to

do with how you see yourself and how others will see you.

7 A second category of self-fulfilling prophecies is *imposed by one person on another*, so that the expectations of one person govern another's actions. The classic example was demonstrated by Robert Rosenthal and Lenore Jacobson in a study they described in their book *Pygmalion in the Classroom*. The experimenters randomly selected 20 percent of a school's population and convinced teachers that the selected students showed unusual potential for intellectual growth. Eight months later these unusual or "magic" children showed significantly greater gains in IQ than did the remaining children, who had not been singled out for the teachers' attention. The change in the teachers' expectations had led to an actual change in the performance of these randomly selected children. In other words, the children did better, not because they were any more intelligent than their classmates, but because they learned that their teachers—significant others—believed that they could.

8 To put this phenomenon in context with the self-concept, we can say that when a teacher communicates to a child the message "I think you're bright," the child accepts that evaluation and changes her self-concept to include it. Unfortunately, we can assume that the same principle holds for students whose teachers send the message, "I think you're stupid."

This type of self-fulfilling prophecy has been shown to be a powerful force for shaping the self-concept and thus the behavior of people in a wide range of settings outside the schools. In medicine, patients who unknowingly use placebos—substances such as injections of sterile water or doses of sugar pills that have no curative value—often respond just as favorably to treatment as those who actually received a drug. The patients believe they have taken a substance that will help them feel better, and this belief actually brings about a "cure." In psychotherapy, Rosenthal and Jacobson describe several studies suggesting that patients who believe they will benefit from treatment do so regardless of the type of treatment they receive. In the same vein, when a doctor believes that a patient will improve, the patient may do so precisely because of this expectation, whereas another person for whom the doctor has little hope often fails to recover. Apparently the patient's self-concept as sick or well—as shaped by the doctor—plays an important role in determining the actual state of health. 9

Reading Comprehension Questions

Vocabulary in Context

_____ 1. In the sentence below, the word *strains* (strānz) means
A. improves.
B. deepens.
C. has no impact upon.
D. injures.

"Such a response strains relationships and can result in exactly what the sensitive person was trying to avoid—rejection." (Paragraph 5)

Central Point and Main Ideas

_____ 2. Which sentence best expresses the central point of the selection?
A. People who expect to like other people usually have no trouble making friends.
B. There are two types of self-fulfilling prophecy, which is what occurs when our expectations of a situation influence what happens.
C. Self-fulfilling prophecies are what determine whether we succeed or fail in life.
D. Children whose teachers have faith in them perform better academically than other children.

_____ 3. The main idea of paragraph 9 is stated in its
A. first sentence.
B. second sentence.
C. third sentence.

Supporting Details

_____ 4. In the experiment described in the book *Pygmalion in the Classroom*,
A. experimenters convinced teachers that certain children were especially bright.
B. experimenters told teachers to give extra attention to their most problematic students.
C. children were allowed to take over their teachers' jobs.
D. experimenters asked teachers to ignore certain students.

_____ 5. Substances known as placebos are
A. experimental drugs not yet approved for general use.
B. a form of antibiotic.
C. substances without curative value that patients believe are medicine.
D. psychiatric drugs that often increase people's self-confidence.

Transitions

_____ 6. The relationship of the second sentence to the first sentence below is one of

A. illustration.
B. cause and effect.
C. addition.
D. comparison.

"Researchers have found that putting a smile on your face, even if you're not in a good mood, can lead to a more positive disposition. Likewise, if you approach a class determined to learn something, you probably will—even if it's how not to instruct students!" (Paragraph 6)

_____ 7. The relationship of the second sentence to the first sentence below is one of

A. illustration.
B. addition.
C. effect.
D. contrast.

"The self-fulfilling prophecy also operates on the job. For instance, salespeople who view themselves as being effective communicators are more successful than those who view themselves as less effective . . . ." (Paragraph 5)

_____ 8. The relationship of the second sentence to the first sentence below is one of

A. illustration.
B. contrast.
C. effect.
D. addition.

"Compared to their more confident peers, they were also more likely to sabotage existing relationships. On the other hand, students who perceived themselves as capable achieved more academically." (Paragraph 5)

Patterns of Organization

_____ 9. The selection mainly

A. defines and illustrates related terms.
B. narrates a series of events in time order.
C. discusses the many causes of a particular effect.
D. lists a variety of types of prophecies.

_____ 10. Paragraph 7 uses definition-example and which two other patterns of organization?
A. Comparison and contrast.
B. List of items and contrast.
C. Comparison and cause-effect.
D. Time order and cause and effect.

Discussion Questions

1. In general, do you accept the premise of this reading: that our expectations have a great deal to do with what we later experience? What evidence have you seen that makes you agree or disagree with the authors' premise?

2. Is it better to expect good things to happen, or to expect the worst and then be pleasantly surprised when things go well? Explain your answer.

3. The authors write about people who are especially sensitive to rejection, and who seem to perceive it where it may not exist. Have you ever witnessed this happening? Why do you think it occurs?

4. How might parents and teachers make use of what was demonstrated by *Pygmalion in the Classroom*?

Note: Writing assignments for this selection appear on page 699.

Check Your Performance — RELATIONSHIPS II

Activity		*Number Right*		*Points*		*Score*
Review Test 1	(5 items)	______	×	2	=	______
Review Test 2	(10 items)	______	×	3	=	______
Review Test 3	(10 items)	______	×	3	=	______
Review Test 4	(10 items)	______	×	3	=	______
				TOTAL SCORE	=	______%

Enter your total score into the **Reading Performance Chart: Review Tests** on the inside back cover.

Name ______________________________ Date __________

Section ____________ SCORE: (Number correct) _______ x 10 = _______ %

RELATIONSHIPS II: Mastery Test 1

A. Fill in each blank with an appropriate transition from the box. Use each transition once. Then, in the spaces provided, write the letter of the transition you have chosen.

A. because	**B.** for example	**C.** in contrast
D. similar	**E.** therefore	

Hint: Make sure that each word or phrase that you choose fits smoothly into the flow of the sentence. Test your choices by reading each sentence to yourself.

_____ 1. [1]The period and the semicolon are marks of punctuation that have a _______________ use. [2]Both can serve to mark the division between two complete thoughts.

_____ 2. [1]Most listeners don't simply absorb your message like human sponges. [2]They send back messages of their own called feedback. [3]_______________, when you phone a friend to say you'll be late, you may hear, "Hey, you really need to get here on time!" [4]That is feedback.

_____ 3. [1]There are actually two types of smog: the London type and the Los Angeles type. [2]The London variety is caused by the burning of fossil fuels, mainly coal with high sulfur content. [3]_______________, Los Angeles smog results when cool ocean air slips under a layer of warmer air and becomes trapped, along with exhaust emissions from automobiles. [4]This type of smog occurs in valleys and other areas with poor air circulation.

_____ 4. [1]The ancient Chinese taught that it was distasteful to serve meat in large pieces that resembled the original animal. [2]_______________, they preferred to cut the meat into bite-size pieces in the kitchen. [3]People then used chopsticks at the table to eat the small morsels of meat.

_____ 5. [1]As a result of millions of years of evolution, people from different racial backgrounds may have similar physical characteristics. [2]American Plains Indians, Ethiopians, and northern Europeans, for example, share the trait of a high-bridged, narrow nose. [3]They all lived in similar cold, dry climates or higher latitudes. [4]A high, narrow nose is an advantage under these conditions _______________ it allows the air in the nasal passage to be moisturized before entering the lungs.

(Continues on next page)

B. Label each item with the letter of its main pattern of organization.

A Definition and example **C** Contrast
B Comparison **D** Cause and effect

_____ 6. [1]In the late nineteenth century, American psychologist William James proposed that much of human behavior was instinctive. [2]Instincts are unlearned, automatic actions that are triggered by external cues. [3]For instance, if you hear a loud noise, you will tend to look toward the source of the noise automatically, perhaps without even realizing you're doing so.

_____ 7. [1]Air pollution has disastrous effects on forests. [2]Trees dying from pollution lose their leaves or needles, allowing sunlight to reach the forest floor. [3]During this process, grass prospers in the increased light and pushes out the native plants and moss, which help to hold rainwater. [4]The soil thus loses absorbency and becomes hard, causing rain and snow to flow over the ground instead of sinking into it. [5]This in turn results in erosion of the soil.

_____ 8. [1]There's an important difference between informative speeches and persuasive speeches. [2]Informative speeches generally concentrate on explaining—telling how something works, what something means, or how to do something. [3]A speaker who gives an informative speech usually tries to give the audience information without taking sides. [4]In contrast, the speaker in a persuasive speech takes a particular position and tries to get the audience to accept and support that position. [5]In a persuasive speech, information is selected according to how well it supports the speaker's point of view, not according to how informative it is.

_____ 9. [1]The atmosphere of Earth resembles a window by letting in light at the same time that it permits us to look out to the stars, planets, and all of space. [2]The atmosphere also serves as a shield to keep out undesirable things. [3]A normal glazed window lets us keep our houses warm by keeping out cold air, and it stops unwanted or harmful elements such as dirt, insects, and animals from coming in. [4]In a similar fashion, Earth's atmospheric window keeps our planet at a comfortable temperature by holding back radiated heat, and it protects us from dangerous levels of ultraviolet light.

_____ 10. [1]Humans differ from other animals in their reactions to drugs. [2]Penicillin is one of the safest, most effective antibiotics in humans. [3]In contrast, it kills hamsters and guinea pigs. [4]Another staple of human medicine, aspirin, produces birth defects in mice and rats and poisons cats. [5]Although they tested safe in nonhuman animals, numerous drugs have been removed from the market after human patients have suffered serious harm, such as paralysis, blindness, or death.

Name ______________________________ Date ____________

Section ____________ SCORE: (Number correct) ________ x 10 = ________ %

RELATIONSHIPS II: Mastery Test 2

Read each paragraph and answer the questions that follow.

A. [1]There are significant differences in the way men and women carry out everyday interactions. [2]According to researchers, men tend to see everyday encounters as competitive situations. [3]Men do not want to have other people "one up" them. [4]This fear of "losing" to others prevents men from asking for help or directions when needed. [5]On the other hand, women go to the opposite extreme. [6]Unlike men, women have been socialized to hold a more subordinate position in day-to-day interactions. [7]Instead of avoiding help, women are likely to seek it out. [8]Ironically, studies have also found that women often seek assistance even when they don't need it.

_____ 1. The main pattern of organization of the paragraph is

A. definition and example. C. comparison.
B. cause and effect. D. contrast.

2. One transition that signals the pattern of organization of this paragraph is ______________________________.

B. [1]A primary group is made up of a small number of people who relate intimately with each other over a long period. [2]The members of such a group know each other personally and behave informally together. [3]Examples of the primary group are families and small circles of friends. [4]Such groups are important units within the larger social structure. [5]In fact, in some traditional small-scale societies, the social structure is based almost totally on primary groups.

_____ 3. The main pattern of organization of the selection is

A. definition and example. C. comparison.
B. cause and effect. D. contrast.

4. The transition that signals the pattern of organization is ____________.

C. [1]Although caffeine is the world's most widely consumed drug, few of its users realize how powerful it is. [2]Caffeine is a drug that acts fast. [3]In less than five minutes after you've drunk a cup of coffee, caffeine is racing to every part of your body. [4]Its effects are many, including increasing the flow of urine and stomach acid, relaxing involuntary muscles, and stepping up the intake of oxygen. [5]In addition, caffeine heightens the pumping strength of the heart. [6]Therefore, too much caffeine can cause an irregular heartbeat. [7]A small dose of caffeine can improve your performance as you type or drive; however, too much caffeine will make you shaky and unsteady.

(Continues on next page)

_____ 5. The main pattern of organization of the paragraph is
A. definition and example. C. comparison.
B. cause and effect. D. contrast.

6. One transition that signals the pattern of organization of this paragraph is _______________.

D. [1]There are interesting similarities between the Renaissance and the present time. [2]The exploration of the Americas during the Renaissance created the same kind of excitement as today's space program: Columbus's voyages were like the astronauts' moon landings or the missions to Mars. [3]The discovery of gunpowder in the Renaissance revolutionized war, just as the atom bomb did at the end of World War II. [4]The invention of the printing press in the Renaissance made more information available to many more people, much as radio, television, and the Internet have done in our day.

_____ 7. The main pattern of organization of the paragraph is
A. definition and example. C. comparison.
B. cause and effect. D. contrast.

8. One transition that signals the pattern of organization of this paragraph is _______________.

E. [1]In the next fifteen years, the population of people over the age of fifty in the United States will soar upward by 75 percent. [2]During the same period, the number of people under the age of fifty will increase by just 2 percent. [3]There are two reasons for this rapid aging of our society. [4]The first is the baby boom that began in the late 1940s. [5]With the end of World War II, men and women quickly settled into family life and, by 1965, had some 75 million babies. [6]This enormous population boom led to the youth culture of the 1960s. [7]And as the baby boomers continue to age, they will produce an "elder boom" which is expected to peak around 2025. [8]The second explanation for the aging of our society is increasing life expectancy. [9]Improvements in medicine and nutrition have resulted in people living longer than ever. [10]Newborns today can expect to live thirty years longer than those born in 1900. [11]The sharp and recent increase in the number of elderly people—here and around the world—supports the surprising fact that more than half of all the elderly people who have ever lived are alive today.

_____ 9. The main pattern of organization of the paragraph is
A. definition and example. C. comparison.
B. cause and effect. D. contrast.

10. One transition that signals the pattern of organization of this paragraph is _______________.

Name ______________________ Date __________

Section __________ SCORE: (Number correct) ______ x 10 = ______ %

RELATIONSHIPS II: Mastery Test 3

A. (1–4.) Arrange the scrambled sentences below into a logical paragraph by numbering them *1, 2, 3,* and *4* in an order that makes sense. Then, in the space provided, write the letter of the main pattern of organization used.

Note that transitions will help you by clarifying the relationships between sentences.

___ Or if you associate a certain group with a particular talent, you may be disappointed when a member of that group cannot do what you expect.

___ For instance, if you believe that a particular group is pushy, you will automatically judge someone who belongs to that group to be pushy—without waiting to see what that person is really like.

___ Stereotyping is holding a set of beliefs about the personal nature of a group of people.

___ It can greatly interfere with our making accurate judgments about others.

_____ 5. The main pattern of organization is
- A. contrast.
- B. comparison.
- C. cause and effect.
- D. definition and example.

B. Read each paragraph and answer the questions that follow.

[1]When life inflicts setbacks and tragedies on optimists, they weather those storms better than pessimists do. [2]Optimists look on the bright side. [3]After a setback, they pick up the pieces and start again. [4]On the other hand, pessimists give up and fall into depression. [5]With their ability to spring back, optimists achieve more at work and in school. [6]Optimists have better physical health and may even live longer. [7]However, even when things go well for pessimists, they are haunted by fears of catastrophe.

_____ 6. The selection mainly
- A. defines and illustrates the terms "optimist" and "pessimist."
- B. shows similarities between optimists and pessimists.
- C. shows differences between optimists and pessimists.
- D. explains the causes of optimism and pessimism.

7. One transition that signals the main pattern of organization of this paragraph is ______________________.

(Continues on next page)

8. Another transition that signals the main pattern of organization of this paragraph is ______________________________.

[1]Cults are religious movements that represent a new or different religious tradition, whereas churches and sects represent the prevailing tradition in a society. [2]From this point of view, all religions begin as cult movements. [3]Early on, today's great world faiths were most assuredly regarded as weird, crazy, foolish, and sinful; they were typically treated with hostility. [4]For example, Roman intellectuals in the first century laughed at the notion that a messiah and his tiny flock in Palestine, an obscure corner of the empire, posed a threat to the mighty pagan temples. [5]But from an obscure cult movement, Christianity arose. [6]Other established religions, including Islam and Buddhism, were once cults. [7]Today they inspire hundreds of millions of faithful followers.

_____ 9. The main pattern of organization of the paragraph is
A. cause and effect.
B. contrast.
C. comparison.
D. definition and example.

10. One transition that signals the pattern of organization of this paragraph is ______________________________.

Name ______________________________ Date __________

Section __________ SCORE: (Number correct) ______ x 10 = ______ %

RELATIONSHIPS II: Mastery Test 4

A. (1–4.) Arrange the scrambled sentences below into a logical paragraph by numbering them *1, 2, 3,* and *4* in an order that makes sense. Then, in the space provided, write the letter of the main pattern of organization used.

Note that transitions will help you by clarifying the relationships between sentences.

___ Also, by the ninth grade, one child in six will have tried marijuana, and one in three will have experimented with alcohol.

___ Last, and worst of all, is the fact that the suicide rate for young people under fifteen has tripled since 1960.

___ Because of peer pressure, some children begin smoking while they are still in grade school.

___ Stresses of the modern world severely affect today's children.

_____ 5. The paragraph lists
A. points of contrast.
B. points of comparison.
C. effects.
D. examples of a defined term.

B. Read each paragraph and answer the questions that follow.

[1]People often feel that domestic cats and their larger relatives, the jungle cats, are very different. [2]In reality, however, cats at home and cats in the wild have many traits in common. [3]Both have eyes suited for night vision, and both prefer to sleep by day and move about at night. [4]Also, just as pet cats use their tails to keep their balance and to signal emotions, so do lions and other large cats. [5]In addition, both kinds of cats can leap great distances. [6]Pet cats are often found on top of bookcases or refrigerators. [7]Similarly, the puma, the champion jumper of the cat family, has been known to jump twenty feet up and forty feet ahead. [8]Finally, little cats are not the only ones that purr; the cheetah, puma, and snow leopard all purr when content.

_____ 6. The main idea is expressed in the
A. first sentence.
B. second sentence.
C. third sentence.
D. last sentence.

(Continues on next page)

_____ 7. The selection mainly
A. defines and illustrates the term *cat*.
B. shows similarities between domestic cats and jungle cats.
C. contrasts domestic cats with jungle cats.
D. explains the effects of different environments on domestic and jungle cats.

8. One transition that signals the main pattern of organization of this paragraph is ______________________.

[1]Perhaps the deepest explanation for the anger so many Americans feel today has economic roots. [2]From the end of World War II through the late 1970s, the economy doubled in size—as did almost everyone's income. [3]Almost all Americans grew together. [4]In fact, those in the bottom fifth of the income ladder saw their incomes more than double. [5]Americans thus experienced upward mobility on a grand scale. [6]Yet for the last three and a half decades, the middle class has been losing ground. [7]The median wage of male workers, adjusted for inflation, is now lower than it was in 1980. [8]In addition, all the mechanisms we've used over the last three decades to minimize the effects of this descent—young mothers streaming into paid work in the late 1970s and 1980s, everyone working longer hours in the 1990s, and then borrowing against the rising values of our homes—are now exhausted. [9]And wages are still dropping; the median is now 4 percent below what it was at the start of the so-called recovery. [10]Meanwhile, income, wealth, and power have become more concentrated at the top than they've been in ninety years. [11]As a result, many have come to believe that the deck is stacked against them. [12]The government bailouts of Wall Street several years ago were, to many, a final piece of evidence that big government and big finance had plotted against the rest of us. [13]The last time Americans felt so angry may have been in the 1920s, another time when income, wealth, and power were similarly concentrated in the hands of a small, uncaring upper class.

_____ 9. The main pattern of organization of the selection is
A. definition and example.
B. cause and effect.
C. comparison.
D. contrast.

10. One transition that signals the main pattern of organization of this paragraph is ______________________.

Name ______________________________ Date __________

Section __________ SCORE: (Number correct) ______ x 10 = ______ %

RELATIONSHIPS II: Mastery Test 5

A. Read the textbook paragraph below. Then answer the question and complete the outline that follows.

[1]Instead of firing workers at times of hardship, some companies slice a few hours off everybody's workweek and pay. [2]Sharing work in this manner has positive effects on workers and the company. [3]Workers are less anxious about being unemployed and feel they are part of a community of people working together. [4]In addition, quality remains high because the company retains all of its experienced workers, rather than firing them to save money. [5]Consequently, because they are fully staffed, companies that have instituted work sharing are better equipped to meet increased demand when business recovers. [6]Also, when times get brighter, workers are more willing to put in long hours for a company that helped them through a tough spell.

_____ 1. The main organizational patterns of the paragraph are list of items and

A. definition and example.
B. cause and effect.
C. comparison.
D. contrast.

2–5. Complete the outline of the paragraph by writing in the four major supporting details.

Main idea: **Work sharing has positive effects on workers and the company.**

Major supporting details:

1. ______________________________

____

2. ______________________________

____

3. ______________________________

____

4. ______________________________

____

(Continues on next page)

B. Read the textbook paragraph below. Then answer the question and complete the map that follows.

[1]Why do people have differing needs for achievement? [2]One researcher found that the need for achievement is related to parental attitudes. [3]Parents who are high achievers themselves usually demand independence from their children. [4]The children must become self-reliant at a relatively early age. [5]As a result, the children develop a sense of confidence and find enjoyment in their own achievements. [6]On the other hand, parents who have low needs for achievement are more protective of their children. [7]They help their children perform everyday tasks, such as dressing and feeding, far more than necessary. [8]The consequence is that children are less independent and often have low achievement needs.

_____ 6. The paragraph

A. defines and illustrates *achievement.*

B. compares two types of parents and their effects.

C. contrasts two types of parents and their effects.

7–10. Complete the map of the paragraph by writing in the missing supporting details.

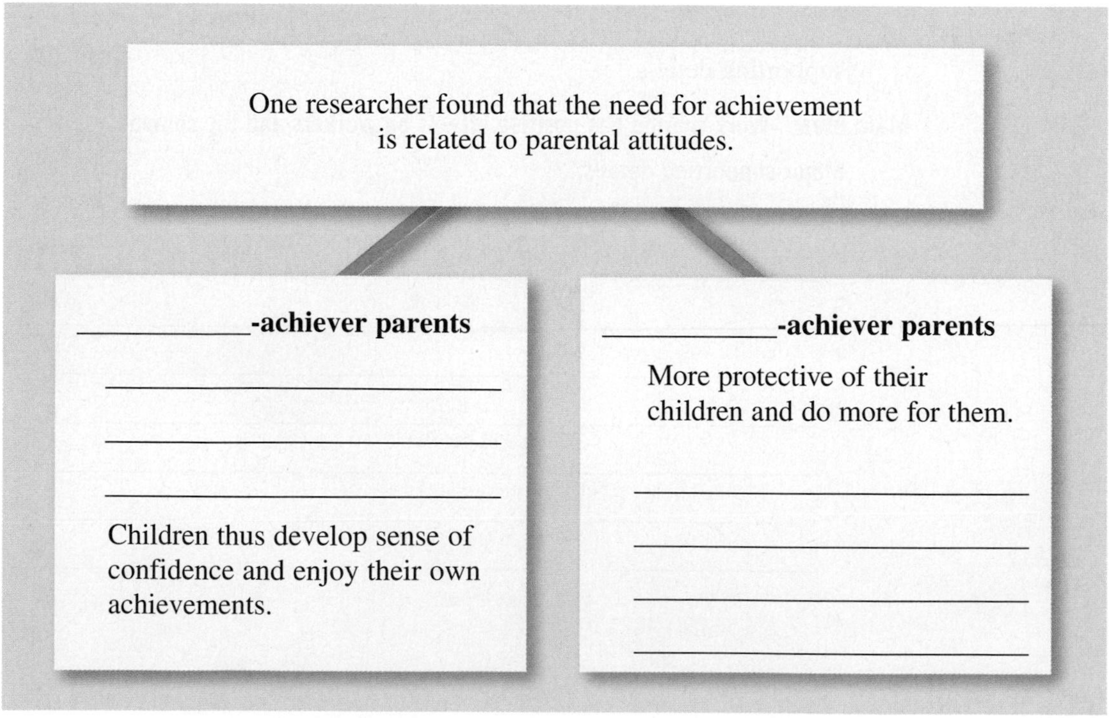

One researcher found that the need for achievement is related to parental attitudes.

___________-achiever parents

____

____

____

Children thus develop sense of confidence and enjoy their own achievements.

___________-achiever parents

More protective of their children and do more for them.

____

____

____

____

Name ______________________________ Date __________

Section __________ SCORE: (Number correct) ______ x 10 = ______ %

RELATIONSHIPS II: Mastery Test 6

A. Read the textbook paragraph below. Then answer the question and complete the outline that follows.

[1]Today's divorce rate is nearly 300 percent higher than it was forty years ago. [2]Why the increase? [3]One reason is that today there is greater social acceptance of divorce. [4]This increased tolerance has resulted from a relaxation of negative attitudes toward divorce among religious denominations. [5]Although divorce is still seen as unfortunate, it is no longer treated as a sin by most religious leaders. [6]An increase in family income has also led to the rise in divorce rates. [7]As couples acquire more wealth, they are more likely to be able to afford the cost of divorce proceedings. [8]Finally, as society provides greater opportunities for women, more and more wives are becoming less dependent on their husbands—both economically and emotionally. [9]Consequently, they are more likely to leave if their marriage seems hopeless.

______ 1. The organizational patterns of the paragraph are list of items and

A. definition and example.
B. comparison and/or contrast.
C. cause and effect.

2–5. Complete the outline of the paragraph by writing in the main idea and three major supporting details.

Main idea: ______________________________

____

1. ______________________________

____

2. ______________________________

____

3. ______________________________

____

(Continues on next page)

B. (6–10.) Read the textbook passage below. Then answer the question and complete the map that follows.

[1]Animal development usually proceeds down one of two quite different paths: indirect development or direct development. [2]In indirect development, the juvenile animal that hatches from the egg differs significantly from the adult, as a caterpillar differs from a butterfly. [3]Animals with indirect development typically produce huge numbers of eggs, and each egg has only a small amount of yolk. [4]The yolk nourishes each developing embryo during a rapid transformation into a small, sexually immature feeding stage called a larva. [5]Numerous larvae hatch.

[6]Other animals, including such diverse groups as reptiles, birds, mammals, and land snails, show direct development, in which the newborn animal, or juvenile, is a sexually immature, miniature version of the adult. [7]These juveniles are typically much larger than larvae, and consequently need much more nourishment before emerging into the world. [8]Two ways of providing such nourishment have evolved: large eggs containing large amounts of yolk (like an ostrich's egg, which weighs several pounds) or nourishing the developing embryo within the body of the mother. [9]Either way, providing food for directly developing embryos places great demands on the mother, and relatively few offspring are produced.

_____ 6. The organizational pattern of the passage is
A. comparison.
B. contrast.
C. cause and effect.

7–10. Complete the map of the passage by writing in the missing supporting details.

Animal development may be either indirect or direct.

______________ **development**

1. Juvenile differs greatly from the adult.
2. Nourishment is a small amount of yolk in a great many eggs.
3. Numerous larvae hatch.

______________ **development**

1. ______________________
____
____
2. Nourishment is either (1) large amounts of yolk or (2) within the mother's body.
3. ______________________
____

TO THE STUDENT

The pages that follow contain three mastery tests that offer additional practice in the skills covered in Chapters 5 and 6:

- Relationships that involve **addition**
- Relationships that involve **time**
- Relationships that involve **illustration**
- Relationships that involve **comparison and/or contrast**
- Relationships that involve **cause and effect**

For ease in reference, the lists of words that show these relationships have been reprinted on the next page.

Addition Words

one	to begin with	also	further
first (of all)	for one thing	in addition	furthermore
second(ly)	other	next	last (of all)
third(ly)	another	moreover	final(ly)

Time Words

before	immediately	when	until
previously	next	whenever	often
first (of all)	then	while	frequently
second (ly)	following	during	eventually
third (ly)	later	as (soon as)	final(ly)
now	after	by	last (of all)

Illustration Words

(for) example	including	(as an) illustration	one
(for) instance	specifically	to illustrate	once
such as	to be specific		

Comparison Words

(just) as	both	in like fashion	in a similar fashion
(just) like	equal(ly)	in like manner	in a similar manner
alike	resemble	similar(ly)	(in) the same way
same	likewise	similarity	(in) common

Contrast Words

but	instead (of)	even though	difference
yet	in contrast	as opposed to	different(ly)
however	on the other hand	in spite of	differ (from)
although	on the contrary	despite	unlike
nevertheless	converse(ly)	rather than	while
still	opposite		

Cause and Effect Words

therefore	so	owing to	because (of)
thus	(as a) result	effect	reason
(as a) consequence	results in	cause	explanation
consequently	leads to	if . . . then	accordingly
due to	since	affect	

Name ______________________________ Date __________

Section __________ SCORE: (Number correct) ______ x 10 = ______ %

RELATIONSHIPS I & II: Mastery Test 1

A. Fill in each blank with an appropriate transition from the box. Use each transition once. Then, in the spaces provided, write the letter of the transition you have chosen.

A. because	B. finally	C. for instance
D. later	E. unlike	

_____ 1. [1]If there is one product that American business can manufacture in large amounts, it is doublespeak. [2]*Doublespeak* is a term applied to the use of words that are evasive, vague, or stilted for the purpose of deceiving or confusing the reader or listener. [3]__________________, a company that decides to fire workers may talk of the need for "re-engineering," "restructuring," or "downsizing" its work force.

_____ 2. [1]Here are some pointers for reading without eyestrain. [2]First, whenever possible, read by natural light. [3]Second, avoid reading in a dark room with light on only your reading material. [4]Third, so that your page-turning hand doesn't cast a shadow across the text, position your reading light to your left if you are right-handed and to your right if you are left-handed. [5]__________________, hold your reading material fourteen to eighteen inches from your eyes.

_____ 3. [1]On average, we sleep one-third of our life. [2]Usually, the amount that we sleep decreases with age. [3]As newborns, we sleep up to 20 hours a day. [4]At age 4 or so, we sleep about 12 hours. [5]By the time we're 10, we sleep about 10 hours. [6]__________________, as adults, we sleep 7–9 hours. [7]Eventually, when we're elderly, we may sleep only 4–6 hours.

_____ 4. [1]Most animal expressions are based in falsehood. [2]Far from being "chicken," hens fiercely defend their chicks, and roosters bravely protect their flock. [3]Instead of sweating or eating "like a pig," pigs lack functional sweat glands and do not overeat. [4]In contrast to human "rats," rats loyally, tenderly, even selflessly assist companions in need. [5]And ______________ a human "wolf," actual wolves are faithful to one mate.

_____ 5. [1]Sunburn is skin damage caused by the sun's ultraviolet rays. [2](Ultraviolet rays do not penetrate glass; consequently, we cannot get sunburned from sunlight shining through a closed window.) [3]When ultraviolet rays destroy skin cells, an increased amount of blood flows to the area, bringing new cells and other repair materials. [4]The red of sunburn results from this increased blood flow. [5]Sunburn hurts __________________ nerve endings in the skin send pain signals in response to cell damage.

(Continues on next page)

B. Fill in each blank with an appropriate transition from the box. Use each transition once. Then, in the spaces provided, write the letter of the transition you have chosen.

A. after	B. instance	C. lastly
D. on the other hand	E. result	

_____ 6. [1]Struggling in quicksand creates a vacuum, which causes a person to sink. [2]But the human body is more buoyant in quicksand than it is in fresh or ocean water, meaning that it is actually easier to float on quicksand than it is in a pool or the ocean. [3]___________ falling into quicksand, a person should slowly spread-eagle and allow the body to gradually come to a back-floating position. [4]By moving cautiously in this position, the quicksand victim can then maneuver back to solid ground and out of danger.

_____ 7. [1]While it's strange but true, white wine is often made from red grapes. [2]In making wine, the grapes are crushed and placed in a large tank. [3]If the skins of the grapes remain in contact with the juice during this step, red wine results. [4]_________________, if the winemaker separates the skins from the juice, then white wine is made.

_____ 8. [1]The catch-and-release way of fishing doesn't really help the fish; in fact, it may _______________ in their death. [2]On a hook and line, fish struggle to breathe. [3]Because of overexertion and inadequate oxygen intake, many fish are brain-damaged, paralyzed, or in shock when released—often fatally. [4]In addition, netting and handling sometimes remove portions of a fish's thin outer skin, leaving it vulnerable to potentially deadly infection.

_____ 9. [1]Voluntary manslaughter is killing that would otherwise be murder, but that occurs after the victim has done something to the killer that would cause a reasonable person to lose self-control or act rashly. [2]In a classic _______________ of voluntary manslaughter, a person discovers his or her spouse with someone else, and that person kills the spouse's lover in a jealous rage. [3]Voluntary manslaughter is punished somewhat less severely than murder as a concession to the frailty of human character.

_____ 10. [1]Psychologist Abraham Maslow theorized that people are motivated by six basic needs which must be fulfilled in turn: three "deficiency" needs and three "growth" needs. [2]The deficiency needs are, first, food, water, and sleep; second, physical and mental stimulation; and third, safety and security. [3]Prompted by their growth needs, people reach outward for love, friendship, and a sense of belonging; seek other people's approval and respect; and, _______________, "self-actualize"—achieve self-fulfillment and realize their full creative potential.

Name ______________________________ Date __________

Section __________ SCORE: (Number correct) ______ x 10 = ______ %

RELATIONSHIPS I & II: Mastery Test 2

Read each selection and answer the questions that follow. Note that paragraphs D and E have **two** patterns of organization.

A. [1]An infomercial is a televised commercial message lasting approximately thirty minutes and used to sell a product by convincing viewers that they must have this product. [2]Kitchen products such as a food dehydrator and a juice extractor are successful goods shown on infomercials. [3]Other examples of products that have made it big on infomercials include a cleaning solution that promises to clean any household surface safely and inexpensively, and a similar product that claims it will shine and polish your car with next to no effort. [4]Infomercials can be very convincing, but viewers are wise to remember the Latin term *caveat emptor:* Let the buyer beware!

_____ 1. The main pattern of organization of the selection is
- A. list of items.
- B. comparison and/or contrast.
- C. definition and example.

2. One transition that signals the pattern of organization of this paragraph is ______________________________.

B. [1]Bats have some fascinating characteristics. [2]For one thing, they are the only mammals that truly fly. [3]Furthermore, they are the only animals that roost hanging upside down. [4]Insect-eating bats have astonishing hearing. [5]Some can hear individual insects walk or flutter their wings. [6]Most insect-eating bats use echo-location to catch insects at night: the bats emit squeaks (too high-pitched for us to hear) that bounce off insects and surrounding objects and echo back, enabling them to follow a moth's zigzag flight or distinguish, say, a mosquito from a gnat. [7]Bats are so adept at locating insects that a single bat may eat several thousand within one night.

_____ 3. The main pattern of organization of the selection is
- A. list of items.
- B. time order.
- C. comparison and/or contrast.

4. One transition that signals the pattern of organization of this paragraph is ______________________________.

C. [1]The flamingo obtains its food through an unusual method. [2]First, it stomps on the ground underwater, using its large webbed feet to churn up food, such as seeds, blue-green algae, and crustaceans, from the muddy bottom. [3]Next, it puts its head into the water so that its beak can collect the particles. [4]Then, using its spiny tongue as a pump, it draws the food past special finger-like projections inside its beak. [5]These projections, called lamellae, act as strainers to separate the bird's meal from the water before it swallows.

(Continues on next page)

_____ 5. The main pattern of organization of the selection is
A. definition and example.
B. time order.
C. comparison and/or contrast.

6. One transition that signals the pattern of organization of this paragraph is ______________________________.

D. [1]For hundreds of years, women were not allowed to sing in church or on the stage; consequently, young boys would sing the high parts. [2]Unfortunately, when the boys reached puberty, their voices would change. [3]By the 1700s, some enterprising Italians came up with a solution to preserve a boy's voice. [4]If the boy was castrated, then he could never go through puberty, and therefore his voice would never change. [5]It was said that these singers, known as the castrati, had voices that could make the angels in heaven cry. [6]Although the Church forbade castration, the voices of the castrati were highly prized at church services. [7]The golden age of this cruel custom began to fade during the 1800s, mostly because it became socially acceptable for women to sing professionally.

_____ 7. The main patterns of organization of the selection are time order and
A. list of items.
B. comparison and/or contrast.
C. cause and effect.

8. One transition that signals the pattern of organization you selected is ______________________________.

E. [1]Because they are similar in size, density, and location (second and third planets from the sun), Venus and Earth have been called "the twin planets." [2]In reality, the two planets radically differ. [3]Earth has climates ranging from subfreezing to tropical. [4]Venus, however, has only one surface temperature: 864ºF, hot enough to melt lead. [5]Nearly three-fourths of the Earth's surface is water. [6]In contrast, Venus has no surface water. [7]Unlike Earth, Venus has no magnetic field. [8]Earth's clouds are composed of water droplets and ice crystals, but Venus's clouds consist mainly of sulfuric acid. [9]Although Earth's atmosphere is primarily nitrogen (77%) and oxygen (21%), Venus's is overwhelmingly carbon dioxide (96%), with relatively small amounts of nitrogen (3.5%) and oxygen (less than 0.5%). [10]Perhaps the most important difference between the two planets is this: Venus is devoid of life.

_____ 9. The main patterns of organization of the selection are list of items and
A. cause and effect.
B. time order.
C. comparison and/or contrast.

10. One transition that signals the pattern of organization you selected is ______________________________.

Name ______________________ Date __________

Section __________ SCORE: (Number correct) ________ x 20 = ________ %

RELATIONSHIPS I & II: Mastery Test 3

Each of the following selections uses **two** patterns of organization. Read each selection and then, in the spaces provided, write the letter of the two patterns of organization.

A. [1]Dinosaurs did not become extinct—not all of them, that is. [2]Most scientists who study fossils now believe that some small, predatory dinosaurs called theropods evolved into birds. [3]In a number of striking ways, birds resemble their probable dinosaur ancestors. [4]Like theropods, birds have light, hollow bones (crucial to bird flight). [5]Theropod forelimbs could pivot similarly to bird wings. [6]Theropods stood erect on two feet, with their ankles held above the ground. [7]Birds stand the same way. [8]Also, theropods had four toes on each foot: three front toes pointing forward and one rear toe pointing backward. [9]So do many birds. [10]Claws are another shared feature. [11]In addition, like all other dinosaurs, theropods laid eggs. [12]Some even had feathers.

_____ 1. The main patterns of organization of the selection are
- A. definition-example and cause-effect.
- B. cause-effect and list of items.
- C. comparison and list of items.

B. [1]Your home is "private territory"—space used by an individual or group for an extended period of time. [2]Your "secondary territory" is any space (such as a classroom) that you use regularly but share with others. [3]Finally, "public territory" is space that is not owned by anyone, but claimed on a first-come, first-served basis. [4]A seat in a waiting room is an example of public territory.

_____ 2. The main patterns of organization of the selection are
- A. definition-example and list of items.
- B. definition-example and cause-effect.
- C. time order and comparison.

C. [1]The aging of our population will have far-reaching implications for what life will be like in the years to come. [2]For one thing, society will need to provide many support services to the frail elderly, because many of them will have outlived their savings and will not be able to pay for their own care. [3]Moreover, as the over-65 population becomes more influential at the polls and in the marketplace, we're likely to see changes in governmental programs, in television programming, in new products, in housing patterns, in population shifts from state to state, and so forth. [4]The effects of this change are virtually infinite.

(Continues on next page)

_____ 3. The main patterns of organization of the selection are
A. definition-example and time order.
B. comparison and time order.
C. list of items and cause-effect.

D. [1]George Washington's famous crossing of the Delaware River on Christmas morning might never have happened if not for John Honeyman, an American spy working in Trenton. [2]In a clever plan he devised with Washington, Honeyman first faked being captured and interrogated by the Americans. [3]Washington then arranged for Honeyman to escape. [4]After returning to Trenton, Honeyman entertained his friends in the British military command with his tale of capture and escape. [5]He told them that he was able to escape only because the American army was weak and undisciplined, and that they wouldn't be able to attack Trenton until spring, if ever. [6]Thus, Washington caught the enemy sleeping off their Christmas Eve celebration, and the result was an important victory.

_____ 4. The main patterns of organization of the selection are
A. definition-example and cause-effect.
B. time order and cause-effect.
C. comparison and list of items.

E. [1]In the book *He Says, She Says,* Lillian Glass shows that, in general, men and women communicate differently. [2]They differ in their body language, facial expressions, displayed emotions, language, and favored topics of conversation. [3]While men gesture away from their bodies and often sit with outstretched limbs, women gesture toward their bodies and usually sit with their arms and legs held close. [4]Men lean back when listening, but women lean forward. [5]While listening, women tend to smile and nod. [6]In contrast, men tend to frown and squint. [7]Women laugh and cry more than men. [8]On the other hand, men shout and curse more than women. [9]Less polite than women, men are more inclined to mumble and interrupt. [10]Women offer more compliments and apologies. [11]Women's speech is more formal and correct than men's, containing less slang and less faulty grammar. [12]Men especially like to joke, talk about their activities, and discuss sports. [13]Women, however, prefer to talk about their feelings and discuss relationships.

_____ 5. The main patterns of organization of the selection are
A. list of items and comparison.
B. time order and contrast.
C. list of items and contrast.

7 Inferences

You have probably heard the expression "to read between the lines." When you "read between the lines," you pick up ideas that are not directly stated in what you are reading. These implied ideas are often important for a full understanding of what an author means. Discovering the ideas in writing that are not stated directly is called **making inferences**, or **drawing conclusions**.

Look at the cartoon below. What inferences can you make about it? Check (✓) the **two** inferences that are most logically based on the information suggested by the cartoon.

___ A. The man was probably working on a home improvement or repair project.

___ B. The man deliberately ruined the woman's pan.

___ C. The woman is upset that the man has used her pan as a hammer.

___ D. The man realizes that the woman is angry at him for using her good pan as a hammer.

Explanation

A. *The man was probably working on a home improvement or repair project.*

Since the man was using a kitchen pan as a hammer, he must be somewhere where there is a kitchen—most likely his and the woman's home. You should have checked this item.

B. *The man deliberately ruined the woman's pan.*

The man's explanation—that he couldn't find his hammer—suggests that he simply needed something to hammer with. While a valuable cooking utensil is not the most intelligent choice, nothing in his response suggests that he intentionally ruined the pan. You should not have checked this item.

C. *The woman is upset that the man has used her pan as a hammer.*

The woman's comment—"I'd like to hammer something"—strongly suggests that she is angry and needs to let out her anger, quite possibly by hammering the person who ruined her good pan. You should have checked this item.

D. *The man realizes that the woman is angry at him for using her good pan as a hammer.*

Nothing in the man's body language or words indicates that he realizes the woman is angry at him. (The fact that he used the pan for a hammer in the first place is a strong indication that he had no idea how she would react.) You should not have checked this item.

Inferences in Reading

In reading, we make logical leaps from information given in a straightforward way to ideas that are not stated directly. As one scholar has said, inferences are "statements about the unknown made on the basis of the known." To make inferences and draw conclusions, we use all the clues provided by the writer, our own experience, and logic.

You have already practiced making inferences in this book. Do you remember the following sentence from "Vocabulary in Context" on page 17?

> The homecoming celebration was *raucous*, with people wildly shouting and cheering, blowing whistles, and pounding on drums.

That sentence does not tell us the meaning of *raucous*, but it does suggest that a raucous celebration involves shouting, cheering, and similar loud noises. So you can infer from this sentence that *raucous* probably means "noisy," and you'd be correct.

You also made inferences in the chapter on implied main ideas. Implied ideas are ones that are not stated directly. Instead, you must infer them from the supporting details.

Check Your Understanding 1

Read the following passage and check (✓) the **two** inferences that are most firmly based on the information given. Then read the explanation that follows.

[1]Jim Johnson panicked when he came home from work to find his neighbor's pet rabbit dead and in the jaws of his German shepherd, Fido. [2]Johnson took the filthy, slightly chewed-up bunny into his house, washed it with care, and then used the blow dryer to restore its fur as best he could. [3]A short time later he secretly put the rabbit back into its outdoor cage.

[4]The next day, Jim's neighbor stopped him as they were both doing yard work. [5]"Did you hear that Thumper died?"

[6]"Uh, no," stammered Johnson.

[7]"We went out a couple days ago and found him dead. [8]What's really weird, though, is that the day after we buried him, we went outside and discovered that someone had dug him up, given him a bath, styled his fur, and put him back into his cage!"

___ 1. Johnson's neighbor had children who took care of the rabbit.

___ 2. Fido had probably dug up the rabbit's grave.

___ 3. The neighbor was convinced Johnson had dug up the rabbit.

___ 4. Jim Johnson assumed his dog had killed the rabbit.

___ 5. The rabbit had been very sick.

Explanation

1. There is no mention of Johnson's children. You should not have checked this item.
2. Since the rabbit had been buried, it is logical to infer that the only way Fido could have gotten it was to dig it up. You should have checked this item.
3. The neighbor, in a matter-of-fact way, told Johnson the story of what happened to Thumper. This suggests he did not suspect Johnson had anything to do with it. You should not have checked this item.
4. Johnson's efforts to cover up what happened to Thumper imply that he believed his dog had killed it. You should have checked this item.
5. There is no suggestion that the rabbit had been sick before the neighbor had found it dead in its cage. You should not have checked this item.

Check Your Understanding 2

Read the following passage and check (✓) the **three** inferences that can most logically be drawn from it. Then read the explanation that follows.

> [1]Early one morning, a man was walking along a sandy, deserted beach. [2]At least he thought it was deserted. [3]As he gazed ahead of him, he noticed that there was another human figure in sight. [4]It was a boy who kept bending down, picking something up, and throwing it into the sea. [5]He repeated the movement again and again and again.
>
> [6]As the man drew near, he saw that the sand surrounding the boy was covered with starfish that had been washed in by the waves. [7]It was these stranded starfish that the boy was throwing into the water.
>
> [8]"Why are you doing that?" the man asked.
>
> [9]Not pausing, the boy replied, "The tide is going out, and the sun is rising. [10]Soon the heat will be too much for the starfish, and they will die."
>
> [11]The man shook his head tolerantly. [12]"My dear boy," he said. [13]"There are miles of beach and hundreds, maybe thousands of starfish. [14]You can't save them all. [15]What you're doing can't make a difference!"
>
> [16]The boy listened politely, then picked up the next starfish and threw it in the water. [17]"It makes a difference for this one," he answered.

___ 1. The boy knows he cannot save all the starfish.

___ 2. The man believes that the boy's efforts are admirable.

___ 3. Many starfish will die despite the boy's efforts.

___ 4. Starfish are very close to extinction.

___ 5. The man decides to help save some of the stranded starfish.

___ 6. The boy believes that a little help is better than nothing.

Explanation

1. This is a logical inference. The boy doesn't show any surprise when the man tells him he can't save all the starfish. Also, the boy's obvious understanding of the shore cycles makes it clear he knew how few starfish he could save. He indicates he still wants to save the ones he can.
2. This is not a logical inference. The man is "tolerant" of what the boy is doing, but he suggests that the boy's actions are pointless.
3. This is a logical inference. As the man points out, there are perhaps thousands of starfish on the beach. The boy cannot save them all.

4. This is not a logical inference. Nothing in the passage suggests that starfish are near extinction.
5. This is not a logical inference. The man does not indicate that he will help save the starfish.
6. This is a logical inference. The boy's efforts to save as many starfish as he can indicate that he does believe a little help is better than none.

Guidelines for Making Inferences in Reading

The exercises in this chapter provide practice in making careful inferences when you read. Here are three guidelines for that process:

1 **Never lose sight of the available information.** As much as possible, base your inferences on the facts. For instance, in the passage about the starfish, we are told that the man questions the boy's efforts, even shaking his head in apparent disapproval. On the basis of those facts, we would not conclude that he sees the boy's efforts as admirable.

It's also important to note when a conclusion lacks support. For instance, the statement that starfish are very close to extinction has no support in the passage. We can infer only that many will die.

2 **Use your background information and experience to help you in making inferences.** For instance, your sense of how much distance there is in a mile helps you conclude that the boy cannot possibly save all the starfish stranded on miles of beach.

The more you know about a subject, the better your inferences are likely to be. So keep in mind that if your background in an area is weak, your inferences may be shaky. If you have a rash and fever, a doctor's inferences about the cause are likely to be more helpful than your inferences.

3 **Consider the alternatives.** Don't simply accept the first inference that comes to mind. Instead, consider all of the facts of a case and all the possible explanations. For example, the doctor analyzing your rash and fever may first think of and then eliminate several possibilities before coming to the right conclusion.

PRACTICE 1

Read the following passages. Then, in the space provided, write the letter of the most logical answer to each question, based on the information given in the passage.

A. [1]If you're a man, at some point a woman will ask you how she looks.

[2]"How do I look?" she'll ask.

[3]You must be careful how you answer this question. [4]The best technique is to form an honest yet sensitive opinion, then collapse on the floor with some kind of fatal seizure. [5]Trust me, this is the easiest way out. [6]Because you will never come up with the right answer.

[7]The problem is that women generally do not think of their looks in the same way that men do. [8]Most men form an opinion of how they look in seventh grade, and they stick to it for the rest of their lives. [9]Some men form the opinion that they are irresistible stud muffins, and they do not change this opinion even when their faces sag and their noses bloat to the size of eggplants and their eyebrows grow together to form what appears to be a giant forehead-dwelling tropical caterpillar.

[10]Women do not look at themselves this way. [11]If I had to express, in three words, what I believe most women think about their appearance, those words would be: "not good enough." [12]No matter how attractive a woman may appear to be to others, when she looks at herself in the mirror, she thinks: woof. [13]She thinks that at any moment a municipal animal-control officer is going to throw a net over her and haul her off to the shelter.

_____ 1. The author (the well-known humorist Dave Barry) suggests that some men
- A. have an unrealistic view of their looks.
- B. don't care about women's looks.
- C. tend to think they look worse than they really do.

_____ 2. The author suggests that women
- A. don't like the way many men look.
- B. are never satisfied with their own looks.
- C. have worse judgment than men.

_____ 3. The author implies that
- A. most men are dishonest with women.
- B. most women, in fact, do not look good enough.
- C. no matter how a man answers a woman's question "How do I look?" she will be unhappy.

_____ 4. We can conclude that the author
- A. is only telling jokes.
- B. is taking something he has observed in real life and exaggerating it.
- C. actually feels that his own looks are "not good enough."

D. [1]Not unlike drugs or alcohol, the television experience allows the participant to blot out the real world and enter into a pleasurable and passive mental state. [2]The worries and anxieties of reality are as effectively put off by becoming absorbed in a television program as by going on a "trip" caused by drugs or alcohol. [3]And just as alcoholics are only imperfectly aware of their addiction, feeling that they control their drinking more than they really do ("I can cut it out any time I want—I just like to have three or four drinks before dinner"), people similarly overestimate their control over television watching. [4]Even as they put off other activities to spend hour after hour watching television, they feel they could easily resume living in a different, less passive style. [5]But somehow or other while the television set is present in their homes, the click doesn't sound. [6]With television pleasures available, those other experiences seem less attractive, more difficult somehow.

[7]A heavy viewer (a college English instructor) observes: "I find television almost irresistible. [8]When the set is on, I cannot ignore it. [9]I can't turn it off. [10]I feel sapped, will-less, weakened. [11]As I reach out to turn off the set, the strength goes out of my arms. [12]So I sit there for hours and hours."

_____ 5. The author (Marie Winn, in her book *The Plug-In Drug: Television, Children and Family*) compares being wrapped up in TV to
- A. the real world.
- B. a drug or alcohol "trip."
- C. more lively activities.

_____ 6. The author thus implies that watching television is
- A. addictive.
- B. easy to control.
- C. not pleasurable.

_____ 7. From the passage we can conclude that the author feels television
- A. is never really interesting.
- B. usually helps us face our problems.
- C. generally takes the place of more worthwhile activities.

_____ 8. From the passage we can conclude that educators
- A. are less likely to be TV addicts.
- B. can be TV addicts.
- C. are more likely to be TV addicts.

C. [1]Following the Civil War, the American pattern of food production and consumption changed dramatically as industrial development brought rural residents to cities, which depended on food from distant sources. [2]As American industry and cities grew, more and more people relied upon the foods produced and preserved by fewer and fewer people. [3]Instead of growing it in their backyards, urban folk got their food from stores. [4]Fewer women spent their days preparing meals "from scratch." [5]Instead, they got jobs and became increasingly dependent on canned and packaged convenience foods from the local market. [6]Today, 92 percent of Americans rely on foods grown and processed by others. [7]Even the remaining 8 percent who are still "down on the farm" don't really feed themselves. [8]They get most of their food from farms and factories hundreds or thousands of miles away. [9]Instead of making a daily trip to the local general store and greengrocer, most Americans shop for food once a week. [10]The food they buy may have left the factory weeks or months earlier, the farm even longer ago than that.

_____ 9. We can conclude that before industrial development, many people
A. got their food from distant sources.
B. grew much of their own food.
C. had very little to eat.

_____ 10. The author suggests that because of industrial development, Americans
A. cook more.
B. buy less food.
C. eat food that's less fresh.

_____ 11. We can infer that American industrial development
A. led to a large food industry.
B. caused cities to shrink.
C. will mean the total disappearance of farms.

_____ 12. We can infer that the "8 percent who are still 'down on the farm' "
A. specialize by growing only one or a few crops.
B. grow a great variety of foods.
C. will soon move to the city.

PRACTICE 2

Read the following textbook passages. Then put a check (✓) by the **three** inferences that are most logically based on the given facts in each passage.

A. Here is an excerpt from an article printed in a women's magazine in the 1950s:

[1]Have dinner ready. [2]Plan ahead, even the night before, to have a delicious meal ready, on time for his return. . . .

[3]Prepare yourself. [4]Take fifteen minutes to rest so you'll be refreshed when he arrives. [5]Touch up your make-up, put a ribbon in your hair, and be fresh-looking. . . . [6]Be a little more interesting for him. [7]His boring day may need a lift, and one of your duties is to provide it. . . . [8]After all, catering for his comfort will provide you with immense personal satisfaction. . . .

[9]Listen to him. [10]You may have a dozen important things to tell him, but the moment of his arrival is not the time. [11]Let him talk first. [12]Remember, his topics of conversation are more important than yours. [13]Make the evening his. . . .

[14]Speak in a low, soothing, and pleasant voice. [15]Don't ask him questions about his actions or question his judgment or integrity. [16]Remember, he is the master of the house and as such will always exercise his will with fairness and truthfulness. [17]You have no right to question him.

[18]A good wife always knows her place.

___ 1. We can infer that the author of the 1950s passage believes a good wife dedicates herself to her husband's comfort and happiness.

___ 2. The author of the 1950s passage suggests that a good wife is intelligent and able to contribute to the family income.

___ 3. The author of the 1950s passage implies that a wife should speak up when her husband's judgment is questionable.

___ 4. The author of the 1950s passage implies that wives should be refreshed and attractive when their husbands return home from work.

___ 5. The author of the 1950s passage suggests that husbands prefer an obedient wife to an intelligent one.

___ 6. After reading the passage, we can conclude that views of the role of a married woman have not changed very much since the 1950s.

B. [1]Cholera is a severe, often fatal disease of the gastrointestinal system. [2]It is caused by bacteria, but before this cause was discovered, cholera epidemics often led to "blaming the victim." [3]During the epidemic of 1813, for example, Americans blamed those who fell ill, describing them as dirty, immoral, drunken, and lazy, and assumed that the disease was a punishment for low character. [4]Some time later, a doctor, John Snow, noticed that in London, victims of cholera were all getting their water from the same system; no one using another water system got sick. [5]Snow concluded, correctly, that the disease was being spread by bad water; but when the next epidemic broke out in America, in 1849, people paid no attention to his idea. [6]When the rich fled to the countryside, where the water was pure, this was taken as proof that clean, virtuous people did not get cholera. [7]In 1862 there was another epidemic, and by then enlightened people were beginning to think about Snow's discovery, but they had little power and little effect. [8]Not until the 1890s, when physicians accepted the germ theory of disease and the first public health laws were passed, would cholera epidemics end in the United States.

___ 1. Most people who fell ill with cholera were in fact dirty, immoral, lazy, and drunken.

___ 2. In the case of cholera, "blaming the victim" was at least partly due to ignorance of how the disease is caused and spread.

___ 3. During the epidemic of 1849, rich people fled to the countryside precisely because they knew the water there was pure.

___ 4. When the germ theory of disease was first proposed, people probably found it hard to believe that something they couldn't see could harm them.

___ 5. Some of the public health laws mentioned in the final sentence may have dealt with ensuring a safe water supply.

___ 6. Today, cholera has been wiped out worldwide.

C. [1]More than two hundred experiments reveal that, contrary to the old proverb about familiarity breeding contempt, familiarity breeds fondness. [2]Mere repeated exposure to all sorts of novel stimuli—nonsense syllables, Chinese characters, musical selections, faces—boosts people's ratings of them. [3]Do the supposed Turkish words *nansoma, saricik,* and *afworbu* mean something better or something worse than the words *iktitaf, biwojni,* and *kadirga*? [4]A researcher found that University of Michigan students preferred whichever of these words they had seen most frequently. [5]Among the letters of the alphabet, people of differing nationalities, languages, and ages prefer the letters appearing in their own name and those that frequently appear in their own language. [6]French students rate capital W, the least frequent letter in French, as their least favorite letter.

[7]Many residents of Grand Rapids, Michigan, were not pleased when presented with their new downtown landmark, a huge metal sculpture created by the artist Alexander Calder. [8]Their reaction? [9]"An abomination," "an embarrassment," "a waste of money." [10]Other people were neutral; few seemed enthusiastic. [11]But within a decade, the sculpture had become an object of civic pride: Its picture adorned bank checks, city posters, and tourist literature. [12]When completed in 1889, the Eiffel Tower in Paris was mocked as grotesque. [13]Today it is the beloved symbol of Paris.

___ 1. Young artists with new ideas are likely to appeal to more people than older artists whose work has been around for many years.

___ 2. University of Michigan students probably preferred Chinese characters to Turkish words.

___ 3. Americans probably tend to prefer the letter *S* to the letter *Y*.

___ 4. Familiarity influences people's taste in art and architecture.

___ 5. We always like someone or something we are familiar with.

___ 6. We may dislike something new just because it's unfamiliar.

Inferences in Literature

Inferences are very important in reading literature. While writers of factual material usually state directly much of what they mean, creative writers often provide verbal pictures that *show* us what they mean. It is up to the reader to infer the point of what the creative writer has said. For instance, a nonfiction writer might write the following:

> The little boy was in a stubborn mood.

But the novelist might write:

> When Todd's mother asked him to stop playing in the yard and come indoors, he didn't even look up but shouted "No!" and then spelled it out, "N . . . O!"

Rather than merely stating that Todd was stubborn, the author *shows* the stubbornness with specific details. To get the most out of literature, you must often infer meanings—just as you do in everyday life.

Now look at the following statement that a nonfiction writer might produce:

> The more English I learned in school, the more separation I felt from my parents.

Compare the above line with the following excerpt from *Hunger of Memory*, a literary autobiography by Richard Rodriguez.

> [1]Matching the silence I started hearing in public was a new quiet at home. [2]The family's quiet was partly due to the fact that, as we children learned more and more English, we shared fewer and fewer words with our parents. [3]Sentences needed to be spoken slowly when a child addressed his mother or father. [4](Often the parent wouldn't understand.) [5]The child would need to repeat himself. [6](Still the parent misunderstood.) [7]The young voice, frustrated, would end up saying, "Never mind"—the subject was closed. [8]Dinners would be noisy with the clinking of knives and forks against dishes. [9]My mother would smile softly between her remarks; my father at the other end of the table would chew and chew his food, while he stared over the heads of his children.
>
> [10]My mother! [11]My father! [12]After English became my primary language, I no longer knew what words to use in addressing my parents. [13]The old Spanish words (those tender accents of sound) I had used earlier—*mamá* and *papá*—I couldn't use anymore. [14]They would have been too painful reminders of how much had changed in my life. [15]On the other hand, the words I heard neighborhood kids call their parents seemed equally unsatisfactory. [16]Mother and Father; Ma, Papa, Pa, Dad, Pop (how I hated the all-American sound of that last word especially)—all those terms I felt were unsuitable, not really terms of address for my parents. [17]As a result, I never used them at home. [18]Whenever I'd speak to my parents, I would try to get their attention with eye contact alone. [19]In public conversations, I'd refer to "my parents" or "my mother and father."

Check Your Understanding

See if you can answer the following inference questions about the excerpt.

_____ 1. From the passage we can infer that
A. the Rodriguez children had never gotten along well with their parents.
B. Rodriguez's father was very strict.
C. Rodriguez's parents were not learning much English.

_____ 2. The passage suggests that
A. the children's learning more English upset their relationship with their parents.
B. the parents were not willing to have their home life disrupted to ensure that their children would fit in with mainstream America.
C. the children were having problems in school.

_____ 3. We can conclude that Rodriguez's father stared over the heads of his children at the dinner table because he
A. preferred not to speak while eating.
B. felt alienated from his children.
C. believed his children should not be speaking English.

_____ 4. The passage suggests that Rodriguez
A. harbored a hatred of America.
B. felt inferior to the other children in his neighborhood.
C. felt some loyalty to the language and culture of his parents.

_____ 5. The passage suggests that Rodriguez's parents
A. were angry and resentful when their children spoke English.
B. patiently accepted their children's new language.
C. were not interested in their children's well-being.

Explanation

1. Rodriguez says that although he and his siblings spoke English slowly to their parents, their parents often did not understand them. This suggests that their parents did not know much English. The correct answer is C.
2. The passage shows that Rodriguez and his parents communicated less as the language gap between them grew. Instead of talking together over dinner, family members ate in silence, unable to share their thoughts. This is evidence that the relationship between parents and children was becoming difficult. Therefore, A is the correct answer.

3. Even if the author's father preferred not to speak while eating, he wouldn't have had to look over his children's heads. That he did so suggests he recognized that he could not interact with his children and thus felt distant, or alienated, from them. So answer A is wrong, and the correct answer is B. Answer C is wrong because there is nothing in the passage showing Rodriguez's father opposing his children going to an English-speaking school.
4. Rodriguez makes no negative comment about America, so answer A is incorrect. Also, he refers to "neighborhood kids" without revealing any sense of being intimidated by them, making answer B incorrect as well. Rodriguez's mention of the "tender accents of sound" of the Spanish words for "mother" and "father" shows he still has emotional ties to his parents' language.
5. At the dining table, Rodriguez's parents cannot understand much of what their children are saying. But Rodriguez says that his mother would "smile softly" and that his father would merely eat in silence. His parents' actions suggest, then, that they are patiently enduring the language changeover. The right answer, then, is B.

The excerpt from *Hunger of Memory* is a small example of how inference skills can increase your appreciation of literary forms—fiction, poetry, autobiography, and other imaginative literature.

Poetry, especially, by its nature, implies much of its meaning. Poets often imply their meanings through comparisons. For example, read the following well-known poem by Carl Sandburg:

The fog comes
on little cat feet.

It sits looking
over harbor and city
on silent haunches
and then moves on.

Here, Sandburg uses a figure of speech known as a metaphor, comparing fog to a cat that makes a sudden, silent, almost mysterious appearance. (More information about metaphors appears on page 295.)

A Note on Figures of Speech

Creative writers often use comparisons known as **figures of speech** to imply their meanings and give us a fresh and more informed way of looking at something. The two most common figures of speech are similes and metaphors.

Simile—a stated comparison, introduced with *like, as,* or *as if.*

"The boss was really angry about the suggestion I made. He chewed me out! I feel like a piece of old bubble gum."

In the cartoon, the man says that because the boss chewed him out, he feels "like a piece of old bubble gum." The simile clearly shows that the man's feelings have been hurt.

Here is another example. Instead of saying, "My stepfather shouted at me," you could express it vividly by saying, "When my stepfather shouted at me, it was like a fist in my face." The simile shows that the stepfather's shout was shocking, violent, and painful. It gives us much more information than the line that simply tells us that the stepfather shouted.

Following are some other similes:

- Many of the players on the football team have arms *as big as tree trunks.*
- In the recently planted garden, I saw tomato plants starting to come out of the ground, curled up *like a hand unfolding.*
- I loved my mother, but she was about *as huggable as a cactus.*

- After I lost my job, my material possessions soon disappeared *like so much dandelion fluff in a wind.*
- When my new boyfriend arrived, my parents stared at him *as if he were a cockroach that had just crawled under the door.*

Metaphor—an implied comparison, with *like, as,* or *as if* omitted.

In this cartoon, the boy, Linus, is using a metaphor when he says that big sisters are "the crab grass in the lawn of life." He means that big sisters (like his own sister, Lucy, who just insulted his cartoon) spoil things and are a nuisance.

In another example, the thought "Life is a struggle" was memorably expressed in metaphor by the ancient writer Plotinus, who wrote: "Be kind, for everyone you meet is fighting a hard battle." His comparison says that even though we may not be aware of it, everyone we meet is dealing with difficulties, just as we are.

Here are some other metaphors:

- From the airplane, I looked down on Manhattan, *an anthill of frantic life.*
- Looking westward, I saw an *army of dark clouds* massed on the horizon.
- Our boss is always a *bear* on Monday morning.
- None of the players on the demoralized football team were strong enough to withstand *the gale-force winds* of the coach's personality.
- My aunt's home was a *pack rat's nest* of everything she had collected during her life.

PRACTICE 3

Use a check (✓) to identify each figure of speech as a simile or a metaphor. Then, in the space provided, answer each inference question that follows.

_____ 1. The head of that corporation needs money as much as a bat needs sunglasses.

___ simile ___ metaphor

You can infer that the head of the corporation
A. is bankrupt.
B. always has been wealthy.
C. doesn't need any more money.

_____ 2. When I emerged from the air-conditioned building, the air hit me in the face like a steaming washcloth.

___ simile ___ metaphor

You can infer that the air outside was
A. cool and dry.
B. hot and humid.
C. hot and dry.

_____ 3. Marlo and Scott's relationship was first a race car, then a stalled sedan, and finally scrap metal.

___ simile ___ metaphor

You can infer that Marlo and Scott's relationship
A. started out strong but fell apart.
B. slowly grew to a strong and lasting one.
C. had a rapid start and an equally rapid end.

_____ 4. My job interview went as smoothly as a drive down a street filled with potholes.

___ simile ___ metaphor

You can infer that the interview went
A. extremely well.
B. fairly well.
C. poorly.

_____ 5 There was nothing uncertain about the voice inside that told me what to do. It spoke with the clearness and certainty of church bells heard on bright Sundays.

___ simile ___ metaphor

You can infer that the author

A. could not make up his mind.

B. felt very sure about what the voice was telling him to do.

C. experienced a moment of insanity.

PRACTICE 4

Following is a short story written by Langston Hughes, a poet and fiction writer who emerged as a major literary figure during the Harlem Renaissance of the 1920s. Read the story, and then write the letter of the most logical answer to each question, based on the information given in the story.

Early Autumn

[1]When Bill was very young, they had been in love. [2]Many nights they had spent walking, talking together. [3]Then something not very important had come between them, and they didn't speak. [4]Impulsively, she had married a man she thought she loved. [5]Bill went away, bitter about women.

[6]Yesterday, walking across Washington Square, she saw him for the first time in years.

[7]"Bill Walker," she said.

[8]He stopped. [9]At first he did not recognize her; to him she looked so old.

[10]"Mary! Where did you come from?"

[11]Unconsciously, she lifted her face as though wanting a kiss, but he held out his hand. [12]She took it.

[13]"I live in New York now," she said.

[14]"Oh"—smiling politely. [15]Then a little frown came quickly between his eyes.

[16]"Always wondered what happened to you, Bill."

[17]"I'm a lawyer. Nice firm, way downtown."

[18]"Married yet?"

[19]"Sure. Two kids."

[20]"Oh," she said.

[21]A great many people went past them through the park. [22]People they didn't know. [23]It was late afternoon. [24]Nearly sunset. [25]Cold.

[26]"And your husband?" he asked her.

[27]"We have three children. [28]I work in the bursar's office at Columbia."

[29]"You're looking very . . . " (he wanted to say old) ". . . well," he said.

[30]She understood. [31]Under the trees in Washington Square, she found herself desperately reaching back into the past. [32]She had been older than he then in Ohio. [33]Now she was not young at all. [34]Bill was still young.

[35]"We live on Central Park West," she said. [36]"Come and see us sometime."

[37]"Sure," he replied. [38]"You and your husband must have dinner with my family some night. [39]Any night. [40]Lucille and I'd love to have you."

[41]The leaves fell slowly from the trees in the Square. [42]Fell without wind. [43]Autumn dusk. [44]She felt a little sick.

[45]"We'd love it," she answered.

[46]"You ought to see my kids." [47]He grinned.

[48]Suddenly the lights came on up the whole length of Fifth Avenue, chains of misty brilliance in the blue air.

[49]"There's my bus," she said.

[50]He held out his hand. [51]"Good-by."

[52]"When . . . " she wanted to say, but the bus was ready to pull off. [53]The lights on the avenue blurred, twinkled, blurred. [54]And she was afraid to open her mouth as she entered the bus. [55]Afraid it would be impossible to utter a word.

[56]Suddenly she shrieked very loudly, "Good-by!" [57]But the bus door had closed.

[58]The bus started. [59]People came between them outside, people crossing the street, people they didn't know. [60]Space and people. [61]She lost sight of Bill. [62]Then she remembered she had forgotten to give him her address—or ask him for his—or tell him that her youngest boy was named Bill, too.

_____ 1. Authors of fiction often choose settings that symbolically reflect their story. In this case, the characters' stage of life is echoed in the author's choices of

A. city and park.

B. season and time of day.

C. transportation and temperature.

_____ 2. Hughes portrayed the awkwardness of the meeting by indicating a contrast between
A. the woman's and Bill's jobs.
B. New York City and Ohio.
C. what Bill said and what he meant.

_____ 3. The suggestion that Bill was still young but the woman was not implies that
A. she was actually many, many years older than he.
B. her life has aged her more rapidly than his life has aged him.
C. he was an exercise buff who had taken especially good care of himself.

_____ 4. The story suggests that Bill
A. did not regret having married someone else.
B. plans on inviting the woman and her husband over for dinner.
C. still wished nothing had come between him and the woman when they were young.

_____ 5. The last few words of the story suggest that
A. the boy was really Bill's son.
B. the woman regretted naming her youngest son Bill.
C. the woman had thought of Bill with so much longing that she named a son after him.

Inferences in Graphs and Tables

You have already tried your hand at making inferences from a picture, the cartoon of the man who used a good pan as a hammer. Many of the cartoons in newspapers and magazines depend on your inference skills. Other "pictures" that require inferences are tables and graphs, which combine words with visual representations. Authors of textbooks, professional and newspaper articles, and other materials often organize large amounts of material into tables and graphs. Very often, the graphs and tables are used to show comparisons and changes that take place over time.

As with other reading material, to infer the ideas presented in tables and graphs, you must consider all the information presented.

Steps in Reading a Graph or Table

To find and make sense of the information in a table or graph, follow a few steps.

1 Read the title. It will tell you what the table or graph is showing in general.

- What is the title of the table below? ______________________________

____

2 Check the source. At the bottom of a table or graph, you will usually find the source of the information, an indication of the reliability of its material.

- What are the sources below? ______________________________

____

3 Read any labels or captions at the top, the side, or underneath that tell exactly what each column, line, bar, number, or other item represents. This information includes such things as quantities, percentages, and years.

- How many student categories are presented in the table? __________
- What do the percentages refer to? ______________________________

____

4 Once you have taken the above steps, you are ready to infer from the table or graph whatever information you seek from it.

The Bingeing Phenomenon

Many college students drink heavily;
shown below is the percentage of students in each category who binge.

AGE	
Under 21	45%
21-23	48
24+	28
COLLEGE RESIDENCES	
Fraternity/sorority	84%
Coed dorm	52
Off-campus housing	40
Single-sex dorm	38

RACE	
White	48%
Hispanic	33
Nat.Amer./Nat.Alask.	34
Asian/Pacific islander	21
African American	16
GENDER	
Male	50%
Female	39

PARTICIPATION IN SPORTS	
Nonparticipant	36%
Participant	54
Team leader	58
ATTITUDE	
Frequent bingers who think they drink lightly/moderately	
Male	91%
Female	78

SOURCES: Harvard School of Public Health, *Journal of American College Health*

Check Your Understanding

See if you can put a check (✓) by the **three** inferences that are most logically based on the table.

___ 1. The older students get, the more they tend to binge.

___ 2. In general, students who live in fraternities or sororities drink more heavily than students who live elsewhere.

___ 3. The percentage of white students who binge is three times as great as the percentage of African American students who binge.

___ 4. Bingeing is not a problem for female students.

___ 5. Bingeing is not popular among college athletes.

___ 6. Most college students who binge are unaware of the true extent of their drinking.

Explanation

1. From the section of the table labeled "Age," we can infer that once students become older than 23, their bingeing decreases—from 48 to 28 percent. So you should not have checked item 1.
2. A glance at the section labeled "College residences" tells us that fraternity and sorority members do drink more heavily than students who live in coed dorms, off-campus housing, and single-sex dorms. You should have checked item 2.
3. The section labeled "Race" tells us that 48 percent of white students and 16 percent of African American students binge. Since forty-eight is three times sixteen, you should have checked item 3.
4. The section labeled "Gender" shows that 39 percent of females binge, so you should not have checked item 4.
5. You also should not have checked item 5. The "Participation in sports" section shows that 54 percent of college athletes and 58 percent of team leaders binge.
6. The section labeled "Attitude" shows that most male and female bingers believe they drink only lightly or moderately. Thus item 6 is the third item you should have checked.

PRACTICE 5

Read the graph below, following the steps on page 300. Then put a check (✓) by the **three** inferences that are most logically based on the graph.

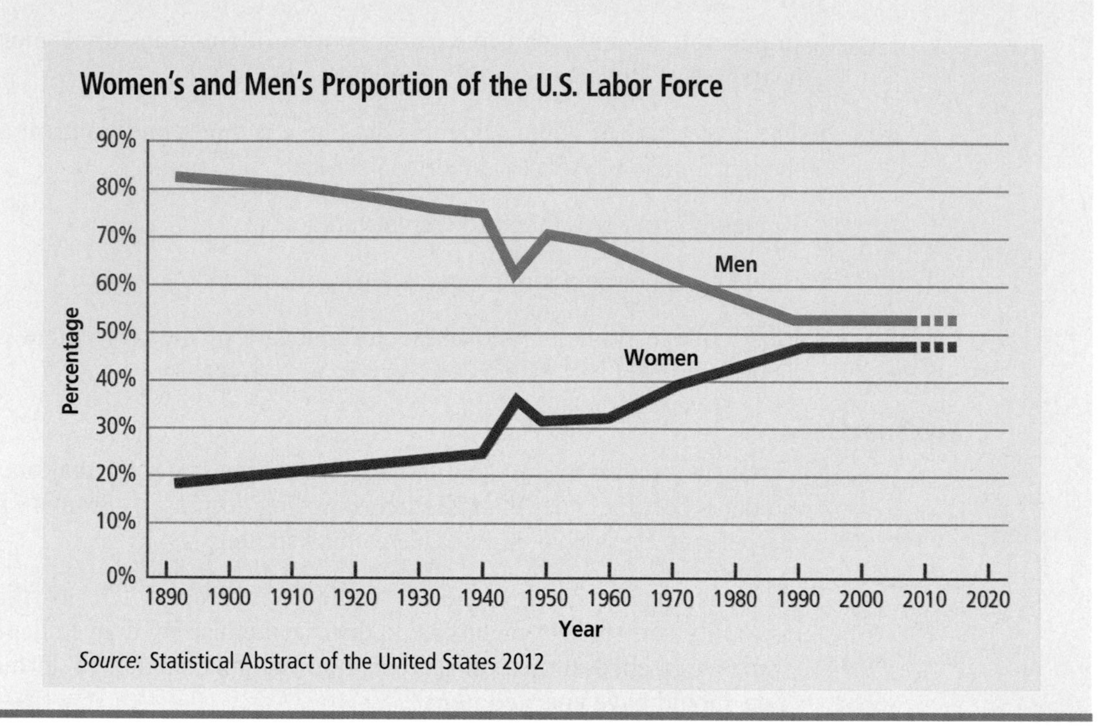

Source: Statistical Abstract of the United States 2012

___ 1. In the next few years, it appears that men will continue to outnumber slightly the number of women in the workforce.

___ 2. In the next few decades, more American women than men will work outside the home.

___ 3. One of the chief characteristics of the U.S. workforce is the steady growth in the numbers of women who work outside the home.

___ 4. Students with some post-secondary education are much more likely to qualify for new jobs than high school dropouts.

___ 5. If it hadn't been for World War II, large numbers of women would have never entered the U.S. workforce.

___ 6. If women had the choice, most would choose to work in the home, not at a paid job.

CHAPTER REVIEW

In this chapter, you learned the following:

- Many important ideas in reading are not stated directly but must be inferred. To make inferences about implied ideas, use the information provided as well as your own experience and logic.
- Inferences are also a key part of reading literature and such visual materials as cartoons, tables, and graphs.

The next chapter—Chapter 8—will help make you aware of an author's purpose and tone.

On the Web: If you are using this book in class, you can visit our website for additional practice in making inferences. Go to **www.townsendpress.com** and click on "Learning Center."

REVIEW TEST 1

To review what you've learned in this chapter, answer each of the following questions about inferences.

1. We make inferences by "reading between the lines" and picking up ideas that are not directly ________________ in what we are reading.

_____ 2. To draw sound inferences we must use
A. all the information provided by the writer.
B. our own experience.
C. logic.
D. all of the above.

3. A reader must make ______________ when determining the meaning of words through context and when deciding on implied main ideas.

4. Creative writers often use comparisons to suggest what they mean. *Similes* are direct comparisons introduced with *like* or *as* or *as if*, and _____________ are implied comparisons with *like* or *as* or *as if* omitted.

5. In textbooks we must often infer the ideas presented in diagrams called graphs and _______________.

REVIEW TEST 2

A. (1–4.) Put a check (✓) by the **four** inferences that are most logically based on the information given in the cartoon.

___ 1. The man in the chair is the supervisor of the man with the glasses.

___ 2. The man with glasses disapproves of his boss's behavior.

___ 3. The man with glasses would like to make his report more attractive.

___ 4. Reducing the type size and running the report through the fax machine will make the print lighter and harder to read.

___ 5. The seated man is using words to obscure, rather than clarify, meaning.

___ 6. Complicated language expresses ideas better than simple language.

___ 7. The cartoonist is criticizing how demanding bosses can be.

___ 8. The cartoonist is making fun of the way business communications are often written.

B. (5–8.) Read the following passage and then put a check (✓) by the **four** inferences that are most logically supported by the information given.

[1]As he lay dying, a friendless miser called to his bedside his doctor, pastor, and lawyer. [2]"They say you can't take it with you," the old skinflint began, "but I will prove them wrong. [3]Under my mattress, I've hidden $90,000. [4]Just before they throw the dirt into my grave, I want each of you to toss in an envelope containing $30,000." [5]At the funeral, the pastor, doctor, and lawyer secretly dropped their envelopes into the grave. [6]As they walked away from the burial plot, the pastor turned to the other two and said, "I have a confession. [7]My church desperately

needs $10,000 to repair the roof, so there was only $20,000 in my envelope." [8]The doctor, moved by the pastor's admission, said, "I have to come clean as well. [9]We need $20,000 to buy equipment for the children's ward at the hospital. [10]So I only threw $10,000 into the grave." [11]The lawyer eyed both of his companions with disdain and said, "I'm appalled, outraged, and ashamed of you both. [12]My envelope contained my personal check for the entire amount."

___ 1. The miser felt he could trust the doctor, pastor, and lawyer.

___ 2. The miser secretly hoped that some of the money would go to a good cause.

___ 3. The doctor and pastor would have taken the money for only a good cause.

___ 4. The lawyer intended to use his $30,000 for a good cause as well.

___ 5. The pastor, doctor, and lawyer did not want anyone else to see them drop envelopes in the grave.

___ 6. Many people attended the funeral, glad the old man had died.

___ 7. The doctor and pastor actually took the remainder of their $30,000 for themselves.

___ 8. The lawyer is not sincere when he says he is "appalled, outraged, and ashamed."

C. (9–10.) Read the following textbook passage and then put a check (✓) by the **two** inferences that are most logically based on the information given.

[1]The amount of eye contact differs from person to person and from setting to setting. [2]We tend to have better eye contact when we discuss topics that we are comfortable with or interested in. [3]Our eye contact also tends to be better when we are trying to influence the other person. [4]In contrast, we tend to avoid eye contact when discussing topics that make us uncomfortable or that we lack interest in. [5]We also tend to avoid eye contact when we are embarrassed, ashamed, or trying to hide something.

___ 1. A child who has "stolen" a cookie is likely to look his mother straight in the eye and deny taking the cookie.

___ 2. Salespeople are likely to have good eye contact with a person they wish to sell something to.

___ 3. A person who has asked his or her friend an important question is likely to have good eye contact when the answer is given.

___ 4. A defendant in court who wishes to be believed innocent should avoid eye contact with lawyers and the jury.

REVIEW TEST 3

A. (1–4.) Read the graph below. Then put a check (✓) by the **four** statements that are most logically supported by the graph.

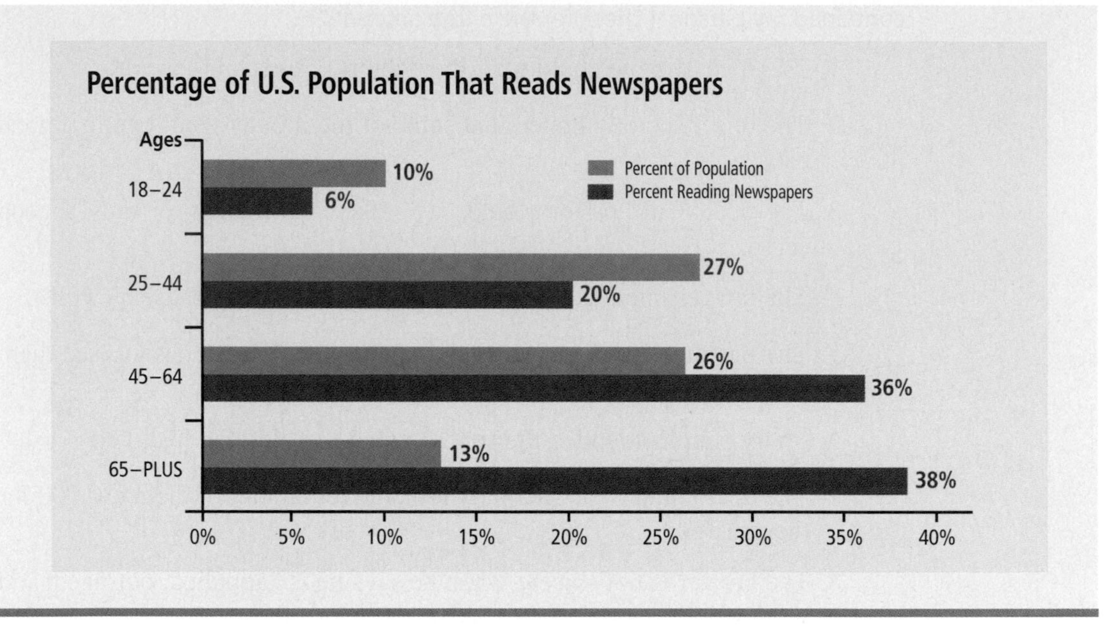

___ 1. Newspaper readership tends to decline with age.

___ 2. Newspaper readership tends to increase with age.

___ 3. Newspaper readership will probably decline over the next decade because few young people today read newspapers.

___ 4. Newspapers are not nearly as profitable as they once were.

___ 5. As young people grow older, they will become newspaper readers.

___ 6. Young people today are not interested in what is going on in the world.

___ 7. An increase in alternative news sources, such as cable TV and the Internet, has probably led to a decline in newspaper readership among the young.

___ 8. If a young person's mother or father reads newspapers, he or she is more likely to become a newspaper reader.

B. Identify each figure of speech as a simile or a metaphor. Then answer each inference question that follows.

_____ 5. The motivational speaker was like a cup of strong coffee for the drowsy audience.
A. simile B. metaphor

_____ 6. You can infer that the speaker in sentence 5 above
A. was funny. B. spoke clearly. C. was energizing.

_____ 7. Paul flatters me so much that I feel as if I'm being force-fed cotton candy.
A. simile B. metaphor

_____ 8. You can infer that the speaker feels Paul's flattery is
A. excessive. B. deserved. C. amusing.

_____ 9. The commissioner's explanations were a dense jungle to his listeners.
A. simile B. metaphor

_____10. You can infer that listeners found the commissioner's explanations to be
A. distasteful. B. unconvincing. C. difficult to understand.

REVIEW TEST 4

Until the year 1947, major-league baseball was "for whites only." It took the willingness of Branch Rickey, and the talent and spirit of Jackie Robinson, to break baseball's color line and to open up professional baseball for all Americans. Robinson, born in the rural South, the son of a sharecropper, was to die prematurely at the age of 52. But his life was a study in courage and achievement, as described in this reading.

To help you continue to strengthen your skills, the reading is followed by questions on what you've learned not only in this chapter but also in previous chapters.

Words to Watch

Below are some words in the reading that do not have strong context support. Each word is followed by the number of the paragraph in which it appears and its meaning there. These words are indicated in the article by a small circle (°).

rampant (6): widespread
staunch (7): strong
raucous (14): harsh-sounding
cantankerous (21): ill-tempered
tumultuous (31): noisy
adulation (31): great admiration

HE WAS FIRST

John Kellmayer

1 Today few people under 70 can remember what it was like *not* to see blacks in professional baseball.

2 But until April 15, 1947, when Jackie Robinson played his first game with the Brooklyn Dodgers, the world of major-league baseball was a whites-only world.

3 The transition was not an easy one. It took place largely because Branch Rickey, owner of the Dodgers, held onto to a dream of integrating baseball and because Jackie Robinson had the character, talent, and support to carry him through an ugly obstacle course of racism.

4 Even before he arrived in professional baseball, Robinson had to combat discrimination. Robinson entered the army with a national college reputation as an outstanding athlete. Still, he was denied permission to play on the football and baseball teams at Fort Riley, Kansas, where he was stationed. He had been allowed to practice with the football team, but when the first game against an opposing team came up, Robinson was sent home on a pass. His exclusion from the baseball team there was more direct. A member of that team recalls what happened: "One day we were out at the field practicing when a Negro lieutenant tried out for the team. An officer told him, 'You have to play with the colored team.' That was a joke. There was no colored team." Robinson walked silently off the field.

5 Eventually, Robinson was granted an honorable discharge, and soon after, he signed a contract to play baseball in the Negro American League.

6 At this time Branch Rickey was waiting for his opportunity to sign a black ballplayer and to integrate major-league baseball. He understood not only that the black ballplayer could be good box office but also that bigotry had to be fought. While involved with his college baseball team, he had been deeply moved by a nasty scene in which his star catcher, an outstanding young black man, was prohibited from registering at a hotel with the rest of the team. Rickey then became determined to do something about the rampant° racism in baseball.

7 By 1944, the social climate had become more accepting of integration, in large part because of the contribution of black soldiers in World War II. Also, when the commissioner of baseball, a staunch° opponent of integration, died in 1944, he was replaced by a man named Happy Chandler. Chandler was on record as supporting integration of the game: "If a black man can make it at Okinawa and go to Guadalcanal, he can make it in baseball."

8 Rickey knew the time had come. He began searching for the special black ballplayer with the mix of talent and character necessary to withstand the struggles to follow. When he learned

about a star player in the Negro American League named Jackie Robinson, he arranged to meet with him.

9 At their meeting, Rickey said, "Jack, I've been looking for a great colored ballplayer, but I need more than a great player. I need a man who will accept insults, take abuse, in a word, carry the flag for his race. I want a man who has the courage not to fight, not to fight back. If a guy slides into you at second base and calls you a black son of a bitch, I wouldn't blame you if you came up swinging. You'd be right. You'd be justified. But you'd set the cause back twenty years. I want a man with courage enough not to fight back. Can you do that?"

10 Robinson thought for a few minutes before answering, "If you want to take this gamble, I promise you there'll be no incidents." The promise was not easily made. Robinson had encountered plenty of racism in his life, and he was accustomed to fighting for black rights. He was known by his teammates in the Negro American League to have a quick temper. Consequently, keeping his promise to Rickey was going to require great personal will.

11 After signing with the Dodgers in October 1945, Robinson did not have to wait long to put his patience to the test. Even before he began to play in the Dodger organization, he and his wife, Rachel, encountered the humiliation of Southern racism.

12 It began when the Robinsons flew from Los Angeles to spring training in Florida, two weeks after they got married. On a stop in New Orleans, they were paged and asked to get off the plane. They later learned that in the South, whites who wanted seats on a flight took preference over blacks already seated. Their places had been given to a white couple. They had to wait a day to get another flight and then were told to get off for yet another white couple at a stop in Pensacola, Florida. The Robinsons then had to take a segregated bus the rest of the way to Jacksonville, where Branch Rickey had a car waiting for them. Of that trip, Rachel Robinson later said, "It sharpened for us the drama of what we were about to go into. We got a lot tougher thereafter."

Soon after, during an exhibition game in Florida, Jackie suffered another humiliation, the first of many more to come on the diamond. During the first inning of that game, a police officer came onto the field and told Jackie, "Your people don't play with no white 13 boys. Get off the field right now, or you're going to jail." Jackie had no choice but to walk quietly off the field. Not one of his teammates spoke up for him then.

14 Robinson's assignment to the Dodger minor-league team in Montreal was evidence of Rickey's careful planning for the breaking of the color barrier, as there was little racism in the Canadian city. That fact became important in supporting the spirits of Jackie and Rachel against the horrible outpouring of hate that greeted him at each stop on the road. Baseball historian Robert Smith wrote that when Robinson first appeared in Syracuse, "the fans reacted in a manner so raucous°, obscene, and disgusting that it might have shamed a conclave of the Ku Klux Klan." It was during this game that a Syracuse player threw a black cat at Jackie and yelled, "Hey, Jackie, there's your cousin." In Baltimore, the players shouted racist insults, threw balls at his head, and tried to spike him. In addition, as would be the case at many stops through the years, Jackie wasn't allowed to stay at the same hotel as the rest of the team.

15 Robinson's manager at Montreal was Clay Hopper, a Mississippi native adamantly opposed at first to the presence of Robinson on his ball club. Rickey once stood near Hopper during a game when Robinson made a superb dive to make an out, and Rickey commented that Robinson seemed "superhuman." Hopper's reply was, "Do you really think he's a human being?"

16 No civil rights legislation could have turned Clay Hopper around the way Jackie Robinson did. By the end of a season in which Robinson led his team to the minor-league World Series, Hopper told Robinson, "You're a great ballplayer and a fine gentleman. It's been wonderful having you on the team." Hopper would later remark to Rickey, "You don't have to worry none about that boy. He's the greatest competitor I ever saw, and what's more, he's a gentleman."

It was clear that Jackie Robinson's 17
next stop was the big leagues, the Brooklyn Dodgers. Not surprisingly, though, the prospect of a black major-league player was not met by all with open arms. Just how much resistance there was, however, could be seen in the meeting of the baseball club owners in January of 1947 in which every owner but Rickey voted against allowing Jackie to play.

Fortunately, commissioner Happy 18
Chandler had another point of view. He later told Rickey, "Mr. Rickey, I'm going to have to meet my Maker some day. If He asked me why I didn't let this man play, and I answered, 'Because he's a Negro,' that might not be a sufficient answer. I will approve of the transfer of Robinson's contract from Montreal to Brooklyn." So the color barrier was broken, and Robinson became a member of the Brooklyn Dodgers.

Robinson's talent meant less to some 19
of the Brooklyn players than race. The prospect of a black teammate prompted a Dodger outfielder, a Southerner by the name of Dixie Walker, to pass among the other Southern players a petition urging Rickey to ban Robinson from

their team. Walker gathered signatures and his petition gained momentum until he approached shortstop Pee Wee Reese, a Kentucky native. Robinson had originally been signed on as a shortstop and could have posed a real threat to Reese's job. Nonetheless, Reese refused to sign the petition. Reese was one of the leaders of the Brooklyn "Bums," so his acceptance of Robinson was of great importance in determining how the rest of the Dodgers would react.

20 As expected, Robinson's presence triggered an ugly racial response. It began with hate mail and death threats against him and his wife and baby boy. In addition, some of his teammates continued to oppose him. Some even refused to sit near him.

21 The opposing teams, however, were much worse, and the hatred was so intense that some of the Dodger players began to stand up for Jackie. In Philadelphia, players cried out such insults as "They're waiting for you in the jungles, black boy," and "Hey, snowflake, which one of you white boys' wives are you dating tonight?" The first Dodger to stand up for Robinson on the field was a Southerner, the cantankerous° Eddie "The Brat" Stanky. When the Phillies pointed their bats at Robinson and made machine-gun-like noises in a cruel reference to the threats on his and his family's lives, Stanky shouted, "Why don't you yell at someone who can answer back?"

22 Other opposing teams were no better. In an early-season game in Cincinnati, for instance, players yelled racial epithets at Jackie. Rex Barney, who was a Dodger pitcher then, described Pee Wee Reese's response: "While Jackie was standing by first base, Pee Wee went over to him and put his arm around him, as if to say, 'This is my man. This is the guy. We're gonna win with him.' Well, it drove the Cincinnati players right through the ceiling, and you could have heard the gasp from the crowd as he did it."

23 In the face of continuing harassment, Jackie Robinson, a hot-tempered young man who had struggled against racism all his life, chose to fight his toughest battle, not with his fists or foul language, but with the courage not to fight back. Instead, he answered his attackers with superior play and electrifying speed.

24 Within the first month of the 1947 season, it became apparent that Robinson could be the deciding factor in the pennant race. His speed on the base paths brought an entirely new dimension to baseball. Robinson used bunts and fake bunts and steals and fake steals to distract opposing pitchers and force basic changes in strategy in the game.

25 Undoubtedly, one reason many Dodger players rallied around Robinson was that they saw him as a critical, perhaps the critical, factor in their pursuit of the pennant. Like Rickey's, their motives reflected a mixture of personal ambition and a genuine concern for doing what was right.

26 And many did do what was right, even off the field. For example, Robinson at first waited until all his teammates had finished their showers before he would take his. One day, outfielder Al Gionfriddo patted Robinson on the butt

and told him to get into the showers with everybody else, that he was as much a part of the team as anyone. Robinson smiled and went to the showers with Gionfriddo.

27 The ballplayers' wives also extended the hand of friendship to Robinson and his wife. Pitcher Clyde King related an incident that was typical of the efforts put forth to make the Robinsons feel part of the Dodger family. At Ebbets Field, an iron fence ran from the dugout to the clubhouse, keeping the fans from the players. After the games, the Dodger wives would be allowed inside the fence to wait for their husbands. Rachel Robinson, reluctant to join the other wives, would wait for Jackie outside the fence among the fans. King remembers that his own wife, Norma, a North Carolina girl, made sure that Rachel joined her and the other Dodger wives inside.

28 For Jackie, a series of such small but significant events may have meant the difference between making it and exploding under the enormous pressure that followed him throughout that first baseball season.

29 As the season passed, he gained the support not only of many of his teammates but of much of the baseball world in general. On September 12, *Sporting News*, the leading publication in baseball, selected Robinson as its Rookie of the Year—the first of many prestigious awards he would receive during his term with the Dodgers.

30 In the article announcing the award, there was a quote from none other than Dixie Walker, the same Dodger who had started the petition in the spring to ban Robinson from playing for Brooklyn. Walker praised Robinson for his contributions to the club's success, stating that Robinson was all that Branch Rickey had said and more.

On September 22, the Dodgers defeated the St. Louis Cardinals to clinch the National League pennant—against a team in whose town Jackie had to stay in a "colored" hotel. Fittingly enough, the following day was proclaimed Jackie Robinson Day at the Dodger ballpark. Robinson was honored with a tumultuous° outpouring of affection from the Brooklyn fans, an unbroken peal of adulation° that shook the very foundations of Ebbets Field. 31

Americans learned something that year about competition and excellence, about character and race. The fire that Jackie Robinson fanned swept across the years to follow, resulting in a permanent change in the makeup of the game. He had demonstrated that not only could blacks play on the same field with white players; they could excel. People brought their families hundreds of miles to see him play. The floodgates opened for the signing of the black ballplayer. The same major-league team owners who had voted against hiring blacks soon followed Rickey's lead. In the next few years came Willie Mays, Ernie Banks, Henry Aaron, and more—an endless list of black stars. 32

For some, Jackie Robinson is simply one of the greatest second basemen of all time. For others, he is much more. He is an individual who stood up and opposed the ugliness of racism with a 33 relentless intensity. He was the first to brave the insults and the ignorance, the first to show that major-league baseball could be raised from the depths of segregation. His victory is a model of what one determined person can accomplish.

Reading Comprehension Questions

Vocabulary in Context

_____ 1. In the sentence below, the word *adamantly* (ăd′ə-mənt-lē) means
A. weakly.
B. stubbornly.
C. secretly.
D. pleasantly.

"Robinson's manager at Montreal was Clay Hopper, a Mississippi native adamantly opposed at first to the presence of Robinson on his ball club." (Paragraph 15)

_____ 2. In the excerpt below, the word *momentum* (mō-mĕn′təm) means
A. a deliberate insult.
B. opposition.
C. forward movement.
D. defeat.

"Walker gathered signatures and his petition gained momentum until he approached shortstop Pee Wee Reese. . . ." (Paragraph 19)

Central Point and Main Ideas

_____ 3. Which sentence best expresses the central point of this selection?
A. Until 1947, there were no blacks in professional baseball.
B. Jackie Robinson, a man of principle and courage, became the best second baseman in baseball.
C. Baseball became integrated because of the courage of Branch Rickey and Jackie Robinson, who proved blacks could excel in major-league baseball.
D. The integration of American society was not easily accomplished.

_____ 4. Which sentence best expresses the main idea of paragraph 7?
A. Happy Chandler became baseball commissioner in 1944.
B. Black soldiers fought for the United States during World War II.
C. A commissioner of baseball who was opposed to integration died in 1944.
D. By 1944, society had become more open to integrating baseball.

Supporting Details

_____ 5. Robinson encountered racism
A. on and off the field in both the North and the South.
B. only during baseball games.
C. mainly in Canada.
D. until he joined the major leagues.

Transitions

_____ 6. The relationship of paragraph 27 to paragraph 26 is one of
A. time.
B. illustration.
C. addition.
D. contrast.

Patterns of Organization

_____ 7. The pattern of organization of paragraph 3 is
A. time order.
B. definition and example.
C. cause and effect.
D. comparison and/or contrast.

Inferences

_____ 8. The author implies that some of Robinson's Dodger teammates
A. resented the intense racism of the opposing teams and fans.
B. taught him a lot about baseball strategy.
C. opposed him more as they won more games.
D. had little influence on how he stood the pressure of his first major-league season.

_____ 9. TRUE OR FALSE? The author implies that the Dodgers won the 1947 National League pennant largely because of Jackie Robinson.

_____10. Which of the following inferences is best supported by paragraph 19?
A. All Southern players were racist.
B. Pee Wee Reese felt threatened by Jackie Robinson.
C. Reese put principle ahead of personal concern.
D. Without Pee Wee Reese, baseball would not have become integrated.

Discussion Questions

1. Kellmayer writes, "By 1944, the social climate had become more accepting of integration, in large part because of the contribution of black soldiers in World War II." Why do you think the contribution of black soldiers in World War II would be such an influence on the progress of integration in the United States?

2. An ongoing question about history is whether individuals cause important changes in society or whether it is circumstances that lead to changes—once the circumstances are right, the right individuals will emerge. In the integration of baseball, how important do you think the times were? How important were the individuals involved?

3. Do you think Branch Rickey was right to make Robinson agree "not to fight back"? Explain your answer.

4. Robinson had to face a great deal of racism. Unfortunately, despite the greater integration of today, racism still exists. Have you experienced any racial insults yourself or seen anyone else treated badly because of the racial or ethnic group he or she belongs to? Tell what happened, and how you or the other person reacted.

Note: Writing assignments for this selection appear on page 700.

Check Your Performance INFERENCES

Activity	*Number Right*	*Points*		*Score*
Review Test 1 (5 items)	______	× 2	=	______
Review Test 2 (10 items)	______	× 3	=	______
Review Test 3 (10 items)	______	× 3	=	______
Review Test 4 (10 items)	______	× 3	=	______
		TOTAL SCORE	=	______%

Enter your total score into the **Reading Performance Chart: Review Tests** on the inside back cover.

Name ______________________________ Date __________

Section __________ SCORE: (Number correct) ______ x 12.5 = _____ %

INFERENCES: Mastery Test 1

A. (1–2.) Put a check (✓) by the **two** inferences that are most logically based on the details in the cartoon below.

___ 1. The children are enjoying themselves.

___ 2. The house was built on stilts so the children could play underneath it.

___ 3. The children probably seldom watch real television.

___ 4. The cartoonist wishes to emphasize how television keeps children from more active play.

___ 5. The cartoonist means to emphasize the children's creativity in building a realistic sand sculpture.

B. (3–4.) Read the passage below. Then check the **two** inferences that are most logically supported by the information given.

[1]"Does the chili have any meat in it?" the woman asked. [2]"No," answered the waiter. [3]"I'll have chili, then." [4]The waiter was disappointed, since chili was one of the restaurant's least expensive items. [5]"The lobster special is delicious," he suggested, "and healthy." [6]The woman shook her head and responded, "Not for the lobster."

___ 1. The woman is a vegetarian.

___ 2. The woman was brought up as a vegetarian.

___ 3. The waiter was hoping to get a larger tip for a more expensive meal.

___ 4. The woman is on a tight budget.

___ 5. The woman was alone.

(Continues on next page)

C. (5–8.) Read the passage below. Then, in the spaces provided, write the letter of the most logical answer to each question, based on the information given in the passage.

[1]Mutual attraction may get us into a love relationship, but it is not the determining factor in making the relationship grow and last. [2]Two factors that make relationships endure have to do with expectations and equity. [3]When two people first fall in love, they often enjoy a mixture of romantic, sexual, and other intense feelings of love. [4]In healthy, lasting relationships this passionate love gradually shifts into compassionate love, which blends friendship, intimacy, commitment, and security. [5]If both people in the relationship anticipate and welcome this shift, the transition is managed comfortably. [6]Expectations are aligned with reality. [7]If not, the relationship can become troubled or even end because of this surprise about the nature of love or any number of other unrealistic expectations that can occur. [8]In addition, each person in the relationship needs to experience a balance between what he/she puts into the relationship and what he/she gets out of it. [9]Each needs to feel that neither too little nor too much is received when compared with what is given. [10]This equity helps make for a happy relationship.

______ 5. We can infer that the author of this passage believes
A. romantic love can be damaging to a relationship.
B. the happiest couples are not physically attracted to one another.
C. physical attraction is often strongest early in a relationship.

______ 6. We can conclude that the author of this passage
A. has learned through personal experience about the uncertainties in relationships.
B. believes that realism about love increases the chance of happiness.
C. believes that love inevitably fades after people have been together a long time.

______ 7. We can infer from this passage that the author believes
A. the changes that people in love go through are sad, but inevitable.
B. compassionate love can be richly rewarding.
C. people should change partners when feelings of romantic love fade.

______ 8. We can conclude from the author's remarks that
A. ideally, people in a relationship will enjoy both giving and receiving.
B. a person who really wants a relationship to succeed will ignore his or her own needs.
C. there is no such thing as receiving too much from a partner.

Name ______________________________ Date __________

Section __________ SCORE: (Number correct) ______ x 10 = ______ %

INFERENCES: Mastery Test 2

A. (1–2.) Put a check (✓) by the **two** inferences that are most logically based on the information suggested by the cartoon.

"But we can't break up. Without you I'd be like a burger without fries."

___ 1. This is the couple's first date.

___ 2. The woman in the cartoon wants to break up with the man.

___ 3. The woman likes the man more than he likes her.

___ 4. The man is a very independent person.

___ 5. The woman may not like the man comparing their relationship to a hamburger and fries.

B. (3–4.) Read the following passage. Then put a check (✓) by the **two** inferences that are most logically based on the information given.

[1]The goal of our lives must be to reach out in kindness, love, and care. [2]We must change the world by our relationships with other people—that will be our immortality. [3]We will not be remembered for job or financial success. [4]There is no gravestone that says, "Effective CEO" or "A Multimillionaire." [5]Hopefully our grave will have words such as "Loving father" or "Devoted daughter" or "Caring husband" or "Beloved sister."

___ 1. Family members should help each other out financially.

___ 2. The writer of this passage is a minister.

___ 3. We will be remembered for how we treated people.

___ 4. Gravestones should describe people's careers.

___ 5. Material success is not the same as human success.

(Continues on next page)

C. (5–10.) Ten statements follow the passage below, taken from *A Son of the Middle Border*, a literary autobiography by Hamlin Garland. The author grew up on a Midwestern farm in the 1860s and 1870s. First read the passage carefully, using the definitions as necessary. Then check (✓) the numbers of the **six** statements which are most logically supported by the information given.

imperative: commanding
impassive: expressionless
countenance: face
resolution: firm determination
mused: thought it over

[1]Slipping from my weary horse, I tied her to the rail and hurried up the walk toward the doctor's bell. [2]I remembered just where the knob rested. [3]Twice I pulled sharply, strongly, putting into it some part of the anxiety and impatience I felt. [4]I could hear its imperative° jingle as it died away in the silent house.

[5]At last the door opened and the doctor, a big blond handsome man in a long nightgown, confronted me with an impassive° face. [6]"What is it, my boy?" he asked kindly.

[7]As I told him, he looked down at my water-soaked form and wild-eyed countenance° with gentle patience. [8]Then he peered out over my head into the dismal night. [9]He was a man of resolution°, but he hesitated for a moment. [10]"Your father is suffering sharply, is he?"

[11]"Yes, sir; I could hear him groan. [12]Please hurry."

[13]He mused° a moment. [14]"He is a soldier. [15]He would not complain of a little thing—I will come."

____ 1. At the time of this narrative, the author is a boy.

____ 2. The author's ride had been a very short one.

____ 3. The author had been to the doctor's house before.

____ 4. The author was very afraid of the doctor.

____ 5. The author did not admire the doctor.

____ 6. The author's errand is an urgent one.

____ 7. The doctor was not expecting a visitor.

____ 8. The doctor did not want to go out at night for a little complaint.

____ 9. The doctor concluded that the soldier's problem deserved immediate attention.

____10. The doctor had been a soldier himself once.

Name ______________________ Date __________

Section __________ SCORE: (Number correct) ______ x 10 = ______ %

INFERENCES: Mastery Test 3

A. (1–2.) Read the passage below. Then check (✓) the **two** statements after the passage which are most logically supported by the information given.

[1]In 1935, Harry S. Truman (who would become president eleven years later) had just been elected to the United States Senate. [2]As a brand-new senator from the Midwest, he was concerned that some of his more experienced colleagues might consider him "a sort of hick politician" who did not deserve to be part of such an important group of lawmakers. [3]But another senator, Ham Lewis, put him at his ease. [4]"Don't start out with an inferiority complex," Lewis told Truman. [5]"For the first six months, you'll wonder how you got here. [6]After that, you'll wonder how the rest of us got here."

___ 1. This was Truman's first elected office.

___ 2. Truman was concerned about what the other senators thought of him.

___ 3. Truman felt he was not qualified to be a senator.

___ 4. Ham Lewis was a close friend of Senator Truman.

___ 5. Ham Lewis felt that after a while, Truman would not feel inferior.

B. (3–6.) Read the passage below. Then check (✓) the **four** statements after the passage which are most logically supported by the information given.

[1]Where does that road go? [2]How does a television set work? [3]What is that tool used for? [4]Answering these questions may have no obvious benefit for you. [5]You may not expect the road to take you anywhere you need to go, or the tool to be of any use to you. [6]Exploration and curiosity appear to be motives activated by the new and unknown and directed toward no more specific a goal than "finding out." [7]Even animals will learn a behavior just to be allowed to explore the environment. [8]The family dog will run around a new house, sniffing and checking things out, before it settles down to eat its dinner.

[9]Animals also seem to prefer complexity, presumably because more complex forms take longer to know and are therefore more interesting. [10]Placed in a maze that is painted black, a rat will explore the maze and learn its way around. [11]The next time, given a choice between a black maze and a blue one, it will choose the blue one. [12]Apparently the unfamiliarity of the unknown maze has more appeal.

___ 1. Curiosity is always stronger than great hunger.

___ 2. We are curious about the unknown.

___ 3. Curiosity is what separates people from animals.

___ 4. Curiosity leads to exploration.

___ 5. Rats are more curious than dogs.

(Continues on next page)

___ 6. Given a choice between a familiar blue maze and an unfamiliar white one, a rat will probably choose the white one.

___ 7. Variety is interesting for its own sake.

C. Read the passage below. Then, in the spaces provided, write the letter of the most logical answer to each question, based on the information given in the passage.

[1]While we say the future depends on our children, we don't feed all of them. [2]While the United States is the wealthiest nation in the world, more than 16 million American children are stuck below the poverty level. [3]Nor do we spend a lot of time with our children. [4]The time that parents spend with their children in meaningful interactions is measured in minutes per day, while the time children spend watching television is measured in hours. [5]We hope that our schools will do the job we aren't doing at home, but we pay schoolteachers a tiny percentage of what we pay professional athletes. [6]We graduate hundreds of thousands of students each year who cannot read their own high-school diplomas.

[7]We isolate our teenagers from the world, quarantining them in school buildings. [8]We give them little responsibility, and demand of them even less. [9]By cutting them off from the adult world, where they could develop a sense of competence and belonging, we leave them alienated and open to joining gangs that will give them a sense of belonging. [10]And many of us have turned away from the human values that have served all the generations that came before us. [11]We act as if enduring values are not important, and then we wonder why our children often seem so morally adrift.

_____ 7. You can infer that this author
- A. thinks society's attitude towards children is often hypocritical.
- B. does not believe our children are "morally adrift."
- C. is opposed to setting expectations for children.

_____ 8. You can infer that the author
- A. believes professional athletes are good role models for children.
- B. blames teachers for not doing a better job of teaching children to read.
- C. believes teachers deserve higher status in our society.

_____ 9. You can conclude that the author
- A. thinks teenagers need to learn to be more self-assertive.
- B. believes teenagers are hungry for a sense of belonging.
- C. does not understand why gangs are attractive to teenagers.

_____10. You can infer that the author of this passage is
- A. cautiously optimistic about the future of society.
- B. indifferent about the future of society.
- C. pessimistic about the future of society.

Name ______________________________ Date __________

Section ___________ SCORE: (Number correct) _______ x 10 = _______ %

INFERENCES: Mastery Test 4

A. Following is one of the most famous passages in the English language, from the play *The Tragedy of Macbeth* by William Shakespeare. Shakespeare has the king, Macbeth, speak the words below upon hearing of the death of his wife. Her death adds to the despair Macbeth feels as his power over the kingdom slips away from him.

First read the passage carefully, noting the definitions as necessary. Then, in the spaces provided, write the letter of the most logical answer to each question on the basis of the information in the passage.

strut: walk pompously
fret: worry

. . . . Out, out, brief candle!
Life's but a walking shadow, a poor player
That struts° and frets° his hour upon the stage
And then is heard no more. It is a tale
Told by an idiot, full of sound and fury,
Signifying nothing.

_____ 1. The metaphor of the "brief candle" that goes out refers to
A. the life of Macbeth's wife.
B. any human life, including Macbeth's.
C. both A and B.

_____ 2. In the metaphor of life as "a walking shadow," Macbeth suggests mainly that life is
A. flimsy and insubstantial.
B. ghostly.
C. too mysterious to understand.

_____ 3. By saying life is a "poor player/That struts and frets his hour upon the stage/And then is heard no more," Macbeth implies that
A. each life is too brief to be very significant.
B. each person's life is of enormous value.
C. he expects to die young.

_____ 4. By saying that life "struts and frets" upon the stage, Macbeth suggests that humanity is
A. full of life and contentment.
B. troubled and vain.
C. important and special.

(Continues on next page)

_____ 5. When he then says that life is "a tale/Told by an idiot, full of sound and fury,/Signifying nothing," Macbeth implies that
A. life is meaningless.
B. people often pretend to care about things when they really do not.
C. people of low intelligence are often angry.

B. (6–10.) Read the graph below. Then check (✓) the **five** statements that are most logically based on the graph.

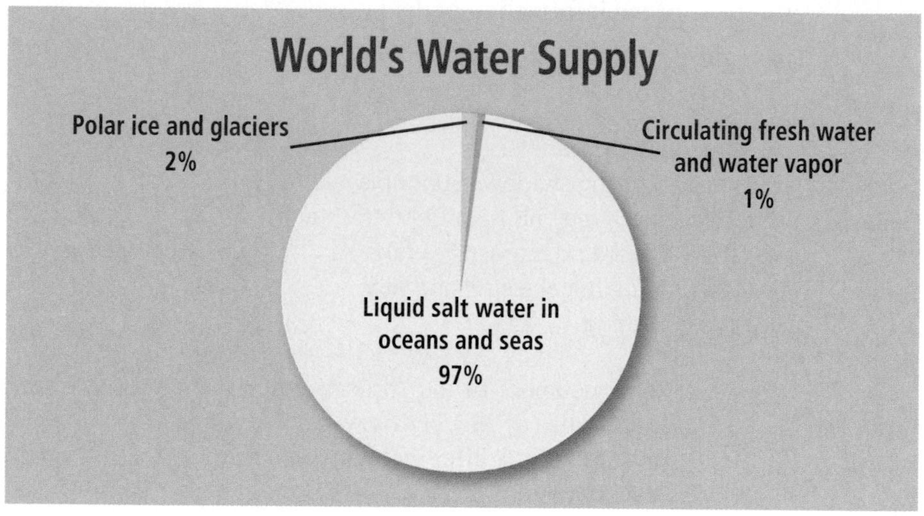

___ 1. By far, the majority of the world's water is salt water.
___ 2. The pie graph represents 50 percent of the world's water supply.
___ 3. The pie graph represents 100 percent of the world's water supply.
___ 4. There is more water in polar ice and glaciers than there is fresh water and water vapor in the world.
___ 5. About 97 percent of the world is covered in water.
___ 6. About 1 percent of the world is covered in water.
___ 7. The water in the Pacific Ocean is part of the 97-percent section of the pie graph.
___ 8. The water that we shower in is represented in the 97-percent section of the pie graph.
___ 9. The humidity in the air is represented by the 2-percent section of the pie graph.
___10. Life processes of the plants and animals on land use the 1 percent of fresh water and water vapor in the world.

Name ______________________ Date __________

Section __________ SCORE: (Number correct) ______ x 10 = ______ %

INFERENCES: Mastery Test 5

A. Read the following textbook passage. Then write the letter of the best answer to each question.

[1]Scholars are limited in charting the details of early human social evolution because of the loss of evidence from natural causes. [2]But owing to the fortunate "airtight" atmospheric conditions in numerous caves of France and Spain, we know that between 33,000 and 12,000 years ago, humans produced some of the most stunning paintings in the entire history of human art. [3]In more than two hundred caves so far discovered (some as recently as 1991 and 1994), the earliest known artists painted breathtaking murals of prancing animals—bison, bulls, horses, stags, and even rhinoceroses. [4]The emphasis in this cave art was on movement. [5]Almost all of the murals depict game species running, leaping, chewing their cud, or facing the hunter at bay. [6]An ingenious device for giving the impression of motion was the drawing of additional outlines to indicate the areas in which the leg or the head of the animal had moved. [7]The cave painters sometimes achieved startling three-dimensional effects by using the natural bumps and indentations of the cave surfaces. [8]All in all, visitors today who are lucky enough to see the cave murals usually find them as stimulating as any paintings hanging in the world's foremost art museums.

______ 1. The "natural causes" mentioned in the first sentence include
- A. religion and art.
- B. early human social evolution.
- C. weather and environmental elements that destroy evidence.
- D. animals that bury evidence.

______ 2. The author refers to the "atmospheric conditions in numerous caves" as being fortunate because those conditions
- A. sheltered the ancient artists.
- B. kept the artwork from being washed away or disintegrating.
- C. were comfortable for the animal models.
- D. created the "natural bumps and indentations" that inspired the artists.

______ 3. The author implies that
- A. artists have learned little throughout the centuries.
- B. the cave artists were creative and talented.
- C. the cave artwork was done quickly.
- D. at the time of the cave painters, interest in art was unusual.

______ 4. The paintings reveal that
- A. hunting was a central activity of the time.
- B. meat was a major food of the time.
- C. rhinoceroses existed at the time in France and Spain.
- D. all of the above.

(Continues on next page)

_____ 5. We can conclude that
A. the cave drawings were the first paintings in the history of humankind.
B. one or two artists made all of the drawings.
C. the natural bumps of the caves may have been used to emphasize an animal's shape.
D. all of the above.

B. (6–10.) Read the chart below. Then put a check (✓) by the **five** inferences that are most logically based on the chart.

The World of Prime-time TV Dramas versus the Real World

Compare the percentages of people and behaviors on American TV network dramas with those in the real world.

Item Viewed	Seen on Television (%)	In the Real World (%)
Female	33	51
Married	10	61
Blue-collar	25	67
Having a religious affiliation	6	88
Implied intercourse: partners unmarried	85	unknown
Beverages consumed: percentage alcoholic	45	16

SOURCE: *Social Psychology*, Sixth Edition (McGraw-Hill)

___ 1. About a third of the characters on prime-time TV are females.
___ 2. About a third of the real-world population is female.
___ 3. TV producers must feel that prime-time audiences are more interested in women than in men.
___ 4. TV producers probably feel that married life is less interesting to prime-time viewers than single life.
___ 5. Almost all of the people in TV dramas drink alcohol.
___ 6. Almost half of all the beverages consumed on TV are alcohol.
___ 7. To prepare this table, someone must have counted the numbers of male and female, married, and blue-collar characters on prime-time shows.
___ 8. The suggestion of sex among single people is avoided on prime-time television.
___ 9. Religion is avoided on prime-time television.
___10. Prime-time TV dramas are a mirror of real life in America.

Name ____________________ Date __________

Section __________ SCORE: (Number correct) ______ x 10 = ______ %

INFERENCES: Mastery Test 6

A. (1–5.) Read the following editorial. Then check (✓) the **five** statements which are most logically supported by the information given.

[1]The American health-care system is clearly in crisis. [2]But only with the Barack Obama administration has the government sought an obvious solution: a nationwide program of universal health care—one that covers every single American—administered by the federal government.

[3]It's not that we could not establish such a system—dozens of countries have already managed to do so, with great success. [4]Americans simply have a gut-level conviction that competition and the profit motive—the free market, in other words—is the only way to maintain the "best health-care system in the world."

[5]The truth of the matter is quite the contrary. [6]The American health-care system has the highest operating expenses (14 percent) among the systems of all other industrialized countries. [7]The obvious reason is that for-profit corporations run most of the system. [8]In contrast, the government system in Canada, often characterized here as "inefficient," runs with exactly 1 percent overhead. [9]Our own Social Security runs on about 2 percent overhead.

[10]You see the overhead when you go to a medical facility and spend more time filling out forms than seeing the doctor; when you count the number of staff talking to insurance companies on the phone, and realize that they rival the number of medical personnel in the office. [11]You see the overhead in the salaries of the CEOs of health-related corporations. [12]In 2000, five top CEOs made annual salaries ranging from $11 million to $54 million. [13]A system is clearly broken that simultaneously produces huge salaries for executives and yet pays nurses' aides salaries that do not allow them to live above the poverty line, or to afford the very health care they are providing.

___ 1. The Canadian health-care system is run on a not-for-profit basis.

___ 2. Most American doctors oppose the idea of a universal health-care program.

___ 3. The current American health-care system is wasteful and inefficient.

___ 4. Executives of American health-related corporations oppose the idea of a universal health-care program.

___ 5. Canadian nurses' aides are more highly paid than American nurses' aides.

___ 6. The American Social Security program is run on a for-profit basis.

___ 7. The American public needs to make a more informed choice about health care.

___ 8. Many working Americans cannot afford health care.

(Continues on next page)

___ 9. The American health-care system helps promote good relationships between patients and doctors.

___ 10. Insurance companies are probably trying to convince the federal government to install a universal health-care system.

B. (6–10.) Read the following textbook passage. Then check (✓) the **five** statements which are most logically supported by the information given.

[1]Humans are characterized by both biologically and socially determined wants. [2]We seek food, clothing, shelter, and the many goods and services associated with a comfortable or affluent standard of living. [3]We are also blessed with aptitudes and surrounded by quantities of property resources—both natural and manufactured. [4]We use available human and property resources—labor and managerial talents, tools and machinery, land and mineral deposits—to produce goods and services which satisfy material wants. [5]This is done through the organizational mechanism we call the economic system.

[6]Quantitative considerations, however, rule out an ideal solution. [7]The blunt fact is that the total of all our material wants is beyond the productive capacity of available resources. [8]Thus, absolute material abundance is not possible. [9]This unyielding fact is the basis for our definition of economics: economics is concerned with the efficient use or management of limited productive resources to achieve maximum satisfaction of human material wants. [10]Though it may not be self-evident, all the headline-grabbing issues of the day—inflation, unemployment, health-care problems, government and international trade deficits, free-trade agreements among nations, poverty and inequality, pollution, and government regulation of business—are rooted in the one issue of using limited resources efficiently.

___ 1. The "biologically . . . determined wants" in paragraph 1 include cars.

___ 2. The "biologically . . . determined wants" in paragraph 1 include food.

___ 3. "Socially determined wants" might include sunshine.

___ 4. "Socially determined wants" might include television sets.

___ 5. Economics is based on absolute material abundance.

___ 6. Economics is based on the need to manage limited resources.

___ 7. Economics can lead to an ideal solution to resource management.

___ 8. Economic issues are rarely discussed in newspapers.

___ 9. The economic system organizes the way members of society share resources.

___ 10. Every society has some kind of economic system.

8 Purpose and Tone

There is an author—a person with thoughts, feelings, and opinions—behind everything you read. Whether this person is a cartoonist, a sportswriter, a newspaper columnist, a novelist, or a friend sending you a letter, he or she writes from a personal point of view. That point of view is reflected in (1) the *purpose* of a piece of writing—to inform, to persuade, or to entertain—as well as (2) its *tone*: the expression of attitude and feeling.

The *purpose* of the above cartoon, like all cartoons, is to entertain. Can you tell what the *tone* of each speaker is? Which one actually means what he or she is saying? Which one does not? After you have decided on your answers, read the explanation that follows.

Explanation

The man means what he is saying. He is asking the woman to go with him on an errand he could easily do on his own, so we can assume he enjoys and desires her company. The woman, on the other hand, does not mean what she is saying. Few people would consider a trip to the drugstore a "fun date," so we can infer she is being sarcastic, saying the opposite of what she means.

Purpose

Authors write with a reason in mind, and you can better evaluate their ideas by determining what that reason is. The author's reason for writing is also called the **purpose** of a selection. Three common purposes are as follows:

- To **inform**—to give information about a subject. Authors with this purpose wish to provide facts that will explain or teach something to readers.

  For example, the author of an informative paragraph about watching television might begin, "American children spend nearly as much time watching TV as they do in school." The author may then go on to provide evidence from research studies that show how many hours children watch TV.

- To **persuade**—to convince the reader to agree with the author's point of view on a subject. Authors with this purpose may give facts, but their main goal is to argue or prove a point to readers.

  The author of a persuasive passage about watching TV might begin, "Parents should not allow their children to watch more than two hours of TV each day." The author might then go on to support that main idea with details about the negative impact of such passive watching and the benefits of spending more time reading, studying, playing outdoors, and so on.

- To **entertain**—to amuse and delight; to appeal to the reader's senses and imagination. Authors with this purpose entertain in various ways, through fiction and nonfiction.

  The author of a humorous paragraph about watching TV might write, "I'm very proud to say that my family always sits down to dinner together; there are five of us, my husband and me, our son and daughter, and the TV set."

While the cover and title of anything you read—books, articles, and so on—don't necessarily suggest the author's main purpose, often they do. On the next page are the covers of three books. See if you can guess the primary purpose of each of these books.

Primary purpose:
A. to inform
B. to persuade
C. to entertain

___ Primary purpose:
A. to inform
B. to persuade
C. to entertain

___ Primary purpose:
A. to inform
B. to persuade
C. to entertain

As you probably concluded, the main purpose of the textbook is to inform; the main purpose of *The Betrayal of the American Dream* is to persuade; and the main purpose of the best-selling horror story *Doctor Sleep* is to entertain.

Check Your Understanding

Read each of the following three paragraphs and decide whether the author's main purpose is to inform, to persuade, or to entertain. Write in your answers, and then read the explanation that follows.

1. Athletes should not earn millions of dollars a year. If they weren't paid so much, then tickets to sports events wouldn't have to be so expensive, and more people could enjoy sports more often. Also, more reasonable pay would make for better role models for young people, many of whom look up to sports figures.

   Purpose: ______________________

2. The bubonic plague, also called the Black Death, swept Europe, Asia, and Africa from 1346 to 1353. So deadly was this disease that it killed one-third of the population of these continents. The plague was spread by fleas infected with bacteria from diseased rats. When it resulted in pneumonia, coughing spread the bacteria directly through the air.

   Purpose: ______________________

3. Men don't even notice 97 percent of the beauty efforts women make. For example, the average woman spends five thousand hours per year worrying about her fingernails. But I have never once, in more than forty years of listening

to men talk about women, heard a man say, "She has a nice set of fingernails!" Many men would not notice if a woman had upward of four hands.

Purpose: ______________________________

Explanation

In the first paragraph, the writer's purpose is *to persuade* readers that "athletes should not earn millions of dollars a year." The word *should* is a clue to the author's persuasive intention. Words like *should, ought,* and *must* are often meant to convince us rather than to inform us.

The purpose of the second paragraph is *to inform.* The author is providing readers with factual details about the Black Death.

In the third paragraph, the playful and exaggerated details about the beauty efforts of women tell us that the author's main goal is *to entertain* with humor.

A Note about Writing with More Than One Purpose

At times, writing may blend two or even three purposes. A persuasive article on the importance of avoiding junk foods, for example, might include a good many facts and even some comic touches.

- What would you say is the main purpose of this book?

A. To inform B. To persuade C. To entertain

If you chose answer A, you're correct—my main purpose is to inform and provide practice. But I also have other purposes at times. For example, in an earlier section, "Some Quick Study Tips" on pages 9–10, what is my main purpose?

A. To inform B. To persuade C. To entertain

My purpose here is both to inform and to persuade you about the importance of four time-proven study hints.

You'll notice, too, that I have included in this book a number of cartoons and amusing passages (for example, the passage on not-so-clever thieves on page 75). What is my purpose in choosing such content?

A. To inform B. To persuade C. To entertain

While my main purpose is to inform, I do at times have a second and even third purpose—to persuade and to entertain. And that is the case for other authors as well. What you need to remember when trying to determine purpose is to ask yourself, "What is the author's *main* purpose here?"

PRACTICE 1

Label each item according to its main purpose: to inform (**I**), to persuade (**P**), or to entertain (**E**).

_____ 1. Nowadays about half of U.S. marriages end in divorce.

_____ 2. American school systems should adopt a year-long schedule in order to become more competitive with schools in other countries.

_____ 3. Many people in my family are seafood eaters. When they see food, they eat it.

_____ 4. More than one-third of American children now live in single-parent families.

_____ 5. I read the obituaries every morning; if I don't find my name, I get dressed and go to work.

_____ 6. Television networks should reduce the number of commercials shown during children's programs.

_____ 7. The seeds of many fruits, including cherries, apples, plums, peaches, and apricots, contain a form of cyanide that can be deadly when eaten in large amounts.

_____ 8. Cosmetic companies that test their products on animals don't deserve your business; please buy from cruelty-free companies instead.

_____ 9. The reason that koala bears appear so calm and sleepy-eyed is that they are slightly drugged from the eucalyptus leaves they feed on.

_____10. Why do they lock gas station bathrooms? Are they afraid someone will clean them?

PRACTICE 2

Following are three passages, one each from a textbook, a humor book, and a collection of essays. In the spaces provided, write the letter of the best description of the purpose of each passage.

_____ 1. [1]To get students to read, give them books they will *want* to read. [2]I have heard more stories than I can remember of school systems that have purchased books they think their students *should* read rather than books their students *will* read. [3]Those books sit largely unused on dusty shelves. [4]I recall being asked to read *A Tale of Two Cities* in high school; I didn't want to read it, and bought a classic comic book instead to do a required book report. [5]That was many years ago, but even today otherwise well-meaning educators ask students to read books that are not about their lives and their worlds. [6]There is a famous line in *Hamlet:* "The readiness is all." [7]If readiness is in fact essential, most students are not ready for the likes of *A Tale of Two Cities*. [8]And few students are going to discover the pleasure of reading if they are forced to read material that doesn't appeal to them.

The main purpose of this passage is to
A. inform readers about books that are required reading in high schools.
B. convince readers that high-school students should be given books that appeal to them.
C. amuse readers with a story about the author's method of avoiding a reading assignment.

______ 2. [1]I have thought about exercise. [2]Read about it. [3]Watched it. [4]Even considered it. [5]Doctors recommend it, especially when they can't think of anything else to say. [6]When you're over fifty you go to the doctor and you're telling him that this hurts and that hurts and that you're tired all the time. [7]You know the doctor just wants to blurt out: "What the blazes do you expect? [8]You're o-l-d. [9]Old!" [10]But they don't say that, because they like to have you keep coming in so they can just kind of look you over and charge you three hundred bucks. [11]At my last checkup, I was complaining about a multitude of maladies visiting my body. [12](Most have since moved in.) [13]And the doctor looked bored—kind of listless, like he might need a checkup himself—and said rotely what he always says, "Are you getting enough exercise?" [14]I replied that I did not exercise at all, which I considered just about the right amount.

The main purpose of this passage is to
A. explain the drawbacks of exercise.
B. persuade people never to trust doctors.
C. entertain with humorous details about aging and doctors.

______ 3. [1]When Julius Caesar landed on the island we now know as Britain almost two thousand years ago, English didn't even exist. [2]Five hundred years later, a form of English called Old English (which was so different from modern English that you and I couldn't even understand it) had emerged, and was spoken by only a few thousand people. [3]By the time William Shakespeare was writing his greatest plays, in the late sixteenth century, English was the native language of five to seven million British people, but was not used anywhere outside of Britain itself. [4]In the four hundred years since then, English speakers such as the Scottish, the Irish, the Americans, and many others have carried their language and culture to all parts of the globe, and English has become the most widely spoken, written, and far-reaching language in human history. [5]Today English is used by roughly a billion people, more than half of whom have learned it as a second language. [6]It has become a global language of business as well as technology, appearing in 75 percent of the world's mail and 80 percent of the information stored in the world's computers.

The main purpose of this passage is to

A. inform readers about events in the history of the English language.

B. persuade readers that English should replace other countries' languages.

C. entertain readers with amusing anecdotes about the spread of English throughout the world.

Tone

A writer's **tone** reveals the attitude that he or she has toward a subject. Tone is expressed through the words and details the writer selects. Just as a speaker's voice can project a range of feelings, a writer's voice can project one or more tones, or feelings: anger, sympathy, hopefulness, sadness, respect, dislike, and so on. Understanding tone is, then, an important part of understanding what an author has written.

Because the purpose of a textbook is to inform, most textbooks are written in a matter-of-fact or objective tone, without any emotional appeal. A textbook author needs to convey information, rather than reveal his or her attitude toward that information. However, other kinds of writing can use any of a variety of tones.

To appreciate the differences in tone that writers can utilize, look at the following statements by employees of fast-food restaurants. Then read them aloud—in the tone of voice appropriate in each case.

> "I hate this job. The customers are rude, the managers are idiots, and the food smells like dog chow." (*Tone:* bitter, angry.)
>
> "I have no doubt that flipping burgers and toasting buns will prepare me for a top position on Wall Street." (*Tone:* mocking, sarcastic.)
>
> "I love working at Burger Barn. I meet interesting people, earn extra money, and get to eat all the chicken nuggets I want when I go on break." (*Tone:* enthusiastic, positive.)
>
> "I'm not excited about wearing fluorescent green polyester uniforms, but the managers are willing to schedule me around my classes, and the company offers scholarships to hard-working employees." (*Tone:* fair-minded, objective.)

PRACTICE 3

Following are five reactions to an aggressive driver weaving his car dangerously in and out of traffic. Label each statement with the tone of voice that you think is present. Choose each tone from the following box, and use each tone only once.

A. angry	B. cautious	C. questioning
D. sarcastic	E. self-pitying	

_____ 1. "Oh my God—I hope he doesn't hit me. This always happens to me. No matter where I go, something like this happens."

_____ 2. "That lousy jerk—he acts like he owns the road! He'd better not try cutting in front of me."

_____ 3. "That man's driving a little dangerously. I'm going to slow down so there's some distance between his car and ours."

_____ 4. "What makes someone drive like that? Are they on drugs? Are they in emotional pain? Are they just flat-out crazy?"

_____ 5. "Well, there's a careful, considerate driver. I want everyone in this car to pay special attention to him, so you can learn how a mature driver acts."

Words That Describe Tone

Below and on the next page are two lists of words commonly used to describe tone. With the exception of the words *matter-of-fact* and *objective*, the words reflect a feeling or judgment. The words in the first list are more familiar ones. Brief meanings are given in *italics* for the words in the second list. Refer to these meanings as needed to learn any words you don't know yet.

Some Words That Describe Tone

admiring	conceited	forgiving	respectful
affectionate	concerned	frightened	self-pitying
amused	critical	grateful	serious
angry	cruel	humorous	sorrowful
apologetic	curious	insulting	sympathetic
ashamed	defensive	joyous	threatening
calming	doubtful	loving	tragic
caring	encouraging	playful	warm
cheerful	excited	praising	worried

More Words That Describe Tone—with Their Meanings

ambivalent	*uncertain about a choice*
arrogant	*full of self-importance; conceited*
bewildered	*confused; puzzled*
bitter	*angry; full of hate*
compassionate	*deeply sympathetic*
depressed	*very sad or discouraged*
detached	*emotionally uninvolved*
disbelieving	*unbelieving*
distressed	*suffering sorrow, misery, or pain*
hypocritical	*false*
impassioned	*filled with strong feeling*
indignant	*angry about something unfair or mean*
instructive	*teaching*
ironic	*meaning the opposite of what is expressed*
lighthearted	*happy and carefree*
matter-of-fact	*sticking to facts; unemotional*
mocking	*making fun of and/or looking down upon something*
nostalgic	*longing for something or someone in the past*
objective	*not influenced by feelings or personal prejudices*
optimistic	*looking on the bright side of things*
pessimistic	*looking on the gloomy, unfavorable side of things*
pleading	*begging*
prideful	*full of pride or exaggerated self-esteem*
remorseful	*guilty over a wrong one has done*
revengeful	*wanting to hurt someone in return for an injury*
sarcastic	*sharp or wounding; ironic*
scheming	*tricky*
scornful	*looking down on someone or something*
self-mocking	*making fun of or looking down on oneself*
sentimental	*showing tender feelings; romantic; overly emotional*
solemn	*involved with serious concerns*
straightforward	*direct and honest*
superior	*looking down on others*
tolerant	*respectful of others' views and behavior; patient about problems*
uncertain	*doubting*

Check Your Understanding

Below are five statements expressing different attitudes about an old car. Five different tones are used:

A. angry	B. disappointed	C. humorous
D. optimistic	E. tolerant	

Label each statement according to which of these five tones you think is present. (Feel free to check the lists on pages 336–337 for the meanings of any unfamiliar tone words.) Use each tone once. Then read the explanation that follows.

_______________ 1. Unfortunately, this car is a lot less reliable than I'd like.

_______________ 2. It's not the greatest car in the world, but it usually takes me where I have to go.

_______________ 3. If car dealers weren't so dishonest, I wouldn't have bought this piece of junk for so much money.

_______________ 4. Even though the car has a problem now and then, I bet it'll keep running forever.

_______________ 5. This car is so old it's eligible for an antique-vehicle license plate.

Explanation

The first item has a disappointed tone because of the words *unfortunately* and *less reliable than I'd like.* In the second item, the phrase *usually takes me where I have to go* shows the writer's accepting attitude, giving the item a tolerant tone. The tone of the third item is angry because of the writer's clearly stated resentment of car dealers, of the car itself, and of its price tag. The bet in the fourth item that the car will "keep running forever" gives that item an optimistic tone. And finally, the obvious exaggeration in the last item imparts a humorous tone.

A Note on Irony

One commonly used tone is irony. When writing has an **ironic** tone, it says one thing but means the opposite. Irony is found in everyday conversation as well as in writing.

Following are a few examples of verbal irony (also known as **sarcasm**); notice that the quotation in each says the opposite of what is meant.

- If the price tag on a shirt you like is double what you'd expect, you might mutter, "What a bargain."
- After sitting through the first session of what is clearly going to be a very boring class, you say to a classmate, "I only hope I can stand all the excitement."
- If someone is unusually attractive and talented, we might remark, "Poor Laura. She's got absolutely nothing going for her."
- After seeing your favorite basketball team play its worst game ever, you might comment, "I knew they wouldn't disappoint me."
- Your sister comes home from a blind date, saying, "It was great once I understood the rules. You see, his job was to talk about himself 100 percent of the time, and my job was to nod."

As you can see, irony is a useful tone for humor and can be used to imply exactly the opposite of what is said or what is done.

Irony also refers to situations in which what happens is the opposite of what we might expect. We would call it ironic, for example, if the arsonist responsible for a string of fires turned out to be a city firefighter, or if a bank is robbed by two guards that were hired to protect it. And in the cartoon below, it is ironic that the father who expects his son to clean his room permits himself to have a very messy environment.

Here are a few more examples of this type of irony:

- An expensive computer system is installed to help a company manage its files. Several weeks later, it crashes, and all the files are lost.
- A doctor tells a man that he'd better exercise if he wants to stay healthy. So the man begins jogging. One day while jogging across a street, he is hit by a truck and dies instantly.

- A woman loved dancing, but her boyfriend did not dance well. So she insisted he take dancing lessons. After he started taking lessons, he fell in love with his dancing instructor.
- After being told they could never have children, a couple adopts a baby. A few months later, the wife becomes pregnant.
- In a story called "The Interlopers," two lifelong enemies are trapped when a tree falls upon them. Injured and helpless, they decide to forget their feud and become friends. Minutes later, they are attacked and killed by wolves.

The five examples above show that irony also describes meaningful situations that are contrary to what is intended or expected.

Check Your Understanding

Look now at the cartoon below. Then identify the quotations from the cartoon as either straightforward or ironic (in which what is said is sarcastically the opposite of what is really meant) by writing the letter of your choice on the line.

_____ 1. "If we know our senior executive is making a bad decision, shouldn't we tell her?"
A. straightforward B. ironic

_____ 2. "Let's end our careers by challenging a decision that won't change. That's a great idea."
A. straightforward B. ironic

_____ 3. "And let's pull our neckties until it hurts."
A. straightforward B. ironic

Explanation

Note the contrast in tone within the cartoon:

1. In the first box, the tone of the words is straightforward—the speaker is serious.
2. What is said in the second box is ironic—it says the opposite of what the speaker really means. For instance, the speaker does not mean, "That's a great idea." The speaker is really saying, "That's a terrible idea."
3. The words on the right in the third box continue the irony by suggesting that causing deliberate pain is as good an idea as challenging the boss's decision.

PRACTICE 4

A. Below are five statements expressing different attitudes about going on a blind date. Five different tones are used:

A. angry	**B.** enthusiastic	**C.** sarcastic
D. pessimistic	**E.** self-pitying	

For each statement, write the letter of the tone that you think is present. Use each tone once.

_____ 1. I just know I'm going to hate this guy my mother's making me go out with. These things never work out.

_____ 2. Me go on a blind date? Oh sure, I've always wanted to meet Dracula's daughter.

_____ 3. No way I'm going on a blind date! You've got a lot of nerve trying to set me up. What do you think I am—desperate?

_____ 4. I'd love it if you'd fix me up with your cousin from out of state. It sounds like a lot of fun.

_____ 5. Oh, I suppose I'll go on a blind date. That's probably the only kind of date I can get.

B. The following conversation between an office worker and his boss involves five of the tones shown in the box below. For each statement, write the letter of the tone that you think is present. Five tones will be left over.

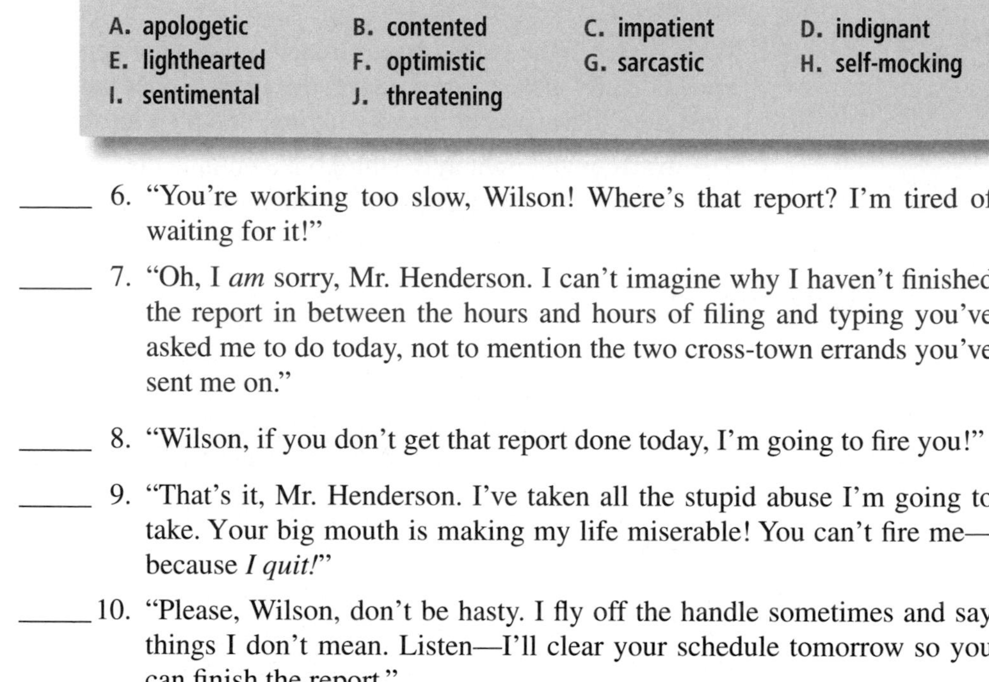

A. apologetic	B. contented	C. impatient	D. indignant
E. lighthearted	F. optimistic	G. sarcastic	H. self-mocking
I. sentimental	J. threatening		

_____ 6. "You're working too slow, Wilson! Where's that report? I'm tired of waiting for it!"

_____ 7. "Oh, I *am* sorry, Mr. Henderson. I can't imagine why I haven't finished the report in between the hours and hours of filing and typing you've asked me to do today, not to mention the two cross-town errands you've sent me on."

_____ 8. "Wilson, if you don't get that report done today, I'm going to fire you!"

_____ 9. "That's it, Mr. Henderson. I've taken all the stupid abuse I'm going to take. Your big mouth is making my life miserable! You can't fire me—because *I quit!*"

_____ 10. "Please, Wilson, don't be hasty. I fly off the handle sometimes and say things I don't mean. Listen—I'll clear your schedule tomorrow so you can finish the report."

PRACTICE 5

Each of the following selections illustrates one of the tones in the box below. In each space, put the letter of the one tone that best applies. Don't use any letter more than once. Three tones will be left over.

Remember that the tone of a selection reflects the author's attitude. To find the tone of a paragraph, ask yourself what attitude is revealed by its words and phrases.

A. admiring	B. bewildered	C. critical	D. hopeful
E. matter-of-fact	F. playful	G. tolerant	H. uncertain

_____ 1. He prayed—it wasn't my religion;
He ate—it wasn't what I ate;
He spoke—it wasn't my language;
He dressed—it wasn't what I wore;
He took my hand—it wasn't the color of mine.
But when he laughed—it was how I laughed,
and when he cried—it was how I cried.

_____ 2. [1]People's behavior is hard to understand. [2]To put it bluntly, every single one of us knows that every other one of us is going to die someday. [3]Our friends, our enemies, our family members, our classmates, our neighbors, our teachers, the guy who serves us our hamburger at McDonald's, ourselves, everybody. [4]Not only are we all aware of our own mortality, but we also know that every human being is dealing with painful, difficult realities of life every day. [5]We're all hurting; we're all struggling in some way or another. [6]Knowing all this, you'd think that people would go out of their way to be as kind and gentle to one another as they possibly could. [7]I mean, we're not here for very long—why not try to be a comfort to each another? [8]Instead, day after day, we beat each other up. [9]We do it on a personal level, on a community level, and certainly on a global level. [10]Why? [11]What is it we think we're gaining by being cruel to one another? [12]Can anyone explain this to me?

_____ 3. [1]Much of the time I look back at this nation's history and think to myself, "Only in America." [2]Only in America could a rag-tag bunch of colonists rise up and defeat the power of the mighty British Empire. [3]Only in America could Abraham Lincoln, a poor boy born in a log cabin, use the power of the presidency to end the horror of slavery. [4]Only in America could endless numbers of immigrants come with almost nothing but the clothes on their backs and then, despite hard times, go on to achieve happy lives for themselves and their families. [5]And only in America could a young senator with the unlikely name of Barack Hussein Obama be elected president, rising above the prejudices and fears in the land to unite a glorious but fractured country. [6]Only in America could our president ride in triumph up Pennsylvania Avenue, passing hotels, theaters, and restaurants where his black ancestors could have entered only as servants. [7]Only in America!

_____ 4. [1]Erik Erikson developed the dreary psychological theory that, from the moment of birth, life consists of a number of stages, each characterized by an issue to be resolved and a "virtue" to be obtained. [2]The task for newborns, to begin with, is to resolve the issue of "basic trust versus mistrust," though probably all they want to do is sleep, eat, and gurgle. [3]Toddlers are supposed to concentrate not on their teddy bears but on working out the issue of "autonomy versus shame and doubt"; preschoolers must take up the task of "initiative versus guilt." [4]And so it goes. [5]Erikson will not even let us die in peace. [6]Old folks, who might prefer just to put their feet up and relax after eighty years of confronting their dismal chores, are expected to resolve "integrity versus despair" before departing this world. [7]Erikson maintains that if we fail a task at any stage, we are in for serious trouble during the next, so those of us who manage to perish before completing this final task will have to face wrath in the afterlife.

_____ 5. Clay comes out to meet Liston
And Liston starts to retreat.
If Liston goes back any further,
He'll end up in a ringside seat.
Clay swings with a left;
Clay swings with a right.
Look at young Cassius
Carry the fight.
Liston keeps backing
But there's not enough room.
It's a matter of time.
There, Clay lowers the boom.
Now Clay swings with a right.
What a beautiful swing.
And the punch raises the bear,
Clear out of the ring.
Liston is still rising
And the ref wears a frown,
For he can't start counting,
Till Sonny comes down.
Now Liston disappears from view.
The crowd is getting frantic,
But our radar stations have picked
him up.
He's somewhere over the Atlantic.
Who would have thought
When they came to the fight
That they'd witness the launching
Of a human satellite?
Yes, the crowd did not dream
When they laid down their money
That they would see
A total eclipse of the Sonny!

(Recited by Cassius Clay, later known as Muhammad Ali, before his first fight with Sonny Liston)

PRACTICE 6

Read the following short essay by noted science and science-fiction author Isaac Asimov (1920–1992). Then answer the questions about purpose and tone that follow.

KP (1): work with the "kitchen police," soldiers who assist the army cooks
bents (2): tendencies
oracles (3): messages from the gods
foist (4): force
arbiter (4): judge
indulgently (6): done to go along with someone's wishes
raucously (6): loudly
smugly (6): in a self-satisfied way

What Is Intelligence, Anyway?

1 What is intelligence, anyway? When I was in the Army, I received a kind of aptitude test that all soldiers took and, against a normal of 100, scored 160. No one at the base had ever seen a figure like that, and for two hours they made a big fuss over me. (It didn't mean anything. The next day I was still a buck private with KP° as my highest duty.)

2 All my life I've been registering scores like that, so that I have the complacent feeling that I'm highly intelligent, and I expect other people to think so, too. Actually, though, don't such scores simply mean that I am very good at answering the type of academic questions that are considered worthy of answers by the people who make up the intelligence tests—people with intellectual bents° similar to mine?

3 For instance, I had an auto repairman once, who, on these intelligence tests, could not possibly have scored more than 80, by my estimate. I always took it for granted that I was far more intelligent than he was. Yet, when anything went wrong with my car, I hastened to him with it, watched him anxiously as he explored its vitals, and listened to his pronouncements as though they were divine oracles°—and he always fixed my car.

4 Well then, suppose my auto repairman devised questions for an intelligence test. Or suppose a carpenter did, or a farmer, or, indeed, almost anyone but an academician. By every one of those tests, I'd prove myself a moron. And I'd *be* a moron, too. In a world where I could not use my academic training and my verbal talents but had to do something intricate or hard, working with my hands, I would do poorly. My intelligence, then, is not absolute but is a function of the society I live in and of the fact that a small subsection of that society has managed to foist° itself on the rest as an arbiter° of such matters.

5 Consider my auto repairman, again. He had a habit of telling me jokes whenever he saw me. One time he raised his head from under the automobile hood to say, "Doc, a deaf-and-dumb guy went into a hardware store to ask for some nails. He put two fingers together on the counter and made hammering motions with the other hand. The clerk brought him a hammer. He shook his head and pointed to the two fingers he was hammering. The clerk brought him nails. He picked out the sizes he wanted, and left. Well, Doc, the next guy who came in was a blind man. He wanted scissors. How do you suppose he asked for them?"

6 Indulgently°, I lifted my right hand and made scissoring motions with my first two fingers. Whereupon my auto repairman laughed raucously° and said, "Why, you dumb jerk, he used his *voice* and asked for them." Then he said, smugly°, "I've been trying that on all my customers today." "Did you catch many?" I asked. "Quite a few," he said, "but I knew for sure I'd catch *you*." "Why is that?" I asked. "Because you're so goddamned educated, Doc, I *knew* you couldn't be very smart."

7 And I have an uneasy feeling he had something there.

_____ 1. In paragraph 4, the author refers to himself with a(n)

A. egotistical tone.
B. tragic tone.
C. humble tone.

_____ 2. When discussing his auto repairman, the author generally uses a(n)

A. loving tone.
B. admiring tone.
C. doubtful tone.

_____ 3. In referring to those who determine what intelligence is (in the last sentence of paragraph 4), the author uses a

A. confused tone.
B. lighthearted tone.
C. critical tone.

_____ 4. In paragraph 6, the comments of the repairman have a

A. straightforward tone.
B. angry tone.
C. superior tone.

_____ 5. Asimov's main purpose in this reading is to

A. inform readers of the traditional view of intelligence tests.
B. persuade readers that the traditional view of intelligence is inadequate.
C. entertain readers with several colorful anecdotes.

CHAPTER REVIEW

In this chapter, you learned that part of effective reading is to do the following:

- Be aware of an author's **purpose**: the reason why he or she writes. Three common purposes are to inform, to persuade, and to entertain.
- Be aware of **tone**: the expression of the author's attitude and feeling about a subject. A writer's tone might be objective—the case in most textbook writing—or it might be lighthearted, sympathetic, angry, affectionate, respectful, or any of the many other tones shown on pages 336–337.
- One important tone to recognize is **irony**: saying one thing but meaning the opposite.

The next chapter—Chapter 9—will explain another part of effective reading: recognizing the point in an argument and evaluating the support for that point.

On the Web: If you are using this book in class, you can visit our website for additional practice in identifying an author's purpose and tone. Go to **www.townsendpress.com** and click on "Learning Center."

REVIEW TEST 1

To review what you've learned in this chapter, answer the following questions by filling in the blank or writing the letter of the correct answer.

_____ 1. The main purpose of a textbook is to
A. inform. B. persuade. C. entertain.

_____ 2. The main purpose of an adventure story, mystery novel, or other work of fiction is to
A. inform. B. persuade. C. entertain.

3. Just as a speaker's voice can project a range of feelings, a writer's voice can project one or more ________________, attitudes, or feelings.

4. If a writer says one thing but means just the opposite, the writer's tone is ________________________.

_____ 5. TRUE OR FALSE? Textbook writing tends to be matter-of-fact and objective in tone, rather than reflecting feelings or judgments.

REVIEW TEST 2: PURPOSE

In the space provided, indicate whether the primary purpose of each passage is to inform (**I**), to persuade (**P**), or to entertain (**E**).

_____ 1. [1]As a TIME subscriber, and one of our most valued customers, you are being extended this unusual invitation:

[2]When you pay early for your next one-year term, you can send a FREE yearlong gift to *anyone* you choose.

[3]You have several things to gain, should you accept:

- [4]The recipient of your gift is sure to appreciate your generosity and good taste.
- [5]The ULTRONIC AM/FM Radio—FREE!
- [6]You'll save 67% off the newsstand price on your own subscription.
- [7]We've also included a FREE gift card (enclosed) to announce your gift personally.

[8]Of course, TIME also has something to gain: the opportunity to acquaint your friend or relative with TIME. [9]We're confident that the person you choose will find that TIME'S perspective on the news is more valuable than ever before. [10]As a regular reader, you know that TIME'S analysis of world events offers unique insights into our ever-changing world so you can better determine how the news impacts your daily life.

[11]So let us hear from you *now*.

_____ 2. [1]Many people who have come close to death from drowning, cardiac arrest, or other causes have described near-death experiences—profound, subjective events that sometimes result in dramatic changes in values, beliefs, behavior, and attitudes toward life and death. [2]These experiences often include a new clarity of thinking, a feeling of well-being, a sense of being out of the body, and visions of bright lights or mystical encounters. [3]Such experiences have been reported by an estimated 30 to 40 percent of hospital patients who were revived after coming close to death and by about 5 percent of adult Americans in a nationwide poll. [4]Near-death experiences have been explained as a response to a perceived threat of death (a psychological theory); as a result of biological states that accompany the process of dying (a physiological theory); and as a foretaste of an actual state of bliss after death (a transcendental theory).

_____ 3. [1]Without question the most important invention in human history, next to frozen yogurt, is the computer. [2]Without computers, it would be virtually impossible for us to accomploiwer xow;gtkc,mg^&)

[3]Hold it, there seems to be a keyboard problem here. [4]Let me just try plugging this cable into . . .

[5]ERROR ERROR ERROR ALL FILES HAVE BEEN DESTROYED YOU STUPID BAZOOTYHEAD

[6]Ha ha! [7]Considering what a wonderful invention computers are, they certainly have a way of making you sometimes feel like pouring coffee into their private parts and listening to them scream. [8]Of course you should not do this. [9]The first rule of data processing is: "Never pour hot beverages into a computer, unless it belongs to somebody else, such as your employer."

______ 4. [1]America—it's been the land of justice and opportunity. [2]It's been the land where you don't have to be born rich or privileged in order to get a fair chance in life. [3]This is the America that I've always believed in. [4]Unfortunately, our politicians in Washington don't seem to share that vision. [5]The handling of the 2008–2009 economic meltdown, a financial catastrophe that swept like a tidal wave from Wall Street through Main Street, is a case in point. [6]As the governmental response to the crisis developed, it became apparent that the banking system and irresponsibly run financial institutions were going to be bailed out, while ordinary Americans were ignored. [7]The fact is that many former politicians and government employees work as well-paid lobbyists for financial firms, including hedge fund firms, investment banks, and the failed mortgage giants Freddie Mac and Fannie Mae. [8]The lobbyists see that the wealthy "haves" are given priority at the expense of the "have nots"—everyday working Americans who struggle to pay their mortgages, feed their families, afford health care, and plan for retirement. [9]Americans who still want to believe their country is the land of justice and opportunity should be outraged that their "leaders" are so willing to sell themselves and their influence to the highest bidders.

______ 5. [1]Mortal combat was one of the most popular sports in ancient Rome. [2]Bouts began with contestants—called gladiators—marching into the arena and acknowledging the Roman leader with the words "Hail, Caesar, we who are about to die salute you." [3]After this formality, the gladiators were given weapons as well as protective clothing. [4]Once armed, they began fighting. [5]Crowds enjoyed a skillful, courageous, and evenly matched fight. [6]If the loser was not killed, the event's sponsor decided his fate. [7]A thumbs-up sign meant the loser would be allowed to heal so he could fight another day. [8]Thumbs down meant that he would immediately have his throat cut by the winner's sword. [9]An actor dressed as a god would then emerge and spear the body to make certain he was dead. [10]The tattered body was then hooked behind a horse and dragged away and the entire arena sprayed with perfume, after which the crowd settled contentedly back for the next contest.

REVIEW TEST 3: TONE

The cartoon and the four passages that follow each illustrate one of the tones in the box below. In the space provided, put the letter of the tone that best applies to each passage. Don't use any letter more than once. Three tones will be left over.

Remember that the tone of a selection reflects the author's attitude. To find the tone of a paragraph, ask yourself what attitude is revealed by its words and phrases.

A. admiring	B. amused	C. encouraging	D. forgiving
E. frightened	F. pessimistic	G. puzzled	H. regretful

_____ 1. What is the tone of the woman in the purple T-shirt in the cartoon below?

"It's such a beautiful day. With our luck, tomorrow will be cold and rainy."

_____ 2. [1]I wished the guy in the seat behind the bus driver would stop looking at me the way he did. [2]He gave me the creeps. [3]I was really glad when my stop came and I could get off the bus. [4]It didn't take me long to realize, however, that he was getting off too. [5]"Please, God, let him go the other way," I thought. [6]I turned toward home. [7]The streets were darker and emptier than I remembered they could be. [8]His footsteps followed mine. [9]When I walked faster, he did too. [10]When I crossed to the other side, he crossed too. [11]Finally, I began to run. [12]My vision was blurred by the tears in my eyes.

_____ 3. [1]Somewhere around midterm, almost every student feels like saying, "I just can't learn anything else. [2]My brain is full!" [3]Well, don't give up so easily—your brain has more room than you think. [4]Scientists believe that memories are stored in the part of the brain called the cerebrum. [5]If you were to store ten bits of information each second of your life, by your one-hundredth birthday, your memory-storage area would be only half full. [6]So the next time you feel your brain is about to short-circuit, take a break and then come back to those books, knowing you've got plenty of room in your head for more learning.

_____ 4. [1]Since the advent of voice mail and then e-mail, the concept of "business hours" has become obsolete. [2]Before these technologies arrived on the scene, we telephoned office workers only between approximately 9 a.m. and 5 p.m. [3]In fact, business etiquette dictated that we shouldn't call before 9:30 in the morning—this was to give the person we were calling time to settle in at his or her desk before having to answer the phone. [4]Nor did a polite person call close to the end of the day, to avoid delaying people who might be clearing off their desks preparatory to going home. [5]It was also thought inconsiderate to telephone during the lunch hour. [6]All that has changed. [7]Callers can now leave voice-mail messages at any time of the day or night, and e-mail and text messages arrive steadily around the clock. [8]This is of course efficient, and a boon for people living and working in different time zones, but it has also meant the end of some practices that were once part of good manners.

_____ 5. [1]The Civil War general Thomas "Stonewall" Jackson had the odd belief that one of his arms was bigger than the other. [2]As a result, he always walked and rode with that arm raised, so that his blood would drain into his body. [3]He was a champion sleeper. [4]More than once he fell asleep at the dinner table with food in his mouth. [5]At one battle, his lieutenants found him all but impossible to awaken and lifted him, still asleep, onto his horse, where he continued to slumber while shells exploded around him. [6]When awake, Jackson would often march his troops all over a battle area in such illogical and unexplainable ways that he earned a reputation among enemy officers for cleverness and cunning. [7]Jackson owes some of his fame to the fact that he had the best nickname any soldier has ever enjoyed. [8]That name may have come from his habit of standing inert, like a stone wall, when a charge was called for.

REVIEW TEST 4

Most of us assume that older people become hard of hearing because they're, well, *old*. Their ears are simply wearing out, right? Actually, new evidence is showing that age has nothing to do with hearing loss. In fact, it's fairly likely that you (regardless of your age) have done something today that may affect your ability to hear many years from now.

To help you continue to strengthen your skills, the reading is followed by questions on what you've learned not only in this chapter but also in previous chapters.

Words to Watch

Below are some words in the reading that do not have strong context support. Each word is followed by the number of the paragraph in which it appears and its meaning there. These words are indicated in the article by a small circle (°).

blithely (3): casually, without any concern
proprietors (6): owners
retrofitted (6): modified, newly equipped
auditory (8): hearing
apparatus (9): equipment
cumulative (11): growing over time
redundancy (11): surplus
aficionados (11): enthusiastic fans
otolaryngology (13): the study of ear, nose, and throat

WHAT CAUSES HEARING LOSS

Jane E. Brody

1 Noise, not age, is the leading cause of hearing loss. Unless you take steps now to protect to your ears, sooner or later many of you—and your children—will have difficulty understanding even ordinary speech.

2 Tens of millions of Americans, including 12 percent to 15 percent of school-age children, already have permanent hearing loss caused by the everyday noise that we take for granted as a fact of life.

3 "The sad truth is that many of us are responsible for our own hearing loss," writes Katherine Bouton in her new book, *Shouting Won't Help: Why I—and 50 Million Other Americans—Can't Hear You*. The cause, she explains, is "the

noise we blithely° subject ourselves to day after day."

4 While there are myriad regulations to protect people who work in noisy environments, there are relatively few governing repeated exposure to noise outside the workplace: portable music devices, rock concerts, hair dryers, sirens, lawn mowers, leaf blowers, vacuum cleaners, car alarms, and countless other sources.

5 We live in a noisy world, and every year it seems to get noisier. Ms. Bouton notes that the noise level inside Allen Fieldhouse at the University of Kansas often exceeds that of a chain saw.

6 After poor service, noise is the second leading complaint about restaurants. Proprietors° believe that people spend more on food and drink in bustling eateries, and many have created new venues or retrofitted° old ones to maximize sound levels.

7 When I'm told about a new restaurant, my first question is, "Is it noisy?" My friends and I will never return to one in which the racket makes it impossible to converse with table-mates. Perhaps the young diners the restauranteurs covet "talk" by texting.

8 The ears are fragile instruments. When sound waves enter the ear, they cause the eardrum to vibrate. The vibrations are transmitted to the cochlea, in the inner ear, where fluid carries them to neatly organized rows of hair cells. These in turn stimulate auditory° nerve fibers, each attuned to a different frequency. These impulses travel via the auditory nerve to the brain, where they are interpreted as, say, words, music, or an approaching vehicle.

Damage to this delicate apparatus° 9
results from both volume and length of exposure to sound. Very loud noises, or chronic exposure to sound even when it is not particularly loud, can wreak havoc on hair cells, causing them to become disarranged and to degenerate.

We are born with a fixed number 10
of hair cells; once they are dead, they cannot be replaced, and auditory sensitivity is permanently lost. Usually, sensitivity to high-frequency sounds is first to go, followed by an inability to hear the frequencies of speech.

Furthermore, the effects of noise 11
exposure are cumulative°, as Robert V. Harrison, an auditory specialist at the University of Toronto, noted recently in *The International Journal of Pediatrics*. Although we start out with a redundancy° of hair cells, with repeated noisy insults, enough are destroyed to impair hearing. Thus, damage to hair cells incurred early in life, as has happened to many rock musicians and rock concert aficionados°, can show up in midlife as difficulty understanding speech.

Sound volume is measured in 12
decibels (dB), and the level at which noise can cause permanent hearing loss begins at about 85 dB, typical of a hair dryer, food processor, or kitchen blender.

Dr. Michael D. Seidman, the director 13
of otolaryngology° at Henry Ford West Bloomfield Hospital in Michigan, told me to use ear plugs when I dry my hair or mow my lawn with a gas-powered mower, and to cover my ears

when an emergency vehicle passes with siren blasting. Ear protection is a must for people who shoot guns as well as those who ride motorcycles or use snow blowers, leaf blowers, hand or pneumatic drills, or chain saws.

14 But even noisier than many of these is the maximum output of some portable music players, which can exceed occupational safety levels and produce sound levels in the ear on a par with that of a jet taking off. If you listen to music with earbuds or headphones at levels that block out normal discourse, you are in effect dealing lethal blows to the hair cells in your ears, Dr. Seidman said.

15 A national study in 2006 by the American Speech-Language-Hearing Association found that among users of portable music devices, 35 percent of adults and up to 59 percent of teenagers reported listening at loud volumes.

16 Dr. Harrison urges purchasers of such "personal entertainment devices" to read and heed the warnings and practical advice on package inserts. Too often people turn up the volume to overcome surrounding noise. A better plan is to set a maximum volume while in a quiet environment and never go above that.

17 In general, if other people can hear what you're listening to, the volume is turned up too high. Many times I've had to change my seat on the subway or bus because the rider next to me was using a music player as if it were a boombox.

18 Some portable listening devices come with the ability to set a maximum volume, which may be worth the added cost to parents concerned about protecting their children's ears.

At a given volume level, earbuds 19
deliver higher noise levels than over-the-ear headphones. If earbuds are used, Dr. Harrison suggests selecting ones that fit loosely and never inserting them tightly into the ear canal. Alternatively, when you are alone and not at risk of missing important environmental cues, like an approaching vehicle, consider using noise-canceling over-the-ear headphones that block out background noise and enable you to listen at a lower volume.

Even toys meant for young children 20
can generate ear-damaging levels of noise. The American Speech-Language-Hearing Association lists as potential hazards cap guns, talking dolls, vehicles with horns and sirens, walkie-talkies, rubber squeaky toys, musical instruments, and toys with cranks. According to the

association, some toy sirens and squeaky rubber toys can emit sounds of 90 dB, as loud as a lawn mower.

21 It suggests that parents with normal hearing test new toys before giving them to a child. "If the toy sounds loud, don't buy it," is the recommendation. For noisy toys already bought, consider removing the batteries or taping over the speaker.

Reading Comprehension Questions

Vocabulary in Context

_____ 1. In the sentence below, the word *myriad* (mĭr′ē-əd) means
A. many.
B. strange.
C. complicated.
D. strict.

"While there are myriad regulations to protect people who work in noisy environments, there are relatively few governing repeated exposure to noise outside the workplace." (Paragraph 4)

Central Point and Main Ideas

_____ 2. Which sentence best expresses the central point of the selection?
A. Our hearing mechanism is very delicate and can be damaged easily.
B. Old age has often been blamed, inaccurately, for hearing loss.
C. Repeated exposure to common noises, not aging, is what damages our hearing.
D. Toys, portable listening devices, and even blow dryers are only a few of the everyday items that can damage hearing.

_____ 3. The implied main idea of paragraphs 3–5 is
A. We live in a noisy world that continues to get noisier.
B. There are very few, if any, laws that protect our hearing outside the workplace.
C. We are each personally responsible for our own hearing loss.
D. Everyday noises can damage hearing, and we need to stay informed if we want to protect our hearing.

_____ 4. The main idea of paragraphs 14–18 is
A. Most people listen to portable music devices too loudly.
B. Listening to portable music devices too loudly can damage hearing.
C. Portable listening devices are dangerous.
D. Those most likely to be affected by hearing loss from portable music devices are teens and children.

Supporting Details

_____ 5. The hair cells in our ears
A. help carry sound waves to the brain.
B. can be destroyed by repeated exposure to noise.
C. cannot be replaced once they are gone.
D. all of the above.

_____ 6. Hair dryers, food processors, and blenders all emit ____ decibels, the level of noise that can cause permanent hearing damage.
A. 25
B. 50
C. 85
D. 100

Inferences

_____ 7. We can infer that the author of this selection
A. has suffered permanent hearing loss due to everyday noise.
B. is careful about exposing her ears to loud everyday noise.
C. feels that portable music devices should be banned.
D. dislikes restaurants, rock concerts, and riding the subway.

____ 8. Paragraphs 6 and 7 suggest that
   A. restaurant owners who think that diners like a loud restaurant are mistaken.
   B. only older people are upset by noise in restaurants.
   C. texting instead of actually talking is becoming more common at restaurants.
   D. maximizing sound in restaurants is important for attracting customers.

Purpose and Tone

9. Which of the following statements best describes the author's purpose?
   A. To persuade the American public to demand safety regulations on everyday noise
   B. To persuade older people to consider past habits that may have caused hearing loss
   C. To inform readers about everyday noise that can create permanent hearing damage
   D. To entertain readers with vivid descriptions of the noises they are forced to listen to on a daily basis

_____10. The author's tone throughout this selection may be characterized as
   A. detached.
   B. optimistic and lighthearted.
   C. superior.
   D. serious and concerned.

Discussion Questions

1. What is the loudest sound you've ever heard? Where were you when you heard it? What did it sound like? Do you think it may have affected your hearing?
2. Brody makes her feelings clear about noise in restaurants. Would you prefer to eat in a quiet restaurant or a noisy one? Why? Are there any situations in which you actually prefer some noise?
3. After reading this article, do you plan to change anything to lessen the impact of the noise you're exposed to? If so, which piece of Brody's advice would you be most likely to follow?
4. In her article, Brody points out that we take our hearing for granted, even though our hearing apparatus is astoundingly complex and fragile. What other things about our bodies do we take for granted? Have you ever suffered an injury or illness that made you more aware of your body's limits? Explain.

Note: Writing assignments for this selection appear on page 700–701.

Check Your Performance

PURPOSE AND TONE

Activity		*Number Right*		*Points*		*Score*
Review Test 1	(5 items)	______	×	2	=	______
Review Test 2	(5 items)	______	×	6	=	______
Review Test 3	(5 items)	______	×	6	=	______
Review Test 4	(10 items)	______	×	3	=	______
			TOTAL SCORE		=	______%

Enter your total score into the **Reading Performance Chart: Review Tests** on the inside back cover.

Name ______________________ Date __________

Section __________ SCORE: (Number correct) ______ x 10 = ______ %

PURPOSE AND TONE: Mastery Test 1

A. In the space provided, indicate whether the primary purpose of each item is to inform (**I**), to persuade (**P**), or to entertain (**E**).

_____ 1. More than half of adult Americans are overweight, and more than a fifth are obese.

_____ 2. Fast-food chains should not be allowed to advertise their high-fat, high-calorie products to children.

_____ 3. I get my exercise every day by lifting weights: my heavy arms and legs.

_____ 4. Medical problems associated with obesity include high cholesterol, high blood pressure, gallbladder disease, arthritis, diabetes, breast cancer, and colon cancer.

_____ 5. My son explained that the healthy vegetable side of his stomach felt full, but that the dessert side was very empty.

B. We usually think of graveyards as solemn places, but gravestone inscriptions can have a variety of tones. Each of the real gravestone inscriptions below illustrates a different tone. In the space provided, write in the letter of the tone that best applies in each case.

A. appreciative	**B.** humorous	**C.** joyous
D. modest	**E.** tender	

_____ 6. On the grave of a dentist:

Stranger, tread this ground with gravity.
Dentist Brown is filling his last cavity.

_____ 7. On the stone for a well-known writer:

Better
Than Anyone Else
He told the truth
About his time.

(Continues on next page)

_____ 8. On the stone for a pioneer woman:
She did what she could.

_____ 9. On the stone for a dead soldier:
Had we a dearest wish
fulfilled
Dearest Daddy
We would ask for you.

_____ 10. On the grave of Dr. Martin Luther King, Jr.:

© Travel Ink—Getty Images

Name ______________________________ Date __________

Section __________ SCORE: (Number correct) ______ x 10 = ______ %

PURPOSE AND TONE: Mastery Test 2

A. In the space provided, indicate whether the primary purpose of each item is to inform (**I**), to persuade (**P**), or to entertain (**E**).

_____ 1. To reduce crime and make the city safer for residents, police must enforce the new curfew and keep teenagers off the streets at night.

_____ 2. My brother says that I was so ugly as a kid that my mother had to tie a pork chop around my neck to get our dog to play with me.

_____ 3. Scientists are almost certain that a catastrophic collision between the Earth and a large meteor will happen sometime in the next fifty thousand years.

_____ 4. When I saw my daughter dumping large amounts of salt on her food, I asked, "Would you like a little dinner with your salt?"

_____ 5. [1]If manufacturers of children's breakfast cereals were honest, they would call their products names like "Too Much Sugar Crisps" and "Fake Fruit Flakes." [2]Breakfast foods targeting children are filled with excess sugars and unnecessary chemical dyes. [3]Such foods condition young children to start their days with sweetened foods, making them more likely to continue eating heavily sugared foods as adults. [4]In addition, these cereals are often more expensive than healthier foods. [5]When shopping for children's breakfast foods, parents should leave these little boxes of sugar chips where they belong—on store shelves.

_____ 6. [1]Students in poor homes don't have much to read. [2]A recent study at the University of Michigan found that the single strongest predictor for a child's future reading ability is the number of books in the home. [3]In middle-income neighborhoods, there are 13 books for every child; in low-income neighborhoods, there is just 1 book for every 300 children!

_____ 7. [1]Imagine a man who spent thirty years of his life in jail. [2]The charge he was convicted of? [3]Fighting to win equal rights for his people. [4]Imagine that the years in prison were harsh. [5]Among the tasks he was forced to do was breaking rocks, and the irritation of stone dust permanently damaged his eyesight. [6]What kind of person would it take to endure this and much more and yet emerge unbroken in mind and spirit? [7]Such a man was Nelson Mandela. [8]And what is hardest of all to imagine is that he would become president of the nation that jailed him and that he would forgive those who did so. [9]Truly, Mandela was an awesome person.

(Continues on next page)

B. Each of the following selections illustrates one of the tones identified in the box below. In each space provided, put the letter of the tone that applies to the selection. (Two tone choices will be left over.)

A. critical	**B.** disbelieving	**C.** encouraging
D. objective	**E.** sarcastic	

______ 8. If you are kind,
People may accuse you of selfish,
ulterior motives;
Be kind anyway.

If you are successful,
You will win some false friends and
some true enemies;
Succeed anyway.

If you are honest and frank,
People may cheat you;
Be honest and frank anyway.

The good you do today,
People will often forget tomorrow;
Do good anyway.

Give the world the best you have,
And it may never be enough;
Give the world the best you've
got anyway.

You see, in the final analysis,
It is between you and God;
It was never between you and
them anyway.

______ 9. [1]General Motors, the company which invented "planned obsolescence"—the decision to build cars that would fall apart after a few years so that the customer would then have to buy a new one—declared bankruptcy in 2009. [2]It refused to build automobiles that the public wanted: cars that got great gas mileage, that were as safe as they could be, that were exceedingly comfortable to drive—and that wouldn't start falling apart after two years. [3]GM stubbornly fought environmental and safety regulations. [4]Its executives arrogantly ignored the "inferior" Japanese and German cars, cars that would become the gold standard for automobile buyers. [5]Beginning in the 1980s, when GM was posting record profits, it moved countless jobs to Mexico and elsewhere, thus destroying the lives of tens of thousands of hard-working Americans. [6]The glaring stupidity of this policy was that, when GM eliminated the income of so many middle-class families, who did it think was going to be able to afford to buy its cars?

______ 10. [1]The barber's red and white spiral-striped pole had its origins in bloodletting. [2]Bloodletting involves removal of small amounts of blood from the body. [3]During the Middle Ages it was considered a remedy for many ailments. [4]Barbers took up bloodletting as a result of their regular trips to monasteries. [5]Besides having the crowns of their heads shaved, medieval monks were required to undergo periodic bloodletting. [6]Barbers simply combined the two services. [7]In villages, barbers placed outside their doors white cloths reddened with blood to indicate the times thought best for bleeding (April, May, and September). [8]Today's barber pole reflects this early form of advertising.

Name ________________________________ Date __________

Section ____________ SCORE: (Number correct) ________ x 10 = ________ %

PURPOSE AND TONE: Mastery Test 3

A. Eight quotations in the story below are preceded by a numbered space. Identify the tone of each italicized quotation by writing, in the space provided, the letter of one of the tones in the box below. (Two tone choices will be left over.)

A. regretful	B. sarcastic	C. apologetic	D. direct
E. uncertain	F. defensive	G. pleasant	H. peacemaking
I. relieved	J. indignant		

In the food court of a busy shopping mall, two couples sat at adjoining tables. One man and woman were in their early 60s. The other couple was young, with a two- and a four-year-old, both in strollers. The older couple was smiling and waving at the friendly children, who grinned and waved back. Then the younger woman passed out the food her husband had just bought for the children. On each stroller tray, she put a chocolate-frosted donut covered with sprinkles. She then divided a giant soft drink between the older child's sippy cup and the baby's bottle.

______ 1. Glancing at the older couple, the young mom smiled and said, *"They get hungry after all that shopping!"*

Then she noticed the horrified look on the older woman's face, and her tone changed. "What's the matter? What are you looking at?" she asked.

______ 2. *"Oh,"* said the older woman. *"I'm sorry. It's just . . . I wonder . . ."*

She trailed off into silence.

"What are you getting at?" the young woman demanded. "If you have something to say, just come out and say it! What is the problem?"

______ 3. *"OK, I will,"* said the older woman. *"I'm worried about all the sugar you're letting your children eat. It's really not good for them."*

"Caroline, honey," the older man said to his wife. "Please don't get into this."

______ 4. Meanwhile, the young mom's face had turned bright red. *"You've got a lot of nerve!"* she said. *"Where do you get off telling me how to feed my kids?"*

______ 5. The older woman looked down. *"I shouldn't have said that,"* she replied. *"You're right. It's none of my business."*

______ 6. *"It's not like I let them eat like this all the time,"* the young mom said. *"It's just that they're really hungry and this is what they like best."*

The young husband had been quiet up until now. But now he said to his wife, "That's no excuse, Tina. It's your job to feed them right. It's going to be your fault if they grow up fat and have diabetes and all that stuff."

"Wait a minute, wait a minute!" said the older man. "Why is it all HER fault? You're their dad—you're responsible for them, too!"

(Continues on next page)

"Yeah!" said Tina. "What's all this 'it's your fault' crap? That's what you always do! Everything's my fault! If you're such an expert, you feed them!"

The older couple hurriedly got up and prepared to leave.

_____ 7. *"I'm sorry,"* said the older woman. *"I didn't mean to start an argument. I should have kept my mouth shut."*

_____ 8. The younger man said, *"That's OK. You're right—we need to watch it with the sugar. We want our babies to be healthy. Right?"* he said to his wife.

"Well, of course we do," she said. "OK, I'll try to do better." She glared at her husband. "But you have to, too!"

B. In the space provided, indicate whether the primary purpose of each passage is to inform (**I**), to persuade (**P**), or to entertain (**E**).

_____ 9. [1]Some students spend their first weeks in college lost in a dangerous kind of fantasy. [2]They feel, "All will be well, for here I am in college. [3]I have a student ID in my pocket, a sweatshirt with the college name on it, and textbooks under my arm. [4]All this proves I am a college student. [5]I have made it. [6]The worst is now behind me." [7]Such students have succumbed to a fantasy we all at times succumb to: the belief that we will get something for nothing. [8]But everyone knows from experience that this hope is a false one. [9]Life seldom gives us something for nothing—and students must understand that school won't either.

_____ 10. [1]A community of nuns living in the Bronx faced a problem when their dog died. [2]There was too much tar and concrete in the Bronx for easy burial, so the nuns decided to put their old German shepherd in a big suitcase. [3]They would take their beloved pet to a convent in Yonkers, New York, where there was land enough for a decent burial. [4]Two of the sisters lugged the heavy suitcase to the subway. [5]At the station a courteous man helped the women in the brown Franciscan habits to lift the load onto the train. [6]On the crowded train, two passengers gave up their seats to the sisters, and the kind man took a position with the suitcase, not far behind them. [7]All seemed to be going well until they arrived at their stop, when a big surprise awaited them. [8]Their suitcase was gone, obviously stolen by the kind man, who was not so kind after all. [9]Happily, their surprise was not the only surprise of the day.

Name ____________________ Date __________

Section __________ SCORE: (Number correct) ______ x 10 = ______ %

PURPOSE AND TONE: Mastery Test 4

A. Eight quotations in the story below are preceded by a blank space. Identify the tone of each italicized quotation by writing in the letter of one of these tones. (Two tone choices will be left over.)

A. admiring	**B.** apologetic	**C.** comforting	**D.** critical
E. downhearted	**F.** horrified	**G.** joking	**H.** relieved
I. scolding	**J.** threatened		

Elena and Dan walked away from the movie theater discussing their reactions to the film they had just seen.

_____ 1. *"Didn't you think the acting was great? I just think the whole cast did a great job,"* Elena said.

_____ 2. *"The movie was short on plot, though. It really had no story at all,"* Dan said.

Before heading down the steps into the subway, Elena reached into her purse for her wallet.

_____ 3. *"Oh no!"* she cried. *"My wallet's gone!"*

_____ 4. *"Now, take it easy. You're probably just not spotting it,"* Dan said soothingly. *"Let's take a better look under the street light."*

"No, it's gone," Elena said after searching. "It must have fallen out when I put my purse down at our seats. We have to hurry back!"

When Elena and Dan arrived back at the theater, only the staff remained. "I've lost my wallet," Elena told an usher. "Please let us into the auditorium. We need to look for it at our seats."

The usher agreed.

_____ 5. *"I'm sorry about this, Dan,"* Elena said with some embarrassment as they searched.

"Hey, it could happen to anybody."

_____ 6. After searching without success, Elena said, *"I've lost thirty dollars and all my I.D. cards. What's most depressing is that somebody took my wallet—not just the money, but everything else too."*

Just then the usher approached them. "Would you describe your wallet for me?" she asked Elena.

"It was denim," Elena answered. "Blue denim with tan trim."

"Then here you are," the usher said with a grin, handing Elena her wallet.

_____ 7. *"That's it! Thank goodness!"* said Elena, beaming.

_____ 8. "Someone turned it in right after the movie." Then the usher giggled. *"I guess you're lucky the movie was* Act of Kindness. *That must have inspired the right emotion."*

(Continues on next page)

B. Read the passage below. Then carefully consider the questions that follow it, and, in the spaces provided, write the letters of the best responses.

[1]The United States has always been a diverse society. [2]In 1673, more than three centuries ago, a visitor to what is now New York City was astonished to find that eighteen languages were spoken among the city's eight thousand inhabitants. [3]By the middle of the nineteenth century, so many people from so many lands had come to the United States that the novelist Herman Melville exclaimed, "You cannot spill a drop of American blood without spilling the blood of the whole world."

[4]One can only imagine what Melville would say today! [5]The United States has become the most diverse society on the face of the Earth. [6]For more than a century, most immigrants to the United States were Europeans—Irish, Germans, English, Scandinavians, Greeks, Poles, Italians, and others. [7]Together with African Americans, they made America the "melting pot" of the world. [8]Today another great wave of immigration—more than one million people a year, mostly from Asia and Latin America—is transforming the United States into what one writer has called the "first universal nation," a multicultural society of unmatched diversity.

_____ 9. The primary purpose of this paragraph is to
- A. inform readers that the United States is and always was a diverse society.
- B. persuade readers that a multicultural society is the best type of society.
- C. entertain readers with colorful facts about the United States.

_____ 10. The tone of this paragraph is one of
- A. distress.
- B. amazement.
- C. tolerance.
- D. compassion.

Name ______________________ Date __________

Section __________ SCORE: (Number correct) ______ x 12.5 = ______ %

PURPOSE AND TONE: Mastery Test 5

Read the paragraphs below. Then carefully consider the questions that follow, and, in the spaces provided, write the letters of the best responses.

A. [1]Habitat for Humanity is a program aimed at eliminating substandard housing and homelessness around the world. [2]Habitat employees and dedicated volunteers work together to build new homes and renovate old ones that are then sold at no profit to families in need. [3]The Habitat volunteers are rewarded with a keen sense of accomplishment and strong bonds of friendship. [4]New volunteers are needed throughout the country to continue the work of this wonderful organization. [5]No special building skills are required. [6]Wouldn't you like to join the thousands who have enabled more than 300,000 people around the world to live in sturdy, decent housing?

_____ 1. The primary purpose of this paragraph is to
- A. inform readers about the existence and work of Habitat for Humanity.
- B. persuade readers to volunteer to help Habitat for Humanity.
- C. entertain readers with details about an interesting organization.

_____ 2. The main tone of this paragraph can be described as
- A. compassionate.
- B. humble.
- C. admiring.
- D. lighthearted.

B. [1]Our country has lost its head when it comes to gun control. [2]When the framers of the United States Constitution said that people have the right to bear arms, they did not mean high-powered rifles and assault weapons. [3]Such guns are designed to kill—not defend. [4]The long range and high power of these weapons jeopardize the safety of people miles away from where the gun is fired. [5]No one is safe as long as these guns are available. [6]And each time another one is manufactured and brought into a neighborhood, America's streets become more dangerous. [7]We have a right to be safe at home, but these weapons do not guarantee safety. [8]They prevent it. [9]Until we outlaw them once and for all, we will have to live like prisoners in our own homes.

_____ 3. The primary purpose of this passage is to
- A. inform.
- B. persuade.
- C. entertain.

_____ 4. The tone of this paragraph can be described as
- A. objective.
- B. impassioned and indignant.
- C. sarcastic and revengeful.
- D. relaxed and chatty.

(Continues on next page)

C. [1]During our daily bouts of pessimism, we can see its constructive role in our lives. [2]In these mild forms, pessimism serves the purpose of pulling us back a bit from the risky exaggerations of our optimism, making us think twice, keeping us from making rash, foolhardy gestures. [3]The optimistic moments of our lives contain the great plans, the dreams, and the hopes. [4]Reality is gently distorted to give the dreams room to flourish. [5]Without these times we would never accomplish anything difficult and intimidating; we would never even attempt the just barely possible. [6]Mount Everest would remain unscaled, the four-minute mile unrun; the jet plane and the computer would be blueprints sitting in some financial vice president's wastebasket.

_____ 5. The primary purpose of this paragraph is to
- A. inform readers about research on pessimism and optimism.
- B. persuade readers of the usefulness of both pessimism and optimism.
- C. entertain readers with inspiring achievements.

_____ 6. The author's tone can be described as
- A. critical but concerned.
- B. lighthearted and amused.
- C. cynical and disbelieving.
- D. serious and positive.

D. [1]More and more, Americans have succumbed to treating their pets like people. [2]Dogs used to be called Rover or Spot or Fido; now they have people's names such as Ingrid, Stuart, or Alexander. [3]Pet food manufacturers no longer stick to dog biscuits—you can now buy your cat or dog a full-course meal that looks just like "people food." [4]Instead of putting plain water in the dog's bowl, you can offer Evian or broth or a soft drink. [5]Pet stores sell Christmas stockings for pets, filled with treats and toys. [6]Proving there is no end to this madness, pet health insurance is available, as is pet dentistry. [7]When your dog or cat becomes a senior citizen, you'll be overjoyed to hear that some veterinarians specialize in geriatrics. [8]And when life draws to a close for your pet, you can seek out a pet cemetery, unless you prefer to keep your pet's ashes at home in a special urn.

_____ 7. The primary purpose of this paragraph is to
- A. inform readers about sensible ways of caring for their pets.
- B. persuade readers that the treatment of pets as people has gone too far.
- C. entertain readers with details about cute animals.

_____ 8. The tone of the passage can be described as
- A. critical.
- B. hypocritical.
- C. bewildered.
- D. matter-of-fact.

Name ______________________________ Date __________

Section __________ SCORE: (Number correct) ______ x 12.5 = ______ %

PURPOSE AND TONE: Mastery Test 6

Read the paragraphs below. Then carefully consider the questions that follow, and, in the spaces provided, write the letters of the best responses.

A. [1]As I turned onto Stanton Street early one Sunday morning, I saw a chicken walking a few yards ahead of me. [2]"Hey, what's this about?" I thought. [3]The chicken seemed to know just where it was going. [4]I started walking faster than the chicken, so I gradually caught up. [5]"I am actually following a chicken," I murmured aloud, shaking my head and smiling to myself. [6]The chicken turned south on Eighteenth. [7]At the fourth house, it turned in at the walk, hopped up the front steps, and rapped sharply on the metal storm door with its beak. [8]After a moment, the door opened, and the chicken went in. [9]I just stood there for a minute, shaking my head and looking at the closed door. [10]This was a story I would definitely remember.

_____ 1. The primary purpose of this passage is to
- A. inform readers about a troubling personal experience.
- B. persuade readers that chickens can be strange.
- C. entertain readers with a story about an unusual chicken.

_____ 2. The tone of the passage can be described as
- A. detached and matter-of-fact.
- B. annoyed but tolerant.
- C. curious and wondering.
- D. disapproving but sympathetic.

B. [1]Dieting habits are heavily linked to culture. [2]In the 1880s, the full-figured actress Lillian Russell was the epitome of beauty. [3]Being overweight then was equated with wealth and success. [4]Today, American culture has gone to the opposite extreme. [5]Research shows that the body weight most American women want to achieve today is 13 to 19 percent below the expected weight for their age and height. [6]Since a body weight below 15 percent of expected weight is one of the criteria for diagnosing anorexia nervosa, what does this say about our ideals? [7]We must do something about those ideals. [8]With extreme slimness as a cultural norm, it is no wonder that fad dieting, surgical fat removal, eating disorders, and fear of fat abound. [9]Every day, magazines, TV, and movies send the message that "thin is in." [10]Unfortunately, this obsession with thinness leads many people to feelings of guilt, despair, and inferiority. [11]Sadly, for some, this struggle ends in death. [12]Isn't it time we taught our children not to emphasize their looks at the expense of their souls?

_____ 3. The primary purpose of this passage is to
- A. inform.
- B. persuade.
- C. entertain.

_____ 4. The tone of the passage can be described as
- A. disbelieving.
- B. admiring and tolerant.
- C. matter-of-fact.
- D. disapproving and distressed.

(Continues on next page)

C. [1]Happiness is not a goal; it is a by-product. . . . [2]Someone once asked me what I regarded as the three most important requirements for happiness. [3]My answer was: "A feeling that you have been honest with yourself and those around you; a feeling that you have done the best you could both in your personal life and in your work; and the ability to love others."

[4]But there is another basic requirement, and I can't understand now how I forgot it at the time: that is the feeling that you are, in some way, useful. [5]Usefulness, whatever form it may take, is the price we should pay for the air we breathe and the food we eat and the privilege of being alive. [6]And it is its own reward, as well, for it is the beginning of happiness, just as self-pity and withdrawal from the battle are the beginning of misery.

_____ 5. The primary purpose of this paragraph is to
A. inform with documented facts.
B. persuade with personal views.
C. entertain with charming anecdotes.

_____ 6. The tone of this paragraph can be described as
A. lighthearted and cheerful.
B. indignant and scornful.
C. serious and caring.
D. concerned and pessimistic.

D. [1]For an outsider, it seems incomprehensible: Why would an abused woman stay with the man who is hurting her? [2]Looking at the situation, observers are quick to say things like, "I'd never put up with that." [3]"The first time he hit me, I'd be gone." [4]"Why doesn't she just walk out?" [5]But typically, abused women do not "just walk out." [6]They stay with their abusers—some for just a short time, but others for many years. [7]Researcher Ann Goetting wanted to understand why some women manage to leave, while so many others do not. [8]She interviewed a number of women who had left abusive relationships. [9]Based upon her findings, she identified several characteristics that set the "leavers" apart. [10]First of all, the women who left had a positive self-image. [11]They believed that they deserved something better than a violent relationship. [12]Also, they had gathered enough money to leave. [13]For some, this meant putting a little aside every week for a long period. [14]And finally, they had a supportive network of family and friends. [15]They could go to that network of people for help and encouragement.

_____ 7. The primary purpose of this paragraph is to
A. inform.
B. persuade.
C. entertain.

_____ 8. The tone of the passage can be described as
A. playful and humorous.
B. curious but mainly objective.
C. impassioned and outraged.
D. detached and critical.

9 Argument

Many of us enjoy a good argument. A good argument is not an emotional experience in which people's feelings get out of control, leaving them ready to start throwing things. Instead, it is a rational discussion in which each person advances and supports a point of view about some matter. We might argue with a friend, for example, about where to eat or what movie to go to. We might argue about whether a boss or a parent or an instructor is acting in a fair or an unfair manner. We might argue about whether certain performers or sports stars deserve to get paid as much as they do. In an argument (such as the one going on in the above cartoon), the two parties each present supporting evidence. The goal is to determine who has the more solid evidence to support his or her point of view.

Argumentation is, then, a part of our everyday dealings with other people. It is also an important part of much of what we read. Authors often try to convince us of their opinions and interpretations. Very often the most important things we must do as critical readers are

1 Recognize the **point** the author is making.
2 Decide if the author's support is **relevant**.
3 Decide if the author's support is **adequate**.

This chapter will give you practice in doing the above, first in everyday arguments and then in textbook material.

The Basics of Argument: Point and Support

A good **argument** is one in which you make a point and then provide persuasive and logical evidence to support it. Here is a point:

Point: Even though the apartment is nice, I don't think you should move there.

This statement hardly discourages us from moving into the apartment. "Why do you say that?" we might legitimately ask. "Give your reasons." Support is needed so we can decide for ourselves whether a valid argument has been made. Suppose the point is followed by these three reasons:

1. The closest washer and dryer are in a laundromat three miles away.
2. Next door to the apartment building is an all-night bar.
3. Several bugs scurried into dark holes when the kitchen sink cabinet door was opened.

Clearly, the details provide solid support for the point. They give us a basis for understanding and agreeing with the point. In light of these details, we may consider looking for another apartment to rent.

We see here a small example of what clear thinking in an argument is about: making a point and then providing support that truly backs up that point. A **valid argument** may also be described as a conclusion supported by logical reasons, facts, examples, and other evidence.

Let's look at another example:

Point: The corner convenience store is run poorly.

We don't yet know if we would agree that the store is run poorly. We might trust the person who made the statement, but we can't judge for ourselves until we learn the supporting details. Here are those details:

1. Milk is routinely kept on the shelves several days after the suggested date of sale.
2. The "fresh" fruits and vegetables are often spotted and wrinkled.
3. At busy times of the day, there's not enough help in the store, so the lines are very long.

Again, the solid support convinces us that a logical point has been made.

The Point and Support of an Argument

In everyday life, of course, people don't simply say, "Here is my point" and "Here is my support." Nor do writers state their basic ideas so directly. Even so, the basic structure of point and support is still at work beneath the surface, and to evaluate an argument, you need to recognize that point.

The following activity will help you distinguish between a point and its support.

PRACTICE 1

In each group, one statement is the point, and the other statement or statements are support for the point. Identify each point with a **P** and each statement of support with an **S**.

> ***Hint:*** If it sounds right to insert the word *because* in front of a sentence, you probably have a statement of support. For example, we could say, "*Because* the closest washer and dryer are three miles away, *because* the apartment building is close to an all-night bar, and *because* several bugs were visible below the kitchen sink, I've come to the conclusion that you should not move into that apartment."

1. _____ A. You should learn how to budget your money.
   _____ B. You're always borrowing money from me.

2. _____ A. Our town ought to require all residents to recycle bottles and cans.
   _____ B. The more the town recycles, the less money it must pay for garbage removal.

3. _____ A. You can use olive oil on your bread instead of butter, which can clog arteries.
   _____ B. You can eat a healthy diet in restaurants with a little care.
   _____ C. You can order sautéed or steamed dishes instead of fatty, high-cholesterol fried foods.

4. _____ A. Our mail carrier often puts our mail in someone else's mailbox.
_____ B. When our mail carrier delivers a package, he leaves it on our front stoop without ringing the doorbell to see if we're home.
_____ C. Our mail carrier is careless about delivering mail.
_____ D. After delivering our mail, the carrier often leaves our mailbox partially open.

5. _____ A. In the 19th century, theatergoers often felt free to "participate" in the performance.
_____ B. It was common for audiences to join in during famous speeches and familiar songs.
_____ C. When audiences particularly enjoyed a song, speech, or scene, they cried aloud, stamped their feet, and often stopped the show to demand an encore.
_____ D. To express disapproval, 19th-century audiences hissed, jeered, and even threw things at the performers.

6. _____ A. Physicians now help people deal with baldness, wrinkles, and sleeplessness.
_____ B. Problems that used to be accepted as part of life are now considered matters for medical attention.
_____ C. Some criminologists have defined antisocial behavior as a medical problem.
_____ D. Some men take prescription drugs in order to increase their sexual potency.

7. _____ A. In the aftermath of World War II, many Americans believed that marriage was an ideal state.
_____ B. In one survey, less than 10 percent of the public believed an unmarried person could be happy.
_____ C. The 1947 best-seller *Modern Woman: The Lost Sex* urged that spinsters be barred from teaching children on the grounds of "emotional incompetence."
_____ D. In the postwar years, more than 95% of the women who came of age got married.

8. _____ A. Affordable daycare facilities often lack professionally trained staff and fail to follow adequate child-safety procedures.
_____ B. It's hard for working parents to find reliable, affordable daycare.
_____ C. Excellent daycare can cost $15,000–$20,000 a year per child.
_____ D. For many working parents, the oldest form of daycare—adult relatives who live nearby—is unavailable.

9. _____ A. According to some medieval philosophers, laughing dishonored humans because it made them look like monkeys.

_____ B. Some medieval theologians believed that all laughing mocked God's creation and therefore endangered the human soul.

_____ C. Many people objected to comedy, believing that laughing encouraged drunkenness and improper behavior.

_____ D. In the Middle Ages, many people considered laughing harmful.

10. _____ A. A bone marrow transplant can increase the chances of survival for thousands of people who are diagnosed with leukemia and other blood-related diseases each year.

_____ B. More people should agree to donate bone marrow if their marrow matches the type of a patient in need.

_____ C. Only about 30 percent of patients can find a match among their own family members.

_____ D. People can donate marrow easily and safely: it can be collected in about forty-five minutes and is naturally replaced by the body within two to three weeks.

Relevant Support

"Potato chips aren't rubbery and blubbery like fat. They're crispy like lettuce. That proves they're diet food!"

Once you identify the point and support of an argument, you need to decide if each piece of evidence is **relevant**—in other words, if it really applies to the point.

The critical reader must ask, "Is this reason relevant support for the argument?" In their enthusiasm for making an argument, people often bring up irrelevant support. For example, the fan of potato chips in the cartoon shown does not offer relevant support for his point that potato chips are diet food. Or as another example: In trying to get your cousin to take you to dinner, you might say, "You just got your paycheck." The fact that she just got her paycheck is beside the point; the question is whether she wants (or is able) to spend any of it on you.

An excellent way to develop your skill in recognizing relevant support is to work on simple point-support outlines of arguments. By isolating the reasons of an argument, such outlines help you think about whether each reason is truly relevant. Paying close attention to the relevance of support will help you not only in your reading, but also in making and supporting points in your own writing.

Check Your Understanding

Consider the following outline. The point is followed by six facts, only three of which are relevant support for the point. See if you can check (✓) the numbers of the **three** relevant statements of support.

Point: Pigs make good pets.

___ 1. When a pig weighs over 180 pounds, it is called a hog.

___ 2. Pigs are friendly and intelligent.

___ 3. In 1965, a pig named "Old Faithful" gave birth to thirty-six piglets in one litter.

___ 4. Pigs are easily housebroken.

___ 5. Pigs, like people, can get sunburn.

___ 6. Pigs can be taught to walk on a leash.

Now read the following comments on the six items to see which numbers you should have checked and why.

Explanation

1. What an animal is called has no bearing on how good a pet it will make. And for many people, the fact that pigs can weigh over 180 pounds is a reason they are *not* good pets. So you should not have checked number 1.
2. People tend to like pets who like them back and with whom they can interact. You should have checked number 2.
3. Admittedly, Old Faithful's accomplishment is nothing to oink at, but how many pet owners want thirty-six more pets than they started out with? You should not have checked number 3.

4. Given modern standards of cleanliness, being easily housebroken is even more attractive to many pet owners than friendliness or a genius IQ. You should have checked number 4.
5. Most people would prefer a pet for whom they wouldn't have to buy a lifetime supply of sunscreen. Therefore, you should not have checked number 5.
6. Since humans enjoy taking walks with their pets, the ability to keep an animal under control outdoors is important. Number 6 is the third number you should have checked.

PRACTICE 2

Each point is followed by three statements that provide relevant support and three that do not. In the spaces, write the letters of the **three** relevant statements of support.

> ***Hint:*** To help you decide if a sentence is relevant or not, ask yourself, "Does this provide logical support for the point being argued?"

1. **Point: Married people have fewer health problems than unmarried people.**
   A. Married people suffer fewer incidents of back pain and headache than single people.
   B. The Centers for Disease Control keeps statistics on health issues affecting various segments of the population.
   C. Married people are more likely to be overweight than single people.
   D. Serious psychological disorders are more common among unmarried people than married people.
   E. High blood pressure afflicts more single people than married people.
   F. On the average, people marry at a later age now than they did a generation ago.

   Items that logically support the point: ________ ________ ________

2. **Point: "Dress-down" Friday in offices has positive effects.**
   A. No one knows exactly how the custom of dressing casually on Fridays started.
   B. Whatever its origins, dressing casually on Fridays has become very widespread.
   C. Dressing casually on Fridays provides a break in the routine, which energizes workers.
   D. Casual dress seems to reduce stress by creating a more relaxed atmosphere.

E. Informality also seems to lead to more friendliness and cooperation between employees.

F. Some employers complain that workers abuse the custom by wearing outfits that belong on the beach—or in the bedroom.

Items that logically support the point: ________ ________ ________

3. **Point: People who do not enjoy flying can do a number of things to make flying less unpleasant.**

A. Fear of flying is a relatively common phobia.

B. People who suffer from motion sickness during air travel can take over-the-counter medications such as Dramamine.

C. Media reports of airline crashes serve to increase people's fear of flying.

D. Fearful flyers can use visualization to feel more in control of the flying experience.

E. Hypnosis has helped some fearful flyers to control their anxiety about air travel.

F. Motion-sickness medication can leave a traveler feeling unpleasantly drugged.

Items that logically support the point: ________ ________ ________

4. **Point: The flu epidemic of 1918 was horrendous.**

A. Worldwide, 40 million people died of the 1918 flu—more than the number killed in World War I.

B. Because of the flu epidemic, in 1918 many public events, including funerals, were restricted or canceled, and bodies piled up in city morgues.

C. The flu strain that swept the world in 1918 was so severe that people would show the first symptoms in the morning and be dead by nightfall.

D. Bubonic plague, another terrible disease, killed about 70,000 people in London between 1664 and 1666.

E. Ordinary flu usually results in fever, coughing, and headache for three or four days.

F. A contagious disease that covers a large part of the world is properly called a "pandemic."

Items that logically support the point: ________ ________ ________

5. **Point: People should consider alternatives to traditional burial practices.**

A. A sympathetic, well-trained funeral director can be very helpful during a difficult time.

B. A biodegradable coffin buried in a plot marked by shrubbery is easier on the environment than a traditional coffin and headstone.

C. People may feel that giving their loved ones anything other than an expensive, conventional burial is somehow disrespectful.

D. Families can avoid the expense of maintaining a cemetery plot by cremating, instead of burying, the dead.

E. Many states permit burial on home property, which can be a more convenient burial location than a cemetery.

F. Burial grounds provide valuable information to genealogists, sociologists, and other people interested in the past.

Items that logically support the point: ________ ________ ________

Relevant Support in Paragraphs

The point, or main idea, of the argument in the paragraph below is stated in the first sentence. One of the other sentences is not relevant support for that point.

Check Your Understanding

Read the paragraph that follows and see if you can find the statement that does **not** support the point of the argument.

> [1]When you go to college, you should live off campus. [2]In a rented apartment you can enjoy the privacy and convenience of your own kitchen and bathroom. [3]If you live off campus, getting to and from classes will take more time. [4]However, off-campus apartments give you more living space than a dormitory room for the same price or less. [5]An off-campus apartment is usually quieter than a dorm. [6]It also gives you a better chance to develop a sense of the larger community, the town or city in which your college is located.

The number of the irrelevant sentence: _____

Explanation

The point of this argument is stated in the first sentence: "When you go to college, you should live off campus." Any statement that doesn't help prove this point is irrelevant. Sentences 2, 4, 5, and 6 provide advantages of living off campus. However, having to spend more time getting to and from classes would generally be considered undesirable since it takes time away from other activities. Therefore, sentence 3 is irrelevant to the argument in this paragraph—it changes the subject to a disadvantage of living off campus.

PRACTICE 3

The point of the argument in each paragraph that follows is stated in the first sentence. One sentence in the paragraph does not support that point. Read each paragraph, and decide which sentence is **not** relevant evidence. Then write its letter in the space provided.

> ***Hint:*** To decide if a sentence is relevant, ask yourself, "Does this *really* provide logical support for the point being argued?"

_____ 1. [1]What people consider masculine and feminine behavior is actually quite variable. [2]Americans, for instance, think of men as naturally stronger and tougher than women and better suited to perform the most strenuous physical labor. [3]In many traditional societies, however, particularly in sub-Saharan Africa and South America, women do most of the heavy work—carrying goods to market, hauling firewood, and constructing houses. [4]Men hunt—and spend a lot of time talking. [5]Americans can learn something from looking at such traditional societies. [6]Among some peoples, agriculture is restricted to men, while in other societies, farming is regarded as women's work. [7]In still other societies, men and women work in the fields side by side.

Which of the following sentences does **not** support the argument that what people consider masculine and feminine behavior can vary?

A. Sentence 3
B. Sentence 4
C. Sentence 5
D. Sentence 6

_____ 2. [1]Cities should give privately run schools a try. [2]Private companies that run school districts are a relatively recent development. [3]Educational companies have done much to upgrade the physical condition of schools that school boards have allowed to decay. [4]One company that was hired to run an East Coast school district, for example, began by immediately painting and repairing local schools that had become so rundown that they challenged any sense of pride that teachers and students might have had in their schools. [5]Graffiti were painted over and kept clean; the only "art work" in hallways was student work and colorful upbeat posters. [6]Furthermore, any nonstudents who used to wander the hallways looking for trouble as well as for customers for drugs were immediately eliminated by a strong disciplinary system that included professional guards. [7]In addition, year-end reading and math scores of students in the privately run schools improved in many cases.

Which of the following sentences does **not** support the argument that cities should give privately run schools a try?

A. Sentence 2
B. Sentence 3
C. Sentence 5
D. Sentence 7

Adequate Support

A valid argument must include not only relevant support but also an **adequate** amount of support—enough to prove the point. For example, it would not be valid to argue "A government tax cut is a bad idea" if one's only support was "My taxes will still be too high." Such an important issue would require more support than one person's tax situation. Arguing a point that doesn't have adequate support is called "jumping to a conclusion."

Check Your Understanding

In the argument below, three supporting reasons are given, followed by four possible conclusions. The evidence (that is, the supporting reasons) adequately supports only one of the points; it is insufficient to support the other three. Choose the **one** point that you think is adequately supported, and put a check mark (✓) beside it.

Support

- Lately Valerie has looked thinner and paler than usual.
- She used to go to all the parties, but now she stays home in the evenings.
- At work, she has been seen crying in the ladies' room.

Which **point** is adequately supported by all the evidence above?

___ A. Valerie is seriously ill.
___ B. Something is troubling Valerie.
___ C. Valerie has broken up with her boyfriend.
___ D. Valerie owes a great deal of money.

Explanation

The correct answer is B. From her behavior, we can safely conclude that something is troubling Valerie, but we have very little evidence about what is troubling her. Answer A is not well supported. The fact that Valerie hasn't been looking well makes us wonder if she's seriously ill, but we have no other evidence for that conclusion.

Answer C is also poorly supported. The fact that Valerie hasn't been going to parties does make us wonder whether or not she's broken up with her boyfriend, but we have absolutely no other evidence to support that conclusion. Finally, except for the evidence showing that Valerie is troubled in some way, answer D has no evidence at all to support it, so it too is a poorly supported conclusion. We simply have insufficient information to decide anything more than this: something is troubling Valerie.

PRACTICE 4

For each group, read the three items of support (the evidence). Then check (✓) the **one** point that is adequately supported by that evidence.

Group 1

Support

- In one study, fifteen of the thirty women who listened to music during childbirth had no need for anesthesia.
- Studies indicate that the body produces pain-reducing hormones when a person listens to enjoyable music.
- Patients who had suffered a stroke gained lasting benefits after listening for three weeks to recorded music.

Point: Which of the following conclusions is best supported by all the evidence above?

___ A. Music can have a role in curing diseases of all types.

___ B. Music can be a helpful tool in dealing with some physical problems.

___ C. Music should be a resource in every medical office.

___ D. Music can also have negative effects on our physical well-being.

Group 2

Support

- "Living out of a suitcase"—being away from home and our familiar routine—and coping with planes, trains, buses, and rental cars can be exhausting.
- While on vacation, we often eat too much, drink too much, get too little sleep, work too hard at sightseeing, and in general overextend ourselves.

- Also, we tend to expect a vacation to be a "dream come true," and so we feel frustrated, angry, and let down if anything is less than perfect.

Point: Which of the following conclusions is best supported by all the evidence above?

___ A. A vacation trip with young children can be very difficult.

___ B. A vacation trip isn't always restful.

___ C. The expense of a vacation trip is a big worry for most people.

___ D. The best vacation is one spent dieting and exercising.

Argument in Textbook Writing

In most textbook writing, argument takes the form of well-developed ideas or theories presented with experiments, surveys, studies, reasons, examples, or other supporting evidence. Textbook arguments generally have solid support, but recognizing the author's point and watching for relevant and adequate support will help you become a more involved and critical reader. Following are two exercises that will give you practice in thinking through the arguments in textbooks.

PRACTICE 5

The point of the argument in each of the textbook paragraphs below is stated in the first sentence. To each paragraph, one sentence has been added that does *not* support the point. Read each paragraph, and then decide which sentence is **not** relevant to the argument. Then, in the space provided, write the letter of that sentence.

To help you decide if a sentence is irrelevant or not, ask yourself, "Does this *really* provide logical support for the point being argued?"

______ 1. [1]Science and technology, while they help solve societal problems, are themselves responsible for many of our problems. [2]Before scientific advances in weaponry, humans were limited to bows and arrows and swords. [3]Now, however, we can kill many more people with the destructive guns and bombs that science has given us. [4]Today we save or extend the lives of countless people because of medical advances that science has provided, but the hazardous waste products that result from medicine pollute our air, streams, and oceans and threaten our health. [5]The world's political leaders must join together to deal with the continuing pollution of our planet. [6]And the tear in the ozone layer caused by gases we've unleashed into the environment through such scientific advances as air conditioning and spray cans allows more ultraviolet rays to reach our skin, resulting in more skin cancer.

Which sentence is **not** relevant support for the argument that science and technology are responsible for many of society's problems?

A. Sentence 3
B. Sentence 4
C. Sentence 5
D. Sentence 6

_____ 2. [1]The safe disposal of toxic chemicals is a huge problem. [2]The amount of hazardous waste produced in the United States rose from about 9 million metric tons in 1970 to 300 million less than 20 years later—enough to fill a line of railroad cars that would stretch around the world, with several thousand miles to spare. [3]Typically, corporations choose the cheapest means of disposal, which are to release the waste products into the air and waterways and to bury the materials in dump sites. [4]Corporations should face heavy fines whenever they are caught favoring profits over public health. [5]In one infamous instance of irresponsible disposal, the Hooker Chemical and Plastics Corporation, over a number of years, dumped 43.6 million pounds of eighty-two different chemical substances into Love Canal, New York, near Niagara Falls. [6]Among the chemicals dumped were 200 tons of trichlorophenol, which included an estimated 130 pounds of one of the most toxic and carcinogenic substances known—dioxin. [7]Three ounces of this substance can kill more than a million people. [8]As a result of exposure to the various chemicals dumped at Love Canal, nearby residents had an unusual number of serious illnesses, a high incidence of miscarriages, and a significant number of children born with birth defects.

Which sentence is **not** relevant support for the argument that safe disposal of toxic chemicals is a huge problem?

A. Sentence 3
B. Sentence 4
C. Sentence 6
D. Sentence 7

PRACTICE 6

In each group, the support is taken from studies reported in a textbook. Check (✓) the point in each case that is adequately supported by that evidence.

Group 1

Support

- An increased amount, or volume, of blood in the circulatory system can elevate blood pressure.

- If the heart is pumping with too much force, that increases blood pressure by straining the circulation.
- The condition of the artery wall is also important: when the wall thickens, the artery becomes narrower, and the pressure of the blood flowing through it rises.

Which **point** is adequately supported by all the evidence above?

___ A. High blood pressure is a mysterious, silent killer.

___ B. Factors in high blood pressure include stress, a fatty diet, and lack of exercise.

___ C. Factors in high blood pressure include the blood, the heart, and the arteries.

___ D. High blood pressure can be controlled by medications and lifestyle changes.

Group 2

Support

- Athletes often privately credit their victories to their own ability and their losses to bad breaks, lousy officiating, or the other team's exceptional performance.
- After receiving poor exam grades, most students in a half dozen studies criticized the exam, not themselves; generally, students interpret good grades to be the result of their own efforts.
- On insurance forms, drivers have explained accidents in such words as these: "An invisible car came out of nowhere, struck my car, and vanished"; "As I reached an intersection, a hedge sprang up obscuring my vision, and I did not see the other car"; "A pedestrian hit me and went under my car."

Which **point** is adequately supported by the evidence above?

___ A. Most people lack the skills they need to perform well at work and school.

___ B. People accept more responsibility for good deeds than for bad ones.

___ C. People tend to perform at a rather high level most of the time.

___ D. People accept more responsibility for successes than for failures.

A Final Note

This chapter has dealt with the basics of argument, including the need for relevant and adequate support. In the next chapter, "Critical Reading," you will learn about some common errors in reasoning—also known as **logical fallacies**—that people may make when advancing an argument.

CHAPTER REVIEW

In this chapter, you learned the following:

- A good argument is made up of a point, or a conclusion, and logical evidence to back it up.
- To critically read an argument, you must recognize the **point** the author is making.
- To think through an argument, you need to decide if each piece of evidence is **relevant**.
- To think through an argument, you also need to decide if the author's support is **adequate**.
- Textbook arguments generally have solid support, but recognizing the author's point and looking for relevant and adequate support will help you become a more involved and critical reader.

The final chapter in Part One—Chapter 10—will explain other aspects of being a critical reader: separating fact from opinion, detecting propaganda, and recognizing errors in reasoning.

On the Web: If you are using this book in class, you can visit our website for additional practice in evaluating arguments. Go to **www.townsendpress.com** and click on "Learning Center."

REVIEW TEST 1

To review what you've learned in this chapter, fill in the blanks.

1. When two people argue a point, the goal is to see who has the more compelling ______________________ for his or her point.

_____ 2. TRUE OR FALSE? A good argument should be more than a rational discussion: it should also be an emotional one as well.

3. It is important to consider whether each piece of evidence in an argument logically supports the point—in other words, that it is (*relevant, adequate*) ______________________________.

4. It is equally important to consider that an argument includes a(n) (*relevant, adequate*) ______________ amount of support—enough to convincingly prove the point.

5. To become a more effective reader (or listener or speaker or writer), you should make a habit of asking yourself two questions: (1) What is the point? and (2) ______________________________?

REVIEW TEST 2

A. Consider the following cartoon and then answer the questions that follow.

"Snow White was poisoned by an apple, Jack found a giant at the top of the beanstalk, and look what happened to Alice when she ate the mushroom! And you wonder why I won't eat fruits and vegetables!?"

1. What is the boy's argument? ______________________________

____

2. What is his support? ______________________________

____

____

_____ 3. Is his support relevant?

A. Yes, the boy effectively argues his point.

B. No, what happens to characters in fairy tales is not necessarily what happens to people in real life.

B. In each group, one statement is the point, and the other statements are support for that point. Write the letter of the point in the space provided.

Hint: If it sounds right to insert the word *because* in front of a sentence, you probably have a statement of support.

_____ 4. A. Ancient Egyptian law protected cats from harm.

B. The ancient Egyptians must have honored cats.

C. Archaeologists have uncovered entire cemeteries in Egypt devoted to mummified cats.

_____ 5. A. In Connecticut in 1830, only one schoolhouse out of forty had ventilation.

B. The average size of a schoolhouse was 18½ feet by 7½ feet, and 7 feet high, and class sizes could be as high as sixty children.

C. In the 1800s, many teachers labored under very primitive conditions.

D. A report in 1848 found that only about half of the schoolhouses in the state offered the luxury of an outhouse.

_____ 6. A. Thirty-five percent of America's endangered species live in tidal wetlands.

B. Tidal wetlands provide a natural way to control flooding and storm damage.

C. Plants that grow only in wetlands are essential to the food chain.

D. Preserving tidal wetlands from overdevelopment should be a national priority.

_____ 7. A. Being poor, being badly nourished, and being overweight often go together.

B. Foods that are high in starch, sugar, or fat tend to be cheaper than lean meats and fresh fruits and vegetables.

C. In low-income neighborhoods, fast-food restaurants are more common than produce markets.

D. High crime rates in poor communities make people reluctant to spend time outdoors getting exercise.

C. The following point is followed by three statements that provide relevant support and three that do not. In the spaces, write the letters of the **three** relevant statements of support.

8–10. **Point: We should use more solar energy.**

A. Unlike oil and coal, energy from the sun is unlimited.
B. The sun nourishes plants and animals.
C. Solar energy is nonpolluting.
D. Wind and water power have been used for centuries.
E. Solar energy is less effective in cloudy climates.
F. Solar energy is extremely cost-effective.

Items that logically support the point: ________ ________ ________

REVIEW TEST 3

A. In the space provided, write the letter of the irrelevant sentence in each paragraph—the sentence that changes the subject.

______ 1. [1]The current generation of young workers will have a better financial future if workers save for retirement instead of counting on the Social Security program. [2]Saving will also provide today's workers with some of the discipline their "I want it all now" generation so sorely needs. [3]Social Security benefits already have been reduced to accommodate a shrinking labor pool and a growing number of retirees. [4]In addition, the government has had to start taxing a percentage of the benefits, lessening them even more. [5]At this rate, if the program isn't completely bankrupt by the early twenty-first century, monthly Social Security checks will be very small.

Which sentence does **not** support the argument that workers must save for retirement instead of counting on Social Security?

A. Sentence 2
B. Sentence 3
C. Sentence 4
D. Sentence 5

______ 2. [1]The death penalty is a vital tool in the fight against crime. [2]Knowing that they will die if they are caught, potential killers will think twice about committing murder. [3]And when murderers are caught, the death penalty is the only sure guarantee that these criminals will not escape or be released to repeat their crimes. [4]Some murderers who have not been executed and instead were released on parole went on to kill other victims. [5]Finally, let us remember that the victims of murder were shown no mercy and given no second chance.

Which of the following is **not** relevant to the author's conclusion that the death penalty is a vital tool in the fight against crime?

A. Sentence 2
B. Sentence 3
C. Sentence 4
D. Sentence 5

______ 3. [1]The quest for the ideal body can become physically unhealthy. [2]At one time or other, almost every American girl undereats for an extended period, sometimes drastically, in order to be thinner. [3]And roughly 5 percent of male high-school seniors use steroids to build up their muscles. [4]These young men risk a variety of serious health problems, especially if they obtain steroids illegally and "stack" one drug with another, as many do. [5]Although one misguided motivation for taking steroids is probably to excel at sports, one survey found that a third of steroid users did not participate at all in interscholastic athletics, apparently taking steroids solely for the sake of appearance. [6]Further, although most adolescents believe that smoking cigarettes puts their health "at risk," at least one in five high-school seniors is a daily smoker, partly because smoking reduces appetite. [7]Interestingly, with most drugs, girls are much more cautious than boys and hence less likely to be users. [8]But largely because of the suppressant effect that smoking has on appetite and weight gain, the rate of cigarette smoking over the past twenty years has been slightly higher among girls than among boys.

Which of the following is **not** relevant to the author's conclusion that the quest for the ideal body can become physically unhealthy?

A. Sentence 2
B. Sentence 6
C. Sentence 7
D. Sentence 8

B. For each group, read the three items of support (the evidence). Then, in the space provided, write the letter of the **one** point that is adequately supported by that evidence.

Remember that the point, or conclusion, should follow logically from the evidence. Do not jump to a conclusion that is not well supported.

Group 1

Support

- The weather bureau said this would be a mild winter, but for weeks, temperatures have been well below normal.
- There was no storm warning in the forecast today, but the winds were so severe that a tree blew down in our neighbor's yard.
- The forecast on the radio said it would be sunny all day, but the ball game was rained out.

_____ 4. Which **point** is adequately supported by all the evidence above?

A. People's poor treatment of the environment affects the ozone layer and causes changes in the weather.
B. Always expect the opposite weather from what the weather reports predict.
C. It is impossible to ever correctly predict the weather.
D. Weather predictions are not always accurate.

Group 2

Support

- "Ring Around a Rosy" is supposedly about the rose-colored rash that was a symptom of the deadly Great Plague; "they all fall down" meant that they died.
- In "Three Blind Mice," the farmer's wife cuts off the mice's tails with a carving knife.
- In "Ladybug, Ladybug," the ladybug is told to fly away home because "your house is on fire, and your children—they will burn."

_____ 5. Which **point** is adequately supported by all the evidence above?

A. Violence on TV can't be so bad for kids.
B. All nursery rhymes are morbid and depressing.
C. Some traditional children's verses refer to gruesome events.
D. Violent criminals are created in early childhood.

REVIEW TEST 4

When does obedience go too far? Here is a chance to apply your understanding of argument to a selection from the textbook *Psychology*, by Mary M. Gergen and others, that addresses that question.

To help you continue to strengthen your skills, the reading is followed by questions not only on what you've learned in this chapter but also on what you've learned in previous chapters.

Words to Watch

Below are some words in the reading that do not have strong context support. Each word is followed by the number of the paragraph in which it appears and its meaning there. These words are indicated in the article by a small circle (°).

critical (1): crucial
solicited (3): sought
confederate (3): associate
sadistic (7): cruel

OBEDIENCE: MILGRAM'S CONTROVERSIAL STUDIES

Mary M. Gergen and others

1 One of the most direct forms of social influence is the demand for *obedience:* people follow orders because an authority figure tells them to. In most societies, obedience plays a critical° role in social control. We obey parents, teachers, police, and other officials. Since many rules, laws, and commands from authority have a positive value, obedience is a major foundation of social life and behavior. However, obedience can go too far! Soldiers in Nazi Germany obeyed the orders of their superiors and, as a result, millions of people were slaughtered. More recently, nine hundred men, women, and children died in a mass suicide in Guyana. The leader of the community, James Jones, gave the order for his followers to drink a poisoned juice, and they did.

In these two instances, we seem to be observing extreme cases of blind obedience. Some might say that instances of blind obedience, where the commands of authority contradict moral and human principles, are extremely 2 rare. But are they? Social psychologist Stanley Milgram set out to find out.

3 In a series of experiments, Milgram solicited° subjects drawn from all walks of life through newspaper advertisements. In the ads, subjects were told they would be paid for participating in a psychology study at Yale University. Volunteers were paired and were told that one would be the "teacher" and the other the "learner" in a study to test the effect of shock on learning. The person designated as learner and the person designated as teacher were seemingly determined by a random draw. Then the learner was seated in an adjoining room, and his arms were strapped to his chair. Electrodes were attached to his arms. At this point, the learner (actually a confederate° of Milgram's) mentioned that he had a slight heart condition.

4 The teacher was then escorted to a separate room and seated in front of an impressive, complicated-looking machine, which the experimenter referred to as a shock generator. The machine had a series of switches with labels from 15 volts ("slight shock") to 450 volts ("danger—severe shock").

5 The teacher was given a somewhat painful sample shock (45 volts) so he or she could have an idea of what the learner would be experiencing. After the sample shock, the experimenter told the teacher to read over the intercom a list of pairs of words so the learner could memorize them. The experimenter then instructed the teacher to read one word of each pair along with four alternatives. It was now the learner's job to pick out the right response. If the response was correct, the teacher was to proceed to the next word. If the response was incorrect, the teacher's task was to give the learner a shock. The teacher was told to start at 15 volts and to proceed up the scale toward 450 volts.

During the experiment, the learner 6 got some items right and others wrong. However, as the experiment progressed, the learner made errors more and more frequently. Each error increased the amount of shock given. In one condition of this experiment, the learner made no response to the shocks until they reached the 300-volt level; then he yelled and complained about the shock and pounded on the wall, shouting "Let me out of here." The learner did this on several occasions.

Finally, he stopped responding to the test. Regardless of what the learner said or did, the experimenter told the teacher to continue to read the words and to test for the right answer; if the learner gave an incorrect answer or no answer, the teacher was instructed to administer the next higher level of shock.

7 As the learner began to scream with pain, the teachers usually became upset and jittery. Many broke out in nervous laughter. Some threatened to quit the experiment. What would you have done? What do you think the average subjects did? Would they go on, or would they stop? Milgram was curious about this question and asked a group of psychiatrists to predict what percentage they thought would obey the experimenter's demands. They estimated that only half of 1 percent (that is, one person in two hundred) of the population would be sadistic° enough to obey. But they were clearly wrong.

8 Readers are usually surprised to learn that 65 percent of the subjects who served as teachers obeyed the experimenter's commands and delivered shocks up to the maximum (450 volts), even though the learner objected, screamed, and begged to be released. Of course, in actuality, the learner was a confederate of Milgram's, never actually received any shocks, and answered the word-pair questions according to a prearranged schedule. However, the confederate was well-trained, and his faked pain and protests were well-staged and seemed quite real to the subject.

9 The finding that two-thirds of the subjects went along with the experimenter's commands suggests that obedience is not just to be found in Nazi Germany or in Jonestown. Rather, obedience seems to be a common response to the commands of authorities. In fact, after examining hundreds of sessions, Milgram failed to find any background, socioeconomic, or personality factors that predicted who would obey the experimenter's commands and who would not.

10 The important question, of course, is why did so many people obey? Milgram thought that people obeyed because they perceived the experimenter to be a legitimate authority; he had the right to dictate behaviors and demands because he was in the role of a scientist. Presumably, obedience to legitimate authorities is something we learn early in life and retain throughout adulthood. As long as we recognize the authority as legitimate, we are subject to its influence.

11 Milgram's research has been strongly criticized for being unethical and misleading. Certain critics have objected to his misuse of people as subjects. They argue that the subjects should not have been led to believe that they may have killed someone. Other critics have suggested that the laboratory experiments were not adequate demonstrations of obedience in real life because the subjects would have felt it was a "science game" and would simply have been playing a cooperative role. However, despite these objections, Milgram's work seems

to have had a substantial social impact. It would appear that people rather readily acquiesce to authority figures, whether they are army officers, religious leaders, or scientists. Given the consequences of obedience, Milgram's works stand out as an important contribution to psychology and as a warning for our society.

Reading Comprehension Questions

Vocabulary in Context

_____ 1. In the sentence below, the words *acquiesce to* (ăk′wē-ĕs′to͞o) mean

A. oppose.
B. obey.
C. question.
D. converse with.

"It would appear that people rather readily acquiesce to authority figures, whether they are army officers, religious leaders, or scientists." (Paragraph 11)

Central Point and Main Ideas

_____ 2. Which sentence best expresses the central point of the selection?

A. Psychological experiments can reveal much about human behavior in various situations.
B. Stanley Milgram has conducted psychological research that has been strongly criticized for being unethical and misleading.
C. An important experiment conducted by Stanley Milgram showed that people will often blindly obey authority.
D. Electrical shocks should not be administered as part of a psychological experiment.

_____ 3. Which sentence best expresses the main idea of paragraph 10?
A. Scientists are authority figures.
B. Milgram concluded that people tend to obey anyone they recognize as a legitimate authority.
C. Milgram wondered why so many people obeyed the experimenter in his experiment.
D. Milgram was surprised to be considered a legitimate authority figure.

Supporting Details

_____ 4. According to the author, obedience to legitimate authority is probably
A. always dangerous.
B. often painful.
C. learned early in life.
D. senseless.

Transitions

_____ 5. The relationship expressed by the sentence below is one of
A. time.
B. addition.
C. contrast.
D. cause and effect.

"Soldiers in Nazi Germany obeyed the orders of their superiors and, as a result, millions of people were slaughtered." (Paragraph 1)

Patterns of Organization

_____ 6. The overall pattern of organization of paragraphs 3–6 is
A. steps in a process.
B. list of items.
C. cause and effect.
D. definition and example.

Inferences

_____ 7. The author suggests that
A. Milgram's research sheds little light on obedience.
B. paid volunteers are more likely to obey than nonpaid volunteers.
C. people should be more questioning of authority figures.
D. there is little reason for obedience in contemporary societies.

Purpose

_____ 8. On the basis of the reading—including its last sentence—we might conclude that the author's intention was
A. only to inform.
B. both to inform and to persuade.
C. to entertain and to persuade.

Argument

Read the three items of support (the evidence). Then, in the space provided, write the letter of the **one** point that is adequately supported by that evidence.

Support

- Most of the "teachers" in Milgram's experiment became nervous and upset as the experiment continued.
- Some of the "teachers" threatened to quit the experiment when they heard the "learners" screaming.
- Two-thirds of the "teachers" continued to inflict shocks up to the maximum, despite the protests of the "learners."

_____ 9. Which **point** is adequately supported by all the evidence above?
A. Milgram's experiment proved that most people enjoy inflicting pain on others.
B. Milgram's experiment proved that experiencing pain helps students learn.
C. The "teachers" in the experiment didn't care if the "learners" were in pain.
D. While "teachers" might have been uncomfortable inflicting increasing amounts of pain, most of them continued to do so.

10. Label the point of the following argument based on the reading with a **P**; label the two statements of support for the point with an **S**. Label with an **X** the one statement that is neither the point nor the support of the argument.

___ A. Participants may have felt that academic researchers would not allow anyone to be genuinely hurt.

___ B. Obedient soldiers in Nazi Germany killed millions of people.

___ C. Milgram's experiment does not represent obedience in real life.

___ D. Participants in the experiment may have felt they were simply cooperating in a "science game."

Discussion Questions

1. Imagine that you were a subject in Milgram's experiment. How do you think you would have responded to the experimenter's commands? Why?

2. The authors write, "Presumably, obedience to legitimate authorities is something we learn early in life and retain throughout adulthood." Why do you think people develop an obedience to authority so early?

3. What might the authors have been thinking of when they wrote that Milgram's experiments "stand out as . . . a warning for our society"? Can you think of any events that reflect unwise obedience to authority?

4. The reading refers to what is negative about obedience to authority. What do you think might be some positive aspects of such obedience?

Note: Writing assignments for this selection appear on page 701.

Check Your Performance — ARGUMENT

Activity		*Number Right*	*Points*		*Score*
Review Test 1	(5 items)	______	× 2	=	______
Review Test 2	(10 items)	______	× 3	=	______
Review Test 3	(5 items)	______	× 6	=	______
Review Test 4	(10 items)	______	× 3	=	______
			TOTAL SCORE	=	______%

Enter your total score into the **Reading Performance Chart: Review Tests** on the inside back cover.

Name ______________________ Date __________

Section __________ SCORE: (Number correct) ______ x 10 = ______ %

ARGUMENT: Mastery Test 1

A. Look at the cartoon below, and then answer the question that follows.

"We do so hire people with disabilities! Dan can't make a decision, Tina is a chronic whiner, Jake is an obsessive compulsive coffee drinker, Katherine has no sense of humor . . ."

_____ 1. TRUE OR FALSE? The woman in the cartoon offers relevant support for her argument.

B. In each group, one statement is the point of an argument, and the other statements are support for that point. In the space provided, write the letter of the point of each group.

_____ 2. A. Horror movies give us a chance to feel smarter than the characters, who often do incredibly stupid things such as investigating the moaning sounds in the dark basement of a haunted house.

B. Horror movies also provide a great bonding experience between friends by allowing us to share screams and grab each other for comfort.

C. Horror movies give us a chance to explore our deepest fears ("There's a crazed killer in the basement!" "There's something horrible lurking in the woods!") while knowing we are safe.

D. Horror movies deserve the popularity they have in American culture.

_____ 3. A. The Internal Revenue Service is the only government agency with the power to take people's property and salaries without a hearing or court order.

B. Legal loopholes allow wealthy, well-connected Americans to avoid paying their fair share of income tax.

C. The U.S. income tax system needs to be reformed.

D. The current tax on interest earned in bank accounts punishes people for saving their money.

(Continues on next page)

_____ 4. A. Requirements should be ended for teacher certification since studies show that whether teachers are certified is irrelevant to their effectiveness.

B. Tenure should be made more difficult to obtain so that weak teachers can be weeded out after two or three years on the job.

C. Bold steps should be taken to improve the U.S. education system and to reduce the gap between the good schools in suburbs and the poor schools in inner cities.

D. Substantial bonuses of $15,000 or more should be awarded annually to good teachers for as long as they teach in schools in low-income areas.

C. Each point is followed by three statements that provide relevant support and three that do not. In the spaces, write the letters of the **three** relevant statements of support.

5–7. **Point: Cats and dogs benefit from being neutered.**

A. Cats and dogs should be taken to a veterinarian at least once a year for a checkup and vaccinations.

B. Neutering reduces the likelihood that a cat or dog will develop certain common forms of cancer.

C. If you adopt an animal from a local shelter, the shelter may neuter your new pet.

D. Neutered cats and dogs tend to be more content to stay at home, where they're safest.

E. On average, neutered cats and dogs live longer than unneutered ones.

F. Purebred cats and dogs are more likely than mixed breeds to suffer from inherited disorders.

Items that logically support the point: _______ _______ _______

8–10. **Point: Many women lack healthy strategies for dealing with their anger.**

A. Women with violent partners often blame themselves for the abuse rather than becoming angry with the man.

B. Men are typically able to express anger with one another without fearing their relationship will be destroyed.

C. Rather than showing anger, many women let anger build up and become very stressful.

D. Being too ready to express one's anger can be as mentally unhealthy as repressing it.

E. Women commit violent, anger-related crimes far less frequently than men.

F. Some women become so afraid of their own anger that they lose the ability to know when they're angry.

Items that logically support the point: _______ _______ _______

Name ______________________________ Date __________

Section ____________ SCORE: (Number correct) ________ x 10 = ________ %

ARGUMENT: Mastery Test 2

A. In each group, one statement is the point of an argument, and the other statements are support for that point. In the space provided, write the letter of the point of each group.

_____ 1. A. A defendant charged with assault and battery would be foolish to show up in the courtroom wearing a black leather jacket, jeans, and boots.

B. The woman who dresses in sweatpants for a job interview with a major retail company isn't likely to be hired.

C. Someone who shows up at a wedding wearing jeans and tennis shoes is likely to be considered rude.

D. People make judgments about us based on the way we dress.

_____ 2. A. Bureaucratic "red tape" may call attention to an undesirable community project so that people can take steps to oppose it.

B. The impersonality of bureaucracy means equal treatment for all who seek benefits.

C. One researcher found that bureaucrats perform at a higher intellectual level than nonbureaucrats.

D. Despite the popular idea of bureaucracies as places where workers are unthinking and nothing gets done, bureaucracies are not all bad.

_____ 3. A. Our schools must spend time dealing with such social problems as substance abuse and teenage pregnancy, which Japanese schools are not expected to do.

B. U.S. schools are not entirely to blame for the lower achievement of their students compared with the skills of Japanese students.

C. Many U.S. teenagers cut back on their study time by taking a part-time job, which is virtually unheard of in Japan.

D. Many U.S. parents work full-time and leave homework decisions to their children, whereas Japanese mothers make sure their children study several hours each night.

_____ 4. A. Some nutritionists believe that dividing food intake into "three square meals a day" is a poor way to fuel metabolism.

B. Many healthcare professionals now consider traditional American eating and activity patterns unhealthy.

C. Heart specialists say today's jobs involve insufficient physical activity.

D. According to healthcare professionals, fast food eaten "on the run" contributes to dangerously high levels of fat and cholesterol and forces the digestive system to work too hard and too fast.

(Continues on next page)

B. Each point is followed by three statements that provide relevant support and three that do not. In the spaces, write the letters of the **three** relevant statements of support.

5–7. **Point: The GPS (Global Positioning System) ankle bracelet is the wave of the future in using technology to fight crime.**

A. The GPS ankle bracelet is not an appropriate means of dealing with violent criminals.

B. Celebrities have been photographed wearing GPS ankle bracelets, generally after committing drug or alcohol offenses.

C. For those under house arrest, a GPS ankle bracelet can alert authorities if the offender leaves the approved location.

D. For people on probation or parole, the GPS ankle bracelet can be programmed with the offender's work schedule and location.

E. The everyday uses of GPS technology include car navigation systems and cell phones.

F. The GPS ankle bracelet frees up prison cells, making space available for violent offenders and allowing courts to keep these offenders in prison longer.

Items that logically support the point: ________ ________ ________

8–10. **Point: High-heeled shoes are a health risk.**

A. It is difficult to walk fast in high-heeled shoes.

B. Although males have worn high-heeled shoes in some cultures and historical periods, they do not wear high-heeled shoes in our society.

C. Long-term wearing of high-heeled shoes increases the likelihood of developing back and foot disorders.

D. Many women wear high-heeled shoes to work.

E. High-heeled shoes increase the risk of falling on a slippery surface.

F. High, narrow heels easily catch in sidewalk cracks and gratings, resulting in falls.

Items that logically support the point: ________ ________ ________

Name ______________________________ Date __________

Section __________ SCORE: (Number correct) ______ x 12.5 = _____ %

ARGUMENT: Mastery Test 3

A. Each point is followed by three statements that provide relevant support and three that do not. In the spaces, write the letters of the **three** relevant statements of support.

1–3. **Point: When naming a baby, parents should consider the effect that a name may have on their child.**

A. Lucas, Sophia, and Emily are among the most popular children's names today.

B. Unusual or out-of-date names such as Barnabas and Hilda may make a child a target for teasing by classmates.

C. Children's initials have been known to have a negative impact on them. Patricia Irene Graham and Anthony Steven Smith are fine names, but when these children's friends realize what the initials spell, Patricia and Anthony may never hear the end of it.

D. Some people change their names when they get older.

E. Names like Buffy and Missy may be perfect for a baby, but they may not inspire confidence in the same person when she or he later runs for Congress or does heart surgery.

F. The most common family name in the world is the Chinese name Chung, shared by at least 104 million people.

Items that logically support the point: ________ ________ ________

4–6. **Point: Cutting down on fats in the diet is not easy.**

A. Fats are flavor carriers, so foods such as baked goods often seem tasteless without fat.

B. Fats satisfy hunger, so people get hungrier more often on a very low-fat diet.

C. Americans, on average, consume far too much fat, as a percentage of total calories.

D. There are several different kinds of fats, some more harmful to health than others.

E. Many popular frozen desserts contain large amounts of fat.

F. Fat cells insulate the body from cold and help protect it from injury.

Items that logically support the point: ________ ________ ________

(Continues on next page)

B. For each group, read the three items of support (the evidence). Then, in the space provided, write the letter of the point that is adequately supported by that evidence.

Group 1

Support

- White settlers in North America were called pioneers rather than invaders; their conquest of the Native Americans' lands was called homesteading, not robbery.
- Whites stereotyped the Native Americans as "lazy," although it was whites who forced them to give up their traditional occupations.
- Whites called Native Americans savages, yet it was whites who slaughtered hundreds of thousands of Native Americans.

_____ 7. Which **point** is adequately supported by all the evidence above?

A. When white people came to North America, they and the Native Americans were always enemies.

B. Contrary to how they were stereotyped, Native Americans were not lazy.

C. Language was used to hide the truth of the unjust treatment of Native Americans by white settlers.

D. Native Americans naturally resisted the invasion of the white "settlers."

Group 2

Support

- In France, no house is given the number 13, and in Italy, the national lottery omits the number 13.
- Friday the 13th is often considered the unluckiest of days; some believe it to be the day that Eve tempted Adam with the apple, the day the Great Flood began, and the day Jesus died.
- In America, many modern skyscrapers, condos, hotels, and apartment buildings skip the number 13; the floor above level 12 is numbered 14.

_____ 8. Which **point** is adequately supported by all the evidence above?

A. Thirteen is an unlucky number, and if you use it, you are just asking for trouble.

B. Everyone is superstitious about something.

C. Many people throughout the world are superstitious about the number 13.

D. Another common superstition is the fear of walking under a ladder.

Name ________________________________ Date __________

Section ____________ SCORE: (Number correct) _______ x 10 = _______ %

ARGUMENT: Mastery Test 4

A. Each point below is followed by three statements that provide relevant support and three that do not. In the spaces, write the letters of the **three** relevant statements of support.

1–3. **Point: Not all stereotypes are negative views of groups.**

A. Asians are often stereotyped as a "model minority," presumably smarter and harder-working than others.

B. Redheaded women are supposed to be sultry, sexy, and gorgeous.

C. On the other hand, redheads are also supposed to be hot-tempered—a negative stereotype.

D. Women in general are stereotyped as having a "maternal instinct" and nurturing: in other words, as good mothers and good caregivers.

E. Other stereotypes of women depict them as being illogical and weak.

F. Most stereotypes are oversimplified at best and outright false at worst.

Items that logically support the point: ________ ________ ________

4–6. **Point: Arranged marriage, as it is still often practiced in India, has its advantages.**

A. The extended family of an arranged couple may be overbearing and meddling.

B. The partners in an arranged marriage are generally compatible in their backgrounds, upbringing, beliefs and values.

C. Strong social pressure may force an arranged couple to stay together, even if one or both are very unhappy.

D. Over the course of their marriage, arranged couples often learn to love each other deeply.

E. If love is absent in the arranged marriage, one or both of the couple may seek it in an affair.

F. Arranged couples generally have plenty of physical and emotional support from their extended families.

Items that logically support the point: ________ ________ ________

(Continues on next page)

B. In the group below, read the three items of support (the evidence). Then, in the space provided, write the letter of the point that is adequately supported by that evidence.

Support

- In the early 1900s, classrooms were crowded, stuffy, poorly lit, and conducive to the spread of disease.
- Classroom "learning" consisted mainly of memorizing questionable facts.
- Physical punishment was considered the best way to teach good behavior.

_____ 7. Which **point** is adequately supported by all the evidence above?

A. A century ago, most education was a very negative experience.
B. Teachers in the early 1900s were poorly trained.
C. Parents a century ago objected to physical punishment of their children.
D. A century ago, few students completed high school.

C. Read the paragraphs below and then answer the questions that follow.

[1]The lack of childcare places women at a disadvantage in the workplace. [2]First of all, women are sometimes prevented from taking paid positions when good childcare is unavailable. [3]Participation in many social activities is also difficult for these same women. [4]In addition, childcare problems force women to stay in part-time jobs with lower pay, little career mobility, and no fringe benefits. [5]Finally, the childcare dilemma discourages women from putting in the time necessary to seek and accept job promotions. [6]Women with childcare responsibilities thus often have no choice but to remain in jobs for which they are overqualified.

_____ 8. Which sentence is the point of the argument?

_____ 9. Which sentence is **not** relevant support for the author's argument?

A. Sentence 2   C. Sentence 4
B. Sentence 3   D. Sentence 5

[1]Animals can be useful in promoting mental stability and health. [2]By forming close relationships with animals, we can demonstrate the kinship of all living things. [3]Experiments in prisons have shown that convicts who are allowed pets become less violent. [4]Also, patients in nursing homes show greater responsiveness and a more positive attitude when they have an opportunity to share affection with dogs and cats. [5]When some autistic children were given the opportunity to interact with dolphins, they made great strides, including speaking for the first time in their lives.

_____ 10. Which sentence is **not** relevant support for the author's argument?

A. Sentence 2   C. Sentence 4
B. Sentence 3   D. Sentence 5

Name ______________________________ Date __________

Section ___________ SCORE: (Number correct) _______ x 20 = _______ %

ARGUMENT: Mastery Test 5

A. In the group below, read the three items of support (the evidence). Then, in the space provided, write the letter of the point that is adequately supported by that evidence.

Support

- The staple food for the Native Americans of the American plains was dried buffalo meat.
- When the Plains Indians killed a buffalo, they transformed its hide into blankets and robes.
- The Indians used buffalo fat to make soap, buffalo horn to make spoons, buffalo hair as stuffing for saddles, and buffalo muscle sinew as strings for their bows.

_____ 1. Which point is supported by all the evidence above?

A. The Plains Indians are to blame for wiping out the country's buffalo.
B. The buffalo is the most useful animal that ever lived.
C. The Plains Indians wasted nothing when they killed a buffalo.
D. Ancient people had to create, rather than purchase, everything they needed to live.

B. Read the paragraphs and answer the questions that follow.

[1]Victimless crimes involving drug use or sexual activity should be decriminalized. [2]These crimes consume an inordinate amount of the time and resources of the criminal justice system and clog already congested courts and jails. [3]Additionally, the laws against drug use and sexual activity almost invariably lead to the development of a black market supplied by organized crime. [4]Victimless crimes are often related to the corruption of police officers and others in the criminal justice system who receive bribes and payoffs from illegal suppliers and practitioners. [5]Of course, if police officers were honest, then bribery would not be a problem. [6]Finally, victimless crime involves acts that are private matters, acts that are not rightfully the concern of government or other people.

_____ 2. Which sentence is the point of the argument?

A. Sentence 1
B. Sentence 2
C. Sentence 3
D. Sentence 4

_____ 3. Which sentence is **not** relevant support for the point of the argument?

A. Sentence 3
B. Sentence 4
C. Sentence 5
D. Sentence 6

(Continues on next page)

[1]The age of required retirement in companies should be raised, and the age at which Social Security begins should be raised. [2]First of all, older workers who remain healthy are valuable workers. [3]Although they may lose some mental speed, their accumulated experience more than compensates for the loss of quickness. [4]In fact, compared with youngsters, older persons may take longer to make a decision, but it is usually a better one. [5]Many studies have shown that the quality of job performance improves with age. [6]Furthermore, raising the retirement age would prevent some of the dire economic consequences that older workers face when they are forced to retire before they need to. [7]Nearly 60 percent of workers in the private sector reach retirement age without any pension from their lifelong work, so they should be allowed to continue working for economic reasons. [8]Luckily, older people don't have to furnish a home, raise children, and pay for educational expenses. [9]Finally, raising the age of required retirement could also mean raising the age that Social Security payments begin. [10]As a result, the cost of one of our country's biggest financial burdens will go down.

______ 4. Which sentence is the point of the argument?
- A. Sentence 1
- B. Sentence 2
- C. Sentence 5
- D. Sentence 9

______ 5. Which sentence is **not** relevant support for the point of the argument?
- A. Sentence 3
- B. Sentence 4
- C. Sentence 5
- D. Sentence 8

Name ______________________ Date ________

Section __________ SCORE: (Number correct) ______ x 10 = ______ %

ARGUMENT: Mastery Test 6

A. For each group, read the three items of support (the evidence). Then, in the space provided, write the letter of the point that is adequately supported by that evidence.

1–3. **Point: Drinking sodas on a regular basis is a poor nutritional choice.**

A. More than a quarter of beverages consumed every day in the U.S. are sodas.

B. Some diet sodas contain aspartame, which has been linked to a variety of health problems.

C. The acids in soda damage tooth enamel, and the sugar in them causes tooth decay.

D. Cola drinks are the most popular soda beverages.

E. Sodas that are non-diet contain the equivalent of about ten cubes of sugar, making them high in "empty" calories.

F. The nation's largest beverage distributors agreed to stop selling non-diet sodas to schools and start serving reduced sizes of other drinks.

Items that logically support the point: ________ ________ ________

4–6. **Point: Wolfgang Amadeus Mozart was a musical genius.**

A. He started composing symphonies at age 9 and by age 13 had written his first opera.

B. Many of Mozart's compositions are universally regarded as masterpieces.

C. Even after being appointed to the prestigious position of concertmaster to the archbishop of Salzburg, Mozart made little money.

D. Mozart composed at superhuman speed; for example, he wrote the overture to his opera *Don Giovanni* the night before its first performance.

E. Mozart was eventually kicked out of the archbishop's palace by the successor to the man who had hired him.

F. Like so many great artists, Mozart died in poverty.

Items that logically support the point: ________ ________ ________

(Continues on next page)

B. Read the paragraphs and answer the questions that follow

[1]The Civil War brought slavery to an end. [2]However, when Reconstruction ended in 1877 with the withdrawal of federal troops from the South, whites in the region regained power and gradually reestablished racial segregation. [3]They enacted a variety of laws that prohibited black citizens from using the same public facilities as whites. [4]During that same time, however, positive milestones such as the founding of the Tuskegee Institute occurred. [5]In *Plessy v. Ferguson* (1896), the Supreme Court endorsed these laws, ruling that "separate" facilities for the two races did not violate the Constitution as long as the facilities were "equal." [6]The *Plessy* decision, in practice, became a justification for the separate and unequal treatment of African Americans. [7]Black children, for instance, were forced into separate schools that rarely had libraries and had few teachers. [8]They were given worn-out books that had been used previously in white schools.

_____ 7. Which sentence is the point of the argument?

A. Sentence 1 C. Sentence 3
B. Sentence 2 D. Sentence 5

_____ 8. Which sentence is **not** relevant support for the point of the argument?

A. Sentence 3 C. Sentence 5
B. Sentence 4 D. Sentence 6

[1]Many Westerners are uncomfortable with silence, which they find embarrassing and awkward. [2]In contrast, Asian cultures have for thousands of years promoted quiet and discouraged the expression of thoughts and feelings. [3]Silence is valued. [4]Asian proverbs support this point of view, saying, "In much talk there is great weariness," and "One who speaks does not know; one who knows does not speak." [5]Unlike Westerners who tend to chatter nervously to fill up silence, Japanese and Chinese believe that remaining quiet is the proper state when there is nothing essential to be said. [6]Of course, individual quirks may make a Westerner very quiet or an Asian person talkative. [7]To Asians, a talkative person is often considered to be showing off or insincere.

_____ 9. Which sentence is the point of the argument?

A. Sentence 1 C. Sentence 5
B. Sentence 3 D. Sentence 7

_____10. Which sentence is **not** relevant support for the point of the argument?

A. Sentence 3 C. Sentence 5
B. Sentence 4 D. Sentence 6

10 Critical Reading

Skilled readers are those who can *recognize* an author's point and the support for that point. **Critical readers** are those who can *evaluate* an author's support for a point and determine whether that support is solid or not. In this book, you have already had practice in evaluating support—deciding when inferences are valid and when they are not (pages 281–302) and determining whether supporting evidence is relevant (pages 375–381) and adequate (pages 381–385).

This chapter will extend your ability to read critically in three ways. It will explain and offer practice in each of the following:

- Separating fact from opinion
- Detecting propaganda
- Recognizing errors in reasoning

Separating Fact from Opinion

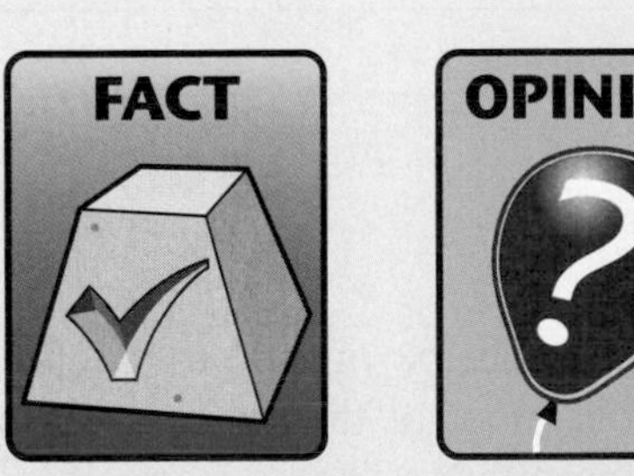

As the illustration suggests, facts are solidly grounded and can be checked for accuracy; opinions are afloat and open to question.

Look at the personals ad below that appeared in a retirement community newspaper in Florida. In the spaces provided, do the following:

1. Write what you think are the **facts** in the ad.
2. Write what you think may be considered the **opinions** in the ad.

> **FOXY LADY**. Blue-haired beauty, 80s, slim 5'4" (used to be 5'6"). Widow who has just buried fourth husband. Has original teeth and new parts including hip, knee, cornea, and valves. A groovy chick who is still the life of the party.

Facts: ______________________________

____

____

____

Opinions: ______________________________

____

____

____

Fact

A **fact** is information that can be proved true through objective evidence. This evidence may be physical proof or the spoken or written testimony of witnesses. The above ad includes these facts: The woman is blue-haired, in her 80s, 5'4" tall; and a recent widow (for the fourth time) who still has her own teeth as well as some new body parts.

Following are some more facts—they can be checked for accuracy and thus proved true.

Fact: My grandfather has eleven toes.

(Someone can count them.)

Fact: In 1841, William Henry Harrison served as president of the United States for only thirty-one days; he died of pneumonia.

(We can check history records to confirm that this is true.)

Fact: Tarantulas are hairy spiders capable of inflicting on humans a painful but not deadly bite.

(We can check biology reports to confirm that this statement is true.)

Opinion

An **opinion** is a belief, judgment, or conclusion that cannot be objectively proved true. As a result, it is open to question. For instance, the woman in the ad says she is "foxy," a "beauty," "slim," and "a groovy chick who is still the life of the party," but we have no way of knowing for sure. These statements are opinions.

Or consider this example: Your friend might visit a new restaurant and report to you that the food was great but the service was terrible. These statements may be reasonable ones with which other people would agree, but they cannot be objectively proved. They are opinions. You might eat at the same restaurant and reach very different conclusions.

Here are some more opinions:

Opinion: My grandfather's feet are ugly.

(There's no way to prove this statement because two people can look at the same thing and come to different conclusions about its beauty. For instance, the speaker's grandmother may have found those feet attractive. *Ugly* is a **value word**, a word we use to express a value judgment. Value words are signals that an opinion is being expressed. By their very nature, these words represent opinions, not facts.)

Opinion: Harrison should never have been elected president in the first place.

(Those who voted for him would not have agreed.)

Opinion: Tarantulas are disgusting.

(Who says? Not the people who keep them as pets.)

Writing Facts and Opinions

To get a better sense of fact and opinion, take a few minutes to write three facts about yourself and then to write three of your opinions. Here, for example, are three facts about me and three of my opinions.

Three facts about me:

- Gray hairs have begun to appear in my beard.
- I work out about five times a week.
- My favorite meal is grilled salmon, mashed potatoes, and asparagus.

Three of my opinions:

- The most important thing about clothes is how comfortable they are.
- Reading for pleasure is one of the joys of life.
- America is a better place with Barack Obama as president.

Now write your facts and opinions in the space below.

Three facts about you:

- ______________________________
  ____
- ______________________________
  ____
- ______________________________
  ____

Three of your opinions:

> ***Hint:*** To make sure that these are opinions, do not begin them with "I." For example, do not write, "I think capital punishment should be outlawed." Simply write, "Capital punishment should be outlawed."

- ______________________________
  ____
- ______________________________
  ____
- ______________________________
  ____

Points about Fact and Opinion

There are several points to keep in mind when considering fact and opinion.

1 Statements of fact may be found to be untrue.

Suppose a new breed of tarantula was discovered whose bite was deadly to humans. The earlier "fact"—that tarantulas inflict a painful but not deadly bite—would then be an error, not a fact. It is not unusual for evidence to show that a "fact" is not really true. It was once considered to be a fact that the world was flat, for example, but that "fact" turned out to be an error. It was originally regarded as a fact that there were weapons of mass destruction in Iraq, but that "fact" also turned out to be an error.

2 **Value words** (ones that contain a judgment) often represent opinions. Here are examples of these words:

Value Words

best	**great**	**beautiful**
worst	**terrible**	**bad**
better	**lovely**	**good**
worse	**disgusting**	**wonderful**

Value words often express judgments—they are generally subjective, not objective. While factual statements *report on* observed reality, subjective statements *interpret* reality. For example, the observation that it is raining outside is an objective one. The statement that the weather is bad, however, is subjective, an evaluation of reality. (Some people—for example, farmers whose crops need water—consider rain to be good weather.)

3 The words *should* and *ought to* often signal opinions. Those words introduce what people think should, or ought to, be done. Other people will disagree.

Couples with young children should not be allowed to divorce.

Parents who abuse their children ought to be put in jail.

4 Don't mistake widely held opinions for facts. Much information that sounds factual is really opinion. A used-car salesman, for example, could say, "This vehicle is an exceptional purchase." Buyers would be wise to wonder what the value word *exceptional* means to this salesman. Or a politician may claim that he fights for working-class people, a statement that at first seems factual. But what is meant by *fights*? If the politician's voting record shows that he voted "yes" on tax cuts for the wealthy and "no"on raising the minimum wage, you might not agree that he has working-class people's interests at heart.

As we will see in later parts of this chapter, advertisers and politicians often try to manipulate us by presenting opinions as if they were facts. For instance, one politician may claim that another will be soft on terrorism or will waste our tax dollars. But accusations are often not facts. Clear-thinking citizens must aim to get below the surface of claims and charges and determine as much factual truth as possible.

5 Finally, remember that much of what we read and hear is a mixture of fact and opinion. Our job, then, is to draw upon existing fact and opinion and to arrive at an informed opinion. On our Supreme Court, for example, nine justices deliberate in order to deliver informed opinions about important issues of our time. But even these justices often disagree and deliver split decisions. The reality is that most of what matters in life is very complex and cannot be separated into simple fact and opinion. Our challenge always is to arrive at the best possible informed opinion, and even then there will be people who disagree with us.

Fact and Opinion in Reading

The amount of fact and opinion in a piece of writing varies, depending on the author's purpose. For example, textbooks, news articles and scientific reports, which are written to inform readers, are supposed to be as factual as possible. On the other hand, the main points of editorials, political speeches, and advertisements—materials written to persuade readers—are opinions. Such writings may contain facts, but, in general, they are facts carefully selected to back up the authors' opinions.

Both facts and opinions can be valuable to readers. However, it is important to recognize the difference between the two.

Check Your Understanding

To sharpen your understanding of fact and opinion, read the following statements and decide whether each is fact or opinion. Put an **F** (for "fact") or an **O** (for "opinion") beside each statement. Put **F+O** beside the **one** statement that is a mixture of fact *and* opinion. Then read the explanation that follows.

> ***Hint:*** Remember that opinions are signaled by value words—words such as *great* or *hard* or *beautiful* or *terrible* that express a value judgment. Take care to note such words in your reading.

_____ 1. No flower is more beautiful than a simple daisy.

_____ 2. In the U.S. presidential election of 2000, the Electoral College—not the direct vote of the people—determined who became president.

_____ 3. It is riskier for a woman to have a first child after age 40 than before.

_____ 4. It is stupid for women over 40 to get pregnant.

_____ 5. Redheads should never wear pink or purple—they look awful in those colors.

_____ 6. In Egypt, 96 percent of the land is desert.

_____ 7. There is too much violence in children's television programs.

_____ 8. Among Americans aged 10 to 24, suicide is the third-leading cause of death (after car accidents and homicides).

_____ 9. It's a fact that parents and teachers must bear the responsibility for not recognizing signs of teenage depression.

_____ 10. Each year, more than 1,600 American teenagers kill themselves, and many of these deaths could be easily prevented.

Explanation

1. This is an opinion. Many people may consider other flowers more beautiful than the daisy. The word *beautiful* is a value word.
2. This is a fact. As reported by the media and in public records, in the 2000 election Governor George Bush won the majority of electoral-college votes (271 to 266), but Vice President Al Gore won the most popular votes (50,922,335 to 50,455,156).
3. This is a fact that can be verified by checking medical statistics.
4. This is an opinion. Some people might admire the woman who has children in her 40s.
5. This is an opinion. As the value words *should* and *awful* suggest, a judgment is being expressed. Many feel that redheads look wonderful in pink and purple.
6. This is a fact, agreed upon and written down by experts who study geography.
7. As the words *too much* suggest, this is an opinion. Some people may conclude there is little harm in children's watching the existing amount of violence in children's shows.
8. All the details here are facts that can be confirmed by looking them up in public records.
9. This is an opinion. Just saying that something is a fact doesn't make it so. Studies show that there are often no warning signs of teenage depression. Even when there are signs, the extent of adult responsibility is a matter of opinion.
10. The first part of the sentence is a fact that can be confirmed by checking records on teen suicides. The second part is an opinion: *easily* is a judgment word—people may differ on how easy or difficult they consider something to be.

PRACTICE 1

Some of the statements below are facts, and some are opinions; in addition, two include fact and opinion. Label facts with an **F**, opinions with an **O**, and the **two** statements of fact *and* opinion with an **F+O**.

_____ 1. The main problem with too many children today is that they have been spoiled by their families.

_____ 2. Most men eat more meat than women, and women eat more fruits and vegetables.

_____ 3. The easiest way to get rich quick is to play the lottery every day.

_____ 4. The odds for hitting one state's $10 million jackpot are 120 million to 1.

_____ 5. Many states that run lotteries also have unfair laws that prohibit other forms of gambling.

_____ 6. The microwave oven is the most useful kitchen appliance ever invented.

_____ 7. A microwave oven heats food by creating a magnetic field that causes the food's water molecules to vibrate more than two billion times per second.

_____ 8. Mark Twain, whose real name was Samuel Clemens, died in 1910.

_____ 9. Mark Twain's novel *The Prince and the Pauper* is about a young king and a look-alike poor boy who get confused with one another.

_____ 10. *The Adventures of Huckleberry Finn*, first published in 1884, is the best birthday present a twelve-year-old boy could receive.

Note: Additional practice in fact and opinion is offered on pages 669–676.

Detecting Propaganda

Advertisers, salespeople, and politicians are constantly promoting their points: "Buy our product," "Believe what I say," and "Vote for me." Often they lack adequate factual support for their points, so they appeal to our emotions by using propaganda techniques.

Part of being a critical reader is having the ability to recognize these propaganda techniques for the emotional fluff that they are. The critical reader strips away the fluff to determine whether there is solid support for the point in question. None of us wants to accept someone else's point as a result of emotional manipulation.

This section will introduce you to six common propaganda techniques:

- Bandwagon
- Testimonial
- Transfer
- Plain Folks
- Name Calling
- Glittering Generalities

While there are other propaganda techniques, the ones described below are among the most common. They all use emotional appeals to distract from the fact that they are not providing solid evidence to support their points.

1 Bandwagon

Old-fashioned parades usually began with a large wagon carrying a brass band. Therefore, to "jump on the bandwagon" means to join a parade, or to do what many others are doing. The **bandwagon** technique tells us to buy a product or support a certain issue because, in effect, "everybody else is doing it."

An ad on a bus tells you to "Become one of the growing number of people who watch *Action News*." Or a TV commercial for an investment company shows a baseball stadium filled with silent fans while the voice-over tells us: "When our financial advisors talk, people listen." Or a political ad may feature people from all walks of life speaking out in support of a certain candidate. The ads imply that if you don't jump on the bandwagon, the parade will pass you by.

Here are two examples of real ads that have used the bandwagon appeal:

> A brand of soap used to advertise: "Aren't you glad you use our soap? Don't you wish everybody did?"
>
> A computer company advertises: "More than half of the companies in North American rely on our computers. Who do you rely on?"

● Check (✓) the ad below that uses the bandwagon appeal.

_____ 1. A magazine ad for Goodbuy Shoes shows a picture of the glamorous movie star Lana Starr. The caption reads: "Why should I spend more when I can get great shoes at Goodbuy?"

_____ 2. An ad for a car dealer shows cattle stampeding across the plains, while the announcer exclaims, "Everybody is rushing to Town Auto Mall!"

2 Testimonial

Famous athletes often appear on television as spokespersons for all sorts of products, from soft drinks to automobiles. Movie and TV stars make commercials endorsing products and political issues. The idea behind the **testimonial** approach is that the testimony of famous people influences the viewers that admire these people.

What consumers must remember is that famous people get paid to endorse products. In addition, these people are not necessarily experts about the products, or the political issues, they promote.

Here are two examples of real ads that have used the appeal of testimonials:

> "This yogurt can help regulate your digestive system in just two weeks," says a famous actress. "And it tastes great."
>
> A former United States senator and one-time candidate for president promotes a product intended to help a man's sexual performance.

● Check (✓) the ad below that uses a testimonial.

_____ 1. Become one of the millions of satisfied customers who control their weight with our diet shakes.

_____ 2. A picture of boxing great Muhammad Ali appears on boxes of a breakfast cereal.

3 Transfer

The most common type of propaganda technique is **transfer**, in which products or candidates try to associate themselves with something that people admire, desire, or love. In the illustration on page 419, we see a political candidate holding a sign saying "Vote for Me" and standing next to a beauty queen wrapped in a U.S.A. banner.

There are countless variations on this ad, in which a beautiful and sexy woman (or an American flag or some other symbol of the U.S.A.) is used to promote a product or candidate or cause. The hope is that we will *transfer* the positive feelings we have toward a beautiful or sexy-looking person to the product being advertised, or that we will *transfer* the patriotism that we feel to a product or candidate. Over the years, advertisers have found that beauty and sex "sell" and that appeals to patriotism often succeed. In short, transfer usually works.

Here are two examples of real ads that have used the appeal of transfer:

> An ad for a hair color product for men shows a beautiful young woman in a short dress running her fingers through a man's hair.
>
> A candidate for Congress is shown sitting at a desk. Standing on either side of him are his wife and family, and there is an American flag behind him.

● Check (✓) the ad below that uses transfer.

_____ 1. A man dressed as Uncle Sam is shown eating a particular brand of hot dog.

_____ 2. A magazine ad shows a film star with a milk mustache. The caption reads: "Drink Milk."

4 Plain Folks

Some people distrust political candidates who are rich or well-educated. They feel that these candidates, if elected, will not be able to understand the problems of the average working person. Therefore, candidates often use the **plain folks** technique, presenting themselves as ordinary, average citizens. They try to show they are just "plain folks" by referring in their speeches to hard times in their lives or by posing for photographs while wearing a hard hat or mingling with everyday people.

Similarly, the presidents of some companies appear in their own ads, trying to show that their giant corporations are just family businesses run by ordinary folks. Also, a company will sometimes show a product being used by ordinary people to suggest that the product appeals to regular folks.

Here are two examples of real ads that have used the appeal of plain folks:

> The chairman of a poultry company is shown leaning on a rail fence in front of a farmhouse. He says, "I'm proud to uphold the values that go back to our company's start on my great-grandfather's farm in 1900."

A presidential candidate is photographed barbecuing ribs and chicken for reporters at his rustic home in the country. Afterward, his wife posts their family recipes on the campaign website.

- Check (✓) the ad below that uses plain-folks approach.

_____ 1. A beautiful woman in an elegant white dress and long white gloves is shown sipping a glass of a certain brand of chardonnay wine.

_____ 2. An average-looking middle-aged couple enjoys an outdoor meal cooked on their new barbecue grill.

5 Name Calling

Name calling is the use of emotionally loaded language or negative comments to turn people against a rival product, candidate, or movement. An example of name calling would be a political candidate's labeling an opponent "soft," "radical," or "wimpy."

Here are two examples of name calling taken from real life:

The opponents of a political candidate say he is a "spineless jellyfish."

A cell phone service advertises: "Unlike some services, we won't rip you off with hidden charges or drop your calls."

- Check (✓) the ad below that uses name calling.

_____ 1. A famous singer tells a television interviewer that a particular candidate for president is "born to run."

_____ 2. A newspaper editorial calls a candidate for town council "a hypocrite and a greedy, ambulance-chasing lawyer."

6 Glittering Generalities

A **glittering generality** is an important-sounding but unspecific claim about some product, candidate, or cause. It cannot be proved true or false because no evidence is offered to support the claim. Such claims use general words such as "great," "magical," or "ultimate." "Simply the best," an ad might say about a certain television set. But no specific evidence of any kind is offered to support such a generality. "The right candidate for our city," a campaign slogan might claim. But what does "right" really mean? It and similar phrases sound good but say nothing definite.

Here are two examples from real ads that use glittering generalities:

A financial advisor says: "True wealth is about more than money. It's about achieving life."

A magazine ad for a line of women's clothing advertises: "Let yourself shine."

- Check (✓) the ad below that uses a glittering generality.

_____ 1. An ad for a body wash invites the reader to "Shower your skin in luxury."

_____ 2. A candidate for the U.S. congress is called "Dr. Millionaire Know-it-all" by his opponent.

PRACTICE 2

In each pair of sentences below, the first sentence does not illustrate a propaganda technique, but the second one does. On the line, write the letter of the propaganda technique used in the second sentence.

A. Bandwagon	**B.** Testimonial	**C.** Transfer
D. Plain folks	**E.** Name calling	**F.** Glittering generalities

_____ 1.
- People's National Bank offers bonus CD/IRA rates, a free standard safe deposit box, and a free investment review.
- Unlike First American Bank, People's National Bank offers bonus CD/IRA rates, a free standard safe deposit box, and a free investment review. So if you want lip service, go to First American. If you want real benefits, choose People's National.

_____ 2.
- The Truflex Revolution Home Gym allows a person to exercise all of the muscle groups.
- "I get a complete full-body workout with the new Truflex Revolution Home Gym," says pro quarterback Brett Casey.

_____ 3.
- Belle Meade is a residential community in Arkansas that attracts retirees.
- Come see for yourself why Belle Meade, in the heart of Arkansas's beautiful Ozark mountains, has become a favorite destination for retirees from everywhere.

_____ 4.
- Westmore runs a chain of comfortable upscale hotels and resorts.
- An ad for a chain of upscale hotels and resorts proclaims, "Westmore. This is how it should feel."

_____ 5.
- Claire Magee gives her children cold medicine when they are ill.
- Working mom Claire Magee says, "By day I'm the president of a multi-million-dollar advertising agency, but in the evening I'm simply a mom who knows she can depend on a cold medicine that's been proven safe and effective for children."

_____ 6. • Milk can be part of a nutritional diet.

• In an ad for milk, actress Glenn Close tells us, "To perform my best, I need to give my body the attention it deserves. That's why I eat right, exercise, and drink milk."

_____ 7. • Nature's Favor Dog Food uses only natural ingredients.

• You'll be surprised to know that many leading dog food brands use glutens, animal by-products, and artificial preservatives—things you wouldn't feed to your dog. But Nature's Favor uses only the finest natural ingredients—the kind you feed your own family.

_____ 8. • Tilex contains ingredients that help control mold, mildew and soap scum.

• A heavily armed SWAT team holds bottles of Tilex as they prepare to enter a bathroom. The caption reads, "Bust the scum. Only Tilex has a full arsenal to combat mold, mildew and soap scum."

_____ 9. • The candidate for mayor supports improving residential neighborhoods.

• The candidate for mayor is shown helping other residents clear trash from an empty lot in his neighborhood.

_____10. • Campbell's Select soups are nutritional.

• An ad for Campbell's Select soups tells us that the product "Satisfies. Restores. Lifts you up."

Recognizing Errors in Reasoning

So far in this chapter, you have gotten practice in separating fact from opinion and in spotting propaganda. In this section you will learn about some common errors in reasoning—also known as **fallacies**—that take the place of the real support needed in an argument. As shown in the illustration, a valid point is based on a rock-like foundation of solid support; a fallacious point is based on a house of cards that offers no real support at all. Regrettably, these fallacies appear all too often in political arguments, often as the result of deliberate manipulation, other times as the result of careless thinking.

You've already learned about two common fallacies in Chapter 9, "Argument." One of those fallacies is sometimes called **changing the subject**. Attention is diverted from the issue at hand by presenting irrelevant support—evidence that actually has nothing to do with the argument. The second fallacy covered in Chapter 9 is sometimes called **hasty generalization**—in which a point is based on inadequate support. To be valid, a point must be based on an adequate amount of evidence. To draw a conclusion on the basis of insufficient evidence is to make a hasty generalization.

Below are six other common fallacies that will be explained in this section.

Three Fallacies That Ignore the Issue

- Circular Reasoning
- Personal Attack
- Straw Man

Three Fallacies That Oversimplify the Issue

- False Cause
- False Comparison
- Either-Or

In all of these fallacies, a point is argued, but no true support is offered for that point.

Fallacies That Ignore the Issue

Circular Reasoning

Part of a point cannot reasonably be used as evidence to support it. The fallacy of including such illogical evidence is called **circular reasoning**; it is also known as **begging the question**.

Here is a simple and obvious example of such reasoning:

Ms. Jenkins is a great manager because she is so wonderful at managing.

The supporting reason ("she is so wonderful at managing") is really the same as the conclusion ("Ms. Jenkins is a great manager"). We still do not know *why* she is a great manager. No real reasons have been given—the statement has merely been repeated.

Can you spot the circular reasoning in the following arguments?

1. Exercise is healthful, for it improves your well-being.
2. Since people under 18 are too young to drive, the driving age shouldn't be lowered below age 18.
3. Censorship is an evil practice because it is so wrong.

Let's look more closely at these arguments:

1. The word *healthful*, which is used in the conclusion, conveys the same idea as *well-being*. We still don't know why exercise is good for us.
2. The idea that people under 18 are too young to drive is both the conclusion and the reason of the argument. No real reason is given for why people under 18 are too young to drive.
3. The claim that censorship "is so wrong" simply restates the idea that it is an evil practice. No explanation is given for why censorship is evil or wrong.

In all these cases, the reasons merely repeat an important part of the conclusion. The careful reader wants to say, "Tell me something new. You are reasoning in circles. Give me supporting evidence, not a repetition."

- Check (✓) the item that contains an example of the circular reasoning fallacy.

_____ 1. Sports cars continue to be popular because so many people like them.

_____ 2. My wife wants to participate in the local amateur theater group, but I don't want all those actors flirting with her.

Personal Attack

This fallacy often occurs in political debate. Here's an example:

> Our mayor's opinions about local crime are worthless. Last week, his own son was arrested for disturbing the peace.

The arrest of his son would probably have embarrassed the mayor, but it has nothing to do with the value of his opinions on local crime. **Personal attack** ignores the issue under discussion and concentrates instead on the character of the opponent.

Sometimes personal attacks take the form of undercutting people's admirable actions. For instance, in the 2000 Republican presidential primary, opponents of Senator John McCain claimed that he had a black daughter whom he had fathered with a black prostitute. In fact, McCain and his wife had adopted the girl from an orphanage in Bangladesh.

- Check (✓) the item that contains an example of personal attack.

_____ 1. Mr. Casey was fined for drinking while driving and should not be allowed to teach math.

_____ 2. Barry cannot make up his mind easily because he is indecisive.

Straw Man

An opponent made of straw can be defeated very easily. Sometimes, if one's real opponent is putting up too good a fight, it can be tempting to build a scarecrow and battle it instead. For example, look at the following excerpt from a political debate between two candidates:

> The candidate for mayor says she'll cut taxes, but do you really want fewer police officers protecting your city?

The candidate does not support having "fewer police officers." Her plan calls for reducing taxes by privatizing the city's trash collection, not by reducing the police force. The **straw man** fallacy suggests that the opponent favors an obviously unpopular cause—when the opponent really doesn't support anything of the kind. Then that made-up position is opposed.

- Check (✓) the item that contains an example of straw man.

  _____ 1. The school board is considering building a swimming pool, but I don't like the idea of kids hanging out there all day and neglecting their studies.

  _____ 2. Pearl is a poor choice for the position of salesperson—she's a lesbian.

Fallacies That Oversimplify the Issue

False Cause

You have probably heard someone say as a joke, "I know it's going to rain today because I just washed the car." The idea that someone can make it rain by washing a car is funny because the two events obviously have nothing to do with each other. However, with more complicated issues, it is easy to make the mistake known as the fallacy of **false cause**. The mistake is to assume that because event B *follows* event A, event B *was caused by* event A.

Cause-and-effect situations can be difficult to analyze, and people are often tempted to oversimplify them by focusing on one "cause" and ignoring other possible causes. To identify an argument using a false cause, look for alternative causes.

Consider this argument:

> The baseball team was doing well before Paul Hamilton became manager. Clearly, he is the cause of the decline.

(*Event A:* Paul Hamilton became manager.
Event B: The baseball team is losing games.)

However, Paul Hamilton has been manager for only a year. What other possible causes could have been responsible for the team's losses? Perhaps the salary policies of the team's owner have deprived the team of some needed new talent. Perhaps several key players are now past their prime. In any case, it's easy but dangerous to assume that just because A *came before* B, A *caused* B.

● Check (✓) the item that contains an example of false cause.

_____ 1. The waiter went off duty early, and then the vase was discovered missing, so he must have stolen it.

_____ 2. In Vermont we leave our doors unlocked all year round, so I don't think it's necessary for you New Yorkers to have three locks on your front doors.

False Comparison

When the poet Robert Burns wrote, "My love is like a red, red rose," he meant that both the woman he loved and a rose are beautiful. In other ways—such as having green leaves and thorns, for example—his love did not resemble a rose at all.

Comparisons are often a good way to clarify a point. But because two things are not alike in all respects, comparisons (sometimes called analogies) often make poor evidence for arguments. In the error in reasoning known as **false comparison**, the assumption is that two things are more alike than they really are. For example, read the following argument:

> When your grandmother was your age, she was already married and had four children. So why aren't you married?

To judge whether or not this is a false comparison, consider how the two situations are alike and how they differ. They are similar in that both involve persons of the same age. But the situations are different in two respects: (1) society, when the grandmother was young, encouraged early marriage; (2) the grandmother was not working outside the home or attending college. The differences in this case are more important than the similarities, making it a false comparison.

● Check (✓) the item that contains an example of the false comparison.

_____ 1. A week after a new building supervisor took over, the elevator stopped working. What a lousy super he is!

_____ 2. All of my friends like my tattoo and pierced tongue, so I'm sure my new boss will too.

Either-Or

It is often wrong to assume that there are only two sides to a question. Offering only two choices when more actually exist is an **either-or** fallacy. For example, the statement "You are either with us or against us" assumes that there is no middle ground. Or consider the following:

> People who support gun control want to take away our rights.

This either-or argument ignores the fact that a person can support gun control *and* believe that hunters and others have the right to own guns. A person may want to keep guns out of the hands of children and criminals. That does not mean the person wants to take away the rights of those who own guns for legitimate reasons.

- Check (✓) the item that contains an example of the either-or fallacy.

_____ 1. Why can't we have a big dog in this apartment? You had a Great Dane when you were growing up on the farm.

_____ 2. Eat your string beans, or you won't grow up strong and healthy.

PRACTICE 3

A. In the space provided, write the letter of the fallacy contained in each argument. Choose from the three fallacies shown in the box below.

> A **Circular reasoning** *(a statement repeats itself rather than providing a real supporting reason to back up an argument)*
>
> B **Personal attack** *(ignores the issue under discussion and concentrates instead on the character of the opponent)*
>
> C **Straw man** *(an argument is made by claiming an opponent holds an extreme position and then opposing that extreme position)*

_____ 1. My sister thinks I should hold onto my job until something better comes along, but what does she know? She's only a department-store clerk.

_____ 2. Tony is a pessimist because he always thinks something bad is about to happen.

_____ 3. My neighbor Brian is against the use of torture as an interrogation tactic. He must feel more sympathy for terrorists than he does for their victims.

_____ 4. Vicky is a daredevil because she enjoys doing dangerous things.

_____ 5. I see that our mayor is now performing same-sex commitment ceremonies. He obviously doesn't care about the sanctity of marriage.

B. In the space provided, write the letter of the fallacy contained in each argument. Choose from the three fallacies shown in the box below.

> A **False cause** *(the argument assumes that the order of events alone shows cause and effect)*
>
> B **False comparison** *(the argument assumes that two things being compared are more alike than they really are)*
>
> C **Either-or** *(the argument assumes that there are only two sides to a question)*

_____ 6. My daughter-in-law wants to put my grandson in day care and go back to work. I didn't go back to work until my son was in high school, so I don't know why she has to.

_____ 7. Did you call our union rep a liar to his face, or did you let him off the hook again?

_____ 8. Shortly after Kevin Fraley took over as mayor, a restaurant and a florist shop went out of business on Main Street. Clearly he doesn't know much about running our town.

_____ 9. In my day, we played with blocks and took naps in kindergarten, so I don't see why they're making kindergartners today learn to read and write.

_____10. There are four fast-food restaurants within a mile of my apartment. That's why I've gained so much weight.

CHAPTER REVIEW

In this chapter, you learned that critical readers evaluate an author's support for a point and determine whether that support is solid or not. Critical reading includes the following three abilities:

- **Separating fact from opinion.** A **fact** is information that can be proved true through objective evidence. An **opinion** is a belief, judgment, or conclusion that cannot be proved objectively true. Much of what we read is a mixture of fact and opinion, and our job as readers is to arrive at the best possible informed opinion. Textbooks and other effective writing provide informed opinion—opinion based upon factual information.
- **Detecting propaganda.** Advertisers, salespeople, and politicians often try to promote their points by appealing to our emotions rather than our powers of reason. To do so, they practice six common propaganda techniques: bandwagon, testimonial, transfer, plain folks, name calling, and glittering generalities.
- **Recognizing errors in reasoning.** Politicians and others are at times guilty of errors in reasoning—**fallacies**—that take the place of the real support needed in an argument. Such fallacies include circular reasoning, personal attack, straw man, false cause, false comparison, and either-or.

On the Web: If you are using this book in class, you can visit our website for additional practice in critical reading. Go to **www.townsendpress.com** and click on "Learning Center."

REVIEW TEST 1

To review what you've learned in this chapter, answer the following questions.

Fact and Opinion

_____ 1. TRUE OR FALSE? A fact can be proved true through objective evidence.

_____ 2. Which of the following is likely to be totally factual?
A. An editorial
B. A movie review
C. A news report

3. Value words are often found in (*facts, opinions, textbooks*)

____.

_____ 4. Direct observation, expert reporting, and research are all sources of
A. facts. B. opinions.

Propaganda Techniques

_____ 5. TRUE OR FALSE? Propaganda is intended to inform readers of the actual worth of a product.

_____ 6. An important difference between a testimonial and a plain-folks appeal is that testimonials feature people who are
A. famous. B. ordinary. C. part of a large group.

_____ 7. Which of the following techniques associates a product with symbols and images that people respect?
A. Bandwagon
B. Transfer
C. Glittering generalities

Fallacies

_____ 8. The fallacy of personal attack
A. presents irrelevant support for a point.
B. ignores the true issue and focuses on the character of the opponent.
C. falsely suggests that the opponent favors an unpopular cause.

_____ 9. TRUE OR FALSE? The fallacy of circular reasoning merely restates the point instead of supporting it.

_____ 10. In the false cause fallacy, the argument ignores the possibility of an additional
A. cause for something happening.
B. side to a question.
C. comparison.

REVIEW TEST 2

A. In the following cartoon, which sentence expresses an opinion?

"This is the world's greatest cellphone. It works as a phone, a camera, and a music player. And if you set the ringer to 'vibrate' and stick it in your sock, it's also a foot massager."

_____ 1. A. Sentence 1 B. Sentence 2 C. Sentence 3

B. Read the following statements and decide whether each is fact or opinion. Put an **F** (for "fact") or an **O** (for "opinion") beside each statement. Put **F+O** beside the **two** statements that are a mixture of fact *and* opinion.

_____ 2. Australia has more types of poisonous snakes and spiders than any other country in the world.

_____ 3. Australia is the most dangerous place in the world to live.

_____ 4. A hamburger doesn't taste right without at least a little salt.

_____ 5. Many canned and frozen vegetables contain salt, so people should eat only fresh vegetables.

_____ 6. Salt, which is now common, was once so rare that Roman soldiers were paid with it.

_____ 7. If you want to learn how to cook well, you should get the new edition of the *Better Homes & Gardens Cookbook*.

_____ 8. The first written recipes were found on a clay tablet from Babylon, dating back to 1500 B.C.

_____ 9. With his homely face and high-pitched voice, Abraham Lincoln could never get elected president if he were alive today.

_____10. Barack Obama was sworn in as president with the same Bible used at the inauguration of Abraham Lincoln.

REVIEW TEST 3

A. Each of the passages below illustrates a particular propaganda technique. On the line next to the passage, write the letter of the technique being used.

_____ 1. A candidate for Congress tells voters, "While I was going to Fulton High, my opponent was attending a fancy prep school. While I was getting my degree from State U., my opponent was at Yale. Vote for someone who understands you. Vote for me, Joe Allen."

A. Plain folks
B. Bandwagon
C. Testimonial
D. Transfer

_____ 2. Against a backdrop of Fourth of July fireworks, an electronics store invites people to declare their independence from boredom by purchasing a new home entertainment system.

A. Glittering generalities
B. Testimonial
C. Name calling
D. Transfer

_____ 3. Actress Kirsti Spelling tells us she lost 36 pounds with Nutrisystem. Now back to size 2, she's the hottest new mom in Hollywood.

A. Transfer
B. Testimonial
C. Plain folks
D. Bandwagon

_____ 4. A TV ad shows a man sitting at a table playing poker with seven other men. Cut to a close-up of his hand—he has drawn an unbeatable hand, a royal flush! Cut back to the man sitting at the table, but now he's alone. He says, "Hey, where'd everybody go?" The announcer states: "They've gone to Betson's Furniture Warehouse."

A. Plain folks
B. Glittering generalities
C. Name calling
D. Bandwagon

_____ 5. A health insurance company claims: "Some hospitals are trying to use misinformation and scare tactics to protect their own profits. Those hospitals are being less than honest with you. They are putting their profits ahead of your good health care."

A. Glittering generalities
B. Transfer
C. Name calling
D. Testimonial

B. In the space provided, write the letter of the fallacy contained in each argument. Choose from the three fallacies shown in the box below.

> A **Circular reasoning** *(a statement repeats itself rather than providing a real supporting reason to back up an argument)*
>
> B **Personal attack** *(ignores the issue under discussion and concentrates instead on the character of the opponent)*
>
> C **Straw man** *(an argument is made by claiming an opponent holds an extreme position and then opposing that extreme position)*

_____ 6. It's ridiculous that Lonnie Maxwell has become a highly paid motivational speaker. Do people forget that she once posed nude in a girly magazine?

_____ 7. The popularity of stock-car racing in America has skyrocketed in the past decade because its audience has increased tremendously.

_____ 8. My opponent is in favor of negotiating with foreign dictators. Do we really need a president without the backbone to stand up to our nation's enemies?

C. Now choose from the three fallacies shown in the box below.

A **False cause** *(the argument assumes that the order of events alone shows cause and effect)*

B **False comparison** *(the argument assumes that two things being compared are more alike than they really are)*

C **Either-or** *(the argument assumes that there are only two sides to a question)*

_____ 9. The crime rate in our state started going up about the same time that more liberal judges were appointed. If we had more conservative judges, the crime rate would go down.

_____10. Are they going to serve veggie burgers at the barbecue, or are they going to serve something that tastes good?

REVIEW TEST 4

How do you handle the conflicts in your life? Whatever your methods, you will probably recognize them in the following excerpt from the widely used textbook *Communicate!* Eighth Edition, by Rudolph F. Verderber.

To help you continue to strengthen your skills, the reading is followed by questions not only on what you've learned in this chapter but also on what you've learned in previous chapters.

Words to Watch

Below are some words in the reading that do not have strong context support. Each word is followed by the number of the paragraph in which it appears and its meaning there. These words are indicated in the article by a small circle (°).

disengagement (9): becoming free of a situation
contention (14): argument
entails (15): involves
coercion (15): force
obscured (16): hidden
degenerate (18): worsen
implement (20): carry out
impracticable (21): impossible to do or carry out

MANAGING CONFLICTS IN RELATIONSHIPS

Rudolph F. Verderber

1 Conflicts include clashes over facts and definitions ("Charley was the first one to talk." "No, it was Mark." or "Your mother is a battle-ax." "What do you mean, a 'battle-ax'?"); over values ("Bringing home pencils and pens from work is not stealing." "Of course it is." or "The idea that you have to be married to have sex is completely outdated." "No, it isn't."); and, perhaps the most difficult to deal with, over ego involvement ("Listen, I've been a football fan for thirty years; I ought to know what good defense is." "Well, you may be a fan, but that doesn't make you an expert.").

2 Although many people view conflict as bad (and, to be sure, conflict situations are likely to make us anxious and uneasy), it is inevitable in any significant relationship. Moreover, conflict is sometimes useful in that it forces us to make choices; to resolve honest differences; and to test the relative merits of our attitudes, behaviors, needs, and goals. Now let's consider methods of dealing with conflict.

METHODS OF DEALING WITH CONFLICT

3 Left to their own devices, people engage in many behaviors, both negative and positive, to cope with or manage their conflicts. The various methods of dealing with conflict can be grouped into five major patterns: withdrawal, surrender, aggression, persuasion, and problem-solving discussion. Let's consider each of these methods in turn.

Withdrawal. One of the most common, and certainly one of the easiest, ways to deal with conflict is to withdraw. When people *withdraw*, they physically or psychologically remove themselves from the situation. 4

Physical withdrawal is, of course, easiest to identify. Suppose Eduardo and Justina get into a conversation about Eduardo's smoking. Justina says, "Eduardo, I thought you told me that whether you stopped smoking completely or not, you weren't going to smoke around the house. Now here you are lighting up!" Eduardo may withdraw physically by saying "I don't want to talk about it" and going to the basement to finish a project he was working on. 5

Psychological withdrawal may be less noticeable but is every bit as common. Using the same example, when Justina begins to talk about Eduardo's smoking in the house, Eduardo may sit quietly in his chair looking at Justina, but all the time she speaks, he is thinking about the poker game he will be going to the next evening. 6

Besides being quite common, both kinds of withdrawal are basically 7 negative. Why? Because they neither eliminate nor attempt to manage the conflict. As researchers Roloff and Cloven note, "Relational partners who avoid conflicts have more difficulty resolving disputes." In the case of the physical withdrawal, Justina may follow Eduardo to the basement, where the conflict will be resumed; if not, the conflict will undoubtedly resurface later—and will probably be intensified—when Justina and Eduardo try to resolve another, unrelated issue. In the case of the psychological withdrawal, Justina may force Eduardo to address the smoking issue, or she may go along with Eduardo's ignoring it but harbor a resentment that may negatively affect their relationship.

8 Another reason why withdrawal is negative is that it results in what Cloven and Roloff call "mulling behavior." By *mulling* they mean thinking about or stewing over an actual or perceived problem until the participants perceive the conflict as more severe and begin engaging in blaming behavior. Thus, in many cases, not confronting the problem when it occurs only makes it more difficult to deal with in the long run.

9 Nevertheless, conflicts do occasionally go away if left alone. There appear to be two sets of circumstances in which withdrawal may work. First, when the withdrawal represents temporary disengagement° for the purpose of letting the heat of the conflict subside, it can be an effective technique for managing conflict.

Consider this example: Bill and Margaret begin to argue over inviting Bill's mother for Thanksgiving dinner. During the conversation, Margaret begins to get angry about what her mother-in-law said to her recently about the way she and Bill are raising their daughter. Margaret says, "Hold it a minute; let me make a pot of coffee. We can both relax a bit, and then we'll talk about this some more." A few minutes later, having calmed down, she returns, ready to approach the conflict more objectively. Margaret's action is not true withdrawal; it's not meant as a means of avoiding confrontation. Rather, it provides a cooling-off period that will probably benefit them both.

10 The second set of circumstances in which withdrawal may work is when a conflict occurs between people who communicate infrequently. Consider Josh and Mario, who work in the same office. At two office gatherings, they have gotten into arguments about whether the company really cares

about its employees. At the next office gathering, Mario avoids sitting near Josh. Again, this form of withdrawal serves as a means of avoiding conflict rather than contributing to it. In this case, Mario judges that it simply isn't that important to resolve the disagreement. It is fair to say that not every conflict needs to be resolved. Withdrawal is a negative pattern only when it is a person's major way of managing conflict.

11 **Surrender.** A second method of managing conflict is to surrender. As you might suspect, *surrender* means giving in immediately to avoid conflict. Although altering a personal position in order to accommodate another can be positive when it's done in the spirit of cooperation, using surrender as a primary coping strategy is unhealthy.

12 Some people are so upset by the prospect of conflict that they will do anything to avoid it. For instance, Juan and Mariana are discussing their vacation plans. Juan would like just the two of them to go, but Mariana has talked with two of their friends who will be vacationing the same week about going together. After Juan mentions that he'd like the two of them to go alone, Mariana says, "But I think it would be fun to go with another couple, don't you?" Juan replies, "OK, whatever you want." Even though Juan really wants the two of them to go alone, rather than describe his feelings or give reasons for his position, he gives in to avoid conflict.

13 Habitual surrender is a negative way of dealing with conflict for at least two reasons. First, decisions should be made on their merits, not to avoid conflict. If one person gives in, there is no testing of the decision—no one knows what would really be best. Second, surrender can be infuriating to the other person. When Mariana tells Juan what she thinks, she probably wants Juan to see her way as the best. But if Juan simply surrenders, Mariana might believe that Juan still dislikes her plan but is playing the martyr. And his unwillingness to present his reasons could lead to even more conflict.

The contention° that surrender is a negative way of dealing with conflict should be qualified to the extent that it reflects a Western cultural perspective. In some cultures, surrendering is a perfectly legitimate way of dealing with conflict. In Japanese culture, for instance, it is thought to be more humble and face-saving to surrender than to risk losing respect through conflict. 14

Aggression. A third method of dealing with conflict is through aggression. *Aggression* entails° the use of physical or psychological coercion° to get one's way. Through aggression, people attempt to force others to accept their ideas or wishes, thereby emerging as "victors" in conflicts. 15

Aggression seldom improves a relationship, however. Rather, aggression is an emotional reaction to conflict. Thought is short-circuited, and the person lashes out physically or verbally. People who use aggression are not concerned with the merits of an 16 issue but only with who is bigger, who can talk louder, who can act nastier, or who can force the other to give in. With either physical or verbal aggression, conflict is escalated or obscured° but not managed.

17 **Persuasion.** A fourth method of managing conflict is by persuasion. *Persuasion* is the attempt to change either the attitude or the behavior of another person in order to seek accommodation. At times during the discussion of an issue, one party may try to persuade the other that a particular action is the right one. Suppose that at one point in their discussion about buying a car, Sheila says, "Don't we need a lot of room?" Kevin might reply, "Enough to get us into the car together, but I don't see why we need more than that." Sheila and Kevin are now approaching a conflict situation. At this point, Sheila might say, "Kevin, we are constantly complaining about the lack of room in our present car. Remember last month when you were upset because we couldn't even get our two suitcases into the trunk and we had to put one of them in the back seat? And how many times have we been embarrassed when we couldn't drive our car with friends because the back seat is too small for even two normal-sized people?" Statements like these represent an attempt at resolving the conflict through persuasion.

18 When persuasion is open and reasonable, it can be a positive means of resolving conflict. However, persuasion can also degenerate° into manipulation, as when a person says, "You know, if you back me on this, I could see to it that you get a few more of the good accounts, and if you don't, well . . ." Although persuasive efforts may fuel a conflict, if that persuasion has a solid logical base, it is at least possible that the persuasion will resolve the conflict.

Discussion. A fifth method of dealing with conflict is *problem-solving discussion*—the verbal weighing and considering of the pros and cons of the issues in conflict. Discussion is the most desirable means of dealing with conflict in a relationship because it provides for open consideration of issues and because it preserves equality. Resolving conflict through discussion is often difficult to accomplish, however, because it requires all parties involved to cooperate: the participants must be objective in their presentation of issues, honest in stating their feelings and beliefs, and open to the solution that proves to be most satisfactory and in the best interests of those involved. 19

Problem-solving discussion includes defining and analyzing the problem, suggesting possible solutions, selecting the solution that best fits the analysis, and working to implement° the decision. In everyday situations, all five steps are not always considered completely, nor are they necessarily considered in the order given. But when two people perceive a conflict emerging, they need to be willing to step back from the conflict and proceed systematically toward a solution. 20

21 Does this process sound too idealized? Or impracticable°? Discussion is difficult, but when two people commit themselves to trying, chances are that they will discover that through discussion they arrive at solutions that meet both their needs and do so in a way that maintains their relationship.

Reading Comprehension Questions

Vocabulary in Context

_____ 1. In the sentence below, the word *harbor* (här′bər) means
- A. hold onto.
- B. avoid.
- C. give up.
- D. pretend.

"Justina may force Eduardo to address the smoking issue, or she may go along with Eduardo's ignoring it but harbor a resentment that may negatively affect their relationship." (Paragraph 7)

Central Point and Main Ideas

_____ 2. Which sentence best expresses the central point of the selection?
- A. Many people have a negative view of conflict.
- B. There are five main ways, both positive and negative, with which people deal with conflict.
- C. Conflicts can force people to make choices and to test their attitudes, actions, needs, and aims.
- D. It is better not to intensify or hide conflict.

_____ 3. The main idea of paragraphs 9 and 10 can be found in the
- A. second sentence of paragraph 9.
- B. third sentence of paragraph 9.
- C. first sentence of paragraph 10.
- D. second sentence of paragraph 10.

Supporting Details

_____ 4. According to the author,
A. withdrawal never works.
B. whether or not surrender is generally a good way to manage conflict is related to one's cultural perspective.
C. aggression is an attempt to change either the attitude or the behavior of another person in order to seek accommodation.
D. discussion is the easiest and most desirable way of dealing with conflict in a relationship.

Transitions

_____ 5. The relationship between the two sentences below is one of
A. comparison.
B. contrast.
C. cause and effect.
D. illustration.

"When persuasion is open and reasonable, it can be a positive means of resolving conflict. However, persuasion can also degenerate into manipulation . . . ." (Paragraph 18)

Patterns of Organization

_____ 6. The main pattern of organization of paragraphs 7 and 8 is
A. time order.
B. definition and example.
C. cause and effect.
D. contrast.

Inferences

_____ 7. We can infer that the author of this selection
A. believes that conflict should be avoided at all costs.
B. feels that conflict is the best way to strengthen a relationship.
C. feels that conflict can be positive if handled appropriately.
D. believes that withdrawal is never an appropriate method of dealing with conflict.

Argument

_____ 8. Three of the items below are supporting details for an argument. Write the letter of the statement that represents the point of these supporting details.

A. People who use aggression are not concerned with the merits of an issue but only with who can force the other person to give in.
B. Aggression usually harms a relationship.
C. In aggression, thought is short-circuited, and the person lashes out physically or verbally.
D. With either physical or verbal aggression, conflict is escalated or obscured but not managed.

Critical Reading

_____ 9. The entire selection is made up of

A. only facts.
B. only opinions.
C. both facts and opinions.

_____ 10. The statement "We need a bigger car because our car is too small" is an example of the logical fallacy of

A. circular reasoning.
B. straw man.
C. personal attack.
D. either-or.

Discussion Questions

1. Which of Verderber's five methods of dealing with conflict do you or people you know typically use? Give examples.
2. Why do you think Verderber regards discussion as "the most desirable means of dealing with conflict in a relationship"? And why might he feel that discussion "is often difficult to accomplish"?
3. Verderber writes that conflict is sometimes useful because it forces us to make choices and test attitudes. When in your life has conflict been a good thing? What did you learn from it?
4. Suggest ways that someone you know could be encouraged to deal effectively with his or her specific conflict.

Note: Writing assignments for this selection appear on page 702.

Check Your Performance — CRITICAL READING

Activity		*Number Right*		*Points*		*Score*
Review Test 1	(10 items)	______	×	1	=	______
Review Test 2	(10 items)	______	×	3	=	______
Review Test 3	(10 items)	______	×	3	=	______
Review Test 4	(10 items)	______	×	3	=	______
				TOTAL SCORE	=	______%

Enter your total score into the **Reading Performance Chart: Review Tests** on the inside back cover.

Name ______________________________ Date __________

Section ____________ SCORE: (Number correct) ________ x 5 = ______ %

CRITICAL READING: Mastery Test 1 (Fact and Opinion)

A. In the following cartoon, which sentence expresses an opinion?

_____ 1. A. Sentence 1 B. Sentence 2

B. Identify facts with an **F, o**pinions with an **O**, and the **one** combination of fact *and* opinion with an **F+O**.

_____ 2. The book most frequently stolen from public libraries is *Guinness World Records.*

_____ 3. One of the most fascinating books in the world to read is *Guinness World Records.*

_____ 4. Without the work of Susan B. Anthony, women would never have gotten the right to vote.

_____ 5. Women were granted the right to vote with the passage of the Nineteenth Amendment in 1920.

_____ 6. It costs the U.S. government nearly two cents to mint each penny.

_____ 7. The U.S. government should stop minting pennies and demand that stores round their prices up to the nearest nickel.

_____ 8. In the United States today, one out of every one hundred people is behind bars.

(Continues on next page)

_____ 9. Clearly, the criminal justice system in the United States is broken and must be repaired.

_____ 10. Charles Schulz, who created the adorable and touching comic strip *Peanuts*, took art lessons by mail because he was too shy to attend regular art classes.

C. Identify facts with an **F**, opinions with an **O**, and the **two** statements of fact *and* opinion with an **F+O**.

_____ 11. People can overcome any handicap if they try hard enough.

_____ 12. Despite being totally blind from the age of seven, Ray Charles went on to become America's most beloved singer.

_____ 13. According to a recent study, over 40 percent of children aged 10–14 are exposed to movies rated R for violence.

_____ 14. Hollywood needs to stop making so many violent movies and concentrate on providing good, wholesome family entertainment.

_____ 15. One of the most spectacular hoaxes ever committed was the radio drama *The War of the Worlds.*

_____ 16. On October 30, 1938, Orson Welles and his Mercury Theater of the Air presented *The War of the Worlds*, a radio drama about Martians invading Earth.

_____ 17. Mozart began to compose music and gave his first public performance at the age of five.

_____ 18. Mozart, who died in 1791 at the age of 35, was certainly the greatest composer who ever lived.

_____ 19. The plain fact is that living together before marriage is a bad idea.

_____ 20. Research shows that the divorce rate for people who move in together before marriage is 46 percent higher than for married couples who don't live together first.

Name ____________________ Date ________

Section ________ SCORE: (Number correct) ______ x 5 = ______ %

CRITICAL READING: Mastery Test 2 (Fact and Opinion)

A. Identify facts with an **F**, opinions with an **O**, and the **two** statements of fact *and* opinion with an **F+O**.

_____ 1. In the 1950s, middle-class American families often had one breadwinner—Dad—and a stay-at-home mom; and the family generally shared a home-cooked meal at the dinner table.

_____ 2. In the 2000s, working mothers, fast foods, divorce, stepparents, and children home alone are daily realities in millions of American households.

_____ 3. In the early 1900s, child-care experts warned mothers that picking up a baby between scheduled feedings would spoil the child.

_____ 4. So-called child-care experts don't know any more about child-rearing than the average person.

_____ 5. The koala, a native of Australia, gets all its nourishment from one tree, the eucalyptus; it does not need to add water to its diet.

_____ 6. It's unfortunate and even shameful that the koala, hunted for both fur and food, is now an endangered species.

_____ 7. It's a fact that the Super Bowl is the most exciting yearly athletic event of any sport.

_____ 8. Margaret Sanger is the most noteworthy figure in the history of family planning.

_____ 9. As a maternity nurse, Sanger sought repeatedly to learn about contraception, but sadly outdated sexual attitudes in American culture made such information almost impossible to get.

_____ 10. Sanger persisted and succeeded in opening the world's first birth control clinic in Brooklyn in 1916.

(Continues on next page)

B. The passage below contains five sentences. Identify each sentence with an **F** (for fact), an **O** (for opinion), or **F+O** (for a combination of fact *and* opinion). Note that **one** sentence combines fact and opinion.

[11]It was by accident that someone invented the air conditioner, one of the world's most important machines. [12]In the summer of 1902, a Brooklyn, New York, printer was having trouble with color printing: the size of paper on the presses was changed enough by the hot, humid air to cause distortions in printing. [13]That problem must have been the printer's worst nightmare. [14]A young engineer named Willis Haviland Carrier, trying to solve the problem, made the discovery that he could reduce the amount of humidity in the air with a machine that blew cool air. [15]Carrier's concept was later used to create the home air conditioner.

_____ 11.

_____ 12.

_____ 13.

_____ 14.

_____ 15.

C. The passage below contains five sentences. Identify each sentence with an **F** (for fact), an **O** (for opinion), or **F+O** (for a combination of fact *and* opinion). Note that **one** sentence combines fact and opinion.

[16]One of the ocean's most fascinating creatures, the octopus, has been taught various skills by scientists testing its intelligence. [17]Octopuses have been taught, for instance, to distinguish squares from crosses and to slip and slide their way through simple mazes. [18]One project provided the most dramatic and interesting evidence yet for the invertebrate's intelligence. [19]In 1992, researchers taught a group of octopuses to grab a red ball instead of a white one; then another group learned the same skill simply by watching the first group. [20]The octopus may well prove to be as intelligent a creature of the sea as the dolphin.

_____ 16.

_____ 17.

_____ 18.

_____ 19.

_____ 20.

Name ______________________ Date __________

Section __________ SCORE: (Number correct) ______ x 10 = ______ %

CRITICAL READING: Mastery Test 3 (Propaganda Techniques)

A. Each pair of items below illustrates a particular propaganda technique. On the line next to each pair, write the letter of the main technique being used.

_____ 1.

- An ad for a nationwide clothing store chain invites you to "find your place in the rhythm of life."
- An ad for granola bars and cereals encourages us to "Come home to goodness . . . Come home to Sunny Valley."

A. Testimonial   C. Bandwagon
B. Transfer   D. Glittering generalities

_____ 2.

- An adorable-looking little girl munches a bologna sandwich in an ad for a brand of lunch meat.
- A handsome, muscular young man wakes up with a smile on his face in an ad for a brand of sleep medication.

A. Testimonial   C. Bandwagon
B. Transfer   D. Glittering generalities

_____ 3.

- An ad for a facial-firming procedure tells us that the procedure is "sweeping America." The ad shows "before" and "after" photos of three women who have had the procedure.
- Eight out of ten women agree: New Silky Cream Oil body lotion feels more moisturizing than their current lotion.

A. Plain folks   C. Bandwagon
B. Transfer   D. Testimonial

_____ 4.

- A multi-millionaire candidate for governor is shown eating a cheesesteak during a street festival in the state's largest city.
- An ad for a foot-care product features an actual elderly couple explaining how the product has helped them stay active.

A. Plain folks   C. Bandwagon
B. Transfer   D. Testimonial

(Continues on next page)

_____ 5. • Actress Melissa Monroe encourages women to try Lovely Tress hair extensions. "With Lovely Tress, they'll never know it's not your own," she tells us.

• Golfer Roger Crandall tells us that TrimLawn riding mowers "make mowing your lawn so quick and easy, you'll have more time for the fun things in life."

A. Plain folks
C. Name calling
B. Transfer
D. Testimonial

_____ 6. • An ad for Sheer Delight pantyhose says, "Unlike other brands of pantyhose that droop by noon, Sheer Delight stays firm and shapely throughout your work day."

• "Tired of the same old greasy fast food you get at Burger Fest? Come to Homestyle Buffet and have a banquet fit for a king!"

A. Plain folks
C. Name calling
B. Transfer
D. Testimonial

B. Below are descriptions of four actual ads. On each line, write the letter of the main propaganda technique that applies to the ad.

A. Bandwagon	**B. Testimonial**	**C. Transfer**
D. Plain folks	**E. Name calling**	**F. Glittering generalities**

_____ 7. In a Viagra commercial, an attractive woman puts her arms around a man on a motorcycle.

_____ 8. Become an Avon representative. And you'll join over five million women who are making their dreams a reality with the world's largest direct seller of beauty products. With Avon, the company for women, you're in business *for* yourself, not by yourself.

_____ 9. An ad for Dillard's Department Stores proclaims Dillard's "The Style of Your Life."

_____ 10. In an ad for Kraft salad dressing, Olympic skating star Michelle Kwan says, "Kraft your salad."

Name ______________________________ Date __________

Section ____________ SCORE: (Number correct) _______ x 10 = _______ %

CRITICAL READING: Mastery Test 4 (Propaganda Techniques)

A. Each pair of items below illustrates a particular propaganda technique. On the line next to each pair, write the letter of the main technique being used.

_____ 1. • The logo of a major oil company is displayed over the main stage of a city's "Welcome America" Fourth of July celebration.

• An ad for a built-in oven shows a beautiful model in an evening dress over the caption, "The Beauty of Power."

A. Plain folks C. Bandwagon
B. Transfer D. Testimonial

_____ 2. • A former world heavyweight boxing champion tells us why we should patronize a chain of automotive repair shops.

• "If you're between the ages of 50 and 85, you can't be turned down!" says game show host Kent McCoy about a brand of life insurance.

A. Plain folks C. Glittering generalities
B. Name calling D. Testimonial

_____ 3. • In a TV commercial, cable company executives are shown plotting how to make it seem as though they offer more channels than Direct Access TV. "You deserve better than cable: Direct Access TV," says the voiceover.

• A candidate for State Assembly suggests that his opponent is a "fat cat lawyer" who got rich filing bogus lawsuits on behalf of greedy clients.

A. Plain folks C. Glittering generalities
B. Name calling D. Testimonial

_____ 4. • You'll feel like a million in a Banks Brothers suit.

• A brand of hair color tells us that their product is "The Color That Changes Everything."

A. Plain folks C. Glittering generalities
B. Transfer D. Bandwagon

(Continues on next page)

_____ 5. • Two middle-aged women in stretch pants and loose-fitting blouses explain the benefits of a particular brand of sewing machine.

• During a power blackout, a balding, middle-aged man turns on his heavy-duty EverLight flashlight.

A. Plain folks C. Bandwagon
B. Transfer D. Testimonial

_____ 6. • An ad for a weight-loss program shows "before" and "after" photographs of twenty people who lost weight on the system.

• A university invites us to join the growing number of professionals who are earning advanced degrees via the university's evening, weekend, and online classes.

A. Plain folks C. Glittering generalities
B. Transfer D. Bandwagon

B. Below are descriptions of four actual ads. On each line, write the letter of the main propaganda technique that applies to the ad.

A. Bandwagon	**B. Testimonial**	**C. Transfer**
D. Plain folks	**E. Name calling**	**F. Glittering generalities**

_____ 7. A beer ad that runs in newspapers during the Memorial Day weekend reads, "A true American holiday deserves a true American beer—Budweiser."

_____ 8. An ad for Extra sugar-free gum tells us, "We've stopped at nothing to give you a breakthrough of the mintiest proportions."

_____ 9. An ad for Dell computers features thumbnail photos of 63 people. "Become a part of the community," it says.

_____ 10. Queen Latifah tells us that "I'm taking the first step to get healthier on the Jenny Craig program. It's a smart choice because it's a proven weight-loss program."

Name ______________________ Date __________
Section ___________ SCORE: (Number correct) _______ x 10 = _______ %

CRITICAL READING: Mastery Test 5 (Errors in Reasoning)

A. Each pair of items below illustrates a particular error in reasoning. On the line next to each pair, write the letter of the logical fallacy contained in both items. Choose from the three fallacies shown in the box below.

> A **Circular reasoning** *(a statement repeats itself rather than providing a real supporting reason to back up an argument)*
>
> B **Personal attack** *(ignores the issue under discussion and concentrates instead on the character of the opponent)*
>
> C **Straw man** *(an argument is made by claiming an opponent holds an extreme position and then opposing that extreme position)*

_____ 1.
- Senator Noonan voted against stricter regulations on imports. I suppose he doesn't care if our children get lead poisoning from toys made in China.
- The school showed the fourth-graders a video on families featuring some same-sex couples. They must be trying to encourage our students to adopt a homosexual lifestyle.

_____ 2.
- The Vermont countryside looks beautiful every spring because it's so scenic.
- Brian is a great salesman because he makes the most sales in the whole company.

_____ 3.
- It's doubtful that Senator Garvey knows anything about family values. I understand his own grandson has become a transsexual.
- I'd never vote for Denise Wyman for Congress. A few years ago, her brother-in-law was convicted of insurance fraud.

_____ 4.
- Pablo Picasso was one of the greatest painters of all time because he had great artistic ability.
- People should be sure to recycle all their plastics, cans, and newspapers because it's the right thing to do.

_____ 5.
- Jane Anderson is in favor of stricter gun control laws. I guess she and others like her won't stop until they make hunting a federal crime.
- Congressman Jeffries supports a ban on logging in Cold Creek Forest. Evidently he likes trees and little furry animals more than he likes people.

(Continues on next page)

B. In the space provided, write the letter of the fallacy contained in each pair of arguments. Choose from the three fallacies shown in the box below.

> **A False cause** *(the argument assumes that the order of events alone shows cause and effect)*
>
> **B False comparison** *(the argument assumes that two things being compared are more alike than they really are)*
>
> **C Either-or** *(the argument assumes that there are only two sides to a question)*

_____ 6. • Unless you become a vegetarian, you're not really serious about lowering your cholesterol.

• There are only two types of women: those who make good mothers and those who do not.

_____ 7. • I nearly bowled a perfect game last night when I wore my striped polo shirt. From now on, I'm wearing that shirt every time I bowl.

• My doctor prescribed an expensive cough medicine, but it didn't make my cough go away. Next time I get sick, I'm going to save my money and buy an over-the-counter medication.

_____ 8. • Grandma said, "Back when I was a girl, nice girls lived at home with their parents until they were married. So I don't see why you need to get your own apartment."

• I worked my way through college. There's no reason you can't do the same.

_____ 9. • My neighbors' son was recently diagnosed as a paranoid schizophrenic. They must have done a poor job of raising him.

• I came down with an awful headache during yesterday's history class. Listening to our professor's boring lecture probably brought it on.

_____10. • If I don't get my poetry published by the time I'm 30, I probably never will.

• Are you going to praise the boss's worthless idea, or are you going to tell him he's dead wrong this time?

Name ______________________________ Date __________

Section __________ SCORE: (Number correct) ______ x 10 = ______ %

CRITICAL READING: Mastery Test 6 (Errors in Reasoning)

A. Each pair of items below illustrates a particular error in reasoning. On the line next to each pair, write the letter of the logical fallacy contained in both items. Choose from the three fallacies shown in the box below.

> A **Circular reasoning** *(a statement repeats itself rather than providing a real supporting reason to back up an argument)*
>
> B **Personal attack** *(ignores the issue under discussion and concentrates instead on the character of the opponent)*
>
> C **Straw man** *(an argument is made by claiming an opponent holds an extreme position and then opposing that extreme position)*

_____ 1.
- My opponent believes the federal government should ensure that all citizens have health coverage. Unlike her, I refuse to accept the notion that Americans would benefit from socialized medicine.
- The fishery council wants to put strict limits on the amount of codfish that fishermen can catch. I suppose those people don't care if fishermen can't feed their families as a result.

_____ 2.
- Senator Hedgely's views on immigration are worthless. He once hired an illegal immigrant to landscape his property.
- It's true my opponent for the Senate received a Purple Heart while serving in Vietnam. But the "wound" he received was no more than a scratch.

_____ 3.
- Governor Brinkman favors building huge wind turbines off our coastline. What does he want to do, kill our summer tourism industry?
- My neighbor Dwayne voted against raising taxes to renovate the high school. I guess he doesn't care if our kids get a third-rate education.

_____ 4.
- My mom thinks it was a big mistake for us to invade Iraq. But what does she know? She never even finished high school.
- Toby Elliot would be a poor choice to become our next mayor. I hear he lives with another man.

_____ 5.
- It's dangerous to ride with Philip because he's an unsafe driver.
- Van Gogh was clearly the greatest artist of modern times, since his paintings are better than anyone else's.

(Continues on next page)

B. In the space provided, write the letter of the fallacy contained in each pair of arguments. Choose from the three fallacies shown in the box below.

> A **False cause** *(the argument assumes that the order of events alone shows cause and effect)*
>
> B **False comparison** *(the argument assumes that two things being compared are more alike than they really are)*
>
> C **Either-or** *(the argument assumes that there are only two sides to a question)*

_____ 6.
- When I was growing up, we went to our family doctor for all our serious illnesses, so I don't see why we have to go to all these fancy specialists today.
- Great Grandpa says, "I don't see why athletes today are paid millions of dollars a year. In my day, they played for the sheer love of the game."

_____ 7.
- Unless you support prayer in our nation's public schools, you can't call yourself a Christian.
- My son wants to get a job at a casino, but I don't want him to become part of that sleazy, gambling-addicted world.

_____ 8.
- When I was young, homosexuality was a taboo subject, so I don't see why gay rights supporters are always blabbing about it today.
- I don't understand why my sons and their wives are always going out to eat. When they were kids, my wife made them good, home-cooked meals every day.

_____ 9.
- Baseball star Andy Hewitt has hit safely in 20 straight games. He says he intends to wear the same socks and underwear until his hitting streak is broken.
- The day after my brother Carl borrowed my car, the fan belt broke. I'll never let him borrow my car again.

_____ 10.
- My daughter is dating a fellow student who wants to be an artist, but I'd prefer that she get involved with someone who will have a serious career.
- A young woman asks her parents, "Are you going to give me a big church wedding, or are you going to be stingy?"

Part Two

Ten Reading Selections

1 The Professor Is a Dropout

Beth Johnson

Preview

After being mistakenly labeled "retarded" and humiliated into dropping out of first grade, Lupe Quintanilla knew she wanted nothing more to do with formal education. Life as a wife and mother would satisfy her . . . and it did, until she saw her own children being pushed aside as "slow learners." Driven to help them succeed, Lupe took steps that dramatically changed her life.

Words to Watch

radical (16): extreme
plant (29): a person put somewhere to spy
renowned (36): famous

1 Guadalupe Quintanilla is an assistant professor at the University of Houston. She is president of her own communications company. She trains law enforcement officers all over the country. She was nominated to serve as an assistant attorney general of the United States. She's been a representative to the United Nations.

2 That's a pretty impressive string of accomplishments. It's all the more impressive when you consider this: "Lupe" Quintanilla is a first-grade dropout. Her school records state that she is retarded, that her IQ is so low she can't learn much of anything.

3 How did Lupe Quintanilla, "retarded" nonlearner, become Dr. Quintanilla, respected educator? Her remarkable journey began in the town of Nogales, Mexico, just below the Arizona border. That's where Lupe first lived with her grandparents. (Her parents had divorced.) Then an uncle who had just finished medical school made her grandparents a generous offer. If they wanted to live with him, he would support the family as he began his medical practice.

4 Lupe, her grandparents, and her uncle all moved hundreds of miles to a town in southern Mexico that didn't even have paved roads, let alone any schools. There, Lupe grew up helping her grandfather run his little pharmacy and her grandmother keep house. She remembers the time happily. "My grandparents were wonderful," she said. "Oh, my grandfather was stern, authoritarian, as Mexican culture demanded, but

Dr. Quintanilla writes at her desk in her Houston home.

they were also very kind to me." When the chores were done, her grandfather taught Lupe to read and write Spanish and do basic arithmetic.

5 When Lupe was 12, her grandfather became blind. The family left Mexico and went to Brownsville, Texas, with the hope that doctors there could restore his sight. Once they arrived in Brownsville, Lupe was enrolled in school. Although she understood no English, she was given an IQ test in that language. Not surprisingly, she didn't do very well.

6 Lupe even remembers her score. "I scored a sixty-four, which classified me as seriously retarded, not even teachable," she said. "I was put into first grade with a class of six-year-olds. My duties were to take the little kids to the bathroom and to cut out pictures." The classroom activities were a total mystery to Lupe—they were all conducted in English. And she was humiliated by the other children, who teased her for being "so much older and so much dumber" than they were.

7 After four months in first grade, an incident occurred that Lupe still does not fully understand. As she stood in the doorway of the classroom waiting to escort a little girl to the bathroom, a man approached her. He asked her, in Spanish, how to find the principal's office. Lupe was delighted. "Finally someone in this school had spoken to me with words I could understand, in the language of my soul, the language of my grandmother," she said. Eagerly, she answered his question in Spanish. Instantly her teacher swooped down on her, grabbing her arm and scolding her. She pulled Lupe along to the principal's office. There, the teacher and the principal both shouted at her, obviously very angry. Lupe was frightened and embarrassed, but also bewildered. She didn't understand a word they were saying.

"Why were they so angry? I don't 8
know," said Lupe. "Was it because I spoke Spanish at school? Or that I spoke to the man at all? I really don't know. All I know is how humiliated I was."

When she got home that day, 9
she cried miserably, begging her grandfather not to make her return to school. Finally he agreed.

From that time on, Lupe stayed at 10
home, serving as her blind grandfather's "eyes." She was a fluent reader in Spanish, and the older man loved to have her read newspapers, poetry, and novels aloud to him for hours.

Lupe's own love of reading flour- 11
ished during these years. Her vocabulary was enriched and her imagination

fired by the novels she read—novels which, she learned later, were classics of Spanish literature. She read *Don Quixote,* the famous story of the noble, impractical knight who fought against windmills. She read thrilling accounts of the Mexican Revolution. She read *La Prensa,* the local Spanish-language paper, and *Selecciones,* the Spanish-language version of *Reader's Digest.*

12 When she was just 16, Lupe married a young Mexican-American dental technician. Within five years, she had given birth to her three children, Victor, Mario, and Martha. Lupe's grandparents lived with the young family. Lupe was quite happy with her life. "I cooked, sewed, cleaned, and cared for everybody," she said. "I listened to my grandmother when she told me what made a good wife. In the morning I would actually put on my husband's shoes and tie the laces—anything to make his life easier. Living with my grandparents for so long, I was one generation behind in my ideas of what a woman could do and be."

13 Lupe's contentment ended when her children started school. When they brought home their report cards, she struggled to understand them. She could read enough English to know that what they said was not good. Her children had been put into a group called "Yellow Birds." It was a group for slow learners.

14 At night in bed, Lupe cried and blamed herself. It was obvious—not only was *she* retarded, but her children had taken after her. Now they, too, would never be able to learn like other children.

15 But in time, a thought began to break through Lupe's despair: Her children didn't seem like slow learners to *her.* At home, they learned everything she taught them, quickly and easily. She read to them constantly, from the books that she herself had loved as a child. *Aesop's Fables* and stories from *1,001 Arabian Nights* were family favorites. The children filled the house with the sounds of the songs, prayers, games, and rhymes they had learned from their parents and grandparents. They were smart children, eager to learn. They learned quickly—in Spanish.

16 A radical° idea began to form in Lupe's mind. Maybe the school was *wrong* about her children. And if the school system could be wrong about her children—maybe it had been wrong about her, too.

17 Lupe visited her children's school, a daring action for her. "Many Hispanic parents would not dream of going to the classroom," she said. "In Hispanic culture, the teacher is regarded as a third parent, as an ultimate authority. To question her would seem most disrespectful, as though you were saying that she didn't know her job." That was one reason Lupe's grandparents had not interfered when Lupe was classified as retarded. "Anglo teachers often misunderstand Hispanic parents, believing that they aren't concerned about their children's education because they don't come visit the schools," Lupe said. "It's not a lack of concern at all. It's a mark of respect for the teacher's authority."

18 At her children's school, Lupe spoke to three different teachers. Two of them

Dr. Quintanilla gets a hug from her daughter, Martha. Martha, an attorney, has served as chief of the Family Violence Division of the Dallas district attorney's office.

told her the same thing: "Your children are just slow. Sorry, but they can't learn." A third offered a glimmer of hope. He said, "They don't know how to function in English. It's possible that if you spoke English at home, they would be able to do better."

19 Lupe pounced on that idea. "Where can I learn English?" she asked. The teacher shrugged. At that time there were no local English-language programs for adults. Finally he suggested that Lupe visit the local high school. Maybe she would be permitted to sit in the back of a classroom and pick up some English that way.

20 Lupe made an appointment with a counselor at the high school. But when the two women met, the counselor shook her head. "Your test scores show that you are retarded," she told Lupe. "You'd just be taking space in the classroom away from someone who could learn."

Lupe's next stop was the hospital where she had served for years as a volunteer. Could she sit in on some of the nursing classes held there? No, she was told, not without a diploma. Still undeterred, she went on to Texas Southmost College in Brownsville. Could she sit in on a class? No; no high-school diploma. Finally she went to the telephone company, where she knew operators were being trained. Could she listen in on the classes? No, only high-school graduates were permitted. 21

That day, leaving the telephone company, Lupe felt she had hit bottom. She had been terrified in the first place to try to find an English class. Meeting with rejection after rejection nearly destroyed what little self-confidence she had. She walked home in the rain, crying. "I felt like a big barrier had fallen across my path," she said. "I couldn't go over it; I couldn't go under it; I couldn't go around it." 22

But the next day Lupe woke with fresh determination. "I was motivated by love of my kids," she said. "I was not going to quit." She got up; made breakfast for her kids, husband, and grandparents; saw her children and husband off for the day; and started out again. "I remember walking to the bus stop, past a dog that always scared me to death, and heading back to the college. The lady I spoke to said, 'I told you, we can't do anything for you without a high-school degree.' But as I left the building, I went up to 23 the first Spanish-speaking student I saw. His name was Gabito. I said, 'Who really makes the decisions around here?' He said, 'The registrar.'" Since she hadn't had any luck in the office building, Lupe decided to take a more direct approach. She asked Gabito to point out the registrar's car in the parking lot. For the next two hours she waited beside it until its owner showed up.

24 Impressed by Lupe's persistence, the registrar listened to her story. But instead of giving her permission to sit in on a class and learn more English, he insisted that she sign up for a full college load. Before she knew it, she was enrolled in four classes: basic math, basic English, psychology, and typing. The registrar's parting words to her were, "Don't come back if you don't make it through."

25 With that "encouragement," Lupe began a semester that was part nightmare, part dream come true. Every day she got her husband and children off to work and to school, took the bus to campus, came home to make lunch for her husband and grandparents, went back to campus, and was home in time to greet Victor, Mario, and Martha when they got home from school. In the evenings she cooked, cleaned, did laundry, and got the children to bed. Then she would study, often until three in the morning.

26 "Sometimes in class I would feel sick with the stress of it," she said. "I'd go to the bathroom and talk to myself in the mirror. Sometimes I'd say, 'What are you doing here? Why don't you go home and watch *I Love Lucy*?'"

But she didn't go home. Instead, she studied furiously, using her Spanish-English dictionary, constantly making lists of new words she wanted to understand. "I still do that today," she said. "When I come across a word I don't know, I write it down, look it up, and write sentences using it until I *own* that word." 27

Although so much of the language and subject matter was new to Lupe, one part of the college experience was not. That was the key skill of reading, a skill Lupe possessed. As she struggled with English, she found the reading speed, comprehension, and vocabulary that she had developed in Spanish carrying over into her new language. "Reading," she said, "reading was the vehicle. Although I didn't know it at the time, when I was a girl learning to love to read, I was laying the foundation for academic success." 28

She gives credit, too, to her Hispanic fellow students. "At first, they didn't know what to make of me. They were eighteen years old, and at that time it was very unfashionable for an older person to be in college. But once they decided I wasn't a 'plant'° from the administration, they were my greatest help." The younger students spent hours helping Lupe, explaining unfamiliar words and terms, coaching her, and answering her questions. 29

That first semester passed in a fog of exhaustion. Many mornings, Lupe doubted she could get out of bed, much less care for her family and tackle her classes. But when she thought of her children and what was at stake for them, 30 she forced herself on. She remembers well what those days were like. "Just a day at a time.That was all I could think about. I could make myself get up one more day, study one more day, cook and clean one more day. And those days eventually turned into a semester."

31 To her own amazement perhaps as much as anyone's, Lupe discovered that she was far from retarded. Although she sweated blood over many assignments, she completed them. She turned them in on time. And, remarkably, she made the dean's list her very first semester.

32 After that, there was no stopping Lupe Quintanilla. She soon realized that the associate's degree offered by Texas Southmost College would not satisfy her. Continuing her Monday, Wednesday, and Friday schedule at Southmost, she enrolled for Tuesday and Thursday courses at Pan American University, a school 140 miles from Brownsville. Within three years, she had earned both her junior-college degree and a bachelor's degree in biology. She then won a fellowship that took her to graduate school at the University of Houston, where she earned a master's degree in Spanish literature. When she graduated, the university offered her a job as director of the Mexican-American studies program. While in that position, she earned a doctoral degree in education.

33 How did she do it all? Lupe herself isn't sure. "I hardly know. When I think back to those years, it seems like a life that someone else lived." It was a rich and exciting but also very challenging period for Lupe and her family. On the one hand, Lupe was motivated by the desire to set an example for her children, to prove to them that they could succeed in the English-speaking academic world. On the other hand, she worried about neglecting her family. She tried hard to attend important activities, such as parents' meetings at school and her children's sporting events. But things didn't always work out. Lupe still remembers attending a baseball game that her older son, Victor, was playing in. When Victor came to bat, he hit a home run. But as the crowd cheered and Victor glanced proudly over at his mother in the stands, he saw she was studying a textbook. "I hadn't seen the home run," Lupe admitted. "That sort of thing was hard for everyone to take."

Although Lupe worried that 34
her children would resent her busy schedule, she also saw her success reflected in them as they blossomed in school. She forced herself to speak English at home, and their language skills improved quickly. She read to them in English instead of Spanish—gulping down her pride as their pronunciation became better than hers and they began correcting her. (Once the children were in high school and fluent in English, Lupe switched back to Spanish at home, so that the children would be fully comfortable in both languages.) "I saw the change in them almost immediately," she said. "After I helped them with their homework, they would see me pulling out my own books and going to work. In the morning, I would show them the papers I had written. As I gained confidence, so did they." By the next year, the children had been promoted out of the Yellow Birds.

Martha and Mario share a laugh with their mother. Martha is an attorney, and Mario is an emergency room physician.

35 Even though Victor, Mario, and Martha all did well academically, Lupe realized she could not assume that they would face no more obstacles in school. When Mario was in high school, for instance, he wanted to sign up for a debate class. Instead, he was assigned to woodworking. She visited the school to ask why. Mario's teacher told her, "He's good with his hands. He'll be a great carpenter, and that's a good thing for a Mexican to be." Controlling her temper, Lupe responded, "I'm glad you think he's good with his hands. He'll be a great physician someday, and he *is* going to be in the debate class."

36 Today, Lupe Quintanilla teaches at the University of Houston, as she has for more than thirty years. "I keep saying I'm going to retire," she says, "but I would miss my students too much!" At the university, she has developed several dozen courses concerning Hispanic literature and culture. Her cross-cultural training for law enforcement officers, which helps bring police and firefighters and local Hispanic communities closer together, is renowned° throughout the United States. She has served on a national board to keep the White House informed of new programs in law enforcement, been named one of Texas's "100 Most Influential Women of the Past Century," represented the U.S. at the United Nations Institute of Justice, been an ambassador to the World Conference on International Issues and Women's Affairs in Austria, and been the author and subject of several books. She has received numerous awards for teaching excellence, and there is even a scholarship named in her honor. Her

Mario and his family live near Dr. Quintanilla in Houston. Here, Mario's daughter and son enjoy a moment with their grandmother.

name appears in the Hispanic Hall of Fame, and she has been co-chair of the White House Commission on Hispanic Education.

37 The love of reading that her grandfather instilled in Lupe is still alive. She thinks of him every year when she introduces to her students one of his favorite poets, Amado Nervo. She requires them to memorize these lines from one of Nervo's poems: "When I got to the end of my long journey in life, I realized that I was the architect of my own destiny." Of these lines, Lupe says, "That is something that I deeply believe, and I want my students to learn it *before* the end of their long journey. We create our own destiny."

38 Her passion for reading and learning has helped Lupe create a distinguished destiny. But none of the honors she has received means more to her than the success of her own children, the reason she made that frightening journey to seek classes in English so many years ago. Today Mario *is* a physician. Victor and Martha are lawyers, both having earned doctor of law degrees. Together with their mother, with her Ed.D., they are four "Dr. Quintanillas"—as she laughingly says, "one retarded, and three slow learners."

Basic Skill Questions

Vocabulary in Context

_____ 1. In the excerpt below, the word *flourished* (flûr′ĭsht) means
A. grew.
B. stood still.
C. was lost.
D. remained.

"Lupe's own love of reading flourished during these years. Her vocabulary was enriched and her imagination fired by the novels she read. . . ." (Paragraph 11)

_____ 2. In the excerpt below, the word *vehicle* (vē′ĭ-kəl) means
A. obstacle.
B. loss.
C. means.
D. place.

"'Reading,' she said, 'reading was the vehicle. Although I didn't know it at the time, when I was a girl learning to love to read, I was laying the foundation for academic success.'" (Paragraph 28)

_____ 3. In the sentence below, the word *instilled* (ĭn-stĭld′) means
A. frightened.
B. established.
C. forced.
D. forgot.

"The love of reading that her grandfather instilled in her is still alive." (Paragraph 37)

Central Point and Main Ideas

_____ 4. Which sentence best expresses the central point of the selection?
A. Lupe, a first-grade dropout, eventually earned a doctoral degree and created a professional career.
B. Lupe Quintanilla's experience proves that the educational system must be set up to accommodate children who speak languages other than English.
C. Through hard work and persistence combined with a love of reading and learning, Lupe has created a distinguished career and helped her children become professionals.
D. In school, Spanish-speaking students may experience obstacles to aiming for a professional career.

_____ 5. Which of the following sentences expresses the main idea of paragraphs 19–24?
A. People at school, a hospital, and a telephone company rejected Lupe's requests for an education.
B. Overcoming rejections and disappointment, Lupe finally found someone who gave her a chance to learn English by enrolling at a college.
C. Lupe discovered that the person who made decisions about who could go to college and who could not was the registrar of the college.
D. The tests Lupe took in first grade indicating that she was retarded were a barrier to her desire to learn English.

_____ 6. Which of the following sentences expresses the main idea of paragraph 34?
A. Lupe's children blossomed in school as she continued to speak English to them and was a role model for them.
B. Lupe was afraid that her children would resent the busy schedule that kept her from spending as much time with them as she would have liked.
C. Wanting her children to know both English and Spanish, Lupe spoke Spanish at home once her children knew English.
D. After helping her children with their homework, Lupe would do her own homework.

Supporting Details

_____ 7. Lupe realized that her children were not retarded when
A. they got good grades at school.
B. they were put in the group called "Yellow Birds."
C. she saw how quickly they learned at home.
D. they read newspapers, poetry, and novels to her.

_____ 8. Lupe's training for law enforcement officers
A. teaches them to speak Spanish.
B. brings police, firefighters, and local Hispanic communities together.
C. offers a scholarship named in her honor.
D. teaches Hispanic literature and culture.

Transitions

______ 9. The relationship between the last sentence below and the two that come before it is one of

A. time.
B. addition.
C. illustration.
D. cause and effect.

"'In Hispanic culture, the teacher is regarded as a third parent, as an ultimate authority. To question her would seem most disrespectful, as though you were saying that she didn't know her job.' That was one reason Lupe's grandparents had not interfered when Lupe was classified as retarded." (Paragraph 17)

______10. The relationship between the two sentences below is one of

A. addition.
B. illustration.
C. contrast.
D. cause and effect.

"When Mario was in high school, . . . he wanted to sign up for debate class. Instead, he was assigned to woodworking." (Paragraph 35)

Patterns of Organization

______11. The pattern of organization of Paragraph 1 is

A. time order.
B. list of items.
C. contrast.
D. comparison.

______12. The main pattern of organization of paragraphs 3–35 is

A. time order.
B. list of items.
C. definition and example.
D. contrast.

Advanced Skill Questions

Inferences

______13. From the sentences below, we might conclude that
- A. although Lupe was not very intelligent at first, she became more intelligent once she learned English.
- B. Lupe really did know English.
- C. there are no IQ tests in Spanish.
- D. an IQ test in a language that the person tested doesn't know is useless.

"Once they arrived in Brownsville, Lupe was enrolled in school. Although she understood no English, she was given an IQ test in that language. Not surprisingly, she didn't do very well." (Paragraph 5)

______14. We might conclude from the reading that
- A. a school system's judgment about an individual is always accurate.
- B. it is often better for a child to stay home rather than attend school.
- C. by paying attention and speaking up, parents may remove obstacles to their children's education.
- D. working parents should accept the fact that they cannot attend important events in their children's lives.

______15. The last line of the reading suggests that
- A. retarded people can become successful professionals.
- B. people should not blindly accept other people's opinion of them.
- C. Lupe's children are smarter than she is.
- D. all of the above.

Purpose and Tone

______16. The author's main purpose is to
- A. inform readers of the struggle Lupe and her children endured to gain an education and accomplish their goals.
- B. persuade readers that the educational system needs to be reformed.
- C. entertain readers with anecdotes about Lupe's adventures in school.

______17. The general tone of the reading is
- A. instructive.
- B. sentimental.
- C. admiring.
- D. uncertain.

Argument

_____ 18. One of the following statements is the point of an argument. The other statements are support for that point. Write the letter of the point of the argument.

A. Lupe and others thought of her as being retarded because an educator gave her an IQ test in a language she didn't know.

B. Putting Mario in a stereotypical career category, one teacher said, "He'll be a great carpenter, and that's a good thing for a Mexican to be."

C. Through lack of insight and perpetuation of stereotypes, educators became obstacles to Lupe's and her children's education.

D. A teacher and principal shouted at young Lupe in a language she didn't understand, bewildering and embarrassing her so much that she dropped out of school.

Critical Reading

_____ 19. The statement below is

A. a fact.

B. an opinion.

C. both fact and opinion.

"Today, Lupe Quintanilla teaches at the University of Houston, as she has for more than thirty years." (Paragraph 36)

_____ 20. The word that makes the statement below an opinion is

A. *reading.*

B. *learning.*

C. *create.*

D. *distinguished.*

"Her passion for reading and learning has helped Lupe create a distinguished destiny." (Paragraph 38)

Summarizing

Add the ideas needed to complete the following summary of "The Professor Is a Dropout."

When Lupe Quintanilla was very young, she and her grandparents moved from Nogales, Mexico, to live with her uncle in a small town in southern Mexico that had no schools. When she was 12, ______________________

____

______________________________. In Brownsville, Lupe was

enrolled in school. After scoring poorly on an IQ test that was given in English, which she did not speak, Lupe was put in first grade. When ____________________

____

______________________________, Lupe begged her grandfather not to send her back to school. Lupe stayed home, where she read newspapers, poetry, and novels to her grandfather. At 16, she married, and within five years, she had three children. When her children were enrolled in school, they were grouped as slow learners, a fact that depressed Lupe—until she realized that at home, they didn't seem like slow learners. That gave her courage to go to school and talk to her children's teachers. When one suggested that ____________________________

________________________ might help her children, Lupe began a search for a way to learn English that ended in attending college and then a university, where she earned a doctoral degree in education. And by speaking English at home, helping her children with their homework, and serving as a good role model, Lupe encouraged her children to do well in school as well. Today, Lupe has a distinguished career as a professor and emphasizes to her students that they create their own destinies. She is also a communications company president and law enforcement trainer. She has been a representative to the United Nations. But what means most to her is ____

____.

Discussion Questions

1. Lupe credits her fellow Hispanic students with being a great help to her in college. Is there anyone in your life—a teacher, family member, or friend—who has helped you through challenging times during your education? Explain what your obstacle was and how this person helped you to overcome it.

2. Lupe found that her school responsibilities conflicted with her duties as wife and mother. What kinds of personal responsibilities have you had to juggle as a student? These may include parenthood, a job, a difficult home situation, extracurricular school activities, or anything else that poses a challenge to your academics. How have you balanced these obligations with your role as student?

3. By the end of Lupe's story, we see the serious mistakes made by those who called her "retarded" and her children "slow learners." Was there ever a time when you felt people misjudged you? What did they say about you that was wrong, and how did it make you feel? Explain how you reacted to their judgments—did you accept their remarks, or did you fight to disprove them?

4. Lupe is an outstanding example of a person who took charge of her life. Would you say that you have taken charge of your life? Describe how, or describe what you think you must yet do to take charge of your life.

Note: Writing assignments for this selection appear on page 702.

Check Your Performance

THE PROFESSOR IS A DROPOUT

Activity	*Number Right*		*Points*		*Score*
Basic Skill Questions					
Vocabulary in Context (3 items)	______	×	4	=	______
Central Point and Main Ideas (3 items)	______	×	4	=	______
Supporting Details (2 items)	______	×	4	=	______
Transitions (2 items)	______	×	4	=	______
Patterns of Organization (2 items)	______	×	4	=	______
Advanced Skill Questions					
Inferences (3 items)	______	×	4	=	______
Purpose and Tone (2 items)	______	×	4	=	______
Argument (1 item)	______	×	4	=	______
Critical Reading (2 items)	______	×	4	=	______
Summarizing (4 items)	______	×	5	=	______
			TOTAL SCORE	=	______%

Enter your total score into the **Reading Performance Chart: Ten Reading Selections** on the inside back cover.

2 Taming the Anger Monster

Anne Davidson

Preview

Many of us have an anger problem. We may snap at slow-moving clerks, swear at aggressive drivers, or steam at the general incompetence that many people (including ourselves) show in the matters of everyday life. Why are we so irritable? Is there anything we can do about it? This article explores the roots of our anger and suggests some ways of coping.

Words to Watch

designated (3): set apart for a particular purpose
petty (5): insignificant
chronic (15): continuous
diffuse (15): not confined to one area; present everywhere
self-perpetuating (15): causing itself to continue
catharsis (15): a release of tension

1 Laura Houser remembers the day with embarrassment.

2 "My mother was visiting from Illinois," she says. "We'd gone out to lunch and done some shopping. On our way home, we stopped at an intersection. When the light changed, the guy ahead of us was looking at a map or something and didn't move right away. I leaned on my horn and automatically yelled—well, what I generally yell at people who make me wait. I didn't even think about what I was doing. One moment I was talking and laughing with my mother, and the next I was shouting curses at a stranger. Mom's jaw just dropped. She said, 'Well, I guess *you've* been living in the city too long.' That's when I realized that my anger was out of control."

Laura has plenty of company. Here are a few examples plucked from the headlines of recent newspapers: 3

- Amtrak's Washington–New York train: When a woman begins to use her cell phone in a designated° "quiet car," her seatmate grabs the phone and smashes it against the wall.
- Reading, Massachusetts: Arguing over rough play at their ten-year-old sons' hockey practice, two fathers begin throwing punches. One of the dads beats the other to death.

- Westport, Connecticut: Two supermarket shoppers get into a fistfight over who should be first in a just-opened checkout line.

4 Reading these stories and countless others like them that happen daily, it's hard to escape the conclusion that we are one angry society. An entire vocabulary has grown up to describe situations of out-of control fury: road rage, sideline rage, computer rage, biker rage, air rage. Bookstore shelves are filled with authors' advice on how to deal with our anger. Court-ordered anger management classes have become commonplace, and anger-management workshops are advertised in local newspapers.

5 Human beings have always experienced anger, of course. But in earlier, more civil decades, public displays of anger were unusual to the point of being aberrant. Today, however, whether in petty° or deadly forms, episodes of unrepressed rage have become part of our daily landscape.

6 What has happened to us? Are we that much angrier than we used to be? Have we lost all inhibitions about expressing our anger? Are we, as a society, literally losing our ability to control our tempers?

WHY ARE WE SO ANGRY?

7 According to Sybil Evans, a conflict-resolution expert in New York City, there are three components to blame for our societal bad behavior: time, technology and tension.

8 What's eating up our time? To begin with, Americans work longer hours and are rewarded with less vacation time than people in any other industrial society. Over an average year, for example, most British employees work 250 hours less than most Americans; most Germans work a full 500 hours less. And most Europeans are given four to six weeks of vacation each year, compared to the average American's two weeks. And to top it all off, many Americans face long, stressful commutes at the beginning and end of each long workday.

Once we Americans do get home from work, our busy day is rarely done. 9
We are involved in community activities; our children participate in sports, school programs, and extracurricular activities; and our houses, yards, and cars cry out for maintenance. To make matters worse, we are reluctant to use the little bit of leisure time we do have to catch up on our sleep. Compared with Americans of the nineteenth and early twentieth centuries, most of us are chronically sleep-deprived. While our ancestors typically slept nine and a half hours a night, many of us feel lucky to get seven. We're critical of "lazy" people who sleep longer, and we associate naps with toddlerhood. (In doing so, we ignore the examples of successful people, including Winston Churchill, Albert Einstein, and Napoleon, all of whom were devoted to their afternoon naps.)

The bottom line: we are time- 10
challenged and just plain tired—and tired people are cranky people. We're ready to blow—to snap at the slow-moving cashier, to tap the bumper of the slowpoke ahead of us, or to do something far worse.

example, it's not sufficient to use your cell phone for phone calls. Now you must learn to use the phone for text-messaging and downloading games. It's not enough to take still photos with your digital camera. You should know how to shoot ultra high-speed fast-action clips. It's not enough to have an enviable CD collection. You should be downloading new songs in MP3 format. The computers in your house should be connected by a wireless router, and online via high-speed DSL service. In other words, if it's been more than ten minutes since you've updated your technology, you're probably behind.

12 In fact, you're not only behind; you're a stupid loser. At least, that's how most of us end up feeling as we're confronted with more and more unexpected technologies: the do-it-yourself checkout at the supermarket; the telephone "help center" that offers a recorded series of messages, but no human help. And feeling like losers makes us frustrated and, you guessed it, angry. "It's not any one thing but lots of little things that make people feel like they don't have control of their lives," says Jane Middleton-Moz, an author and therapist. "A sense of helplessness is what triggers rage. It's why people end up kicking ATM machines."

13 Her example is not far-fetched. According to a survey of computer users in Great Britain, a quarter of those under age 25 admitted to having kicked or punched their computers on at least one occasion. Others confessed to yanking out cables in a rage, forcing the computer to crash. On this side

11 Technology is also to blame for the bad behavior so widespread in our culture. Amazing gadgets were supposed to make our lives easier—but have they? Sure, technology has its positive aspects. It is a blessing, for instance, to have a cell phone on hand when your car breaks down far from home or to be able to "instant message" a friend on the other side of the globe. But the downsides are many. Cell phones, pagers, fax machines, handheld computers and the like have robbed many of us of what was once valuable downtime. Now we're *always* available to take that urgent call or act on that last-minute demand. Then there is the endless pressure of feeling we need to keep up with our gadgets' latest technological developments. For

of the Atlantic, a Wisconsin man, after repeated attempts to get his daughter's malfunctioning computer repaired, took it to the store where he had bought it, placed it in the foyer, and attacked it with a sledgehammer. Arrested and awaiting a court appearance, he told local reporters, "It feels good, in a way." He had put into action a fantasy many of us have had—that of taking out our feelings of rage on the machines that so frustrate us.

14 Tension, the third major culprit behind our epidemic of anger, is intimately connected with our lack of time and the pressures of technology. Merely our chronic exhaustion and our frustration in the face of a bewildering array of technologies would be enough to cause our stress levels to skyrocket, but we are dealing with much more. Our tension is often fueled by a reserve of anger that might be the result of a critical boss, marital discord, or (something that many of today's men and women experience, if few will admit it) a general sense of being stupid and inadequate in the face of the demands of modern life. And along with the annoyances of everyday life, we now live with a widespread fear of such horrors as terrorist acts, global warming, and antibiotic-resistant diseases. Our sense of dread may be out of proportion to actual threats because of technology's ability to so constantly bombard us with worrisome information. Twenty-four-hour-a-day news stations bring a stream of horror into our living rooms. As we work at our computers, headlines and graphic images are never more than a mouse click away.

THE RESULT OF OUR ANGER

Add it all together—our feeling of 15
never having enough time; the chronic° aggravation caused by technology; and our endless, diffuse° sense of stress—and we become time bombs waiting to explode. Our angry outbursts may be briefly satisfying, but afterward we are left feeling—well, like jerks. Worse, flying off the handle is a self-perpetuating° behavior. Brad Bushman, a psychology professor at Iowa State University, says, "Catharsis° is worse than useless." Bushman's research has shown that when people vent their anger, they actually become more, not less, aggressive. "Many people think of anger as the psychological equivalent of the steam in a pressure cooker. It has to be released, or it will explode. That's not true. The people who react by hitting, kicking, screaming, and swearing just feel more angry."

Furthermore, the unharnessed 16
venting of anger may actually do us physical harm. The vigorous expression of anger pumps adrenaline into our system and raises our blood pressure, setting the stage for heart attack and strokes. Frequently angry people have even been shown to have higher cholesterol levels than even-tempered individuals.

HOW TO DEAL WITH OUR ANGER

Unfortunately, the culprits behind much 17
of our anger—lack of time, frustrating technology, and mega-levels of stress—are not likely to resolve themselves

anytime soon. So what are we to do with the anger that arises as a result?

18 According to Carol Tavris, author of *Anger: The Misunderstood Emotion*, the keys to dealing with anger are common sense and patience. She points out that almost no situation is improved by an angry outburst. A traffic jam, a frozen computer, or a misplaced set of car keys is annoying. To act upon the angry feelings those situations provoke, however, is an exercise in futility. Shouting, fuming, or leaning on the car horn won't make traffic begin to flow, the screen unlock, or keys materialize.

19 Patience, on the other hand, is a highly practical virtue. People who take the time to cool down before responding to an anger-producing situation are far less likely to say or do something they will regret later. "It is true of the body as of arrows," Tavris says, "that what goes up must come down. Any emotional arousal will simmer down if you just wait long enough." When you are stuck in traffic, in other words, turn on some soothing music, breathe deeply, and count to ten—or thirty or forty, if need be.

20 Anger-management therapist Doris Wild Helmering agrees. "Like any feeling, anger lasts only about three seconds," she says. "What keeps it going is your own negative thinking." As long as you focus on the idiot who cut you off on the expressway, you'll stay angry. But if you let the incident go, your anger will go with it. "Once you come to understand that you're driving your own anger with your thoughts," adds Helmering, "you can stop it."

21 Experts who have studied anger also encourage people to cultivate activities that effectively vent their anger. For some people, it's reading the newspaper or watching TV, while others need more active outlets, such as using a treadmill, taking a walk, hitting golf balls, or working out with a punching bag. People who succeed in calming their anger can also enjoy the satisfaction of having dealt positively with their frustrations.

22 For Laura Houser, the episode in the car with her mother was a wake-up call. "I saw myself through her eyes," she said, "and I realized I had become a chronically angry, impatient jerk. My response to stressful situations had become habitual—I automatically flew off the handle. Once I saw what I was doing, it really wasn't that hard to develop different habits. I simply decided I was going to treat other people the way I would want to be treated." The changes in Laura's life haven't benefited only her former victims. "I'm a calmer, happier person now," she reports. "I don't lie in bed at night fuming over stupid things other people have done and my own enraged responses." Laura has discovered the satisfaction of having a sense of control over her own behavior—which ultimately is all any of us can control.

Basic Skill Questions

Vocabulary in Context

_____ 1. In the sentence below, the word *aberrant* (ă-bĕr′ənt) means
- A. amusing.
- B. abnormal.
- C. common.
- D. beneficial.

"But in earlier, more civil times, public displays of anger were unusual to the point of being aberrant." (Paragraph 5)

_____ 2. In the sentence below, the word *discord* (dĭs′kôrd′) means
- A. disagreement.
- B. harmony.
- C. absence.
- D. energy.

"Our tension is often fueled by a reserve of anger that might be the result of a critical boss, marital discord, or (something that many of today's men and women experience, if few will admit it) a general sense of being stupid and inadequate in the face of the demands of modern life." (Paragraph 14)

Central Point and Main Ideas

_____ 3. Which sentence best expresses the central point of the selection?
- A. People today have lost their ability to control their anger and behave in a civil fashion.
- B. Our out-of-control anger has understandable causes, but common sense and patience are more satisfying than outbursts of rage.
- C. Anger would last only a few seconds if we didn't keep it going with negative thinking.
- D. While technology has its positive aspects, it has made us constantly available to others and challenged us to master the endless new developments.

_____ 4. The main idea of paragraph 9 is expressed in its
- A. first sentence.
- B. second sentence.
- C. third sentence.
- D. fourth sentence.

_____ 5. Which sentence best expresses the implied main idea of paragraph 11?
A. Cell phones, computers, and other technological gadgets can be very convenient.
B. We would all be better off living without technological gadgets.
C. Despite their good points, technological gadgets have added stress to our lives.
D. Cell phones, digital cameras, and computers need to be made simpler to use.

Supporting Details

_____ 6. Sybil Evans says that the three forces to blame for our anger are
A. finances, technology, and tension.
B. technology, marital discord, and money.
C. time, technology, and tension.
D. tension, incompetence, and critical employers.

_____ 7. A number of respondents to a survey of computer users in Great Britain admitted that
A. they had kicked or punched their computers.
B. their computers made them feel stupid.
C. they often sent and received personal e-mails at work.
D. they had accidentally deleted important work files and lied about it.

_____ 8. According to psychology professor Brad Bushman,
A. "blowing off steam" is a psychological necessity.
B. people who do not express their anger become seriously depressed.
C. the emotion of anger lasts only a few seconds.
D. venting our anger does us more harm than good.

Transitions

_____ 9. The relationship of the second sentence below to the first is one of
A. time order.
B. cause and effect.
C. illustration.
D. comparison.

"Unfortunately, the culprits behind most of our anger . . . are not likely to resolve themselves anytime soon. So what are we to do with the anger that arises as a result?" (Paragraph 17)

_____10. What is the relationship of the second sentence below to the first?
A. Contrast
B. Illustration
C. Comparison
D. Cause and effect

"[Tavris] points out that almost no situation is improved by an angry outburst. . . . Patience, on the other hand, is a highly practical virtue." (Paragraphs 18 and 19)

Patterns of Organization

_____11. The pattern of organization of paragraph 2 is
A. comparison.
B. list of items.
C. definition and example.
D. time order.

_____12. The section "Why Are We So Angry?" (paragraphs 7–14)
A. compares people's reasons for being angry.
B. presents a series of steps in the process of becoming angry.
C. lists and discusses causes of the angry behavior in our society.
D. contrasts time with technology.

_____13. Paragraph 22
A. explains changes that Laura has made and the effects of those changes.
B. contrasts Laura's and her mother's ways of handling anger.
C. lists ways that Laura has changed her behavior.
D. defines *patience* and illustrates the term.

Advanced Skill Questions

Inferences

_____14. From paragraph 2 we can infer that
A. Laura's mother was a bad-tempered woman.
B. Laura's mother was proud of her daughter's behavior.
C. Laura's mother knew the driver of the car ahead of them.
D. Laura had not always been so quick-tempered.

______15. In paragraph 11, the author suggests that
A. it is nearly impossible to keep up with technological advances.
B. only lazy people ignore the wonderful advantages of technology.
C. text messaging is a waste of time.
D. most digital cameras and cell phones do not work very well.

______16. We can infer from the excerpt that follows that
A. being well-informed about bad news gives us a sense of control.
B. we would be less worried about problems if we were not constantly reminded of them.
C. the news media deliberately exaggerate the problems in the world.
D. it is irresponsible not to keep up with world news.

"Our sense of dread may be out of proportion to actual threats because of technology's ability to so constantly bombard us with worrisome information. Twenty-four-hour-a-day news stations bring a stream of horror into our living rooms. As we work at our computers, headlines and graphic images are never more than a mouse click away." (Paragraph 14)

Purpose and Tone

______17. The main purpose of this selection is to
A. entertain readers with anecdotes about people whose tempers are out of control.
B. inform readers about the epidemic of anger and ways to handle anger.
C. persuade readers to get more sleep at night and to nap during the day.

______18. The author's tone when discussing technology is largely
A. admiring.
B. amused.
C. concerned.
D. thankful.

Argument

_____19. Three of the items below are supporting details for an argument. Write the letter of the statement that represents the point of these supporting details.

A. Modern technological gadgets often make us feel stupid or inadequate.
B. A hundred years ago, most people got several hours more sleep a night than people do today.
C. Twenty-four-hour news sources keep us constantly aware of scary or worrisome stories.
D. Modern-day people have to deal with sources of anger that earlier people did not.

Critical Reading

_____20. Paragraph 8 is made up of

A. facts.
B. opinions.
C. a mixture of facts and opinions.

Outlining

Complete the outline by filling in the four missing major details.

Central point: There is an epidemic of anger in today's society, but people can learn to deal with their anger.

A. Introduction: Laura Houser anecdote and other examples of widespread public anger

B. Causes of our anger

1. ______________________________
2. ______________________________
3. ______________________________

C. Solutions to our anger

1. ______________________________
2. Finding activities that vent our anger

Discussion Questions

1. What kinds of things make you most angry? Is your anger directed mostly at others, or at yourself? What steps do you think you should take, or what steps have you taken, to control anger?
2. Of the three sources of our anger identified in the reading—time, technology, and tension—which do you think is the greatest problem for you? Why?
3. If you were teaching a class to students on what they should do to control anger, what would be your advice?
4. Do you agree with Carol Tavris, author of *Anger: The Misunderstood Emotion*, that almost no situation is improved by an angry outburst? Is anger ever helpful? Explain your answer.

Note: Writing assignments for this selection appear on page 703.

Check Your Performance

TAMING THE ANGER MONSTER

Activity	*Number Right*	*Points*	*Score*
Basic Skill Questions			
Vocabulary in Context (2 items)	______	× 4 =	______
Central Point and Main Ideas (3 items)	______	× 4 =	______
Supporting Details (3 items)	______	× 4 =	______
Transitions (2 items)	______	× 4 =	______
Patterns of Organization (3 items)	______	× 4 =	______
Advanced Skill Questions			
Inferences (3 items)	______	× 4 =	______
Purpose and Tone (2 items)	______	× 4 =	______
Argument (1 item)	______	× 4 =	______
Critical Reading (1 item)	______	× 4 =	______
Outlining (4 items)	______	× 5 =	______
		TOTAL SCORE =	______%

Enter your total score into the **Reading Performance Chart: Ten Reading Selections** on the inside back cover.

3 Young and Isolated

Jennifer M. Silva

Preview

Is the so-called American Dream dying? For young working-class men and women, the dream already appears to be dead. There was a time when education and hard work naturally translated to a bright future. But for many of today's young people, there seems to be no hope for any kind of decent future at all.

Words to Watch

affluent (4): wealthy
embody (5): represent
deindustrialization (5): removal or reduction of industry
venture (11): project, undertaking
milquetoast (11): someone who can be easily controlled
rendered (13): made
empathy (15): understanding
virulent (16): bitter
solidarity (18): unity

1 In a working-class neighborhood in Lowell, Mass., in early 2009, I sat across the table from Diana, then 24, in the kitchen of her mother's house. Diana had planned to graduate from college, marry, buy a home in the suburbs, and have kids, a dog and a cat by the time she was 30. But she had recently dropped out of a nearby private university after two years of study and with nearly $80,000 in student loans. Now she worked at Dunkin' Donuts.

2 "With college," she explained, "I would have had to wait five years to get a degree, and once I get that, who knows if I will be working and if I would find something I wanted to do. I don't want to be a cop or anything. I don't know what to do with it. My manager says some people are born to make coffee, and I guess I was born to make coffee."

3 Young working-class men and women like Diana are trying to figure out what it means to be an adult in a world of disappearing jobs, soaring education costs, and shrinking social support networks. Today, only 20 percent of men and women between 18 and 29 are married. They live at home longer, spend more years in college, change jobs more frequently, and start families later.

4 For more affluent° young adults, this may look a lot like freedom. But

for the hundred-some working-class 20- and 30-somethings I interviewed between 2008 and 2010 in Lowell and Richmond, Va., at gas stations, fast-food chains, community colleges, and temp agencies, the view is very different.

5 Lowell and Richmond embody° many of the structural forces, like deindustrialization° and declining blue-collar jobs, that frame working-class young people's attempts to come of age in America today. The economic hardships of these men and women, both white and black, have been well documented. But often overlooked are what the sociologists Richard Sennett and Jonathan Cobb in 1972 called their "hidden injuries"—the difficult-to-measure social costs borne by working-class youths as they struggle to forge stable and meaningful adult lives.

6 These are people bouncing from one temporary job to the next; dropping out of college because they can't figure out financial aid forms or fulfill their major requirements; relying on credit cards for medical emergencies; and avoiding romantic commitments because they can take care of only themselves. Increasingly disconnected from institutions of work, family, and community, they grow up by learning that counting on others will only hurt them in the end. Adulthood is not simply being delayed but dramatically reimagined along lines of trust, dignity, and connection and obligation to others.

Take Jay, for example. He was 7
expelled from college for failing several classes after his mother suffered a severe mental breakdown. He worked for a year, then went before the college administration and petitioned

to be reinstated. He described it as a humiliating experience: "It's their jobs to hear all these sob stories, you know, I understand that, but they just had this attitude, like you know what I mean, 'Oh, your mom had a breakdown and you couldn't turn to anyone?'"

8 Jay got back in and graduated (after a total of seven years of college). But when I talked to him, he was still working food-service and coffee-shop jobs at 28, baffled about how to turn his communications major into a professional job. He felt as if he was sold fake goods: "The world is at my fingertips, you can rule the world, be whatever you want, all this stuff. When I was 15, 16, I would not have envisioned the life I am living now. Whatever I imagined, I figured I would wear a suit every day, that I would own things. I don't own anything."

9 I heard many people express feeling betrayed by the major institutions in their lives, whether colleges, the health care system, employers, or the government.

10 Christopher, who was 25, stated simply, "Well, I have this problem of being tricked." He explained: "Like, I will get a phone call that says, you won a free supply of magazines. And they will start coming to my house. Then all of a sudden I am getting calls from bill collectors for the subscriptions to *Maxim* and ESPN. It's a runaround: I can't figure out who to call. Now I don't even pick up the phone, like I almost didn't pick up when you called me." He described isolation as the only safe path; by depending on no one, Christopher protected himself from trickery and betrayal.

These fears seep into the romantic sphere, where commitment becomes yet another risky venture°. Kelly, a 28-year-old line cook, spent 10 years battling depression and living off and on in her car. She finally had a job and an apartment of her own. But now she was worried about risking that hard earned sense of security by letting someone else into her life. "I like the idea of being with someone," she said, "but I have a hard time imagining trusting anybody with all of my personal stuff." She said she would "rather be alone and fierce than be in a relationship and be milquetoast°." 11

Men often face a different challenge: the impossibility of living up to the male provider role. Brandon, who worked the night shift at a clothing store, described what he thought it would be like to be in a relationship with him: "No woman wants to sit on the couch all the time and watch TV and eat at Burger King. I can only take care of myself." 12

It is not that these men and women don't value family. Douglas, then 25, talked about loss: "Trust is gone. The way people used to love is gone." Rather, the insecurities and uncertainties of their daily lives have rendered° commitment a luxury they can't afford. 13

But these young men and women don't want your pity—and they don't expect a handout. They are quick to blame themselves for the milestones they have not achieved. Julian, an Army vet from Richmond who was unemployed, divorced, and living with 14 his mother at 28, dismissed the notion that his lack of success was anyone's fault but his own: "At the end of the day, looking in the mirror, I know where all my shortcomings come from. From the things that I either did not do or I did and I just happened to fail at them." Kelly echoed that: "No one else is going to fix me but me."

15 This self-sufficiency, while highly prized in our culture, has a dark side: it leaves little empathy° to spare for those who cannot survive on their own.

16 Wanda, a young woman with big dreams of going to college, expressed virulent° anger toward her parents, a tow-truck driver and a secretary, for not being able to pay her tuition: "I feel like it's their fault that they don't have nothing." Rather than build connections with those who struggled alongside her, Wanda severed relationships and willed herself not to be "weak-minded" like her parents: "If my mentality were different, then most definitely I would just be stuck like them."

Working-class youths come to 17
believe that if they have to make it on their own, then everyone else should, too. Powerless to achieve external markers of adulthood like marriage or a steady job, they instead measure their progress by cutting ties, turning inward, and numbing themselves emotionally.

We don't want to go back to the 18
1950s, when economic stability and social solidarity° came at the cost of exclusion for many Americans. But nor can we afford the social costs of going forward on our present path of isolation. The social and economic decline of the American working class will only be exacerbated as its youngest members make a virtue out of self-blame, distrust, and disconnection. In order to tell a different kind of coming-of-age story, we need to provide these young men and women with the skills and support to navigate the road to adulthood. Our future depends on it.

Basic Skill Questions

Vocabulary in Context

_____ 1. In the following sentence, the word *forge* (fôrj) means to

A. imagine.
B. decide on.
C. build.
D. copy.

"But often overlooked are what the sociologists Richard Sennett and Jonathan Cobb in 1972 called their 'hidden injuries'—the difficult-to-measure social costs borne by working-class youths as they struggle to forge stable and meaningful adult lives." (Paragraph 5)

_____ 2. In the following excerpt, the word *exacerbated* (ĭg-zăs′ər-bāt′ĭd) means
A. made worse.
B. improved.
C. prevented.
D. explained.

"But nor can we afford the social costs of going forward. The social and economic decline of the American working class will only be exacerbated as its youngest members make a virtue out of self-blame, distrust, and disconnection." (Paragraph 18)

Central Point and Main Ideas

_____ 3. Which sentence best expresses the central point of the entire selection?
A. Today's working-class young people often blame themselves for not being more successful.
B. A shortage of blue-collar jobs is making it difficult for many young people to live on their own.
C. Because working-class young people are having such a hard time finding good jobs, they are putting off getting married and starting families.
D. Our society needs to help young working-class men and women who are struggling to build meaningful lives.

_____ 4. The implied main idea of paragraphs 5–6 is that
A. Lowell and Richmond are two communities that have been hard hit by deindustrialization and a lack of blue-collar jobs.
B. because so many young people today are struggling economically, they are becoming less able to lead traditional adult lives.
C. there have been many studies done on the economic problems of today's working-class youths.
D. many young people today take temp jobs, drop out of college, use credit cards to pay for medical emergencies, and avoid commitments.

Supporting Details

_____ 5. To obtain the information presented in the selection, the author
A. studied research reports about young working-class people.
B. interviewed over a hundred working-class young people in two American cities.
C. conducted an online survey of young people who were employed in various low-paying jobs.
D. interviewed community college students throughout the United States.

_____ 6. According to the selection, the percentage of people between the ages of 18 and 29 who are married is
A. 5 percent.
B. 10 percent.
C. 20 percent.
D. 30 percent.

_____ 7. The author presents which of the following as an example of a structural force that shapes people's lives?
A. The fact that many young people are putting off marriage
B. A decline in the willingness to trust others
C. A refusal to accept personal responsibility for mistakes
D. A decline in the number of blue-collar jobs

_____ 8. According to the author, many of today's working-class young people
A. blame the government for their problems.
B. don't value family the way earlier generations did.
C. still believe that their situations will improve over time.
D. blame only themselves for their problems.

Transitions

_____ 9. How are the following three sentences related?
A. Comparison
B. Time
C. Illustration
D. Addition

"Diana had planned to graduate from college, marry, buy a home in the suburbs and have kids, a dog and a cat by the time she was 30. But she had recently dropped out of a nearby private university after two years of study and with nearly $80,000 in student loans. Now she worked at Dunkin' Donuts." (Paragraph 1)

Patterns of Organization

_____10. In general, the selection
A. lists reasons that so many working-class young people are unable to find well-paying jobs.
B. provides examples of young people who are struggling in a time of economic insecurity.
C. contrasts the attitude toward marriage of working-class youth today with the attitudes of earlier generations.
D. compares the challenges young men face in today's economy with the challenges young women face.

Advanced Skill Questions

Inferences

_____11. We can infer from paragraphs 1 and 2 that Diana
- A. enjoys working at Dunkin' Donuts.
- B. was afraid of going into even deeper debt if she had stayed in college.
- C. will go back to college after paying off her debts.
- D. will one day manage a Dunkin' Donuts.

_____12. The reading suggests that today's working-class young people
- A. recognize that their lives are being shaped by forces beyond their control.
- B. find a sense of freedom in putting off marriage.
- C. don't realize that social forces beyond their control are making life more difficult for them.
- D. are willing to help out those less fortunate than they are.

_____13. Paragraphs 7 and 8 suggest that Jay
- A. would not be working food-service if he hadn't been expelled from college.
- B. should not have gone back to college.
- C. feels bitter and frustrated about his life so far.
- D. believes that his life will improve sometime soon.

_____14. We can infer from paragraphs 14–17 that today's working-class young people
- A. will eventually succeed if they try hard enough.
- B. aren't succeeding, no matter how hard they try.
- C. aren't as mentally strong as their parents' generation.
- D. refuse to look honestly at their own shortcomings.

_____15. What audience did Silva have in mind when she wrote this article?
- A. Social scientists who study how economic hardships affect the lives of young people
- B. Working-class young people who are unemployed or underemployed
- C. General readers who may not be aware of the social costs of deindustrialization on young working-class people
- D. Politicians and other civic leaders who are working to lower unemployment rates

Purpose and Tone

_____16. In general, the author's main purpose for writing this article was to
A. inform readers about the growing divide between today's working-class adults and the rest of society.
B. persuade readers to help young adults who are struggling to build meaningful lives.
C. entertain readers with a surprising description of an alienated segment of society.
D. inform readers about the struggles facing young people who have both graduated and dropped out of college.

_____17. The tone of the last paragraph of the selection is
A. detached.
B. matter-of-fact.
C. frightened.
D. concerned.

Argument

18. Label the point of the following argument with a **P** and the two statements of support with an **S**. Label with an **X** the one statement that is neither the point nor the support of the argument.

___ A. Diana is not living the life she once imagined she'd be living by the time she was in her 20s.

___ B. Diana thought she would graduate from college, but she had to drop out and now owes $80,000 in loans.

___ C. Diana lives with her parents and works at an unskilled job for low pay.

___ D. Diana's boss thinks Diana was "born to make coffee."

_____19. Three of the items below are supporting details for an argument. Write the letter of the statement that represents the point of these supporting details.
A. Many young people feel betrayed by major institutions such as colleges, the government, or employers.
B. As more and more jobs disappear in the United States, these young people are forced to work at low-paying, unskilled jobs.
C. Many working-class young people are struggling to live fulfilling adult lives.
D. Often, there is a mistrust or fear of commitment, making the possibility for a relationship slim for many of these young adults.

Critical Reading

_____20. This selection is made up of
- A. only facts.
- B. only opinions.
- C. both facts and opinions.

Outlining

Circle the letter of the outline notes that best cover "Young and Isolated."

A. Increasingly, young working-class adults are struggling to build meaningful lives.
1. Diana
   a. Lives at home
   b. Dropped out of school
   c. Works at Dunkin' Donuts
2. Jay
   a. Doesn't know how to use his degree to get a job
   b. Feels betrayed by college
   c. Doesn't own anything
3. Christopher
   a. Feels everyone is out to trick him
   b. Thinks isolation is the only safe path
4. Kelly/Brandon/Douglas
   a. Are afraid to let someone into their lives
   b. Think no one would want to be with them
   c. Think loving someone makes you weak
5. Wanda
   a. Blames her parents
   b. Has severed relations with parents rather than working alongside them

B. Young working-class adults are unhappy with their lives for several reasons.
1. Education did not help them.
2. They blame themselves for the lives they lead.
3. They work at unskilled, low-paying jobs.
4. Some of them do not get along with their parents.
5. They have few belongings.
6. Many are distrustful of their bosses, government, and colleges.
7. They are reluctant to get in relationships.

C. Increasingly, young working-class adults are struggling to build meaningful lives for several reasons.
   1. They are unprepared to make a decent living.
      a. Many are either unable to afford college, finish college, or use the degrees they've gotten.
         Examples: Diana, Jay, and Wanda
      b. Some owe substantial student loans.
      c. They move from low-paying job to low-paying job.
   2. There is a sense of being tricked or betrayed by major institutions.
         Example: Christopher
   3. Many are reluctant to be in relationships with others.
      a. Romantically, they feel they cannot offer enough or that love cannot be trusted.
         Examples: Kelly, Brandon, Douglas
      b. Some are angry/estranged from their own families.
         Example: Wanda
   4. Many blame themselves for the lives they are leading.

Discussion Questions

1. Sometimes an author will choose a title that has more than one meaning. What are two possible meanings of the word *isolated* in "Young and Isolated"?

2. Overall, the author presents a pretty grim picture of the lives of today's working-class young people. Do you think her picture is accurate? Why or why not?

3. In the selection, a young man named Christopher describes isolation as "the only safe path." Another young person, Kelly, says that she would "rather be alone and fierce than be in a relationship and be milquetoast." Might there be any negative consequences to becoming isolated? If so, what might they be?

4. According to the author, many working-class young people believe that "if they have to make it on their own, then everyone else should, too." Do you agree that it's up to the individual to make it on his or her own? Or are there things that society can do to help? Explain.

Note: Writing assignments for this selection appear on pages 703–704.

Check Your Performance — YOUNG AND ISOLATED

Activity	*Number Right*		*Points*		*Score*
Basic Skill Questions					
Vocabulary in Context (2 items)	______	×	4	=	______
Central Point and Main Ideas (2 items)	______	×	4	=	______
Supporting Details (4 items)	______	×	4	=	______
Transitions (1 item)	______	×	4	=	______
Patterns of Organization (1 item)	______	×	4	=	______
Advanced Skill Questions					
Inferences (5 items)	______	×	4	=	______
Purpose and Tone (2 items)	______	×	4	=	______
Argument (2 items)	______	×	4	=	______
Critical Reading (1 items)	______	×	4	=	______
Outlining (1 item)	______	×	20	=	______
			TOTAL SCORE	=	______%

Enter your total score into the **Reading Performance Chart: Ten Reading Selections** on the inside back cover.

4 My Father's Hands

Calvin R. Worthington

Preview

The man described in the following selection is strong, kind, intelligent—and illiterate. Looking back on his father's life, Calvin Worthington paints an unforgettable picture of a good man whose life—and death—were tragically shaped by his inability to read.

Words to Watch

upside (1): on (slang)
hunkering down (1): squatting close to the ground
lair (1): den
towhead (2): someone with light blond hair
unsurpassed (5): unequaled
infidel (9): someone who does not believe in the religion of the speaker or writer
nitroglycerin (12): a medicine used to combat the effects of heart disease
brow (13): the top edge of a hill
gnarled (13): twisted
anguish (16): pain and suffering

1 His hands were rough and exceedingly strong. He could gently prune a fruit tree or firmly wrestle an ornery mule into harness. He could draw and saw a square with quick accuracy. He had been known to peel his knuckles upside° a tough jaw. But what I remember most is the special warmth from those hands soaking through my shirt as he would take me by the shoulder and, hunkering down° beside my ear, point out the glittering swoop of a blue hawk, or a rabbit asleep in its lair°. They were good hands that served him well and failed him in only one thing: they never learned to write.

2 My father was illiterate. The number of illiterates in our country has steadily declined, but if there were only one I would be saddened, remembering my father and the pain he endured because his hands never learned to write. He started first grade, where the remedy for a wrong answer was ten ruler strokes across a stretched palm. For some reason, shapes, figures, and recitations just didn't fall into the right pattern inside his six-year-old towhead°. Maybe

he suffered from some type of learning handicap such as dyslexia. His father took him out of school after several months and set him to a man's job on the farm.

3 Years later, his wife, with her fourth-grade education, would try to teach him to read. And still later I would grasp his big fist between my small hands and awkwardly help him trace the letters of his name. He submitted to the ordeal, but soon grew restless. Flexing his fingers and kneading his palms, he would declare that he had had enough and depart for a long, solitary walk.

4 Finally, one night when he thought no one saw, he slipped away with his son's second-grade reader and labored over the words, until they became too difficult. He pressed his forehead into the pages and wept. "Jesus—Jesus—not even a child's book?" Thereafter, no amount of persuading could bring him to sit with pen and paper.

5 From the farm to road building and later factory work, his hands served him well. His mind was keen, his will to work unsurpassed°. During World War II, he was a pipefitter in a shipyard and installed the complicated guts of mighty fighting ships. His enthusiasm and efficiency brought an offer to become line boss—until he was handed the qualification test. His fingers could trace a path across the blueprints while his mind imagined the pipes lacing through the heart of the ship. He could recall every twist and turn of the pipes. But he couldn't read or write.

6 After the shipyard closed, he went to the cotton mill, where he labored at night, and stole from his sleeping hours the time required to run the farm. When the mill shut down, he went out each morning looking for work—only to return night after night and say to Mother as she fixed his dinner, "They just don't want anybody who can't take their tests."

It had always been hard for him 7
to stand before a man and make an "X" mark for his name, but the hardest moment of all was when he placed "his mark" by the name someone else had written for him, and saw another man walk away with the deed to his beloved farm. When it was over, he stood before the window and slowly turned the pen he still held in his hands—gazing, unseeing, down the mountainside. I went to the springhouse that afternoon and wept for a long while.

Eventually, he found another 8
cotton-mill job, and we moved into a millhouse village with a hundred look-alike houses. He never quite adjusted to town life. The blue of his eyes faded; the skin across his cheekbones became a little slack. But his hands kept their strength, and their warmth still soaked through when he would sit me on his lap and ask me to read to him from the Bible. He took great pride in my reading and would listen for hours as I struggled through the awkward phrases.

Once he had heard "a radio 9
preacher" relate that the Bible said, "The man that doesn't provide for his family is worse than a thief and an infidel° and will never enter the kingdom of Heaven." Often he would ask me to read that part to him, but I was never able to

find it. Other times, he would sit at the kitchen table leafing through the pages as though by a miracle he might be able to turn to the right page. Then he would sit staring at the Book, and I knew he was wondering if God was going to refuse him entry into heaven because his hands couldn't write.

10 When Mother left once for a weekend to visit her sister, Dad went to the store and returned with food for dinner while I was busy building my latest homemade wagon. After the meal he said he had a surprise for dessert, and went out to the kitchen, where I could hear him opening a can. Then everything was quiet. I went to the doorway and saw him standing before the sink with an open can in his hands. "The picture looked just like pears," he mumbled. He walked out and sat on the back steps, and I knew he had been embarrassed before his son. The can read "Whole White Potatoes," but the picture on the label did look a great deal like pears.

11 I went and sat beside him, and asked if he would point out the stars. He knew where the Big Dipper and all the other stars were located, and we talked about how they got there in the first place. He kept that can on a shelf in the woodshed for a long while, and a few times I saw him turning it in his hands as if the touch of the words would teach his hands to write.

12 Years later, when Mom died, I tried to get him to come live with my family, but he insisted on staying in his small frame house on the edge of town with a few farm animals and a garden plot. His health was failing, and he was in and out of the hospital with several mild heart attacks. Old Doc Green saw him weekly

and gave him medications, including nitroglycerin° tablets to put under his tongue should he feel an attack coming on.

13 My last fond memory of Dad was watching as he walked across the brow° of a hillside meadow, with those big, warm hands—now gnarled° with age—resting on the shoulders of my two children. He stopped to point out confidentially, a pond where he and I had swum and fished years before. That night, my family and I flew to a new job and new home, overseas. Three weeks later, he was dead of a heart attack.

14 I returned alone for the funeral. Doc Green told me how sorry he was. In fact, he was bothered a bit, because he had written Dad a new nitroglycerin prescription, and the druggist had filled it. Yet the bottle of pills had not been found on Dad's person. Doc Green felt that a pill might have kept him alive long enough to summon help.

15 An hour before the chapel service, I found myself standing near the edge of Dad's garden, where a neighbor had found him. In grief, I stopped to trace my fingers in the earth where a great man had reached the end of his life. My hand came to rest on a half-buried brick, which I aimlessly lifted and tossed aside, before noticing underneath it the twisted and battered, yet unbroken, soft plastic bottle that had been beaten into the soft earth.

As I held the bottle of nitroglycerin 16
pills, the scene of Dad struggling to remove the cap and in desperation trying to break the bottle with the brick flashed painfully before my eyes. With deep anguish° I knew why those big warm hands had lost in their struggle with death. For there, imprinted on the bottle cap, were the words, "Child-Proof Cap—Push Down and Twist to Unlock." The druggist later confirmed that he had just started using the new safety bottle.

I knew it was not a purely rational 17
act, but I went downtown and bought a leather-bound pocket dictionary and a gold pen set. I bade Dad good-bye by placing them in those big old hands, once so warm, which had lived so well, but had never learned to write.

Basic Skill Questions

Vocabulary in Context

_____ 1. In the sentence below, the word *ornery* (ôr′nə-rē) means

A. agreeable.
B. stubborn.
C. very young.
D. gentle.

"He could gently prune a fruit tree or firmly wrestle an ornery mule into harness." (Paragraph 1)

_____ 2. In the excerpt below, the word *ordeal* (ôr-dēl′) means
A. a pleasant experience.
B. a practical joke.
C. a physical examination.
D. a difficult or painful experience.

"Years later, his wife, with her fourth-grade education, would try to teach him to read. And still later I would grasp his big fist between my small hands and awkwardly help him trace the letters of his name. He submitted to the ordeal, but soon grew restless." (Paragraph 3)

Central Point and Main Ideas

_____ 3. Which sentence best expresses the main point of this selection?
A. Worthington's father worked hard all his life, but developed heart disease when he grew older.
B. Although Worthington's father never completed first grade, he was a skilled pipefitter and later worked in cotton mills.
C. Worthington's father, an illiterate, had unusually strong and capable hands.
D. Worthington's father's inability to read or write caused him great suffering and eventually led to his death.

_____ 4. Which sentence expresses the main idea of paragraphs 3–4?
A. As a married man, Worthington's father hated learning to read and write.
B. Although his wife and son tried to teach him to read and write, Worthington's father grew discouraged and stopped trying to learn.
C. Worthington once saw his father cry over his inability to read his second-grade reader.
D. Worthington's father preferred going for long, solitary walks to learning to read and write.

Supporting Details

_____ 5. The students in Worthington's father's first-grade class
A. all had difficulty learning to read and write.
B. laughed at Worthington's father for not knowing the correct answer.
C. were struck with a ruler for giving the wrong answer.
D. received extra help when they had difficulty learning.

_____ 6. Worthington's father was embarrassed when
A. his son caught him reading from a second-grade book.
B. he mistook a can of potatoes for a can of pears.
C. he was fired from his job as a pipefitter.
D. his grandchildren learned he was illiterate.

Transitions

_____ 7. The sentences below express a relationship of
A. contrast.
B. comparison.
C. time order.
D. cause and effect.

"After the shipyard closed, he went to the cotton mill, where he labored at night, and stole from his sleeping hours the time required to run the farm. When the mill shut down, he went out each morning looking for work . . . ." (Paragraph 6)

_____ 8. The relationship between the two sentences below is one of
A. illustration.
B. comparison.
C. addition.
D. contrast.

"The blue of his eyes faded; the skin across his cheekbones became a little slack. But his hands kept their strength, and their warmth still soaked through when he would sit me on his lap and ask me to read to him from the Bible." (Paragraph 8)

Patterns of Organization

_____ 9. Paragraph 1 primarily
A. lists several things that Worthington's father could do with his hands and the one thing he couldn't.
B. contrasts the good things Worthington's father did with his hands with the bad things he did with them.
C. presents things that Worthington's father did in time order.
D. provides a reason why Worthington's father never learned to write.

_____10. On the whole, the reading is organized as a
A. series of events, in time order, in the life of Worthington's father.
B. contrast between past attitudes and current attitudes toward disabilities.
C. list of details about the various jobs that Worthington's father held.
D. comparison between the author's life and that of his father.

Advanced Skill Questions

Inferences

_____11. In paragraph 2, Worthington implies that
A. his father was punished for having a learning disability.
B. we know more about learning disabilities now than when Worthington's father was a boy.
C. it was wrong of Worthington's grandfather to take his son out of school in the first grade.
D. all of the above.

_____12. We can infer from paragraph 5 that
A. people who cannot read or write may be highly skilled in other ways.
B. Worthington's father never became a line boss because he was illiterate.
C. Worthington's father was a valuable worker.
D. all of the above.

_____13. We can infer from paragraphs 10–11 that Worthington
A. was very disappointed that he could not have pears for dessert.
B. was trying to get his father's mind off the mistake he made about the can of potatoes.
C. did not respect his father because he could not read or write.
D. knew that his father would quickly forget the mistake he made in buying a can of potatoes rather than pears.

Purpose and Tone

_____14. The main purpose of this selection is to
A. inform readers of how being illiterate affected one man's life.
B. entertain us with a heartwarming life story of a beloved parent.
C. persuade us to support efforts to stamp out illiteracy.
D. predict how those with learning handicaps will be helped in the future.

_____15. In general, the author's tone is
A. objective.
B. loving.
C. lighthearted.
D. indignant.

Argument

_____16. Write the letter of the statement that is the point of the following argument. The other statements are support for that point.
A. Worthington's father was an excellent pipefitter during World War II.
B. Worthington's father could draw and saw a square with quick accuracy.
C. Worthington's father was skilled in work that required him to use his hands.
D. Worthington's father could gently prune a fruit tree or wrestle a mule into harness.

_____17. Which item does **not** support the following point?

Point: Worthington's father suffered because he could not read or write.

A. In first grade, he was hit with a ruler for giving the wrong answer.
B. He wept when he could not read his son's second-grade reader.
C. He worked as a pipefitter at a shipyard during World War II.
D. He died because he could not read the instructions on the bottle of nitroglycerin pills.

Critical Reading

_____18. The statement below is
A. a fact.
B. an opinion.
C. both fact and opinion.

"In grief, I stopped to trace my fingers in the earth where a great man had reached the end of his life." (Paragraph 15)

_____19. Which of the following is a statement of opinion?
A. He started first grade, where the remedy for a wrong answer was ten ruler strokes across a stretched palm.
B. During World War II, he was a pipefitter in a shipyard and installed the complicated guts of mighty fighting ships.
C. "The man that doesn't provide for his family is worse than a thief and an infidel and will never enter the kingdom of Heaven."
D. His health was failing, and he was in and out of the hospital with several mild heart attacks.

_____20. The following statement illustrates the logical fallacy of
A. circular reasoning.
B. false cause.
C. false comparison.
D. either-or.

"Our elementary school building is at least 70 years old. No wonder our kids aren't learning to read and write!"

Summarizing

Add the ideas needed to complete the following summary of "My Father's Hands."

His hands were strong and capable, but one thing Worthington's father could not do with them was write. When he struggled in first grade, his father pulled him out of school and put him to work on the family farm. Years later, his wife and son tried to teach him to read and write, but ____. During World War II, he became a pipefitter in a shipyard. Although he was an enthusiastic and efficient worker, he could not get promoted to line boss because ____. When the shipyard closed, he worked in a cotton mill. When that closed, he had a difficult time finding another job because of his illiteracy. In the meantime, he had to sell the family farm. Later, he got a job in another cotton mill and moved into a millhouse village. Although he always provided for his family, he wondered ____.

Years later, after Worthington's father had suffered several mild heart attacks, his doctor gave him nitroglycerin tablets to put under his tongue if he felt an attack coming on. When he died of another heart attack, Worthington found the unopened bottle of pills where he had fallen. Looking at the cap, which said "Child-Proof Cap—Push Down and Twist to Unlock," he realized that ____.

Discussion Questions

1. Why do you think that Worthington and his mother were unable to persuade Worthington's father to try to learn to read and write? Can you think of anything they could have done that might have had better results?

2. Worthington's father's first experience of learning to read was a bad one. Were your earliest experiences of learning to read generally positive—or negative? What made them so? Do you think these early experiences have influenced your present attitude toward reading? Explain.

3. How have attitudes toward people with learning disabilities changed since Worthington's father's time? Overall, do you think today's teachers are more helpful toward students who find reading difficult? Or is our educational system still failing them?

4. In your opinion, is illiteracy still a major problem in the United States? What evidence can you give for your answer? If you knew someone who you suspected might be illiterate, what could you do to help him or her?

Note: Writing assignments for this selection appear on page 704.

Check Your Performance — MY FATHER'S HANDS

Activity	*Number Right*	*Points*		*Score*
Basic Skill Questions				
Vocabulary in Context (2 items)	______	× 4	=	______
Central Point and Main Ideas (2 items)	______	× 4	=	______
Supporting Details (2 items)	______	× 4	=	______
Transitions (2 items)	______	× 4	=	______
Patterns of Organization (2 items)	______	× 4	=	______
Advanced Skill Questions				
Inferences (3 items)	______	× 4	=	______
Purpose and Tone (2 items)	______	× 4	=	______
Argument (2 items)	______	× 4	=	______
Critical Reading (3 items)	______	× 4	=	______
Summarizing (4 items)	______	× 5	=	______
		TOTAL SCORE	=	______%

Enter your total score into the **Reading Performance Chart: Ten Reading Selections** on the inside back cover.

5 Motivation and Needs

Virginia Quinn

Preview

If you had to choose between friendship and achievement, which would you pick? And how much security would you give up in order to avoid boredom? According to psychologist Abraham Maslow, we all would answer these questions in more or less the same way—because we all share the same basic human needs. In this selection from her textbook *Applying Psychology*, Virginia Quinn explains Maslow's view of human motivation and needs.

Words to Watch

hierarchy (2): a group arranged in order of rank
et al. (7): an abbreviation of a Latin phrase meaning "and others"
apathetic (7): having little interest
dispirited (7): discouraged
novelty (10): something new
fluctuate (10): alternate
affiliation (13): social connection
superficial (13): shallow
implications (15): inferences
refraining from (15): not using
capitalize on (18): take advantage of
spontaneous (31): behaving freely

1 Whether their motivation is conscious or unconscious, people have a broad range of needs. Some needs are shared by everyone. For example, everyone is motivated to stay alive and survive. Food, rest, oxygen, and other necessities for life are common to all people. Other needs vary from one person to the next. For example, some people need to drive a fancy sports car and wear designer clothes. Others may need to travel to far-off lands and live among different cultures. Undoubtedly, you have heard of individuals who had a need to climb high mountains or do missionary work in underdeveloped countries. Strangely, some people even feel a need to write psychological books!

2 Trying to sort and organize every possible need seems like a monstrous

task. Yet Abraham Maslow, one of the most important contributors to the field of motivation, managed to classify human needs or motivations into a pyramid-like hierarchy°. In order to progress upward to the top of the pyramid, you need to satisfy each need along the way.

3 At the base of his pyramid, Maslow placed everyday physiological needs required for survival—needs for food, drink, rest, elimination, etc. On the next level, Maslow put need for stimulation and escape from boredom. The need to explore and satisfy curiosity would be included on this second level. Safety and security needs follow. As you continue up his pyramid, you develop a need for love and a sense of belonging. At this fourth level, friendships become important. As you move to the upper levels of the hierarchy, you need to feel respected by others. The final level is reached by very few people. It involves carrying out one's total potential. Maslow labeled the top step of his hierarchy "self-actualization."

4 Maslow felt that people move up and down this pyramid throughout their lives. Indeed, people can move to different steps or needs on the pyramid within a single day. His pyramid is like a ladder you climb throughout your life. You must step on each rung to reach the next. But suppose a person is on a high rung. For example, a woman may have progressed to the point where she is looking for approval and self-esteem. Suddenly, a man points a gun at her. She will abruptly descend the hierarchy to satisfy her need for safety and security. Whenever a rung in the hierarchy "breaks," the person must return down to that level to satisfy the need. However, usually the person's progress back up to the higher level will occur rapidly.

In the next sections, you will focus 5
on what specifically is encountered at each step of Maslow's hierarchy of needs.

SURVIVAL NEEDS

Most Americans experience only a mild 6
form of survival need. Survival needs are biological necessities required to continue living. You may have believed yourself starving or dying of thirst. But chances are your needs were minimal when compared with people who had beyond doubt been without water or food for days.

During World War II, Keys et al.° 7
studied men who had been fed just enough to stay alive. They found that the men became preoccupied with food thoughts and fantasies. The men delighted in reading cookbooks and exchanging favorite recipes. They forgot about wives, girlfriends, and sex. They became apathetic°, dispirited°, and irritable.

There has been considerable evi- 8
dence that thirst needs are even stronger than hunger needs. When any physiological needs are not satisfied, personality changes generally result. Persons who have been without sleep for extended periods have been known to become anxious and hallucinate. Have you ever been in steady, persistent pain for a prolonged time? You probably noticed your own personality change.

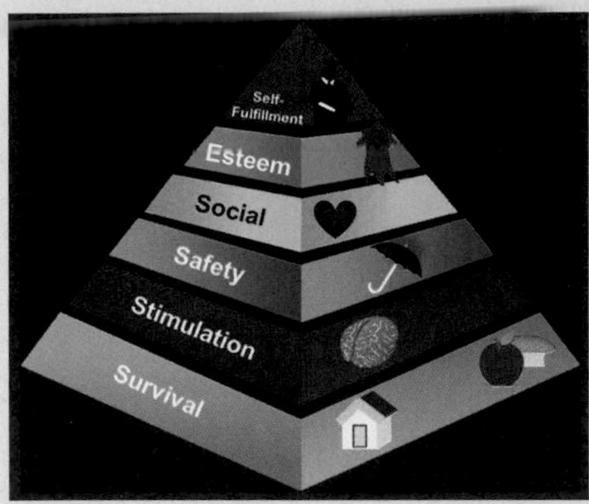

In all likelihood, you were easily irked and had difficulty concentrating. Your interest and motivation were concentrated on how to relieve yourself of some pain and become more comfortable.

9 Newborn infants are motivated on this lowest level of Maslow's hierarchy. Initially their concerns are biological. If newborn infants are provided with food, drink, and comfortable, restful surroundings where they are free from pain, their motivational needs will be satisfied. But not for long! Once this step is met, the infant quickly progresses to the next level, stimulation needs.

STIMULATION NEEDS

10 Just as the infant who is fed, rested, and comfortable begins to look for something of interest, all children and adults also seek ways to escape boredom. However, as you might have suspected, the rattles and mobiles that satisfy the infant's need for novelty° and stimulation rarely, if ever, excite interest in adults. As you grow older, your interests and stimulation needs change and fluctuate°. Maslow would consider that sexual interest, curiosity, and pleasure were stimulation needs. Although sexual activity is biological or physiological in nature, it is not essential for survival. Consequently, the need for sex is on the second step of Maslow's hierarchy and is classified as a stimulation or psychological need.

SAFETY AND SECURITY NEEDS

Chances are you take many precautions to be certain you are safe and secure. You live in some type of shelter, whether it be an apartment, a house, a teepee, or a barn. This shelter protects you from rain, snow, and other unfavorable elements. But undoubtedly, your motivations and concerns for safety and security extend well beyond your need for shelter. Do you have locks on your doors and windows? How about flashlights and hurricane lanterns? If you keep a spare tire in your car and maintain health and auto insurance, you are responding to your motivation to satisfy safety and security needs. Our country supports a national military force; towns and cities have police and fire departments. These people in uniform all attest to our needs for safety and security. 11

LOVE AND BELONGINGNESS NEEDS

The first three levels of Maslow's hierarchy may have seemed selfish to you. Indeed, the needs described are basic, self-centered, and narrow. Physiological, curiosity, and security needs may be satisfied without calling on other people. However, these basic needs must be met before the need for 12 other individuals can be recognized and accepted.

13 The needs for love and belongingness are sometimes called "affiliation° needs." If you have ever felt lonely or isolated, you have experienced a need to affiliate. Affiliation is not limited to romantic or parental love. You also need friends who accept you. There are immense differences in affiliation needs. Some people are satisfied with one or two close, deep friendships. Others crave superficial° relationships with large groups. Some fluctuate between group and individual friendships. Selection of friends usually changes with development.

14 At this level of the hierarchy, people look for ways to please others and win their approval. Most are selective, seeking acceptance from only certain friends and associates. It would clearly be impossible to win everyone's approval!

15 Clubs such as Alcoholics Anonymous and Weight Watchers are designed to motivate people through their need for affiliation and social approval. Many individuals drink or eat because they feel unwanted or lonely. Although eating and drinking are physiological needs, they are often also associated with affiliation. Whether we are enjoying a formal dinner party or a few beers with some friends, the purpose is not solely satisfying hunger and thirst needs. Alcoholics Anonymous and Weight Watchers recognize the social implications° of eating and drinking. The groups were formed to approve refraining from° alcohol and excessive food. To win acceptance from the groups, you must keep sober and thin.

Just as there are differences in the 16
type and number of friends needed, there are also wide variations in the intensity and strength of the need to belong and be accepted by others. Crowne and Marlowe developed a test to measure the need for social approval. They then used subjects who had either extremely high or extremely low scores on their tests. Next, the high and low scorers were asked to do a chore. They were told to put twelve spools in a box, lifting only one at a time. When the box was full, they had to empty it and repeat placing each spool back in the box. Sound like fun? Interestingly, the subjects who had high scores on the need-for-approval test claimed they enjoyed the task. They were also far more enthusiastic about the scientific usefulness of the experiment than were the low scorers. High scorers even stated they had learned something from the experiment. Evidently the low scorers had less need to be approved and could recognize a dull chore!

High needs for approval and 17
affiliation can also be identified through clothes. Sorority and fraternity pins, team or club windbreakers, and dressing alike are ways of demonstrating a need to belong. Adolescents often show remarkable conformity in their dress. Men and women who frequent singles bars or attend every mixer and dance usually have strong affiliation needs.

Advertisers capitalize on° the need 18
for love and belongingness. Many ads

begin with a negative appeal. Jim is lonely and disapproved of by everyone. He has either dandruff, messy hair, bald spots, bad breath, a bad odor, or ill-fitting underwear. However, after he uses the advertised product, his problem is solved and he gains popularity. The advertisers are appealing to your need for approval. They hope you will believe their product will gain you the same popularity as Jim. Check magazines, newspapers, and your television for this type of ad.

ESTEEM AND SELF-ESTEEM NEEDS

19 Once you feel approved of and accepted by others, you are prepared to progress to the next step in the hierarchy, esteem and self-esteem. At this level you seek what both Rodney Dangerfield and Charlie Brown never get, namely, "respect." To satisfy the need for esteem, you need more than acceptance and belonging. You have to be held in high regard and have some status in your group.

20 How can you convince others that you are worthy of their respect? Usually an outstanding achievement will win some praise and prestige. If you score a goal in a soccer game, win a beauty contest, create an outstanding mural, or produce a perfect exam paper, you will usually win the esteem of others. Achievements also improve your own self-esteem. When you convince others that you deserve respect, you also convince yourself.

21 **The need to achieve.** Clearly, esteem and self-esteem needs are related to each other. And achievements are a key way to satisfy the need for both. Achievements can be any accomplishment, from getting an office with a view or a personal secretary to maintaining the clearest complexion on campus. An achievement is a demonstration of success. Think of some achievements that you felt gave you status among others. Did you ever receive the highest grade on an exam or earn enough money for a car or an unusual vacation? Perhaps you have won a contest!

Some contests require an accomplishment, while others are based strictly on luck. Often people feel a sense of achievement in winning contests based more on chance than on actual accomplishments. Bingo and sweepstake addicts delight in the possibility of winning huge sums of money easily. Studies have shown that only rarely are these individuals strong achievers at work. Strong achievers usually want to feel personally responsible for their own success. 22

Games of chance do not require individual efforts. According to McClelland, people with strong needs for achievement like to use their own skills and want to improve themselves. They prefer tasks that require some effort but are not impossible. If they have control of their jobs and set their own goals, they feel more satisfied with themselves. A high achiever would prefer a game of chess to a game of poker. 23

Achievers usually set goals for themselves that everyone else will believe are 24 symbols or signs of success. They want to do well and enjoy getting positive feedback from others. Men and women with strong needs for achievement like to get pats on the back. Feedback from others is more important than money. Adams and Stone reported that high achievers will even spend their leisure time in activities that will reflect achievement.

25 Why do some people have strong needs for achievement? McClelland found that the need for achievement is related to parents' attitudes. Parents who are high achievers themselves usually demand independence from their children. The children must become self-reliant at a relatively early age. As a result, the children develop a sense of confidence and find enjoyment in their own achievements.

26 On the other hand, parents who have low needs for achievement are more protective of their children. They help their children perform everyday tasks such as dressing and feeding far more than necessary. Their children have less freedom and usually have low achievement needs.

27 **Fear of success.** What about people who are afraid to achieve? Psychologists believe the fear of success is usually related to a lower need, the need for love and belongingness. People who fear success are afraid they will lose valued friendships and affection if they become successful.

28 Horner was a pioneer in the study of fear of success in women. She gave college students one sentence and asked them to complete an essay. Male students were given the sentence: "After first-term finals, John finds himself at the top of his medical school class." Female students were given the same sentence, with the name "Ann" substituted for "John." The men had a positive attitude toward "John." Only about 10 percent of the male students had any negative comments. Interestingly, almost two-thirds of the women had a negative attitude toward "Ann." They described her as either unpopular and rejected, or a guilty cheat, or a hoax.

Recent studies by Maccoby and Jacklin and Monahan and Shaver have supported Horner's findings. In our society, fear of success is common among women. Successful competitive women are often not socially acceptable. Although more prevalent in women, fear of success has also been found to occur in men. Many men feel insecure about achieving and losing the friendship of their coworkers and their acquaintances in their own economic group. Again, from Maslow's point of view, unless the need for love and belonging is met fully, achievement will not be possible. 29

SELF-ACTUALIZATION

At last to the top of the pyramid! But only when every imaginable need has been met is a person ready for the maximum growth through self-actualization. Maslow himself had difficulty finding a precise definition for self-actualization. He felt that all people have some inner talents or abilities that they want to use or actualize. If all lower 30 needs are met, people can grow and develop by using these abilities. This growth is a continuous process that allows individuals to find self-fulfillment and realize their full potential.

31 In his attempt to identify some characteristics of people who have reached the level of self-actualization, Maslow studied the lives of forty-nine people that he believed to be self-actualizers. Among those studied were Albert Einstein, Eleanor Roosevelt, Abraham Lincoln, Thomas Jefferson, William James, and Jane Addams. Among the common characteristics of self-actualizers were:

- ***Honesty*** They have an ability to be objective and do not show selfish interest.
- ***Creativity*** They are spontaneous° and natural and enjoy trying new approaches.
- ***Acceptance*** They have total acceptance of themselves and are willing to accept others for what they are.
- ***Appreciation*** They possess an ability to become fully absorbed, enjoying even simple and basic experiences.
- ***Sense of humor*** They can recognize cleverness and whimsy and will laugh easily.
- ***Sensitivity*** They experience a deep feeling of sympathy for other people.

According to Maslow, self- 32
actualization is extremely rare. He screened about three thousand students and found only one self-actualized person. Although self-actualization is slightly more likely among older individuals, it is far from common. Most people never move above the level of esteem. They never reach self-actualization and fully develop their potential.

Slightly more common than self- 33
actualization are what Maslow called "peak experiences." A peak experience is an extremely brief, momentary sense of total happiness or fulfillment. For a few seconds or perhaps a minute, you have a sense of self-actualization. This feeling could come from such experiences as watching a spectacular sunset, holding a baby, running a marathon, creating a sculpture, or greeting a returned love. Peak experiences give the same feeling of aliveness and wholeness that self-actualizers encounter. However, the feeling ends abruptly.

Basic Skill Questions

Vocabulary in Context

_____ 1. In the excerpt below, the word *irked* (ûrkt) means
A. pleased.
B. informed.
C. annoyed.
D. entertained.

"Have you ever been in steady, persistent pain for a prolonged time? . . . In all likelihood, you were easily irked and had difficulty concentrating." (Paragraph 8)

_____ 2. In the excerpt below, the words *attest to* (ə-tĕst′ to͞o) mean
A. are evidence of.
B. remain ignorant.
C. become silent.
D. make complaints.

". . . towns and cities have police and fire departments. These people in uniform all attest to our needs for safety and security." (Paragraph 11)

Central Point and Main Ideas

_____ 3. Which sentence best expresses the central point of the selection?
A. Everyone has various needs to satisfy.
B. Motivation can be conscious or unconscious.
C. Maslow classified human motivations into six levels through which people progress.
D. The most fundamental needs, according to Maslow, are physiological survival needs.

_____ 4. Which sentence best expresses the main idea of paragraph 1?
A. Our motivations may be conscious or unconscious.
B. Some needs, such as the need to stay alive and survive, are shared by everyone.
C. Some needs, such as the need to drive a fancy sports car, vary from one person to the next.
D. People have a broad range of needs, some of which are shared by everyone and some of which vary from person to person.

_____ 5. The main idea of paragraph 18 is stated in its
A. first sentence.
B. second sentence.
C. third sentence.
D. last sentence.

Supporting Details

_____ 6. The first three levels of Maslow's hierarchy
A. depend on other people.
B. are self-centered.
C. are always fully met.
D. result in "peak experiences."

_____ 7. TRUE OR FALSE? According to Maslow, most people never reach the level of self-actualization.

Transitions

_____ 8. The transition beginning paragraph 26 signals
A. addition.
B. time.
C. contrast.
D. cause and effect.

_____ 9. The relationship of the second sentence below to the first is one of
A. addition.
B. illustration.
C. contrast.
D. cause and effect.

"The children must become self-reliant at a relatively early age. As a result, the children develop a sense of confidence and find enjoyment in their own achievements." (Paragraph 25)

Patterns of Organization

_____10. The pattern of organization of paragraph 31 is
A. a series of events.
B. steps in a process.
C. list of items.
D. cause and effect.

11. The term being defined in paragraph 33 is "____________________."

The paragraph provides *(how many?)* ________ examples of that term.

Advanced Skill Questions

Inferences

_____12. We can infer that Maslow's hierarchy is considered to be like a ladder because

A. ladders come in different heights.
B. Maslow was influenced by house-building techniques.
C. one can begin with the top need and work downward.
D. one must "climb" from the lower needs to the higher ones.

_____13. Paragraph 3 implies that Maslow felt

A. the need for love is as important as the need for survival.
B. a person is more likely to seek friendship than security.
C. curiosity is more fundamental than the need for safety.
D. people will seek respect before they seek food and drink.

_____14. From the reading we can conclude that

A. people's needs for esteem can be met in different ways.
B. upbringing greatly influences how people meet their needs for esteem.
C. people who have not met all their esteem needs may still enjoy peak experiences at times.
D. all of the above.

_____15. TRUE OR FALSE? From paragraphs 27–29, we might conclude that children who gain a strong sense of being loved and belonging are more likely than other children to seek success as adults.

Purpose and Tone

_____16. The main purpose of this selection is to

A. inform.
B. persuade.
C. entertain.

______17. From the tone of paragraph 2, we can infer that the author
A. is critical of Maslow's pyramid.
B. is amused by Maslow's pyramid.
C. accepts Maslow's pyramid.
D. rejects Maslow's pyramid.

Argument

18. Label the point of the following argument with a **P** and the two statements of support with an **S**. Label with an **X** the one statement that is neither the point nor the support of the argument.

___ A. Sexual interest and curiosity help fulfill adults' stimulation needs.

___ B. Sexual activity is not essential for survival.

___ C. Well-fed, comfortable babies may meet their stimulation needs with rattles and mobiles.

___ D. Our stimulation needs change throughout our lives.

Critical Reading

______19. The author's statement that Abraham Maslow is "one of the most important contributors to the field of motivation" (paragraph 2) is a statement of
A. fact.
B. opinion.

______20. TRUE OR FALSE? The statement below is an opinion.
"Some contests . . . are based strictly on luck." (Paragraph 22)

Mapping

Complete the map of "Motivation and Needs" by filling in the missing major and minor details. The missing items are listed in random order below the outline.

Central point: According to Abraham Maslow, there are six levels of human needs, each of which must be satisfied before proceeding to the next level.

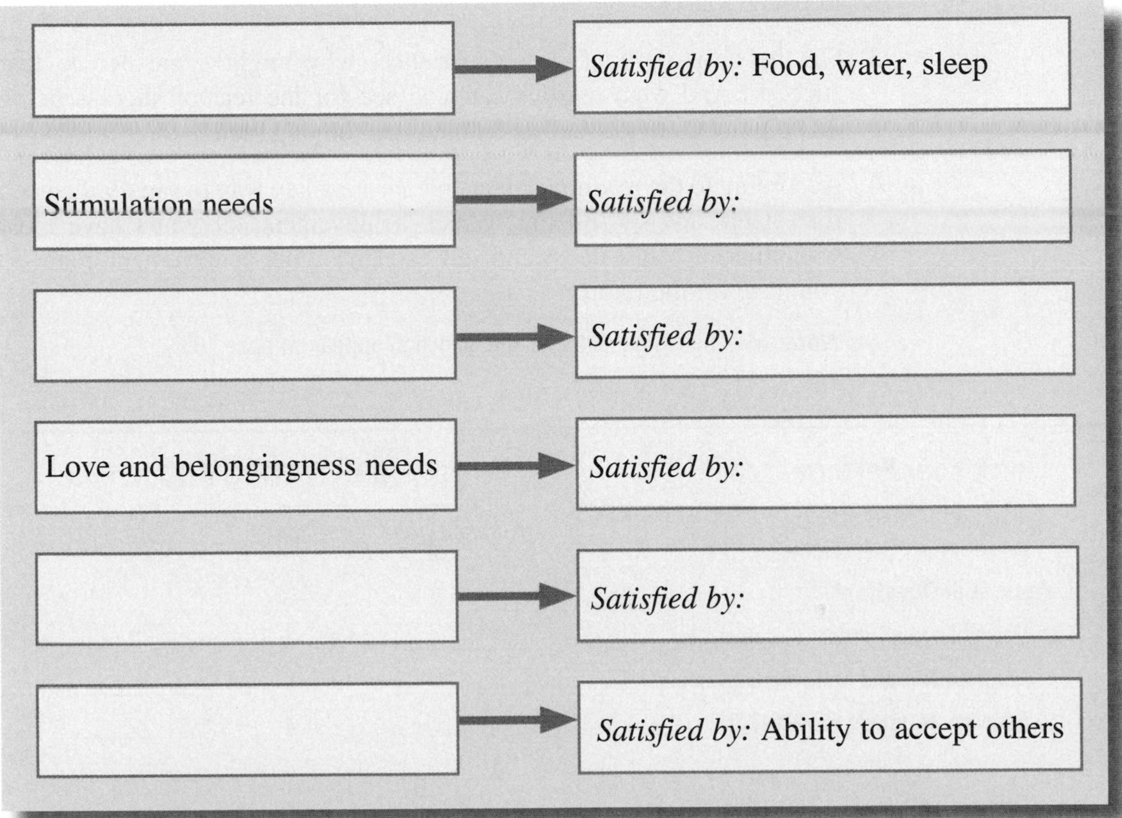

Items missing from the map:

- Self-actualization needs
- A baby's rattle
- Locks on doors
- A high grade on a test
- Survival needs
- Joining a club
- Safety and security needs
- Esteem and self-esteem needs

Discussion Questions

1. Do you know a workaholic, a compulsive gambler, a television addict, or a joiner? Which of Maslow's needs do you think each of these people is trying to meet?
2. What ads have you seen recently that appeal to our need for approval? Which ones begin with a "negative appeal," like the one Quinn describes in paragraph 18?
3. On the basis of your own experience, why might some people fear success? And what reasons can you see for the fear of success being much more common among women than among men?
4. According to the reading, achievements are a key way to satisfy the need for esteem and self-esteem. Which achievements of yours have most strengthened your esteem and self-esteem? What achievement goals do you have for the future?

Note: Writing assignments for this selection appear on page 705.

Check Your Performance — MOTIVATION AND NEEDS

Activity	*Number Right*	*Points*	*Score*
Basic Skill Questions			
Vocabulary in Context (2 items)	______	× 4 =	______
Central Point and Main Ideas (3 items)	______	× 4 =	______
Supporting Details (2 items)	______	× 4 =	______
Transitions (2 items)	______	× 4 =	______
Patterns of Organization (2 items)	______	× 4 =	______
Advanced Skill Questions			
Inferences (4 items)	______	× 4 =	______
Purpose and Tone (2 items)	______	× 4 =	______
Argument (1 item)	______	× 4 =	______
Critical Reading (2 items)	______	× 4 =	______
Mapping (8 items)	______	× 2.5 =	______
		TOTAL SCORE =	______%

Enter your total score into the **Reading Performance Chart: Ten Reading Selections** on the inside back cover.

6 Effects of the Automobile

James M. Henslin

Preview

"Well, of course cars have had an effect on society," you may be thinking. "They've allowed us to move from place to place much more easily." But like most important technological breakthroughs, the automobile has affected society in far more subtle ways than meet the eye. When you read this excerpt from the textbook *Sociology: A Down-to-Earth Approach*, you may be surprised to learn all the ways that the world we live in has been shaped by the automobile.

Words to Watch

in earnest (2): seriously
prospect (2): possibility
cumbersome (6): awkward
flourishing (6): thriving
urban sprawl (9): the spread of urban development into areas adjoining the city's edge
trysting (9): meeting
forays (12): attempts to leave one's usual area

1 If we try to pick the single item that has had the greatest impact on social life in the twentieth century, among the many candidates the automobile stands out. Let us look at some of the ways in which it changed U.S. society.

2 The automobile gradually pushed aside the old technology, a replacement that began in earnest° when Henry Ford began to mass-produce the Model T in 1908. People immediately found automobiles attractive. They considered them cleaner, safer, more reliable, and more economical than horses. Cars also offered the appealing prospect° of lower taxes, for no longer would the public have to pay to clean up the tons of horse manure that accumulated in the city streets each day. Humorous as it sounds now, it was even thought that automobiles would eliminate the cities' parking problems, for an automobile took up only half as much space as a horse and buggy.

The automobile also replaced a 3
second technology. The United States had developed a vast system of urban transit, with electric streetcar lines

radiating outward from the center of our cities. As the automobile became affordable and more dependable, Americans demonstrated a clear preference for the greater convenience of private transportation. Instead of walking to a streetcar and then having to wait in the cold and rain, people were able to travel directly from home on their own schedule.

4 The decline in the use of streetcars actually changed the shape of U.S. cities. Before the automobile, U.S. cities were web-shaped, for residences and businesses were located along the streetcar lines. When freed by automobiles from having to live so close to the tracks, people filled in the area between the "webs."

5 The automobile also stimulated mass suburbanization. Already in the 1920s, U.S. residents had begun to leave the city, for they found that they could commute to work in the city from outlying areas where they benefited from more room and fewer taxes. Their departure significantly reduced the cities' tax base, thus contributing to many of the problems that U.S. cities experience today.

6 The automobile had a profound impact on farm life and villages. Prior to the 1920s, most farmers were isolated from the city. Because using horses for a trip to town was slow and cumbersome°, they made such trips infrequently. By the 1920s, however, the popularity and low price of the Model T made the "Saturday trip to town" a standard event. There, farmers would market products, shop, and visit with friends. As a consequence, farm life was altered; for example, mail-order catalogs stopped being the primary source of shopping, and access to better medical care and education improved. Farmers were also able to travel to bigger towns, where they found a greater variety of goods. As farmers began to use the nearby villages only for immediate needs, these flourishing° centers of social and commercial life dried up.

7 The automobile's effects on commercial architecture are clear—from the huge parking lots that decorate malls like necklaces to the drive-up windows of banks and restaurants. But the automobile also fundamentally altered the architecture of U.S. homes. Before the car, each home had a stable in the back where the family kept its buggy and horses. The stable was the logical

place to shelter the family's first car, and it required no change in architecture. The change occurred in three steps. First, new homes were built with a detached garage located, like the stable, at the back of the home. Second, as the automobile became a more essential part of the U.S. family, the garage was incorporated into the home by moving it from the backyard to the side of the house, and connecting it to the house by a breezeway. In the final step, the breezeway was removed and the garage integrated into the home so that Americans could enter their automobiles without even going outside.

8 By the 1920s, the automobile was used extensively for dating. This removed children from the watchful eye of parents and undermined parental authority. The police began to receive complaints about "night riders" who parked their cars along country lanes, "doused their lights, and indulged in orgies." Automobiles became so popular for courtship that by the 1960s about 40 percent of marriage proposals took place in them.

9 In 1925 Jewett introduced cars with a foldout bed, as did Nash in 1937. The Nash version became known as "the young man's model." Since the 1970s, mobile lovemaking has declined, partly because urban sprawl° (itself due to the automobile) left fewer safe trysting° spots, and partly because changed sexual norms made beds more accessible.

10 The automobile may also lie at the heart of the changed role of women in U.S. society. To see how, we first need to see what a woman's life was like before the automobile. Historian James Flink described it this way:

> *Until the automobile revolution, in upper-middle-class households, groceries were either ordered by phone and delivered to the door or picked up by domestic servants or the husband on his way home from work. Iceboxes provided only very limited space for the storage of perishable foods, so shopping at markets within walking distance of the home was a daily chore. The garden provided vegetables and fruits in season, which were home-canned for winter consumption. Bread, cakes, cookies, and pies were home-baked. Wardrobes contained many home-sewn garments.* 11
>
> *Mother supervised the household help and worked alongside them, preparing meals, washing and ironing, and house cleaning. In her spare time she mended clothes, did decorative needlework, puttered in her flower garden, and pampered a brood of children. Generally, she made few family decisions and few forays° alone outside the yard. She had little knowledge of family finances and the family budget. The role of the lower-middle-class housewife differed primarily in that far less of the household work was done by hired help, so that she was less a manager of other people's work, more herself a maid-of-all-work around the house.* 12

Because automobiles required skill rather than strength, women were able to drive as well as men. This new mobility freed women physically from the narrow confines of the home. 13

As Flink observed, the automobile changed women "from producers of food and clothing into consumers of national-brand canned goods, prepared foods, and ready-made clothes. The automobile permitted shopping at self-serve supermarkets outside the neighborhood, and in combination with the electric refrigerator made buying food a weekly rather than a daily activity." When women began to do the shopping, they gained greater control over the family budget, and as their horizons extended beyond the confines of the home, they also gained different views of life.

14 In short, the automobile changed women's roles at home, including their relationship with their husbands, altered their attitudes, transformed their opportunities, and stimulated them to participate in areas of social life not connected with the home.

With changes this extensive, it would not be inaccurate to say that the automobile also shifted basic values and changed the way we look at life. No longer isolated, women, teenagers, and farmers began to see the world differently. So did husbands and wives, whose marital relationship had also been altered. The automobile even transformed views of courtship, sexuality, and gender relations. 15

No one attributes such fundamental changes solely to the automobile, of course, for many historical events, as well as other technological changes, occurred during this same period, each making its own contribution to social change. Even this brief overview of the social effects of the automobile, however, illustrates that technology is not merely an isolated tool but exerts a profound influence on social life. 16

Basic Skill Questions

Vocabulary in Context

_____ 1. In the sentence below, the word *confines* (kŏn′fīnz′) means

A. thrills.
B. limits.
C. bedrooms.
D. emotional attachments.

"This new mobility freed women physically from the narrow confines of the home." (Paragraph 13)

Central Point and Main Ideas

_____ 2. Which sentence best expresses the central point of the selection?
A. The automobile has been the source of all social change during the twentieth century.
B. Automobiles are responsible for the decline of traditional farm communities.
C. The automobile has had a profound impact on American culture and society.
D. Women's liberation could never have occurred without the automobile.

_____ 3. The main idea of paragraphs 2 and 3 is stated in the
A. first sentence of paragraph 2.
B. last sentence of paragraph 2.
C. first sentence of paragraph 3.
D. second sentence of paragraph 3.

_____ 4. The main idea of paragraph 4 is
A. stated in its first sentence.
B. stated in its second sentence.
C. stated in its third sentence.
D. unstated.

_____ 5. The main idea of paragraph 6 is stated in its
A. first sentence.
B. second sentence.
C. third sentence.
D. last sentence.

_____ 6. Which sentence best expresses the implied main idea of paragraph 7?
A. The automobile had numerous important effects.
B. The automobile affected both commercial and home architecture.
C. The automobile led to huge parking lots and drive-up windows.
D. At first, the stable was the logical place to keep the automobile.

_____ 7. Which sentence best expresses the implied main idea of paragraph 13?
A. Being physically strong is not a necessity when it comes to driving a car.
B. Before the invention of the car, women produced more of their own food.
C. Men's authority was not affected as the result of the automobile.
D. The automobile transformed women's lives in several ways.

Supporting Details

_____ 8. According to the author, the automobile changed the shape of U.S. cities because

A. cars severely damaged the old cobblestone and dirt streets.
B. auto accidents required the installation of traffic lights.
C. many buildings were demolished in order to build wider streets.
D. cars enabled residents to settle in areas away from streetcar tracks.

_____ 9. Villages near farming families lost their place as "centers of social and commercial life" because

A. farmers could not afford to shop in those centers after buying cars.
B. farmers used mail-order catalogs instead of shopping in the nearby villages.
C. once they had cars, farmers could drive to the city both to socialize and to shop.
D. there wasn't enough room in the nearby villages to park the farmers' cars.

Transitions

_____10. The relationship expressed in the sentence below is one of

A. comparison.
B. illustration.
C. contrast.
D. cause and effect.

"Their departure significantly reduced the cities' tax base, thus contributing to many of the problems that U.S. cities experience today." (Paragraph 5)

Patterns of Organization

_____11. The selection mainly

A. presents a definition with many kinds of examples.
B. narrates a series of events in time order.
C. discusses many different effects that had the same cause.
D. compares and contrasts the automobile with other new technologies.

_____12. Paragraph 2 in large part

A. compares the use of horses and cars.
B. contrasts people's views of horses and cars.
C. lists modes of transportation.
D. defines and illustrates a new term.

Advanced Skill Questions

Inferences

_____13. From the sentences below, we might conclude that
- A. before the 1920s, arranged marriages were common in the U.S.
- B. before the 1920s, most dating was done in the home.
- C. people married at a younger age before the 1920s than after it
- D. the practice of dating was almost unknown before the 1920s.

"By the 1920s, the automobile was used extensively for dating. This removed children from the watchful eye of parents and undermined parental authority." (Paragraph 8)

_____14 We might conclude after reading paragraph 13 that
- A. women were at first reluctant to try out the new automotive technology.
- B. men welcomed the changes that the automobile created in women's lives.
- C. the introduction of the car made women less dependent on their husbands.
- D. women grew more socially conservative as a result of the introduction of the car.

Purpose and Tone

_____15. The author's main purpose is to
- A. inform readers of ways in which the introduction of the automobile affected U.S. society.
- B. persuade readers that the automobile was the only important influence on social life in the twentieth century.
- C. entertain readers with anecdotes about why people loved the automobile when it first appeared.

_____16. From the tone of paragraphs 10 and 13, we can conclude that the author
- A. is skeptical about Flink's conclusions.
- B. disagrees with Flink's observations.
- C. is scornful of Flink's scholarship.
- D. accepts Flink's observations.

Argument

17. The following argument is based on the reading. Label the point of the argument with a P and the two statements of support with an S.

   ___ A. The automobile has made people less community-oriented and more independent.

   ___ B. People travel outside their neighborhoods for shopping and entertainment.

   ___ C. Instead of using public transportation to commute to work with their neighbors, people drive alone in cars.

______18. The point below is followed by four statements, three of which logically support the point. Which of the statements does **not** support the point of the argument?

Point: The automobile affected the way that the United States looks.

A. Houses are now built with garages attached.
B. Shopping centers are surrounded by huge parking lots.
C. Once they could drive, women began to make more family decisions.
D. Suburban developments have grown to house people who commute long distances to work.

Critical Reading

______19. The sentence below is
A. a fact.
B. an opinion.
C. both fact and opinion.

"Already in the 1920s, U.S. residents had begun to leave the city, for they found that they could commute to work in the city from outlying areas where they benefited from more room and fewer taxes." (Paragraph 5)

______20. An ad for Toyota Camry that calls it the best-selling car in America is using the propaganda technique of
A. transfer.
B. plain folks.
C. glittering generalities.
D. bandwagon.

Summarizing

Add the five ideas needed to complete this summary of "Effects of the Automobile." Read the entire passage before deciding what fits in each blank.

The automobile quickly replaced two technologies: ______________________ ______________________. The decline of streetcars affected the appearance of cities because residents no longer had to live close to streetcar lines. Many residents left the cities for the suburbs, attracted by the suburbs' greater space and ______________________. The lives of farmers were dramatically changed, as they could now easily travel to distant towns to market products, shop, or visit friends. As a result, local villages dried up. The automobile affected both commercial and residential architecture. For instance, businesses installed large parking lots and drive-up windows. Houses were now built with attached garages. By the 1920s, the car was used extensively for dating, thus increasing freedom for young people and undermining the authority of ______________________. The automobile may also lie at the heart of the changed role of women in U.S. society. Before the advent of automobiles, women did their shopping on a daily basis at stores that were within walking distance of their homes. They produced a good deal of their own food and often sewed the family's clothes. The use of the automobile changed ______________________ from producers of food and clothing into consumers of store-bought food and clothing. As a result, women gained greater control over the family budget. The automobile led to the end of isolation for women, teenagers, and farmers, thus illustrating that changes in ______________________ have a profound effect on social life.

Discussion Questions

1. The author lists numerous effects of the automobile, but does he think any of those effects are positive or negative? Look at the reading and try to determine the author's opinion of the various effects he describes.

2. Most people's lives would be different without the automobile and its automotive "relatives," such as the van, truck, bus, tractor, and motorcycle. How would your life change if there were suddenly no automobiles?

3. The selection explains that domestic chores were greatly changed with the introduction of the car and the electric refrigerator. Give some examples of other technological inventions that have changed domestic chores.

4. The passage argues that the automobile stands out as a candidate for the "single item that has had the greatest impact on social life in the twentieth century." Can you think of another item that has also had—or will have—a tremendous impact on society? What is it, and what are some of its more important effects?

Note: Writing assignments for this selection appear on page 705.

Check Your Performance

EFFECTS OF THE AUTOMOBILE

Activity	*Number Right*	*Points*		*Score*
Basic Skill Questions				
Vocabulary in Context (1 item)	______	× 4	=	______
Central Point and Main Ideas (6 items)	______	× 4	=	______
Supporting Details (2 items)	______	× 4	=	______
Transitions (1 item)	______	× 4	=	______
Patterns of Organization (2 items)	______	× 4	=	______
Advanced Skill Questions				
Inferences (2 items)	______	× 4	=	______
Purpose and Tone (2 items)	______	× 4	=	______
Argument (2 items)	______	× 4	=	______
Critical Reading (2 items)	______	× 4	=	______
Summarizing (5 items)	______	× 4	=	______
		TOTAL SCORE	=	______%

Enter your total score into the **Reading Performance Chart: Ten Reading Selections** on the inside back cover.

7 Two Main Forms of Scientific Inquiry

Neil A. Campbell, Jane B. Reece, and others

Preview

In the attempt to understand the mysteries of our world (and beyond), we typically do two things. We observe to make discoveries, and then we experiment to explain our observations. However, science is not always as straightforward as these two types of "scientific inquiry" would suggest. Sometimes we have to think outside the experimental box.

Words to Watch

genome (2): a set of chromosomes, often studied by scientists to understand genetics
distill (3): condense and extract
diversification (9): the creation of many different types
extrapolate (12): to use known facts in order to draw conclusions about something unknown
criteria (14): standards for judging things
scenario (16): situation

1 The word *science* is derived from a Latin verb meaning "to know." Science is a way of knowing about the natural world. It developed out of our curiosity about ourselves, other life forms, our planet, and the universe. Striving to understand seems to be one of our basic urges.

2 At the heart of science is **inquiry**, a search for information and explanation, often focusing on specific questions. Inquiry drove Darwin to seek answers in nature for how species adapt to their environments. And today inquiry drives the genome° analyses that are helping us understand biological unity and diversity at the molecular level. In fact, the inquisitive mind is the engine that drives all progress in biology.

There is no formula for successful 3
scientific inquiry, no single scientific method with a rule book that researchers must rigidly follow. As in all quests, science includes elements of challenge, adventure, and luck, along with careful planning, reasoning, creativity, cooperation, competition, patience, and

the persistence to overcome setbacks. Such diverse elements of inquiry make science far less structured than most people realize. That said, it is possible to distill° certain characteristics that help to distinguish science from other ways of describing and explaining nature.

4 Biologists use two main types of scientific inquiry: discovery science and hypothesis-based science. Discovery science is mostly about *describing* nature. Hypothesis-based science is mostly about *explaining* nature. Most scientific inquiries combine these two research approaches.

DISCOVERY SCIENCE

5 Sometimes called descriptive science, **discovery science** describes natural structures and processes as accurately as possible through careful observation and analysis of data. For example, it is discovery science that has built our understanding of cell structure, and it is discovery science that is expanding our databases of genomes of diverse species.

Types of Data

6 Observation is the use of the senses to gather information, either directly or indirectly with the help of tools such as microscopes that extend our senses. Recorded observations are called **data**. Put another way, data are items of information on which scientific inquiry is based.

7 The term *data* implies numbers to many people. But some data are *qualitative*, often in the form of recorded descriptions rather than numerical measurements. For example, Jane Goodall spent decades recording her observations of chimpanzee behavior during field research in a Gambian jungle. She also documented her observations with photographs and movies. Along with these qualitative data, Goodall also enriched the field of animal behavior with volumes of *quantitative* data, which are generally recorded as measurements. Skim through any of the scientific journals in your college library, and you'll see many examples of quantitative data organized into tables and graphs.

Induction in Discovery Science

Discovery science can lead to important conclusions based on a type of logic called induction, or **inductive reasoning**. Through induction, we derive generalizations from a large number of specific observations. "The sun always rises in the east" is an example. And so is "All organisms are made of cells." The latter generalization, part of the so-called cell theory, was based on two centuries of biologists discovering cells in the diverse biological specimens they observed with microscopes. The careful observations and data analyses of discovery science, along with the generalizations reached by induction, are fundamental to our understanding of nature. 8

HYPOTHESIS-BASED SCIENCE

The observations and inductions of discovery science stimulate us to seek natural causes and explanations for those observations. What *caused* the diversification° of finches on the Galapagos Islands? What *causes* the roots of a plant seedling to grow 9 downward and the leaf-bearing shoot to grow upward? What *explain*s the generalization that the sun always rises in the east? In science, such inquiry usually involves the proposing and testing of hypothetical explanations — that is, hypotheses.

The Role of Hypotheses in Inquiry

10 In science, a **hypothesis** is a tentative answer to a well-framed question—an explanation on trial. It is usually an educated guess, based on experience and on the data available from discovery science. A scientific hypothesis leads to predictions that can be tested by making additional observations or by performing experiments.

11 We all use hypotheses in solving everyday problems. Let's say, for example, that your flashlight fails during a camp-out. That's an observation. The question is obvious: Why doesn't the flashlight work? Two reasonable hypotheses based on your experience are that (1) the batteries in the flashlight are dead or (2) the bulb is burnt out. Each of these alternative hypotheses makes predictions you can test with experiments. For example, the dead-battery hypothesis predicts that replacing the batteries will fix the problem. **Figure 1.24** [on the next page] diagrams this campground inquiry. Of course, we rarely dissect our thought processes this way when we are solving a problem using hypotheses, predictions, and experiments. But hypothesis-based science clearly has its origins in the human tendency to figure out by trial and error.

Deduction: The "If ... Then" Logic of Hypothesis-Based Science

A type of logic called deduction is built 12
into the hypothesis-based science. Deduction contrasts with induction, which, remember, is reasoning from a set of specific observations to reach a general conclusion. In **deductive reasoning,** the logic flows in the opposite direction from the general to the specific. From general premises, we extrapolate° to the specific results we should expect if the premises are true. If all organisms are made of cells (premise 1), and humans are organisms (premise 2), then humans are composed of cells (deductive prediction about a specific case).

In hypothesis-based science, 13
deductions usually take the form of predictions of experimental or observational results that will be found if a particular hypothesis (premise) is correct. We then test the hypothesis by carrying out the experiments or observations to see whether or not the results are as predicted. This deductive testing takes the form of "*If ... then*" logic. In the case of the flashlight example: *If* the dead-battery hypothesis is correct, and you replace the batteries with new ones, *then* the flashlight should work.

A Closer Look at Hypotheses in Scientific Inquiry

The flashlight example illustrates 14
two important qualities of scientific hypotheses. First, a hypothesis must be *testable*; there must be some way to check the validity of the idea. Second, a hypothesis must be *falsifiable*;

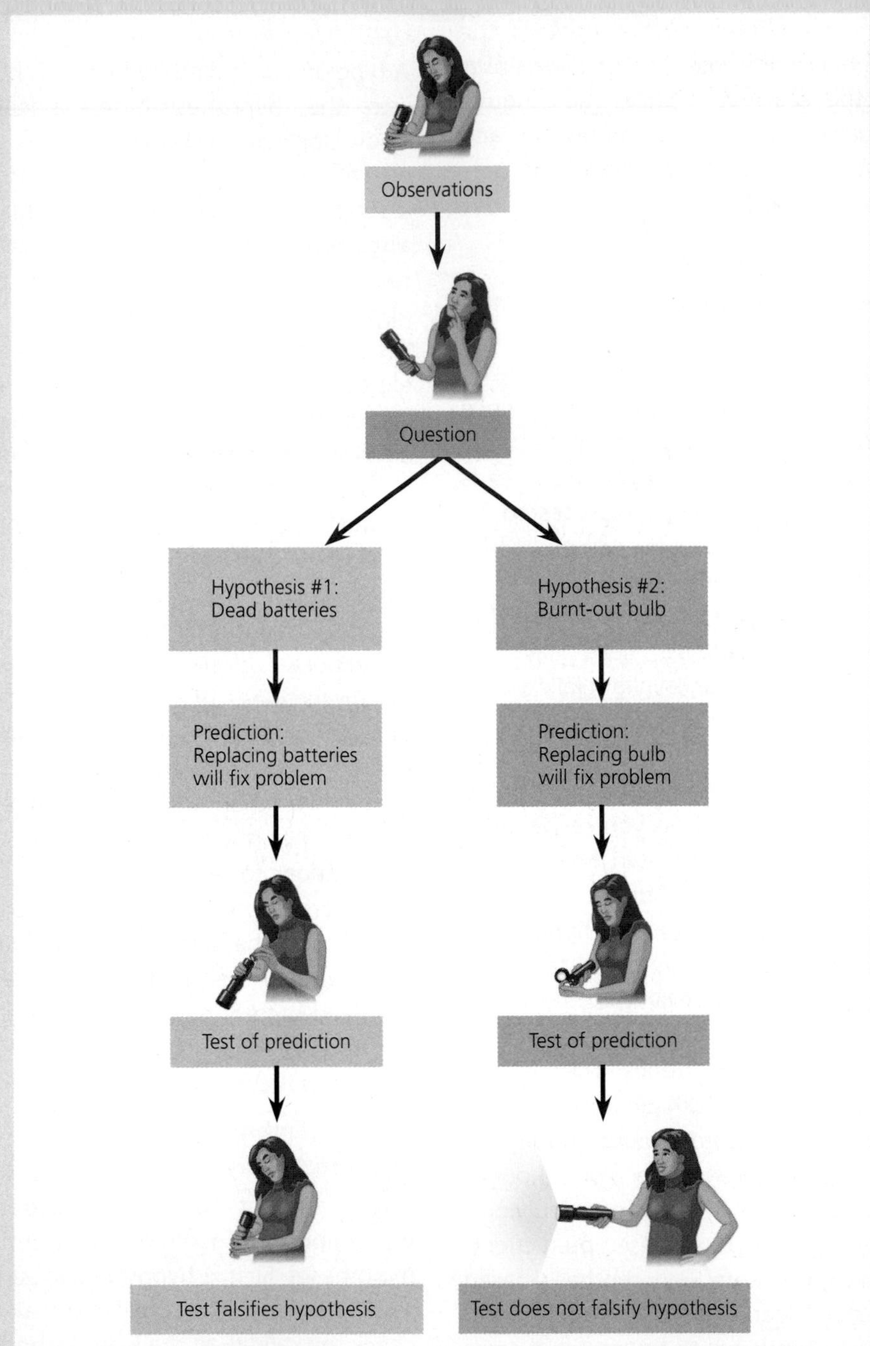

Figure 1.24 A campground example of hypothesis-based inquiry.

there must be some observation or experiment that could reveal if such an idea is actually not true. The hypothesis that dead batteries are the sole cause of the broken flashlight could be falsified by replacing the old batteries with new ones and finding that the flashlight still doesn't work. Not all hypotheses meet the criteria° of science: Try to devise a test to falsify the hypothesis that invisible campground ghosts are fooling with your flashlight!

15 The flashlight inquiry illustrates another key point about hypothesis-based science. The ideal is to frame two or more alternative hypotheses and design experiments to falsify those candidate explanations. In addition to the two explanations tested in Figure 1.24, another of the many possible alternative hypotheses is that *both* the batteries *and* the bulb are bad. What does this hypothesis predict about the outcome of experiments in Figure 1.24? What additional experiment would you design to test this hypothesis of multiple malfunction?

16 We can mine the flashlight scenario° for still one more important lesson about hypothesis-based science. Although the burnt-out bulb hypothesis stands up as the most likely explanation, notice that the testing supports that hypothesis not by proving that it is correct, but by not eliminating it through falsification: Perhaps the bulb was simply loose, and the new bulb was inserted correctly. We could attempt to falsify the burnt-out bulb hypothesis by trying another experiment—removing the bulb and carefully reinstalling it. But no amount of experimental testing can *prove* a hypothesis beyond a shadow of doubt, because it is impossible to test *all* alternative hypotheses. A hypothesis gains credibility by surviving attempts to falsify it while testing eliminates (falsifies) alternative hypotheses.

The Myth of the Scientific Method

The flashlight example of Figure 17
1.24 traces an idealized process of inquiry called the *scientific method.* We can recognize the elements of this process in most of the research articles published by scientists, but rarely in such structured form. Very few scientific inquiries adhere rigidly to the sequence of steps prescribed by the "textbook" scientific method. For example, a scientist may start to design an experiment, but then backtrack upon realizing that more observations are necessary. In other cases, puzzling observations simply don't prompt well-defined questions until other research places those observations in a new context. For example, Darwin collected specimens of the Galapagos finches, but it wasn't until years later, as the idea of natural selection began to gel, that biologists began asking key questions about the history of those birds.

Moreover, scientists sometimes 18
redirect their research when they realize they have been asking the wrong question. For example, in the early 20th century much research on schizophrenia and manic-depressive disorder (now called bipolar disorder) got sidetracked by focusing too much on the question of how life experiences

might cause these serious maladies. Research on the cases and potential treatments became more productive when it was refocused on questions of how certain chemical imbalances in the brain contribute to mental illness. To be fair, we acknowledge that such twists and turns in scientific inquiry become more evident with the advantage of historical perspective.

19 There is still another reason that good science need not conform exactly to any one method of inquiry: Discovery science has contributed much to our understanding of nature without most of the steps of the so-called scientific method.

20 It is important for you to get some experience with the power of the scientific method—by using it for some of the laboratory inquiries in your biology course, for example. But it is also important to avoid stereotyping science as lock-step adherence to this method.

Basic Skill Questions

Vocabulary in Context

_____ 1. In the excerpt below, the word *tentative* (tĕn′tə-tĭv) means

A. definite.
B. reluctant.
C. possible.
D. complicated.

"In science, a **hypothesis** is a tentative answer to a well-framed question—an explanation on trial. It is usually an educated guess, based on experience and on the data available from discovery science. A scientific hypothesis leads to predictions that can be tested by making additional observations or by performing experiments." (Paragraph 10)

_____ 2. In the excerpt below, *credibility* (krĕd′ə-bĭl′ĭ-tē) means

A. believability.
B. confusion.
C. momentum.
D. popularity.

"We could attempt to falsify the burnt-out bulb hypothesis by trying another experiment—removing the bulb and carefully reinstalling it. But no amount of experimental testing can *prove* a hypothesis beyond a shadow of doubt, because it is impossible to test *all* alternative hypotheses. A hypothesis gains credibility by surviving attempts to falsify it while testing eliminates (falsifies) alternative hypotheses." (Paragraph 16)

_____ 3. In the excerpt below, the words *lock-step adherence* (lŏk stĕp ad-hêr′əns) mean

A. looking up.
B. giving in.
C. referring loosely.
D. sticking strictly.

"It is important for you to get some experience with the power of the scientific method—by using it for some of the laboratory inquiries in your biology course, for example. But it is also important to avoid stereotyping science as lock-step adherence to this method." (Paragraph 20)

Central Point and Main Ideas

_____ 4. Which sentence below best expresses the central point of this selection?

A. Although there are two definite forms of scientific inquiry, most scientists feel there should be more than two.
B. When it comes to science, we discover things by observing and experimenting.
C. Scientific inquiry is defined as using discovery or hypothesis methods.
D. Use of hypotheses and the "scientific method" are important to learn, but we shouldn't stereotype science by thinking that's all science is.

_____ 5. The main idea of paragraphs 3 and 4 is that

A. although there is no set "rule book" for scientific inquiry, scientists tend to use two main types of inquiry.
B. methods for scientific exploration and discovery are actually quite a bit less structured than most people think.
C. most questions about the world around us are approached by combining discovery science and hypothesis-based science.
D. many people are surprised to realize that science involves elements of adventure, luck, challenge, and creativity.

_____ 6. The main idea of paragraphs 14 and 15 is that

A. if it is impossible for a hypothesis to be proven false, then that hypothesis does not meet the criteria of science.
B. a hypothesis must be both testable and falsifiable.
C. you must be able to test and falsify a hypothesis in order to hope to prove it, and sometimes the answer lies in several tests and falsifications.
D. the flashlight scenario is an oversimplified example of using the hypothesis method, since the answers to most scientific questions are far more complex.

Supporting Details

_____ 7. ___________ reasoning reaches a conclusion by going from the general to the specific, while ___________ reasoning examines specific details in order to reach a general conclusion.
A. scientific, hypothetical
B. deductive, inductive
C. logical, illogical
D. credible, false

_____ 8. TRUE OR FALSE? In her study of chimpanzees, Jane Goodall recorded numerous descriptions of the animals, but she did not create any charts or graphs measuring the physical qualities of chimps.

_____ 9. A hypothesis must be
A. testable and falsifiable.
B. proven and unquestionable.
C. tentative and credible.
D. considered true until proven false.

Transitions

_____10. The relationship of the third sentence below to the first two is one of
A. contrast.
B. comparison.
C. addition.
D. illustration.

"The flashlight example illustrates two important qualities of scientific hypotheses. First, a hypothesis must be *testable*; there must be some way to check the validity of the idea. Second, a hypothesis must be *falsifiable*; there must be some observation or experiment that could reveal if such an idea is actually not true." (Paragraph 14)

_____11. The two sentences below express a relationship of
A. contrast.
B. comparison.
C. cause and effect.
D. illustration.

"It is important for you to get some experience with the power of the scientific method—by using it for some of the laboratory inquiries in your biology course, for example. But it is also important to avoid stereotyping science as lock-step adherence to this method." (Paragraph 20)

Patterns of Organization

_____12. The main pattern of organization of paragraphs 4–8 of the selection is
A. list of items.
B. cause and effect.
C. definition and example.
D. time order.

Advanced Skill Questions

Inferences

_____13. This selection suggests that
A. science can be more interesting and, possibly, more successful when one does not follow *only* the exact steps of scientific method.
B. scientists are often reluctant to search for more than two falsifiers when testing a hypothesis.
C. generally speaking, discovery science is not as successful as hypothesis-based science in making advances in science.
D. the "if . . . then" logic of hypothesis-based science is often flawed and should be avoided.

_____14. On the basis of paragraph 7, we can infer that
A. research into animal behavior is best done in the animal's natural environment.
B. Good scientists back up their observations with documentary proof.
C. Goodall made an important contribution to the field of animal behavior.
D. all of the above.

Purpose and Tone

_____15. TRUE OR FALSE? The main purpose of this selection is, primarily, to inform readers about the two main types of scientific inquiry and, secondarily, to persuade them not to conform to any one method of inquiry.

_____16. The authors' tone in the sentence below is
A. serious.
B. curious.
C. critical.
D. lighthearted.

"Not all hypotheses meet the criteria of science: Try to devise a test to falsify the hypothesis that invisible campground ghosts are fooling with your flashlight!" (Paragraph 14)

Argument

_____17. Write the letter of the statement that is the point of the following argument. The other statements are support for that point.
A. There is no single formula for successful scientific inquiry.
B. Discovery science has contributed much to our understanding of nature without most of the steps of the so-called scientific method.
C. A scientist may start to design an experiment, but then backtrack upon realizing that more observations are necessary.
D. Scientists sometimes redirect their research when they realize they have been asking the wrong question.

Critical Reading

_____18. TRUE OR FALSE? A hypothesis is an opinion based upon as many relevant facts as possible.

_____19. The sentence below is
A. a fact.
B. an opinion.

"Jane Goodall spent decades recording her observations of chimpanzee behavior during field research in a Gambian jungle." (Paragraph 7)

_____20. A scientist notes that a certain species of fish has disappeared from a lake not long after a tornado occurred and then states, "The fish were thriving before the tornado. Clearly, the tornado caused the disappearance of this species." Which logical fallacy does her statement contain?
A. False comparison
B. Straw man
C. Circular reasoning
D. False cause

Mapping

Complete the map of "Two Main Forms of Scientific Inquiry" by filling in the missing details.

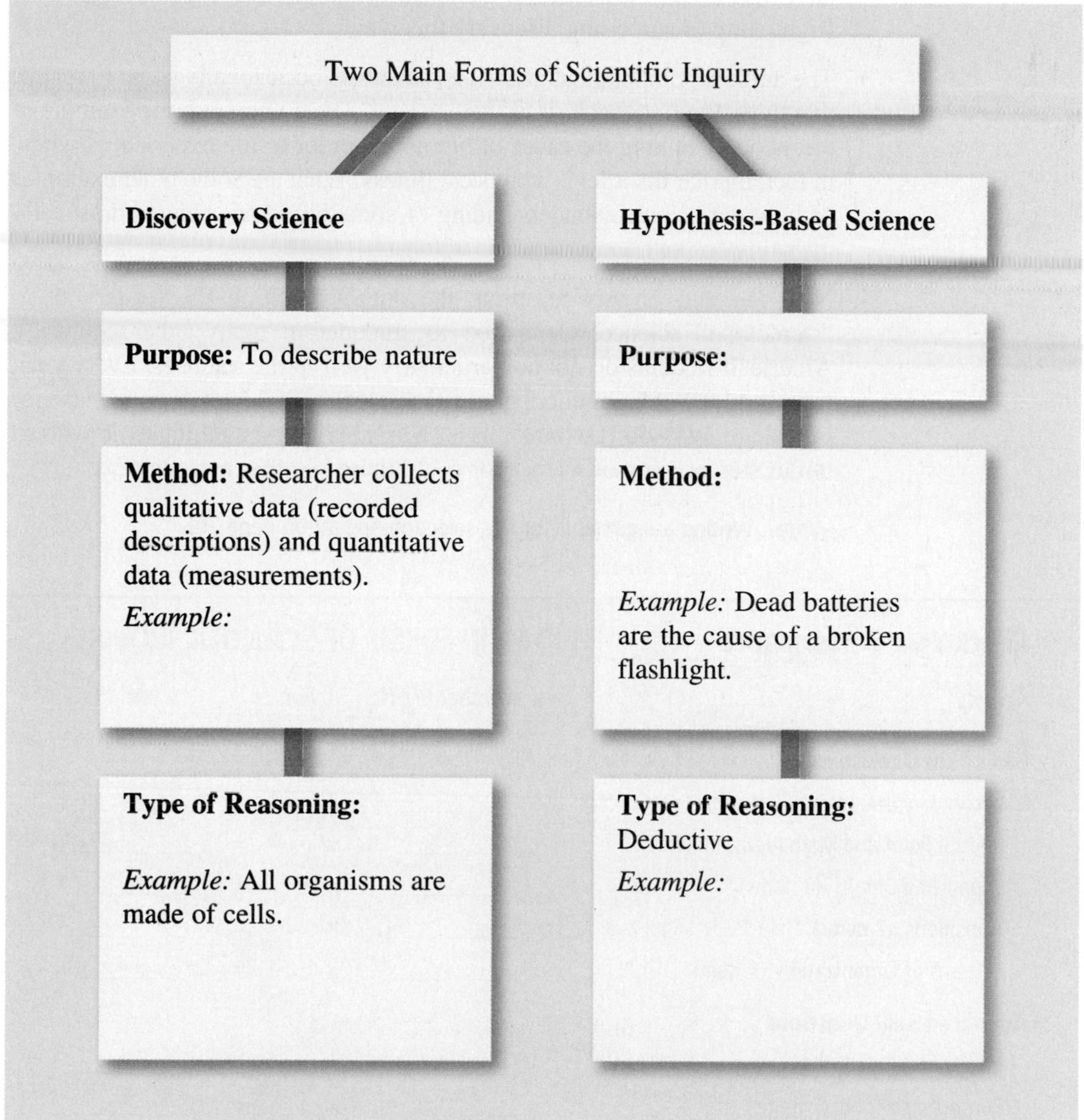

Discussion Questions

1. What are some everyday problems that require you to form a hypothesis and then test your hypothesis in order to solve the problem? Can you think of a time when you had to test and falsify several different possible answers before finding the solution?

2. Whether or not we're collecting scientific information, we've all participated in discovery science by way of observation. The authors describe observation as "the use of the senses to gather information." When and how have you used your senses to gather information? Have you ever made a frightening or surprising discovery this way?

3. The authors point out that over time, scientists occasionally come to realize that their original conclusions were wrong. The authors use the example of erroneously linking the cause of bipolar disorder to life experiences when, in fact, bipolar disorder is a physical illness. What are some other examples of how our scientific understanding of something has changed drastically over time?

4. Near the end of this selection, the authors caution the reader not to "stereotype" science. Compared to students in many other countries, American students do not do particularly well in the sciences. Every year, fewer and fewer high school graduates are interested in majoring in science in college. Why do you think this is? Might it have something to do with an unfair stereotyping of science, or could there be other reasons? Explain.

Note: Writing assignments for this selection appear on page 706.

Check Your Performance

TWO MAIN FORMS OF SCIENTIFIC INQUIRY

Activity	*Number Right*		*Points*		*Score*
Basic Skill Questions					
Vocabulary in Context (3 items)	______	×	4	=	______
Central Point and Main Ideas (3 items)	______	×	4	=	______
Supporting Details (3 items)	______	×	4	=	______
Transitions (2 items)	______	×	4	=	______
Patterns of Organization (1 item)	______	×	4	=	______
Advanced Skill Questions					
Inferences (2 Items)	______	×	4	=	______
Purpose and Tone (2 items)	______	×	4	=	______
Argument (1 item)	______	×	4	=	______
Critical Reading (3 items)	______	×	4	=	______
Mapping (5 items)	______	×	4	=	______
			TOTAL SCORE	=	______%

Enter your total score into the **Reading Performance Chart: Ten Reading Selections** on the inside back cover.

8 Bad Managers

Michael W. Drafke and Stan Kossen

Preview

We often hear about workers who make life hard for their managers in various ways—coming in late, leaving early, taking no pride in their work. But just as there are bad workers, there are bad managers as well, and they come in various forms. In this reading from *The Human Side of Organizations*, Seventh Edition, Michael W. Drafke and Stan Kossen describe various troublesome behaviors of bad managers. See if any of these bosses sound familiar to you.

Words to Watch

laterally (1): to a position at a similar level
entrenched (3): securely established
dysfunctional (3): not working normally or correctly
anticlimactic (8): disappointing after a big buildup
malicious (9): deliberately harmful
manifests (9): makes known
Machiavellian (14): characterized by selfishness and deceit, from Niccolò Machiavelli, who described in his book *The Prince* (1513) a king who gained and kept power with no concern for moral principles

1 The incompetent manager is a victim of the Peter Principle or a psychological deficiency. The Peter Principle states that people are promoted to their level of incompetence. In other words, when people do well in a job, they are rewarded with a promotion. If they do well in the next job, they are promoted again. The cycle repeats itself until they are placed in a job that they can't perform. Then they are demoted, moved laterally°, or fired. The level at which the Peter Principle applies is different for each person. Some people reach competence with an entry-level position; others reach it after ten promotions.

2 Some managers are incompetent not because of a lack of ability but because of a psychological defect. The

only result of their actions that they foresee is failure. They are unable to decide because they are convinced that whatever they choose will be wrong. Several warning signs can identify the psychologically impaired incompetent manager:

- denial
- playing it by the numbers
- buck passing
- abdication
- obfuscation
- delaying tactics
- escaping

Managees should be alert to these warning signs, for it is hard for a managee to do his or her job, much less progress, with an incompetent manager.

3 Managers using denial will insist that there are no problems. Problems brought to their attention either don't exist, will go away by themselves, or were solved long ago. If there are no problems, no decision needs to be made or action taken. Managers playing it by the numbers always consult the rule book. If the answer is in the book, then they do not have to devise any solutions, and if the problem is not in the book, then it is not a problem. This can often be seen in the firmly entrenched°, and dysfunctional°, bureaucratic mind.

Buck passing (passing a problem 4
along to someone else) is a strong sign of incompetence, but it may also be a characteristic of new managers. Sometimes a manager has not been managing or is so new to the organization that he or she really doesn't know the answer and must pass the decision along. If the manager is experienced, then buck passing can be a sign of incompetence. The issue may be passed to other areas or departments, or it may be passed up to the manager's manager. In either case, the incompetent manager can never seem to decide anything on his or her own authority.

An incompetent manager who can't 5
give a problem to another manager may try giving it to managees. Whereas buck passing removes the decision from one manager to another, abdication passes authority off to others with less power or with no official power. Abdication can involve passing authority to a committee, to subordinates, or to a third party. Passing authority to subordinates may look like participative management, but a behavioral manager acts as a group leader, not an absent leader.

When unable to form a committee and when unable to have managees make decisions, the abdicator may bring in consultants. Whatever form of abdication is chosen, there are two goals: avoid making the decision, and ensure that there is someone else to blame if things go wrong.

6 Some incompetent managers use obfuscation, clouding and confusing the issue to the point that people walk away too embarrassed to admit they are confused, or they give up in frustration. If the problem cannot be clouded or given to someone else, then the incompetent manager may try to delay any involvement. Managers have a number of effective delaying tactics. One reason many of them are effective is that sometimes there are valid excuses for waiting. However, delaying tactics become warning signs of incompetence when they constantly recur. One common delaying tactic is to ask for the problem in writing. This works quite often. Sometimes managees are reluctant to create evidence that they are afraid may be used against them, or they may believe that writing the incident down will be a waste of time because nothing will happen anyway (which with incompetent managers is usually true). This reinforces the manager's mental problems because the manager can now rationalize the avoidance of decision making by saying that it couldn't have been much of a problem if the managee wasn't willing to put it in writing.

7 Caution is another delaying tactic used by incompetent managers. Here the manager always warns managees that "We'd better not move too quickly. Slow and steady wins the race." Another form of using caution to delay is to wait for new technology. But because technology is always improving, the manager is always waiting and never has to decide. Another delaying tactic involves insisting that problems must be handled on a first-come, first-served basis. Because this manager still has his or her first problem to decide, this in effect bars all future decisions until the past ones are decided. Sometimes the problem is insufficient information. Therefore, the situation will have to be studied and some research done. Of course the information is never gathered, or there is always more to get.

The final signal that a manager 8
may be incompetent is escaping, or running away from the entire situation. Some managers escape by leaving for a business trip, going home, arranging to be too busy or always in a meeting, or going on vacation. In one situation involving an abusive health-care managee, the day finally came when physicians, an outside agency, co-managees, and a particularly spine-less manager were to present a large volume of information, and the managee was to be fired. As the appointed hour on a Wednesday afternoon came, all were gathered except the manager. After several minutes of this high-tension atmosphere, the manager's secretary came in to announce that the manager had just called to say he had decided to start a vacation that day. About two months after the abusive managee was

fired, many of the same people and top administrators gathered for the firing of the manager (for this and other acts of incompetence). The event was somewhat anticlimactic° because the manager had taken an unannounced "personal day."

9 Incompetent managers are just one type of generally poor managers; other bad managers can actually be classified as malicious°. Malicious managers actively cause harm or distress to managees. Typically this is mental distress, but sometimes sexual and physical harassment is involved. Whatever stressful behavior is exhibited by these managers, they can be classified by the manner in which the maliciousness manifests° itself. Some of the mostly unsuccessful malicious managers are:

- clueless
- Janus-type
- grumps
- spineless

Three other types are often highly successful, but their tactics are typically unnecessarily harsh or stressful. These types can be classified as:

- first-in, last-out managers
- perfectionists
- intimidators

If you are being managed, learn to differentiate between these types because your responses should differ depending on the type.

10 Clueless managers are living in the Dark Ages. They have missed or ignored behavioral management, women's rights, diversity and minority rights, and the Americans with Disabilities Act. Clueless managers may stun you with behavior so out of date that you have no immediate response. Sexual advances; stereotypical comments concerning race, gender, or ability; and a lack of any sense of what is appropriate in the workplace are symptoms of managerial cluelessness. Typically, the clueless manager is consistently clueless, whereas the Janus types are unpredictable.

Janus, the Roman god of gates and doorways, had two faces. Janus-type managers have two faces, and managees never know which to expect, the good side or the bad side. The disturbing aspect to Janus-type behavior is that the mood can change from day to day or even from hour to hour. Many consider Janus-types to be more difficult than grumps, who are always in a bad mood. They seem to hate everything and almost everybody, seem to never be happy, and think that nothing is ever going to improve or to work properly. However, at least the grumps are consistent. You know what you are getting when you have to talk with one. People fear the unknown, and the Janus-types touch this with their unpredictability. . . . 11

Spineless managers choose to avoid issues and deny problems, and they are quite adept at it. To avoid being held accountable later, the spineless never take a stand or express a strong opinion. These managers seem to walk around holding their breath, fearful that someone might ask them a 12 pointed question. Once, during a heated discussion involving much yelling and gesturing, two people who were arguing turned to a third colleague, each looking for support. The colleague was almost totally spineless even though the outcome of the argument was going to affect him directly. Instead of choosing sides, offering a compromise, or even offering a third option, he just stood there staring at the floor. After more than a few moments with no response, the two that had been arguing looked at him, looked at each other, looked at him again, and looked at each other once more; finally one said, "Hello? Anyone home?" The entire argument stopped cold while Mr. Spineless stared at the floor. Finally the two settled the argument and things broke up. Later Mr. Spineless said that he was so shocked to see the other two yelling that he couldn't respond. The problem was that he couldn't decide who was going to win, and rather than take a chance or try to figure out who was right, he pretended that his brain had locked up on him.

13 Because of their insecurities, the spineless will not commit to things and will not direct people in what to do. As with the other signs of maliciousness, this one is self-evident. Because this behavior is seen, the incompetence of spineless managers eventually is exposed, and few last long in any one place. This is not to say that they can't, for reasons strange and bizarre, be found in upper management. They can. However, you would not find as many of these as you would the next three types.

Some successful managers can still be classified as malicious. This is so because, when dealing with other people, sometimes "It's not whether you win or lose; it's how you play the game." Some malicious people (Hitler, Attila the Hun, Stalin) had what they would argue was some degree of success. We typically reject a Machiavellian° world in which anything goes in the name of winning (winning typically meaning that the individual gets what he or she wants regardless of what happens to others). The ends do not justify the means. An example of one who sometimes succeeds is the FILO manager. 14

FILO is an accounting term meaning "first in, last out." FILO managers are the first to arrive and the last to leave. They often work on Saturdays, Sundays, and holidays. This would be fine, except that most FILO managers expect their managees to do the same. One FILO manager put up cots in the workplace to remind people that their twelve-to-fourteen-hour workdays could be worse—they could be twenty-four-hour workdays. Worse yet, FILOs seem to travel in groups. Entire organizations can be composed of these workaholics, so it is important to know whether or not you can fit in with these people before making a major commitment to what is essentially an entire lifestyle. . . . 15

Perfectionists seem to think that everyone must share in their compulsion. The malicious perfectionist with power often victimizes managees with numerous, highly detailed questions that it is unlikely any one person could answer. Other perfectionists may make 16 completely unreasonable demands of managees and then berate them publicly for not being able to complete the task. One perfectionist who sometimes screams at people with veins popping out of his head and fists banging on the desk until they leave in tears has a sign on the wall, "Be realistic. Demand the impossible." Although we should strive to do the job right, perfectionists' standards are unrealistically high, and they perceive anything less, no matter how close to perfect it comes, as failure. In school, these people consider missing one item on a test with fifty or one hundred questions a failure. It is not just their having high standards that stresses other people, but rather the anything-less-is-totally-unacceptable attitude that accompanies it that seems to push these people into the poor manager category.

17 The final general type of malicious manager includes behavior that is often exhibited with that of other types. Whether as a means to push their perfectionist ideals or as part of mind games or to make up for their own deficiencies or mental inadequacies, some managers may become intimidators. Intimidators do not lead (at least not in the typical way); they do not persuade; they do not request. Instead, they bully people. They yell, insult, or scream to get what they want. Some intimidators return work they don't like, torn into tiny pieces. Others throw things, make managees stay in meetings past midnight, withhold paychecks, or keep people waiting simply to demonstrate their power. A few even work with a partner. While one plays the bad guy, screams and yells and stomps out of the room, the other plays good guy, staying behind and remaining calm so as to smooth over the intimidation of the one playing the bad guy. The intimidators are not just intelligent or tough; they can be either or both, and they want to display their power and position. Maybe they like to be bullies; maybe they can't think of another, more civil way to act; or maybe they don't believe other tactics will work. In any case, they and the other malicious and incompetent managers need to be dealt with.

Basic Skill Questions

Vocabulary in Context

_____ 1. In the excerpt below, the word *managee* (măn-ə-jē′) means
- A. someone who works under a manager.
- B. an incompetent worker.
- C. a highly competent worker.
- D. a manager.

"... it is hard for a managee to do his or her job, much less progress, with an incompetent manager." (Paragraph 2)

_____ 2. In the excerpt below, the word *rationalize* (răsh′ə-nə-līz) means
- A. explain away.
- B. predict.
- C. notice.
- D. imitate.

"This reinforces the manager's mental problems because the manager can now rationalize the avoidance of decision making by saying that it couldn't have been much of a problem ...." (Paragraph 6)

Central Point and Main Ideas

_____ 3. Which sentence best expresses the central point of the selection?
- A. It is hard for a managee to do his or her job with an incompetent manager.
- B. Incompetent and malicious managers can be identified by a number of warning signs, which managees should learn to identify.
- C. Denial, buck-passing, abdication, and escaping are all signs of incompetence in managers.
- D. Many managers are placed in jobs that they're not capable of performing.

_____ 4. Which sentence best expresses the main idea of paragraph 4?
- A. Buck-passing is passing a problem along to someone else rather than solving it oneself.
- B. Although buck-passing is understandable in new managers, it can be a sign of incompetence in an experienced manager.
- C. Managers who are new should not be expected to deal with problems that go beyond their experience.
- D. Buck-passing may involve passing the problem along to other areas or up to the manager's manager.

_____ 5. Which of these sentences best expresses the main idea of paragraph 7?

A. There are no valid reasons to warn employees against moving too quickly.

B. If a manager insists on a "first-come, first-served" policy but never deals with the first problem, the later problems will never be addressed either.

C. There are several ways an incompetent manager can justify using "caution" as a reason not to address a problem.

D. Because technology is constantly changing, a manager can put off a decision for a long time while waiting for "new technology."

Supporting Details

_____ 6. Write the letter of the best general outline of the reading.

A. 1. Victims of the Peter Principle
   2. Incompetent managers
   3. Warning signs
   4. Escaping

B. 1. Incompetent managers
      a. Victims of the Peter Principle
      b. Victims of a psychological deficiency, who can be identified by various warning signs
   2. Malicious managers
      a. Unsuccessful malicious managers
      b. Successful malicious managers

C. 1. Denial, playing it by the numbers, buck passing, abdication
   2. Obfuscation, delaying tactics, escaping
   3. Clueless, Janus-type, grumps, spineless
   4. First-in, last-out managers; perfectionists; intimidators

_____ 7. Managers who "play by the numbers"

A. pass authority along to others with less power.

B. deny that a problem exists if they can't find it in the rule book.

C. are generally less experienced than other managers.

D. rewrite the rule book so that it reflects their own preferences.

_____ 8. The authors refer to managers who bully managees by yelling, insulting, and screaming as

A. clueless.

B. spineless.

C. grumps.

D. intimidators.

Transitions

_____ 9. The relationship of the second sentence below to the first is one of
A. contrast.
B. time.
C. addition.
D. illustration.

"One reason many of them are effective is that sometimes there are valid excuses for waiting. However, delaying tactics become warning signs of incompetence when they constantly recur." (Paragraph 6)

_____10. The sentence below expresses a relationship of
A. illustration.
B. addition.
C. comparison.
D. cause and effect.

"The event was somewhat anticlimactic because the manager had taken an unannounced 'personal day.'" (Paragraph 8)

Patterns of Organization

_____11. The main pattern of organization of "Bad Managers" is
A. list of items.
B. time order.
C. cause and effect.
D. comparison-contrast.

_____12. The main patterns of organization of paragraph 2 are
A. cause-effect and list of items.
B. definition-example and comparison.
C. cause-effect and contrast.
D. definition and example.

Advanced Skill Questions

Inferences

_____13. We can infer that the manager in the anecdote in paragraph 8
A. believed the managee to be fired was not truly abusive.
B. had planned his vacation weeks in advance.
C. began his vacation in order to avoid being involved in the firing.
D. believed that the firing would be less painful for the managee if he was not present.

_____14. The selection suggests that
A. managers who are psychologically impaired often become more competent as time goes on.
B. working for an incompetent manager can be difficult.
C. all managers suffer from some degree of psychological impairment.
D. managees can usually find ways to effectively deal with an incompetent manager and so find great satisfaction in working under him or her.

Purpose and Tone

_____15. TRUE OR FALSE? The main purpose of this selection is to inform the reader about psychological impairment or maliciousness in various types of poor managers.

_____16. Which sentence reveals a persuasive element in the reading?
A. "The level at which the Peter Principle applies is different for each person."
B. "Managers using denial will insist that there are no problems."
C. "Some managers escape by leaving for a business trip, going home, arranging to be too busy or always in a meeting, or going on vacation."
D. "If you are being managed, learn to differentiate between these types because your responses should differ depending on the type."

_____17. The authors' tone in the discussion of malicious managers (paragraphs 14–17) is
A. tolerant.
B. threatening.
C. critical.
D. curious.

Argument

_____18. TRUE OR FALSE? The authors support their point that managers may be incompetent or malicious by explaining specific types of incompetence and malice.

Critical Reading

_____19. In the sentence below, words that reflect opinions are
A. *managers, type.*
B. *one, other.*
C. *just, be classified.*
D. *poor, bad, malicious.*

"Incompetent managers are just one type of generally poor managers; other bad managers can actually be classified as malicious." (Paragraph 9)

_____20. The reading is
A. all fact.
B. all opinion.
C. both fact and opinion.

Mapping

Complete the map of "Bad Managers" by filling in the rest of the main idea and the missing major and minor supporting details.

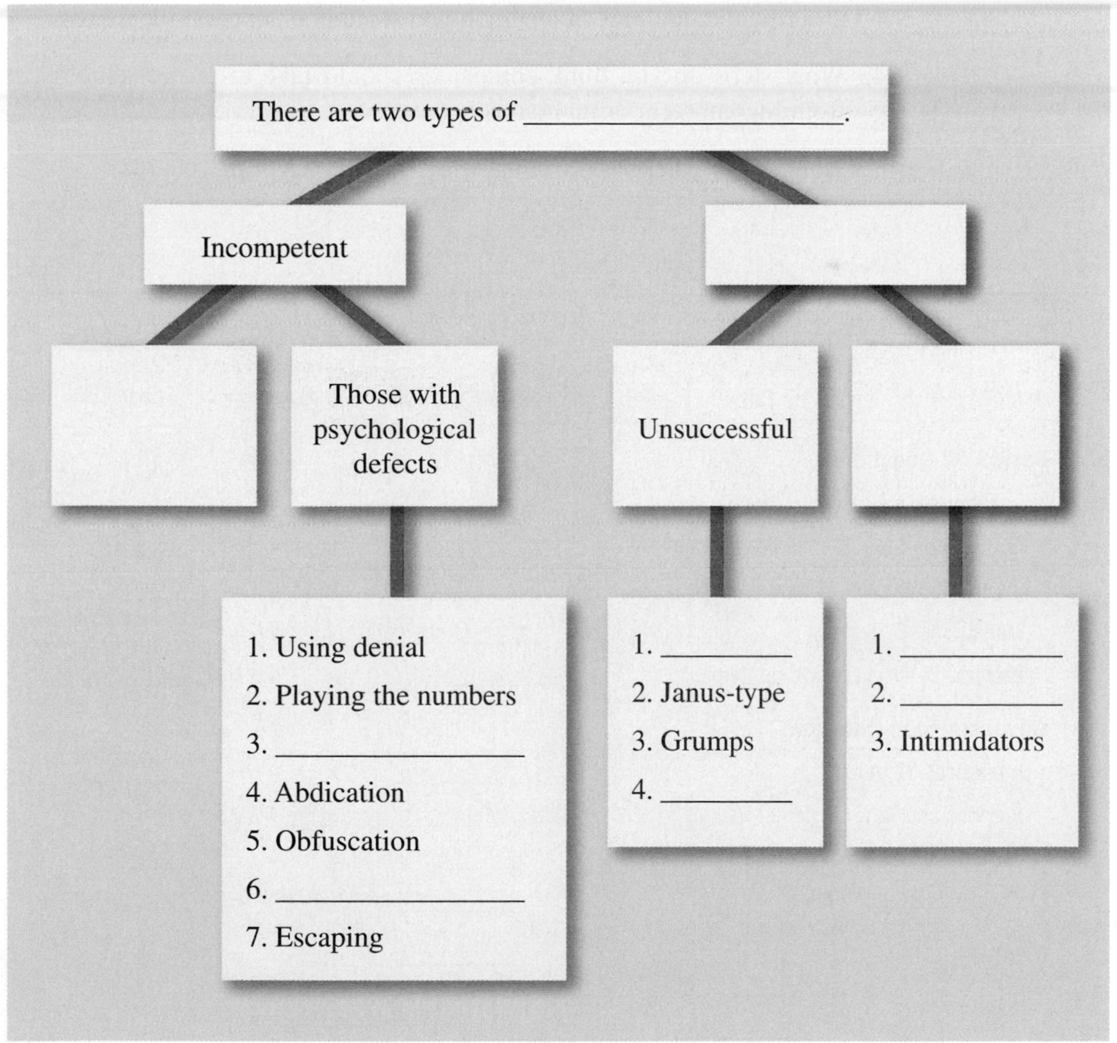

Discussion Questions

1. Describe the worst boss you ever had. Which of the behaviors described in this selection did your boss exhibit? How did those behaviors affect you and other employees?

2. The reading describes problem managers but gives no advice on how workers should deal with them. Select one of the incompetent or malicious managers described in the reading. What advice would you give to someone who was trying to deal with such a boss?

3. On the basis of the information in this article and your own experience, describe the qualities of a person you would consider an ideal boss.

4. What steps do you think companies should take to protect employees from incompetent or malicious bosses?

Note: Writing assignments for this selection appear on pages 706–707.

Check Your Performance — BAD MANAGERS

Activity	*Number Right*		*Points*		*Score*
Basic Skill Questions					
Vocabulary in Context (2 items)	_______	×	4	=	_______
Central Point and Main Ideas (3 items)	_______	×	4	=	_______
Supporting Details (3 items)	_______	×	4	=	_______
Transitions (2 items)	_______	×	4	=	_______
Patterns of Organization (2 items)	_______	×	4	=	_______
Advanced Skill Questions					
Inferences (2 items)	_______	×	4	=	_______
Purpose and Tone (3 items)	_______	×	4	=	_______
Argument (1 item)	_______	×	4	=	_______
Critical Reading (2 items)	_______	×	4	=	_______
Mapping (10 items)	_______	×	2	=	_______
			TOTAL SCORE	=	_______%

Enter your total score into the **Reading Performance Chart: Ten Reading Selections** on the inside back cover.

9 Better, More Affordable Colleges Start Online

L. Rafael Reif

Preview

When we think of college, we tend to think of four years spent in classrooms, either living on campus or commuting to it daily. But according to L. Rafael Reif, president of the Massachusetts Institute of Technology, it may be time to change the way we think. Online learning, once considered a second-best option to classroom learning, is proving to be as good as (and often better than) time spent sitting in a room full of other students.

Words to Watch

innovators (1): leaders, trendsetters
endowments (1): donations
subsidizing (1): supporting financially
unsustainable (1): weak, unable to support itself
eminent (4): well-known
exploit (4): take advantage of
quantify (5): to count or measure
credentialing (10): giving credit or, in this case, a diploma

1 Everyone would like a solution to the problem of rising college costs. While students worry that they cannot afford a college education, U.S. colleges and universities know they cannot really afford to educate them either. At a technology-intensive research university like the Massachusetts Institute of Technology, it now costs three times as much to educate an undergraduate as we receive in net tuition—that is, the tuition MIT receives after providing for financial aid. To push the research frontier and educate innovators° in science and engineering demands costly instrumentation and unique facilities. Even for institutions with substantial endowments°, subsidizing° a deficit driven by these and other costs is, in the long run, unsustainable°.

2 Some wonder whether today's online technologies—specifically, massive open online courses, or MOOCs, which can reach many thousands of students at a comparatively low cost—could be an answer. I am convinced that

digital learning is the most important innovation in education since the printing press. Yet if we want to know whether these technologies will make a college degree less expensive, we may be asking the wrong question. I believe they will; we are assessing this possibility at MIT even now. But first we should use these tools to make higher education better—in fact, to reinvent it. When the class of 2025 arrives on campuses, these technologies will have reshaped the entire concept of college in ways we cannot yet predict. Those transformations may change the whole equation, from access to effectiveness to cost.

3 To understand the potential, it's important to focus on what digital learning is good for. At least at the moment, it is surely not very good at replacing a close personal connection with an inspiring teacher and mentor. However, it is incomparably good at opening possibilities for billions of human beings who have little or no other access to higher learning. The global appetite for advanced learning is enormous: MIT OpenCourseWare—the initiative we started in 2002 to post virtually all our course materials for free online—has attracted 150 million learners worldwide. Today learners from every state in America and every nation on earth are actually taking MIT online classes; the edX platform we launched with Harvard 17 months ago has enrolled 1.25 million unique learners—10 times the number of living MIT graduates. With our edX partner institutions, we see an immense opportunity to help people transform their lives.

Yet digital learning also offers 4
surprising advantages even for students with access to the best educational resources. First, digital technologies are remarkably good at teaching content: the basic concepts of circuits and electronics, the principles of chemistry, the evolution of architectural styles. At an online-learning summit at MIT, one eminent° professor of physics from a peer university explained that although he loves lecturing and receives top ratings in student reviews, he recently came to rethink his entire approach. Why? Because testing indicated that many students did not come away from his lectures ready to apply the concepts he aimed to teach. By contrast, comparable students taught through online exercises—including immediate

practice, feedback and reinforcement—retained the concepts better and were better prepared to put them into practice. With so much introductory material moving online, instructors can take time that was previously reserved for lectures and use it to exploit° the power of innovative teaching techniques. A 2011 study co-authored by physics Nobel laureate Carl Wieman at the University of British Columbia showed the benefits: when tested on identical material, students taught through a highly interactive "flipped classroom" approach did nearly twice as well as peers taught via traditional lectures.

5 Digital learning technologies offer a second advantage, which is harder to quantify° but is deeply appealing to both students and faculty: flexibility. Just as college traditionally requires four years at the same academic address, traditional courses require large groups of students to regularly gather at the same time and place. By making it possible to break the course content into dozens of small conceptual modules of instruction and testing, digital learning allows students to engage the material anytime, any day, as often as they need to, anywhere in the world. A student can now spend a year immersed in remote field research on an important problem while staying in sync with the courses in her major. A team of students working on a project can now reach for a new concept just at the moment they need it to solve a problem—the most powerful learning incentive of all.

6 And we are only beginning to benefit from a third advantage of digital learning: the ability to analyze and gain information from the vast data we are generating about how people actually learn best. By providing, on a huge scale, a systematic, data-driven way to learn about learning, online technologies will provide testable conclusions that could improve teaching methods and strategies for both online and in-person instruction.

For all the strengths of today's digital technologies, however, we know that some things—perhaps the most important elements of a true education—are transmitted most effectively face-to-face: the judgment, confidence, humility, and skill in negotiation that come from hands-on problem solving and teamwork; the perseverance, analytical skill, and initiative that grow from conducting frontline lab research; the skill in writing and public speaking that comes from exploring ideas with mentors and peers; the ethics and values that emerge through being apprenticed to a master in your field and living as a member of a campus community. 7

Online learning may not help students arrive at such lessons directly—but it may serve to clear the way. At MIT, faculty members experimenting with online tools to convey content in their courses are finding that it allows them more time to focus on education: detailed discussions, personal mentorship, project-based learning. They are developing a blended model that uses online tools strategically—and they are making education more 8 engaging and more effective for more students than it has ever been before.

9 Digital learning technologies present us with a tremendous opportunity to examine what college is good for, to imagine what colleges might look like in the future, and to strive for ways to raise quality and lower costs. To teach what is best learned in person, do we need four years on campus, or could other models be even more effective? Could the first year of course work be conducted online as a standard for admission? Or could online tools allow juniors to spend a year working in the field? Then there's the question of our physical campuses. MIT has about 200 lecture halls. How many will we need in 20 years—and what different learning spaces should campuses include instead? Should we develop a new kind of blended education that combines the best of online and in-person learning? Would this lead to a new, more customized and valuable model of residential education—and what changes should we make to maximize that value?

10 Once we answer these questions, the college experience could look quite different in 10 or 20 years. I expect a range of options, from online credentialing° in many technical fields all the way to blended online and residential experiences that could be more stimulating and transformative than any college program in existence now. Higher education will have the tools to engage lifelong learners anywhere, overturning traditional ideas of campus and student body. I believe these experimental years will produce many possibilities, so that future learners will be able to choose what is best for them. If you're wondering how much these options will cost, a better question might be, How much will these options be worth? I strongly believe that by capitalizing on the strengths of online learning, we will make education more accessible, more effective, and more affordable for more human beings than ever before.

Basic Skill Questions

Vocabulary in Context

_____ 1. In the excerpt below, the word *transformations* (trăns′fər-mā′shənz) means

A. problems.
B. changes.
C. questions.
D. mysteries.

"When the class of 2025 arrives on campuses, these technologies will have reshaped the entire concept of college in ways we cannot yet predict. Those transformations may change the whole equation, from access to effectiveness to cost." (Paragraph 2)

_____ 2. In the sentence below, the word *massive* (măs′ĭv) means

A. expensive.
B. very large.
C. secret.
D. challenging.

"Some wonder whether today's online technologies—specifically, massive open online courses, or MOOCs, which can reach many thousands of students at a comparatively low cost—could be an answer." (Paragraph 2)

Central Point and Main Ideas

_____ 3. Which sentence best expresses the central point of this selection?

A. There are various aspects of live, in-person teaching and learning that cannot be replaced by online learning.
B. Online learning is becoming more popular primarily because it is less expensive and more convenient.
C. For several reasons, online learning may transform the way we think about acquiring a college education.
D. Because of the flexibility of online learning, people who thought they didn't have the time to go to college are now able to work toward a degree.

_____ 4. Which sentence best expresses the main idea of paragraph 3?

A. MIT has developed a popular program of online classes.
B. Online learning has dramatically changed the lives of people worldwide.
C. MIT has launched an online program that actually has more users than MIT has living graduates.
D. Although online learning cannot replace a live teacher, it provides learning opportunities for people worldwide.

_____ 5. Which sentence best expresses the main point of paragraph 5?

A. A main advantage of online learning is flexibility.
B. Students taking online classes are free to learn whenever they want.
C. Traditional learning forces students to gather in classrooms, but online learning does not.
D. With online learning, a student can be doing research in a foreign land and still take classes.

Supporting Details

_____ 6. A recent study revealed that students taught through an online course

A. did not do as well as students taught through traditional lectures.
B. did almost twice as well as students taught through traditional lectures.
C. paid only half as much as they would have paid for an on-campus course.
D. did not tend to complete the course as quickly.

_____ 7. It is difficult for online learning to replace skills acquired from
A. face-to-face negotiation.
B. experience in public speaking.
C. values acquired from working with a master in your field.
D. all of the above.

_____ 8. Digital technologies are particularly good at teaching
A. basic content.
B. foreign students.
C. advanced and complex courses.
D. students how to organize their time.

Transitions

_____ 9. The sentence below expresses a relationship of
A. cause and effect.
B. comparison.
C. addition.
D. illustration.

"Just as college traditionally requires four years at the same academic address, traditional courses require large groups of students to regularly gather at the same time and place." (Paragraph 5)

_____10. The relationship of the second sentence below to the first sentence is one of
A. contrast.
B. addition.
C. comparison.
D. cause and effect.

"At least at the moment, [digital learning] is surely not very good at replacing a close personal connection with an inspiring teacher and mentor. However, it is incomparably good at opening possibilities for billions of human beings who have little or no other access to higher learning." (Paragraph 3)

Patterns of Organization

_____11. Two main patterns of organization in this selection are
A. cause and effect / comparison and contrast.
B. series of events / cause and effect.
C. list of items / comparison and contrast.
D. definition and example / cause and effect.

Advanced Skill Questions

Inferences

_____12. This selection suggests that
- A. most students would rather take classes online than in a classroom.
- B. online learning is more interesting than face-to-face learning.
- C. online learning is going to change the college experience in the next decade or so.
- D. teachers who are in favor of online teaching are probably not particularly good teachers.

_____13. In paragraph 9, when the author asks questions such as, "Could the first year of course work be conducted online as a standard for admission? Or could online tools allow juniors to spend a year working in the field?" and "Should we develop a new kind of blended education that combines the best of online and in-person learning?" we can infer that
- A. the author would probably answer "yes" to the questions.
- B. the author would probably answer "no" to the questions.
- C. the author doesn't know the answers to the questions.
- D. the next article the author writes will answer these questions.

_____14. In the final paragraph, the author states, "If you're wondering how much these options will cost, a better question might be, How much will these options be worth?" This statement suggests that
- A. the online options will be fairly inexpensive.
- B. the online options will be very expensive.
- C. the value of the online education will outweigh the cost.
- D. an online education will not be worth much.

Purpose and Tone

_____15. The main purpose of this selection is to
- A. entertain readers with an unusual and innovative approach to college education.
- B. inform readers of the progressive actions taken by MIT.
- C. inform readers of how accessible, effective, and affordable online education could be.
- D. persuade readers to demand more online options at their schools.

_____16. The general tone of the entire selection is
- A. somewhat doubtful and skeptical.
- B. mainly positive and optimistic.
- C. mostly impatient and critical.
- D. somewhat alarmed and warning.

Argument

_____17. Write the letter of the statement that is the point of the following argument. The other statements are support for that point.
- A. Online learning makes college courses available to millions of people worldwide who would not be able to attend college otherwise.
- B. Studies have shown that digital courses are actually more effective for teaching basic content than traditional classroom lectures.
- C. Digital learning is the most important innovation in education since the printing press.
- D. Online classes make it possible for students to do field research in other parts of the world while still working toward their degrees.

_____18. TRUE OR FALSE? The author supports his point that online learning gives us important data on how people learn by referring to past research on this topic.

_____19. The author supports his point that online learning is effective in teaching content by
- A. referring to a 2011 study on this topic.
- B. citing the comments of a professor of physics.
- C. explaining the blended course approach being developed at MIT.
- D. all of the above.

Critical Reading

_____20. Which sentence below expresses a fact, not an opinion?
- A. "If you're wondering how much these options will cost, a better question might be, How much will these options be worth?"
- B. "MIT has about 200 lecture halls."
- C. "Digital learning technologies present us with a tremendous opportunity to examine what college is good for."
- D. "I expect a range of options . . . that could be more stimulating and transformative than any college program in existence now."

Outlining

Complete the outline of paragraphs 4–6 of the selection by filling in the missing major and minor details. The missing items are listed in random order below.

Items Missing from the Outline

- Digital learning offers flexibility.
- A student doing field research can stay in sync with the courses in her major.
- Analyzing the data could provide conclusions that could improve teaching methods.
- Students test twice as well as their peers taught via traditional lectures.

Main idea: **There are three main advantages to the innovation of online learning.**

A. Digital technologies are remarkably good at teaching basic content.
   1. Students taught online retain concepts better.
   2. Teaching basic courses online frees up time for professors to develop new teaching techniques.
   3. ____

B. ____
   1. Students can study any time, any day, anywhere in the world.
   2. ____
   3. Students working on a project can reach for a new concept at the moment they need it to solve a problem.

C. Digital learning helps us gain information about how people learn best.
   1. It provides data on a huge scale.
   2. ____

Discussion Questions

1. Given the option, would you prefer to "attend class" online—or in person? Why?
2. The author points out that studies have revealed that students who take basic courses online retain material better and test better than students who sit in a classroom and listen to a professor lecture. Why do you think a student might absorb information differently in an online setting?
3. The author wonders what "learning spaces" might look like in the future. If, in the future, colleges offer half or more of their courses online, how might a college campus change? What would a futuristic college that blends virtual and live education look like?
4. Some may argue that the negative aspects of online learning, such as the absence of human interaction and the lack of opportunity to develop interpersonal skills, outweigh any positive aspects. Would you agree—or disagree? Explain.

Note: Writing assignments for this selection appear on pages 707–708.

Check Your Performance

BETTER, MORE AFFORDABLE COLLEGES START ONLINE

Activity	*Number Right*	*Points*	*Score*
Basic Skill Questions			
Vocabulary in Context (2 items)	______	× 4 =	______
Central Point and Main Ideas (3 items)	______	× 4 =	______
Supporting Details (3 items)	______	× 4 =	______
Transitions (2 items)	______	× 4 =	______
Patterns of Organization (1 item)	______	× 4 =	______
Advanced Skill Questions			
Inferences (3 items)	______	× 4 =	______
Purpose and Tone (2 items)	______	× 4 =	______
Argument (3 items)	______	× 4 =	______
Critical Reading (1 item)	______	× 4 =	______
Outlining (4 items)	______	× 5 =	______
		TOTAL SCORE =	______%

Enter your total score into the **Reading Performance Chart: Ten Reading Selections** on the inside back cover.

10 Into the Light

Tanya Savory

Preview

What would you do if you were convinced that people would reject, even despisc you if they knew who you really were? Would you dare to be yourself and risk their condemnation? Or would you do your best to conform to their expectations? In this selection, Tanya Savory tells how she came to terms with her identity as a gay woman.

Words to Watch

commonplace (15): routine
heterosexuality (18): desire for someone of the opposite sex
murky (23): dark and gloomy
boycotted (23): stayed away from
prissy (24): overly prim and proper
orientation (27): direction

1 One night in April when I was barely seven years old, my mother told me to put on my Sunday dress—Dad was taking the family to a church across town. None of this made sense to me. After all, it was a Thursday, it was nearly bedtime, and our church was right next door. Dad was the minister, so all we did was walk across a parking lot to get to church. Why were we going across town?

2 After what seemed like an endless drive, we were winding slowly through a neighborhood I'd never seen before. Suddenly we were in front of a big wooden building with no windows. Streams of people were pouring in, all of them quiet and many of them hugging or holding hands. When our family walked into the church, many people turned to stare at us for a moment—nearly everyone in the church was black, and we were white. But then a friend of my father's, a young black minister, rushed over to greet us and led us to a pew.

Throughout that evening, the tall black woman sitting next to me turned to smile at me again and again even though there were tears in her eyes. I was amazed by her hat full of flowers and even some bird feathers, so I smiled back. No one wore hats like that in our church. I gazed at her hat until I became 3 drowsy and drifted in and out of sleep, occasionally waking up to hear voices joined in song. Many songs were sung that night that I knew, but at the end of the service everyone joined hands and sang a slow, moving song that I'd never heard before: *We shall overcome, we shall overcome, we shall overcome some day* . . . The tall woman next to me put one arm around me and lifted the other into the air, tears streaming down her face.

4 It was April 4th, 1968, and Martin Luther King Jr. had been shot and killed just five hours earlier.

5 When I was a senior in high school, I sat on the front porch with my dad one warm South Carolina afternoon and asked him about that night.

6 "Weren't you afraid?" I asked.

7 "Afraid? Of what?" my dad asked, giving me a kind of funny look.

8 "Well, you know," I said awkwardly, "afraid of the kind of white people who hate blacks. What if they had found out that we were at that service that night? Weren't you afraid of what they might think or do?"

9 My dad stared at me for a long moment before he answered. "Your mother and I have never been *afraid* of what bigots think of us. And we certainly weren't going to be bullied into hiding the way we felt just because some racists thought we were wrong."

10 "Yeah, but when everyone found out, you lost a lot of friends. Even Aunt Jo still doesn't speak to you," I pointed out.

11 "Not a lot of friends—a few. But that's a small price to pay to be true to yourself. I'm sorry to lose some friends, but I'd be sorrier to be living my life according to how other people think I should live it."

"Really? I asked. "You really think that?" 12

"Yes. I really *know* that," my dad answered. 13

That night I lay awake for hours thinking about what my dad had said. I knew he was right, but I was 100% afraid to be true to myself. I was in a small town in the South in 1978, and I was afraid, very afraid, that I was someone that even open-minded people would despise. Someone who, if I *were* true to myself, would be laughed at, abandoned by my friends, and worse. Someone whose own mother and father might turn against her. I was afraid I was gay. 14

This was decades before gay characters on TV or in the movies had become commonplace°. The words "gay marriage" would only have been heard in a punch line to a joke, and, in fact, most people still believed that homosexuality was a mental illness or a crime. In the town where I grew up, it was illegal to be gay—police used to stake out a little rundown cinderblock bar on the other side of the tracks where, supposedly, gay men gathered. It was not uncommon for the police to rough up and handcuff men they saw coming out of this bar. Then they were thrown in the jail for the night for little or no real reason. Most of the townspeople thought this was a good idea. 15

Every day in the halls at school, I would wonder and worry if my classmates could tell by looking at me. 16

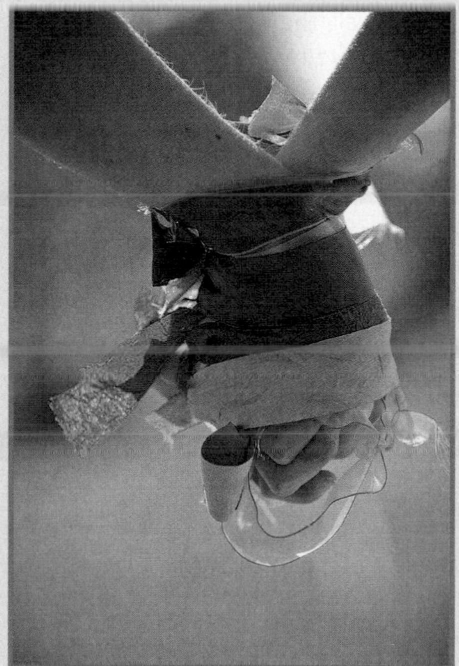

I pretty much looked and acted like any other seventeen-year-old girl. I passed notes in geometry, wore too much mascara, and worried about what I would wear to the prom in April. And like most of my friends, I had a boyfriend that I loved. But something had begun to creep into my consciousness about a year earlier—something like the slightest pinprick of light that had grown just a bit brighter every day until I was sure that everyone could see it like a spotlight on me: I didn't love my boyfriend, Mark, the same way I loved my best friend, Karla. I loved her more—I was *in* love with her. Midway through my senior year in high school, I became so afraid and confused about how I felt that I simply made the choice to stop being friends with Karla. The way I saw it, if I turned off the spotlight, no one would be able to see the real me.

In the darkness, it was easier to hide. I made new friends that I didn't really care too much about. I lost interest in anything that was special or unique about me, not wanting to draw attention to who I was. I went entirely overboard in my devotion to Mark, even suggesting that we get married as soon as we graduated from high school. College and my future no longer mattered to me. All that mattered was escaping the light, the fear of who I really was. It didn't matter that I was confused and miserable as long as I was hidden. 17

Strange as it may sound today, I was actually relieved when, one Sunday morning, I came across a short and angry article in a Christian magazine that insisted that homosexuality was a sin and that it was a choice. Apparently, all one had to do was change his or her mind about who they loved, *choose* to hate that kind of love, and everything would be okay. Supposedly it was as simple as deciding not to rob a bank or choosing not to eat too much pie. Choose heterosexuality° and you get heaven. Otherwise, you get hell. I had made the right choice! In a burst of satisfaction, I decided to tell my father everything I had been through and how I had made the right decision. After all, he was a minister. Surely he'd be proud of me. 18

Thankfully, he was not. 19

"Is your decision based on who you really are or who you want people to think you are?" was my dad's first question. 20

21 I was stunned. This was not how I had expected my father to respond at all. No one I knew had ever said anything about it being okay to be gay. In fact, no one ever talked about it at all except to make fun of it. I paused for a long time before answering. Finally, I quietly said, "I'm not sure."

22 I don't remember what else was said, but my father hugged me. And that was a great turning point, a great source of light in my life.

23 Decades later, I look back on that year as a strange, murky° time full of confusion about myself and about the world around me. Luckily, I had parents who, though they worried about how the world around me would treat me, did not try to change me. They never once suggested that there was anything "wrong" with me. But most of the gay people I know who grew up in that same era were not so lucky: One friend tells a story of his 75-year-old grandmother chasing him down the street with a shotgun when she found out he was gay. "She thought I'd be better off dead," he explained. "Luckily, her aim was bad." Another friend describes how her parents changed the locks on the doors, leaving a note that simply read, "Don't come back." Perhaps worst of all was a friend whose own family boycotted° his funeral when he died of AIDS.

24 It's hard to imagine where that kind of hate comes from. What is it about love between two people of the same sex that creates such anger and hostility? Some people, like my friend's 75-year-old grandmother, have an uninformed idea of what gay people are like. They believe all the ridiculous stereotypes that they've read about or seen on TV or in the movies. The stereotypes are frightening to them—and fear is always one step away from hate. To them, gay people are a big group of creepy and weird outcasts full of prissy° men who wear dresses and angry women who look like lumberjacks. In reality, of course, gay people are no different from anyone else. We work in the same jobs, eat the same foods, have the same worries, and experience the same joys and sorrows as any other human beings.

25 Other people, like the parents who locked their daughter out of their house, feel that it is immoral—that it is just plain wrong for two people of the same sex to fall in love. They feel that it is best to just lock it out and hope it goes away. This, in fact, was the same way many people felt about black and white people falling in love years ago. It just seemed wrong, and it made people feel uneasy. They didn't want to have to see it or think about it. So until 1948, it was against the law in the United States for interracial couples to marry. But laws designed to keep people from loving one another, and labeling something "immoral" just because it makes some people uncomfortable, are always bad ideas.

26 Still other people, like the family that refused to attend their own son's funeral, claim that God doesn't approve of homosexuality. Like the author of the article I had read so many years ago, they feel it's a sin. There is rarely any argument one can present that can change the minds of people who point to the Bible

as their reason for disliking, even hating, gay people. But using religion to justify the way we can mistreat other people, however, is nothing new. In the past, the Bible has been used to justify slavery, segregation, and even denying women the right to vote. As the daughter of a minister, all of this seems strange to me. Like my father, I would like to think that religion is better suited to promoting love—not hate.

27 Luckily, attitudes are changing fast. Today, the world is far from the dark and mysterious place for a young gay person that it was when I was seventeen. It is definitely no longer considered funny or socially acceptable to make fun of gay people or tell jokes about them based on their sexual orientation°. In fact, the majority of young people in the United States agree that making fun of gay people isn't cool.

28 And though it was pretty much unthinkable when I was growing up, now more and more states are making it legal for gay couples to marry. In only a handful of decades, gay Americans have gone from being afraid to carefully hold hands in a darkened movie theater to publicly (and legally) celebrating a wedding! That's some incredible progress. By law, marriage can no longer be defined as being only between a man and a woman. Many feel and hope that it will not be long before gay marriage is legal throughout the entire country. After all, gay marriage is already legal in more than a dozen countries, including our next-door-neighbor, Canada.

29 Even so, there is still plenty of progress to be made. In nineteen states, it is still perfectly legal to discriminate against a person for being gay. This means that, by law, you can fire someone, refuse to hire someone, and even deny housing to someone just because you don't approve of whom they love. These are the same states that will certainly fight against legalizing gay marriage with everything they've got. And beyond all the legalities, there are still many Americans who dislike, even hate, gay people. As was proven with the Civil Rights Movement, changing laws is easier than changing the hearts and minds of people who hate others for who they are.

Not long ago, I read a story that 30
made me very angry. In a small town in the Midwest, an elderly woman named Sarah had just lost her partner of forty-two years, Laura, to leukemia. As Laura lay dying in the hospital, Sarah pleaded with the hospital staff to allow her to see Laura, but the staff refused. Sarah and Laura lived in one of those states where gay people can still be denied rights. Only family was allowed in the rooms of critical patients. That was the law. Laura died alone, and Sarah never got to tell her goodbye.

Within a couple days of Laura's 31
death, Laura's only surviving relative, a nephew who hadn't seen his great-aunt in twenty years, came to claim possession of the home Sarah and Laura had shared for decades. The home was in Laura's name, so now the law said it belonged to the nephew. Additionally, the nephew was happy to be legally entitled to all of the home's possessions and all of the money in his aunt's

savings. Sarah was left with nothing—no laws protected her because no laws recognized her relationship with Laura. Legally, Sarah and Laura were no more than strangers to one another. Sarah would spend her remaining years in a rundown facility for penniless elderly people.

32 And, legally, Sarah could even have been denied the right to attend her partner's funeral if the nephew hadn't wanted her there. However, the nephew had no interest in attending the service once he secured the deed to Laura's house.

33 On a cold April morning, Sarah and a handful of friends gathered at Laura's gravesite. But just as the service began, shouts were heard. Ten members of an anti-gay hate group had gathered across the road from the rural cemetery. Somehow, they had gotten wind of the fact that a gay person was about to be buried. Standing in a line and holding signs with slogans such as "Fags Burn in Hell" and "God Hates Homos," the group shouted cruel and angry comments throughout the funeral service. *Legally*, they had the right to do this.

34 As I read this story and looked at the pictures of the faces of those holding the signs and yelling, I felt hate. I felt like jumping in my car and driving nonstop to that little town and giving them a dose of their own darkness.

35 But then, near the end of the story, a comment by the elderly woman, Sarah, stopped me in my tracks. Reporters, who had crassly rushed to the scene, asked Sarah how she felt about the group picketing across the street. "Well," she had said, "I'm sorry they feel that way. But it won't do no good to hate them back."

36 And suddenly, Sarah's words were like a light—a light that seemed to shine all the way back to nearly forty years ago. It shone on a night in April amidst a group of mourners who chose to sing and hold hands in response to hate and violence—a group that was certainly angry and weary of being treated unfairly. And surely, somewhere during that evening, the young black minister who had led us to a seat must have reminded the congregation of Dr. King's own words: "Darkness can not drive out darkness; only light can do that. Hate can not drive out hate; only love can do that."

Basic Skill Questions

Vocabulary in Context

______ 1. In the excerpt below, the word *hostility* (hŏ-stĭl′ĭ-tē) means
- A. envy.
- B. discomfort.
- C. sadness.
- D. strong opposition.

"It's hard to imagine where that kind of hate comes from. What is it about love between two people of the same sex that creates such anger and hostility?" (Paragraph 24)

______ 2. In the excerpt below, the word *crassly* (krăs′lē) means
- A. rudely.
- B. sensitively.
- C. violently.
- D. cleverly.

"Reporters, who had crassly rushed to the scene, asked Sarah how she felt about the group picketing across the street. 'Well,' she had said, 'I'm sorry they feel that way. But it won't do no good to hate them back.'" (Paragraph 35)

Central Point and Main Ideas

______ 3. Which sentence best expresses the main idea of the selection?
- A. The author had a difficult time growing up in a small town in the South.
- B. Attitudes toward homosexuality have changed over the past few decades.
- C. Over time, the author learned to accept her gayness and love her enemies.
- D. Gays have often been the target of cruel and unfair treatment.

______ 4. Which sentence best expresses the main idea of paragraph 16?
- A. During high school, Savory looked and acted like any other seventeen-year-old girl.
- B. During high school, Savory had a boyfriend, but realized she was in love with her best friend, Karla.
- C. Midway though her senior year, Savory decided to stop being friends with Karla.
- D. During high school, Savory was afraid and confused that she might be gay.

_____ 5. Which sentence best expresses the main idea of paragraph 31?
A. Despite their long-term relationship, Sarah was left with nothing after Laura died.
B. Laura's nephew, not Sarah, inherited her house and money.
C. Laura's only surviving relative was a nephew who hadn't seen his great-aunt in twenty years.
D. Sarah spent her remaining years in a rundown facility for penniless elderly people.

Supporting Details

_____ 6. Savory first became aware that she might be gay
A. when she was seven years old.
B. when she was seventeen.
C. as a college student.
D. in her early thirties.

_____ 7. According to this selection, the majority of Americans
A. still despise homosexuals.
B. think that gays will always be outcasts.
C. believe in gay marriage.
D. think gays should be treated the same as anyone else.

_____ 8. The hospital staff told Sarah she could not see her partner Laura because
A. Laura had a highly contagious disease.
B. Sarah was not a family member.
C. Sarah was gay.
D. Laura didn't want any visitors.

Transitions

_____ 9. The relationship of the second sentence below to the first is one of
A. addition.
B. comparison.
C. contrast.
D. illustration.

"And, legally, Sarah could even have been denied the right to attend her partner's funeral if the nephew hadn't wanted her there. However, the nephew had no interest in attending the service once he secured the deed to Laura's house." (Paragraph 32)

_____10. The sentence below expresses a relationship of
A. addition.
B. time.
C. cause and effect.
D. comparison.

"Like the author of the article I had read so many years ago, they feel it's a sin." (Paragraph 26)

Patterns of Organization

_____11. The main pattern of organization of paragraphs 1–4 is
A. list of items.
B. time order.
C. contrast.
D. comparison.

_____12. In paragraph 28, the author mainly
A. compares American and Canadian attitudes toward gay marriage.
B. provides reasons that American attitudes toward gay marriage have changed.
C. contrasts how gay marriage would have been perceived when she was growing up with how it is perceived now.
D. lists examples of how attitudes toward gay marriage have changed.

Advanced Skill Questions

Inferences

_____13. We can infer that Savory's father took his family to the black church the night of Martin Luther King's assassination
A. to prove to bigots that he wasn't afraid of them.
B. because he was in the habit of visiting different churches.
C. to learn more about black church services.
D. to show their support for the black community.

_____14. On the basis of paragraphs 18–23, we can infer that the author's father
A. believed that people could choose to be gay or heterosexual.
B. did not think homosexuality was sinful.
C. had little to do with his daughter after she came out as a gay woman.
D. knew a lot of gay people.

_____15. In telling the story of Sarah and Laura, the author implies that
A. Sarah should have inherited Laura's home, possessions, and money.
B. Laura's nephew didn't care about Laura; all he cared about was her money.
C. Sarah is a forgiving person.
D. all of the above.

Purpose and Tone

_____16. TRUE OR FALSE? One of the author's purposes is to inform readers how she came to accept the fact that she was gay.

_____17. The word that best describes the tone of the last paragraph of the selection is
A. light-hearted.
B. ironic.
C. apologetic.
D. forgiving.

Argument

_____18. Write the letter of the statement that is the point of the following argument. The other statements are support for that point.
A. It is no longer socially acceptable to make fun of gay people.
B. By law, marriage can no longer be defined as being only between a man and a woman.
C. Attitudes toward and rights for gay people have changed since Savory was seventeen.
D. More and more states in the United States are legalizing gay marriage.

Critical Reading

_____19. The sentence below is
A. a fact.
B. an opinion.

"So until 1948, it was against the law in the United States for interracial couples to marry." (Paragraph 25)

_____20. Someone who says "It is just plain wrong for two people of the same sex to fall in love because it is immoral" is illustrating the logical fallacy of
A. false cause.
B. false comparison.
C. either/or.
D. circular reasoning.

Summarizing

Add the ideas needed to complete the following summary of "Into the Light."

When Tanya Savory was seven years old, her minister father took the family to a black church a few hours after Martin Luther King Jr. was shot and killed. Later, when Savory was a high-school senior, she asked her father ______________________________ ______________________. He replied that he hadn't been, and that he was not willing to live his life according to how other people thought he should live it. As Savory thought this over, she realized that she was 100% afraid to be true to herself. Fearing that she was gay, she stopped being friends with her best friend Karla, with whom she was in love, and went overboard in her devotion to her boyfriend, Mark. Later, when she came across an anti-gay article in a Christian magazine, she was glad that ______________________________. But when she told her told her father of her decision, he asked ________ ______________________________ ______________________. After a stunned silence, Savory said, "I'm not sure." Fortunately for Savory, her parents never suggested there was anything wrong with her. But she met many gay people who had been rejected by their families. To people who hold stereotypical views of gays, Savory points out that gay people are no different from anyone else. Unlike people who use religion to mistreat others, Savory believes ____________ ______________________________. While Savory is glad that things have improved for gays, she tells of reading one story that made her very angry. When an elderly woman named Sarah lost Laura, her longtime partner, Laura's nephew, not Sarah, inherited her house and money. This was because ______________________________ ______________________. Later, an anti-gay hate group shouted cruel and angry comments at Laura's funeral. Savory was tempted to spew venom right back at this group. But when she read that Sarah had said, ". . . it won't do no good to hate them back," she remembered the church service the night of Dr. King's murder and Dr. King's own words: "Darkness can not drive out darkness; only light can do that. Hate can not drive out hate; only love can do that."

Discussion Questions

1. How does Savory's attitude toward homosexuality change in the course of the selection? What incident marks the turning point in her attitude toward her own sexuality?
2. What comparison does Savory draw between the treatment of blacks and the treatment of gays? In your view, is this comparison convincing? Explain.
3. What did Savory feel was so unjust about the story of Sarah and Laura? If you agree with her attitude toward the couple, what steps could be taken to make sure that unfortunate situations like these no longer occur?
4. In paragraph 28, Savory states, "Many feel and hope that it will not be long before gay marriage is legal throughout the entire country." Do you agree? What are your feelings about gay marriage?

Note: Writing assignments for this selection appear on page 708.

Check Your Performance — INTO THE LIGHT

Activity	*Number Right*	*Points*	*Score*
Basic Skill Questions			
Vocabulary in Context (2 items)	______	× 4 =	______
Central Point and Main Ideas (3 items)	______	× 4 =	______
Supporting Details (3 items)	______	× 4 =	______
Transitions (2 items)	______	× 4 =	______
Patterns of Organization (2 items)	______	× 4 =	______
Advanced Skill Questions			
Inferences (3 items)	______	× 4 =	______
Purpose and Tone (2 items)	______	× 4 =	______
Argument (1 item)	______	× 4 =	______
Critical Reading (2 items)	______	× 4 =	______
Summarizing (5 items)	______	× 4 =	______
		TOTAL SCORE =	______%

Enter your total score into the **Reading Performance Chart: Ten Reading Selections** on the inside back cover.

Part Three

Relationships and Combined-Skills Tests

1 Relationships Tests

Understanding relationships between ideas is a key part of good comprehension. The tests that follow will give you practice at mastering the common types of relationships that have been explained in Chapters 5 and 6 of this book.

RELATIONSHIPS: Test 1

For each pair of sentences below, answer the question about the relationship between the sentences.

_____ 1. ● In different cultures, people consider some very unusual foods to be treats.

● People eat huge fried spiders on special occasions in parts of Asia.

What does the second sentence do?

A. It establishes a cause and effect relationship.
B. It presents an event that happened later in time than the event in the first sentence.
C. It gives an example to support what is stated in the first sentence.
D. It contrasts with the first sentence.

_____ 2. ● Super-compact cars are becoming increasingly popular due to their impressive gas mileage.

● Very small cars are death traps because they provide very little protection and are unsafe on interstate highways.

What is the relationship between the two sentences?

A. They contradict each other.
B. They repeat the same idea.
C. They provide a cause and an effect.
D. They compare similar situations.

_____ 3. • Due to global warming, some drastic changes are taking place on our planet.

• Melted glacial ice could raise sea levels as much as 23 inches by the year 2100.

What does the second sentence do?

A. It sums up the point made in the first sentence.
B. It gives evidence to support the claim made in the first sentence.
C. It contrasts with the first sentence.
D. It gives contradictory information.

_____ 4. • Serving sizes in restaurants have increased dramatically in the past thirty years.

• On average, Americans weigh twenty pounds more today than they did thirty years ago.

How are the two sentences related?

A. They repeat the same idea.
B. They provide a cause and an effect.
C. They contradict each other.
D. They present two events in the order in which they happened.

_____ 5. • In the 1400s, armored knights raised their visors to identify themselves when they rode by their king.

• Later, this custom became the modern military salute.

What is the relationship between the two sentences?

A. Addition
B. Comparison
C. Contrast
D. Time order

_____ 6. • A cockroach can live three weeks with its head cut off.

• The cockroach is an amazingly resilient insect.

What does the second sentence do?

A. It gives contradictory information.
B. It provides an example of what is stated in the first sentence.
C. It draws a conclusion about what is stated in the first sentence.
D. It repeats information given in the first sentence.

_____ 7. ● Texting while driving has been found to be just as dangerous as driving drunk.
● Most states now have laws against texting and driving, and offenders can be charged as much as $100 for a first offense.

What does the second sentence do?

A. It reinforces a claim made in the first sentence.
B. It states a result.
C. It provides an example of what is stated in the first sentence.
D. It gives unrelated information.

_____ 8. ● Playing online games like *Scrabble* and *Sudoku* is beneficial because it can help keep memory and problem-solving skills sharp.
● Spending too much time playing online games may lead to an addiction that can be harmful to one's work productivity, social life, and even health.

How are the two sentences related?

A. They state a cause and an effect.
B. They contradict each other.
C. They repeat the same information.
D. The second sentence supports claims made in the first sentence.

_____ 9. ● Although women are paid more fairly than they used to be, they still receive less pay than men.
● In 2011, American women were paid only 77 cents for every dollar that American men earned.

What does the second sentence do?

A. It sums up the points made in the first sentence.
B. It explains the effect of a cause mentioned in the first sentence.
C. It gives evidence to support the claim made in the first sentence.
D. It gives unexpected information.

_____ 10. ● When he was president, Abraham Lincoln often told jokes about himself in order to put people he met at ease.
● Lincoln found that if he made fun of himself, strangers meeting him for the first time were not so nervous.

What does the second sentence do?

A. It gives unexpected information.
B. It provides an example of what is stated in the first sentence.
C. It repeats the information given in the first sentence.
D. It sums up the points made in the first sentence.

_____ 11. ● Grizzly bears are often thought to be aggressive and quick to attack and kill.

● Grizzlies prefer to avoid people, and when they meet a human, they tend to bluff and threaten rather than attack.

What does the second sentence do?

A. It states an effect.
B. It gives unexpected information.
C. It repeats the information given in the first sentence.
D. It supports the claims made in the first sentence.

_____ 12. ● Some animals that normally live in the woods have adapted to urban living.

● In Chicago, coyotes have made themselves at home in public parks and among apartment complexes and industrial buildings.

What does the second sentence do?

A. It gives an example to support what is stated in the first sentence.
B. It presents an event that happened later in time than the event in the first sentence.
C. It establishes a cause and effect relationship.
D. It contrasts with the first sentence.

_____ 13. ● Most people see bright streaks across the night sky and think they are falling stars.

● "Falling stars" are nothing more than particles of dust drifting into our atmosphere.

How are the two sentences related?

A. They repeat the same information.
B. They present two events in the order in which they occurred.
C. They state a cause and an effect.
D. They contradict each other.

_____ 14. ● Poverty is extreme in some parts of Cambodia.

● Some of the poorest Cambodians live in the city dump and dig through the trash for items to resell.

What does the second sentence do?

A. It states a result.
B. It draws a comparison.
C. It repeats information.
D. It gives contradictory information.

_____ 15. ● Sharks were not considered particularly dangerous until the summer of 1916, when four people were killed by sharks near the New Jersey shoreline.

● By the mid-1920s, sharks were hated and feared and killed regularly for sport.

What is the relationship between the two sentences?

A. Comparison
B. Addition
C. Time order
D. Statement and example

_____ 16. ● The designs on American paper money are amazingly intricate.

● On the back of a five-dollar bill, the top of the Lincoln Memorial contains the names of all fifty states.

How are the two sentences related?

A. They state a cause and an effect.
B. They contradict each other.
C. The second sentence repeats the information given in the first sentence.
D. The second sentence supports the claim made in the first sentence.

_____ 17. ● More and more people are concerned about nutrition and calories when they go out to eat.

● Increasingly, restaurants are putting nutritional information in their menus.

What does the second sentence do?

A. It explains an effect of the cause stated in the first sentence.
B. It repeats the information given in the first sentence.
C. It presents an event that happened later in time than the event in the first sentence.
D. It gives unexpected information.

_____ 18. ● Negative emotions such as anxiety and depression can weaken the immune system, leading to all sorts of illnesses.

● You are more likely to become physically ill when you are going through periods of great emotional stress.

What is the relationship between the two sentences?

A. They draw a comparison.
B. They contradict each other.
C. They repeat the same information.
D. They present two events in the order in which they occurred.

_____ 19. ● A giraffe has two small horns on top of its head that no longer serve any purpose.

● Scientists suspect that wisdom teeth used to be necessary, but today, we no longer need them.

How are the two sentences related?

A. They compare similar situations.
B. They state a cause and an effect.
C. They contradict each other.
D. They contain a statement and an example.

_____ 20. ● Many women wear eye makeup in an attempt to look younger, more glamorous, and better rested.

● Certain eye makeup ingredients can cause eye infections, puffiness, and even gradual loss of vision.

What does the second sentence do?

A. It repeats the information given in the first sentence.
B. It contrasts with the first sentence.
C. It presents an event that happened later in time than the event in the first sentence.
D. It gives evidence to support the claim made in the first sentence.

_____ 21. ● Billions of dollars in productivity are lost every year due to employees wasting time on the Internet when they should be working, a pastime known as "cyberslacking."

● Many companies have blocked computer access to social network sites, personal e-mail, and chat rooms.

What does the second sentence do?

A. It presents an effect of the cause stated in the first sentence.
B. It provides an example of the statement in the first sentence.
C. It repeats the information given in the first sentence.
D. It compares spending time on social network sites to reading e-mails.

_____ 22. ● We celebrate July 4th as the day the Declaration of Independence was signed.

● Only John Hancock and Charles Thomson signed the Declaration on the 4th of July—most of the other signatures were not added until August 2.

What is the relationship between the two sentences?

A. They contain a statement and an example.
B. They state a cause and an effect.
C. They compare similar situations.
D. They contradict each other.

_____23. ● Fifty years ago, privacy was very important, and people rarely aired their personal problems publicly, preferring to keep private matters behind closed doors.

● Today, reality TV shows—that expose other people's personal problems, from obesity to infidelity—are a major form of entertainment.

What is the relationship between the two sentences?

A. Statement and example
B. Time order
C. Comparison
D. Cause and effect

_____24. ● Road rage is an outburst of anger that usually has far less to do with what's actually happening on the road than it does with what's going on in the life of the person expressing the rage.

● Quite often, domestic violence is triggered by a meaningless argument that has nothing to do with the violence that follows.

How are the two sentences related?

A. They contain a statement and an example.
B. They state a cause and an effect.
C. They compare similar situations.
D. They contradict each other.

_____25. ● Before there were safer procedures and stricter safety regulations, building large structures such as dams and bridges was exceedingly dangerous work.

● In the 1930s, nearly 100 men were killed during the construction of the Hoover Dam, and 11 men died during the building of the Golden Gate Bridge.

How are the two sentences related?

A. They contradict each other.
B. They provide a cause and an effect.
C. The second sentence provides an example of the statement in the first sentence.
D. They compare similar situations.

RELATIONSHIPS: Test 2

For each pair of sentences below, answer the question about the relationship between the sentences.

_____ 1. ● Personal need or desire is what drives many inventors to create a new invention.
● For instance, Thomas Edison, the inventor of the light bulb, was afraid of the dark.

What is the relationship between the two sentences?

A. Cause and effect
B. Contrast
C. Statement and example
D. Time order

_____ 2. ● Before dogs were domesticated, they often traveled in packs and slept in tight circles for warmth and protection.
● Because of this history, dogs maintain the ancient habit of circling several times before lying down to sleep.

What is the relationship between the two sentences?

A. Addition
B. Contrast
C. Comparison
D. Cause and effect

_____ 3. ● It's healthier—and less messy—to eat meals at a table rather than in a car.
● Furthermore, eating while driving is a distraction that can lead to an accident.

What is the relationship between the two sentences?

A. Comparison
B. Contrast
C. Addition
D. Time order

_____ 4. ● Many people claim that the feeling of being in love is like the feeling they get when eating chocolate.
● Both love and chocolate release chemicals called endorphins, which create a feeling of happiness and well-being.

What is the relationship between the two sentences?

A. Addition
B. Comparison
C. Contrast
D. Statement and example

_____ 5. ● There is a reason that babies, kittens, and puppies bring us such pleasure and make us want to take care of them.
● Our brains are hard-wired to respond, with caring and loving feelings, to large heads, large eyes, and soft features—characteristics associated with infancy.

What is the relationship between the two sentences?

A. Time order
B. Addition
C. Comparison
D. Cause and effect

_____ 6. ● The earliest Spanish explorers of Florida and the Gulf Coast called the large, toothy creature they encountered there "el largarto," or "the lizard."

● Then along came English-speaking settlers, who adopted the Spanish name but changed it to "alligator" so it would be easier for them to pronounce.

What is the relationship between the two sentences?

A. Time order
B. Addition
C. Cause and effect
D. Statement and example

_____ 7. ● When interviewing for a job, it's always important to present yourself as confident and knowledgeable.

● But it's never a good idea to be aggressive or attempt to show off to the interviewer.

What is the relationship between the two sentences?

A. Cause and effect
B. Time order
C. Contrast
D. Addition

_____ 8. ● Fewer people are smoking today due to awareness of how deadly cigarettes can be.

● Also, because cigarettes are so expensive, many young people don't begin smoking in the first place.

What is the relationship between the two sentences?

A. Addition
B. Cause and effect
C. Statement and example
D. Comparison

_____ 9. ● In the 1700s, people did not associate dirt with disease, and baths were actually thought of as being a threat to health.

● As a result, illness caused by infection and bacteria was significantly more common than it is today.

What is the relationship between the two sentences?

A. Statement and example
B. Cause and effect
C. Comparison
D. Contrast

_____ 10. ● Because written communication today is primarily electronic, the postal service has seen a steady decline in deliveries and revenue.

● Likewise, companies that produce paper and writing instruments have also seen sales go sharply downhill.

What is the relationship between the two sentences?

A. Time order
B. Statement and example
C. Contrast
D. Comparison

_____ 11. • The flight abilities of dragonflies are really quite remarkable.
• Specifically, dragonflies can fly in six different directions and reach speeds of close to 60 miles per hour.

What is the relationship between the two sentences?

A. Cause and effect
B. Contrast
C. Statement and example
D. Addition

_____ 12. • Escape artist Harry Houdini was able to free himself from handcuffs and chains, due in part to his small wrists and hands.
• In addition, Houdini was unusually strong, allowing him to tense his muscles tightly enough to squeeze his limbs through tight bindings.

What is the relationship between the two sentences?

A. Comparison
B. Addition
C. Statement and example
D. Cause and effect

_____ 13. • Fortune cookies are served in Chinese restaurants, and we associate them with Chinese culture.
• However, the fortune cookie was created in the United States; it is mostly unknown in China.

What is the relationship between the two sentences?

A. Addition
B. Contrast
C. Cause and effect
D. Time order

_____ 14. • Female grizzly bears give birth to their cubs in January or February while hibernating in a dark den.
• After three months, the young cubs leave the den and see sunlight for the first time.

What is the relationship between the two sentences?

A. Time order
B. Statement and example
C. Addition
D. Cause and effect

_____ 15. • Bears will tear apart even the toughest of containers and backpacks to get to food.
• Therefore, many campsites provide a system of poles and wires that allows hikers to hang bags of food in midair, where a bear cannot get to them.

What is the relationship between the two sentences?

A. Contrast
B. Statement and example
C. Addition
D. Cause and effect

_____ 16. ● A baby hawk can eat an entire rabbit and two rats in a single day.
● Similarly, a baby robin ingests 14 feet of earthworms every 24 hours.

What is the relationship between the two sentences?

A. Addition C. Comparison
B. Cause and effect D. Statement and example

_____ 17. ● Nearly half of all Americans claim to believe in the existence of ghosts.
● Yet barely 25 percent of those people claim to have actually ever seen a ghost.

What is the relationship between the two sentences?

A. Contrast C. Statement and example
B. Addition D. Comparison

_____ 18. ● In her final attempt to fly around the world in 1937, Amelia Earhart radioed that her airplane was running out of gas just after sunrise on July 2nd.
● Two hours later, Earhart's plane disappeared somewhere over the Pacific Ocean, and even today, her disappearance remains a mystery.

What is the relationship between the two sentences?

A. Contrast C. Time order
B. Addition D. Comparison

_____ 19. ● Authorities at Grand Central Station in New York City have devised ways to make sure passengers get to their trains on time.
● One of these methods is to show, on the schedule boards, earlier departing times—by about 2 minutes—than when trains really depart.

What is the relationship between the two sentences?

A. Cause and effect C. Contrast
B. Statement and example D. Comparison

_____ 20. ● While human noses contain about 5 million receptors for smell, dogs have more than *300 million* receptors, making their sense of smell unbelievably sensitive.
● Consequently, dogs' sense of smell is used to track criminals, sniff out drugs and bombs, and even detect cancer.

What is the relationship between the two sentences?

A. Time order C. Comparison
B. Statement and example D. Cause and effect

_____ 21. ● In folktales and children's stories, trolls are grumpy creatures who enjoy causing mischief.

● In similar fashion, Internet trolls are people who post obnoxious or off-topic messages on chat rooms, forums, or blogs in order to disrupt online discussions.

What is the relationship between the two sentences?

A. Addition
B. Statement and example
C. Comparison
D. Contrast

_____ 22. ● The Chinese had discovered the properties of natural gas by 200 B.C., when they were already piping it through bamboo chutes for cooking, heating, and lighting.

● It wasn't until the 1800s that people in the West began to use natural gas for street lighting.

What is the relationship between the two sentences?

A. Cause and effect
B. Comparison
C. Statement and example
D. Time order

_____ 23. ● The human body is physically connected to the earth in many ways.

● Human blood contains elements found in the earth, including iron, zinc, salt, and copper.

What is the relationship between the two sentences?

A. Comparison
B. Cause and effect
C. Statement and example
D. Addition

_____ 24. ● In the 1800s, mining towns in the American West had higher rates of homicide than today's big American cities.

● On the other hand, because nearly everyone carried a gun, the rates of robberies and burglaries was lower than those of Eastern cities at the same time.

What is the relationship between the two sentences?

A. Cause and effect
B. Contrast
C. Addition
D. Time order

_____ 25. ● Because ancient oceans once covered much of what is now the United States, the soil of some coastal states is very sandy.

● Moreover, fossils of such sea creatures as whales and giant sharks have been found as far inland as Kansas.

What is the relationship between the two sentences?

A. Comparison
B. Addition
C. Statement and example
D. Cause and effect

2 Combined-Skills Tests

Following are twenty-five tests that cover many of the skills taught in Part One and reinforced in Part Two of this book. Each test consists of a short reading passage followed by questions on any of the following: vocabulary in context, central points and main ideas, supporting details, relationships, inferences, purpose and tone, argument, and critical reading.

COMBINED SKILLS: Test 1

Read the passage below. Then write the letter of the best answer to each question that follows.

[1]Many years ago, waiting to meet a colleague, I was sitting in the lobby of Hahnemann Hospital, my briefcase on my lap, drinking a cup of coffee—when a woman in an obvious hurry walked by and put a dollar in my cup! [2]She clearly didn't see a man in a wheelchair. [3]She saw someone who was "different," and responded quickly.

[4]I tell this story frequently because it teaches us so much about ourselves. [5]Our brains are hard-wired to react instantly to members of our species who don't look or behave the way they "should." [6]When we encounter someone with a disfigured body or acting in ways that don't fit the expected norm, we feel distress.

[7]It happens so fast that we don't even know what we're feeling. [8]Our first instinct, however, is to find a way to diminish our distress. [9]That's why, when I go into a restaurant, the hostess will often ask my companion, "Where would he like to sit?" [10]The hostess makes eye contact with my companion in order to lessen the stress of facing someone who is "different."

[11]Sometimes our reaction to the distress takes the form of anger or harsh judgment. [12]Parents of children on the autism spectrum tell me that when their child becomes agitated in a public place, they frequently get critical looks or even patronizing comments. [13]The reason: Affixing blame can help diminish distress caused by the unusual behavior of others. [14]It makes the world feel more orderly.

[15]There is a price, however, and not only for the person who is judged or ignored. [16]Stress is a symptom; diminishing it by judging, criticizing or ignoring others is merely a form of symptom relief, like having a stiff drink.

[17]So what can we do? [18]Since stress is hard-wired, allow yourself to simply experience the stressful feelings without trying to avoid them. [19]Make eye contact if you can. [20](This gets easier with practice, as anyone who works with disabled people can tell you.)

[21]I have always believed that if you look in someone's eyes, you can find their humanity—and in that process, you can learn more about your own. [22]If that woman in Hahnemann's lobby had been able to look into my eyes, she would have seen a fellow human, a quadriplegic who in fact has a great deal in common with her.

_____ 1. In sentence 12, the word *patronizing* means
A. intended as humorous.
B. intelligent.
C. treating with respect.
D. looking down upon.

_____ 2. According to the author, people often ignore or criticize those who are "different" because

A. that is how their parents taught them to behave.

B. such behavior helps them to diminish the distress they feel.

C. they feel that people who are different from them are dangerous.

D. they are basically rude, angry people.

_____ 3. The main pattern of organization used in the passage is

A. time order.

B. definition and example.

C. comparison and contrast.

D. cause and effect.

_____ 4. We can infer that the woman who gave the author a dollar

A. believed he was begging for handouts.

B. felt she was being kind.

C. had little or no experience with disabled people.

D. all of the above.

_____ 5. The passage suggests that

A. the author knows a great deal about psychology.

B. the author is unemployed.

C. the author often gets angry at total strangers.

D. all of the above.

_____ 6. The tone of the passage is mainly

A. bitter and self-pitying.

B. defensive.

C. detached.

D. tolerant and instructive.

_____ 7. Sentence 21 is a statement of

A. fact.

B. opinion.

_____ 8. Which sentence best states the central point of the selection?

A. Disabled people have to put up with a lot of rude behavior.

B. Because we are hard-wired to react instantly to people who don't look or act the way they "should," we feel distress in their presence.

C. Although our instinctive reaction is to feel distress when noticing people whose appearance or behavior is different from ours, we should try to get to know them as fellow human beings.

D. Affixing blame on those who look different or act differently from us makes the world feel more orderly.

COMBINED SKILLS: Test 2

Read the passage below. Then write the letter of the best answer to each question that follows.

[1]Just as the automobile changed dating culture in the early 1900s by giving young people more freedom and privacy, texting is altering the current American dating scene. [2]According to a recent survey, roughly a third of participants agree that it's less intimidating to ask for a date by texting than by using the phone. [3]To avoid the stress of phoning, one can simply text, "I'm here with a group of people. [4]Show up if you want to." [5]Texting for dates also ties in with the preference young people today have for socializing in packs.

[6]In addition, the survey found that more men (44%) than women (37%) say mobile devices make it easier to flirt and get to know someone. [7]"Texting is kind of an ongoing conversation," says Alex Pulda, 27, a product researcher in San Francisco. [8]"It's not like text conveys a ton of emotion, but you are getting a little more comfortable with each other." [9]He adds, "I don't love phone calls. [10]They have all the downsides and don't have the benefit of face-to-face communication. [11]It's kind of this in-between. [12]And part of it is, it's a lot more work than to text."

[13]Furthermore, it can be time-efficient to text for dates. [14]Ruthie Dean, 28, the co-author of *Real Men Don't Text,* says, "Guys are using text messages to send the same message to multiple women. [15]'Hey, do you want to hang out tonight?' [16]They're kind of fishing for a response."

[17]Clinical psychologist Beverly Palmer has studied flirting and non-verbal behavior. [18]She says that texting can make ending a relationship quicker because text doesn't establish the same level of intimacy that voice does. [19]"In texting, a man can pull back quickly if he gets rejected, and it's easier to say 'no' to the guy because you're not having to confront the guy."

[20]According to linguistics professor Naomi Baron, telephone calls are often thought of as an intrusion, while texting offers a way of "controlling the volume." [21]She uses this term to describe the sense of control that text gives users that they can't get with a voice conversation.

[22]Ruthie Dean sees more of a downside to texting. [23]"We have our heads down in our smartphones a lot," she says. [24]"We don't know how to express our emotions, and we tend to hide behind technology, computers, and social media. [25]People are uncomfortable using the phone. [26]A text message is easier."

[27]Whatever one's feelings about texting versus calling, texting is here to stay. [28]About 764 text messages per person were sent or received each month in the USA in 2012, compared with about 165 mobile calls per month.

_____ 1. In sentence 1, the word *altering* means
- A. improving.
- B. changing.
- C. relaxing.
- D. making more difficult.

_____ 2. Which of the following is **not** mentioned in this passage as an advantage of texting for dates?
A. It's less intimidating to text for a date than to call to arrange one.
B. Texting for dates saves time.
C. Texting can make ending relationships easier.
D. Texting is more intimate than phoning.

_____ 3. According to the selection, one of the disadvantages of texting for dates is that texting
A. is a lot more work than phoning.
B. is more time-consuming than phoning.
C. doesn't give people practice in expressing emotions.
D. lets young people socialize in packs.

_____ 4. The relationship of the first part of sentence 1 to the second part is one of
A. addition.
B. comparison.
C. cause and effect.
D. contrast.

_____ 5. In general, this selection
A. compares dating in the early 1900s with dating today.
B. lists reasons why texting is popular.
C. illustrates ways in which texting is changing the American dating scene.
D. provides a brief history of American dating since the early 1900s.

_____ 6. We can infer from the selection that
A. more men than women text.
B. in the future, almost no one will make phone calls.
C. you can get to know someone just as easily by texting them as by talking with them face-to-face.
D. young people today like to keep first dates casual.

_____ 7. The main purpose of this selection is to
A. inform readers that texting is changing the American dating scene.
B. persuade readers that they should stop texting and go back to phoning for dates.
C. entertain readers with amusing "true life" dating experiences.
D. predict that in the future, texting will become the only form of communication for young people.

_____ 8. Which is the most appropriate title for this selection?
A. Changes in American Dating Since 1900
B. Why Shy Guys Text for Dates
C. Socializing in Packs
D. How Texting Is Changing the Way Americans Date

COMBINED SKILLS: Test 3

Read the passage below. Then write the letter of the best answer to each question that follows.

[1]Ah, potato chips. [2]Bet you can't eat just one! [3]And that's unfortunate, because potato chips are truly one of the unhealthiest foods imaginable.

[4]To begin with, they're made of . . . potatoes. [5]Compared to most other vegetables, potatoes are high in both calories and carbohydrates. [6]They're pretty much starch bombs, exploding in your system to turn into abdominal fat, spike your blood sugar, and encourage the development of Type 2 diabetes. [7]And that's when they're simply baked or boiled. [8]The process of turning them into potato chips makes them far more unhealthy.

[9]First, of course, frying them increases their calorie count substantially. [10]And most potato chips are fried in oil containing trans fats, the "bad" fats that clog arteries and can lead to heart disease. [11]In addition, what are potato chips without a generous sprinkling of salt? [12]Unfortunately, most Americans already consume far more sodium than is good for them, and when you add the salty crunch of potato chips to your diet, you're increasing your risk of high blood pressure, heart disease, kidney stones, and other health problems.

[13]Additionally, there is evidence that chips' seductive blend of fat, salt, and sugar (plant sugar, naturally occurring in the potato) may be literally addictive. [14]Lab rats allowed unlimited access to potato chips will eat them to the exclusion of almost any other food. [15]Brain imaging performed on those rats shows that the "addiction centers" in their brains are lit up like video arcades, just as they would be if the rats were ingesting cocaine.

[16]Finally and most disturbingly, when potato slices are fried at high temperatures to turn them into chips, they release a chemical called acrylamide. [17]Acrylamide is linked to the development of heart disease and several types of cancer. [18]Two recent studies have shown that women who regularly ate potato chips were 43 percent more likely to develop breast cancer and twice as likely to develop ovarian cancer, when compared with non-potato-chip eaters. [19]The Environmental Protection Agency has set limits for acrylamide in drinking water, but it has set no such limits for the foods we consume.

[20]So if there is one snack food that you should consider permanently banning from your diet, it is potato chips.

[21]Easier said than done, you say? [22]Well, if you truly can't do without a salty snack, try air-popped popcorn. [23]It has a low acrylamide level, since it doesn't require the high heat of oil-popped popcorn. [24]In addition, it's much lower in fat than potato chips. [25]Nuts are another healthier alternative to chips.

_____ 1. In sentence 15, the word *ingesting* means
A. craving.
B. adjusting to.
C. consuming.
D. withdrawing from.

_____ 2. The relationship of sentence 16 to the sentences that come before it is one of
A. comparison.
B. illustration.
C. cause and effect.
D. addition.

_____ 3. Sentences 9–20 mainly
A. contrast potato chips with other types of potato products.
B. discuss research findings about potato chips in time order.
C. list ways that potato chips harm people's health.
D. illustrate how difficult it can be to stop eating potato chips.

_____ 4. According to the selection, acrylamide
A. leads to increased abdominal fat and Type 2 diabetes.
B. contributes to the build-up of trans fats that clog arteries.
C. leads to addiction in the same way that cocaine does.
D. has been linked to the development of several types of cancer.

_____ 5. On the basis of this selection, we might conclude that the author
A. believes that consuming French fries is healthier than consuming potato chips.
B. eats potatoes that are baked or boiled but not potato chips.
C. is a health-care professional.
D. believes that the makers of potato chips want people to become addicted to eating their products.

_____ 6. The tone of this passage is
A. sarcastic and scornful.
B. concerned and instructive.
C. angry and vengeful.
D. detached and objective.

_____ 7. Which statement best expresses the central point of the selection?
A. Most snack foods are unhealthy, but potato chips are the worst.
B. It's better to consume potatoes than potato chips.
C. Potato chips are bad for your health.
D. American consumers need to pay more attention to what foods they eat.

_____ 8. The author's main purpose is to
A. inform readers about potato chips.
B. persuade readers not to eat potato chips.
C. entertain readers with horror stories about food addictions.
D. predict that legislation will be passed outlawing the sale of potato chips.

COMBINED SKILLS: Test 4

Read the passage below. Then write the letter of the best answer to each question that follows.

[1]Today most modern people agree that bathing and showering are essential to cleanliness. [2]Yet, beginning in the mid-fourteenth century, most Europeans went out of their way *not* to bathe. [3]This was the period when the bubonic plague was sweeping Europe, killing at least one out of three people. [4]The Black Death, as it was called because of the characteristic dark, festering lumps in the groins, armpits, and necks of its victims, originated in Asia and was transported to Europe by flea-infested rats. [5]In 1348, King Philippe VI of France asked the medical faculty of the University of Paris to investigate the origins of the plague. [6]The professors concluded that the plague was the result of a disastrous alignment of the planets, which caused infected vapors to rise out of the earth and waters and poison the air. [7]Susceptible people breathed the poisonous air, became ill, and died. [8]In addition, the professors identified a new health risk—hot baths. [9]In their view, once heat and water created openings through the skin, the plague could easily invade the entire body. [10]For the next 200 years, whenever the plague threatened, people were warned against bathing. [11]Sadly, the best medical advice of the day probably doomed many people, for the dirtier people were, the more likely they were to harbor plague-carrying fleas. [12]The alarming image of the deadly effects of bathing continued into the 18th century. [13]Even when a plague did not threaten, people remained suspicious of water. [14]This fear affected even the highest levels of society: Queen Elizabeth I of England bathed once a month, as she said, "whether I need it or not." [15]Her successor, James I, reportedly washed only his fingers. [16]In France, King Louis XIII once boasted, "I take after my father; I smell of armpits." [17]It wasn't until the middle of the 18th century, when the plague had finally receded as a threat, that people again began to view bathing as beneficial, not life-threatening.

_____ 1. In sentence 17, the word *receded* means

A. lessened.
B. increased.
C. got louder.
D. emerged.

_____ 2. In the 1300s, people believed that the plague was caused by

A. rats.
B. fleas.
C. poisonous air.
D. dirty people.

___ 3. The relationship of sentence 2 to sentence 1 is one of
A. contrast.
B. cause and effect.
C. comparison.
D. time.

___ 4. During the mid-fourteenth century, the bubonic plague killed
A. one out of two people.
B. one out of three people.
C. three out of four people.
D. one out of five people.

___ 5. The passage suggests that
A. kings and queens differed from common people in their attitudes toward bathing.
B. the idea that bathing is dangerous can have tragic consequences.
C. some people *did* get the plague as a result of breathing poisonous air.
D. it is often unwise to listen to medical advice.

___ 6. We can infer that in the mid-fourteenth century
A. university professors were not respected.
B. most people understood that germs caused disease.
C. medical advice could be more dangerous than helpful.
D. wealthy people took baths while poor people didn't.

___ 7. The author's main purpose in writing the selection is to
A. warn people against following the advice of so-called experts.
B. persuade people of the importance of bathing regularly.
C. entertain readers with stories about the foolish behavior of kings and queens.
D. inform readers why Europeans were once suspicious of bathing.

___ 8. Which sentence best states the main idea of the passage?
A. Due to mistaken beliefs about bathing, many Europeans failed to keep themselves clean.
B. In the mid-fourteenth century, the bubonic plague spread from Asia to Europe, where it killed at least one out of three people.
C. Professors at the University of Paris wrongly believed that the bubonic plague was caused by the influence of the planets on the earth's air.
D. For hundreds of years, Europeans feared bathing because they mistakenly believed it exposed the body to disease.

COMBINED SKILLS: Test 5

Read the passage below. Then write the letter of the best answer to each question that follows.

[1]Recently, two University of Chicago professors, Richard Thaler and Cass Sunstein, suggested that people sometimes have to be given hints to do the right thing. [2]As an example, they point to the city of San Marcos, California. [3]When people there received energy bills showing how much energy they used compared to their neighbors, heavy users quickly lowered their consumption, even though no one asked them to. [4]According to Thaler and Sunstein, this energy reduction policy succeeded because of the deep-seated human need to conform, even when conformity is irrelevant. [5]Another example of invisibly encouraging good behavior while still giving people a choice can occur in school cafeterias. [6]Putting healthful food at the front of a cafeteria line leads kids to take more of it, even with nothing to stop them from picking the chips and cookies farther down.

[7]Thaler has been putting these ideas to work for years in corporate retirement-savings plans. [8]Some 30% of people eligible for such plans fail to sign up, even though companies often match contributions. [9]As a result of Thaler's work, many firms have switched to automatic enrollment. [10]People who don't wish to enroll must choose not to. [11]That turns people's tendency to stick with the default option—whether or not it's a good one—into an advantage. [12]The authors believe that the same strategy could be used to bolster the nation's ranks of organ donors. [13]In one survey, only 64% of people wishing to be organ donors had marked that choice on their driver's license. [14]If, instead of making people choose to donate, states asked them to check a box if they chose *not* to, participation rates would skyrocket—from 42% to 82% in one experiment. [15]Even just forcing people to make a decision one way or another (with no default) boosts participation to 79%. [16]More lives saved, and more people following through on a desire to be donors. [17]That's a hint that can pack a punch.

_____ 1. In sentence 12, the word *bolster* means
- A. increase.
- B. lower.
- C. improve.
- D. influence.

_____ 2. In San Marcos, California, heavy energy users lowered their energy consumption
- A. after their neighbors objected to how much energy they were using.
- B. after they were fined for using too much energy.
- C. when they learned how much energy they used compared to their neighbors.
- D. after installing solar panels on their roofs.

_____ 3. In one survey, the percentage of people wishing to be organ donors who had actually marked that choice on their driver's license was

A. 30%. C. 64%.
B. 42%. D. 79%.

_____ 4. The author has developed this passage by

A. providing a series of steps in the process of reducing energy consumption.
B. contrasting people who want to do the right thing with those who do not.
C. giving examples of ideas that encourage people to do the right thing.
D. comparing one city's energy reduction policy to corporate retirement plans.

_____ 5. The author would probably agree with which of the following statements?

A. Heavy energy users should be forced to lower their energy consumption.
B. School cafeterias should offer only healthy foods.
C. People should have to choose *not* to register to vote rather than choose to register.
D. It's always best to stick with the default option when choosing a corporate retirement-savings plan.

_____ 6. The author's tone can be described as

A. critical. C. lighthearted.
B. straightforward. D. compassionate.

_____ 7. The author's main purpose in writing this selection is to

A. persuade readers that they should pay more attention to the choices they make.
B. inform readers of how people can be influenced to make good decisions.
C. entertain readers with the tricky ways that some people are using to manipulate the public.
D. predict how many American citizens will make wise decisions in the future.

_____ 8. Which sentence best states the central point of the selection?

A. Research suggests that giving people hints about the right thing to do will lead them to make better decisions.
B. People need to be forced to make the right decision.
C. Both the government and private industry should encourage people to use less energy, eat healthier foods, and become organ donors.
D. Research suggests that many people fail to make choices that would benefit themselves and others.

COMBINED SKILLS: Test 6

Read the passage below. Then write the letter of the best answer to each question that follows.

[1]The Amazon rain forest in South America is a showcase for the diversity of life on Earth. [2]Colorful birds, insects, and other animals live among a myriad of trees, shrubs, vines, and wildflowers, and an excursion along a waterway or a forest path typically reveals a lush variety of plant life. [3]Visitors traveling near the Amazon's headwaters in Peru are therefore surprised to come across tracts of forest that are almost completely dominated by a single plant species—a willowy flowering tree called *Duroia hirsuta.* [4]Travelers may wonder if the garden is planted and maintained by local people, but the indigenous people are as mystified as the visitors. [5]They call these stands of *Duroia* trees "devil's gardens," from a legend attributing them to an evil forest spirit.

[6]Seeking a scientific explanation, a research team recently solved the "devil's garden" mystery. [7]The researchers showed that the "farmers" who create and maintain these gardens are actually ants that live in the hollow stems of the *Duroia* trees. [8]The ants do not plant the *Duroia* trees, but they prevent other plant species from growing in the garden by injecting intruders with a poisonous chemical. [9]In this way, the ants create space for the growth of the *Duroia* trees that serve as their home. [10]With the ability to maintain and expand its habitat, a single colony of devil 's garden ants can live for hundreds of years.

[11]The chemical the ants use to weed their garden turns out to be formic acid. [12]This substance is produced by many species of ants and in fact got its name from the Latin word for ant, *formica.* [13]In many cases, the formic acid probably serves as a disinfectant that protects the ants against microbial parasites. [14]The devil's garden ant is the first ant species found to use formic acid as a herbicide. [15]This use of a chemical is an important addition to the list of functions mediated by chemicals in the insect world. [16]Scientists already know that chemicals play an important role in insect communication, attraction of mates, and defense against predators.

[17]Research on devil's gardens is only one example of the relevance of chemistry to the study of life. [18]Unlike a list of college courses, nature is not neatly packaged into the individual natural sciences—biology, chemistry, physics, and so forth. [19]Biologists specialize in the study of life, but organisms and their environments are natural systems to which the concepts of chemistry and physics apply. [20]Biology is a multi-disciplinary science.

_____ 1. In sentence 4, the word *indigenous* means
A. constantly moving.
B. highly creative.
C. unfriendly.
D. native to the area.

_____ 2. The ants create space for *Duroia* trees by
A. killing insects that attack the *Duroia* trees
B. poisoning the soil with formic acid so that only *Duroia* trees will grow.
C. using formic acid to protect the *Duroia* trees against microbial parasites.
D. killing other plant species by injecting them with poison.

_____ 3. Ants protect *Duroia* trees because
A. they are their chief source of food.
B. shade from the trees protects the ants against the hot jungle sun.
C. the ants live in *Duroia* trees.
D. all of the above.

_____ 4. The "farmers" mentioned in this selection are
A. indigenous people.
B. settlers who have recently arrived in the Amazon rain forest.
C. scientists who have raised and studied colonies of devil's garden ants.
D. devil's garden ants.

_____ 5. In the first paragraph, the author mainly
A. compares visitors to the Amazon with the indigenous inhabitants of the region.
B. lists reasons why the Amazon rainforest is one of the most beautiful places on earth.
C. contrasts the diversity of most of the Amazon rain forest with sections that are dominated by *Duroia* trees.
D. narrates a voyage to the headwaters of the Amazon River in Peru.

_____ 6. The relationship between the first part of sentence 8 and the second part is one of
A. comparison.
B. cause and effect.
C. contrast.
D. addition.

_____ 7. The passage suggests that
A. the devil's garden ant is harming the natural environment and should be destroyed.
B. scientists who solved the devil's garden mystery should receive an important prize in science.
C. ants are the most destructive insect species.
D. studying the natural world requires more than just a strong background in biology.

_____ 8. Which title best summarizes the passage?
A. Biology, the Multi-disciplinary Science
B. Solving the "Devil's Garden" Mystery
C. The Legend of *Duroia* Trees
D. The Amazing Rain Forest

COMBINED SKILLS: Test 7

Read the passage below. Then write the letter of the best answer to each question that follows.

[1]Monkey researchers have observed the process by which behavioral innovations spread from individual to individual and become part of a troop's culture independently of genetic transmission. [2]Consider the case of Imo, a two-year-old female monkey. [3]Imo and her troop of free-ranging monkeys live on the small Japanese island of Koshima, a high, wooded mountain with a surrounding beach. [4]Researchers enticed Imo and a number of other younger monkeys out of the forest by leaving sweet potatoes on a stretch of open beach. [5]In due course Imo began doing something that no other monkey had done. [6]She would carry her sweet potatoes to a freshwater pool, dip them in the water with one hand, and brush the sand off with the other. [7]Soon her companions began copying her. [8]The behavior spread to the playmates' siblings and mothers. [9]However, adult males, who rarely participated in the group's behavior, did not acquire the habit. [10]When the young females who engaged in potato-washing matured and had offspring of their own, all of the offspring learned to wash potatoes from their mothers. [11]Then Imo undertook another new behavior. [12]She took the potatoes that she had cleaned in the fresh water and washed them anew in the sea. [13]Imo apparently liked the flavor of the salt water. [14]Within ten years, the practice of washing sweet potatoes in the sea had spread to two-thirds of the monkeys.

_____ 1. In sentence 1, *behavioral innovations* means
A. noisy behaviors.
B. old behaviors.
C. new behaviors.
D. genetic behaviors.

_____ 2. Imo's practice of washing her potatoes in fresh water was first copied by
A. fathers of the group.
B. Imo's children.
C. mothers of the group.
D. Imo's companions.

_____ 3. What is the relationship of sentence 9 to sentence 8?
A. Addition
B. Contrast
C. Illustration
D. Time

_____ 4. Sentence 10 is a statement of
- A. fact.
- B. opinion.
- C. fact and opinion.

_____ 5. From this passage, you could infer that
- A. monkeys are solitary animals by nature.
- B. most monkeys dislike the taste of salt.
- C. Imo was a monkey of average intelligence.
- D. the monkeys learned by watching.

_____ 6. The purpose of this passage is mainly to
- A. inform.
- B. entertain.
- C. persuade.

_____ 7. Which title best summarizes the selection?
- A. Genetic Influences on Animal Cultures
- B. A Diet for Monkeys: Sweet Potatoes
- C. How a Young Monkey Changed Her Troop's Culture
- D. Animal Researchers and Subjects in Native Environments

_____ 8. Which of the following is the best outline of the selection?
- A. Scientists observed behaviors among members of a monkey troop in Japan.
  1. Young and female monkeys copied a young female monkey's ideas in preparing sweet potatoes for eating—washing the potatoes in fresh water and then in salt water.
  2. Adult male monkeys did not copy the new behaviors, presumably because they rarely participated in the group's behaviors.
- B. Monkeys' innovative behavior
  1. Japanese island of Koshima
     - a. a high, wooded mountain
     - b. a surrounding beach
  2. Imo and her troop of free-ranging monkeys
- C. New behaviors have been observed to spread from individual to individual to become part of a group's culture.
  1. Imo's washing of sweet potatoes in fresh water became a common behavior in her monkey troop.
  2. Imo's practice of washing sweet potatoes a second time in salt water also spread throughout much of the troop.

COMBINED SKILLS: Test 8

Read the passage below. Then write the letter of the best answer to each question that follows.

[1]Our first year in New York we rented a small apartment with a Catholic school nearby, taught by the Sisters of Charity, hefty women in long black gowns and bonnets that made them look peculiar, like dolls in mourning. [2]I liked them a lot, especially my grandmotherly fourth-grade teacher, Sister Zoe. [3]I had a lovely name, she said, and she had me teach the whole class how to pronounce it. [4]*Yo-lan-da.* [5]As the only immigrant in my class, I was put in a special seat in the first row by the window, apart from the other children so that Sister Zoe could tutor me without disturbing them. [6]Slowly, she enunciated the new words I was to repeat: *laundromat, corn flakes, subway, snow.*

[7]Soon I picked up enough English to understand a threat of war was in the air. [8]Sister Zoe explained to a wide-eyed classroom what was happening in Cuba. [9]Russian missiles were being assembled, trained supposedly on New York City. [10]President Kennedy, looking worried too, was on television at home, explaining we might have to go to war against the Communists. [11]At school, we had air-raid drills: an ominous bell would go off and we'd file into the hall, fall to the floor, cover our heads with our coats, and imagine our hair falling out, the bones in our arms going soft. [12]At home, Mami and my sisters and I said a rosary for world peace. [13]I heard new vocabulary: *nuclear bomb, radioactive fallout, bomb shelter.* [14]Sister Zoe explained how it would happen. [15]She drew a picture of a mushroom on the blackboard and dotted a flurry of chalkmarks for the dusty fallout that would kill us all.

[16]The months grew cold, November, December. [17]It was dark when I got up in the morning, frosty when I followed my breath to school. [18]One morning as I sat at my desk daydreaming out the window, I saw dots in the air like the ones Sister Zoe had drawn—random at first, then lots and lots. [19]I shrieked, "Bomb! Bomb!" [20]Sister Zoe jerked around, her full black skirt ballooning as she hurried to my side. [21]A few girls began to cry.

[22]But then Sister Zoe's shocked look faded. [23]"Why, Yolanda dear, that's snow!" [24]She laughed. [25]"Snow."

[26]"Snow," I repeated. [27]I looked out the window warily. [28]All my life I had heard about the white crystals that fell out of American skies in the winter. [29]From my desk I watched the fine powder dust the sidewalk and parked cars below. [30]Each flake was different, Sister Zoe had said, like a person, irreplaceable and beautiful.

_____ 1. In sentence 6, *enunciated* means

A. knew.
B. shouted.
C. pronounced.
D. listened to.

_____ 2. The author was seated apart from the other children
A. to punish her for not speaking English.
B. because she had trouble hearing the teacher otherwise.
C. so the teacher could give her special help.
D. because she was afraid of the other children.

_____ 3. During an air-raid drill, the children
A. crouched under their desks.
B. ran to their homes.
C. said a rosary for world peace.
D. went into the hall and covered themselves with their coats.

_____ 4. When Yolanda mistook snow for radioactive fallout, Sister Zoe
A. laughed and reassured her.
B. scolded her for frightening the others.
C. burst into tears.
D. announced an air-raid drill.

_____ 5. The main pattern of organization used in this passage is
A. time order.
B. definition and example.
C. comparison and contrast.
D. cause and effect.

_____ 6. We can infer from this passage that
A. Sister Zoe resented having to deal with an immigrant student.
B. the author's fellow students made fun of her inability to speak English.
C. the Cuban government supported President Kennedy.
D. before moving to New York City, the author had never seen snow.

_____ 7. It is reasonable to conclude that Sister Zoe
A. spoke Yolanda's native language.
B. was a kind and caring teacher.
C. had not been a nun very long.
D. was an immigrant herself.

_____ 8. Which of the following is the best title for the selection?
A. Sister Zoe and My First Snowfall
B. The Sisters of Charity
C. Air-Raid Drills
D. The Cuban Missile Crisis

COMBINED SKILLS: Test 9

Read the passage below. Then write the letter of the best answer to each question that follows.

[1]Humans generally spend more time working than do other creatures, but there is greater variability in industriousness from one human culture to the next than is seen in subgroups of any other species. [2]For instance, the average French worker toils for 1,646 hours a year; the average American for 1,957 hours; and the average Japanese for 2,088.

[3]One reason for human diligence is that people, unlike animals, can often override the impulses they may feel to slow down. [4]They can drink coffee when they might prefer a nap or flick on the air-conditioning when the heat might otherwise demand torpor. [5]Many humans are driven to work hard by a singular desire to gather resources far beyond what is required for survival. [6]Squirrels may collect what they need to make it through one winter, but only humans worry about college bills, retirement, or replacing their old record albums with compact discs.

[7]"Among other primates, if you don't need to travel around to get food for that day, you sit down and relax," said Dr. Frans de Waal of Emory University in Atlanta. [8]"It's typically human to try to accumulate wealth and get more and more."

[9]Much of the acquisitiveness is likely to be the result of cultural training. [10]Anthropologists have found that most hunter-gatherer groups, who live day to day on the resources they can kill or forage and who stash very little away for the future, generally work only three to five hours daily.

[11]Indeed, an inborn temptation to slack off may lurk beneath even the most work-obsessed people, which could explain why sloth ranks with lust and gluttony as one of the seven deadly sins.

_____ 1. The word *torpor* in sentence 4 means
A. increased activity.
B. extreme heat.
C. industriousness.
D. inactivity.

_____ 2. The relationship of sentence 2 to sentence 1 is one of
A. time.
B. illustration.
C. contrast.
D. cause and effect.

_____ 3. According to the author, humans are so industrious because
A. they are stronger and better protected than animals.
B. they can overcome the impulse to slow down, and they work for gains beyond survival.
C. they have an inborn temptation to take it easy.
D. they need much more than animals need in order to survive.

_____ 4. The pattern of organization of the passage is a combination of contrast and
A. a series of events.
B. steps in a process.
C. definition and example.
D. cause and effect.

_____ 5. Sentence 2 is a statement of
A. fact.
B. opinion.
C. both fact and opinion.

_____ 6. The author implies that most hunter-gatherer groups
A. have not been culturally conditioned to desire many possessions.
B. often go hungry.
C. would be happier if they worked more hours each day.
D. are more industrious than many French people.

_____ 7. The tone of this passage is
A. critical and anxious.
B. disbelieving and excited.
C. straightforward and analytical.
D. ambivalent yet optimistic.

_____ 8. Which title best summarizes the selection?
A. Sloth: One of the Seven Deadly Sins
B. Work among Humans and Animals
C. The Accumulation of Wealth
D. Cultural Training

COMBINED SKILLS: Test 10

Read the passage below. Then write the letter of the best answer to each question that follows.

[1]If you have read Nathaniel Hawthorne's *The Scarlet Letter,* you know about shaming. [2]Hester Prynne, who committed adultery, a serious offense at the time, because it struck at the community's moral roots, had to wear a red "A" on her clothing. [3]For life, wherever she went, she was marked as a shameful adulteress. [4]Now it appears that some judges and other officials are bringing back shaming in a different form. [5]Recently, a judge ordered thieves to wear sandwich boards that said, "I stole from this store." [6]They had to parade back and forth outside the stores they stole from. [7]Similarly, a Texas judge ordered a piano teacher who pleaded guilty to molesting his young students to give away his prized $12,000 piano and to not play the piano for 20 years. [8]If you don't think this was harsh, consider the shaming that accompanied this punishment. [9]He had to post a sign prominently on the door of his home declaring himself a child molester.

[10]Judges have ordered drunk drivers to put bright orange bumper stickers on their cars that say, "I am a convicted drunk driver. [11]Report any erratic driving to the police."

[12]The Minneapolis police department has even organized "shaming details." [13]Prostitutes and their johns must stand handcuffed in front of citizens who let loose with "verbal stones," shouting things like "You're the reason our children aren't safe in this neighborhood!"

[14]Kansas City has tried a different approach to prostitution. [15]"John TV" shows the mug shots of men who have been arrested for trying to buy sex and of the women who have been arrested for selling it. [16]Their names, birth dates, and hometowns are displayed prominently.

[17]Rosters of convicted sex offenders are available at the click of a mouse. [18]On your computer screen, you can see the individual's photo, name, date of birth, conviction, and in some instances, even the offender's current address and clickable neighborhood map. [19]While this information is supposed to be intended to alert citizens to potential danger, it certainly is a shaming device.

[20]Does shaming work? [21]No one knows whether it reduces law-breaking. [22]But shaming certainly can be powerful. [23]A woman convicted of welfare fraud was ordered to wear a sign in public that said, "I stole food from poor people." [24]She chose to go to jail instead.

_____ 1. The word *prominently* in sentences 9 and 16 means
- A. quietly.
- B. noticeably.
- C. gently.
- D. sloppily.

_____ 2. The main pattern of organization used in this passage is
A. comparison.
B. cause and effect.
C. list of items.
D. time order.

_____ 3. According to the passage, which of the following would **not** be a shaming device?
A. Having to wear a sandwich board saying, "I stole from this store"
B. Being shown on "John TV"
C. Being forced to display a bright orange bumper sticker that says, "I am a convicted drunk driver"
D. Being ordered not to play the piano for 20 years

_____ 4. We can infer from the selection that
A. in the United States, adultery is no longer an offense that would result in public shaming.
B. the judge who sentenced the child molester was being easy on him.
C. most people believe that prostitution is a victimless crime.
D. these days, very few people have heard of *The Scarlet Letter*.

_____ 5. It is reasonable to conclude that the author
A. has experienced shaming himself.
B. might favor shaming if it was shown to reduce law-breaking.
C. prefers shaming criminals to imprisoning them.
D. doubts that shaming actually reduces law-breaking.

_____ 6. The overall tone of the passage is
A. critical and distressed.
B. light-hearted and amused.
C. sympathetic and concerned.
D. straightforward and instructive.

_____ 7. The author's main purpose in this passage is to
A. inform readers about the reappearance of shaming as a form of punishment.
B. persuade readers that they should be careful not to break the law.
C. entertain readers with amusing anecdotes about some outrageously harsh punishments.
D. predict that shaming will be used as a punishment much more extensively in the future.

_____ 8. The central point of the selection is stated in sentence
A. 1.
B. 2.
C. 3.
D. 4.

COMBINED SKILLS: Test 11

Read the passage below. Then write the letter of the best answer to each question that follows.

[1]South Pole explorer Ernest Shackleton never reached his goal of crossing Antarctica, but the circumstances that prevented him from reaching that goal pushed him to achieve an even more amazing feat. [2]In January 1915 Shackleton's ship *Endurance* became trapped in ice off Antarctica. [3]He and his crew of twenty-seven lived on the ship trapped in the ice floes for nine months, until they had to abandon ship when the ice crushed the boat. [4]The day the boat sank, Shackleton wrote his new goal: "The task is to reach land with all members of the Expedition." [5]The group camped on the ice floes for six months, until the ice broke up and they took small lifeboats to nearby uninhabited Elephant Island. [6]During their time on the boat, ice, and island, Shackleton's group endured temperatures as low as twenty degrees below zero and had no daylight from May to July. [7]They had to hunt scarce seals and penguins for food, and were hunted themselves by killer whales and sea leopards, which would rise through the ice in search of prey. [8]Throughout this time, Shackleton demonstrated his leadership by rationing food, rotating use of the warmer sleeping bags, and keeping a calm, positive attitude that helped morale. [9]He also showed great courage as he and five of his men crossed eight hundred miles of dangerous ocean to the nearest inhabited island to seek help. [10]Despite no maps and terrible weather, Shackleton's small boat reached the island where Shackleton and an even smaller group crossed unexplored, jagged mountains to reach a whaling station. [11]He organized a rescue party to retrieve the rest of his crew, and despite the perils of living in south polar waters for almost two years, all twenty-seven men came back from the expedition. [12]Shackleton never crossed the South Pole, but he completed the task of bringing back all of his crew alive.

_____ 1. Shackleton and his men had to abandon the *Endurance* when
- A. killer whales attacked the ship.
- B. the ship ran aground on Elephant Island.
- C. they ran out of food and had to leave to hunt for more.
- D. ice crushed the ship.

_____ 2. The "more amazing feat" referred to in sentence 1 is Shackleton's
- A. ability to withstand severe cold.
- B. managing to get all crew members back alive.
- C. crossing jagged, unexplored mountains.
- D. crossing eight hundred miles of ocean.

_____ 3. The main pattern of organization used in the passage is one of
A. list of items.
B. definition and example.
C. time order.
D. cause and effect.

_____ 4. Sentence 1 is made up of
A. fact.
B. opinion.
C. fact and opinion.

_____ 5. The author's main purpose in this passage is to
A. inform readers about the facts of the Shackleton expedition.
B. persuade readers that Shackleton was responsible for the failure of the expedition.
C. entertain readers with anecdotes about the hardships of the Shackleton expedition.

_____ 6. The author's tone is
A. detached.
B. admiring.
C. doubtful.
D. sentimental.

_____ 7. The author implies that
A. Shackleton's men were generally cowardly and poor sailors.
B. Shackleton carelessly began the voyage without adequate preparation.
C. he considers Shackleton's voyage a failure because it did not reach the South Pole.
D. Shackleton's men would likely have perished if not for his courage.

_____ 8. The main idea of the passage is
A. stated in sentence 1.
B. stated in sentence 4.
C. stated in sentence 8.
D. not stated.

COMBINED SKILLS: Test 12

Read the passage below. Then write the letter of the best answer to each question that follows.

[1]The 2008 Democratic presidential primary race was unique since, for the first time ever, a woman and a black man were major candidates. [2]Both Barack Obama and Hillary Clinton faced prejudice as they struggled to disprove the notion that only white men are qualified to become president. [3]Yet recent experiments indicate that it may be easier for political candidates to overcome racism than to overcome sexism. [4]For example, one experiment found it easy for whites to admire African American doctors; they just mentally categorized them as "doctors" rather than as "blacks." [5]In another experiment, researchers put blacks and whites in sports jerseys as if they belonged to two basketball teams. [6]People looking at the photos logged the players in their memories more by team than by race, recalling a player's jersey color but not necessarily his or her race. [7]But only very rarely did people forget whether a player was male or female. [8]It appears that, in this instance, gender trumps race.

[9]The challenge for women competing in politics or business has much to do with unconscious sexism: Americans don't dislike women, but they do often stereotype them as warm and friendly. [10]This bias creates a mismatch with the stereotype we hold of leaders as tough and strong. [11]So voters (women as well as men, though a bit less so) may feel that a woman isn't a good fit for a tough leadership job. [12]In addition, women face a related challenge: Those viewed as tough and strong are also typically viewed as cold and unfeminine. [13]Many experiments have found that women have trouble being viewed as both nice and competent. [14]"Clinton ran the risk of being seen as particularly cold, particularly uncaring, because she didn't fit the mold," said Joshua Correll, a psychologist at the University of Chicago. [15]"It probably was something a man doesn't deal with."

[16]But prejudicial beliefs can change. [17]Research subjects who were asked to think of a strong woman then showed less implied bias about men and women. [18]And students exposed to a large number of female professors also experienced a reduction in gender stereotypes. [19]So maybe the impact of the 2008 presidential primary contest won't be measured just in national policies, but also in progress in the deepest recesses of our own minds.

_____ 1. As used in sentence 8, the word *trumps* means
- A. is more important than.
- B. influences.
- C. is less important than.
- D. challenges.

_____ 2. According to the passage, Americans tend to stereotype women as
A. strong and friendly.
B. warm and friendly.
C. tough and strong.
D. cold and unfeminine.

_____ 3. When people look at photos of black and white men in sports jerseys, they tend to categorize them
A. by race.
B. by team.
C. by age.
D. by body type.

_____ 4. Students exposed to a large number of female professors
A. tended to be less racist than other students.
B. got higher grades than other students.
C. praised their female professors as warm and friendly.
D. experienced a reduction in gender stereotypes.

_____ 5. The relationship of sentence 5 to sentence 4 is one of
A. addition.
B. illustration.
C. time.
D. comparison.

_____ 6. The author implies that Hillary Clinton had to go out of her way to appear
A. both feminine and caring.
B. both feminine and competent.
C. both tough and strong.
D. both cold and uncaring.

_____ 7. The author implies that Hillary Clinton
A. may have paved the way for other women presidential candidates.
B. lost to Barack Obama because she was a woman.
C. was cold and unfeminine.
D. was actually more competent than Barack Obama.

_____ 8. The central point of the selection is stated in
A. sentence 1.
B. sentence 2.
C. sentence 3.
D. sentence 9.

COMBINED SKILLS: Test 13

Read the passage below. Then write the letter of the best answer to each question that follows.

[1]Late in the year, we tackled the informal essay. [2]"The essay, don't you see, is the . . ." [3]My mind went numb. [4]Of all the forms of writing, none seemed so boring as the essay. [5]Naturally we would have to write informal essays. [6]Mr. Fleagle distributed a homework sheet offering us a choice of topics. [7]None was quite so simple-minded as "What I Did on My Summer Vacation," but most seemed to be almost as dull. [8]I took the list home and dawdled until the night before the essay was due. [9]Sprawled on the sofa, I finally faced up to the grim task, took the list out of my notebook, and scanned it. [10]The topic on which my eye stopped was "The Art of Eating Spaghetti."

[11]This title produced an extraordinary sequence of mental images. [12]Surging up out of the depths of memory came a vivid recollection of a night in Belleville when all of us were seated around the supper table—Uncle Allen, my mother, Uncle Charlie, Doris, Uncle Hal—and Aunt Pat served spaghetti for supper. [13]Spaghetti was an exotic treat in those days. [14]Neither Doris nor I had ever eaten spaghetti, and none of the adults had enough experience to be good at it. [15]All the good humor of Uncle Allen's house reawoke in my mind as I recalled the laughing arguments we had that night about the socially respectable method for moving spaghetti from plate to mouth.

[16]Suddenly I wanted to write about that, about the warmth and good feeling of it, but I wanted to put it down simply for my own joy, not for Mr. Fleagle. [17]It was a moment I wanted to recapture and hold for myself. [18]I wanted to relive the pleasure of an evening at New Street. [19]To write it as I wanted, however, would violate all the rules of formal composition I'd learned in school. . . .

[20]Two days passed before Mr. Fleagle returned the graded papers, and he returned everyone's but mine. [21]I was bracing myself for a command to report to Mr. Fleagle immediately after school for discipline when I saw him lift my paper from his desk and rap for the class's attention.

[22]"Now, boys," he said, "I want to read you an essay. [23]This is titled 'The Art of Eating Spaghetti.'"

[24]And he started to read. [25]My words! [26]He was reading *my words* out loud to the entire class. [27]What's more, the entire class was listening. [28]Listening attentively. [29]Then somebody laughed; then the entire class was laughing. . . .

[30]When Mr. Fleagle finished, he put the final seal on my happiness by saying, "Now that, boys, is an essay, don't you see. [31]It's—don't you see—it's of the very essence of the essay, don't you see. [32]Congratulations, Mr. Baker."

______ 1. The word *exotic* in sentence 13 means

A. boring.
B. well-known.
C. favorite.
D. excitingly unfamiliar.

_____ 2. Sentences 10–12
A. define a term.
B. compare two things.
C. describe a cause-effect relationship.
D. list several items.

_____ 3. According to the author, the choices for an essay topic
A. featured "What I Did on My Summer Vacation."
B. were hard to choose from because so many were interesting.
C. were mostly about food.
D. seemed quite dull at first.

_____ 4. When Mr. Fleagle returned the students' papers, he
A. held back several of the best ones.
B. congratulated Baker as he handed him his paper.
C. held back only Baker's.
D. announced that Baker had gotten the only A.

_____ 5. From reading this passage, one can conclude that
A. Mr. Fleagle was an extraordinarily good teacher.
B. Baker had always enjoyed writing essays.
C. a simple experience can be a good topic for an essay.
D. it was painful for the author when the entire class laughed.

_____ 6. Young Baker
A. had expected Mr. Fleagle to like his essay.
B. enjoyed the dinner at his aunt's, and his essay showed that enjoyment.
C. invented many of the details that appeared in his essay.
D. did not intend his essay to be amusing.

_____ 7. From the passage, we can conclude the author would agree that
A. students should not be required to write informal essays.
B. students should not be subjected to hearing their work read aloud in front of a class.
C. people who are not "born writers" will never learn to enjoy writing.
D. one key to good writing is finding the right topic.

_____ 8. Which statement best expresses the central point of this selection?
A. An interesting assignment and others' approval gave the author a joyful writing experience.
B. The informal essay is more useful than the formal essay for getting students excited about their assignments.
C. A writing assignment brought to the author's mind a funny spaghetti dinner at his aunt's house.
D. Teachers should create interesting writing assignments if they expect their students to care about writing.

COMBINED SKILLS: Test 14

Read the passage below. Then write the letter of the best answer to each question that follows.

[1]Optimism predisposes a positive approach to life. [2]"The optimist," notes researcher H. Jackson Brown, "goes to the window every morning and says, 'Good morning, God.' [3]The pessimist goes to the window and says, 'Good God, morning.'" [4]Many of us, however, have what researcher Neil Weinstein terms "an unrealistic optimism about future life events." [5]At Rutgers University, for example, students perceive themselves as far more likely than their classmates to get a job, draw a good salary, and own a home, and as far less likely to experience negative events, such as developing a drinking problem, having a heart attack before age 40, or being fired. [6]In Scotland, most late adolescents think they are much less likely than their peers to become infected by the AIDS virus. [7]After experiencing the 1989 earthquake, San Francisco Bay area students did lose their optimism about being less vulnerable than their classmates to injury in a natural disaster, but within three months their illusory optimism had rebounded.

[8]Another researcher notes how illusory optimism increases our vulnerability. [9]Believing ourselves immune to misfortune, we do not take sensible precautions. [10]In one survey, 137 marriage license applicants accurately estimated that half of marriages end in divorce, yet most assessed their chance of divorce as zero percent. [11]Sexually active undergraduate women who don't consistently use contraceptives perceive themselves, compared with other women at their university, as much less vulnerable to unwanted pregnancy. [12]Those who cheerfully shun seatbelts, deny the effects of smoking, and stumble into ill-fated relationships remind us that blind optimism, like pride, may, as the ancient proverb warns, go before a fall.

[13]Optimism definitely beats pessimism in promoting self-efficiency, health, and well-being. [14]Yet a dash of realism can save us from the perils of unrealistic optimism. [15]Self-doubt can energize students, most of whom—especially those destined for low grades—exhibit excess optimism about upcoming exams. [16](Such illusory optimism often disappears as the time approaches for receiving the exam back.) [17]Students who are overconfident tend to underprepare. [18]Their equally able but more anxious peers, fearing that they are going to bomb on the upcoming exam, study furiously and get higher grades. [19]The moral: Success in school and beyond requires enough optimism to sustain hope and enough pessimism to motivate concern.

_____ 1. In sentences 7 and 8, *illusory* means

A. proven.
B. carefully considered.
C. helpful.
D. based on error.

_____ 2. The relationship of sentence 8 to the several sentences before it is one of
A. time.
B. cause-effect.
C. addition.
D. contrast.

_____ 3. Which of the following is in a contrast relationship to the sentence preceding it?
A. Sentence 10
B. Sentence 11
C. Sentence 12
D. Sentence 14

_____ 4. The third paragraph
A. lists several causes of optimism.
B. contrasts optimism with realism and pessimism.
C. defines and illustrates optimism.
D. all of the above.

_____ 5. The passage suggests that
A. many people unrealistically think themselves safe from harm.
B. both optimism and pessimism are useful.
C. unrealistic optimism can create problems.
D. all of the above.

_____ 6. The author of this passage would probably agree with which of the following statements?
A. Children should be encouraged to be as optimistic as possible.
B. It is better to be 100 percent realistic.
C. Negative experiences make people temporarily more realistic.
D. Optimists are more likely than pessimists to take precautions.

_____ 7. Which sentence best expresses the central point of the selection?
A. Sentence 1
B. Sentence 8
C. Sentence 15
D. Sentence 19

_____ 8. Which title best summarizes the passage?
A. Optimism Affects Grades
B. A Dash of Realism
C. Unrealistic Optimism
D. Think Positive!

COMBINED SKILLS: Test 15

Read the passage below. Then write the letter of the best answer to each question that follows.

[1]Those with closed minds refuse to consider any contradictory facts, and they proceed with their planned course of action, full speed ahead, with their "minds made up" and tightly shut. [2]As an illustration, consider the situation in 1986, prior to the space shuttle *Challenger's* disastrous launch that killed all seven astronauts aboard. [3]There was a heated telephone debate between two engineers for the company that produced the shuttle booster rockets and top officials of NASA (the federal government's space agency). [4]The engineers insisted that the flight was too risky because of freezing temperatures at the Florida launch site. [5]They explained that some of the seals on the fuel tanks were not designed to withstand such low temperatures and might leak under pressure, thus endangering the craft and crew.

[6]Despite the pleas to abort the flight, officials at NASA overruled the engineers, who were best qualified to make judgments about the complex technical problems of space flight. [7]What caused the officials to ignore the engineers? [8]Several flights had already been postponed, and it would not look good to postpone another. [9]It would be bad public relations to disappoint the crowds of people and news reporters waiting for the launch. [10]Top government officials were ready to appear on national television and take the credit for another safe flight. [11]As a result, with their minds absolutely closed to the facts presented by the engineers, NASA officials ordered the *Challenger* to take off. [12]Seventy-three seconds later, the spacecraft was enveloped in flame.

[13]Incredibly, seventeen years later, the lesson of the *Challenger* disaster was repeated. [14]In 2003, the space shuttle *Columbia* broke apart while re-entering the earth's atmosphere, killing another crew of seven. [15]During the shuttle's liftoff, a piece of foam insulation had broken off, hitting the shuttle's wing at five hundred miles per hour. [16]Lower-level engineers at NASA begged for photographs of the *Columbia* in orbit, which might have shown the extent of the damage, but their closed-minded superiors ignored their requests. [17]It was the damage caused by the 1.7-pound chunk of insulation that doomed the *Columbia*.

[18]There is no virtue in ignoring contradictory facts and "sticking to your guns" when the course taken shows all the signs of being the wrong one. [19]Closed minds are especially noticeable in political campaigns and debates. [20]Many people line up to support one candidate or another and won't listen to any facts presented by the opposing candidate.

[21]All those with an open mind say is this: "I don't know everything, so I'd better keep my mind, eyes, and ears open to any new facts that may come along." [22]The world would be a much better and safer place if everyone had this attitude.

_____ 1. In sentence 6, the word *abort* means
A. take. C. watch.
B. rush. D. stop.

_____ 2. The pattern of organization used in the second paragraph is
A. cause and effect. C. definition and example.
B. comparison. D. contrast.

_____ 3. The *Challenger*'s weak point was
A. its crew. C. the fuel tanks' seals.
B. the fuel. D. the size of its rockets.

_____ 4. The author implies that
A. the *Columbia* disaster was impossible to foresee.
B. incompetent engineers were to blame for the *Columbia* explosion.
C. the *Columbia*'s damaged wing could not withstand the stress of re-entering the earth's atmosphere.
D. the *Columbia* was deliberately sabotaged.

_____ 5. The author of this passage would probably agree with which of the following statements?
A. People with open minds make more responsible citizens than those with closed minds.
B. NASA should abandon its space-shuttle campaign.
C. Once a person makes a decision, he or she should stick to it.
D. The *Challenger* and *Columbia* explosions may have been caused by deliberate foul play.

_____ 6. The author's main purpose is to
A. inform readers about what an open mind is.
B. entertain the reader with two stories of tragedies in space.
C. persuade readers of the importance of an open mind.

_____ 7. The tone of the second and third paragraphs can be described as
A. amused. C. revengeful.
B. critical. D. uncertain.

_____ 8. Which sentence best expresses the central point of the passage?
A. There is a great deal of closed-minded thinking in the federal government.
B. One is more likely to see closed-minded thinkers in science and politics.
C. An open mind is more logical and safer than a closed mind.
D. Closed-minded thinking is a widespread phenomenon.

COMBINED SKILLS: Test 16

Read the passage below. Then write the letter of the best answer to each question that follows.

[1]It is clear that advertisements work. [2]Attention is caught, communication occurs between producers and consumers, and sales result. [3]It turns out to be difficult to detail the exact relationship between a specific ad and a specific purchase, or even between a campaign and subsequent sales figures, because advertising is only one of a host of influences upon consumption. [4]Yet no one is fooled by this lack of perfect proof; everyone knows that advertising sells. [5]If this were not the case, then tightfisted American businesses would not spend a total of fifty billion dollars annually on these messages.

[6]But before anyone despairs that advertisers have our number to the extent that they can marshal us at will and march us like automatons to the checkout counters, we should recall the resiliency and obduracy of the American consumer. [7]Advertisers may have uncovered the softest spots in our minds, but that does not mean they have found truly gaping holes. [8]There is no evidence that advertising can get people to do things contrary to their self-interests. [9]Despite all the finesse of advertisements, and all the subtle emotional tugs, the public resists the vast majority of the petitions. [10]According to the marketing division of the AC Nielsen Company, a whopping 75 percent of all new products die within a year in the marketplace, the victims of consumer disinterest, which no amount of advertising could overcome. [11]The appeals in advertising may be the most captivating there are to be had, but they are not enough to entrap the wily consumer.

[12]The key to understanding the discrepancy between, on the one hand, the fact that advertising truly works, and, on the other, the fact that it hardly works, is to take into account the enormous numbers of people exposed to an ad. [13]Modern-day communications permit an ad to be displayed to millions upon millions of individuals; if the smallest fraction of that audience can be moved to buy the product, then the ad has been successful. [14]When 1 percent of the people exposed to a television advertising campaign reach for their wallets, that could be one million sales, which may be enough to keep the product and the advertisements coming.

_____ 1. In sentence 3, the word *host* means a
- A. lack.
- B. question.
- C. fear.
- D. large number.

_____ 2. The word *discrepancy,* in sentence 12, means
- A. similarity.
- B. inconsistency.
- C. marketing.
- D. delay.

3. According to the passage, the American consumer is
   A. a sucker for ads.
   B. stingy.
   C. willing to try anything new.
   D. motivated by self-interest.

_____ 4. The reading
   A. contrasts advertisements with consumers.
   B. discusses the effectiveness of ads.
   C. lists reasons for advertising.
   D. narrates a series of events in the history of advertising.

_____ 5. According to the AC Nielsen Company, the percentage of new products that survive their first year in the marketplace is
   A. 15.
   B. 25.
   C. 50.
   D. 75.

_____ 6. The passage suggests that an ad may be considered successful if it
   A. makes people laugh or cry.
   B. moves 1 percent of viewers to buy the product advertised.
   C. is remembered by 75 percent of the viewers.
   D. costs a great deal.

_____ 7. One can conclude from reading this passage that
   A. advertisements aren't worth their enormous cost.
   B. advertising is the single most important influence on a consumer's decision to buy.
   C. an ad cannot get people to buy a product they aren't otherwise interested in.
   D. companies are generally reluctant to spend money on advertising.

_____ 8. Which title best summarizes the passage?
   A. The Role of Advertising in Modern Life
   B. Advertising: Effective but Not Foolproof
   C. Why Advertising Fails
   D. What Makes for a Good Advertisement?

COMBINED SKILLS: Test 17

Read the passage below. Then write the letter of the best answer to each question that follows.

[1]We tend to think of America's early European settlers, who came seeking religious freedom, as solemn, sober folk. [2]So it is surprising to learn that in the seventeenth and eighteenth centuries, beer consumption was a big part of daily life, and it is even more surprising to learn that beer was considered a health drink! [3]In the seventeenth century, even adult Quakers (religious refugees from England who were known for their devout and simple lifestyle) typically drank three to four quarts of beer a day. [4]Their children drank one to two quarts of "small beer"—a very weak brew with a low alcohol content. [5]Large estates, such as the home of wealthy William Penn, Pennsylvania's founder, included a brew house. [6]In humbler households, the housewife brewed beer in a big iron kettle in the yard. [7]The colonists considered beer a necessity because they believed it was healthier than water—and indeed it was, though for reasons that were not understood at the time. [8]In early American towns and homesteads, wells were not lined. [9]As a result, drinking water was often contaminated with animal manure and human waste. [10]The early settlers did not know that their water was full of bacteria; it was not until the mid-nineteenth century that scientists began to understand that invisible germs cause much disease, and that boiling water kills these germs. [11]The colonists did not realize that the several rounds of boiling that are part of the brewing process sterilized their dirty water. [12]But they did realize that they stayed healthier drinking beer than drinking well water. [13]Tea—also made with boiled water—was also considered a healthy drink; but tea was an expensive product imported from China or India, out of reach of many homesteaders, and reserved for guests and special occasions even in wealthy homes. [14]Thus, while the colonists condemned and punished public drunkenness, it is likely that they frequently went about their business feeling something of an alcohol "buzz"—which they undoubtedly preferred to the stomach sickness they might have gotten from a plain glass of their unsanitary well water.

_____ 1. According to the passage,
A. rich settlers had their own brew houses.
B. rich households drank only tea rather than beer.
C. wealthy settlers usually lined their wells and drank water.
D. non-wealthy settlers could afford only "small beer."

_____ 2. Beer actually was healthier than water in colonial times because
A. the alcohol in the beer killed bacteria.
B. the boiling involved in the brewing process killed bacteria.
C. the linings of wells polluted the water with lead.
D. high-quality ingredients for brewing beer were imported from China and India.

_____ 3. The relationship between sentences 8 and 9 is one of
A. time order.
B. cause and effect.
C. comparison.
D. contrast.

_____ 4. The relationship of sentence 12 to sentence 11 is one of
A. time order.
B. cause and effect.
C. comparison.
D. contrast.

_____ 5. The author's tone can be described as
A. admiring and amused.
B. objective and informal.
C. scholarly, but critical.
D. unkind and sarcastic.

_____ 6. The author implies that
A. drunkenness was unknown in the colonies.
B. the Quakers did not realize beer could lead to intoxication.
C. beer was simply considered a beverage, not a sure way to become intoxicated.
D. the beer the colonists brewed contained little water.

_____ 7. Which is the most appropriate title for this selection?
A. The Surprising Quakers
B. Life in the Early Colonies
C. Beer Consumption in Colonial America
D. Benefits of Beer and Tea

_____ 8. Which of the following statements best expresses the main idea of the passage?
A. Quakers, religious refugees from England known for their devout and simple lifestyle, drank a lot of beer.
B. The American colonists knew that drinking water was unhealthy, but they didn't know why.
C. The well water in early American towns and homesteads was often contaminated by manure and human waste.
D. Early American colonists found beer to be more healthful than water.

COMBINED SKILLS: Test 18

Read the passage below. Then write the letter of the best answer to each question that follows.

[1]Why are some rich and powerful men generous while others are misers? [2]New evidence reveals that the mere presence of female family members—even infants—can lead men to become more generous. [3]In a recent study conducted in Denmark, researchers found that chief executives paid their employees about $100 less after becoming fathers. [4]Apparently, it's common for a male chief executive to claim a larger share of "his firm's resources for himself and his growing family, at the expense of his employees." [5]The twist to the study was that the chief executives reduced wages after having a son but not after having a daughter. [6]Researchers theorize that as fathers care for their daughters, they become gentler and more empathetic. [7]In other words, daughters bring out their fathers' caretaking tendencies.

[8]In a second study, participants were asked to choose between two options: either you get $25 and your partner gets $10, or you get $20 and your partner gets $30. [9]The latter option is the more generous because it involves sacrificing a small amount to increase your partner's gains by a much larger amount. [10]In this study, the people who chose the second option were 40 percent more likely to have sisters than the people who made the less generous choice. [11]Another study has shown that men who have grown up with sisters spend more time raising their own children. [12]Social scientists believe that the caring, empathetic behaviors of sisters rub off on their brothers. [13]For example, psychologist Alice Eagly at Northwestern University has conducted studies that demonstrate that women tend to do more giving and helping in close relationships than men. [14]It might also be that boys feel the need to protect their sisters. [15]Additionally, research has found that men are significantly more likely to help women than to help men.

[16]Some of the world's most charitable men have acknowledged that the women in their lives have inspired them to become more generous. [17]According to Bill Gates, his mother Mary "never stopped pressing me to do more for others." [18]And Bill's wife Melinda has played a pivotal role in guiding much of the Bill and Melinda Gates Foundation's philanthropy. [19]These women have been a major reason that Gates has donated more than $28 billion over the years while other billionaires have been relatively tight-fisted about charitable giving.

[20]Given the opportunity, women could also exert a beneficial effect in the boardroom. [21]When women join top management teams, they could encourage male colleagues to treat employees more generously and to share information more freely. [22]Increases in motivation, cooperation, and innovation in companies may be fueled not only by the direct actions of female leaders, but also by their influence on male leaders.

_____ 1. In sentences 6 and 12, the word *empathetic* means
A. emotional. C. reliable.
B. kindhearted. D. committed.

_____ 2. In the second study described in the passage, the participants who chose the more generous option were more likely to
A. be only children. C. have sisters.
B. be parents of sons. D. be men.

_____ 3. The relationship of sentence 13 to sentence 12 is one of
A. addition.
B. cause and effect.
C. illustration.
D. contrast.

_____ 4. In general, the selection
A. illustrates the idea that women influence men to become more generous.
B. contrasts generous men with men who are not generous.
C. explains why women tend to be more giving and helpful in close relationships than men.
D. lists reasons why it's important to be charitable.

_____ 5. The author would probably agree with which of the following statements?
A. Women are too caring to be successful on top management teams.
B. Because Bill Gates is so rich, he should donate more of his fortune to philanthropy.
C. American businesses would benefit if more women took part in executive decision-making.
D. When women become successful in business, they sometimes become less empathetic.

_____ 6. On the basis of the last paragraph of the selection, we can infer that
A. female leaders can help corporations become more profitable.
B. men on top management teams tend to be cut-throat.
C. men currently outnumber women in the boardroom.
D. all of the above.

_____ 7. The tone of this selection is
A. impassioned and pleading.
B. concerned and uncertain.
C. detached and objective.
D. instructive and optimistic.

_____ 8. Which statement best expresses the central point of the passage?
A. Fathers who have daughters are often more generous than fathers who have sons.
B. Because women tend to make men more generous, women should play a greater role in both charitable ventures and the business world.
C. Researchers have spent a great deal of time studying what causes men to become more generous.
D. The empathetic behavior of sisters can cause their brothers to become more caring.

COMBINED SKILLS: Test 19

Read the passage below. Then write the letter of the best answer to each question that follows.

[1]Recently there have been several highly publicized incidents in which adolescent boys have killed themselves after being tormented with accusations of being "gay," "faggots," or "queer." [2]One victim, a Massachusetts boy who hanged himself, was only 11. [3]In Ohio, a similarly bullied 17-year-old shot himself. [4]Their offenses, it seems, ranged from getting good grades to liking theater, playing the piano, and being unenthusiastic about sports. [5]The hateful scenario is a familiar one in almost any middle school or high school in America. [6]Most such situations, fortunately, do not have consequences as tragic as suicide, but such tormenting inevitably leaves deep and lasting emotional scars. [7]Strangely, being called a "fag" today has almost nothing to do with actually being homosexual. [8]In many schools, any boy who is perceived as more than usually gentle, or caring about books or music or clothes, or open about his feelings, risks being so labeled. [9]Why? [10]In an era where civil rights for gay adults have made significant progress, why is there such a poisonous boy-culture in our schools? [11]Why does that culture celebrate thuggish behavior and punish boys who are perceived as artistic or nerdy or caring or bookish? [12]Some observers theorize that boys today are struggling in a new way to define what "masculine" means. [13]In the past, many boys expected to follow their fathers and grandfathers into "men's work" in factories and other blue-collar jobs. [14]Now with factories closing down and blue-collar jobs vanishing from the American landscape, that clear path to manhood has been obliterated. [15]As a result, these boys try to prove their "manhood" by tormenting others who are more vulnerable. [16]Perhaps parents who misguidedly push their sons to be "tough" and "manly" are contributing to the problem, suggesting that to be soft or caring is to be unaccepted and unloved. [17]Whatever the cause, the need to throw such words as "gay" and "faggot" and "queer" around reveals some sort of terrible fear and uncertainty at the core of the boys doing the tormenting. [18]What is it that so threatens them about others who do not fit their limited idea of what it is to be a man?

_____ 1. In sentence 14, the word *obliterated* means
- A. made easier.
- B. refused.
- C. destroyed.
- D. outlawed.

_____ 2. According to the passage, boys today
- A. can expect to do the same sort of work their fathers and grandfathers did.
- B. may feel threatened by other boys who are artistic, gentle, and studious.
- C. are not as tough as they used to be.
- D. have parents who are unloving.

_____ 3. On the basis of the selection, we can infer that
- A. only gay boys get tormented in school.
- B. only the toughest and manliest boys torment others.
- C. parents play no part in how their sons behave in school.
- D. the decline of blue-collar jobs may have made bullying in schools worse.

_____ 4. The passage suggests that
- A. being called "gay" or "queer" in school is not an important issue.
- B. girls are never called "gay" or "queer."
- C. the adolescent boys who killed themselves were gay.
- D. the adolescent boys who killed themselves didn't know how to stand up to bullying.

_____ 5. The author of this passage would probably agree with which of the following statements?
- A. Teenage boys who try to prove their manhood by tormenting others are actually very fearful.
- B. Parents who push their sons to be "tough" and "manly" bear some responsibility if their sons become bullies.
- C. It's fine for boys to be gentle and care about such things as books, clothes, and music.
- D. all of the above.

_____ 6. The author's tone can be described as
- A. sentimental.
- B. matter-of-fact.
- C. uncertain.
- D. concerned.

_____ 7. Sentence 17 is a statement of
- A. fact.
- B. opinion.

_____ 8. Which statement best expresses the main idea of the passage?
- A. In many schools, young men who prefer books or music to sports are often bullied.
- B. Boys who torment other boys by calling them "fag" or "queer" do so because they are trying to prove their own masculinity.
- C. Today's parents often push their sons to be "tough" and "manly."
- D. The decline of American industry has caused many changes in American life.

COMBINED SKILLS: Test 20

Read the passage below. Then write the letter of the best answer to each question that follows.

[1]Resources are the things or services used to produce goods, which then can be used to satisfy wants. [2]Economic resources are scarce; free resources, such as air, are so abundant that they can be obtained without charge. [3]The test of whether a resource is an economic resource or a free resource is price: scarce economic resources command a price; abundant free resources do not. [4]The number of free resources is actually quite limited. [5]For instance, although the Earth contains a huge amount of water, it is not a free resource to typical urban or suburban homeowners, who must pay a local water authority for providing and maintaining their water supply. [6]In a world where all resources were free, there would be no economic problems, since all wants could be satisfied.

[7]Economic resources can be classified into three categories:

Land. [8]A shorthand expression for natural resources, land includes minerals as well as plots of ground. [9]Clearly, land is an important and valuable resource in both agriculture and industry. [10]Think of the fertile soil of Iowa or Kansas, which produces such abundant crops. [11]Or consider Manhattan Island, which supports the skyscrapers, shops, and theaters in the heart of New York. [12]In addition, land is an important part of our environment, and it provides enjoyment above and beyond its contribution to agricultural and industrial output.

Labor. [13]Human efforts, both physical and mental, are included in the category of labor. [14]Thus, when you study for a final examination or make out an income tax return, this is as much labor as if you were to dig a ditch. [15]In 2003, over 140 million people were employed (or looking for work) in the United States. [16]This vast labor supply is, of course, an extremely important resource, without which our nation could not maintain its current output level.

Capital. [17]Buildings, equipment, inventories, and other nonhuman producible resources that contribute to the production, marketing, and distribution of goods and services all fall within the economist's definition of capital. [18]Examples are machine tools and warehouses; but not all types of capital are big and bulky: for example, a hand calculator, or a pencil for that matter, is a type of capital. [19]Workers in the United States have an enormous amount of capital to work with. [20]Think of the oil refineries in New Jersey and Philadelphia, the electronics factories near Boston and San Francisco, the aircraft plants in California, and all of the additional types of capital we have and use in this country. [21]Without this capital, the nation's output level would be a great deal less than it is.

_____ 1. In sentence 3, the word *command* means

A. give an order.
B. have authority over.
C. escape.
D. can get.

_____ 2. Labor is defined as
A. a form of capital.
B. mental and physical efforts.
C. only physical efforts.
D. excluding persons looking for work.

_____ 3. According to the passage, the number of free resources is
A. limited.
B. determined by the availability of labor.
C. the same the world around.
D. growing.

_____ 4. The passage lists several
A. definitions and examples.
B. comparisons.
C. events in time order.
D. causes and effects.

_____ 5. The relationship of sentence 5 to sentence 4 is one of
A. addition.
B. comparison.
C. contrast.
D. illustration.

_____ 6. The author's main purpose is to
A. inform.
B. persuade.
C. entertain.

_____ 7. Sentence 3 is a statement of
A. fact.
B. opinion.
C. fact and opinion.

_____ 8. Which statement best expresses the central point of the passage?
A. Economic resources are scarce and cost money, unlike free resources such as air.
B. Economic resources—resources that aren't free—can be classified into three categories: land, labor, and capital.
C. Resources are things and services used to produce goods, which may then be used to fulfill wants.
D. Such things as buildings, equipment, and pencils are among the nonhuman producible resources that contribute to the economy.

COMBINED SKILLS: Test 21

Read the passage below. Then write the letter of the best answer to each question that follows.

[1]Today no country that employs the death penalty can be admitted to the European Union, and the practice dwindles daily. [2]Nonetheless, Texas and a handful of other states continue to take their place among such paragons as North Korea, China, and Iran in the club of those who administer the death penalty as a form of "justice." [3]Indeed, Texas has executed nearly 500 people since the Supreme Court reinstated the death penalty in 1976. [4]That ruling overturned an earlier court ruling that the death penalty was "cruel and unusual punishment."

[5]Why shouldn't we execute people? [6]One reason is that black people are disproportionately represented on death row, as are blacks imprisoned throughout the United States. [7]Many would say (or whisper) that black people are more prone to crime and violence than are white people.

[8]But I know that there was a time when my people—Irish-Americans—were deemed to be more prone to crime and violence than were others. [9]This was in the years after the potato famines of the 1800s that brought so many desperately poor Irish people to these shores. [10]The police in New York City so frequently arrested Irishmen that they began to call the van they threw the arrestees into "the Paddy Wagon"—a name that has stuck ever since.

[11]But who today would dare to claim that the Irish are prone to criminal behavior? [12]Irish immigrants were more likely to become criminals not because of some genetic inheritance, but because they were so very poor, so neglected, so abandoned. [13]When I see a vagrant today, snoring on a park bench, I think to myself: Whatever happened to this guy, no one loved him enough when he was a child. [14]His parents, if he had parents, were too taken up with the struggle for survival to tend to him adequately, if at all. [15]No one came to rescue this child, to give him the love and security that everyone needs in order to grow.

[16]Our society has largely ignored such people. [17]Many other Western societies devote considerable resources to keeping poor families from despair. [18]As an American friend of mine who lives in Denmark says, "In Denmark we tax the rich, but everyone is comfortable." [19]Not everyone is comfortable in the United States. [20]Millions of children live below the poverty line, without enough food or adequate shelter and with almost no attention to their educational and emotional needs.

[21]If we would pay attention to the needs of all our children, our world would change overnight. [22]We would certainly not need our electric chairs and nooses and lethal injections. [23]We could then say what the poet-priest John Donne said in 1623, "Any man's death diminishes me because I am involved in mankind."

_____ 1. In sentence 1, the word *dwindles* means

A. becomes milder.
B. decreases.
C. becomes more widespread.
D. intensifies.

_____ 2. The relationship of sentence 2 to sentence 1 is one of

A. cause and effect.
B. contrast.
C. comparison.
D. time order.

_____ 3. According to the selection, Irish immigrants in the 19th century
- A. were the most violent ethnic group ever to immigrate to the U.S.
- B. were more likely to be arrested due to prejudice on the part of the police.
- C. were more likely to commit crimes because they were worse off than other ethnic groups.
- D. had a genetic abnormality that made them more violent than other ethnic groups.

_____ 4. We can conclude from this selection that
- A. some ethnic and racial groups will always be more likely to commit violent crimes than others.
- B. there are parallels between the experiences of Irish-Americans in the 1800s and African Americans today.
- C. if Texas stopped executing people, its murder rate would go up.
- D. the author often gives handouts to vagrants who sleep on park benches.

_____ 5. The author of this selection would probably agree with which of the following statements?
- A. Rich Americans should pay higher taxes so that everyone in the United States can be comfortable.
- B. The death penalty should be abolished in the United States.
- C. If our society took better care of poor people, our violent crime rate would drop.
- D. All of the above.

_____ 6. Sentence 10 is a statement of
- A. fact.
- B. opinion.
- C. both fact and opinion.

_____ 7. Which statement best expresses the central point of the selection?
- A. Just as some people accuse blacks today of being more prone to crime and violence than whites, people in the 19th century accused Irish immigrants of being more prone to crime and violence than others.
- B. In contrast to Denmark, not everyone in the U.S. is comfortable.
- C. Although most industrialized countries have eliminated the death penalty, Texas and some other states continue to put people to death.
- D. Because most violent crime is caused by poverty, we should take steps to reduce poverty and abolish the death penalty.

_____ 8. Which of the following would be the best title for this passage?
- A. The Hardships of Poverty
- B. Why We Should Stop Executing People
- C. How Paddy Wagons Got Their Name
- D. America and Denmark: Similarities and Differences

COMBINED SKILLS: Test 22

Read the passage below. Then write the letter of the best answer to each question that follows.

[1]Memorial Day, which originated during the Civil War to honor the Union and Confederate dead, has over the ages become an occasion to also celebrate current members of the armed forces and veterans.

[2]Unfortunately, however, the observance, like Veterans Day in the fall, means more to many people for providing an extra day off. [3]It's when they go to the Shore for the unofficial start of summer. [4]Little time is spent thinking about the war dead, soldiers, or veterans, unless someone in your family fits one of those distinctions.

[5]It's interesting that, after after 12 years of perpetual war in Iraq and Afghanistan, Americans have found myriad ways to pay superficial homage to their soldiers, sailors, airmen, and Marines. [6]They get to board airliners first, are provided shopping and other discounts, and are often serenaded by applause and shouts of "Thank you for your service." [7]And many of these expressions of gratitude are heartfelt.

[8]But just how much this country cares about its military men and women may be better measured by how well they are coping in the high-pressure environment of a military installation, or upon their return to civilian life after a final tour of duty in combat situations.

[9]Here's a statistic that suggests veterans aren't getting all the attention they deserve: Every day in America, about 22 veterans kill themselves. [10]That's a 20 percent increase in veteran suicides since 2007. [11]Even in the context of an overall increase in suicides in this country, the number for veterans is disturbing. [12]It indicates not only a lack of effective mental-health programs for veterans, but also insufficient emphasis on the problem by the Department of Veterans Affairs.

[13]Unemployment among veterans needs more attention, too. [14]U.S. Chamber of Commerce members have pledged to hire more than 200,000 veterans over the next five years. [15]But the pace needs to pick up. [16]The unemployment rate among veterans still hovers about 2 percentage points above the 7.5 percent national rate. [17]Too many vets are running out of money before they find a job. [18]Too many are living on the streets, some contemplating suicide because they have been unable to make the transition back to civilian life.

[19]In the days of an all-volunteer military, this nation should make an even stronger commitment to help those who step up, often multiple times, to serve their nation in uniform. [20]It's not asking too much that they be treated with more respect upon the completion of their service. [21]That includes finding them jobs and tending to their health.

_____ 1. In sentence 5, the word *myriad* means

A. unrecognized.
B. costly.
C. many.
D. informal.

_____ 2. According to the selection, which of the following does **not** contribute to the high suicide rate among veterans?

A. The need for better mental-health programs
B. Problems with returning to civilian life
C. A lack of official recognition for their service
D. The difficulty of finding a job

_____ 3. The relationship of sentence 2 to sentence 1 is one of
A. cause and effect.
B. time order.
C. addition.
D. contrast.

_____ 4. We can logically infer from the selection that
A. most veterans don't care at all about boarding airliners first and receiving store discounts.
B. veterans of Iraq and Afghanistan are receiving more help than veterans of other conflicts.
C. only a tiny minority of veterans are experiencing difficulty returning to civilian life.
D. the ways that Americans currently express their gratitude toward veterans don't address the real problems these veterans face.

_____ 5. The author of this selection would probably agree with which of the following statements?
A. Once a veteran leaves the armed forces, he or she should be guaranteed a high-paying job.
B. The advantages of serving in the military outweigh the disadvantages of doing so.
C. We have a special responsibility to veterans of Iraq and Afghanistan because they've borne the brunt of these extended conflicts.
D. To ease the burden on our troops, we should eliminate the all-volunteer military and reinstitute the draft.

_____ 6. The author's main purpose is to
A. inform readers about the original purpose of Memorial Day and Veterans Day.
B. inspire readers with stories of the heroic sacrifices made by veterans.
C. persuade readers that we need to provide veterans with more meaningful support.
D. persuade readers that we should avoid becoming involved in wars that last a long time.

_____ 7. The tone of this selection is best described as
A. pleading and regretful.
B. calm and instructive.
C. compassionate and straightforward.
D. objective and optimistic.

_____ 8. Which statement best expresses the central point of the selection?
A. The Department of Veterans Affairs needs to do a better job of caring for veterans with mental health issues.
B. Americans need to show their respect for veterans by helping them find jobs and caring for their health.
C. Because many Iraq and Afghanistan veterans have faced multiple deployments, they face greater challenges than veterans of other wars.
D. Having a family member in the military makes people more likely to honor veterans in meaningful ways.

COMBINED SKILLS: Test 23

Read the passage below. Then write the letter of the best answer to each question that follows.

[1]In seeking to explain belief in witchcraft, historians agree that the idea took shape toward the end of the Middle Ages. [2]Peasant culture throughout the Middle Ages included belief in the possibility of sorcery. [3]In other words, most simple rural people assumed that certain unusual individuals could practice good, or "white," magic in the form of healing, divination for lost objects, and fortunetelling; or perhaps also evil, "black" magic that might, for example, call up tempests or ravage crops. [4]But only in the fifteenth century did learned authorities begin to insist, on theological grounds, that black magic could be practiced only as a result of pacts with the devil. [5]Naturally, once this belief became accepted, judicial officers soon found it urgent to prosecute all "witches" who practiced black magic because warfare against the devil was paramount to Christian society and "the evil one" could not be allowed to hold any sway. [6]Accordingly, in 1484 Pope Innocent VIII ordered papal inquisitors to root out alleged witchcraft with all the means at their disposal, and the pace of witch-hunts gained momentum in the following decades. [7]Nor were witch trials curtailed in areas that broke with Rome, for Protestant reformers believed in the insidious powers of Satan just as much as the Catholics did.

[8]The victims were most frequently women, no doubt in part because preachers had encouraged their flocks to believe that evil had first come into the world with Eve and in part because men in authority felt psychologically most ambivalent about members of the opposite sex. [9]Pure sadism certainly cannot have been the original motive for such proceedings, yet once trials began, horrendous sadism very often was unleashed. [10]Thus old women, young girls, and sometimes even mere children might be brutally tortured by having needles driven under their nails, fires placed at their heels, or their legs crushed under weights until marrow spurted from their bones, in order to make them confess to having had filthy orgies with demons. [11]The final death toll will never be known, but in the 1620s there was an average of one hundred burnings a year in the German cities of Würzburg and Bamberg, and around the same time it was said the town square of Wolfenbüttel "looked like a little forest, so crowded were the stakes."

______ 1. As used in sentence 5, *paramount* means
A. reasonable.
B. discouraging.
C. questionable.
D. of greatest importance.

______ 2. Example context clues for the word *sadism,* in sentence 9, are in sentence
A. 8.
B. 9.
C. 10.
D. 11.

_____ 3. One reason women were most often accused of witchcraft is that
A. they were cruel more often than men.
B. they were linked through the story of Eve to the entry of evil into the world.
C. they could find lost objects more easily than men could.
D. their ability to care for the sick made others suspicious.

_____ 4. According to the passage, people suspected of witchcraft were
A. driven from their homes.
B. excluded from the church.
C. forced to be "converted" by the church.
D. tortured until they confessed.

_____ 5. The relationship of sentence 4 to sentence 3 is one of
A. addition.
B. comparison.
C. contrast.
D. example.

_____ 6. Sentence 6 is a statement of
A. fact.
B. opinion.
C. fact and opinion.

_____ 7. It is reasonable to conclude that before the fifteenth century,
A. the idea of "black magic" was unknown in most of Europe.
B. people who practiced "black magic" were not thought to have made pacts with the devil.
C. sorcery was practiced in almost all households.
D. witch-hunts were banned by law throughout Europe.

_____ 8. Which statement best expresses the central point of the passage?
A. Peasants throughout the Middle Ages believed in the possibility of sorcery.
B. Educated authorities of the 1400s stated that black magic took place only as a result of pacts with the devil.
C. A belief in black magic that began during the Middle Ages led the church to cause the hunting and torture of so-called witches.
D. During and after the Middle Ages, people believed in magic and witches, both good and evil.

COMBINED SKILLS: Test 24

Read the passage below. Then write the letter of the best answer to each question that follows.

[1]Human populations tend to go through stages which are tied to economic development. [2]In the first stage, both birth rates and death rates are high. [3]Because the two rates more or less balance each other, the population is fairly stable, neither growing nor declining rapidly. [4]This was the stage of the populations in Western Europe in 1650, before industrialization. [5]During the second stage, the birth rate remains high but the death rate declines sharply. [6]This stage occurred in Western Europe after it became industrialized, and it is occurring today in many developing nations. [7]The introduction of modern medicine, along with better hygiene and sanitation, has decreased the death rates in developing countries. [8]But the economies and values of these countries are still essentially traditional, so their birth rates remain high. [9]As a result, their populations grow rapidly. [10]During the third stage, both birth rates and death rates decline. [11]Western countries found themselves in this stage after they reached a rather high level of industrialization. [12]Today, Taiwan, South Korea, and Argentina are among the developing nations that have reached this stage. [13]The birth rates in these countries have declined significantly. [14]In this stage, the population still grows because the birth rate continues to exceed the death rate, but growth is slower than during the second stage. [15]The fourth stage is marked by a low birth rate and a low death rate. [16]Only the most industrialized nations of Western Europe, the United States, and Japan have reached this stage. [17]They have fairly stable populations and are moving close to zero population growth. [18]At least 40 countries, such as Italy, Spain, and Germany, have already fallen below zero population growth, with birth rates lower than death rates; in other words, the fertility rate is less than the replacement level.

_____ 1. According to the selection, countries with traditional economies and values tend to experience

A. declining birth rates.
B. high birth rates.
C. zero population growth.
D. a decline in fertility.

_____ 2. According to the selection, shortly after Western Europe became industrialized,

A. its population rapidly declined.
B. both its birth rate and death rate slowly declined.
C. its birth rate remained high, but its death rate declined sharply.
D. both its birth rate and its death rate rose sharply.

_____ 3. The relationship of sentence 9 to sentence 8 is one of
A. contrast.
B. comparison.
C. cause and effect.
D. time.

_____ 4. On the basis of this selection, we can conclude that
A. Italy, Spain, and Germany are no longer industrialized countries.
B. Italy, Spain, and Germany are still essentially traditional countries.
C. Taiwan, South Korea, and Argentina have reached zero population growth.
D. the population of countries such as Italy, Spain, and Germany will decline if these countries do not admit immigrants.

_____ 5. This selection suggests that
A. only Western nations are moving close to zero population growth.
B. as societies become wealthier, people tend to have fewer children.
C. the introduction of modern medicine was the most important factor in declining death rates.
D. the United States is a traditional society.

_____ 6. The tone of the passage is
A. worried.
B. doubtful.
C. indignant.
D. objective.

_____ 7. The author's main purpose is to
A. persuade readers that all countries should move closer to zero population growth.
B. inform readers about stages of human population.
C. entertain the reader with interesting facts about other countries.
D. predict that eventually, more countries will achieve zero population growth.

_____ 8. The author would probably agree with which of the following statements?
A. Industrialization resulted in more people living longer.
B. Women in developed countries are selfish for not having more children.
C. Better hygiene and sanitation are the most important factors enabling people to live longer lives.
D. All of the above.

COMBINED SKILLS: Test 25

Read the passage below. Then write the letter of the best answer to each question that follows.

[1]All living cells in an animal's body require energy to power the various chemical processes going on inside them. [2]This energy is ultimately supplied by the food that animals eat. [3]These chemical processes are collectively referred to as *metabolism*, and one of the byproducts of metabolism is heat. [4]Metabolic rates vary significantly between species. [5]Warm-blooded animals (birds and mammals) have metabolic rates about five to ten times higher than those of similarly sized cold-blooded ones (reptiles, amphibians, and fishes). [6]And it is precisely because birds and mammals have such high metabolic rates that they are able to keep their bodies warm.

[7]The terms *warm-blooded* and *cold-blooded* are still in everyday use, but they are not entirely precise. [8]Anyone who has handled a snake knows this because a snake's body actually feels quite warm. [9]But very little of the snake's body heat originates internally, from its cells, most of it having been supplied from the outside, either by the sun or by a heat lamp. [10]Instead of referring to reptiles as cold-blooded, they are best described as *ectothermic*, meaning "outside heat." [11]Similarly, birds and mammals are said to be *endothermic*, meaning "inside heat."

[12]There are advantages and disadvantages to each thermal strategy. [13]Reptiles are usually sluggish first thing in the morning, their body temperatures having dropped during the cool of the night. [14]Accordingly, they have to bask in the sun to raise their body temperatures, but once they have warmed up sufficiently, they can go about their business. [15]By alternating between the sun when they are too cool, and the shade when they are too warm, many reptiles are able to maintain their body temperatures at optimum levels of about 95°F or more. [16]Endotherms, on the other hand, maintain temperatures of about 98°F all the time, so they are always ready for action.

[17]I used to keep a small crocodile. [18]He had very sharp teeth, and I had to be careful how I handled him during the daytime, when he was warm. [19]But I could do whatever I wanted at night, when he was cold, without any fear of being bitten. [20]The obvious disadvantage of being ectothermic is that the animal's activity levels are dependent upon the environment. [21]But its low metabolic rates mean that it requires far less food, which is an advantage. [22]I used to feed the crocodile a tiny piece of liver once a week, while the family cat demanded three meals every day. [23]We should therefore not think that reptiles are inferior to mammals and birds; they are just different.

_____ 1. In sentence 12, the word *thermal* means

A. related to hunting.
B. inactive.
C. related to mammals.
D. having to do with heat.

_____ 2. In sentence 15, the word *optimum* means

A. most desirable.
B. low.
C. always necessary.
D. high.

_____ 3. According to the author, the term *cold-blooded* is misleading because "cold-blooded" animals
A. always have a high body temperature.
B. cannot survive cold temperatures.
C. are more affected by heat than by cold.
D. often have a body temperature comparable to that of warm-blooded animals.

_____ 4. The main organizational patterns of the passage are cause-effect and
A. comparison.
B. contrast.
C. time order.
D. list of items.

_____ 5. The author's attitude toward reptiles seems to be
A. fearful.
B. appreciative.
C. distasteful.
D. suspicious.

_____ 6. Which of the following best expresses the unstated main idea of the last paragraph?
A. The author enjoyed keeping exotic pets.
B. The author's crocodile demonstrated the advantages and disadvantages of being ectothermic.
C. Crocodiles and other reptiles are less dangerous during the night, when they are cold and inactive.
D. An ectothermic animal is cheaper to keep than a mammal, as it eats only rarely.

_____ 7. The author implies in the last paragraph that
A. endothermic animals are more intelligent than ectothermic ones.
B. snakes are not actually ectothermic animals.
C. maintaining a high metabolic rate requires a lot of fuel in the form of food.
D. a low metabolic rate is an advantage in a cold climate.

_____ 8. Which is the most appropriate title for this selection?
A. Endotherms and Ectotherms
B. The Advantages of Ectothermism
C. Common Misconceptions about Reptiles
D. Birds and Mammals

Sample Answer Sheet

Use the form below as a model answer sheet for the twenty-five combined-skills tests.

Name ______________________________ Date __________

Section __________ SCORE: (Number correct) ______ x 12.5 = _____ %

COMBINED SKILLS: Mastery Test ____

1. _____
2. _____
3. _____
4. _____
5. _____
6. _____
7. _____
8. _____

Part Four

For Further Study

1 More about Summarizing and Outlining

This section of the book adds to what you have learned about summarizing and outlining on pages 105–110 and 113–118. It will help you take better study notes on your textbook reading assignments. Although everyone agrees that summarizing and outlining are valuable skills, they are all too seldom taught. To cite a personal example, while I was asked in high school to prepare summaries and outlines of books, stories, and articles, I was never actually taught how to do so. All of my teachers seemed to assume that someone else was responsible for helping me learn these sophisticated skills.

When I got to college, I had to do even more summarizing and outlining. For instance, many essay exam questions required summaries, that is, brief accounts of large amounts of material. I also had to summarize and outline when writing papers and giving reports, studying class lecture notes, and preparing study sheets on textbook reading assignments. Through necessity, then, I gradually learned how to summarize and outline effectively.

Understanding Summaries

All of us often summarize in everyday life. For example, in response to someone's question, we might summarize our day by saying:

> "I had a good day" or "I had a bad day."

Or we might offer a slightly more specific summary:

> "I had an exciting day" or "I had a depressing day" or "I had a busy day."

Or our summary might be even more detailed:

> "I had a busy day. I had three classes at school this morning, spent the afternoon in the library doing homework, and then worked at my part-time job for five hours in the evening."

When we make such general statements, we are providing summaries. A **summary** can be defined as the reduction of a large amount of information to its most important points. Just as we can offer a summary of the numerous details of our day, so we can prepare summaries of the numerous details in our college course materials.

Read the following two textbook passages, and then look at the summary that follows each.

Passage 1

[1]Psychologists have developed a number of suggestions for controlling anger. [2]A sense of humor can often defuse intense anger. [3]By finding something amusing in a situation, you can make tension crumble. [4]Physical exercise has also been effective in controlling anger. [5]Using the added physical strength that intense emotions produce can help to release some pressure. [6]Jogging, racquetball, hitting punching bags, and lifting weights are effective ways to use up physical energy. [7]Relaxation exercises have also been beneficial in controlling anger. [8]One type of relaxation exercise stresses tensing and relaxing muscles in various parts of your body: your arms, your legs, your feet, and even your nose and tongue. [9]Another relaxation exercise emphasizes deep breathing.

Summary of Passage 1

To control anger, psychologists suggest a sense of humor as well as physical and relaxation exercises.

Passage 2

[1]Compromise is a common and effective way of coping directly with conflict or frustration. [2]We often recognize that we cannot have everything we want and that we cannot expect others to do just what we would like them to do. [3]We then compromise, deciding on a more realistic solution or goal since an ideal solution or goal is not practical. [4]A young man who loves animals and greatly wishes to become a veterinarian may discover that he has less aptitude for biology than he had hoped and that dissecting is so distasteful to him that he could never bring himself to operate on animals. [5]By way of compromise, he may decide to become an animal technician, a person who works as an assistant to a veterinarian.

Summary of Passage 2

Compromise is a direct way of coping in which we decide on a more realistic solution or goal since an ideal solution or goal is not practical. For example, a person not good in biology or opposed to dissection may decide to be an animal technician rather than a veterinarian.

Important Points about Summarizing

1 A summary typically includes the main idea and often the major supporting details of a selection. In the summary of the first passage on the previous page, the main idea and the major details have been combined in one sentence. In the second summary, the main idea is the definition of *compromise*; it is followed by a brief example that helps make the definition clear. *Note that textbook summaries will often include definitions of key terms followed by condensed examples.*

2 At times a summary may consist of the main idea and only one or no major details; at other times, the summary may consist of a main idea followed by several major details. In other words, the length of a summary will depend upon your purpose. As a general guideline, though, a paragraph might be reduced to a sentence or two; an article might be reduced to a paragraph; an entire textbook chapter might be reduced to about three pages of notes.

3 A summary should *never* include more than one statement of the main idea. Authors—especially textbook authors—often repeat main ideas to make them as clear as possible. When summarizing, you must eliminate such restatements.

To avoid repetition, you must do the clear thinking necessary to truly understand the basic idea or ideas in a selection. You must "get inside" the material and realize fully what it says before you can reduce it to its essentials.

4 Depending on your purpose, a summary can be in the words of the author, or in your own words, or a combination of the two. If you are summarizing textbook material or a class lecture, you may be better off using the author's words or your teacher's words, especially where definitions of important terms are involved. (Notice in the second passage summarized on the previous page that the author's definition of *compromise* is used in the summary.) If you are summarizing a story or article as part of a written report, you will be expected to use your own words.

5 Your understanding of patterns of organization can often help you in summarizing material. For example, if a selection is basically a list of items, then you know your summary will also list items. If a selection is mainly a narrative (first this happened, then that happened), then your summary will briefly narrate a series of events. If a selection is mainly a series of definitions and examples, then your summary will provide both, with a focus on selecting and condensing the examples.

A Helpful Step in Summarizing: Recognizing Basic Ideas

Summarizing requires the ability to notice when an author is restating a main idea, rather than presenting another idea on the same topic. As already mentioned, textbook authors and other writers often restate ideas. By doing so, they help ensure clear communication. If the reader does not understand—or only partly understands—one wording of an idea, he or she may understand the idea when it is expressed again, in slightly different words. Effective readers and thinkers develop the ability to recognize such restatements of ideas.

Read the following passage. Then see if you can underline the two topic sentences—the sentences that express the main idea.

> [1]Our attention is selective—we focus on aspects of our environment that are most important to us or that we expect to see. [2]Thus we notice our doctor's receptionist, the office hours, and the number of people sitting ahead of us in the waiting room. [3]We may fail to see the piece of modern art that is displayed on a wall. [4]We expect our boss to give us negative feedback, so we miss hearing the nice things he or she has to say. [5]We expect a friend to be a poor cook, so we notice the parts of the meal that are poorly prepared. [6]In the process, we fail to appreciate the parts of the meal that were tasty. [7]The significant issues in our lives and our beliefs act as filters on our environment, greatly determining what will and will not get our attention.

The main idea is first presented in sentence 1; it is then restated in sentence 7. The restatement emphasizes and clarifies the main idea. Keep in mind, then, that different sentences can state pretty much the same idea. For example, the main idea above could be worded in yet another way: "What we notice and what we ignore in our environment are largely determined by what is important to us and by our expectations."

Check Your Understanding

To develop your ability to distinguish a restatement of the main idea from a basically different idea on the same topic, read the following sentence:

> **One reason we don't always listen carefully is that we're often wrapped up in personal concerns that are of more immediate importance to us than the messages others are sending.**

Now decide which three of the six statements on the following page are basically the same in meaning as the statement above and which three are basically different. Put the letter **S** (for *Same*) next to the **three** statements whose meaning is basically the same. After labeling each statement, read the explanation that follows.

____ 1. Some people listen much more carefully than others.

____ 2. One way to improve your listening skills is to look the speaker in the eye.

____ 3. Because of personal distractions, we do not always pay close attention to a speaker.

____ 4. The messages that others convey to us are sometimes very distracting.

____ 5. We sometimes don't listen carefully because our minds are on personal issues.

____ 6. Being preoccupied with our own concerns is one cause of our poor attention to what others are saying.

Explanation

1. Statement 1 compares *how* people listen—some listen much more carefully than others. In contrast, the boldfaced statement is about *why* we don't always listen carefully. Although both statements are about listening carefully, they say basically different things about that topic.

2. Statement 2 is also basically different from the boldfaced statement. Rather than explaining why we do not listen carefully, it is about a way to improve one's listening.

3. Both statement 3 and the boldfaced sentence express the idea that personal distractions are one reason we don't always listen carefully. Therefore, statement 3 means basically the same as the boldfaced sentence.

4. Statement 4 is about how distracting other people's messages can be, but the boldfaced sentence is about personal distractions. The two sentences have two different meanings.

5. Like the boldfaced sentence, statement 5 explains that personal concerns sometimes keep us from listening carefully. Thus this sentence means basically the same thing as the boldfaced sentence.

6. Statement 6 also explains that personal ("our own") concerns can keep us from listening carefully. It too is basically the same as the boldfaced sentence.

The following practice will help you develop the ability to recognize multiple statements of the main idea.

PRACTICE 1

Carefully read each opening statement (set off in **boldface**). Then decide whether each numbered statement that follows is basically the same in meaning or basically different in meaning from the opening statement. Write **S** (for *Same*) next to the **three** statements whose meaning is closest to the original statement.

1. **Not everything that is faced can be changed, but nothing can be changed until it is faced.**

    ____ 1. There's no guarantee that a bad situation will improve, but it certainly will not unless it is confronted.

    ____ 2. People are generally not willing to ask for help in solving their problems.

    ____ 3. If a problem is to have a chance to be solved, it must be honestly acknowledged.

    ____ 4. Since many problems are impossible to solve, it's just as well to ignore them.

    ____ 5. All problems can be solved if the people involved will honestly face the situation.

    ____ 6. Even a problem that is solvable will not be solved unless it is faced.

2. **We may be motivated to eat by "internal cues," such as hunger pangs or low blood glucose, or "external cues," including attractive food, the time of day, or commercials for food.**

    ____ 1. Overweight people are overly influenced by external cues to eat.

    ____ 2. There are two types of cues that motivate us to eat: internal and external.

    ____ 3. When people are not hungry, external cues to eat have no effect.

    ____ 4. The motivators that cause people to eat can be categorized as either "external cues" or "internal cues."

    ____ 5. External cues are even more powerful motivators to eat than internal cues are.

    ____ 6. We may get the urge to eat because of inner physical conditions or from signals in our environment.

3. **Once we form an opinion of someone, we tend to hang on to it and make any conflicting information fit our image.**

    ____ 1. Our first impression of another person is quickly displaced by a second, more accurate impression.

____ 2. First impressions are very powerful. Even as we learn more about a person, we assume that our first impression was basically correct.

____ 3. It's important not to allow ourselves to form an immediate impression of someone we've just met.

____ 4. First impressions are difficult to change even if we learn new information that contradicts them.

____ 5. First impressions tend to be lasting.

____ 6. Our first impressions of people will almost invariably be proved correct by what we later learn about them.

Summarizing Short Passages

As stated earlier, many passages of paragraph length can often be reduced to the main idea and one or more major supporting details. This section will give you practice in writing passage-length summaries. It will also review outlining, which can be a helpful step in writing a summary.

Read the passage below. Then decide which of the four statements that follow accurately summarizes the essential information of the passage.

> [1]For some people, the need to achieve is low because they actually fear becoming successful. [2]Research by Matina Horner and others shows that this fear of success occurs in both men and women. [3]Why should someone display anxiety over getting ahead in life? [4]Several factors seem to be involved. [5]Horner implies that some individuals may fear that success will bring social rejection. [6]They fear losing their close friends or having people reject them because "now he or she is better than I am." [7]Herb Goldberg suggests that guilt is another factor. [8]People may feel guilty because they somehow "do not deserve to be better than other people." [9]This reaction is sometimes observed in children who are more successful than their parents. [10]John Sisk indicates that anxiety over losing control may also be important. [11]Successful people typically acquire a lot of money and other material goods. [12]Sisk believes that "affluence, like passion, means a loss of control." [13]As one gets more success, money, and material things, there is a risk that such things will control what we do. [14]Some people probably worry that they will lose the freedom to act independently.

____ Write the letter of the statement that best summarizes the passage.

A. Some men and women have a low need to achieve because they fear that success will bring social rejection, guilt, or loss of control.

B. Some people fear that they will lose the freedom to act independently because of social rejection, guilt, and loss of control.

C. Some people may fear that acquiring a lot of money will mean a loss of freedom to act independently.

D. The low need to achieve is sometimes caused by the fear that success will bring social rejection.

Here is how you could have determined the best answer on the previous page—and how you can go about summarizing any passage:

1 First read the entire passage through once. Then reread it, asking yourself, "What is the topic of this passage, and what point is being made about the topic?"

2 As you reread the passage, you'll note that the topic is fear of success: the first several sentences all refer to a fear of success. You'll note also what is said about the topic: that several factors seem to be involved in this fear of success. You are now ready to put together the implied main idea: "Some people have a low need to achieve because they fear success for various reasons."

3 At almost the same time that you are asking yourself, "What is the topic?" and "What is the point being made about the topic?" you should ask, "What are the major details that support the point?" Further study of the passage reveals that it is basically a list of items—it lists the three reasons, or factors, behind people's fear of success. (Notice that two transition words in the passage—*another* and *also*—help signal that a list is being provided.) The major supporting details of the passage are the three factors: fear of social rejection, feelings of guilt, and anxiety over losing control.

You may find it very helpful while summarizing to do a mini-outline of the passage by numbering the supporting points. On scratch paper or in the textbook margin or simply in your head, you might create the following:

Point: People fear success for various reasons.

Support:
1. Fear of social rejection
2. Feelings of guilt
3. Anxiety over losing control

Such an outline will help you understand the content and basic relationships in a passage. You can then proceed with summarizing the material.

4 For the passage on the previous page, you should have chosen statement A as the best summary—it is a one-sentence combination of the main idea and the three major supporting details. Statement B is incorrect because the main idea is about the fear of success, not the fear of losing the freedom to act independently. Statement C is incorrect because it covers only one minor detail. And finally, statement D is incorrect because it is about only one of the three major details.

PRACTICE 2

Write the letter of the statement or statements that best summarize each selection that follows. Your choice should provide the main idea; it may include one or more major supporting details as well.

_____ 1. [1]Working conditions in the nineteenth century seem barbaric today: twelve-to-fourteen-hour workdays; six- and seven-day weeks; cramped, unsafe factories; marginal wages; and no legal protection. [2]Yet employers seldom had problems motivating their workers; Poverty and unemployment were so widespread that any job was welcome.

A. Working conditions in the nineteenth century were difficult and even dangerous.
B. Workers in the nineteenth century were more highly motivated than workers are today.
C. Widespread poverty and unemployment made nineteenth-century workers willing to put up with terrible working conditions.
D. Legal protection and wages have improved sharply since the barbaric conditions that prevailed in the nineteenth century.

_____ 2. [1]The hallmark of representative democracy is that all citizens have the fundamental right to vote for those who will administer and make the laws. [2]Those in power have often defied this principle of democracy by minimizing, neutralizing, or even negating the voting privileges of blacks. [3]Although the Fourteenth Amendment gave blacks the right to vote after the Civil War, the white majority in the Southern states used a variety of tactics to keep them from voting. [4]Most effective was the strategy of intimidation. [5]Blacks who tried to assert their right to vote were often beaten and were sometimes lynched, or their property was destroyed.

A. All citizens of a democracy have a right to vote for those who will administer and make laws, and nobody should try to interfere with that right.
B. Those in power have often interfered with the constitutional voting rights of blacks through various tactics, the most effective being cruel intimidation.
C. After the Civil War, blacks who tried to vote were often beaten.
D. Those in power have often defied the principles of democracy in order to further their own selfish ends.

_____ 3. [1]All family systems can be roughly categorized into one of two types. [2]The *extended family* is one in which more than two generations of the same kinship line live together, either in the same house or in adjacent dwellings. [3]The head of the entire family is usually the eldest male, and all adults share responsibility for child rearing and other tasks. [4]The extended family, which is quite commonly found in traditional preindustrial societies, can be very large: sometimes it contains several adult offspring of the head of the family, together with all their spouses and children. [5]In contrast, the *nuclear family* is one in which the family group consists only of the parents and their dependent children, living apart from other relatives. [6]The nuclear family occurs in some preindustrial societies and is the usual type in virtually all modern industrialized societies. [7]In fact, the growing dominance of the nuclear family is transforming family life all over the world.

A. There are two types of families. In the extended family, in which more than two generations of family live together, the head of the family is the eldest male and all adults share in family tasks. This type of family is common in preindustrial societies.

B. There are various types of families. The nuclear family is the most common among modern industrialized societies. The dominance of the nuclear family is transforming family life worldwide.

C. An extended family consists of two generations of family living together. A nuclear family consists of parents and their dependent children. It occurs in some preindustrial societies and is the usual type of family in just about all modern industrialized societies.

D. There are two basic types of families. The extended family, which is more than two generations living together, is common in preindustrial societies. The nuclear family, made up of parents and their dependent children, is usual in modern industrialized societies.

Understanding Outlines

Very often a good way to summarize something is to outline it first. An **outline** is itself a summary in which numbers and letters are often used to set off the main idea and the supporting details of a selection. For example, the passage on page 644 about controlling anger could have been outlined as follows:

Psychologists suggest several ways to control anger.

1. Sense of humor
2. Physical exercise
3. Relaxation exercises

Outlines and visual outlines, called **maps**, are described in this book on pages 105–113.

Important Points about Outlining

1 Both outlines and summaries are excellent thinking tools that will help you with all your reading and study assignments. Both demand that you work to identify the main idea of a selection and to understand the relationship between it and the major details that develop the idea. *The very act of outlining or summarizing will help you understand and master the material.*

2 With class lecture notes and textbook reading assignments in particular, outlines and summaries are excellent review materials. Studying an outline or a summary is easier and more productive than repeated rereading of an entire set of notes or entire textbook chapters.

Following are tips for outlining and summarizing textbook material, with practice activities.

Outlining and Summarizing a Textbook Chapter

I will never forget two early college courses for which I had to read and study a great deal of material. For a history course and an introductory psychology course, I had teachers who lectured a great deal in class. I typically filled up ten or so notebook pages per class, leaving my head spinning and my hand cramped. I remember using up several Bic pens that semester. Besides having to know the lecture material, students were also responsible for textbook chapters not covered in class.

Several weeks into the semester, I sat down on a Saturday to study for my first psychology exam. With all the class material to cover, I knew I would have to study very efficiently, getting as much out of my time as possible. I spent most of the day reading three required textbook chapters, and that same evening I started to study the chapters. After about two hours of work I had reread and studied the material on the first four pages of the first chapter; I still had almost ninety-two pages to go. I also had a pile of lecture notes to study.

When I realized my problem, I just sat at my desk for a while, wondering what to do. It was then that my roommate, who himself faced a mountain of material to study, suggested we order a pizza. I quickly agreed. I felt like a dying man, so I figured it wouldn't hurt to have a last meal. But the pizza went down in heavy lumps. I knew my days in college were numbered unless I came up with a system for organizing and condensing all the material I had to study.

Here in a nutshell is what I learned to do with the chapters in my psychology book (I used a similar system with my extensive lecture notes):

1 I previewed and read each chapter, marking off all the definitions of key terms, along with an example in each case that made each definition clear for me. Specifically, I would put *DEF* in the margin for a definition and *EX* in the margin for an example. I also numbered *1, 2, 3* . . . major lists of items—especially lists in which a series of subheadings fit logically under a main heading.

2 Then I outlined the material, making sure that basic relationships were clear. I did this mainly by looking for relationships between main headings and subheadings within each chapter. For instance, one of the headings in the first chapter was "Methods of Psychology." I wrote down that heading and then wrote down and numbered all the subheadings that fit under it:

Methods of Psychology

1. Naturalistic-Observation Method
2. Experimental Method
3. Correlational Method

3 As part of my outline, I wrote down the definitions and examples. For example, I wrote down each method of psychology and an example of the method. I also wrote down what seemed to be other important details about each method.

4 Then I recorded the next main heading and the subheadings under it. In cases where there were no subheadings, I tried to convert the heading into a basic question and answer the question. For example, one heading in my psychology text chapter was "The Social Relevance of Psychology." I turned that into the question "What *is* the social relevance of psychology?" and then wrote a summary of the textbook author's answer to that question. When I was done, I had reduced thirty-two pages in the textbook chapter to three pages of notes. I had, in effect, used a combination of outlining and summarizing to condense a large amount of information down to its most important points.

In a nutshell, then, my study method was as follows. First, I previewed and read all the material through once, marking off definitions and examples and numbering major lists of items. Then I took notes on the material by writing down definitions and examples and major lists of items. I also asked basic questions about the headings and wrote down condensed answers to those questions. Finally, I concentrated on studying my notes, testing myself on them until I could recite the material without looking at it. With my systematic preparation, I managed to score a low B on that test; and as I became better at outlining and summarizing, my scores on later tests were even better.

Check Your Understanding

To get a sense of how to outline and summarize textbook material, read the following passage. Then circle the letter—A, B, or C—of the notes that most accurately reflect the content of the passage.

> [1]Anxiety becomes a disorder when fears, ideas, and impulses are exaggerated or unrealistic. [2]A person suffering from *anxiety disorder* often has such physical symptoms as sweating, shaking, shortness of breath, and a fast heartbeat. [3]*Phobias*, the most common form of anxiety disorder, are continuing unrealistic fears that interfere with normal living. [4]For instance, instead of fearing only threatening animals, a phobic person may fear all animals, even those that are docile and friendly. [5]People with this phobia may panic at the sight of a harmless snake or mouse.
>
> [6]Eating problems are another form of anxiety disorder. [7]One eating disorder, *anorexia nervosa*, generally begins when young girls grow anxious about becoming overweight. [8]Although they initially want to eat, they eventually completely lose their desire for food. [9]They diet continually, even when they are so underweight that their lives are threatened. [10]The sight of food makes them nauseated. [11]In a related disorder, *bulimia*, the person goes on eating binges and then uses laxatives or vomits to purge herself. [12]Bulimia is believed to be most common among college-age women.
>
> [13]There are also obsessive-compulsive anxiety disorders. [14]*Obsessions* are persistent ideas or impulses that invade people's minds against their will and cannot be gotten rid of by reasoning. [15]One common obsession is an intense fear of germs. [16]Someone with this obsession refuses to shake hands or otherwise come into contact with others. [17]Obsessions often lead to *compulsions*, which are persistent behaviors. [18]Feeling they are never clean, for instance, people obsessed with fears of contamination may become compulsive about hand-washing.

A. Anxiety disorder—an exaggerated or unrealistic fear, idea, or impulse, often with physical symptoms such as shaking or fast heartbeat.

Types:

1. Phobias—unrealistic fears that interfere with daily living, such as fear of a harmless animal
2. Eating disorders—unrealistic fear of gaining weight
   a. Anorexia nervosa—loss of desire for food
   b. Bulimia—eating binges followed by purging
3. Obsessive-compulsive disorders—exaggerated, unrealistic ideas and impulses
   a. Obsession—persistent idea, such as fear of being contaminated by germs
   b. Compulsion—persistent behavior, such as constant hand-washing

B. Anxiety disorder—often includes physical symptoms such as sweating, shaking, shortness of breath, and a fast heartbeat

Types:
1. Phobias—fears that interfere with daily living
2. Anorexia nervosa—loss of desire for food
3. Bulimia—eating binges followed by purging
4. Obsession—persistent idea, such as fear of being contaminated by germs
5. Compulsion—persistent behavior, such as constant hand-washing

C. Anxiety disorder—an exaggerated or unrealistic fear, idea, or impulse, often with physical symptoms such as shaking or fast heartbeat

Types:
1. Phobias
   a. Fears that interfere with daily living, such as fear of a harmless animal
   b. Anorexia nervosa—loss of desire for food
   c. Bulimia—eating binges followed by purging
2. Obsessive-compulsive disorders
   a. Obsession—persistent idea, such as fear of being contaminated by germs
   b. Compulsions—persistent behavior, such as constant hand-washing

Explanation

To find the best of the three sets of notes, you must do the same thing you would do if you were outlining the passage yourself—identify the main idea and major and minor details. A careful reading of the passage reveals that the main idea of the passage is: "There are various types of anxiety disorders, which are exaggerated or unrealistic fears, ideas, and impulses that often cause such physical symptoms as sweating, shaking, shortness of breath, and a fast heartbeat." The major details are the three types of anxiety disorder listed: phobias, eating disorders, and obsessive-compulsive disorders. Thus the outline that best reflects the passage will define and explain *anxiety disorders* and then go on to name and explain the three types listed.

Having analyzed the passage, let's turn to the sets of notes above. Set A defines and explains *anxiety disorder* and goes on to list and explain the three types of anxiety disorder. The important minor details have been listed as well. Set A, then, is a pretty good condensation of the passage.

In contrast, set B does not account for two of the major-detail categories: eating disorders and obsessive-compulsive disorders. In set C, the category of eating disorders has been skipped, and anorexia nervosa and bulimia are incorrectly identified as phobias.

PRACTICE 3

Read each of the selections that follow. Then write the letter of the notes that best outline and summarize the material in each selection.

______ 1. [1]Erik Erikson divided adulthood into three stages. [2]In his view, the central task of the first stage, young adulthood, is that of achieving *intimacy*. [3]The young person who has a firm sense of identity is eager and able to fuse his or her identity with another person's in a loving relationship, without fear of competition or loss of self. [4]A young person who avoids commitment may experience isolation. [5]In middle age, personal and social concerns merge. [6]Adults who feel they have contributed something of value to society and who are involved in guiding the next generation (as parents or in other roles) experience *generativity*. [7]Those who do not experience stagnation—the sense of going nowhere, doing nothing important. [8]Generativity lays the foundation for *integrity* in old age, a sense of a life well lived. [9]Older people who have achieved integrity are satisfied with the choices they made and feel that had they a second life to live, they would "do it all over again." [10]They see death as the final stop in a meaningful journey.

A. Erikson's three stages of adulthood
   1. Intimacy—a fusion with another in a loving relationship
   2. Generativity—feeling of contributing something of value
   3. Integrity—a sense of a life well lived

B. Erikson's stages of adulthood
   1. Intimacy
   2. Isolation
   3. Generativity
   4. Stagnation
   5. Integrity

C. Erikson's stages of adulthood
   1. Young adulthood
      a. Intimacy achieved in a loving relationship
      b. Avoidance of commitment may result in isolation
   2. Middle age
      a. Generativity achieved by those contributing to society and guiding the young
      b. Stagnation experienced by those who don't contribute
   3. Old age—integrity achieved through a sense of a life well lived

_____ 2. [1]Across the life span we find ourselves immersed in countless relationships. [2]Few are more important to us than those we have with our **peers**—individuals who are approximately the same age. [3]Peer groups serve a variety of functions. [4]First, they provide an arena in which children can exercise independence from adult controls. [5]Next, peer groups give children experience with relationships in which they are on an equal footing with others. [6]In the adult world, in contrast, children occupy the position of subordinates, with adults directing, guiding, and controlling their activities. [7]Third, peer groups afford a social sphere in which the position of children is not marginal. [8]In them, youngsters can acquire status and achieve an identity in which their own activities and concerns are paramount. [9]And last, peer groups are agencies for the transmission of informal knowledge, sexual information, deviant behaviors, superstitions, folklore, fads, jokes, riddles, and games. [10]Peers are as necessary to children's development as adults are; the complexity of social life requires that children be involved in networks both of adults and of peers.

A. Children need relationships with both adults and peers.
   1. Peer groups provide an arena in which children exercise independence from adult controls.
   2. Peer groups provide adolescents with an impetus to seek greater freedom.
   3. Peer groups give children experience with relationships in which they are on an equal footing with others.
   4. Adult-child relationships allow adults to direct, guide, and control children's activities.
   5. Peer groups provide a social sphere in which children don't have a marginal position.
   6. Peer groups transmit informal knowledge.

B. Peer groups, made up of individuals who are about the same age, serve various functions.
   1. Provide an arena in which children can exercise independence from adult controls
   2. Give children experience of being on an equal footing with others, allowing for experiences different from adult-child relationships
   3. Provide a social sphere in which children don't have a marginal position
   4. Transmit useful knowledge

C. Across the life span we find ourselves immersed in countless relationships.
   1. Peer relationships—with individuals who are approximately the same age
   2. Adolescent-adult relationships
   3. Adult-child relationships
   4. Networks of both adults and peers

______ 3. [1]Our capacity to learn from watching as well as from doing means that the mass media have important socialization consequences for us. [2]The mass media are those organizations—television, radio, motion pictures, newspapers, and magazines—that convey information to a large segment of the public. [3]All the mass media educate. [4]The question is: What are they teaching? [5]The good news from research is that prosocial (positive and helpful) models can have prosocial effects. [6]Children who view a prosocial television diet, including such programs as *Sesame Street* and *Mister Rogers' Neighborhood*, exhibit greater levels of helping behaviors, cooperation, sharing, and self-control than children who view a neutral or violent diet. [7]Moreover, these programs have a positive effect on language development.

[8]The bad news from television research is that there is a link between the mayhem and violence in children's programs and aggressive behavior in children. [9]Although televised violence does not harm every child who watches it, many children imitate the violent attitudes and behaviors they see. [10]Prime-time programs depict about five violent acts per hour, and Saturday morning cartoons average twenty to twenty-five violent acts per hour. [11]By the time most young people leave high school, they have spent more time before a television screen than in the classroom. [12]In the process they will have witnessed some 13,000 murders. [13]Television not only provides opportunities for children and adults to learn new aggressive skills; it also weakens the inhibitions against behaving in the same way. [14]And television violence increases the toleration of aggression in real life—a "psychic numbing" effect—and reinforces the tendency to view the world as a dangerous place.

A. The mass media have important socialization consequences for us.
   1. The mass media convey information to a large segment of the public.
      a. television
      b. radio
      c. motion pictures
      d. newspapers
      e. magazines

2. TV research reveals a link between TV violence and aggressive behavior in children.
   a. Violence on TV makes children more aggressive and violent.
   b. TV violence increases toleration of real-life aggression.
   c. TV violence reinforces the tendency to view the world as a dangerous place.

B. The mass media influence the public.
   1. Researchers have found positive influences.
      a. Prosocial models can have prosocial effects.
      b. Children's programs help language development.
   2. Researchers have found negative influences.
      a. Violence on TV makes children more aggressive and violent.
      b. TV violence increases toleration of real-life aggression.
      c. TV violence reinforces the tendency to view the world as a dangerous place.

C. The mass media influence the public.
   1. Prosocial models can have prosocial effects.
      — Programs such as *Sesame Street* and *Mister Rogers' Neighborhood* encourage helping behavior in children who watch.
   2. Children's programs help language development.
   3. Prime-time programs depict about five acts of violence an hour.
   4. TV violence increases toleration of real-life aggression.
      — By the end of high school, most young people have spent more time before a TV than in the classroom.
   5. TV violence reinforces the tendency to view the world as a dangerous place.
      — By high school, children will have witnessed some 13,000 murders on TV.

REVIEW TEST 1

To review what you've learned in this chapter, answer the following questions.

1. Summarizing is a way to (*predict, outline, condense*) ______________ material.

2. A summary will always include (*the main idea, all the major details, several minor details*) ______________________________.

_____ 3. TRUE OR FALSE? The author's study method included reading through all the material, marking off definitions and examples and lists of items.

_____ 4. TRUE OR FALSE? One note-taking step that the author does **not** recommend is turning textbook headings into questions and summarizing in notes the answers to the questions.

_____ 5. TRUE OR FALSE? Writing an outline can be a helpful step toward writing a summary.

REVIEW TEST 2

A. Carefully read each opening statement (set off in **boldface**). Then decide whether each numbered statement that follows is basically the same in meaning or basically different in meaning from the opening statement. Write **S** (for *Same*) next to the **two** statements whose meaning is closest to the original statement.

1–2. **Adults who were mistreated as children have a greater tendency to be violent than those who were not mistreated.**

____ 1. Children should never be yelled at.

____ 2. Children who are mistreated have little choice but to become violent adults.

____ 3. Violent adults tend to be people who were mistreated as children.

____ 4. The tendency toward violence, while powerful, can be controlled.

____ 5. A mistreated child is more likely to become a violent adult than is a child who is not mistreated.

____ 6. We could overcome the problem of violence in our society if only we tried harder.

3–4. **Compensation is stressing a strength in one area to hide a shortcoming in another.**

____ 1. We need to defend ourselves against people who try to make their weaknesses less noticeable than their strengths.

____ 2. Compensation involves having strengths and shortcomings in about equal amounts.

____ 3. Compensation cannot turn a shortcoming into a strength.

____ 4. In order to hide a personal flaw, we may emphasize one of our strengths; this is called compensation.

____ 5. There are various ways in which we can conceal our weak points and emphasize our strong points.

____ 6. We are said to be using compensation when we emphasize a strength of ours in order to hide a defect.

5–6. **Tension headache, a condition common among people who suppress their emotions (and thus build up tension in their bodies), is usually caused by a tightening of the muscles of the head and neck.**

____ 1. Headaches of all kinds are caused by the tightening of muscles in the head and neck, a common symptom among people who suppress their emotions.

____ 2. Learning to relax will not affect the pain of a tension headache.

____ 3. People who suffer from tension headaches tend to have very aggressive personalities.

____ 4. Tension headaches are usually caused by tight head and neck muscles, common among those who hold back their emotions and thus tighten their muscles.

____ 5. When people bottle up their emotions, the stress they feel tends to tighten the muscles in their heads and necks.

____ 6. Tension headaches usually have a physical cause—tight head and neck muscles. That muscle tightness, in turn, has a psychological cause—the restraining of emotions.

B. (7.) Circle the letter of the answer that best summarizes the selection that follows.

[1]Of all major ethnic groups in the United States, Japanese Americans are the most economically successful. [2]There seem to be two major factors involved in the Japanese American "success story." [3]The first factor is educational achievement. [4]On the average, both male and female Japanese Americans complete more years of schooling than the general population. [5]For example, while 13 percent of all U.S. males complete college, 19 percent of Japanese American males do. [6]The second factor that helps explain Japanese Americans' economic success is their assimilation into the larger society. [7]Their high intermarriage rate is evidence of that assimilation. [8]About 40 percent of third-generation Japanese Americans marry non-Japanese Americans. [9]Such merging into mainstream culture helps ensure that the doors of economic opportunity swing open for many Japanese Americans.

A. Because of their high assimilation rate, Japanese Americans are the most economically successful of all major ethnic groups in the United States. Their high intermarriage rate is evidence of their assimilation.

B. Of all major ethnic groups in the United States, Japanese Americans are the most economically successful.

C. While 13 percent of all U.S. males complete college, 19 percent of Japanese American males do.

D. Japanese Americans are the most economically successful of all major ethnic groups in the United States because of their high level of educational achievement and their high rate of assimilation into the larger society.

C. (8.) Circle the letter of the outline notes that best summarize the selection that follows.

[1]According to Margaret Mead, children typically pass through three stages in developing a self: an imitation stage, a play stage, and a game stage. [2]In the first stage, children imitate other people without understanding what they are doing. [3]They may "read" a book, but the behavior lacks meaning for them. [4]Even so, such imitation is important because children are preparing themselves to take the stance of others and act as others do. [5]In the play stage, children act such roles as mother, police officer, teacher, Mrs. Elliot, and so on. [6]They take the role of only one other person at a time and "try on" the person's behavior. [7]The model, typically a person central to the child's life, is termed by sociologists a significant other. [8]For instance, a two-year-old child may examine a doll's pants, pretend to find them wet, and reprimand the doll. [9]Presumably the child views the situation from the perspective of the parent and acts as the parent would act.

[10]Whereas in the play stage children take the role of only one other person at a time, in the game stage they assume many roles. [11]Much as in a baseball game, a person must take into account the intentions and expectations of several people. [12]For instance, if the batter bunts the ball down the third-base line, the pitcher must know what the catcher, the shortstop, and the first, second, and, third basemen will do. [13]In the game, children must assume the roles of numerous individuals in contrast to simply the role of one other person. [14]To do so, they must abstract a "composite" role out of the concrete roles of particular people. [15]These notions are extended to embrace all people in similar situations—the "team." [16]In other words, children fashion a generalized other—they come to view their behavior from the standpoint of the larger group or community.

A. Margaret Mead's stages of child self-development
   1. Imitation stage—imitating others' behavior that has no meaning for child
   2. Preparation for the mature attitude and behavior of others
   3. Play stage—acting the role of one other person at a time
   4. "Trying on" the behavior of a significant other
   5. Game stage—assuming and taking into account many roles
   6. Viewing one's behavior from the standpoint of a larger group or community

B. How children develop
  1. They prepare themselves to take the stance of others and act as others do.
  2. They take the role of only one other person at a time and "try on" the person's behavior.
  3. They assume many roles.

C. Margaret Mead's view of child self-development: three stages
  1. Imitation stage—imitating behavior that has no meaning for child
     a. Function: preparation for the mature attitude and behavior of others
     b. Example: a child "reads" a book
  2. Play stage—acting the role of one other person at a time
     a. Function: "Trying on" the behavior of a significant other
     b. Examples: Acting like mother, police officer, teacher
  3. Game stage—assuming and taking into account many roles
     a. Function: viewing one's behavior from the standpoint of a larger group or community
     b. Example: baseball pitcher interacting with other team members

REVIEW TEST 3

A. Carefully read each opening statement (set off in **boldface**). Then decide whether each numbered statement that follows is basically the same in meaning or basically different in meaning from the opening statement. Write **S** (for *Same*) next to the **two** statements whose meaning is closest to the original statement.

1–2. **People are comfortable making statements of fact and opinion, but they rarely disclose their feelings.**

____ 1. People are less comfortable about conveying their feelings than they are about expressing facts and opinions.

____ 2. Facts and opinions are far more reliable predictors of people's actions than feelings are.

____ 3. As people get to know one another better, they talk less in terms of facts and opinions and more in terms of feelings.

____ 4. It is easier for people to talk about emotions than to discuss facts and opinions.

____ 5. People who keep their emotions bottled up tend to be very opinionated.

____ 6. People rarely express how they feel, being much more comfortable expressing facts and opinions.

3–4. **A self-fulfilling prophecy is one that comes true because someone's expectations of an event have helped to bring it about.**

____ 1. If a person believes strongly that a certain event is going to happen, he or she may actually influence that event to occur. Such a belief, or prediction, is known as a self-fulfilling prophecy.

____ 2. The idea of the self-fulfilling prophecy is based upon a person's certain knowledge ahead of time of how a situation will end.

____ 3. A situation is more likely to end well if a person gets help from others in achieving that desired end.

____ 4. People only imagine that they have any influence over most situations.

____ 5. When people act in ways that cause a situation to end in the manner they expect, their expectation becomes a self-fulfilling prophecy.

____ 6. A person's expectations of an event cannot change its outcome, but they may change the person's perception of that outcome.

5–6. **If only there were evil people somewhere treacherously committing evil deeds, we could separate them from the rest of us and destroy them; but the line dividing good and evil cuts through the heart of every human being.**

____ 1. People who appear to be good are in reality only hiding the evil that they have done.

____ 2. Since every human being has the potential to do good and evil, we can't get rid of evil simply by getting rid of all the so-called evil people.

____ 3. Because the world is not divided between good people and evil people, there's no way to identify and eliminate the evil ones; rather, all people are made up of both good and evil.

____ 4. Evil people look so much like the rest of us that it is impossible to identify them.

____ 5. Destroying the evil people in the world would make life much safer for the rest of us.

____ 6. Some people have nothing but good in their hearts; some people are entirely evil.

B. (7.) Circle the letter of the answer that best summarizes the selection that follows.

[1]Money does not guarantee victory in a political campaign, but it does guarantee the *opportunity* for victory. [2]Without good financing, potential candidates do not become candidates. [3]With good financing, potential candidates can hire consultants—media experts, pollsters, direct mailing specialists, voice coaches, statisticians, speech writers, and make-up artists—to give their campaigns appeal. [4]Not only do the consultants charge a lot (perhaps $250 per hour), but the technology they employ—computers, interviews, and television—is costly. [5]Because consultants need success in order to build their reputations, they shun underfunded candidates. [6]One student of consulting concludes that "you need $150,000 just to get in the door to see a consultant."

[7]Indeed, consultants are now as important to candidates as are political parties. [8]Not only have they supplemented the role of parties in the campaign (volunteer doorbell-ringers and phone-callers are now only one means of connecting with voters), but they also encourage candidates to de-emphasize issues and concentrate on image. [9]The "three p's"—polling, packaging, and promotion—are as vital as parties, grassroots support, and the development of strong positions on the issues.

A. Political candidates require good financing for various expenses. Money buys candidates such consultants as media experts, pollsters, direct mailing specialists, voice coaches, statisticians, speech writers and make-up artists.

B. Today's political candidates require money to hire expensive consultants and the technology they use, including computers, interviews, and television. Consultants' emphasis on "polling, packaging, and promotion" has reduced the importance of parties, grassroots support, and strong positions on the issues.

C. Today's political campaigns are a fraud. They require the candidates to shun genuine grassroots support and strong positions in favor of know-nothing, high-tech media consultants and expensive surveys. The consultants themselves care more about building their reputations than they do about electing qualified candidates.

D. Political parties are far less important today than ever. Owing to the influence of consultants and the demands of media-centered campaigns, candidates de-emphasize issues and concentrate on image. "Polling, packaging, and promotion" have become more important than parties, grassroots support, and strong positions on the issues.

C. (8.) Circle the letter of the outline notes that best summarize the selection that follows.

[1]The autonomic nervous system is composed of all the neurons that carry messages between the central nervous system and all the internal organs of the body. [2]The autonomic nervous system consists of two branches: the sympathetic and parasympathetic divisions. [3]These two divisions act in almost total opposition to each other, but both are directly involved in controlling and integrating the actions of the glands and the smooth muscles within the body.

[4]The nerve fibers of the sympathetic division are busiest when you are frightened or angry. [5]They carry messages that tell the body to prepare for an emergency and to get ready to act quickly or strenuously. [6]In response to messages from the sympathetic division, your heart pounds, you breathe faster, your pupils enlarge, and digestion stops.

[7]Parasympathetic nerve fibers connect to the same organs as the sympathetic nerve fibers, but they cause just the opposite effects. [8]The parasympathetic division says, in effect, "Okay, the heat's off, back to normal." [9]The heart then goes back to beating at its normal rate, the stomach muscles relax, digestion starts again, breathing slows down, and the pupils of the eyes get smaller. [10]Thus, the parasympathetic division compensates for the sympathetic division and lets the body rest after stress.

A. The body's response to emergencies: the sympathetic division and the parasympathetic division
   1. Function: prepares body for emergency when someone is frightened or angry
   2. Physical responses: pounding heart, faster breathing, enlarged pupils, halted digestion
   3. After the emergency: the parasympathetic division
      a. Function: normalizes the body after an emergency
      b. Physical responses: return to normal heart rate, relaxed stomach muscles, resumed digestion, normalized breathing, reduced pupil size

B. The autonomic nervous system: two-branched system that controls and integrates the work of the glands and smooth muscles through neurons carrying messages between the central nervous system and all the internal organs
   1. Sympathetic division
      a. Function: prepares body for emergency when someone is frightened or angry
      b. Physical responses: pounding heart, faster breathing, enlarged pupils, halted digestion

2. Parasympathetic division
   a. Function: normalizes the body after an emergency
   b. Physical responses: return to normal heart rate, relaxed stomach muscles, resumed digestion, normalized breathing, reduced pupil size

C. The sympathetic division of the autonomic nervous system prepares the body for emergencies when the person is frightened or angry.
1. When someone is frightened or angry, the nerve fibers are busiest; they then carry messages.
   a. This prepares the body for an emergency.
   b. This prepares the body to act quickly or strenuously.
   c. In response, your body changes in various ways.
      1) Your heart pounds.
      2) You breathe faster.
      3) Your pupils enlarge.
      4) Your digestion stops.
2. After the emergency, the parasympathetic division causes the body to relax.
   a. Your heartbeat normalizes.
   b. Your breathing slows down.
   c. Your pupils get smaller.
   d. The stomach muscles relax.

Check Your Performance — SUMMARIZING AND OUTLINING

Activity	*Number Right*		*Points*		*Score*
Review Test 1 (5 items)	______	×	4	=	______
Review Test 2 (8 items)	______	×	5	=	______
Review Test 3 (8 items)	______	×	5	=	______
	TOTAL SCORE			=	______%

2 Additional Tests on Fact and Opinion

Name ______________________________ Date __________

Section __________ SCORE: (Number correct) ______ x 5 = ______ %

FACT AND OPINION: Mastery Test 1

A. Identify facts with an **F**, opinions with an **O**, and the **one** combination of fact and opinion with an **F+O**.

_____ 1. While mating, a female praying mantis eats the head of the male.

_____ 2. Violence in the insect world is far worse than violence in the human world.

_____ 3. It is a fact that the Republican Party would do a better job of defending America from terrorists seeking to overthrow our country.

_____ 4. It is a fact that the Democratic Party would do a better job of defending America from its enemies, both foreign and domestic.

_____ 5. Dracula has been the subject of more films than any other fictional character.

_____ 6. No horror film is more scary and entertaining to watch than a movie that features vampires.

_____ 7. The best way to share photos with other members of your family, no matter where they are living, is to put them on Facebook.

_____ 8. Facebook is one of the most-trafficked websites in the world, with more than one billion active users.

_____ 9. When the Egyptian pyramids were first constructed, around 2500 B.C., they were paper-white and as smooth as glass.

_____ 10. Even though invaders stripped the pyramids of their smooth limestone surface around 500 A.D., the pyramids deserve to be regarded as one of the great wonders of the world.

(Continues on next page)

B. Identify facts with an **F**, opinions with an **O**, and the **one** combination of fact and opinion with an **F+O**.

_____ 11. The fear of the number 13 is so great that some hotels skip the number 13 when numbering rooms.

_____ 12. Students who are not good at math should not be required to take advanced math in high school.

_____ 13. Before the invention of mass-marketed shampoos, households made their own shampoos from watery soap.

_____ 14. It's a waste of money to buy expensive hair care products because inexpensive ones work just as well.

_____ 15. Bill Clinton's affair with Monica Lewinsky, which resulted in his impeachment, was the most disgraceful act ever committed by an American president.

_____ 16. Bill Clinton left office with an approval rating of 65%, the highest end-of-presidency approval rating of any president who came into office after World War II.

_____ 17. Before his death, Charles Schulz was the most widely syndicated cartoonist in history; his comic strip, *Peanuts*, appeared in more than 2,600 newspapers in 75 countries.

_____ 18. *Peanuts* is by far the most heartwarming comic strip ever created.

_____ 19. The fastest growing segment of the American economy is self-storage units, with one in 11 households now renting self-storage space.

_____ 20. Americans should stop spending so much money on stuff they don't really need and contribute more to charity.

Name ______________________ Date ________

Section __________ SCORE: (Number correct) ______ x 5 = ______ %

FACT AND OPINION: Mastery Test 2

A. Identify facts with an **F**, opinions with an **O**, and the **one** combination of fact and opinion with an **F+O**.

_____ 1. If Barbie were a real woman, she'd measure 36-18-33 and would lack the 17–22 percent of body fat required for good health.

_____ 2. It would be better for girls' self-esteem if the fashion dolls they play with looked more like real, everyday women.

_____ 3. It seems likely that our planet will receive visitors from other galaxies in the not-too-distant future.

_____ 4. Scientists estimate that the universe contains over 100 billion galaxies.

_____ 5. George Washington, our first president, was the only one of the Founding Fathers to free his slaves.

_____ 6. George Washington was the only American president who did not live in Washington, D.C.

_____ 7. George Washington must be regarded as the greatest of all American presidents.

_____ 8. George Washington was the only president who was unanimously elected, running unopposed for both terms.

_____ 9. Russia won the most medals at the 2014 Olympic Games held in Sochi, Russia.

_____ 10. Sochi, a warm-weather resort city with a subtropical climate, located near the Black Sea and famous for its mild winters, was a poor choice for the snow and ice events of the Winter Olympics.

(Continues on next page)

B. Identify facts with an **F**, opinions with an **O**, and the **one** combination of fact and opinion with an **F+O**.

_____ 11. There are two reasons that ads for watches nearly always show the hands at roughly 10 minutes past 10: to set off the watch company's logo and to make the watch look as if it is smiling.

_____ 12. The finest watches in the world are made by the Swiss manufacturer Rolex.

_____ 13. Because the infant mortality rate was so high, frontier parents often left their infants nameless for many months rather than "waste" a name.

_____ 14. With all our wealth, America's infant mortality rate, which is one of the highest in the world, should be the lowest in the world.

_____ 15. The best way to conduct any kind of research is to start with the search engine Google.

_____ 16. Google, the Internet search company, got its name from the word "googol," which represents the number 1 followed by one hundred zeroes.

_____ 17. In the Middle Ages, people believed that washing with water would lead them to contract diseases through the pores in their skin.

_____ 18. The discovery that germs cause disease was the greatest scientific breakthrough ever.

_____ 19. Universal Studios Florida in Orlando is the most exciting amusement park in the world.

_____ 20. The first American amusement parks were built near the end of the 19th century by trolley companies, which constructed them at the end of their lines to increase business on the weekends.

Name ______________________________ Date __________

Section __________ SCORE: (Number correct) ______ x 5 = ______ %

FACT AND OPINION: Mastery Test 3

A. Identify facts with an **F**, opinions with an **O**, and the **two** combinations of fact and opinion with an **F+O**.

_____ 1. Any baseball player who tests positive for steroids should be permanently banned from the game, since steroids give him an unfair advantage over other players.

_____ 2. In 2007, a government report named 89 major league baseball players who were alleged to have taken steroids or other drugs.

_____ 3. Animals will die just as quickly from sleep deprivation as from food deprivation.

_____ 4. Countries ought to be permitted to deprive terror suspects of sleep in order to get them to reveal information that may save lives.

_____ 5. In ancient Rome, the sweat, dirt, and oil that a famous athlete or gladiator scraped off himself was sold to his fans in small vials.

_____ 6. People today are foolish to spend money on a product just because it has been endorsed by a sports celebrity.

_____ 7. Parents should strictly limit the number of soft drinks their children consume in a day.

_____ 8. Children who eat lots of salty snacks also tend to drink more sugary soft drinks to quench their thirst.

_____ 9. Although it is legal in a number of European countries, prostitution should not be legalized in America because it is sinful.

_____ 10. Nevada and Rhode Island are the only two states in the United States that have legalized prostitution.

(Continues on next page)

B. Identify facts with an **F**, opinions with an **O**, and the **two** combinations of fact and opinion with an **F+O**.

_____ 11. Most doctors are not very good at making their patients feel comfortable during routine physical exams.

_____ 12. A study found that one out of four patients diagnosed with high blood pressure in a doctor's office had normal blood pressure when measured away from the doctor's office.

_____ 13. The average budget for a wedding in the United States is estimated to be $25,000.

_____ 14. With nearly half of all American marriages ending in divorce, couples should be discouraged from spending a lot of money on a wedding.

_____ 15. There are more Chinese restaurants in the United States—over 41,000—than all the McDonald's, Burger Kings, Wendy's, Domino's, and Pizza Hut restaurants combined.

_____ 16. It's more enjoyable to eat at a Chinese restaurant than at a fast-food joint.

_____ 17. The harp, one of the oldest of musical instruments, can be found in countries all over the world.

_____ 18. Harp music, which has been found to lower the heart rates and anxiety levels of humans and animals alike, should be used more in office background music.

_____ 19. Although they resemble pigs, the hippo's closest living relatives are whales and dolphins.

_____ 20. With their funny, rounded features, frighteningly huge mouths, and incredible bulk, hippos are among the most fascinating of wild animals.

Name ______________________________ Date __________

Section ____________ SCORE: (Number correct) _______ x 5 = _______ %

FACT AND OPINION: Mastery Test 4

A. Identify facts with an **F**, opinions with an **O**, and the **two** combinations of fact and opinion with an **F+O**.

_____ 1. Every homeless person in America who is mentally ill should be identified and placed in an institution.

_____ 2. About one-quarter of homeless Americans have serious mental illnesses, and it is wrong for so many people to be prejudiced against them.

_____ 3. Research has found that men tend to lie to make themselves look better, while women are more likely to lie to make the other person feel better.

_____ 4. It is always best to tell the truth, whatever the circumstances.

_____ 5. In 1898, Bayer marketed heroin as a cough and cold remedy. When reports of extreme addiction became known, it stopped making the medicine in 1918.

_____ 6. Pharmaceutical companies today care more about profits than about whether the products they market are safe.

_____ 7. Geologists believe that the Himalaya Mountains were formed about 70 million years ago when the Indian subcontinent collided with Asia.

_____ 8. It's foolish for any but the most skilled mountaineers to attempt to climb Mt. Everest, which, at 29,000 feet, is the tallest mountain in the world.

_____ 9. Fashion magazines need to stop featuring stick-like models and focus more on average-build or even full-figured women.

_____ 10. One hundred years ago, the ideal of feminine beauty was Broadway star Lillian Russell, who stood 5'6" and weighed about 180 pounds.

(Continues on next page)

B. Identify facts with an **F**, opinions with an **O**, and the **two** combinations of fact and opinion with an **F+O**.

_____ 11. It is a fact that women are superior to men.

_____ 12. Women have a longer life expectancy than men.

_____ 13. During the early years of the Great Depression, President Herbert Hoover became so unpopular that at a campaign stop in Kansas, voters threw tomatoes at his train.

_____ 14. President Herbert Hoover has to rank as the worst president in American history.

_____ 15. With their shiny black bodies, twitching antennae, and athletic hind legs, crickets are among the most repulsive-looking insects on the planet.

_____ 16. If you count how many times a cricket chirps in 15 seconds and add 37, you will get an approximation of the outside temperature.

_____ 17. In Shakespeare's day, all women's parts were played by men, since it was considered improper for women to appear on the stage.

_____ 18. Examples of brilliant movie actors who did an amazing job playing women include Dustin Hoffman in *Tootsie*, Robin Williams in *Mrs. Doubtfire*, and Jack Lemmon in *Some Like It Hot*.

_____ 19. In Japan, the average corporate executive makes 11 times what the average factory worker makes; in the United States, the average corporate executive makes 475 times what the average factory worker makes.

_____ 20. It is a disgrace that our corporate executives are so highly paid when they perform so poorly.

3 Three Additional Readings

The three short selections that follow come from a variety of current college texts. Using the skills you have learned in this book, see if you can take notes on the important ideas in each selection.

BABY LOVE

Mary M. Gergen and others

1 At the base of an infant's social life is its first experience of love. During the first two years, infants normally acquire a basic sense of attachment. By **attachment**, we mean a feeling of dependence, trust, and the desire to be physically close to the major caregiver, usually the mother. Developmentalists such as Erik Erikson believe that the basic trust formed during this period provides the foundation for all other social and emotional development.

2 We do not know how quickly infants develop attachment. Psychologists had once believed that infants in the first few weeks of life were not yet able to distinguish their mother from other people, but recent research indicates that they are able to. By six months or so, they have clearly developed attachment. One indication of this is that many infants will cry if their mothers disappear from sight. Also, children often will show fear and distress in the presence of a stranger. The presence of a caretaker will soothe them.

3 What is the basis of the infant's attachment to its mother? Some learning theorists believe that the attachment between mother and child develops because of the child's ability to cry and smile. Crying and smiling are innate responses in infants; these responses reflect the child's need states, which the child communicates in a primitive way to parents. The child cries when in distress, and the parent relieves the distress. At this point, the child smiles (which in a sense rewards the parent's actions). The behaviors of parents and infants are mutually reinforcing—the infant provides smiles and the parent provides food and care—so both parties become attached.

4 For some time, psychologists thought that the nourishment provided by the parent was the principal reinforcer for infants, but research suggests that the physical comfort provided by parents may be even more important. Harry and Margaret Harlow conducted several experiments on infant monkeys who were separated from their mothers at birth and reared with surrogate, or substitute, mothers. In some cases, the surrogate mother was made of wire with a wooden block for a head. This was not a very cozy mother to cuddle up to. In other cases, the surrogate mother had a soft, cuddly, terry-cloth body. In one experiment, the infant monkeys were raised in a cage with both the terry-cloth "mother" and the wire "mother." However, only the wire mother was equipped with a milk bottle, so nourishment came from the wire mother alone.

5 The Harlows and their associates observed the behavior of the infants and discovered an important tendency. The infant monkey had become attached to the terry-cloth mother, even though the wire mother provided the food. If an infant monkey was frightened (by sounds, lights, or a new object), it would seek the security of the terry-cloth mother. It would feed from the wire mother's bottle, but it spent most of its time with the cloth-covered mother. Also, when an infant monkey proceeded to investigate the cage, it would keep one foot on the terry-cloth mother and would return and cling to this surrogate mother whenever frightened. These results suggest that contact comfort is in many ways more important for attachment than nourishment.

Even though the terry-cloth mothers provided the infant monkeys with security, these monkeys did not develop into normal adults. While they were less disturbed than monkeys raised only with wire mothers, as adults they exhibited disturbed behavior. They constantly rocked, sucked on themselves, and behaved in an aggressive manner when released into a group of monkeys. This behavior lasted through their adult lives. 6

Obviously, the terry-cloth and wire mothers were not enough. Attachment to real monkeys seemed important for the young monkeys to develop into proper adults. But need the mother be present for this to occur? Harry Harlow looked at this question as well. He found that infant monkeys that were separated from their mothers and raised with other infants showed more clinging behavior and tended to be more timid as adults than normally reared monkeys. These infants showed some negative effects of being raised without a mother, but they were not so badly affected as infants who were raised completely isolated from other monkeys. 7

Of course, you may have doubts about generalizing to humans from experiments with monkeys. This is a reasonable doubt. But we should note that apes and monkeys are our closest nonhuman relatives. Thus, we may suspect that some similarities might 8 exist. Also, studies of children brought up in orphanages show that those who are not given the opportunity to form strong attachments to caregivers suffer from social and emotional difficulties.

9 Harlow also tested whether or not the effects of early isolation could be reversed. In one study, he placed young monkeys who had not been isolated with older monkeys that had been isolated. The younger monkeys showed a lot of clinging behavior, and very little aggressive behavior. The usual response of the younger monkeys was to cling and attach themselves to the older monkeys. Over time, the isolates reciprocated this behavior, and after six months the isolates behaved much like the younger monkeys. The younger monkeys apparently provided nonthreatening models to the isolates.

10 Studies of young children in orphanages have shown that giving loving attention and care to formerly neglected babies improves their lives significantly. Listless, dull babies became lively, normal youngsters when they were lovingly cared for. In one study, the children who did not receive loving care became mentally retarded and remained institutionalized all of their lives, while the others who were cared for developed into normal adults living in the community. We should point out that this series of studies merely observed some orphanages; it was not an experiment. It would appear that the effects of the early experience of isolation may be correctable. Recently, a review of twenty studies on early separation of mothers from their children indicated that children do not usually suffer permanent harm from this experience. What seems to matter is that someone gives loving care to the infants.

We have emphasized attachment 11
to the principal caretaker, but typically by one year of age children extend their attachments to others, such as the father, grandparents, and other caretakers. Also at this time the fear of strangers, which peaks around eight months, begins to decrease, and will be reduced markedly by the time the child is eighteen months old. The attachment to others provides the foundation for future social relationships.

LABELING AND THE ONSET OF OLD AGE

James M. Henslin

1 You probably can remember when you thought a twelve-year-old was "old"—and anyone older beyond reckoning, just "up there" someplace. You probably were 5 or 6 at the time. Similarly, to a twelve-year-old someone 21 seems "old." At 21, 30 may mark that line, and 40 may seem "very old." And so it keeps on going, with "old" gradually receding from the self. To people who turn 40, 50 seems old; at 50, the late 60s look old (not the early 60s, for at that point in accelerating years they don't seem too far away).

2 At some point, of course, an individual must apply the label "old" to himself or herself. Often, cultural definitions of age force this label on people sooner then they are ready to accept it. In the typical case, the individual has become used to what he or she sees in the mirror. The changes have taken place very gradually, and each change, if not exactly taken in stride, has been accommodated. (Consequently, it comes as a shock, when meeting a friend one has not seen in years, to see how much that person has changed. At class reunions, each person can hardly believe how much older the others appear!)

3 If there is no single point at which people automatically cross a magical line and become "old," what, then, makes someone "old"? We can point to several factors that spur people to apply the label of "old" to themselves.

The first factor is biology. One 4
person may experience "signs" of aging much earlier than another: wrinkles, balding, aches, difficulty in doing some things that he or she used to take for granted. Consequently, one person will feel "old" at an earlier or later age than others, and only at that time adopt the rules of an "old person," that is, begin to act in ways old people in that particular society are thought to act.

Personal history or biography is 5
a second factor that influences when people consider themselves old. An accident that limits mobility may make one person feel old sooner than others. Or a woman may have given birth at 16 to a daughter, who in turn has a child at 18. When this woman is 34, she is a biological grandmother. It is more unlikely that she will begin to play any stereotypical role—spending the day in a rocking chair, for example—but knowing that she is a grandmother has an impact on her self-concept. At a minimum, she must deny that she is old.

A third factor in determining when 6
people label themselves old is gender age, the relative value that a culture places on men's and women's ages. For example, around the world, compared with most women, most men are able to

marry much younger spouses. Similarly, on men graying hair and even some wrinkles may be signs of "maturing," while on women those same features are likely to be interpreted as signs of "old." "Mature" and "old," of course, carry quite different meanings in Western cultures—the first is desired, while the second is shunned. Two striking examples of gender age in U.S. society are found in the mass media. Older male news anchors are likely to be retained, while female anchors who turn the same age are more likely to be transferred to a less visible position. Similarly, in movies older men are much more likely to play romantic leads—and opposite much younger rising stars.

7 Many individuals, of course, are exceptions to these patterns. Maria, for example, may marry Bill, who is fourteen years younger than she. But in most marriages in which there is a fourteen-year age gap between husband and wife, around the world the odds greatly favor the wife's being the younger of the pair. Biology, of course, has nothing to do with this socially constructed reality.

The fourth factor is timetables, the 8 signals societies use to inform their members that they are old. Since there is no automatic age at which people become "old," these timetables vary around the world. One group may choose a particular birthday, such as the sixtieth or the sixty-fifth, to signal the onset of old age. Other groups may not even have birthdays, making such numbers meaningless. Only after they moved to the reservations, for example, did Native Americans adopt the white custom of counting birthdays. For traditional Native Americans, the signal for old age is more the inability to perform productive social roles than any particular birthday. Consequently, those unable to continue in these roles tend to think of themselves as old, regardless of their age. In one survey, for instance. a Native American woman with many disabilities described herself as elderly, although she was only 37.

NONVERBAL COMMUNICATION

Michael W. Drafke and Stan Kossen

1 Nonverbal communication accounts for 55 percent of the total message we can deliver. It is so powerful that when the verbal and tonal portions conflict with the nonverbal portion, people believe the nonverbal message. This reinforces the old saying "Actions speak louder than words." The following section investigates the details of nonverbal communication.

THE BODY SPEAKS

2 Whether you realize it consciously or not, you're communicating each time you make a gesture or glance at a person. The motions people make with their body (or sometimes don't make) often communicate messages. Body language isn't always accurate or effective, but it is communication nonetheless. For example, assume that after you arrive at your job one morning, you pass a coworker in the hallway who gives you an unusual glance or at least a glance that appears to you to be strange. You might wonder for the rest of the day what that glance meant. Some employees seldom greet others that they pass in hallways or work areas. Instead, their faces seem frozen. Sometimes a person might think that a frozen stare is an indication of displeasure.

3 Once again, a word of warning: Some people are misled by body language. We already are aware that we have plenty of difficulties interpreting correctly the verbal symbols of others, even when we've had training in listening. We can also be easily misled by body language. For example, your listener's crossed arms may not necessarily mean a lack of receptivity to your message. Instead, it could merely mean that the person feels cold.

FUNCTIONS OF NONVERBAL COMMUNICATION

Nonverbal communication (NVC) has five basic functions. Nonverbal communication can accent, complement, contradict, regulate, or substitute for verbal communication. 4

When nonverbal communications punctuate verbal communications, the NVC is performing an **accenting** role. Poking a finger into someone's chest is an example of accenting. Punctuating a message with a sweeping motion of the hand at chest level with the palm facing out says that the conversation is over. 5

Complementing nonverbal communications reinforce the spoken message; complementing NVC would not convey the same message if used alone. The distance between two people is an example of complementing NVC. Standing four feet away from someone might indicate that this person is a stranger. When the person is your boss 6 and you are four feet away and you present her with a formal salutation ("Good morning, Ms. Smith"), then the distance reinforces the message that the boss is of higher rank and the two of you have an unchallenged authority relationship.

7 Of the more interesting nonverbal communications are those that contradict the verbal message. **Contradicting** NVCs convey messages that are opposite to the verbal messages. Often this is the way people reveal their true feelings or send the wrong or an unintended message. Even though people say that they are paying attention, if they give less eye contact than they receive (that is, if they look off into the distance rather than at the speaker), they send a contradicting nonverbal message. The message they send is that they are bored or uninterested. When verbal and nonverbal messages conflict, people believe the *nonverbal* ones.

8 A **regulating** nonverbal communication controls the course of a conversation. Raising your hand with the index finger extended indicates that you want the other person to wait a minute or to stop speaking. Tapping a coworker's shoulder twice with your index finger while she is walking away from you indicates that you want her to stop or to wait for you so you can speak to her. Touching someone's arm while he speaks also performs a regulating function by indicating to him that you wish to speak.

We use **substituting** nonverbal communications to replace a verbal message. This use is quite common because sometimes it is not practical or politically wise to state out loud what we are thinking. When two people are in a hurry and pass in a busy hall, they may not have the time to speak to one another, or the crowd may be too large for a spoken word to be heard unless one shouts. Instead, we often substitute an "eyebrow flash" for a spoken "How you doin', Fred?" We can't talk, but we don't want to be rude to our colleague, so we raise both eyebrows as a silent, substitute salutation. Or you may be standing behind a boss who comes down hard on a coworker for a minor transgression. It would not be politically smart to disagree verbally with this boss, but you also want to let your coworker know that you think the boss is going too far. So you shake your head back and forth in a silent "no" that is unseen by the boss. 9

Although there are just five functions of nonverbal communications, there are many types and hundreds of examples of these types. Most nonverbal messages are learned automatically, but it is still important to study them; for although many are innate, one can accidentally send an incorrect or overly revealing nonverbal message if one is not knowledgeable and careful. 10

4 Understanding Bias

Bias refers to a subjective view—in other words, a view that is either positive or negative. It contrasts with an objective view—one that is neutral. You have already learned about bias in two previous chapters. In "Purpose and Tone," you learned that a selection with an objective tone is not biased and that a selection with a subjective tone is at least partly biased—it represents the writer's point of view. In "Critical Reading," you learned that speakers and writers often include their point of view—that is, their opinion—in what they communicate. What they say is therefore at least partly biased. That bias is sometimes revealed through value words, such as *best* and *worst* and *great* and *terrible.* In this chapter, you will get more practice in recognizing biased language.

Biased Language

Look at the following sentences:

1. Phil spends very little money.
2. Phil is thrifty.
3. Phil is a cheapskate.

Each of these three sentences describes the same person and behavior. The first one is strictly factual. It simply tells what Phil does without making a judgment about it. The second sentence, by using the word *thrifty,* hints that Phil should be praised for his careful money management. By using the word *cheapskate,* the third sentence strongly suggests that Phil's behavior is undesirable.

Just by choosing one word rather than another, an author expresses a viewpoint. In choosing the phrase *spends very little money,* the writer of the first sentence remained *objective*—neither for nor against Phil. The writer of the second sentence expressed a bias in Phil's favor, and the writer of the third sentence expressed a bias against him. Word choices like the positive word *thrifty* and the negative word *cheapskate* are sometimes called "emotionally loaded" or simply "loaded" words. The writer uses them to express a positive or negative attitude toward a subject.

Check Your Understanding

Suppose you were writing the sentence below and had to choose between the two words in parentheses. One word makes a factual statement about Cindy's work; the other expresses a bias, a positive or negative view of her work. Decide which word suggests a bias and write it in the blank.

Cindy performed her work *(faster, better)* ____________________ than her coworkers.

Explanation

The biased word is *better*. The other word, *faster*, simply describes Cindy's pace. Anyone who pays attention to how fast Cindy and her coworkers work will have to agree that Cindy works faster—it's a fact. However, *better* makes a positive judgment about the quality of Cindy's work. Others may or may not agree with this opinion.

PRACTICE 1

Each sentence below can be completed in two ways, one neutral and the other biased. For each sentence, choose the biased word, and write it on the line.

1. The *(student, nerd)* _______________ asked permission to turn his research paper in early.

2. I sat up most of the night *(remembering, regretting)* _______________ my date with Linda.

3. There were hundreds of unusual *(treasures, items)* _______________ for sale at the flea market.

4. Climbing stairs provides *(some, good)* _______________ aerobic exercise.

5. Americans *(typically, unfortunately)* _______________ eat an average of 134 pounds of sugar each year.

Bias in Longer Passages

Longer passages may contain a whole series of words that work together to suggest a bias in the writer's point of view.

Check Your Understanding

The following passage is someone's description of supermarket tabloids. After reading the passage, write the letter of the group of words that reveals the writer's bias about the tabloids. Then write the letter of the statement that expresses the writer's point of view.

> [1]The suckers who take seriously supermarket tabloids like the *Enquirer* or the *Globe* should wise up to the fact that reporters are writing entertainment, not news. [2]The editorial policy for these rags seems to be "anything goes." [3]The stories are often pure fantasy, as in the article "Spirit of Elvis Haunts Widow's Microwave," or gossip reported by unreliable sources, such as plumbers of Hollywood celebrities. [4]Read as entertainment, tabloids are good for a laugh, but nobody should base a decision on the obvious misinformation found in these publications.

_____ 1. The biased words are
- A. *supermarket, policy, stories, Hollywood.*
- B. *reporters, sources, decision, publications.*
- C. *suckers, rags, unreliable, misinformation.*

_____ 2. The author expresses a bias against
- A. Elvis Presley.
- B. Hollywood entertainment.
- C. tabloids as a source of news.

Explanation

The words *suckers, rags, unreliable,* and *misinformation* are all "loaded" or biased words—they show that the writer is not objective about the topic of tabloids. Noticing which words are biased will help you pinpoint the nature of the writer's bias. In this case, such words as *unreliable* and *misinformation* leave us in little doubt that the writer feels supermarket tabloids are undependable sources of news. Thus the correct answer to question 2 is C.

PRACTICE 2

Read the passages below to see if you can detect the words that reveal each author's bias. Also, think about the direction of that bias. Then answer the questions that follow.

A. [1]The New Jersey Pine Barrens, 650,000 acres of wilderness, represent a vast ecological wealth of rare plants and animals, as well as a priceless reservoir of natural water. [2]Irresponsible land developers, however, are threatening to rape parts of the Barrens and replace them with shopping malls and condominiums.

_____ 1. The biased words are
- A. *Jersey, wilderness, water, malls.*
- B. *wealth, priceless, irresponsible, rape.*
- C. *acres, represent, plants, developers.*

_____ 2. The author's bias is against the
- A. New Jersey Pine Barrens.
- B. land developers.
- C. rare plants and animals.

B. [1]The Hopi Indians of northern Arizona have admirably withstood the United States government's attempts to blend them into America's melting pot. [2]The Hopis are rightly more concerned with seeking harmony within themselves and with their environment than they are with adopting conventional American ways. [3]Thus their worthy culture still survives.

_____ 3. The biased words are
- A. *Hopi, Arizona, environment, ways.*
- B. *admirably, rightly, worthy.*
- C. *government's, seeking, culture.*

_____ 4. The author expresses a bias in favor of the
- A. United States government.
- B. melting pot.
- C. Hopis.

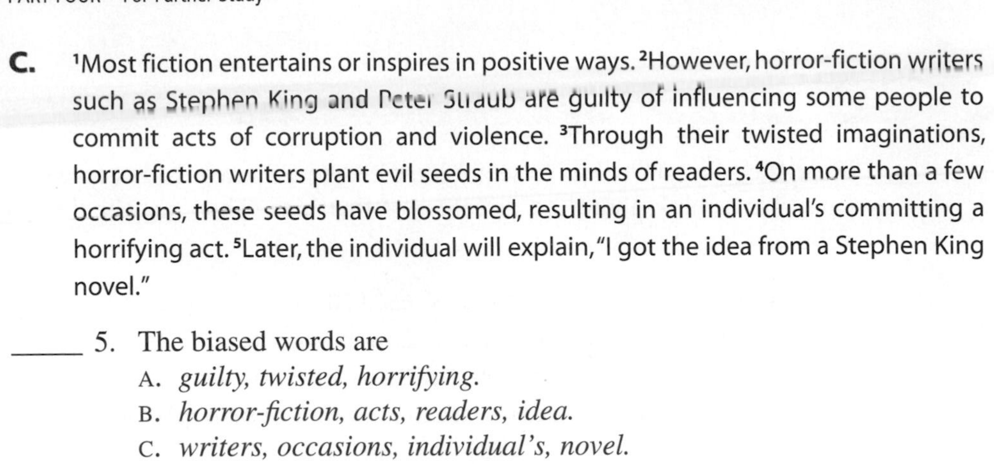

C. [1]Most fiction entertains or inspires in positive ways. [2]However, horror-fiction writers such as Stephen King and Peter Straub are guilty of influencing some people to commit acts of corruption and violence. [3]Through their twisted imaginations, horror-fiction writers plant evil seeds in the minds of readers. [4]On more than a few occasions, these seeds have blossomed, resulting in an individual's committing a horrifying act. [5]Later, the individual will explain, "I got the idea from a Stephen King novel."

_____ 5. The biased words are
   A. *guilty, twisted, horrifying.*
   B. *horror-fiction, acts, readers, idea.*
   C. *writers, occasions, individual's, novel.*

_____ 6. The author expresses a bias against
   A. readers.
   B. fiction.
   C. horror-fiction writers.

D. [1]With frequent droughts, numerous anti-watering ordinances, and a polluted environment, it's obvious that large grassy lawns are outdated. [2]A big spread of grass may look pretty, but it has real drawbacks. [3]In order to keep their grass green and weed-free, many homeowners use chemicals that harm the larger ecosystem. [4]Also, keeping all that grass healthy requires a lot of water that could be put to better use. [5]Preferable alternatives to a lawn include wide walkways, flowerbeds, vegetable beds, and the use of ground covers. [6]Another commendable option is to use only drought-tolerant plants that thrive in a particular area. [7]In the southwestern United States, for instance, extended patios surrounded by cactus work well. [8]In other areas, drought-tolerant plants such as ornamental grasses, native wildflowers, "hens and chickens," and aloe can take the place of grass. [9]Wherever they live, people can choose sensible lawn alternatives.

_____ 7. The biased words include
   A. *obvious, outdated, preferable, commendable, sensible.*
   B. *polluted, environment, ecosystem, drought-tolerant.*
   C. *chemicals, cactus, ornamental grasses, wildflowers, aloe, lawn alternatives.*

_____ 8. The author expresses a bias in favor of
   A. the southwestern United States.
   B. alternatives to lawns.
   C. keeping lawns healthy and weed-free.

REVIEW TEST 1

To review what you've learned in this chapter, answer each question with **T** or **F** or by writing the letter of the answer you choose.

_____ 1. TRUE OR FALSE? An author may express a bias in his or her choice of words.

_____ 2. TRUE OR FALSE? A biased point of view is objective.

_____ 3. A subjective statement expresses
- A. a fact.
- B. an opinion.
- C. a question.

_____ 4. A biased point of view can be
- A. negative.
- B. positive.
- C. either of the above.

_____ 5. An example of a biased word is
- A. *round.*
- B. *money.*
- C. *selfish.*
- D. *recent.*

REVIEW TEST 2

Write the letter of the answer to each question that follows the passages below.

A. [1]Alternative education programs for disruptive students have been established in some states. [2]While disruptive behavior in schools is a serious concern, why should taxpayers have to foot the bill for educating young delinquents? [3]These troublemakers should either follow the rules or be expelled. [4]If students are too rowdy to function in the traditional classroom setting, let them quit school and get a job.

_____ 1. The biased words include
- A. *alternative, bill, students.*
- B. *delinquents, troublemakers, rowdy.*
- C. *education, function, classroom, job.*

_____ 2. The author has a bias against
- A. the traditional classroom setting.
- B. special treatment for disruptive students.
- C. taxpayers.

B. [1]A writer for *Fortune* magazine described a conversation he had after reading the autobiography of Sam Walton, founder of Wal-Mart. [2]He told his friend how incredibly active Walton had been as a kid—"president of this, football team, newspaper boy, more, more, more." [3]The writer's friend commented, "Nowadays they would have put him on that calming medication, Ritalin."

[4]The scary thing is that he may be right. [5]Chances are Sam Walton was not always an easy kid to deal with. [6]He was brilliant, energetic, bursting with new ideas and activities. [7]He probably drove his parents and teachers crazy at times. [8]Can't you just picture some all-too-rigid teacher today calling his mother to say, "Mrs. Walton, Sam is rather disruptive in class. [9]I think he has Attention Deficit Disorder. [10]We ought to see if he responds to medication"? [11]If that had regrettably happened and the Ritalin had "worked," would anyone know Sam Walton's name today?

_____ 3. The biased words include
- A. *conversation, autobiography, medication.*
- B. *scary, all-too-rigid, regrettably.*
- C. *active, calming, energetic.*

_____ 4. The author is biased against
- A. students who disrupt classes.
- B. teachers.
- C. medicating difficult students.

C. [1]George Washington was not a tactician of the quality of Caesar or Robert E. Lee. [2]His lack of genius made his achievements all the more impressive. [3]He held his forces together in adversity, avoiding both useless slaughter and catastrophic defeat. [4]People of all sections, from every walk of life, looked on Washington as the embodiment of American virtues. [5]He was a man of deeds, rather than words. [6]He was a man of substance, accustomed to luxury, yet capable of enduring great hardships stoically; a bold patriot, quick to take arms against British tyranny, yet eminently respectable. [7]The Revolution might have been won without Washington, but it is unlikely that the free United States would have become so easily a true nation had he not been at its call.

_____ 5. The biased words are
- A. *impressive, bold patriot, eminently respectable.*
- B. *forces, substance, arms.*
- C. *Robert E. Lee, Revolution, United States.*

_____ 6. The author expresses a bias in favor of Washington's
- A. lack of genius.
- B. being accustomed to luxury.
- C. achievements during the American Revolution.

D. [1]The hospice movement was begun in the 1960s by two women physicians: Elisabeth Kübler-Ross and Cicely Saunders. [2]They wanted to change medicine so that it would better meet the needs of dying patients and their families. [3]In an ordinary hospital, death is the enemy, and doctors and nurses feel that their job is to fight death off as long as possible and by any means possible. [4]A hospice, by contrast, does not attempt to fight or delay death, but instead simply makes the dying patient as comfortable as possible. [5]A hospice rightly strives for death with dignity and tries to give patients as much control as possible over their final months, weeks, or days of life. [6]When the movement first began, hospices were separate facilities, but now the emphasis is on letting dying patients stay home, with most treatment delivered by visiting nurses and physicians. [7]As a result of Kübler-Ross's and Saunders's admirable work, other physicians have also become more aware of the special needs of dying patients, especially the relief of pain; and in-home care, including hospice care, is today one of the fastest-growing areas of medicine.

_____ 7. The biased words include
A. *change medicine, ordinary hospital, visiting nurses and physicians.*
B. *better, rightly, admirable.*
C. *women physicians, special needs, fastest-growing.*

_____ 8. The author's bias is in favor of
A. treating the dying in ordinary hospitals.
B. hospice care for the dying.
C. fighting off death by any means possible.

REVIEW TEST 3

Write the letter of the answer to each question that follows the passages below.

A. [1]Alcohol-related highway deaths are the number-one killer of young people. [2]Misguided individuals advocate counseling for teens with a drinking problem. [3]They argue that the peer pressure teens face leads them to drink, which is sheer nonsense. [4]With ten thousand young people dying each year from suicides, accidents, and injuries all related to alcohol, the solution is clear: get tough with spineless underaged drinkers. [5]Throw the book at them, and we'll see that they'll suddenly be able to resist peer pressure without counseling.

_____ 1. The biased words include
A. *highway, individuals, peer pressure.*
B. *misguided, nonsense, spineless.*
C. *young, problem, alcohol.*

_____ 2. The author's bias is against
A. teen drinkers.
B. young people.
C. the legal system.

B. [1]Relaxation techniques have proved remarkably effective in reducing anxiety and increasing an individual's ability to resist stress. [2]The best-known of the relaxation techniques is transcendental meditation (TM), which can produce almost miraculous results. [3]An overworked and out-of-shape businessman, for example, can decrease his oxygen consumption and respiratory and heart rates if he practices transcendental meditation on a regular basis. [4]For the TM center nearest you, check your Yellow Pages.

_____ 3. The biased words include
A. *remarkably effective, miraculous.*
B. *anxiety, respiratory, regular.*
C. *stress, oxygen, transcendental meditation.*

_____ 4. The author's bias is in favor of
A. oxygen consumption.
B. transcendental meditation.
C. businessmen.

C. [1]In Pittsburgh, a high-school administration has decided to take a strong stand against the flashy, expensive clothes worn by students. [2]No longer will the students at River Heights High be allowed to show off all the latest designer clothes and accessories. [3]This fall, a dress code was established that will limit the type and amount of jewelry worn and eliminate the overly revealing miniskirt. [4]The new code was designed with the hope of ending the ridiculous amount of student competition concerning clothes. [5]This competition, administrators feel, distracts students from their class work.

_____ 5. The biased words include
A. *flashy, overly revealing, ridiculous.*
B. *clothes, jewelry, administrators.*
C. *high-school administration, students, class work.*

_____ 6. The author's bias is in favor of
A. the dress code.
B. the miniskirt.
C. student competition concerning clothes.

D. [1]During the Great Depression, President Hoover dined each night at the White House in regal splendor. [2]He had thought about cutting back but decided it would be bad for the morale of the country. [3]If he changed his habits one bit, it would seem a sign of lost confidence. [4]So each evening Hoover entered the dining room in black tie, ready to consume seven full courses. [5]Buglers in uniform heralded his arrival and departure with glittering trumpets, even when the only guest was his wife.

[6]Such behavior earned Hoover the reputation of being insensitive, but that was not the case. [7]He never visited a bread line or a relief shelter because he could not bear to see suffering. [8]When the press criticized him, he withdrew, wounded and hurt. [9]Rumors that circulated about him were as painful as they were ridiculous. [10]It was said, for instance, that dogs instinctively disliked him; that he had masterminded the kidnapping and murder of Charles Lindbergh's infant son; that roses wilted in his hands. [11]Hoover was doing all he could to promote recovery, more than any earlier president. [12]Yet he was scorned. [13]His natural sullenness turned to self-pity. [14]"You can't expect to see calves running in the field the day after you put the bull to the cows," Calvin Coolidge reassured him. [15]"No," said an exasperated Hoover, "but I would expect to see contented cows."

______ 7. The biased words include
- A. *the Great Depression, his wife, recovery.*
- B. *the White House, relief shelter, calves running in the field.*
- C. *not the case, doing all he could, more than any earlier president.*

______ 8. The author's bias is in favor of
- A. a sign of lost confidence.
- B. the critical press.
- C. Hoover.

Check Your Performance — UNDERSTANDING BIAS

Activity	Number Right		Points		Score
Review Test 1 (5 items)	______	×	4	=	______
Review Test 2 (8 items)	______	×	5	=	______
Review Test 3 (8 items)	______	×	5	=	______
			TOTAL SCORE	=	______%

5 Writing Assignments

To the Instructor: Before assigning any of the following topics, you might want to go over with your students the guidelines that appear below and on the next page.

A Brief Guide to Effective Writing

Here in a nutshell is what you need to do to write effectively.

Step 1: Explore Your Topic through Informal Writing

To begin with, explore the topic that you want to write about or that you have been assigned to write about. You can examine your topic through **informal writing**, which usually means one of three things.

First, you can **freewrite** about your topic for at least ten minutes. In other words, write, for ten minutes, whatever comes into your head about your subject. Write without stopping and without worrying at all about spelling or grammar or the like. Simply get down on paper all the information about the topic that occurs to you.

A second thing you can do is to **make a list of ideas and details** that could go into your paper. Simply pile these items up, one after another, like a shopping list, without worrying about putting them in any special order. Try to accumulate as many details as you can think of.

A third way to explore your topic is to **write down a series of questions and answers** about it. Your questions can start with words like *what, why, how, when,* and *where*.

Getting your thoughts and ideas down on paper will help you think more about your topic. With some raw material to look at, you are now in a better position to decide on just how to proceed.

Step 2: Plan Your Paper with an Informal Outline

After exploring your topic, plan your paper, using an informal outline. Do two things:

- **Decide on and write out the main point (main idea) of your paper.** It is often a good idea to begin your paragraph with this point, which is also known as the *topic sentence*. If you are writing an essay of several paragraphs, you will probably want to include your main point somewhere in your first paragraph. In a paper of several paragraphs, the main point is called the *central point, central idea*, or *thesis*.
- **List the supporting reasons, examples, or other details that back up your point.** In many cases, you should have at least two or three items of support.

Step 3: Use Transitions

Once your outline is worked out, you will have a clear "road map" for writing your paper. As you write the early drafts of your paper, use **transitions** to introduce each of the separate supporting items (reasons, examples, or other details) you present to back up your point. For instance, you might introduce your first supporting item with the transitional words *first of all*. You might begin your second supporting item with words such as *another reason* or *another example*. And you might indicate your final supporting detail with such words as *last of all* or *a final reason.*

Step 4: Edit and Proofread Your Paper

After you have a solid draft, edit and proofread your paper. To evaluate your paper, ask yourself these questions:

1. Is the paper **unified**? Does all the material in the paper truly support the main point?
2. Is the paper **well supported**? Is there plenty of specific evidence to back up the main point?
3. Is the paper **clearly organized**? Does the material proceed in a way that makes sense? Do transitions help connect ideas?
4. Is the paper **well written**? When the paper is read aloud, do the sentences flow smoothly and clearly? Has the paper been checked carefully for grammar, punctuation, and spelling mistakes?

Writing Assignments for the Twenty Readings

Note: The discussion questions accompanying the twenty readings can also make good topics for writing. Some of the writing assignments here are based on these questions.

Part One Readings

All Washed Up?

1. Write a paragraph about your own policy of handwashing. What was your policy in the past? Did that policy change over the last couple of years as our culture became more sensitive to the ways that people can be infected with germs? Will your policy change after reading this article on hand-washing? If so, in what specific ways will it change?

2. As this essay notes, "Did you wash your hands?" is a question most of us grew up hearing more times than we can count. What were some of the other behavior-related reminders you grew up with? They may have come from parents or grandparents, teachers, or babysitters. Write a paragraph in which you reminisce about some of the reminders you frequently heard as a child.

3. Washing one's hands is a small thing that can have a big impact on one's health. And yet many people neglect doing it. Write a paper in which you describe in detail several other relatively easy things people can do to benefit their health, but often don't do. In your conclusion, present your theory or theories about why people neglect such simple health practices.

How Dual-Earner Couples Cope

1. Today, the dual-earner couple is the norm. In contrast, a generation ago it was far more common to have the man working outside the home while the woman attended to the house and children. What effects did that arrangement typically have on a marriage and family? Write a paragraph in which you explain what you believe were the good and bad points of the old pattern, in which the man was typically the only wage earner.

2. The authors describe women who experience stress because of the conflicting demands of their work (where they are expected to be aggressive and competitive) and home (where they are looked to for compassion and nurturing). Think of a time when you have felt torn by conflicting demands. Perhaps your friends expected certain behavior from you while your parents

wanted something else. Or you were torn between the demands of a romantic significant other and your old crowd. Write a paragraph that describes the stress you experienced and how you handled it.

3. Papalia and Olds divide dual-earner couples into three categories: conventional, modern, and role-sharing. On the basis of your observations of friends with dual-income marriages (or your own marriage), what are the pros and cons of each of those three patterns? Which of the three do you think is closest to ideal? Write an essay sharing your thoughts.

Now More Than Ever: Community Colleges

1. Like Miranda, many of us have big dreams that don't work out exactly as we'd planned. Write a paragraph about a dream you've had that either didn't come true or, as in Miranda's situation, came true in a way different from what you had imagined. In your paragraph, describe your dream, and then describe the reality of what happened. Conclude your paragraph by pointing out what you learned from the experience.

2. The author points out that the "moral of the story" is definitely *not* that it's a bad idea to go to college. Nonetheless, there are some people who believe that college is a waste of time and money. Have you ever known someone who disapproved of college or thought that it was unnecessary? What was that person like? What was his or her life like? Why, in particular, was this person opposed to college? Write a paragraph that describes this person and his/her viewpoint.

3. Imagine that you are a high-school counselor. Write an essay for seniors that presents what you believe are the three most important bits of advice to consider before heading to college. Before writing, think about Miranda's experience. She left for a university 1500 miles away without considering that she would not be able to visit home more than once a year, and she became homesick. She didn't enjoy living with someone she had never met. And she clearly had not carefully considered her choice of major or how expensive college life would be.

   There are, of course, many other unexpected problems that college freshmen might run into. Choose three problems, and devote a paragraph to each one. In each paragraph, present the problem, and then suggest ways to be prepared for it or ways to handle the problem when it comes up.

Forget What You Know about Good Study Habits

1. Of the study techniques suggested in this article, which one or ones are you most likely to try yourself? Write a paragraph explaining what they would be and how you would put that technique or techniques into practice.

2. Carey's article details how "some of the most hallowed advice on study habits is flat wrong." For example, he states that studying in the same place every time is not the best idea. And spacing out studying is far more likely to help you actually *learn* something than spending an entire night cramming for an exam. On the basis of what you've learned from the article, write a one-paragraph summary of study tips that would benefit today's students.

3. As Carey points out, excellent teachers are far from all alike. Write an essay about three teachers whom you considered to be excellent. (Alternatively, write about two teachers you thought were very good and one you thought was *not* good.) Explain how their particular approaches to teaching helped (or did not help) you learn effectively.

Soft Addictions

1. Bashard ends his article by pointing out that "knowledge is power," and, therefore, we should all ask ourselves if we might have some kind of soft addiction. In other words, we can all have more power over our own lives if we are honest and acknowledge an everyday habit we have that disrupts our lives. Do you have a soft addiction? Write a paragraph about it. In the paragraph, be sure to answer the following questions:
   - What is the addiction?
   - How much time do you devote to it each day?
   - How does this habit make you feel?
   - How does this habit disrupt your life?
   - How might you free yourself from this addiction?

2. Imagine going for an entire day without looking at your computer or your smartphone. How would doing without this contact affect you? Write a paragraph describing how you'd feel, how different your day might be, and why being without your phone or the Internet for 24 hours would be a good or a bad thing.

3. Imagine that you are a counselor writing an article for students on how to break three soft addictions. Choose from the habits described in Bashard's essay or from the following list:

- shopping
- eating
- procrastinating
- texting
- talking on the phone
- dating

You can also discover other bad habits by Googling "soft addictions" or "harmful bad habits." Then write the article, devoting one paragraph in the body of your essay to each addiction. Briefly describe the addiction, and then give advice on how to control it. In your conclusion, explain to students how much better they will feel about themselves once they've "kicked" these habits.

If you need information about how to work on breaking these soft addictions, a simple search along the lines of "how to stop shopping/eating/texting so much" should bring up hundreds of ideas.

The Influence of the Self-Fulfilling Prophecy

1. The "Pygmalion in the Classroom" experiment suggests that a teacher's expectations of a student have a great deal to do with his or her success. Write a paragraph about a teacher who seemed to have especially high or low expectations for you. How did you perform in his or her classroom? What effect do you think the teacher's expectations had upon you?

2. Think of a person who, in your opinion, continually sabotages his or her chances for happiness or acceptance. Write a paragraph in which you give that person some advice. Explain what you see the person doing to himself or herself, and suggest how he or she could change the self-sabotaging behavior.

3. Describe a time when you went into a situation expecting something bad to happen—or, at least, expecting not to enjoy yourself. Write an essay in which you compare or contrast what happened with what you believed would happen. As you consider that situation now, do you think that your attitude might have influenced what happened? Do you now feel, after reading the selection on self-fulfilling prophecies, that things might have been different if you had been more positive or less negative?

He Was First

1. Pee Wee Reese used his position as a team leader to stop the anti-Robinson momentum. When have you seen an individual stand up to a group and speak up for another point of view? Write a paragraph that describes the mood of the group, the actions of the individual, and how the group responded.

2. If you had been Jackie Robinson, do you think you could have agreed to Branch Rickey's request not to fight back when you were insulted? If so, do you believe you could have honored that request in the face of what Robinson experienced? Write a paragraph in which you tell what your response to Rickey would have been and how you believe you would have handled the pressure of Robinson's experience.

3. What do you think drives people to commit the kind of vicious attacks that were directed against Jackie Robinson, as well as other "hate crimes" against racial minorities and homosexuals that we read about in the papers every day? Why do some people react to others whom they perceive as "different" with such violent hatred? Write an essay in which you discuss several possible explanations for hate crimes. An example of a central point for this paper is "I believe that people who commit hate crimes are driven by their upbringing, their fears, and their desire to impress their friends."

What Causes Hearing Loss

1. As this article points out, our world is a noisy place. Most of us have gotten so used to the noise that we hardly even notice it anymore. Think about all the everyday noises that you are subjected to on a regular basis. Take some time to listen to the world around you. Then write a paragraph that describes the noises that you hear, starting in the morning and ending at night. Be as creative as you can be.

2. Brody writes about never returning to noisy restaurants and having to move away from people whose music is turned up too loudly in their headphones. Have you ever complained about—or even had to get away from—someone or something that was too loud or irritating? Perhaps it was an audience member talking in a movie theater or an all-night party in your apartment building or even a coughing and sniffling classmate during an exam. Write a paragraph about that experience. Describe the noise/sound problem and what you did about it.

3. What are the *best* sounds you've ever heard? Think of all the wonderful things you've heard in your life, and write an essay about the top three. Take some time to consider what constitutes a "best sound" to you. It could be a voice, a song, ocean waves from a memorable vacation, certain words from someone important to you, the engine of your car starting when you thought you were stranded in the middle of nowhere, or even the sound of silence after a long and noisy day.

   Your thesis statement can be as simple as this: "There are three sounds I've heard in my life that were so wonderful that I'll never forget them."

Obedience: Milgram's Controversial Studies

1. What do you think of Milgram's experiment? Was it ethical? Do its results suggest what people would do in a "real-life" situation? Write a paragraph telling how you responded to the experiment and why.

2. Have you ever found yourself automatically obeying an order from someone in authority, then later wondering if you'd done the right thing? Write a paragraph describing what happened and how you later wished you had responded.

3. Few people would question the need for children to learn to obey. Children who do not obey their parents endanger themselves ("Don't use the hairdryer in the bathtub") and alienate their community ("Don't play ball in Ms. Mitchell's garden"). Yet this passage suggests that some people learn to obey all too well, abandoning their own morals and good sense as they follow orders. How can parents encourage their children to be appropriately obedient and still teach them to think for themselves? Write an essay in which you make suggestions to parents on how to help their children achieve a healthy balance. Include examples to illustrate what can happen when a child is raised with too much or too little emphasis on obedience.

Managing Conflicts in Relationships

1. Think of a person you know whom you would define as one of the following: a withdrawer, a surrenderer, an aggressor, or a persuader. Write a paragraph in which you describe this person and his or her approach to dealing with conflict. Include at least one specific example of his or her behavior.

2. What advice would you give to Eduardo and Justina, the couple in the reading who are in conflict about Eduardo's smoking? What do you think Eduardo should do? What should Justina do? Write a paragraph advising the couple on how to handle their problem.

3. When have you and another person had an important conflict you needed to deal with? (To be "important," the conflict need not be earth-shattering. It is sufficient that it was a conflict you were unwilling to ignore.) Write a paper that describes the nature of the conflict, then takes the reader through the process that occurred as you and the other person dealt with it. Use transitional words such as *first*, *next*, and *finally* to help the reader follow the action. In the final paragraph, provide a conclusion that states how satisfied or dissatisfied you felt about the process.

Part Two Readings

The Professor Is a Dropout

1. When Lupe ran into obstacle after obstacle in her search to learn English, she nearly gave up. Write a paragraph about a time you felt extremely discouraged. What had brought you to that point? How did you proceed?

2. Write a paragraph about a class that you initially found difficult but that turned out to be not as bad as you expected. (Or write about a class you first thought would be easy but turned out to be hard.) Describe the process you went through as your perception of the class changed.

3. What are your memories of reading in your preschool days? What kind of reading did you do throughout your school years? And what kind of a reader are you today? Write a paper in which you describe your life as a reader in those three periods. You will add interest to your paper if you include titles of favorite books and memories of what particular books or stories meant to you. Alternatively, write an essay about the reasons that you have never become a regular reader.

Taming the Anger Monster

1. Write a paragraph in which you narrate a recent event that made you angry. Give plenty of details so that the reader can picture exactly what happened and how you reacted. Include dialog, if appropriate. Conclude by saying how you felt about yourself after the incident.

2. Laura Houser, the woman mentioned at the beginning and end of this selection, implied that her anger had simply become a bad habit that she was able to change, once she recognized it. What is a bad habit of yours that you would like to change? What would be a healthier habit to replace it with? Write a paragraph in which you identify your bad habit, explain how it affects your life, and describe how you might break it.

3. In this selection, the author identifies three sources of anger: time, technology, and tension. Write an essay in which you identify three things that particularly anger you. Explain typical situations in which you are likely to encounter each of these three anger-producers, why they irritate you so much, and how you respond to them.

Young and Isolated

1. In the selection, a young woman named Kelly states that "No one else is going to fix me but me." Do you agree with the idea that it is always up to the individual to "fix" whatever the problem is with him or her? Write a paragraph in which you explain your view, using examples from your own experience or the experiences of people you know to support your point of view.

2. When Jay was a teenager, he envisioned his future as being very different from the life he now leads. Write a paragraph in which you compare and contrast what you once envisioned your future to be and what it is like now. Overall, is your life very different or similar to what you envisioned? Do you think it will still turn out as you had envisioned?

3. In the selection, the author suggests that society as a whole bears responsibility for helping working-class youth overcome the challenges they face. In your opinion, should government play a role in helping individuals overcome the obstacles they are facing, or should responsibility rest with the individual? Write an essay supporting your position. Your thesis might be similar to one of these: "Government should play a leading role in helping young people overcome economic hardships" or "Whatever life brings, it is primarily up to the individual to look after himself or herself."

To support your thesis statement, describe three specific situations in which people face serious challenges. These challenges may involve lack of a job, housing, education, natural disasters, medical emergencies, providing for the elderly, and so on. Explain in each case what role you envision the individual playing and what role (if any) you envision the government playing. You may discuss either situations that have actually occurred or ones that might occur.

My Father's Hands

1. Worthington's father was uneducated and not economically successful. Yet his son refers to him as "a great man." As you read this essay, what reasons can you find that explain why Worthington thought so highly of him? Using evidence from the essay, write a paragraph in support of this statement: "I can understand why Calvin Worthington admired his father."

2. When Worthington's father had trouble learning to read as a child, he was punished and removed from school. It is easy to imagine that the negative experience made him think he could never be successful. However, if a teacher had been kind and patient with him, he might have done better in school. Write a paragraph about a time that you tried something new and felt like either a failure or a success. For example, you might have been playing a sport or a musical instrument for the first time, speaking a new language, or trying your hand at a craft. In your paragraph, explain what it was that you attempted, what encouragement or discouragement you received, whether or not you continued to try, and how you felt about the experience.

3. Judging from this essay, Worthington's father was profoundly illiterate—unable even to tell the difference between the words *pears* and *potatoes.* Imagine that you wake up one day and discover you are illiterate—unable to read even a newspaper headline or a street sign. Write a paper describing what your day would be like. Go into detail about the obstacles you would encounter as you attempted such tasks as getting ready for work, doing your job, communicating with friends, or grocery shopping; and explain how you would try to overcome those obstacles.

Motivation and Needs

1. Think of an advertisement that appeals to a person's need for approval. Write a paragraph that describes the ad in detail and then explains which human need the advertisement touches and how the ad promises to fulfill that need.

2. Quinn writes, "A peak experience is an extremely brief, momentary sense of total happiness or fulfillment." Have you ever had such a peak experience—or a time of really special happiness? Write a paragraph that describes that time. What brought it about? How did it make you feel? How long did it last?

3. Quinn writes, "There are immense differences in affiliation needs. Some people are satisfied with one or two close, deep friendships. Others crave superficial relationships with large groups. Some fluctuate between group and individual friendships." Write a paper about what satisfies your affiliation needs and how your needs have either changed or stayed the same through the years. Use specific examples of your friendships and what roles they have played at different stages of your life.

Effects of the Automobile

1. Clearly, the automobile has had an enormous effect on society. What is another invention that you believe has had a comparable impact on modern life? Write a paragraph about your choice. Explain some of the ways you believe it has shaped our society and influenced our lives.

2. What is the downside of the automobile and its effects on society? (Focus on societal change, not on physical problems such as air pollution or accidents.) Write a paragraph explaining the negative impact of the automobile on individuals, families, or communities.

3. Imagine that last night as you slept, automobiles everywhere disappeared. Write a paper describing how your day today would be affected by their absence. Include details from the time you woke up in the morning to the time you will go to bed. How would your activities be limited? How would your world look, smell, and sound different? How would you cope?

Two Main Forms of Scientific Inquiry

1. Many people think of serious, formal, and, frankly, often boring experimental processes when they think of "science." However, as the authors suggest, science can be fascinating and exciting. Similarly, we sometimes find that what we *thought* a class or subject would be like turns out to be nothing like our preconceived ideas. Write a paragraph about a class that turned out to be far more interesting than you thought it would be. Why was this class so interesting? What did you do in the class? What was your teacher like?

   Conversely, you could write a paragraph about a class that you signed up for with high hopes and anticipation, but that really disappointed you afterward. What happened? Why were you disappointed?

2. Scientific discovery is an ongoing process. On Earth, we have explored less than *5 percent* of the oceans that cover over 70 percent of our planet. Every year, we discover new living creatures and solve more of the mysteries of our own brains and bodies. And beyond our own planet lies an entire universe. If you could explore any area, what would you want to research or discover? Write a paragraph about it. Why are you interested in this field? How would you investigate it? What would you hope to find?

3. A hypothesis-based experiment is basically the process of figuring something out by asking "What caused this?" or "What is the explanation for this?" As the authors point out, we form hypotheses (sometimes referred to as "educated guesses") nearly every day in some form or fashion when trying to figure something out. Write an essay about your own hypothesis-based experiment. It can be as ordinary as trying to figure out what was wrong with your car when it broke down—or as unusual as trying to explain those creepy sounds in your house late at night.

   In the body of your essay, devote one paragraph to explaining the problem or mystery, another to how you tested your hypothesis, and a third to what you concluded or discovered.

Bad Managers

1. When have you had a boss (or supervisor, or instructor) whom you considered incompetent? Write a paragraph in which you describe this less-than-competent person. If he or she fell into one of the categories described in the selection, name it. If not, come up with your own term for his or her particular brand of incompetence. Provide at least one example of the person's behavior that demonstrates his or her incompetence.

2. The selection refers to managers who are unable to make decisions because they believe whatever they choose will be wrong. Write a paragraph about a time you faced a difficult decision, one in which every option seemed flawed. What were the issues involved? What were the good points and bad points of each of the options you could have chosen? What did you finally decide to do?

3. Many of the types of incompetence described in this selection involve a manager's refusal to take responsibility for a problem. Instead, he or she attempts to blame someone else for the problem or passes the responsibility on to another person. Think about instances that you have observed (or heard about) of people avoiding responsibility. They could be minor, as when a child doesn't take responsibility for keeping his room clean, or major, as when young parents abandon their baby rather than care for it. Write a paper that describes several instances you've observed of people not accepting responsibility. Make clear what you believe their responsibility is and how they are avoiding it.

Better, More Affordable Colleges Start Online

1. Have you ever taken an online course? Was it an enjoyable experience, a negative experience, or a little of both? Write a paragraph that is a "review" of your online class. Imagine that you're writing this review for others who might be interested in taking the same online class. Use specific details when explaining what was both good and bad about your experience.

2. The author points out that "we know that some things—perhaps the most important elements of a true education—are transmitted most effectively face-to-face." Think about your own years of gaining an education. What is one particularly memorable experience that could not be duplicated with online learning? This could be a challenging experience (for example, public speaking) or a personal experience (for example, the support of a teacher) or any other kind of unforgettable educational experience that involved human interaction. Write a paragraph describing this experience and why it was memorable for you.

3. Near the beginning of this article, the author claims that online learning could be the most important innovation for learning since the printing press. It could change how we learn, where we learn, and our ability to learn. Think of your experience in either high school or college. What are three things you would change to improve the experience you had (or have) there? These can be educational, social, or day-to-day (such as cafeteria, classrooms, parking lot, etc.) experiences. Be creative when thinking of how you would change

or update these experiences. Then write an essay that explores your three suggested changes. In each paragraph, describe why something needs to be updated and how you would go about implementing the changes you are suggesting. You might want to conclude your essay by pointing out how these changes will affect future students.

Into the Light

1. Although, as Savory points out, gay people are now more accepted by society than they once were, gay marriage is still a controversial topic. Write a paragraph either in support of or in opposition to the idea of gay marriage. Explain the reasons you have for your position.

2. Savory was outraged by the picketers who appeared at Laura's funeral. Although most of us have probably not experienced this level of hatred, we've all seen or heard about situations which have awakened our sense of injustice. Write a paragraph about a situation you've experienced or learned about whose injustice outraged you. Describe in detail what happened, your reaction, and why you reacted as you did.

3. Clearly, Savory's minister father was an important figure in her life. Not only did he show her that it was important to stand up for her beliefs and to treat others with respect, but he also made it easier for her to accept her own sexual orientation. Write an essay about a person in your life who has had a positive influence on you. Provide whatever background information is necessary for the reader to understand your relationship with this person. Your thesis will be a general statement that summarizes the person's impact on your life, such as this one: "_________ helped me in several ways that greatly affected my life." Then continue your introduction by listing three specific ways that person influenced you, and write about each way in a separate paragraph. An example of such a plan-of-development sentence might be: "He helped me to believe in myself, showed me that it was important to listen to others, and taught me the value of hard work."

Appendixes

Pronunciation Guide

Each word in Chapter 1, "Vocabulary in Context," is followed by information in parentheses that shows you how to pronounce the word. (There are also pronunciations for the vocabulary items that follow the readings in Parts One and Two.) The guide below and on the next page explains how to use that information.

Long Vowel Sounds

ā	pay
ē	she
ī	hi
ō	go
o͞o	cool
yo͞o	use

Short Vowel Sounds

ă	hat
ĕ	ten
ĭ	sit
ŏ	lot
o͝o	look
ŭ	up
yo͝o	cure

Other Vowel Sounds

â	care
ä	card
îr	here
ô	all
oi	oil
ou	out
ûr	fur
ə	ago, item, easily, gallop, circus

Consonant Sounds

b	big
d	do
f	fall
g	dog
h	he

Consonant Sounds

j	jump
k	kiss
l	let
m	meet
n	no
p	put
r	red
s	sell
t	top
v	have
w	way
y	yes
z	zero
ch	church
sh	dish
th	then
th	thick
zh	usual

Note that each pronunciation symbol above is paired with a common word that shows the sound of the symbol. For example, the symbol ā has the sound of the *a* in the common word *pay*. The symbol ă has the sound of the *a* in the common word *hat*. The symbol ə, which looks like an upside-down *e* and is known as the schwa, has the unaccented sound in the common word *ago*. It sounds like the "uh" a speaker often says when hesitating.

Accent marks are small black marks that tell you which syllable to emphasize as you say a word. A bold accent mark (**′**) shows which syllable should be stressed. A lighter accent mark (′) in some words indicates a secondary stress. Syllables without an accent mark are unstressed.

Limited Answer Key

An important note: To strengthen your reading skills, you must do more than simply find out which of your answers are right and which are wrong. You also need to figure out (with the help of this book, the teacher, or other students) *why* you missed the questions you did. By using each of your wrong answers as a learning opportunity, you will strengthen your understanding of the skills. You will also prepare yourself for the review and mastery tests in Parts One and Four, the reading comprehension questions in Part Two, and the combined-skills tests in Part Three, for which answers are not given here.

Answers to the Practices in Part One

1 Vocabulary in Context

Practice 1: Examples

1. Examples: *glared at each other, refused to stay in the same room together;* C
2. Examples: *cutting the police force in half, reducing the pay of all city employees;* B
3. Examples: *a trembling mugging victim, a crying lost child;* A
4. Example: *discovered, to my humiliation, that some of the blueberry pie I had eaten for lunch was still on my front teeth;* A
5. Examples: *sequins, feathers, gold trim;* B
6. Examples: *a broken leg is noticeably thinner when the cast is removed, a patient bedridden for too long will lack the lower-body strength needed to stand up;* C
7. Examples: *the cactus and the camel in the desert, the polar bear and the seal in the Arctic;* C
8. Examples: *eating tomatoes, taking a bath, letting a baby kick its legs;* B
9. Examples: *knowledge and beliefs, rules of behavior and values, signs and language;* B
10. Examples: *the Napoleonic wars of 1800–1815, the revolutions of 1848, the Crimean War in the 1850s, the Franco-Prussian War of 1870;* A

Practice 2: Synonyms

1. reveal
2. clear
3. irritating
4. serious
5. touching
6. worst
7. quacks
8. skillful
9. cast out
10. disturbing

Practice 3: Antonyms

1. Antonym: *scarce;* C
2. Antonym: *genuine;* B
3. Antonym: *harsh;* A
4. Antonym: *useful;* B
5. Antonym: *Those who agreed;* C
6. Antonym: *Physically active;* B
7. Antonym: *whose power is limited;* C
8. Antonym: *approval;* B
9. Antonym: *sped up;* B
10. Antonym: *varied;* C

Practice 4: General Sense

1. B
2. B
3. C
4. A
5. C
6. B
7. A
8. A
9. C
10. B

2 Main Ideas

Practice 1

1. S G S S
2. G S S S
3. S S S G
4. S S S G
5. S G S S
6. S G S S
7. S S S G
8. S S G S
9. S S G S
10. S S S G

Practice 2

Answers will vary.

Practice 3

1. S S P S
2. S S S P
3. S S P S
4. S S S P

Practice 4

1. S S P S
2. S P S S
3. P S S S
4. S P S S

Practice 5

1. S S S P
2. S S P S
3. S P S S
4. S S S P

Practice 6

Group 1
A. SD
B. T
C. MI
D. SD

Group 2
A. SD
B. SD
C. MI
D. T

Group 3
A. SD
B. T
C. SD
D. MI

Group 4
A. T
B. SD
C. SD
D. MI

Practice 7 *(Wording of topics may vary.)*

Paragraph 1
1. *Topic:* Cannibalism [in the animal world]
2. *Main idea:* Sentence 1

Paragraph 2
1. *Topic:* The Great Wall of China
2. *Main idea:* Sentence 1

Paragraph 3
1. *Topic:* Chaperones
2. *Main idea:* Sentence 1

Paragraph 4
1. *Topic:* Cardiovascular disease
2. *Main idea:* Sentence 2

Practice 8

1. Sentence 2
2. Sentence 3
3. Sentence 1
4. Sentence 14

Practice 9

Central point: Sentence 2

3 Supporting Details

Practice 1 *(Wording of answers may vary.)*

A. **Main idea:** Researchers have identified four kinds of intimacy.
   1. One kind of intimacy is physical.
   2. Intimacy can come from intellectual sharing.
   3. Another kind is emotional.
   4. Intimacy can come from shared activities.

B. **Main idea:** . . . four basic types of crowds.

1. Casual crowd—people with little in common except for participating in a common event
   Minor detail: People looking through a department-store window
2. Conventional crowd—people who have assembled for a specific purpose
   Minor detail: People attending a baseball game or concert
3. Expressive crowd—people who have gotten together for self-stimulation and personal satisfaction
   Minor detail: People attending a religious revival or rock concert
4. Acting crowd—an excited, explosive collection of people
   Minor detail: People engaged in rioting, looting, or other aggressive behavior

Practice 2 *(Wording of answers may vary.)*

A. 1. Act as matchmaking institutions
   2. Establish social networks
   3. Provide employment
   4. Stabilize employment

B. 1. *Minor detail:* Plow fields and pull carts
   2. *Major detail:* Benefit when die naturally
   3. *Minor detail:* Used as fertilizer and cooking fuel
   4. *Major detail:* Easy to raise

Practice 3

A. B
B. C

Practice 4 *(Examples may vary.)*

A. A Pyrrhic victory—a victory won at enormous cost.
Example—The Greek general Pyrrhus defeated a Roman army, but his own army suffered terrible losses.

B. Suppression—a deliberate attempt to avoid stressful thoughts.
Example—To not think about an argument with his girlfriend, Jeff spends a lot of time with his buddies.

4 Implied Main Ideas

Practice 1

Paragraph 1
1. A
2. D

Paragraph 2
1. B
2. C

Paragraph 3
1. C
2. D

Practice 2

1. C
2. C
3. D

Practice 3 *(Wording of answers may vary.)*

A. *Topic:* Fashions
Implied main idea: There are several reasons why fashions occur.

B. *Topic:* Hurricanes and tornadoes
Implied main idea: Hurricanes and tornadoes are different kinds of storms.

C. *Topic:* The American Revolution (**or:** The British army vs. the American colonial army)
Implied main idea: During the American Revolution, there were many important differences between the British army and the American colonial army.

Practice 4

Implied central idea: B

5 Relationships I

Practice 1 *(Answers may vary.)*

1. Another
2. also
3. In addition
4. second
5. Furthermore

Practice 2 *(Answers may vary.)*

1. frequently
2. After
3. During
4. until
5. Before

Practice 3 *(Wording of answers may vary.)*

A. Main idea: "Regrettable comments" fall into five general categories.

1. Blunder
2. Direct attack
3. Negative group reference
4. Direct and specific criticism
5. Saying too much

B. Main idea: . . . putting preventive medicine into practice.

1. Primary prevention—keep disease from occurring at all
   Example—Childhood vaccinations against polio, measles, smallpox
2. *Example*—Self-examination by women for breast cancer
3. Tertiary prevention—prevent further damage from already existing disease
   Example—Keeping diabetic on insulin; controlling pneumonia so it does not lead to death

Practice 4 *(Wording of answers may vary.)*

Main idea: Four significant events led up to World War II.

1. Hitler was named chancellor of Germany.
2. Hitler moved troops to French border.
3. Germany seized control of Austria.
4. Hitler invaded Poland.

Practice 5 *(Wording of answers may vary.)*

Main idea: The scientific method consists of four stages.

1. Formulation of a problem
2. Observation and experiment
3. Interpretation
4. Testing the interpretation

Practice 6 *(Wording of answers may vary.)*

Main idea: You can take several steps to gain control of a heavy workload.

1. List quickly everything that needs to get done.
2. Divide tasks into three groups: do now, do by next week, postpone till later.
3. Break each task into exact steps needed to get it done.

Practice 7

1. B
2. A
3. A
4. B
5. A
6. A
7. B
8. A
9. B
10. A

6 Relationships II

Practice 1 *(Answers may vary.)*

1. for instance
2. including
3. For example
4. Specifically
5. such as

Practice 2 *(Wording of answers may vary.)*

A. *self-handicapping strategy*; *definition*—1;
   example 1—3;
   example 2—5

B. *Loss leader; definition*—1;
   example 1—2;
   example 2—3

Practice 3 *(Answers may vary.)*

1. like
2. in the same way
3. Just as
4. Likewise
5. Similarly

Practice 4 *(Answers may vary.)*

1. However
2. Although
3. Unlike
4. On the other hand
5. Nevertheless

Practice 5 *(Wording of answers may vary.)*

A. Contrast: work and play

B. Comparison and contrast: First World War and Second World War

Practice 6 *(Answers may vary.)*

1. reason
2. result
3. consequence
4. cause
5. Because

Practice 7 *(Wording of answers may vary.)*

A. *Effect:* Shoplifting
   Cause: Poverty
   Cause: Frugal customers
   Cause: Sense of excitement and fun
   Cause: Desire for social acceptance

B. **Main idea** *(the effect):* Earth's population continues to rise dramatically.
Major supporting details (the causes):
1. Technology
2. Changing rates of deaths and births

Practice 8

1. C
2. B
3. A
4. C
5. A
6. B
7. C
8. B
9. A
10. C

7 Inferences

Practice 1

A. 1. A
2. B
3. C
4. B

B. 5. B
6. A
7. C
8. B

C. 9. B
10. C
11. A
12. A

Practice 2

A. 1, 4, 5
B. 2, 4, 5
C. 3, 4, 6

Practice 3

1. C, simile
2. B, simile
3. A, metaphor
4. C, simile
5. B, metaphor

Practice 4

1. B
2. C
3. B
4. A
5. C

Steps in Reading a Graph or Table

- *Title:* The Bingeing Phenomenon
- *Sources:* Harvard School of Public Health; *Journal of American College Health*
- *Student categories:* Six
- *Percentages refer to:* The students in each category who binge

Practice 5

1, 3, 5

8 Purpose and Tone

Practice 1

1. I
2. P
3. E
4. I
5. E
6. P
7. I
8. P
9. I
10. E

Practice 2

1. B
2. C
3. A

Practice 3

1. E
2. A
3. B
4. C
5. D

Practice 4

A. 1. D
2. C
3. A
4. B
5. E

B. 6. C
7. G
8. J
9. D
10. A

Practice 5

1. G
2. B
3. A
4. C
5. F

Practice 6

1. C
2. B
3. C
4. C
5. B

9 Argument

Practice 1

1. A. P
B. S

2. A. P
B. S

3. A. S
B. P
C. S

4. A. S
B. S
C. P
D. S

5. A. P
B. S
C. S
D. S

6. A. S
B. P
C. S
D. S

7. A. P
B. S
C. S
D. S

8. A. S
   B. P
   C. S
   D. S

9. A. S
   B. S
   C. S
   D. P

10. A. S
    B. P
    C. S
    D. S

Practice 2

1. A, D, E
2. C, D, E
3. B, D, E
4. A. B. C
5. B, D, E

Practice 3

1. C
2. A

Practice 4

Group 1: B
Group 2: B

Practice 5

1. C
2. B

Practice 6

Group 1: C
Group 2: D

10 Critical Reading

Practice 1

1. O
2. F
3. O
4. F
5. F+O
6. O
7. F
8. F
9. F
10. F+O

Detecting Propaganda

- *Bandwagon:* 2
- *Testimonial:* 2
- *Transfer:* 1
- *Plain Folks:* 2
- *Name Calling:* 2
- *Glittering Generalities:* 1

Practice 2

1. E
2. B
3. A
4. F
5. D
6. B
7. E
8. C
9. D
10. F

Fallacies That Ignore the Issue

- *Circular Reasoning:* 1
- *Personal Attack:* 1
- *Straw Man:* 1

Fallacies That Oversimplify the Issue

- *False Cause:* 1
- *False Comparison:* 2
- *Either-Or:* 2

Practice 3

A. 1. B
   2. A
   3. C
   4. A
   5. C

B. 6. B
   7. C
   8. A
   9. B
   10. A

Answers to the Practices in Part Four

1 More about Summarizing and Outlining

Practice 1

1. 1, 3, 6
2. 2, 4, 6
3. 2, 4, 5

Practice 2

1. C
2. B
3. D

Practice 3

1. C
2. B
3. B

4 Understanding Bias

Practice 1

1. nerd
2. regretting
3. treasures
4. good
5. unfortunately

Practice 2

A. 1. B
   2. B

B. 3. B
   4. C

C. 5. A
   6. C

D. 7. A
   8. B

Acknowledgments

Text Credits

Adler, Ronald B. "The Influence of the Self-Fulfilling Prophecy." *From Looking Out, Looking In*, 10th ed. Copyright © 2002 Wadsworth, a part of Cengage Learning, Inc. Reproduced by permission. www.cengage.com/permissions.

Alvarez, Julia. Selection on page 604. From *How the Garcia Girls Lost Their Accents*. Copyright © 1991 by Julia Alvarez. Published by Plume, an imprint of Dutton Signet, a division of Penguin USA and originally in hardcover by Algonquin Books of Chapel Hill.

Asimov, Isaac. "What Is Intelligence, Anyway?" Copyright © by the Estate of Isaac Asimov.

Auth, Tony. Cartoon on page 317. From *The Philadelphia Inquirer Sunday Magazine*, May 31, 1992. Reprinted by permission of Tony Auth.

Baker, Russell. Selection on page 614. From *Growing Up*. Copyright © 1982 by Russell Baker.

Bashard, Tim. "Soft Addictions." Reprinted by permission.

Brody, Jane E. "What Causes Hearing Loss." From *The New York Times*, March 26, 2013, © 2013 *The New York Times*. All rights reserved.

Campbell, Neil A., Jane B. Reece, and others. "Two Main Forms of Scientific Inquiry." From *Biology*, 8th ed. Copyright © 2008. Reprinted by permission of Pearson Education, Inc., Upper Saddle River, NJ.

Carey, Benedict. "Forget What You Know about Good Study Habits." From *The New York Times*, September 7, 2010, © 2010 *The New York Times*. All rights reserved.

Davidson, Anne. "Taming the Anger Monster." Reprinted by permission.

Drafke, Michael W., and Stan Kossen. "Bad Managers" and "Nonverbal Communication." From *The Human Side of Organizations*, 8th ed. Copyright © 2002. Reprinted by permission of Pearson Education, Inc., Upper Saddle River, NJ.

Garland, Hamlin. Selection on page 320. From *A Son of the Middle Border* by Hamlin Garland. Copyright © 1917 by Hamlin Garland; copyright renewed 1945 by Mary I. Lord and Constance G. Williams.

Gergen, Mary M., and others. "Baby Love" and "Obedience: Milgram's Controversial Studies." From *Psychology: A Beginning*, 1st ed. © 1989 South-Western, a part of Cengage Learning, Inc. Reproduced by permission. www.cengage.com/permissions.

Hansen, Sara. "All Washed Up?" Reprinted by permission of the author.

Henslin, James M. "Effects of the Automobile" and "Labeling and the Onset of Old Age." From *Sociology: A Down-to-Earth Approach*, 3rd ed. Copyright © 1997 by James M. Henslin. Reprinted by permission of Pearson Education, Inc., Upper Saddle River, NJ.

Hughes, Langston. "Early Autumn." From *Short Stories* by Langston Hughes. Copyright © 1996 by Ramona Bass and Arnold Rampersad. Reprinted by permission of Hill and Wang, a division of Farrar, Straus, and Giroux, LLC.

Johnson, Beth. "The Professor Is a Dropout." Reprinted by permission.

Kellmayer, John. "He Was First." Reprinted by permission.

Papalia, Diane E., and Sally Wendkos Olds. "How Dual-Earner Couples Cope." From *Human Development*, 7th ed. Copyright © 1998 by The McGraw-Hill Companies, Inc. Reproduced by permission of McGraw-Hill Education, LLC.

Quinn, Virginia. "Motivation and Needs." Adapted from *Applying Psychology*. Copyright © 1993 by McGraw-Hill, Inc. Reproduced by permission of McGraw-Hill Education, LLC.

Reif, L. Rafael. "Better, More Affordable Colleges Start Online." *Time*, September 26, 2013. Reprinted by permission of the author.

Savory, Tanya. "Into the Light." Reprinted by permission.

Silva, Jennifer M. "Young and Isolated." From *The New York Times*, June 22, 2013, © 2013 *The New York Times*. All rights reserved.

Verderber, Rudolph E. "Managing Conflicts in Relationships." From *Communicate!* 8th ed. Copyright © 1996 Wadsworth, a part of Cengage Learning, Inc. Reproduced by permission. www.cengage.com/permissions

Winn, Marie. Selection B on page 287. From *The Plug-In Drug: Television, Children, and Family.* Copyright © 1977 by Marie Winn. Published by Viking-Penguin, Inc.

Wister, Daniel. "Now More Than Ever: Community Colleges." Reprinted by permission.

Worthington, Calvin R. "My Father's Hands." A *Reader's Digest* Story. Condensed from *New York Sunday Magazine*, November 30, 1978. Reprinted by permission of the author.

Photo Credits

Part One

Chapter 1, p. 37 © matty/Alamy; Chapter 2, p. 86 © UpperCutImages/Alamy; Chapter 3, p. 126 © Peter Casolino/Alamy; Chapter 4, p. 166 © PhotoAlto/SuperStock; Chapter 5, p. 210 © Monkey Business-Fotolia.com; Chapter 6, p. 256 © DW Images/Alamy; Chapter 7, p. 309 © AP Photo; Chapter 8, p. 354 © Kzenon-Fotolia.com; Chapter 9, p. 393 © moodboard-Fotolia.com; Chapter 10, p. 438 © Catchlight Visual Services/Alamy.

Part Two

Chapter 1, pp. 460, 462, 465, 466 courtesy Guadalupe Quintanilla; Chapter 2, p. 476 © Blend Images/Alamy; Chapter 3, p. 486 © Frances Roberts/Alamy; Chapter 4, p. 498 © AgStock Images Inc./Alamy; Chapter 5, p. 508 © SlideGeeks.com; Chapter 6, p. 520 © Darren Baker-Fotolia.com; Chapter 8, p. 542 © darkbird-Fotolia.com; Chapter 9, p. 554 © Pixellover RM 1/Alamy; Chapter 10, p. 565 © Jack Young-People/Alamy.

Index